T0318586

Human Resource Management Systems

Human Resource Management Systems

Strategies, Tactics, and Techniques

by

Vincent R. Ceriello
with *Christine Freeman*

Jossey-Bass Publishers • San Francisco

Jossey-Bass books and products are available through most bookstores. To contact Jossey-Bass directly, call (888) 378-2537, fax to (800) 605-2665, or visit our website at www.josseybass.com.

Substantial discounts on bulk quantities of Jossey-Bass books are available to corporations, professional associations, and other organizations. For details and discount information, contact the special sales department at Jossey-Bass.

Library of Congress Cataloging-in-Publication Data
Ceriello, Vincent R.
    Human resource management systems : strategies, tactics, and techniques / Vincent R. Ceriello with Christine Freeman.
        p. cm. — (The Jossey-Bass business and management series)
    Originally published: Lexington, Mass. : Lexington Books, c1991.
    Includes bibliographical references and index.
    ISBN (invalid) 0-7879-4536-6 (pbk.)
    1. Personnel management—Data processing. 2. Personnel management—Computer programs. 3. Microcomputers—Programming. I. Freeman, Christine (Christine Mary) II. Title. III. Series: Jossey-Bass business & management series.
HF5549.5.D37C47 1998
658.3'00285—dc21   98-20009

PB Printing 10 9 8 7 6 5 4

To my wife, Kathy, a very special person who successfully coped with my highs and lows, and to my children, Kara, Michael, and Linda. I stole lots of hours from them, spending many nights and weekends writing, editing, reviewing, teaching, and attending numerous meetings related to this project. My parents, Victor and Elena, were a source of constant encouragement. I wish my father had lived long enough to share in my achievement. For all my family's love and support, I dedicate this book to them.

—Vincent R. Ceriello

To my husband, Mike, and my children, Justin and Meredith, who granted me the time, flexibility, and support this work has required. And to my parents, Roger and Emily, who inspired me to love words and to value the effort required to forge them into meaning.

—Christine Freeman

Contents

III HRMS Applications 363

IV   HRMS Trends and Resources   693

22.   Emerging Trends and the Future of HRMS   695

Epilogue   735

HRMS Resources   737

Figures

Preface

The challenges facing management today are many: financial, technological, organizational, and competitive. The biggest challenge of all, that blankets all of the others, is the management of the "people" resource. With regulatory and legislative mandates, the dynamic nature of human resources management, the emphasis on increased productivity and reduced expenditure, and expanding computer literacy, no enterprise can meet these challenges without timely and accurate information. That is the reason why human resources management systems (HRMS) exist. Trite as it may sound, information is power.

The term *human resources management system* was coined by me in 1973. Prior to that time, computer applications in this field were referred to as personnel data systems or employee information systems. Practitioners in this new field emphasized computer technology and how it increased the efficiency of record-keeping and reporting processes. The game has changed. The business world has become more comfortable with computers and has accepted their involvement in almost every public and private enterprise. Executives are coming to understand more clearly that an effective HRMS involves much more than the computer and its data. It encompasses thorough system planning, properly selected and trained staff, user support, policies and procedures, and interfaces with other systems.

This shift in perceptions has combined with other factors to expand the information needs of HRMS professionals. For instance, as people have become less intimidated by computers, many have become confused about the abundance of new technologies. As HRMS managers have gained expertise with implementation, they have become more interested in developing comprehensive approaches to HRMS implementation and maintenance. Human resources itself has become more complex as a result of regulatory changes, increased business competitiveness, and growing financial concerns.

To meet these challenges, HRMS professionals often look for guidelines and suggestions. Over the course of more than twenty years, I have dealt with more than two hundred public and private enterprises working to build effective systems that properly utilize staff, users, technology, and financial resources. During this period, I have observed that firms that want to be independent often wind up needing resources to provide them with HRMS education because they cannot find comprehensive background material.

Because an HRMS contains so many disparate components, few sources have yet to provide a broad but practical guide to HRMS planning, development, implementation, and maintenance. The most common sources of this information are magazine articles that offer current information, but no single article can provide sufficient information to guide planners or decision makers. Until recently, the few books available on HRMS have been either technically oriented or out of date. Only now do standard procedures and structures have general application in a wide variety of circumstances.

This book provides general guidelines for people interested or involved in HRMS. I conceived the idea for this book back in 1985 and truly believed that we could complete it in a year. After all, I had written more than twenty articles that I thought we could simply organize into a readable book. Five years later, I realize how naive this view was. Several false starts, as well as the need to continue making a living and directing the activities of a growing consulting practice, contributed to the time between conception and birth.

I owe a great deal to my coconspirator, Christine Freeman. She has been more than a coauthor; she has been my conscience, my wordsmith, and an absolute pleasure to work with. We did not always agree, but in matters of grammar, word usage, and consistency, I usually bowed to her advice and she was inevitably correct. She also was able to apply subtle pressure to keep me working on this project when consulting engagements, teaching, and other diversions got in my way. This book would not have been possible without her collaborative efforts and attention to detail.

The most difficult thing about writing this book was how to organize the wealth of background information available. It was an embarrassment of riches. If anything, we had too much information to include in a book of reasonable length and scope. We decided to organize our effort into four parts.

In Part I, we present the background and evolution of HRMS. Automated applications in support of human resources are more than twenty-five years old. They have evolved in some rather unusual ways. What was state-of-the-art in 1965 would be considered antediluvian today. Nonetheless, since the past is prologue, we consider it important that our readers understand just how HRMS have developed. Part I continues with some basic and timeless concepts for planning and designing an HRMS and describes the current trends in hardware and software.

Once planners have concluded that an HRMS is technically, functionally, and economically feasible, how do they ensure that the department winds up with a system that suits its needs? Part II begins with the acquisition of software, but the process of vendor evaluation is only the beginning. Because an HRMS will be around for a long time, we also cover contract negotiations, use of consultants, implementation strategies, system maintenance, and management concepts. These factors are at least as important as the system selection process.

Part III covers specific application areas, describing the data requirements and possible outputs for each. Our treatment of these topics is broad rather than deep. We emphasize how the system can support the functional area discussed. This part of the book illustrates the extent to which HRMS have become an excellent training ground for individuals who want to make a career of human resources.

In Part IV, we discuss emerging technologies and strategic trends in HRMS. We also include several appendixes on resources available to HRMS professionals. When making a list of emerging trends or a compendium of resources, an author always fears that one or more trends may no longer apply once the book is published or that a resource will dissolve, merge with another, or change its name and no longer be available. Nonetheless, we trust that the material in this section will serve as a useful starting point for those who want to study the present and future of HRMS.

—Vincent R. Ceriello

Although the subject of this book has many technical components, we do not consider technicians to be our primary audience. Rather, we wish to provide a kind of translation service for professionals whose primary interest is in human resources but whose work prompts them to become involved with computer systems.

Some seasoned professionals may wish that we had discussed certain subjects in more detail. We hope that our readers will bear in mind that the heart of this book deals not with computer systems per se or with the intricacies of human resources but with the intersection of these two areas. We have tried to include all the topics that we considered appropriate, though a few are covered in summary form. Because the field of HRMS is developing so rapidly, additional issues arise frequently. This book cannot serve as a complete HRMS encyclopedia, but we have tried to cover the most important subjects in a useful way.

Occasionally, someone may react to a presentation in the book by saying, "But that's not how *we* do things!" We had to make choices about how to organize, divide, and present material; others might have made different selections. We intend our material to serve as guidelines, not rigid prescriptions. Every human resources department has different needs, priorities, and resources. Decision makers should base their actions on more resources than this book can possibly provide.

Although Vince and I never expected the writing of this book to require the better part of three years, we did have a great time working on it. Vince would hand me a stack of background material, I would build a chapter outline, and we would engage in long discussions on each topic. Then the actual writing would begin. In reviewing my drafts, Vince unfailingly clarified concepts that I did not understand. He added neglected material. He shed invaluable light on differences between theory and practice. He raised challenging points of meaning and style in a lively, informal, but professional manner. We are both enthusiastic about this coauthorship experience and process; we recommend such partnerships to individuals who have high standards and a sense of humor. We hope you enjoy and benefit from our joint endeavor.

—Christine Freeman

Acknowledgments

We owe our thanks to many people. Although most of this book is directly from Vince's more than twenty-five years of experience in HRMS, we are grateful for the support of a number of people who reviewed various parts of the book, provided constructive criticism, and generally encouraged me to complete the project. We wish to thank the many human resources professionals who took time from their busy schedules to review chapters. Your valuable suggestions saved us from numerous errors and omissions (though any remaining imperfections are certainly ours alone).

These friends and reviewers included Paul Kreider, wine maker extraordinaire, brother-in-law, and independent human resources consultant who really knows the employment business and has published his own books on the subject; Fred Brooks, compliance manager, Equal Employee Opportunity Commission, whose staff reviewed the EEO chapter from a factual point of view, and Dr. Donna Wiley, professor, California State University–Hayward, who reviewed it functionally; Art Handy, principal, Mercer-Meidinger-Hansen, who has probably forgotten more about compensation and HRMS than most people will ever know; Jim Shea, benefits expert, who had the misfortune of knowing Section 89 too well; Dr. Lynn Turner, professor and chairman of the School of Business, California State Polytechnic University–Pomona, who not only reviewed the employee and industrial relations chapter but also used drafts of the book in his classes; Dr. Michael Marx, president of Selection Sciences, who reviewed training and development; Dick Frantzreb, president, Advanced Personnel Systems, who knows the theory and practice of human resources planning and the burgeoning field of microcomputer-based HRMS as well as anyone; Barbara Keyes, manager, Safety Division, an occupational health and safety expert at the University of Cincinnati; and Jerry Stanton, western division director of The Consulting Team, who reviewed the chapter on payroll.

We would like to acknowledge Dick Kaumeyer, vice president of Fuchs, Cuthrell & Company; Gary Meyer, personnel data administrator, University of Cincinnati; Mel King, managing director of INFOHRM, Melbourne, Australia; and Bob Michaels, free-lance technical writer and illustrator, who provided invaluable advice on content, format, and structure and on how to deal with our publisher. We also need to acknowledge Bill Oliver, our literary agent, who connected us with Lexington Books and supported our efforts.

A special note of thanks to Dr. William C. Bessey, associate professor and chairman of the Department of Management, Golden Gate University, San Francisco, for supporting the book's first exposure to the test of classroom distribution and use. Thanks also to Vince's graduate students in the HRMS classes at Golden Gate University for their many suggestions, criticisms, and patience in coping with our rewrites and revised versions.

We would also like to thank the secretary for the VRC Consulting Group, Darlene Kinchen, who handled deadlines and incessant changes with great efficiency and patience. She was able to balance the urgency of finishing the book with myriad duties related to my consulting practice. Her facility with several word processors, the nuances of desktop publishing, and the creative development of charts, graphs, and tables sometimes bordered on the incredible. Her skills allowed her to react promptly and efficiently to make sure this book was produced on time.

Finally, a special thanks to Vince's mother, Elena Ceriello, who handled literally tens of thousands of individual sheets of paper as we incorporated revisions in the text and bibliographies and the insertion of almost two hundred charts, tables, and graphs for the students in Vince's Golden Gate University classes.

Numerous trademarked products are referenced in this book, and many are acknowledged where the product is mentioned. Those not otherwise noted are included in the following list. These names are trademarks or registered trademarks of the organizations indicated.

Macintosh, A/UX (Apple Computer, Inc.)

Intellect (Artificial Intelligence, Inc.)

MS-DOS, Excel (MicroSoft Corp.)

IBM, AIX, AS/400, DB/2, OS/2, PS/2, SQL/DS, SAA, and OS/2, Office Vision (International Business Machines Corp.)

Focus (Information Builders, Inc.)

dBase (Ashton-Tate Corp.)

Unix (American Telephone & Telegraph Company)

Lotus 1-2-3 (Lotus Development Corp.)

SuperCalc (Sorcim Corp.)

Vectra, NewWave (Hewlett Packard Co.)

MicroVax (Digital Equipment Corp.)

Xenix (Intel Corp.)

NextStep (NeXt, Inc.)

R:base (Microrim, Inc.)

Rolodex

Informix

Part I
HRMS Planning

"Imagination is the beginning of creation; you imagine what you desire; you will what you imagine; and at last you create what you will."

—George Bernard Shaw

The opportunity to introduce a new information system to an organization sends some human resources managers into shock, overwhelmed by visions of chaos, conflict, and information breakdown. Others rub their hands together with glee, envisioning new capabilities, new reliability, and increased productivity through more and better human resources information. In truth, most skilled managers have mixed feelings about the prospect. Although new systems offer many advantages, they require thousands of hours of strategic planning, information gathering, priority setting, and decision making. To minimize disappointments and maximize success, managers must engage in thorough system planning.

No book can provide the ideal plan for human resources management systems (HRMS). Each organization must develop its own HRMS plan. Cultures and priorities differ, as do skills, staff resources, and financial options. Some organizations can buy a simple system off the shelf; others require a customized system with interfaces to other systems. No matter how simple or complex a plan is, it should include some specific steps and issues. The major steps in HRMS planning are as follows:

- Requirements definition or needs analysis
- Feasibility analysis
- Functional and technical system design
- Software selection, adaptation, or development
- System implementation

This book covers each step in the planning process in some detail. It then addresses the issues of what to do with an HRMS. This is followed by a general discussion of the uses or applications to which the HRMS can be put. Finally, there is a section on resources—where and to whom to go for help.

1
Human Resources and HRMS

> There is nothing more difficult to take in hand, more perilous to conduct, or more uncertain in its success, than to take the lead in the introduction of a new order of things.
> —Nicolo Machiavelli, *The Prince*

Machiavelli's statement of almost five hundred years ago may seem a bit abstract today, but suppose you were to substitute "system" for "new order of things." The basic precept still holds. Creating a new system can be fraught with the perils and uncertainties of which Machiavelli spoke. In business, developing a successful system is no accident. Successful human resources management requires mastery of a tremendous amount of well-organized information.

Traditionally all such information resided in files and on paper. In the 1980s, more and more corporate and public entities adopted the data management capabilities of computers to aid them in attracting, retaining, and promoting individuals who could help make their organizations more productive.

Developing Role of Human Resources

Until the 1970s, most organizations referred to the departments that handled employee hiring, firing, and tracking as personnel. These record-keeping and reporting procedures concentrated on personnel transactions. Through them, the company learned who had been hired, fired, promoted, or transferred. Staff could determine how many full-time, part-time permanent, and temporary employees worked in a particular section, unit, department, division, region, or company. They could report on the present, and, to some degree, on the past, but these procedures did not aid significantly in developing strategic or tactical plans.

In the 1970s, several factors added to the department's data collection and analysis responsibilities. New government regulations required specific attention to equal employment opportunity (EEO), occupational health and safety, pension and retirement plan accounting, and privacy of personnel records. Demographic and economic changes combined to increase frequency of job changes in the population. Even smaller companies offered more benefits and

The Emergence of Human Resources

From the simple, early days of personnel administration, human resources management has emerged as a more powerful and active participant in organizational program development and decision making. This includes the following evolutionary changes:

Traditional Personnel Administration		Contemporary Human Resources Management
Reacting to problems	$\longrightarrow$	Developing new programs
Nonprotective	$\longrightarrow$	Protection of employee rights
Limited authority	$\longrightarrow$	Multiple functions
Little government involvement	$\longrightarrow$	Much regulatory influence
Local operations	$\longrightarrow$	Multinational operations
Record keeping	$\longrightarrow$	Information resource management

more complex benefits choices. As management increasingly recognized the importance of hiring internal staff for critical positions, specialties such as succession planning and manpower forecasting emerged.

Many human resources departments began performing more planning and analysis to support top management requirements for decision-support information. To incorporate such management-level functions, many personnel departments took on the name human resources. In addition to all routine, largely operational personnel functions, a human resources department also included staff and compensation planning, management and career development, affirmative action, productivity measurement, and turnover analysis.

Senior management, recognizing the importance of improving integration of the human resources department with the strategic business direction of the entire organization, endorsed the creation of new, complex, and expensive human resources systems. Key decision makers were asking their human resources departments to assume a more proactive management role in productivity improvement, performance-based compensation programs, manpower planning and forecasting, and cost containment. To meet these expectations, the human resources department needed more management-level information and support.

All these data management pressures, coupled with the increasing accessibility of more powerful computers, have led to widespread growth of computer applications within human resources. These new computer systems are known as human resources management systems.

Growing Significance of the Computer in Human Resources

Until the 1980s, only the largest and most prosperous organizations could justify investing in the mainframe computers that human resources automation required. With the advent of microcomputers, record automation became accessible to most businesses, public institutions, and other employers. Microcomputers became commonplace business and management tools, with

---

A Brief History of Human Resources Systems

1960s. HRMS began as the province of very large companies that had vast amounts of computer power and the resources and motivation to invest in automating human resources. IBM, AT&T, General Electric, Remington Rand (then Sperry, now Unisys), Ford, and a few others developed the earliest systems. Other large, labor-intensive organizations with special needs soon developed human resources systems. Such groups included banks (Manufacturers Hanover Trust, Chemical Bank, Bank of America) and retailers (Sears & Roebuck, Montgomery Ward) that had to cope with high staff turnover, a number of manufacturing companies with large work forces and labor unions, and utility companies that could pass on the costs of automation to their customers. In this decade, pressure grew for social reform, and extensive government social programs at the federal, state, and local levels began to emerge. These factors contributed to the need for HRMS, but most HRMS were fueled by enlightened self-interest, bidding on government contracts, participating in the space race, and vestiges of the Great Society programs promulgated under the Kennedy and Johnson administrations. During the 1960s, few vendors offered commercial software packages. Those that did exist had limited responsiveness. Most HRMS were custom designed and were, correspondingly, very expensive.

1970s. During the 1970s, HRMS became more powerful. The push for growth arose from more comprehensive labor and equal employment opportunity (EEO) laws, the Occupational Safety and Health Act (OSHA) of 1970, the Employment Retirement Income Security Act (ERISA) of 1975, and lawsuits. This decade saw the beginnings of on-line, distributed processing, telecommunications, and data base management. At least 30 to 50 vendors opened their doors during this period.

1980s. During this decade, computer power came within the reach of every business through stand-alone microcomputers, local area networks (LANs), and fourth-generation languages (4GLs). The human resources field itself became increasingly complex, with higher compensation and benefits costs, more sophisticated employee benefits, monitoring and testing of safety hazards and the work environment, higher training and development costs, and omni-present demands for government compliance. A whole new series of regulations emerged that impact the human resources function, such as COBRA, TEFRA, and TSCA. Hundreds of new HRMS vendors emerged, particularly in the area of microcomputer applications. Scores of systems support every conceivable human resources application.

---

corresponding growth in human resources-related software. Today most organizations are planning or have already undertaken some human resources automation. But system selection and maintenance requires large investments of money and time. The number and complexity of hardware, software, and operational choices present human resources and systems planners with a formidable challenge. They must create and maintain an HRMS that meets information needs efficiently and successfully.

Defining Human Resources Systems

The term *human resources management system* is a mouthful even for those who work with them every day. Some people use the term *HRMS* for short. Some refer to this type of a system as a human resources information system (HRIS), a personnel data system, an employee information system, or a staff data system. Whichever term they use, more and more professionals who are responsible for employee-related record keeping are including computers as an integral part of their management process. All these terms refer to the application of computers not only to employee-related record keeping and reporting but also to management decision making.

As with any other computer system, an HRMS is more than a high-technology black box. The basic HRMS consists of the following parts:

- Data on employees organized into a set of files known as the employee master data base (Data become information when they are organized, sequenced, reported, and ready for logical analysis.)

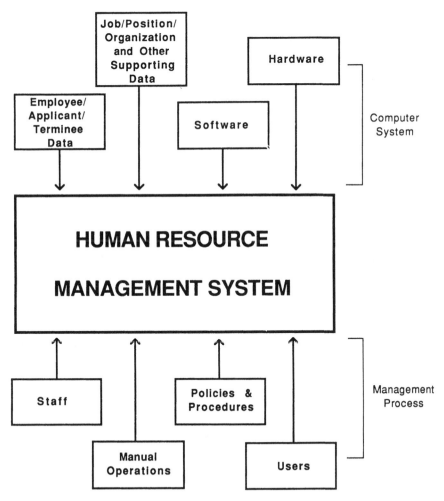

Figure 1–1. Components of an HRMS. A well-functioning HRMS is a combination of the computer system and the management process. The absence of any of these components can make the HRMS incomplete and unresponsive.

- Other data bases and files that provide human resources-related information, such as wage-rate tables, organization tables, and job classification tables
- Software—programming instructions that order and control data storage and manipulation, plus the documentation, training, and procedural support to use the system properly.
- Hardware—the electronic and mechanical equipment that performs the ordered functions, including peripheral equipment and consumables
- Staff—managers, programmers, analysts, technical support, data base administrators, security experts, information center (IC) staff, data entry staff, and legal, auditing, and procurement staff
- Manual operations—generally procedures that support computerized activities but also operations in which security, privacy, or technological limitations mandate activity that does not involve the computer
- Policies and procedures—standards for automated and manual processes that may describe how to handle specific data entry, transaction updates, report generation, system maintenance, and related activities
- Users—the values, needs, abilities, experience, and skills of both designers and users; includes all users from neophytes to experts, both within human resources and outside

Most people tend to think of a computerized HRMS as a simple and easy method of personnel record keeping. A well-designed and carefully implemented system does much more than that. The master data base that results from the HRMS planning process makes it practical to provide many types of analyses at a reasonable cost. Some systems, responding to users who have low-level demands, provide basic record-keeping functions; others come loaded with a dozen or more applications to support higher-level needs. In some form or another, an HRMS can support every functional area of human resources.

Almost every HRMS is different. Some are small enough to run on a microcomputer with an off-the-shelf program that is difficult to modify. Some require a mainframe, a network of remote or distributed terminals, and a staff of computer programmers and analysts. Some human resources departments try to integrate all human resources software applications into one computer system. The applications share a common data base, and authorized users may access and compare data from several human resources functions simultaneously. Others maintain separate systems for various human resources functions, creating interfaces for electronic data transfer or for linking with other systems. Some keep functions completely separate, with only manual data exchange. For instance, payroll often uses a stand-alone or interfaced system, with occasional data exchange with the HRMS. An HRMS may start as a stand-alone microcomputer application for one function, typically to support

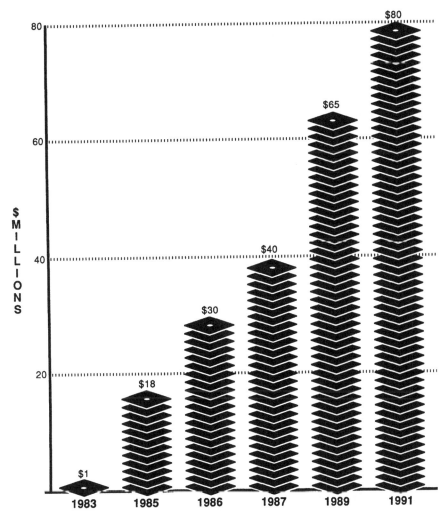

Figure 1–2. **Growth of HRMS microcomputer software. Sales of human Resources software for microcomputers have risen sharply and constantly since their introduction to business environments in the mid-1980s.**
(Source: *Business Computer Systems*, Reed Publishing USA, May 1986. Reprinted with permission.)

employment or applicant tracking. This system then expands as other human resources staff and corporate management recognize the advantages of computerizing human resources.

Large organizations usually have a sizable, often highly compartmentalized, HRMS, which is a microcosm of the organization. Such a system includes software for numerous human resources applications and serves users who are specialists in areas such as executive compensation, strategic human resources planning, plant security, and so forth. Some large companies with a number of locations use a centralized HRMS that is simultaneously accessible to headquarters and divisions. Headquarters makes high-level policy and strategic decisions based on HRMS information, and the divisions perform operational activities. Other large organizations with decentralized human resources have a completely independent HRMS for each region or location; each has its own data base and a full complement of human resources applications software. The separate units input transactions or changes of status (hires, promotions, transfers, and terminations) to update the central HRMS and may provide the central system with summary information.

A small company may have only one location and so require a less sophisticated HRMS, but users may need generalist skills to work with multiple human resources functions on the system. Some smaller firms have special needs that are as complex as those of larger organizations.

HRMS Record Keeping and Reporting

Human resources administration is largely an information-handling business, so straightforward record keeping and reporting are its most basic jobs. Human resources professionals may require information on subjects such as the following:

- Personal employee information
- Wages and salaries
- Review dates
- Benefits
- Education and training
- Attendance
- Performance appraisal

The range of such topics demonstrates the scope of the personnel function and the need for an automated system. Users can view this information on-screen and in reports. Depending on the capability of the individual application, a report may come in any of several forms—text, tables, graphics, or a combination of these. Common reports include the following information:

- Profiles and listings of individual employees
- Summary reports on groups of employees or the entire population
- Historical trends in work-related information
- Person-position comparisons

- Individualized employee communications
- Reports required by external agencies
- Trend analysis and time series comparisons

Basic record-keeping and reporting systems emphasize the accuracy of records. Most of these systems can provide only basic listings, rosters, directories, and other single-detail reports. Some record-keeping and reporting systems have more sophisticated capabilities, such as graphics and ad hoc reporting, and their price tags reflect it. It is not unusual to see costs exceeding

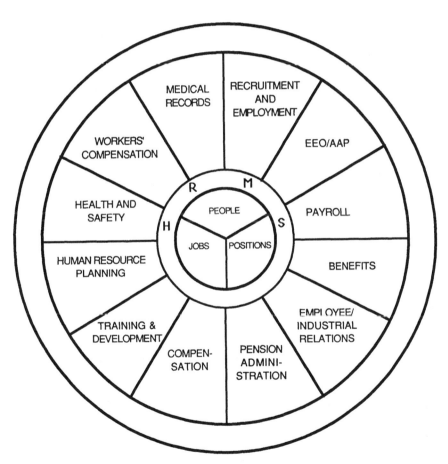

Figure 1–3. An HRMS tracks people, jobs, and positions. These three basic types of data, shown in the inner ring, provide most of the information needed by the wide variety of possible HRMS applications, some of which are shown in the outer ring.

$500,000 for comprehensive human resources systems, although some excellent record-keeping systems for microcomputers cost less than $1,000.

The scope of a new system depends on an organization's financial resources, growth pattern, staffing availability and experience, organizational needs, and productivity of current procedures. Basic record-keeping and reporting systems are most likely to meet the needs of start-up companies, small organizations with a stable work force or little prospect of rapid growth, and firms with limited, predictable, and traditional human resources needs.

Regardless of specific needs, most successful HRMS share several characteristics: They are

- Able to accommodate data initiated by employees (marital status, beneficiaries, address) or by employer (job code, location, salary)
- Responsive to changes in regulations, organization policies, and business conditions
- Time-consuming to develop
- Expensive to implement
- Allow only authorized users access to sensitive data
- Expandable, so human resources can add new applications later
- More transaction-driven than computational

Human Resources as a Business Partner

Some large organizations have spent millions of dollars on an HRMS without being satisfied with the results. They wanted to go far beyond personnel record keeping and reporting. They demanded features such as management succession planning, manpower forecasting, and executive compensation administration. An organization that expects its computer system to perform high-level analysis must first master basic functions such as personnel record keeping and reporting. Absent or unreliable data cannot support high-level functions. To perform management activities, the HRMS must include special tools that handle sophisticated analyses, not just transaction-based data processing.

Some human resources management activities involve use of general business applications such as advanced data base technology, statistical packages, spreadsheets, and other modeling software. Other tasks work best via software tailored specifically for human resources, such as succession planning programs or position control programs. Sophisticated systems should allow for flexible reporting structures as well as full integration with a variety of activities, such as word processing, graphics, mail-list maintenance, and import of external data bases.

Systems with these features require not only additional software (and possibly hardware) and staff training but also careful attention to make sure each component performs well in concert with the others. These projects can benefit greatly from the advice and guidance of external resources, such as consultants and specialists.

To perform more sophisticated analyses, human resources also needs access to corporate data provided by the finance, marketing, and production departments. With integration in, or interfacing with, other computer systems in the organization, the HRMS becomes less a human resources-owned commodity and more a corporate asset for all. In the long term, the human resources systems group will follow in the footsteps of human resources and become more closely tied to business activities and information. This will result in greater respect for human resources and the HRMS in the information systems (IS) community.

Advantages of Automating Human Resources

Computerization brings numerous benefits to a human resources department. Each human resources function finds its own special blessings in automation. In virtually every case, the automation of human resources records will do the following:

- Increase data accuracy
- Increase processing speed
- Create more useful, sophisticated results
- Increase productivity

Increase Data Accuracy

Computers do not make errors; they can, however, malfunction. Humans can make errors. Unlike a human clerk, a computer always gets the right answer to the question asked. It makes no computational errors. It always looks for data in the right table and in the right part of the table. When asked to select or order employees according to particular values, it includes every file, sorts accurately every time, and flags any problems or inconsistent records. Computer systems usually include critical edit and validation rules; these instructions allow the system to accept only data entries that meet selected criteria for a particular data field. For instance, a computer system will reject the date November 31 or the birth date 1853 for a current employee. Moreover, because it processes data faster than manual systems, users are working with more current, and therefore more accurate, data. Computers answer the exact question asked. Users still must take responsibility for providing good data and making meaningful inquiries.

HRMS Development Goals .

Regardless of scope, content, or complexity, every HRMS shares certain basic goals:

Goal 1: To provide complete, timely, and accurate information for personnel administration and analysis. The primary function of an HRMS, whether computer-based or manual, is to function as an efficient, responsive system for managing a firm's human resources. Data should meet high standards for accuracy and completeness. Entry and updating methods should ensure up-to-date information.

Goal 2: To match its own capabilities with the needs, skills, and interests of human resources staff and other users. Systems should mirror the sophistication level of their designers and users. Users who have outgrown a simple system need more sophisticated tools and training to maintain their support of the HRMS and to maximize their productivity. A system whose complexity exceeds the capacity of its users is providing answers for which no one has asked the right questions. Human resources staff who are familiar with record keeping but not with sophisticated management planning might begin HRMS development with straightforward operations. They can add more advanced capabilities later after adjusting to the process of computerization and the specific system's characteristics.

Goal 3: To foster comfort and trust among its intended users. An HRMS succeeds only to the extent that users truly incorporate the system's capabilities into their daily routines. The most important aspect of a new HRMS is not that it performs every possible operation but that it performs reliably the functions it does undertake. It should use procedures that are as clear and simple as possible.

Increase Processing Speed

Many people think of speed as the computer's biggest advantage. Computers certainly can perform data entries, updates, calculations, sorting, and report generation faster than manual operators. Once set up, customized form letters require little time and human intervention. The computer can make reports on special employee populations available as needed in a timely manner. As mentioned earlier, this speed is a great advantage, as it increases the extent to which human resources staff can access completely up-to-date information. Although an HRMS can eliminate some of the drudgery of manual clerical work, some mundane work remains. For example, the file clerk becomes a data-entry clerk with responsibility for feeding the computer.

Create More Useful, Sophisticated Results

The faster computers work, the more people ask them to do. Computers perform more complex statistical operations and modeling than a manual operator could handle practically. Because an HRMS can easily sort, calculate, and correlate variables, users can obtain more detailed information about human resources issues. A few examples follow:

- Computer-assisted applicant screening
- Comprehensive population demographics
- Costs of benefits
- Work-related factors in injuries and illnesses
- Career planning options
- Succession planning
- Organization charting

Many computer applications offer automatic flagging, which also helps human resources staff perform more effectively. This function marks or lists data or patterns outside a defined range. For instance, the system might flag the records of all employees whose last performance review took place more than one year ago. It might list reviews due or overdue and even issue reminders to supervisors to minimize the number of overdue reviews. Human resources staff use such information to resolve conflicts and solve problems earlier, and usually more simply, than if they waited for complaints by employees, management, or government agencies.

Finally, many systems keep records of every data addition or change. Human resources auditors can use these transaction files to trace the source of problem data in the event of discrepancies, security violations, or disputes.

Increase Productivity

The chief executive of a major bank once said, "I don't need to know where my bank is going; I want to know where it can go. Where are our strengths that we can use as the nucleus for new products and services, and what are our weak links?" In certain contexts, he might have been talking about managing money or constructing new facilities, but in this case, he was talking about his bank's human resources.

How an HRMS Enhances Productivity

Increases Work Force Quality

- More appropriate hiring
- Better training and development
- Improved retention of desired employees

Eases Regulatory Compliance

- Equal employment opportunity (EEO) reports
- Consolidated Omnibus Budget Reconciliation Act (COBRA) and other benefits reports
- Occupational Safety and Health Administration (OSHA) safety reports

Controls Expenses

- More thorough salary/benefits administration tracking and analysis
- More appropriate training and development
- Ad hoc reports to answer queries
- More user independence

Consider some of the statements about human resources that appear in annual reports or are heard at high-level conferences: "A company is its people" or "The very survival of our company depends on better human resources management." Senior executives ask key personnel professionals, "Are we filling the gaps that will be created by the increasing incidence of early retirement?" "Do we really have quantitative shortages of people, or do we have people in the wrong slots?" "Are we in compliance with the disclosure provisions of all government regulations such as EEO, COBRA, and OSHA?" Such questions show that executives recognize the role of human resources in running a successful organization.

A responsive HRMS increases the quality of the employee population by helping the human resources department hire, support, develop, and retain the most qualified employees. A trained HRMS user can perform a computer search for data much more thoroughly and efficiently than a manual search. The same efficiency occurs with file updating, data analysis, and report creation. Moreover, in a multifunction system, all human resources units can share

"You're right . . . at one time, the buck did stop here, but lately, thank God, it's been cruising right on by, down to Gunderson, in Personnel!"

Figure 1–4. (Source: Bradford Veley. *Personnel Journal*, September 1985. Reprinted with permission.)

information quickly and thoroughly. In such ways, well-conceived human resources automation improves the overall productivity and competitiveness of the organization.

For instance, a good applicant tracking module can preselect the most qualified applicants, produce the necessary analysis of candidates, schedule them for interviews, and create offer letters, thus facilitating the hiring process. The system also can track performance and career development needs. It can flag opportunities for managers, employee relations staff, and others to take steps to correct, encourage, reward, and develop employees appropriately. With computerized data tracking and reporting, users can obtain useful internal and government reports more easily.

Limits of Computer Systems for Human Resources

Only ten or fifteen years ago, many people viewed computers as a panacea for personnel managers' problems. Many thought it would revolutionize human resources management. Although a computer can improve the accuracy and timeliness of personnel records, automation itself does not automatically make a human resources department successful. Many systems have improved human resources operations immensely, but even an excellent system provides only part of what a productive human resources department needs. Some human resources processes are still handled by human resources staff manually, with little or no computer involvement. These processes primarily include interpersonal activities such as counseling, interviewing, supervision, and surveillance. An HRMS cannot substitute for sound management policies and procedures that deal with applicants, employees, and retirees. Computerization is no substitute for management and communication skills.

Many users expect the system to be a panacea even if all they have done is automate their file cabinets. Human resources still must maintain checks of data accuracy. Although the system may prevent a user from entering November 31 as a valid date, if the user enters December 12 but meant to enter

---

Why Human Resources Systems Often Cannot Do the Job

Unclear goals and objectives

System solves the wrong problems

Started too big; aimed too high

Improper vendor/product selection

Low level of user involvement

Planning overlooks impact on clerical procedures

Lack of human resources expertise with computers

Management has unrealistic expectations

Lack of overall plan for human resources record management

Lack of flexibility and adaptability

Misinterpretation of HRMS specifications

Poor communication between human resources and IS

Underestimation of conversion effort

Improper testing of the HRMS

December 21, the computer would not block this incorrect entry. Moreover, a computer has no way of judging the truthfulness or fairness of data entered. Human resources staff must make sure that performance ratings, salary reviews, and other evaluative material entered into the system reflect high professional and ethical standards.

Some departments have become disenchanted with their human resources systems. The major causes for such failures have been inappropriate management of user expectations, poor system selection, and inadequate training—all situations that good planning could have prevented.

Human resources staff often can identify and resolve many issues without a new computer system. The real need may be to reorganize the human resources department or to consolidate information. Some organizations find that they need to produce a summary report and use better procedures to process transactions and document flow. Resolution of every issue does not require automation; for those issues that do, an already efficient personnel function with good communication paths fares best.

Neither management nor users should expect a new human resources system to solve organizational problems or to eliminate all data disputes, employee inquiries, or the inevitable queuing for reports. Any department must make some compromises in system selection, and HRMS managers need to prioritize projects. Vendor promises also can contribute to unrealistic expectations. Some less-than-candid software vendors may oversell their packages with marketing masterpieces that bear little resemblance to reality. Planners must compare their needs with the proven functions of potential software.

Management must be able to tell computer technicians what they need from the HRMS. For instance, human resources staff and computer technicians often speak quite different languages. As shown in figure 1–5, each group has its own "alphabet soup" of acronyms, as well as many other specialized terms. Participants should ask about words they do not know and explain special terms that they use. Careful consideration of the needs of the two cultures can improve communication and results.

Systems meet the needs of users only to the extent that users and managers can define those needs during the planning stage. If technicians do not understand what users want, they may pass on incorrect specifications to the supplier, vendor, or in-house IS. This leads to an unresponsive and unreliable system that is poorly implemented, without proper testing or validation. If the HRMS lacks important data or functions or has insufficient capacity, it cannot produce the desired results. If the HRMS provides more information than is required, users may tend to overanalyze results. Only careful screen and report design avoids providing interesting but useless output.

In such cases, one cannot blame the hardware or software. Computers are electronic marvels, but they perform only as instructed. Computer success depends on proper planning, particularly adequate communication among users, planners, consultants, and vendors.

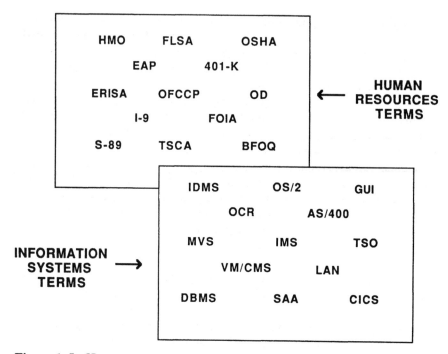

Figure 1–5. Human resources and IS alphabet soup. Human resources
professionals generally understand most of the human
resources terms, but people outside that function often find
the acronyms and abbreviations bewildering. IS staff can
work more effectively with human resources if they
understand these terms. Similarly, high-technology areas
such as IS are filled with abbreviations and acronyms.
Computer technicians developing an HRMS cannot assume
that human resources staff and management understand their
terminology. Programmers, system analysts, vendors, and
consultants have the responsibility to inform human
resources staff what the acronyms stand for and briefly
explain the technology involved.

Steps in Computerizing Human Resources

An organization cannot simply clone the system of some other group. To have
an effective HRMS, the human resources department must ascertain the most
appropriate scope, content, structure, and procedures for computerizing its
operations. To make appropriate decisions, an organization must follow a set
of time-consuming but constructive steps. The resulting HRMS can contrib-

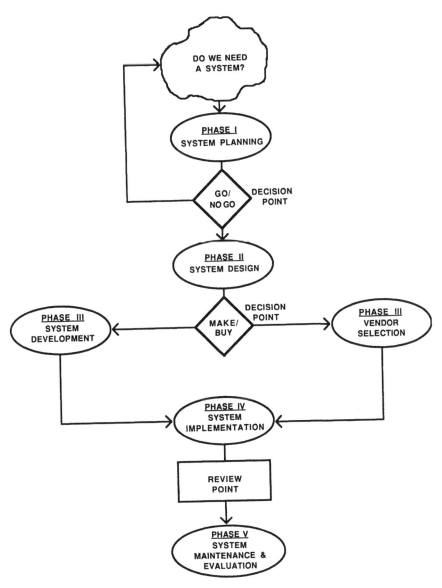

Figure 1-6. The five phases of HRMS development.

ute to the productivity of virtually every function of human resources. Creating a successful HRMS requires five distinct phases of effort:

1. System planning
2. System design
3. Vendor selection
4. System implementation
5. System maintenance and evaluation

Each phase requires information gathering, issue resolution, and decision making. These phases are described in detail later in this book. The information that follows provides an overview of the process from conception to ongoing system maintenance.

System Planning

Planning is the most important phase in the process of creating an HRMS. Actually, planning is often a two-step process—requirements definition and feasibility analysis. Each step may consume several months of effort and cost many thousands of dollars in internal resources or external consulting fees. In spite of this relatively high financial cost, many organizations that skimp on planning live to regret it. As shown in the accompanying sidebar entitled "Why Human Resources Systems Often Cannot Do the Job," most poor HRMS performance stems from poor planning.

The first step, a requirements definition, involves several types of investigation to determine what kinds of data, analysis, security, reports, and other features users need. Planners consider current trends in personnel administration and human resources management, interview key users and other staff who will subsequently interact with the system, examine existing internal systems, and prepare findings and recommendations.

The next step, feasibility analysis, estimates the resources required to achieve those objectives. This analysis should consider not only hardware costs, vendor charges for software, and facilities requirements but also consultant time, custom software development, documentation revisions, and user training. It includes financial costs, human resource allocation, and a projected schedule for implementation.

System Design

The design phase includes development of the product that will eventually make up the system itself. Designers investigate commercial software to decide whether to make or buy the needed software. They must determine to what

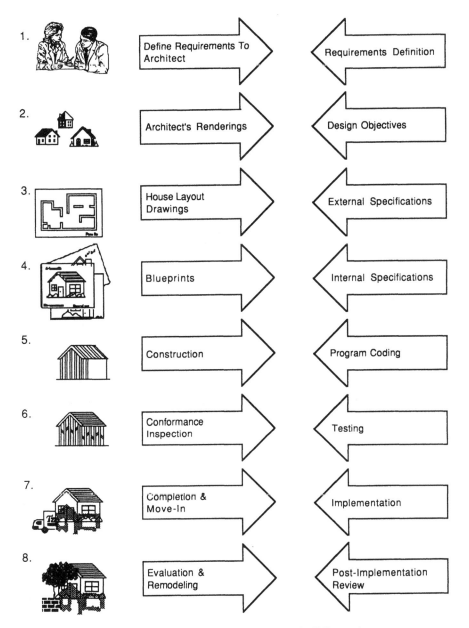

Figure 1–7. Building a system is like building a house.

extent their project can succeed with commercial packages and to what extent they should consider creating custom software or adapting commercial packages.

Organizations often can use packaged software for some applications, such as applicant tracking, payroll, or benefits. For other applications, such as a payroll/personnel interface, career planning, or safety, the design team must plan to tailor software to the needs of users and the organization.

Even commercially available software often needs programming-level adaptation to define data fields, create screens, and build report formats. Some of the tasks involved are highly technical and may require special expertise. These include structuring the data base, developing code lists, defining transaction flow, developing report requirements, and determining requirements for additional modules.

As part of this process, the project team must specify hardware that is compatible with the software as well as with the organization's current technological environment and future goals.

Vendor Selection

In HRMS planning, the term *vendor* generally refers to the software provider. Vendor evaluation involves developing or constructing specifications and a request for proposal (RFP). The RFP may cover both hardware and software requirements, though software requirements usually require more careful planning and negotiation, especially if hardware already exists or must integrate with existing equipment. On the basis of the RFP, vendors can propose and bid on a system. Management can then select the most appropriate vendor and develop contracts and maintenance agreements.

System Implementation

Implementation transforms the HRMS from a plan to a functioning system. This process may take two months to two years or more depending on whether the system will operate on a mainframe, a midrange computer, or a microcomputer. Installing the software is probably the simplest part of system implementation. Getting the software to run smoothly involves more complicated steps, such as data transfer, interfaces with existing systems, and acceptance testing. Perhaps the most important part of implementation is staff training. Several groups require training, including system operators, users, analysts, administrators, and managers. The vendor generally provides training, but such training is usually generic rather than tailored to a specific firm. It does not take into account the organization's culture, its specific operating characteristics, or the sophistication of its users.

System Maintenance and Evaluation

System maintenance and evaluation occur throughout a system's life cycle, since the organization, its data and reporting needs, and the field of human resources software are constantly evolving. In fact, a very large proportion of an organization's IS budget goes toward maintaining operational systems. Of the overall cost of building and operating a system, maintenance consumes over 60 percent of the resources. Some studies indicate that maintenance can be as high as 80 percent.

Maintenance includes any work done on the system after delivery and operational acceptance. Most maintenance involves the software, but procedures also may be involved. To assess problems and needs, HRMS staff regularly conduct audits and evaluations with users, consultants, and systems staff. Based on these results, they (or the users) may refine procedures and data collection methods, revise cost-benefit estimates, adjust staffing and budgeting for system operation, interface with other "people" systems, and deal with administrative, organizational, policy, and procedural issues. In this process, HRMS staff modify, add to, and reconcile aspects of the system design or installation that may cause problems. At every step, staff should compare actual results with the requirements established during the first phase of system development. The final HRMS maintenance task is to recognize when additional "fixes" cannot mask the fact that the system has outlived its usefulness. At this point, planning for a new generation of system should begin.

Glossary

Application A set of related activities that may be served by a specific software package. In HRMS, computer applications often correspond to human resources functions or specific responsibilities of those functions. For instance, common HRMS applications include equal employment opportunity, payroll, benefits administration, and compensation.

Data Numbers, words, or phrases that, when processed on a computer, can produce information.

Data base The aggregate set of collected data on a population, such as that contained in the HRMS master file; the set of individual data elements on which the system can collect, sort, or output data.

Feasibility analysis An analysis of the alternatives for HRMS development, including building, buying, or a combination of the two. An estimate of the resources required to achieve a particular HRMS plan. This analysis includes the extent to which each plan or alternative meets the organization's needs, as well as its financial costs, staff and other resource requirements, and projected schedule for implementation. It may include a formal cost-benefit-value analysis.

Hardware   The central processing unit (CPU), disk drives, tape drives, console, video display terminals (VDTs), printers, and other physical components of a computer system. All but the CPU are referred to as peripherals.

HRMS   See *Human resources management system.*

Human resources   The function within an organization that facilitates the hiring, retention, and promotion of qualified individuals as employees. Some businesses still refer to this function as personnel administration or personnel relations. The term human resources has evolved as a way to present this department as having equal status with other business resources, such as financial resources, marketing resources, facilities, and production.

Human resources management system (HRMS)   The software, hardware, support functions, and system policies and procedures for a computer system designed to support the activities of the human resources department. This system is also known as an employee information system (EIS), personnel data system (PDS), personnel management system (PMS), and automated personnel management reporting system (APMRS).

Implementation   The process of transforming an HRMS from a set of programs and modules to a fully functioning system. It includes hardware installation, software installation, data conversion and transfer, acceptance testing, and staff training.

Information   Data organized, formatted, sequenced, and presented in a logical form ready to be analyzed and interpreted by an end user.

Information systems (IS)   The department or unit that manages and maintains an organization's computer systems. Sometimes called data processing (DP) or electronic data processing (EDP). In the HRMS context, IS usually refers to a central staff who develop and maintain non-human resources computer applications but also may have responsibility for the HRMS.

IS   See *Information systems.*

Maintenance   The process of evaluating HRMS needs and performance that leads to system or programming modifications such as screen and report changes, data base additions and deletions, new or enhanced applications, hardware upgrading, or policy and procedure changes designed to optimize and enhance the existing system.

Module   A portion of the HRMS dedicated to the data needs and computer operations of particular HRMS functions, such as benefits, compensation, or safety. A module may contain a single software package or an integrated multiprogram package.

Requirements definition   A determination of the needs for data, analysis, security, reports, and other features that a new system should include in the context of the organization's goals and objectives.

Vendor   In the HRMS context, a firm that sells packaged computer software, specifically for human resources applications. In a more general context, the term vendor may refer to a seller of hardware, bundled systems, which include both hardware and software, or of services such as training, specialized design and development, or maintenance.

Discussion Points

1. What is human resources? What are the major differences between human resources and personnel administration?

2. In what ways might an HRMS in a large organization differ from one in a small organization?

3. What factors contribute to the continued growth of human resources complexity and importance? How does each affect the HRMS?

4. In what ways can computerization increase data accuracy? Give several examples of how this improved accuracy benefits human resources departments.

5. Describe several ways in which an HRMS can improve an organization's productivity.

6. To what extent do people still retain responsibility for human resources operations even with a sophisticated HRMS?

7. Under what circumstances might development of a new HRMS not be the most effective solution to human resources department's needs?

8. What are the responsibilities of human resources in each phase of HRMS development? What are the responsibilities of information systems (IS)?

Further Reading

Amico, Anthony M. "Critical Human Resource Issues of the 1980s." *Human Resource Planning*, Vol. 6, No. 2, 1983.

Anderson, Kirk J. "HRS Life Cycle." *Journal of Human Resource Systems Management*, September 1986.

Awad, Elias M., and Wayne F. Cascio. *Human Resource Management: An Information Systems Approach*. Reston, VA: Reston Publishing Company, Inc., 1981.

Balicki, Richard J. "Evolution of Human Resource Management Systems." *Infosystems*, August 1983.

Bassett, Glen A., and Harvard Y. Weatherbee. *Personnel and Data Management*. New York: American Management Association, 1971.

Bennison, M. "Computers in Personnel: The Crunch Issues." *Personnel Journal*, September 1982.

Berry, William E. "What a Personnel EDP System Should Do." *Personnel*, January/February 1969.

Brown, P. "The Computer and Personnel Management." *Personnel Management*, July 1971.

Burack, Elmer H. *Personnel Management: Human Resource Systems Approach*. New York: John Wiley & Sons, 1982.

Campbell, Charles R. "HRMS Features, Functions Fairly Easy to Identify." *Personnel Journal*, March 1983.

Carolin, Brian, and Alastair Evans. "Computers as a Strategic Personnel Tool." *Personnel Administrator*, July 1988.

Carrell, Michael R., Frank Kuzmits, and Norbert Elbert. *Personnel: Human Resource Management*. Columbus, OH: Merrill Publishing, 1989.

Ceriello, Vincent R. "Human Resource Management Systems: Toy or Tool?" *Journal of Systems Management*, May 1980.

———. "Human Resource Management Systems: Part I." *Personnel Journal*, October 1982.

———. "How to Make the Least of Planning." *NCHRC Quarterly*, Winter 1987.

Cheek, Logan M. "Personnel Computer Systems: Solutions in Search of a Problem." *Business Horizons*, August 1971.

Dukes, Carlton W. "Computer Technology/Systems and Human Resource Management." *Personnel Management*, June 1978.

Dyer, L. "Studying Strategy in Human Resource Management: An Approach and an Agenda." Industrial Relations 23, 1984.

Famularo, Joseph J. "The Computer in Personnel Administration." In *Handbook of Modern Personnel Administration*, edited by Joseph J. Famularo. New York: McGraw-Hill, 1972.

Flamholtz, Eric G. *Human Resource Accounting: Advances in Concepts, Methods, and Applications*. San Francisco: Jossey-Bass, 1985.

Gallagher, M. *Computing and Personnel Management*. London: William Heinemann, Ltd., 1986.

Heisler, William J., W. David Jones, and Phillip O. Benham, Jr. *Managing Human Resources Issues*. San Francisco: Jossey-Bass, 1988.

Hoffman, Frank O. "Identity Crisis in the Personnel Function." *Personnel Journal*, March 1978.

Ive, Tony. *Personnel Computer Systems*. New York: McGraw-Hill, 1982.

Jenkins, Michael L., and Gayle Lloyd. "How Corporate Philosophy and Strategy Shape the Use of HR Information Systems." *Personnel*, May 1985.

Kavanaugh, Michael J., H. G. Gueutal, and S. I. Tannenbaum. "Government: Who Needs an HRIS?" Computers in Personnel, Winter 1987.

Krebs, Valdis. "HR Says the M Word." *Computers in Personnel*, Spring 1989.

Lee, Sang M., and Cary D. Thorp, Jr., eds. *Personnel Management: A Computer Based System*. Princeton, NJ: Petrocelli Books, Inc., 1978.

Mitsch, Robert J. "A Brief History of the Computer in Personnel." *Personnel Journal*, July 1980.

Muller, Donald L. "Computers: A Boon for HRM." *Personnel Administrator*, May 1987.

Saari, B. "New and Emerging Boardroom Concerns and HRIS Implications." HRSP Review, Fall 1988.

Sewell, Gary. "Why Are Human Resources Last to Be Automated?" *The Office*, November 1987.

Tomeski, Dr. Edward A., and Dr. Harold Lazerus. *People-Oriented Computer Systems*. New York: Van Nostrand Reinhold, 1975.

Walker, Alfred. "A Brief History of the Computer in Personnel." Personnel Journal, July 1980.

Webb, David R. "The Computer in Personnel Administration." In *Handbook of Modern Personnel Administration*, edited by Joseph J. Famularo. New York: McGraw-Hill, 1972.

Wille, Edgar, and Valerie Hammond. *The Computer in Personnel Work*. New York: Renouf USA, 1981.

Windsor, David Burns. *Developing a Computerized Personnel System*. Sussex: Institute of Personnel Management, 1986.

2
Planning an HRMS

If we could first know where we are, and whither we are tending, we
could better judge what to do, and how to do it.
—Abraham Lincoln

Some refer to HRMS planning as the "pay me now, pay me later" syndrome. Whether the organization chooses to do a proper planning study, engage a consultant to do it, or bypass the step entirely, it will eventually pay a price. Often management believes that a new HRMS will solve all the organization's problems. Perhaps some managers or technicians want others to perceive them as current; perhaps the organization has a periodic but difficult to define deficiency in management information reporting. The drive for a new system should come from two related bases: (1) understanding the current business, organizational, and environmental conditions that require correction or enhancement, and (2) understanding what computer systems for human resources can and cannot do.

Although planning alone cannot produce an effective HRMS, the best systems result from the best planning. To succeed, human resources management must make sure that the HRMS project team carefully performs each step in the planning process. Briefly, these steps are as follows:

- Establishing the project team
- Defining system requirements
- Performing a feasibility analysis
- Obtaining support for the HRMS

Those involved in HRMS planning should remember that planning itself is not the goal. These steps should aim to provide management with the information needed to authorize proceeding with the design phase of the HRMS project and to choose the direction that phase should take.

Establishing the Project Team

Successful HRMS development requires a full-time project manager. A specific person or people should have direct responsibility for turning human

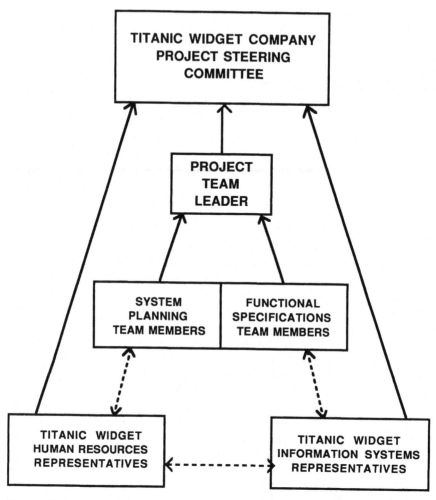

Figure 2–1. Reporting responsibilities of the HRMS project team. Solid lines indicate the flow of authority, or the reporting relationship. Dotted lines indicate the functional flow, or dependence.

resources automation into reality. Working together as an HRMS project team, they can give each other feedback and support.

The HRMS project team takes responsibility for system planning, design, and implementation. The team's planning tasks include requirements definition and feasibility analysis. The team also facilitates development of technical specifications during the design phase. At implementation, team members supervise installation, vendor involvement, data conversion, program modification, testing, and training. The project team may carry out all these functions itself, use subordinates or peers from human resources and IS, and/or use consultants. The project team usually acts as a liaison with any consultants involved in HRMS design and development.

The Team Leader

Whether or not human resources will be the prime system user, the leader of the development effort should be from that department. This firmly establishes user ownership from the beginning. The project team leader reports to the human resources department, ideally to the director, though this is not often the case. The leader should have well-developed project management and communication skills and work comfortably with top management. He or she should have a thorough understanding of the human resources department's operations, including the responsibilities of each area and the interaction among the various functions. Of course, the leader will probably not have thorough knowledge of every human resources area, but the rest of the user community can provide this perspective.

In some cases, human resources staff may lack a full appreciation of IS concepts and the limitations of automation. They tend to be people oriented rather than systems oriented. In spite of this, assigning project ownership to the human resources department usually works best, as this department is the

---

Tips for Practical Project Management

- Distribute tasks of appropriate size and scope, then check that subordinates complete their tasks.
- Assign individual, rather than joint, responsibility for tasks; no more than two persons should share responsibility.
- Maintain consistent priorities; make sure everyone is properly notified if priorities change.
- Start every task as soon as possible; many will take longer than planned and require additional staff.
- Develop a procedure for requesting and authorizing project changes; make all participants aware of this procedure.
- Make only those promises that you can keep; where possible, qualify every promise and state assumptions.
- Use charts, diagrams, and graphs whenever possible; a picture *is* worth a thousand words.

---

driving force behind the development of the HRMS and is definitely the owner of the system. Before taking on a system development project, human resources staff must recognize the critical nature of issues inherent in areas such as project management, data processing, and system development.

Sometimes management considers assigning project ownership to the IS function because of the IS staff's technical orientation and experience in project management and system implementation. IS may, however, fail to consider significant human resources needs and practices. Their technical orientation also may impair the enthusiasm with which human resources users greet the new system. In addition, if there are any underlying antagonism between payroll and human resources, primary project ownership by the payroll function may create tension that will limit the project's success.

Team Members and Communication

Having received authorization from management to explore HRMS development, human resources assembles the project team and appoints a leader if it has not already done so. The leader should make sure that each team member receives a project assignment appropriate to his or her background, skills, and experience. When technically difficult challenges arise, the people with the most relevant experience and problem-solving skills should address these issues. If some individuals shy away from sticky situations, the team leader

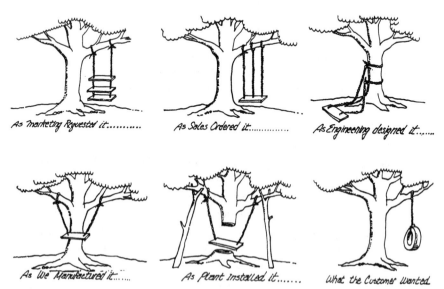

As *Marketing Requested* it..........   As *Sales Ordered* it..............   As *Engineering designed* it.......

As *We Manufactured* it.......   As *Plant Installed* it.......   *What the Customer Wanted*

Figure 2–2. What happens to projects without good communication.

should help them understand that they may consult with other team members or outside resources as needed to compensate for limitations in skills, experience, or availability.

The scope of the proposed HRMS plays a key role in determining the size of the project team. If the project is relatively small, the project team may have only one full-time member, with others handling specific tasks as required. Even the most active team member may have ongoing responsibilities for other existing human resources work. If a small firm can afford only one person for project development, this person must have functional knowledge and also be computer literate.

For larger projects, team members may include representatives from key human resources functions, finance, and IS, as well as HRMS consultants. The level of technical sophistication necessary depends on the project's scope and complexity. The project team should include people who understand both the primary business of the organization, such as manufacturing, banking, or retailing, and the functions of human resources, such as employment, compensation, benefits, and training.

If the project team is small, the entire team should meet regularly and frequently. For larger teams, a smaller, representative steering committee should be formed to support the team. The committee's job is to coordinate all elements of the project and keep the project running smoothly. Many policy issues relating to data ownership, access, reporting responsibilities, and timing will arise naturally as diverse yet overlapping human resources functions begin to share the project. The steering committee should address and resolve any and all policy issues as they arise. In addition to informing all interested parties of the project's status, the steering committee bonds the various user groups to the HRMS.

A large project may have a general project executive who handles high-level management interactions and strategic planning; a project manager who takes care of daily management tasks; and, reporting to the manager, two or more team leaders in charge of functional issues and technical issues. The project executive and project manager should participate in regularly scheduled steering committee meetings.

Team Building

The HRMS project team should start out fairly small. In this way, at least a few people can get an overview of the project before becoming too specialized. This broad view is valuable later when the team and the project grow larger and more complex.

The entire human resources department should know of the existence of the project team and its members. Everyone in the organization, not just the project team, should know who is in charge of the project. Team responsibilities should be included in each team member's job assignment rather than having them added to the member's daily routine without any adjustment of other responsibilities.

To carry out the planning phase appropriately, the team should establish a schedule, budget, and technical standards for the work involved. Regularly scheduled meetings, planned far enough in advance that members can easily avoid schedule conflicts, should be held. The project team leader or a facilitator should prepare an agenda in advance and distribute it several days before the meeting so members can come prepared.

The project leader should facilitate meetings so that everyone has an opportunity to present his or her point of view. Conflicts inevitably will arise within the team (between the team and management or peers in other departments) and between users and technical specialists. The team should discuss conflict resolution and intervention procedures before problems arise so that members are prepared to handle conflicts promptly and constructively. When conflicts do occur, the project leader should help those involved identify the underlying issues, keep all disagreements on a professional level, and emphasize the common values and goals of all participants.

Most important, the project team leader should acknowledge the progress and contributions of each participant. When schedules get tight and everyone is feeling pressured, many managers focus only on problem areas. The leader can help the team to feel as positive as possible by providing positive reinforcement to individual team members and to the team as a whole.

Management Steering Committee

Depending on the scope of the HRMS project, the team may find a management-level steering committee useful. Committee members are not strictly human resources or IS managers but central decision makers in the organization. They should include or represent top management, finance, strategic planning, and line functions of the organization. This committee should meet periodically to resolve high-level policy issues, review the feasibility of the proposed HRMS, and monitor project progress. Monthly meetings often work well. During implementation, the steering committee should continue to meet, though less frequently, to resolve problems that may arise. Often this committee meets jointly with the HRMS project team. Having several members of management involved in the HRMS project often is an advantage in obtaining authorization to proceed with acquisition and implementation.

Planning and Design Issues

The three major HRMS development phases—planning, design, and implementation—address basically the same issues: obtaining quality information;

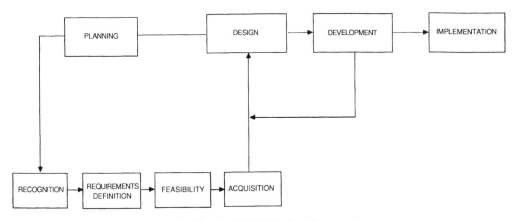

Figure 2–3. Typical HRMS development process.

high system functionality; sufficient input, processing, and output capability; and user appropriateness.

The project team explores these issues many times during the course of the project. During the planning phase, the project team develops overall system requirements and strategies. During design, the team considers each issue in greater detail, constructing more finely honed schemes for maximizing performance within acknowledged limits. During implementation, the team must resolve any unanswered questions.

At every phase, the project team should use quantitative measures to address the issues whenever possible. Such measures allow both management and the project team to make valid comparisons of various alternatives, as well as of the planned system and the implemented system. The project team should try to assign quantifiable values to attributes such as timely, accurate, flexible, and reliable. For instance, instead of "timely reports," the definition could be "produce all standard reports according to an established schedule and all ad hoc reports within 1 to 2 hours of request." Instead of "reliable," the definition could be "has no more than 4 hours of downtime per month during regular business hours."

Criteria for Quality Information

The success of the HRMS as an information-gathering tool depends on having an effective requirements analysis and continuing communication with human resources information users at all levels of the organization throughout the planning and design processes, as well as during implementation and maintenance. The planning and design process succeeds only if developers maximize the quality of data incorporated into and created by the system being designed. An HRMS succeeds not just by providing vast amounts of data from a rather large data base, but also by providing the right data in the right form to the right audience at the right time.

Differences between Data and Information. Data and information are not the same. "Data" refers to a collection of facts, figures, numbers, or other symbols not organized or presented in any meaningful format. "Information" results when data are formatted, structured, sequenced, and made ready for interpretation and analysis. This interpretation forms the basis for conclusions about the meaning of the data in relation to the goals and objectives of the organization. Data become quality information when the content is reliable, timely, comprehensive, readable, and relevant to the audience.

Reliable Information. Reliable information tells management and users what they need to know in a consistent way. This develops trust and confidence in the HRMS. What really constitutes reliable information? Many people would argue that information can be reliable only if every piece of data is accurate. In fact, reliability depends on the nature of the information, the type of report in which it appears, company standards, and user expectations.

For example, human resources staff may reasonably consider a detailed list of annual salary increases and performance ratings unreliable if it contains an unacceptable amount of inaccurate information. Users concerned with detail may have a very low error tolerance level.

Tolerance of errors depends on the nature of the inaccuracy. Users can accept, within reason, inaccuracies due to operator error or omissions, especially when they are correctable. However, no operation should tolerate inaccuracies due to faulty or missing edit and validity checks in the HRMS. This type of inaccuracy can discredit not only the information but also the entire system because it indicates bad planning.

Human resources staff may need to accept a higher tolerance for errors in information presented in summary fashion. Users interested in summary-level information should not be overly concerned with inaccuracies in the specific data that form the basis for the information—unless data inaccuracy is widespread. A few inaccurate pieces of data have an insignificant impact on a summary. A data base that is missing ten employee records will not significantly change a yearly head count trend line for a high-growth company having 1000 employees.

From the point of view of computer systems, the definition of information reliability depends on the application and the expectations of the users. In this regard, HRMS staff should manage user expectations, as this will determine their standards for information reliability.

Timely Information. Timeliness means that users have information when they need it. This attribute depends on how and when individuals plan to use the information. In extreme cases, even a one-hour delay in delivery may render information useless. In some cases, timeliness has less leeway than reliability.

To facilitate timeliness, a system should contain only the data and routines that users are most likely to need, thus reducing the need for custom operations to obtain information. To achieve these results, the project team must question users about their needs and develop efficient report creation, tracking, and retrieval procedures. These techniques are discussed in more detail in chapter 3.

Comprehensive Information. Comprehensive information can provide more complete answers to users' immediate questions. To achieve this quality, the project team must examine both input and output requirements. What information do users need and in what form? Evaluating the comprehensiveness of a detail report is relatively easy, as the criteria are simply the extent to which the report includes all data on all relevant employees. In contrast, evaluation of the comprehensiveness of a summary report may involve interviewing the management staff who use these reports. Could they make management decisions based on the information included? Did the reports include all relevant categories of data? Did managers need to take additional steps that the system could have performed more efficiently?

Readable Information. Quality information allows users to see its key message or messages quickly and then draw appropriate conclusions. It presents the information in a visually pleasing way that allows users to focus on the message, not the medium.

Significant and Relevant Information. Users often fail to make maximum use of an HRMS if they do not find the information they need either displayed on a screen or via reports. Users may receive information for which they have no use, or they may fail to receive information for which they have a legitimate need. To attain quality information, HRMS staff must perform an initial requirements analysis, keep up on changing information requirements, and audit human resources information practices on a regular basis.

Perhaps the greatest obstacle to making information significant and relevant is that users do not know how to ask the right questions. Of course, the human resources systems center (HRSC) manager should take responsibility for this connection. The manager must understand the business, the human resources department, and the technical environment within which the HRMS operates. Based on this knowledge, the manager should make suggestions and recommendations regarding the collection of data and the use of information. Successful managers often help human resources and business managers develop appropriate choices about information needs by offering helpful hints based on what other organizations are doing and by generating reports that anticipate user questions.

Functionality

Modularity. In computer terms, *modularity* refers to a building block approach to system creation, having a separate module for each human resources application instead of establishing a system in one large piece. Ideally, an organization implements an HRMS in bite-size chunks, or modules, to achieve an effective system within an acceptable time frame. Whether a project team follows this approach or not, the members must carefully examine the needs for interdependence and independence among the affected human resources functions. Normally, human resources data are functionally interdependent. Some data are specific to one function, but most basic data will be required by all functions. In addition, though some functions may need more specialized data, even these data could overlap several functions. In some cases, however, the needs and priorities of each functional area of human resources may dictate an approach whereby each function is looked at separately.

A well-planned HRMS data base can satisfy the major information requirements in all functional areas, even those outside the original implementation scheme. As future projects add data to support new functions, existing functions will benefit. A modular approach provides the systems designer with greater control and flexibility. After installation, human resources can change the system more quickly and with less chance of damage. Planners should try to avoid situations in which operations people must shut down the system to make one change.

To avoid premature obsolescence, the system must be able to adapt to changes in business conditions, government regulations, and management policy with minimal disruption. A good system can retrieve ad hoc and varied information and should contain built-in analytical routines for calculations and summations.

Utility Functions. The requirements definition should identify the system's ancillary support capabilities, including graphics, word processing, telecommunications, and other decision support functions. During the design process, such needs can be integrated into the main HRMS capabilities, often by adding compatible auxiliary programs to the main HRMS package.

Integration and Interfacing. The team should consider interfacing existing equipment and programs with the new system. Even if the department has no existing human resources software, programs for payroll, labor cost management, office automation, or other operations may be used. Organizations using

A CHECKLIST FOR PLANNING A
HUMAN RESOURCE MANAGEMENT SYSTEM

Organization Name (Division/Region Name)	Industry (SIC Code)
Address	Locations to be Covered
City/State/Zip	
Primary Contact/Title/Telephone	

Total Number of Staff _____

Salaried–Exempt - regular _____
Salaried–Nonexempt - regular _____
Salaried - part time/temporary _____
Other Categories (specify) _____

Hourly - regular _____
Hourly - part time/temporary _____
Unionized _____
Non-unionized _____

CURRENT & PLANNED STATUS - HUMAN RESOURCE APPLICATIONS (Check Appropriate Boxes)

Application	Current Status				Priority			
	Manual	Automated	Comb.	Vendor	Need Now	Need Later	Nice To Have	Not Critical
Employee Recordkeeping								
Applicant Recordkeeping								
Terminee Recordkeeping								
Wage & Salary Administration								
Benefits Administration								
Flexible Benefits								
ERISA Reporting								
EEO/Affirmative Action								
HR Planning/Forecasting								
Skills Inventory/Career Planning								
Performance Appraisals								
Labor Cost Distribution								
Job Requisitions/Job Posting								
Attendance/Timekeeping								
Retirement Benefit Administration								
Succession Planning								
Training								
Payroll								
Labor/Industrial Relations								

Figure 2–4. Checklist for planning an HRMS. Many organizations manually handle numerous activities that a computer system could deal with much more easily. As part of the needs analysis process, the HRMS project team may ask users to complete a form similar to this one. No one person has all the information required for the needs assessment. Moreover, individuals often have differing views on what the system needs depending on their experience and role.

WHICH FUNCTION IS MORE IMPORTANT

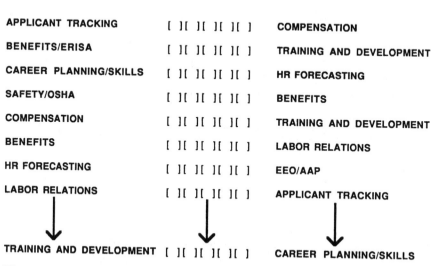

Figure 2–5. **Human resources functional rankings questionnaire. Some HRMS project teams distribute this type of questionnaire to help determine which human resources functions to include in the HRMS. Each respondent indicates the relative importance of each horizontal pair of functions. For example, by checking the first column on the first line, users indicate that applicant tracking is much more important to them than compensation. Checking the third column indicates that the two identified functions have equal importance. Checking box 4 indicates that the right-hand choice is somewhat more important than the one on the left.**
(Source: Copyright © 1990. Wyvern Research Associates, Inc. All rights reserved.)

external service bureaus for payroll must consider how the external and internal systems will interconnect.

Input and Processing Capability

Speed. Just because a system can hold a large volume of records does not mean that it can process changes to all those records speedily. Some human resources operations demand systems that are capable of a quick turnaround between data entry and finished report. After consulting with users, the project team, possibly with technical help, can estimate the number of records the system must handle within a particular processing cycle. For instance, payroll has specific timing requirements; in most organizations, each employee's earnings and deductions must be entered, calculated, recorded, and generated within a few days. Most organizations have other standard or periodic reports with short turnaround times and tight production schedules.

Efficiency. This term refers to the internal organization and handling of data to maximize speed and capabilities. The system should allow programmers to designate certain calculated fields, which are based on other fields into which users enter data. For example, entering the transaction effective date of a salary change should automatically trigger calculations of changes in months since last salary change and projected date of next scheduled review.

This efficiency should extend to alphanumeric fields. For instance, the internal routines of the system should automatically build a chronological stack of employment history when key data elements in the employee's work status change. Whenever a change takes place in salary, job, or organization code, the old system transfers the old status to a stack maintained in descending order of effective date. This keeps such transactions protected from loss. Other general features that demonstrate internal efficiency include accumulators for year-to-date totals, pending transactions that remain in suspense until the system interrogates the internal clock, and automatic triggers that generate lists of eligibility or actionable items when a critical date approaches.

Information Retrieval. An HRMS requires a high level of retrievability. Users must be able to retrieve grouped data, such as a list of all employees in the marketing department, or to find the average length of service of department managers. The system also should facilitate retrieval of an individual employee's record for a single element of data or to review the entire record as a profile.

One example of a technique that maximizes retrievability is an accumulator procedure. With this feature, the system automatically maintains and updates a separate file of totals from every occurrence of a particular data field in all designated records. For instance, an accumulator file may track federal income tax withholdings for all employees, which provide the basis for calculating gross-to-net pay and payroll tax payments.

Data Integrity. A good system includes several types of procedures that maximize the accuracy of the data it contains. Most data errors occur in the data entry process through miscoding or operator carelessness. Edit and validation processes limit the types of data accepted in a particular field. For instance, a date field may accept only numeric data; the month portion of that field may accept only the numbers 01 through 12. Clear, descriptive on-screen error messages also help users identify, avoid, and correct problems. Because the potential for human error is high, the system must be easy to use and include reliable field and record validation, such as verification of valid job codes.

Data Base Size and Format. As part of determining internal requirements, the project team must estimate the amount of data the system needs to accommodate. Most HRMS projects concentrate on the information needs of the main human resources users. System design usually focuses on the basic employee, job, and work history portions of the master file. It also should eventually include the data needed to record compensation, skills, training, career planning, benefits, payroll, and other areas of a comprehensive system. To estimate data base size, the project team makes a preliminary estimate of the number of records, types of data fields, number of fields per record, lengths and types of fields, sources of data, and supporting codes and tables involved. The data base may include records on all current employees as well as information on applicants, terminated employees, retirees, those on leave or furlough, and other former employees and their dependents. Such calculations must consider record retention requirements. This information is discussed more thoroughly in chapter 3.

Several different estimates may emerge, each of which reflects the participation and data needs of different human resources functions. For instance, a system that tracks only basic employee, job, and organization data generates a smaller data base than one that also supports human resources training, employee relations, planning and forecasting, and safety. Since most functions have overlapping data requirements, however, these estimates are not necessarily additive. The project team should consider the potential efficiencies of combining data bases of several human resources functions.

Output Capabilities

Printing and Report Design. The project team should assess users' reporting needs, including reports to management, human resources staff, employees, and government agencies. For example, exchanges of data sometimes occur between the payroll and general ledger systems or between sales and incentive compensation. This process begins with a list of current and future reporting needs, then lists each data element needed in each report.

Security. The human resources department often tracks applicant and employee information that requires restricted access for legal, ethical, or business reasons. For instance, specific legal restrictions apply to dissemination of information such as ethnicity, handicap, religious beliefs, criminal record, and medical history. Most companies want to have tight control of compensation information, particularly in situations involving discretionary salaries and highly paid executives. The requirements definition process helps identify which data require special security, as well as the circumstances under which human resources staff must have access to those data.

Distribution Needs. The team should address the form in which users need to exchange information. Options may include electronic mail, batch data exchange with external service bureaus, use of external data bases, distributed or off-line printing at multiple locations, and other telecommunications options.

User Appropriateness

User Sophistication. The project team must consider the human resources community's familiarity with computers. Human resources staff who have not worked with computer systems on an ongoing basis have quite different requirements from those who have a fair amount of computer literacy. Beginning users must have basic training in computer use, clear documentation, self-explanatory screens, and other computer-user interfaces. A rapidly growing company should expect that a fair number of human resources staff will start as computer novices. If intended users include staff with significant computer experience, human resources may benefit from selecting a system that allows those users to apply their expertise and work independently. Such users will value features such as report generators and screen handlers that allow operational flexibility and full system utilization.

Coding. Ultimately a system can work only as well as users can interpret the data it provides, a quality known as accessibility or readability. Many systems use coding structures for information, such as 1 = day shift, 2 = swing shift, and 3 = night shift. Although codes save space on a form or screen, they may impede a user's ability to read an employee's record. New systems tend to be more accessible than their predecessors. They may use coding, but most have logical, mnemonic codes that are much easier to interpret. In the preceding example, designers may substitute the codes D, S, and N for 1, 2, and 3. Other features of readability include menus, submenus, navigation paths, on-line help, and forced-choice data selection. Most of these are discussed in greater detail in chapter 3.

Documentation. Any system or subsystem should include complete, well-written documentation about every term, function, operation, and error message. This includes not only commercial software but custom applications and interfaces as well. Human resources may need several types of documentation—one for users, one for technical staff, one for operations, and so on. Many modern systems also offer a substantial amount of documentation on-line and available for display on demand.

Creating the Requirements Definition

No matter what kind of HRMS an organization considers, users, planners, and managers need a common starting point. To find answers to the question "What should the system do?" some organizations use a needs analysis and others a requirements definition. People often use these terms interchangeably, but they have distinct meanings. A *needs analysis* looks at the users' current needs for data and reports. A *requirements definition* provides a more comprehensive background for project planning, including both present and future needs. It differentiates more clearly between required features and desired features. A requirements definition is more likely to detail attributes and operations, such as specifying the differences between applicant flow and applicant tracking and those between recruitment analysis and internal placement. This phase emphasizes system objectives rather than how the system will meet those objectives.

Techniques for Requirements Definitions

Approaches to creating requirements definitions vary widely. To gather enough of the right kind of information, most successful project teams use more than one information-gathering and evaluation tool. Common approaches include evaluating the current HRMS, evaluating someone else's system, conducting user interviews and surveys, performing business system analysis, developing scenarios, and prototyping. Designers can determine what a system should do by making sure that it meets end users' needs.

Evaluating Current Systems. Many organizations have some type of computer-based system (or several systems) to support human resources applications. These systems may store skeleton records added to an earlier payroll system, or each application may use a stand-alone microcomputer. Some systems can make the task of maintaining personnel records more difficult because they maintain and report data inefficiently or in a nonstandard form. At the other extreme, an existing system may be a technical masterpiece that uses all the latest technology but fails to meet the needs of the human resources community. The requirements analysis should include an audit of the current human resources system. Because periodic audits are an important part of ongoing system maintenance, the audit process is described in more detail in chapter 10.

An operational audit of human resources and business practices can uncover the warning signals that the department needs an automated HRMS. These signals may include:

- Heavy reliance on indispensable individuals for information
- Heavy reliance on outside computer service bureaus
- Complex, costly manual processes
- Inadequate current information support to human resources and other functions
- Heavy reliance on spreadsheet applications
- Proliferation of unauthorized user-developed systems
- A technically or functionally obsolete HRMS

Sometimes significant modifications to an existing system can correct such shortcomings, but other times the problems are so ingrained that the only efficient solution is a new HRMS.

Evaluating Another HRMS. Occasionally a firm may have access to another organization's HRMS for evaluation purposes. This often occurs with nonprofit groups, government entities, and semiautonomous subsidiaries of a conglomerate. This analysis may resemble the analysis of a firm's own existing system. To the extent feasible, this analysis should involve systems that resemble the alternatives under consideration.

User Interviews and Surveys. The project team should interview or survey users about their needs. Topics should include the normal work flow of each function: data collected, used, and maintained; reports generated, used, and received; and time and processing cycle requirements. The team also should inquire about user experience with computer systems. Helpful hints may emerge from this experience.

Business Systems Analysis. The organization's decision makers always need information from the HRMS, so their input is vital in developing an accurate and complete requirements definition. The project team should ask management to identify the most important human resources information needs in terms of the organization as a whole. Because this interview process may raise managers' expectations about the entire HRMS project, project team members should be well organized and prepared. Above all, they must learn to manage management's expectations.

Business strategists have developed numerous methodologies for determining organizational needs. Detailing such management approaches is beyond the scope of this book. An HRMS project team should examine

Achieving Consensus on HRMS Requirements

The following material is excerpted from an exercise given to human resources staff whose department was planning a new applicant and employment tracking system. This exercise illustrates the importance and difficulty of achieving consensus on HRMS requirements.

Attached is a list of HRMS requirements in the applicant and employee tracking function. For each stated requirement, allocate one of the following weights:

1. Must have in the initial system (critical need)
2. Must have but can wait a year after implementation
3. Nice to have but not critical to current operations
4. Do not need

The system/module allows for recruiter/interviewer input on quality of résumé, cover letter, or application.

——— The system captures "position applied for" data.

——— The system tracks efforts of recruiters and interviewers.

——— The system maintains data on applicant's previous work experience.

——— The system provides a "skills bank" for active applicants.

——— The system generates candidate lists for common positions.

——— The system offers an applicant status profile via on-line query.

——— The system provides analysis/tracking of agency effectiveness.

——— The system automatically creates a new-hire record.

——— The system provides for automatic purging of applicant data.

——— The system keeps an inventory of open requisitions.

The Critical Success Factor Approach to Executive HRMS Planning

Many business professionals use the Critical Success Factor (CSF) approach to help define information requirements at senior management levels. This approach focuses on strategic management issues. As applied to HRMS planning, it has three basic steps:

1. Learn more about the business by reviewing strategic short-term and long-term plans established by management.
2. Interview key managers and executives to determine their business plans, goals, and means of success.
3. Translate the business plans, goals, and critical success factors into human resources and HRMS measurements to facilitate definition of system requirements.

The CSF approach offers many advantages in defining HRMS requirements:

- The team obtains results with minimal interaction with hard-to-reach top management staff.
- The team can develop true business requirements, since its efforts focus on the strategic and tactical planning for the organization.
- Top management has a framework through which to specify the information requirements that will help the organization achieve its goals.
- The human resources system center (HRSC) learns more about how the business functions at higher management levels.

Examples of CSFs for a human resources department include the following:

- Attract and retain quality employees
- Good reputation in employment markets
- High employee morale
- Employees free to act and innovate
- Line managers with effective personnel skills
- Cost-effective human resources programs

Scenario Analysis

Scenario analysis works well in developing requirements definitions for certain applications, such as EEO. The following scenario rephrases an actual case of an organization's dealings with a specific EEO issue:

> The U.S. Supreme Court found that an employer violated equal pay provisions of the Fair Labor Standards Act by paying male night-shift inspectors more than female day-shift inspectors. The employer did not cure its violation either by permitting women to work as night-shift inspectors or by equalizing day-shift and night-shift inspector wage rate.

How could an HRMS help track this situation? How could it help alleviate the situation? What data must the HRMS contain for the organization to work effectively and efficiently to resolve these issues?

(Source: Labor Relations Reporter, Vol. 86, No. 9, The Bureau of National Affairs, Inc., June 1, 1974. Reprinted with permission.)

alternatives before interviewing the chief executive officer (CEO) and other high-ranking executives. The sidebar titled "The Critical Success Factor Approach to Executive HRMS Planning" briefly describes one approach that aids in obtaining management's input on HRMS priorities.

Scenario Analysis. The interview approach can include scenarios to help the team come up with a set of requirements. A scenario is merely a simulation of a potential real-world issue acted out by potential end users. The sidebar titled "Scenario Analysis" presents a real-world situation that one company used to help users identify criteria for an EEO/affirmative action (EEO/AA) module.

Prototyping. Sometimes, an organization with an existing HRMS and a fairly experienced HRMS staff may use a prototype approach to defining system needs. In this approach, the team builds a working model through several iterations of user definitions and system functions. The organization may either buy a simple system and adapt it or build a system from scratch, starting with a general structure and expanding its functions over the course of several months. The prototype allows users to react to a system, change what they do not like, and add missing features. Prototyping has special advantages in complex environments, particularly those mixing mainframes, midrange computers, and microcomputers. For instance, one human resources department may use prototyping to try human resources applications on new equipment being purchased for non-human resources applications. Another may prototype new software applications on existing systems or microcomputers before committing to buying expensive new equipment. The prototyping concept is described further in chapter 10.

Support for the Requirements Definition

When the project team has determined the organization's HRMS requirements, it should seek a sign-off from the user community. The team should present a written report of its process, findings, and recommendations. All project team members should receive a copy, as should human resources management, heads of each human resources function, IS management, and other management decision makers. Every organization will have its own report structure, but a typical outline might include the following headings:

- Overview of the HRMS project
- Requirements definition methodology
- Analysis of current system
- Definition of user needs
- Recommended technical solutions
- Findings and recommendations
- Supporting documentation

The project team then holds progress review meetings to present and discuss the requirements definition. Attendees may include the entire project team, human resources management, IS development staff, representatives from other affected departments, central corporate management, external consultants, and representative users. Ideally, the project team should issue a preliminary report, solicit feedback via one or more meetings with interested parties, then issue a final report. Based on this work, the project team finalizes HRMS criteria and optimum approaches, then begins the more detailed feasibility analysis.

Performing the Feasibility Analysis

Having described the ideal system, the project team's next step is to determine the extent to which the organization needs a new system and at what cost. This feasibility analysis may develop and consider several different alternatives, such as keeping the existing system, buying a low-end inflexible system, or buying an expensive but expandable system. The analysis includes technical, administrative, and economic evaluations of each option.

The chapters on design, software, hardware, and implementation discuss many of the issues that arise during the feasibility analysis. These range from the relative costs of various hardware configurations to the pros and cons of in-house development versus purchase of a commercial system. To accumulate information about the alternatives, team members often work with prospective hardware and software vendors, HRMS consultants, in-house IS staff, and others skilled in project management. This effort may involve technically experienced people in the development of time schedules and resource allocation estimates. The feasibility analysis should consider factors outside the human resources department that might affect the project. These may include organizational budgeting cycles, pending reorganization or management changes, regulatory or tax changes, and expected changes in organizational strategy or direction. Having gathered and analyzed all the relevant information, the team can prepare a feasibility report for review by key decision makers.

Only rarely can an organization afford to bypass a feasibility analysis entirely or take only a cursory approach to this step. Skipping a formal feasibility analysis usually works only if the firm is relatively small and has significant computer expertise and if the head of the organization is actively involved with and supportive of the HRMS project.

Technical Evaluation

The technical evaluation considers the functional and technological aspects of the system. It begins with a review of the existing system and vendor market to determine the extent to which current and commercial software can fulfill defined requirements. It evaluates the ease of performing internal or external adaptation of such software to meet the organization's additional requirements. It addresses conflicts between standard software and the organization's culture. On the basis of the technical analysis, the project team usually determines specific technological approaches to meeting the requirements. Depending on the circumstances, these choices may include manual versus automated approaches, separate versus integrated or interfaced systems, making or buying a system, and the products of several different HRMS vendors.

In a feasibility analysis report, the project team presents the technical strengths and weaknesses of each approach. Sometimes the report summarizes this information in chart form. It addresses the extent to which each alternative meets the technical criteria identified in the requirements definition. The technical portion of the feasibility report may describe the techniques that each alternative uses to achieve those objectives.

If retaining the existing system is one alternative under consideration, the feasibility study usually includes a discussion of possible improvements to that system. The project team may determine what steps might improve system performance and capabilities, such as performance optimization, streamlining reports, and changing the data base structure, tables, screens, and so forth.

Although the technical aspects of the feasibility study require the efforts of those project team members with the most computer expertise, human resources staff who want to become familiar with the HRMS will benefit greatly by participating in this process.

Administrative Evaluation

The administrative analysis investigates the impact of the corporate climate, the organizational structure, management support, business cycles, competing priorities, and resource availability on staffing, training, scheduling, and other procedural aspects of the project.

Staffing. The project team should estimate the number, qualifications, and availability of staff needed for development and implementation of each HRMS alternative. The team should include staffing needs for the human resources information center (HRIC) and for the human resources functions affected by the HRMS. Members may address the possible roles of each participant, including consultants, IC staff, and human resources staff, during all project phases. The economic evaluation can then derive direct and indirect labor costs from these estimates of staffing requirements.

The study must address whether the organization has qualified people available to undertake the tasks. Although this question applies to the acquisition of a vendor-developed system, it has particular importance for alternatives that propose in-house development or adaptation. In some circumstances, the study will list key individuals expected to play significant roles in these phases and describe their qualifications. This portion of the study may address the opportunity costs of having staff devote their time to the HRMS project. Management and others should understand what work these people may forgo to participate in the HRMS project.

Training. The feasibility study should identify the training requirements of each system option. It should list the types of training, persons requiring training, and days of training required. It should compare possible sources of training, such as vendor contract, internal staff training, and computer-based training. These figures form the basis for estimating training costs during the economic analysis.

Vendors. The HRMS project team also should ascertain the availability of qualified vendors and obtain vendors' expressions of interest in the project. The major routes for locating vendors, along with information on vendor evaluation criteria and the selection process, are described in chapter 6.

Schedule. Realistic timetables are critical to the success of any project. Timetables can help the organization monitor progress, provide incentives to stay on target, and give early warning signals of impending problems. T' - project team must establish and acknowledge priorities not only for the project itself but also for all the resources that may be involved, particularly in-house staff. Once the project team allocates available resources on a priority basis, it can develop an HRMS implementation schedule. It is important to leave enough time in the schedule to allow for inevitable delays and changes in priorities.

The feasibility report should include a schedule for each alternative. The team may use Gantt charts, project evaluation and review technique (PERT) or critical path method (CPM) diagrams, or other scheduling techniques. The schedule should list work periods and deadlines for system design, vendor selection, installation, training, conversion, testing, and other points in the HRMS development and implementation process.

Planners must consider the extent to which speed of implementation is a priority. A quick, successful implementation allows users to begin experiencing the benefits of the new system sooner, but the rush to meet an unnecessary or unrealistic deadline can cause design compromise and user frustration. Such setbacks can lead to a less than successful HRMS.

Economic Evaluation

Organizations generally cannot justify upgrading to the next generation of HRMS software solely on technical grounds. Many HRMS projects live or die by the project team's ability to demonstrate an adequate return on investment. The economic evaluation portion of the feasibility study provides a cost-benefit-value analysis for the various options under consideration. This economic evaluation usually has two steps. In the first step, the team establishes the costs, benefits, and values of the existing system. As mentioned earlier, the HRMS requirements analysis or the feasibility study should include an evaluation or audit of the existing HRMS, even if retaining the system is not an initially attractive alternative. Second, the team measures the costs, benefits, and values of the proposed system against those of the existing system.

The project team may want to develop a cost-benefit worksheet or checklist for each alternative. It could establish assumptions, such as unit cost, unit value, or costing period, for each line item. Team members working on estimates for different alternatives (including the current system) can use this worksheet to confirm that everyone is using the same line items, units, inflation factors, and other variables.

The project team should agree on the expected life cycle of the current and potential HRMS. Unfortunately, the fast pace of evolution in technology, microcomputers, government regulations, and personnel management policies and practices makes the life of an HRMS all too brief. If different options have different life-cycle projections, calculations for those having shorter life cycles must include costs and benefits to the end of the life cycle of the longer-lived options. The study should include estimates of inflation, salary and wage increases, and other changes in costs over the life cycles of the systems.

Costs. Costs fall into three categories:

- Acquisition and development costs, including hardware, software, salaries for the project team, and consultant fees
- Implementation costs, including conversion, training, staff salaries, and design and printing of forms
- Operating costs, including ongoing staff salaries, training, outside services, forms, maintenance, and upgrades

The study should include the terms of any purchase or lease agreements involved in acquisition and implementation. As appropriate, it may divide equipment and software categories into items owned, leased, and made available by a service bureau or time-share arrangement.

In labor calculations, the study should include total person-hours (or days) used in each job classification, especially where salary or wage rates differ significantly. If the project will require overtime, the team can either price it separately at the appropriate rates or convert it to equivalent straight-time hours, then price it according to standard hours and standard rates.

An in-house project normally requires more staffing than a purchased system. Such a project has an economic advantage only if staff costs fall significantly below those of the HRMS vendor. Often internal staff rates do not differ substantially from those of the vendor except for the vendor's profit margin. For example, the in-house cost of programmers and analysts may be $50 and $75 per hour, respectively (including all overhead), while the vendor's rates are $75 and $100. Because the vendor has more experience and training, the vendor's staff can probably complete the project in less time. Comparing an in-house charge of $50 per hour for 1,000 hours with a vendor's charge of $75 per hour for 750 hours yields similar costs. But the vendor often works faster, and so, all other things being equal, achieves the same or a superior result sooner.

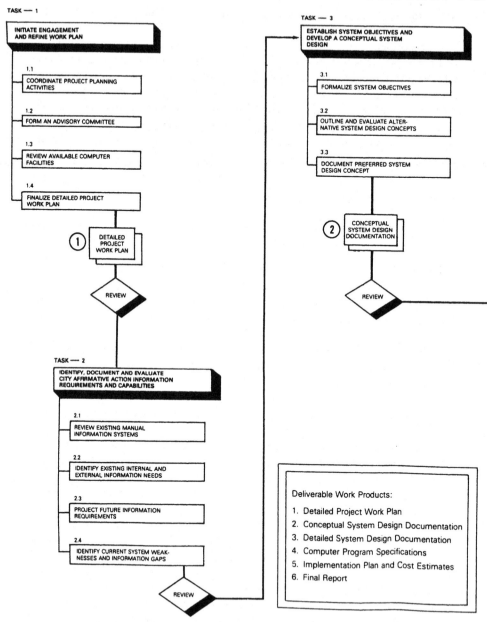

Figure 2-6. Project plan and schedule for an in-house system. Most tasks are the same as for a purchased system, but in-house development requires more attention to specifications and to implementation plans. Each box represents a distinct activity during project planning, design, or development.
(Source: Arthur Andersen & Company. Reprinted with permission.)

ND SCHEDULE

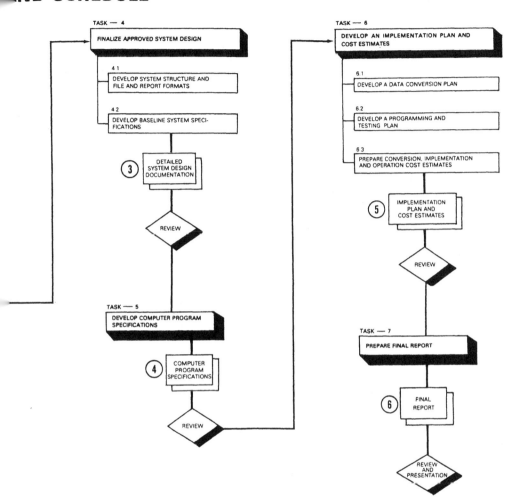

TASK — 4

FINALIZE APPROVED SYSTEM DESIGN

4 1
DEVELOP SYSTEM STRUCTURE AND
FILE AND REPORT FORMATS

4 2
DEVELOP BASELINE SYSTEM SPECI-
FICATIONS

(3) DETAILED
SYSTEM DESIGN
DOCUMENTATION

REVIEW

TASK — 5

**DEVELOP COMPUTER PROGRAM
SPECIFICATIONS**

(4) COMPUTER
PROGRAM
SPECIFICATIONS

REVIEW

TASK — 6

**DEVELOP AN IMPLEMENTATION PLAN AND
COST ESTIMATES**

6.1
DEVELOP A DATA CONVERSION PLAN

6.2
DEVELOP A PROGRAMMING AND
TESTING PLAN

6 3
PREPARE CONVERSION, IMPLEMENTATION
AND OPERATION COST ESTIMATES

(5) IMPLEMENTATION
PLAN AND
COST ESTIMATES

REVIEW

TASK — 7

PREPARE FINAL REPORT

(6) FINAL
REPORT

REVIEW
AND
PRESENTATION

PRELIMINARY PROJECT PLAN — WEEK OF	1 Feb 5	2 Feb 12	3 Feb 19	4 Feb 26	5 Mar 5	6 Mar 12	7 Mar 19	8 Mar 26	9 Apr 2	10 Apr 9	11 Apr 16	12 Apr 23	13 Apr 30	14 May 7	15 May 14	16 May 21	17 May 28	18 Jun 4	19 Jun 11	20 Jun 18	21 Jun 25	22 Jul 2	23 Jul 9	24 Jul 16	25 Jul 23	26 Jul 30
Project Initiation	X																									
Interviews/Data Gathering		X	X	X																						
Policy & Procedure Review			X	X	X																					
Technical Review				X	X	X	X	X	X																	
Database Design									X	X	X	X	X													
Cost/Benefit/Value Analysis										X	X	X														
Technical/Functional Alternatives											X	X	X	X												
Vendor Evaluation														X	X	X	X	X	X	X	X					
Request For Proposal																X	X	X	X							
Reference Checking																		X	X	X						
Site Visits																			X	X						
Implementation Planning																				X	X	X	X			
Final Planning Report																							X	X	X	
Management Presentation																								X		X
Progress Review Meetings				X			X				X				X					X				X	X	X

Figure 2–7. **Gantt chart for HRMS project planning and design. This chart is taken from an actual plan. This kind of planning tool helps clarify not only when particular activities take place but also which activities take place simultaneously and which can take place only after the completion of others.**

The study should categorize operating costs and state them in terms of a unit of time—per hour, per day, per month, or per year. The data should be expressed in terms of the total system and also in terms of subsystems, organizational units, or units produced. Units produced, in turn, could show the cost required to produce a report or to process a transaction. To obtain accurate information on operating costs of the existing system, operators should track these costs monthly, using a standard form. The HRMS project team should update this form as new applications are added.

An adequate feasibility study must include maintenance costs, since most of the cost of an HRMS occurs after it becomes operational. Every newly installed HRMS has bugs, which may require a great deal of time and effort to correct. Over time, the HRMS will require updates to remain in compliance with regulatory changes. Moreover, as users become comfortable with the system, they may want it to operate faster or to process new calculations. Too often planners overlook or underestimate maintenance staffing costs, but maintenance and enhancement usually require in-house staff for development

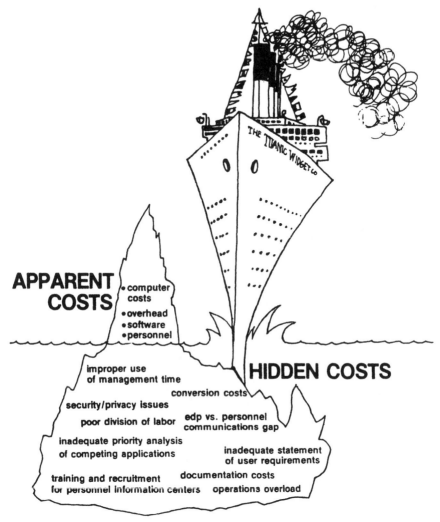

Figure 2–8. Beware of hidden costs. Most project teams can develop a fairly accurate estimate of the apparent costs of developing a new system, but many organizations overlook the hidden costs, which results in conflict and compromise later on. By working with professionals who have had experience with HRMS implementation, the team can recognize and estimate hidden costs.

and additional training. One West Coast bank has more than fifty people involved in HRMS maintenance and enhancement. Although that company has a large system, even a smaller-scale HRMS requires some support.

With purchased HRMS packages, planners can forecast costs and completion dates more accurately. In most cases, however, a new HRMS requires substantial modification. For any project, estimates of costs and schedules may change due to unexpected events. The team must allow for a contingency budget to cover unanticipated costs.

Benefits. Staff can usually pinpoint HRMS costs relatively easily, but ascertaining benefits is more difficult. HRMS benefits fall into three general categories:

- Direct savings, including reductions in staff, facility space, outside services, and consumables (such as paper and ribbons)
- Cost avoidance, including current system inflation, maintenance of unauthorized systems, additional staff, hardware maintenance, and potential lawsuits
- Intangible benefits, including productivity improvements, better information and decision making, greater accuracy, more timely response, higher reliability, and increased flexibility

Intangible benefits, also known as values, have a special role in HRMS evaluation. The value of a new HRMS reflects the extent to which the system can fulfill its objectives. A new HRMS may offer reduced legal and safety risks, increased worker satisfaction, improved community relations, and smoother interactions with government agencies. Some have begun using the term *cost-benefit-value analysis* to acknowledge the special significance of intangible benefits.

The project team should pay particular attention to benefits that reflect objectives originally developed for the HRMS during the requirements analysis. Factors such as system efficiency, accuracy, timeliness, economy, and productivity should be considered. As with costs, the team can use worksheets as guidelines, making sure terms and units are used consistently to describe and quantify benefits. The team can quantify factors such as computer run times, volume of transactions processed, and error rates. A scale (poor, fair, good, excellent) may work well for factors for which numerical quantification seems impractical. In many cases, an HRMS yields considerable benefits that may be difficult to forecast precisely. Neither prospective users nor project team members may be able to quantify some HRMS values. Nonetheless, the cost-benefit-value analysis should include and even emphasize these expected benefits.

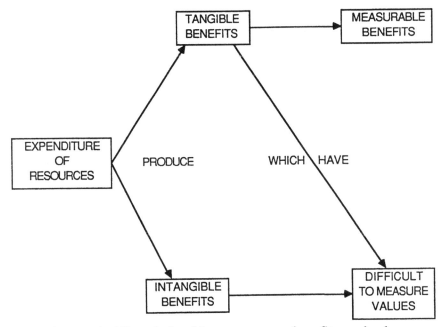

Figure 2–9. The relationship among costs, benefits, and values.

Economic Conclusions. The team may evaluate total costs and benefits for the HRMS under consideration from several different perspectives. Most feasibility studies focus on life-cycle costs. This approach compares the total of all the costs and benefits accrued from inception to a particular point in time for all the alternatives. It avoids penalizing a system that has a high initial cost but will result in greater productivity in the long run.

Some systems are so expensive to operate that their acquisition may have a measurable impact on the company's profit and cash flow. Conversely, their benefits may save the firm from potentially disastrous inefficiencies. In such cases, some teams use a profit-and-loss approach to economic evaluation. They consult with management about the organization's current financial condition. This may involve use of documents such as current and future budgets, capital expenditure plans, and marketing and operating projections.

Getting Support for the HRMS

If management does not perceive the need for a system and is only looking for dollar savings, those interested in HRMS development may have difficulty convincing managers to support the project. Including a cost-benefit analysis of the present system in the feasibility study report often provides powerful evidence of the relative benefits of the proposed system or improvements. The challenge is to make management understand and appreciate the intangible advantages of the proposed HRMS. Management needs to see that the greatest benefits come not through staff reduction (which is rare) but increased decision support and that HRMS benefits accrue not only to human resources but also to the entire organization.

Everyone involved should understand that the feasibility study report provides estimates of time and costs but not guarantees. Most planners tend to underestimate the total time and costs of any in-house HRMS development project. Over a project cycle of 12 to 18 months, unexpected problems such as the following often arise:

- Unexpected employee turnover, particularly on the HRMS project team
- Lack of vital information concerning the project
- Poor communication between IS staff and users
- Project team members do not adequately understand HRMS requirements and computer technology
- Changing management demands; redefinition of goals and priorities
- New security and privacy issues
- New government regulations

Because the people who are contributing to the analysis base their estimates on certain assumptions, those assumptions must be included in the feasibility report. This frees the HRMS project team from appearing to make promises that it may not be able to keep.

Glossary

Administrative evaluation The process of investigating the impact of corporate culture, organizational structure, management support, business cycles, competing priorities, and resource availability on staffing, training, scheduling, and other procedural aspects of a project.

Business systems analysis Any of several strategic planning techniques by which management identifies the most important human resources information needs.

Cost-benefit-value analysis A systematic process of determining and comparing costs and benefits (both tangible and intangible) of planning, developing, implementing, and maintaining various HRMS alternatives.

CPM A planning and scheduling technique for managing complex projects. It is used to predict and measure relationships between relative costs and alternative completion dates. The critical path is the graphic representation of the sequence of events representing the minimum time necessary for project completion. See also PERT

Critical success factors (CSF). An evaluation technique in which tasks and activities considered to be critical to the success of a project.

Data integrity The extent to which data have a high degree of accuracy, completeness, and consistency. Often referred to as *reliability*.

Economic evaluation The process of investigating and comparing the costs, benefits, and values of the present system and of various project development options. This evaluation usually includes both implementation and maintenance costs.

Efficiency In terms of computer systems, the internal management and handling of data to maximize speed and throughput.

Feasibility study An analysis to determine the viability and practicality of alternatives in terms of technical, administrative, and economic variables.

Gantt chart A particular type of project planning and scheduling chart. A Gantt chart lists tasks vertically and time increments horizontally. Marks next to each task delineate the time period during which that task should take place, showing start and end dates but not relationships among tasks.

Input Data entered into the system for system processing or storage. Inputting occurs via a keyboard, disk or tape transfer, or some other electronic transfer device. Also refers to the process of entering data into the system.

Intangible benefits An identifiable but not easily quantifiable improvement resulting from some action. Intangible benefits of a new HRMS often include improved productivity, greater data accuracy, and more well-informed decision making. Also referred to as *value*.

Integration The process by which multiple programs, applications, or systems can share data on an ongoing basis without loss of content or formatting. In human resources integration, updating data in one application automatically updates dependent data in other integrated applications or systems.

Integrity The completeness and accuracy of the HRMS data base, which is protected by procedures for on-line processing, edit and validation, data security, and data recovery.

Interface A link between two systems, pieces of equipment, or software programs so that instructions and data from one can be interpreted by and transferred to the other; a portion of computer storage used by two or more computer programs; the hardware or software needed to connect one system to another.

Life-cycle costing Economic evaluation that considers not only initial costs but also estimates the expected life span of development options and projects costs throughout that life span. Underscores the inherent differences between development costs and maintenance costs.

Mnemonic A Greek word meaning "sounds like." Thus, a code for mechanical engineering might be Mech Eng or ME and be readily understood by even the most casual user.

Modularity A building block approach to putting a system together, as opposed to establishing a system in one large piece. A modular system can implement several human resources applications at one time, then add others during a later phase.

Needs analysis The process of analyzing the current data and reporting needs of users.

Output Data transferred from system memory or storage to a form interpretable by a user or another system. The most common forms of output are disk or tape storage and other electronic transfers.

PERT Project Evaluation and Review Technique. A project scheduling and control methodology that provides graphic displays that identify and order project tasks and activities, relationships among activities, estimated start and completion times for individual tasks, and elapsed time for the entire project. See also CPM.

Project team The group of people charged with attaining a specific goal. An HRMS project team works toward development and implementation of a new system.

Prototyping The process of building a working model of a system through several iterations of user definition and system coding.

Requirements definition A systematic approach to determine functional and technical requirements, including what is legally mandated, what the organization needs, and what would be nice to have.

Scenario analysis A simulation of a real-world issue acted out by potential end users. A technique used to help users identify important system features, functions, and data elements.

Tangible benefits Identifiable, quantifiable improvements resulting from some action, including direct savings and cost avoidance.

Technical evaluation The process of assessing the functional and technological aspects of various system options in terms of project goals and objectives.

Discussion Points

1. What are some of the differences between needs analysis and requirements definition? Describe how this difference might affect an organization's view of the ideal system.

2. Define the types of feasibility an HRMS project team should consider and the components of each.

3. What line items should an HRMS cost-benefit-value analysis include?

4. Why are the benefits of a new HRMS difficult to quantify? What techniques help to overcome this challenge?

5. What values may accrue from an HRMS that transcend its tangible costs and benefits?

6. What are the differences between data and information? Why is it important for HRMS planners to keep these differences in mind?

7. What procedures and activities help build team cohesiveness among those working on the HRMS project?

8. Describe ways of obtaining management support for the HRMS project.

Further Reading

Ceriello, Vincent R. "Computerizing the Personnel Department: Make or Buy?" *Personnel Journal*, September 1984.

Durbin, Gary. "Off the Rack: The Case for Packaged Software." *Computers in Personnel*, Spring 1987.

Kustoff, Marc. "Pinpointing Personnel's Systems Needs: A Practical Guide to the Preliminaries." *Computers in Personnel*, Fall 1986.

Lederer, Albert L. "Planning and Developing a Human Resource Information System." *Personnel Administrator*, August 1984.

Munn, R. W. "HRIS: Towards an Effective Requirements Analysis." *Personnel Administrator*, May 1985.

Nardoni, Ren. "The Building Blocks of a Successful Microcomputer System." *Personnel Journal*, January 1985.

Richards-Carpenter, Colin. "One User's Grumbles About Computers in Personnel." *Personnel Management*, August 1987.

———. "Proper Planning Demands Good Information." *Personnel Management*, April 1988.

Simon, Sidney H. "Selling Management on an HR System." *Personnel Journal*, December 1986.

Smith, R. D. "The Design and Implementation of Human Resource Information Systems." In Management of Human Resources, edited by E.L. Miller, E. Burack, and M. Albrecht. Englewood Cliffs, NJ: Prentice-Hall, 1980.

Stambaugh, Robert H. "HRMS: Performing a Needs Analysis." *Personnel Administrator*, March 1985.

Sudman, S., and N. M. Bradburn. Asking Questions: A Practical Guide to Questionnaire Design. San Francisco: Jossey-Bass, 1983.

Walker, Alfred J. "How Large Should the HR Staff Be?" *Personnel*, October 1988.

Wolfe, Julie W. "Software Success: A Proactive Plan of Attack." *Personnel Administrator*, January 1988.

Sudman, S., and N. M. Bradburn. Asking Questions: A Practical Guide to Question-naire Design. San Francisco: Jossey-Bass, 1983.

Walker, Alfred J. "How Large Should the HR Staff Be?" *Personnel*, October 1988.

Wolfe, Julie W. "Software Success: A Proactive Plan of Attack." *Personnel Administrator*, January 1988.

3
Designing an HRMS

It is better to err on the side of daring than on the side of caution.
—Alvin Toffler

The requirements definition created during the planning phase should provide sufficient information about data requirements to allow the project team to proceed with design. The design process has three primary components:

1. Define data needs by designing data structure, content, and control.

2. Select, create, or adapt software that will store, process, and provide those data as required.

3. Select hardware on which that software will function properly or locate software that will run on hardware already in place.

In an ideal situation, system design proceeds from data base to software to hardware. In reality, preexisting hardware or software may influence the data base design process. Sometimes a human resources department already has hardware that is new and powerful enough for the project team to build its data and software specifications around. Sometimes new software must interface or integrate with existing applications. Selecting compatible software may limit data options that otherwise might be available.

Although no aspect of system design is isolated from the others, this book focuses on each step in turn. This chapter concentrates on data base design; chapters 4 and 5 deal with software and hardware, respectively. Other aspects of system design include vendor selection (chapter 6) and testing, training, and implementation (chapter 9). In whatever order a project team tackles these issues (sometimes separate task groups may work on them simultaneously), team members should understand all the issues involved before beginning decision making in one area.

The Data Base Design Process

The core element of system design is the data base. If you cannot put the information in, you cannot get it out. The project team must make certain that the system design considers every aspect of data collection, utilization, analysis, and reporting that human resources functions require. This time-consuming, exacting task is critical in determining whether a system will meet the organization's goals. If the organization winds up buying a system, their planning and design efforts form the basis for evaluating which vendor's system best meets their information needs. If they build or adapt a system, they will have to perform more detailed design analysis to specify the building blocks for programmers.

During the planning phase, team members define the input, output, and analytical functions needed. HRMS developers then base system design on the requirements definition.

The Design Team

To be effective, the HRMS design process must include the project team as a whole, not just its technical members. The members who are not experts in systems development are excellent sounding boards for whether the ideal technical design will work well when nonexperts use it. In each organization, the division of tasks depends on the skills, experience, and availability of staff and (in some cases) consultants. Internal human resources and IS departments may have staff with considerable technical knowledge, but they rarely have individuals who have designed and installed an HRMS. For the most economical results, many companies have a consultant concentrate on design and development areas in which prior experience plays an important role.

For example, because data base content and format are relatively straightforward, client staff can usually specify these functional requirements without much help from a consultant. Consultants often design the structure of the data base, however, determining the interdependency of data elements and the code structures that support them. As the HRMS project progresses, the team may use a combination of internal and outside resources to develop forms, reports, screens, documentation, training, testing protocols, and the like. Proper project management, task delegation, and accountability ultimately ensure satisfactory results.

The Design Process

The objectives of the design process depend on the extent to which the human resources department already knows whether it will buy a system or build one. A team that will be buying a system need not create all the definitions and limits for the data base and its support, but team members should understand the definitions and limits they require in packaged programs. If the project team will supervise creation of an in-house system, the members must use the design process to establish specific definitions, criteria, limits, formats, and procedures for every aspect of data flow in the HRMS. Programmers will use those specifications to build the system.

In either case, the design team bases its work on the requirements definition developed during the planning phase. To detail data base design, the project team uses techniques such as examination of existing systems (both manual and automated), analysis of existing forms and reports, and data base mapping (a process of defining data elements and their relationships). The team also works closely with vendors to compare data requirements with what vendors offer.

The project team develops draft specifications based on numerous meetings, discussions, reviews, and analyses. These specifications may include samples of visual elements, such as screen layouts and report formats, as well as lists of tables, volume requirements of records of various types, and calculation routines. The project team distributes these draft specifications for review by consultants, data base administrators, security specialists, and human resources management as appropriate. Based on review comments, the team then performs further investigation as needed and produces a final set of specifications.

If the department intends to purchase a system, the specifications often take the form of a document for distribution to potential vendors. This document, known as a request for proposal (RFP), gives vendors the guidelines that any proposed system must achieve. As the next part of the purchase phase, the team engages in the RFP and negotiations processes, which are discussed in chapters 6, 7 and 8.

To build a system internally, the team must spend considerably more time on specifications. For instance, project team members or HRMS users may complete a special form for each data element. The project team leader relies on programmers and other technical specialists assigned to the project to create functioning computer programs. Although this programming activity is beyond the scope of this book, human resources professionals and HRMS developers will be better prepared to interact with such a process by understanding the design issues and activities discussed in this chapter.

Defining the Data Base

Compared with the hardware and software aspects of the HRMS, the data base is much closer to the basic responsibilities of the human resources department—managing information about employees, applicants, and former employees. This data base works like a matrix of information. It includes a list of subjects (such as individual employees) and information about each subject (such as the employee's home address, birth date, job class, title, and current salary).

HRMS vendors and other professionals use the term *data base* in two ways. First, they use it to refer to the set of topics on which the system will collect and maintain information; each topic is known as a data element or field. Second, they use the term to refer to the aggregate set of data on the population contained within the master file. This is the "live" data entered to correspond with the data elements for each subject. In the following table, the headings are the data elements and the table body the live data:

Name	Birth Date	Job Class	Annual Salary
Davis, S.	06/04/49	42911	$44,000.00
Jones, J.	10/11/50	43107	$27,500.00
Marks, M.	03/01/53	42880	$21,300.00

Thus, the data base is a collection of the names of the data elements as well as the content of each data element. Developing a data base requires consideration of several factors, including the scope of records to include, data elements pertaining to those records, coding for those data elements, organization of data by each human resources function, data sources, and frequency of use.

Data Organization

Early in the design process, the project team establishes a basic data organization scheme. Designers categorize data according to the type of files in which the data will be stored.

Employee Files. Sometimes referred to as master files, these files contain all the data elements that pertain to each individual. Each record may contain hundreds of data elements; the master file usually groups data elements according to the human resources function or activity to which it primarily pertains. Many human resources systems use a special grouping for *core data*— employee data used by all or most human resources functions. The core data segment includes headings such as name, address, social security number, position code, date of hire, and other widely used data. Typical master file organization is shown in the accompanying sidebar.

Master File Organization

A basic HRMS comprises the following categories of data. A typical system may have as few as one or as many as forty categories of data:

Personal	Benefits
Job/position	Employee/industrial relations
Education and training	Organization/location
Compensation	Work history
Payroll	Time reporting

Additional categories of data that may be considered for inclusion in the HRMS master file include the following:

Skills and experience	Safety and health
Job posting	Labor cost distribution
Planning and forecasting	Management development
Pension administration	Applicant tracking

Job Classification Files. These files contain all the HRMS data on each job in the system. This information pertains to the job, not to the individual. Files hold information such as title, job grade, union, EEO code, Fair Labor Standards Act (FLSA) code, and exposure to toxic substances. In turn, each individual employee's file may indicate a job classification code.

Other Tables. Many kinds of tables play important and useful roles in an HRMS. A comprehensive HRMS may have eighty to one hundred tables, each of which usually contains information supporting a specific human resources function or activity. These may include wage and salary scales, injury and accident codes, organization codes, EEO categories, education and training programs, and so forth. Chapters 12 through 21 describe how to use these and other tables in specific human resources functions and activities.

Many data in employee records are based at least partially on table data. The HRMS uses calculation routines known as algorithms to pull particular table data into an employee's file or to calculate data for that employee's record. For instance, if an employee is in job grade 15 and has two years of service, the system will check the corresponding wage-rate table to determine that this employee's wage rate should be $12.50 per hour. Moreover, when wage rates change, such as might occur through collective bargaining agreements, changing the wage-rate tables automatically updates wage rates listed in the record of each affected employee. Thus, the appropriate use of tables allows staff to maximize data consistency and timeliness with a minimum of effort.

File Keys. In any data base, one field controls identification of each file or record. This file key is typically the person's social security number, employee number, time card number, job class code, or organization code. Many systems use file keys to link one type of record with another. For instance, an employee record could use employee number as its file key but contain organization code as a data element. That organization code could, in turn, serve as file key for the file on departments or organization entities. The file key links employee records to information such as department, supervisor, site, state, and so forth without the user having to enter this information in each employee record.

Number and Scope of Records

Early in the design stage, the project team must decide how many records the system will maintain. A record consists of the set of data that pertains to one unit of a data base, such as an employee. A firm of 2,000 people may actually have to maintain records on 3,000 to 4,000 individuals. The extra records would include applicants, terminations and replacements, and population growth. An annualized turnover of 25 percent on a base population of 2,000 would include 500 terminated employees plus 500 replacements. This translates to a total of at least 2,500 records in one year's time, plus normal retirements, layoffs and recalls, and growth. Including applicants or employee dependents increases the number dramatically. One major airline maintains records on more than 60,000 active employees, 250,000 dependents of employees, and 500,000 applicants.

In defining the population on which the HRMS will maintain data, designers must know whether users want the system to maintain records of active employees only or active employees plus applicants and open requisitions. All active employees eventually become inactive, either temporarily through layoffs or leaves of absence or permanently through terminations or resignations. The project team must determine how long the HRMS should maintain inactive records. Many firms keep such records as active files for one or two years and as archived files for five to ten years. Many organizations are subject to federal regulations regarding employee record retention.

Most organizations have several categories of employees. For example, many firms have some full-time staff and some part-time, as well as some regular (permanent) employees and some temporary. This creates at least four separate categories of employees. Taking into account categories such as hourly versus salaried or FLSA exempt versus nonexempt employees increases the number of possibilities even more.

Data Elements

Data elements are the individual fields of information that the files maintain. Most commonly, this term refers to the information required about each individual. In a process sometimes referred to as data mapping, system designers compile a list of data elements based on the requirements definition and analysis of existing forms and reports, later cross-referencing this with new requirements. Designers should consider whether they want this process to include all human resources functions or only those under consideration for initial implementation.

HRMS designers may start with a list of possible data elements and ask users to indicate which ones their function will find useful. An example is shown in the sidebar entitled "Building a Data Base." The questionnaire may include items such as the following:

- Do you report EEO data via EEO-1 or EEO-4?
- Which insurance coverage options do you offer?
- What aspects of prior work experience are important to you?
- What factors do you use in computing turnover rates?

This process helps the design team anticipate the requests and questions that human resources and management users will pose when actually using the HRMS. In so doing, the team will increase the system's timeliness, or the speed with which users can extract needed information.

Based on this survey, the manager determines a tentative list of data elements to use as a factor in vendor selection or system design. Some human resources data, such as employee name and hire date, are universal. They are useful in some manner to almost every personnel function. Others, such as race and sex, are useful only to specific functions. Designers must identify which are core data and which are required by only one or two functions.

If the project team decides to pursue a packaged system, it should share this list with prospective vendors. This detailed list of data elements forms the basis for selecting appropriate vendor software that can handle all required data, or at least an acceptable proportion. If human resources decides to create or adapt an in-house system, the team needs to specify each data element in more detail. To build this more concrete data specification based on the nontechnical input from users, many HRMS designers use some type of data element definition form. On this form, they define each element and specify its

Building a Data Base

In many cases, several human resources functions require access to the same data elements. Here are some common examples:

	Empl	Trng	Comp	Bene	ER	Payroll
Employee name	X	X	X	X	X	X
Former name	X			X		
Home address	X			X		X
Citizenship	X			X	X	
Birth date				X		
Race					X	
Sex				X	X	
Job title	X	X	X		X	
Organization	X				X	
Location	X	X				X
Salary/wage	X		X			X
Education	X	X				
Pay basis			X			X
Insurance coverage				X		X
Beneficiary				X		
Dependents				X		
Hire date	X	X	X	X	X	X

relationship to other elements in the system. The form should include the following categories:

- Data element name
- Description
- Size of field (fixed or variable; number of characters)
- Type of field (alphabetic, numeric, or alphanumeric)
- Source of input (existing systems, employees, or other)
- Input method (direct input, calculated, or derived)
- Supporting codes or permissible values
- Editing rules to be applied
- Links to other file
- Expected use or applications
- Retention requirements
- Comments or descriptive information

Sample HRMS Data Base Definition

Although the full list of data elements may include as many as 1000 fields, the following chart lists basic information about a representative selection. Numerical entries in the column marked "Code/Comments" tie the affected field to a corresponding table of codes. This system might contain 50 to 100 code lists; this chart includes several such lists.

	Field Type[a]	Field Size	Code Comments	Priority[b]
Last name	A	16		1
First name	A	12		1
Middle name	A	12		2
First/middle initials	A	2		1
Familiar name	A	10		3
Former last name	A	16		3
Street address	A/N	24		1
City	A	22		1
State/zip code	A/N	8	CA, AZ, NV, etc.	1
Home telephone number	N	10		1
Office telephone number	N	10		2
Supplemental address (c/o)	A/N	24		2
Race	A	1	1	1
Sex	A	1	2	1
Marital status	A	1	3	2
Handicap	A/N	2	4	2
Birth date	N	6	MMDDYY	1
Date of hire	N	6	MMDDYY	1
Seniority date	N	6	MMDDYY	2
Date of full-time status	N	6	MMDDYY	2
Anniversary date	N	6	MMDDYY	3
Recruitment source	N	2		3
Shift	N	1		3
Employee category/status	N	2	6	1
Citizenship	A	2	5	2
Work hours	N	4		2

[a]A = alphabetic; N = numeric; A/N = alphanumeric.
[b]Priority refers to the relative importance of the data element.

Code 1: Race
    0. White
    1. Black
    2. Asian American
    3. American Indian
    4. Hispanic

Code 2: Sex
> F. Female
> M. Male
> U. Unspecified

Code 3: Marital Status
> S. Single
> M. Married
> D. Divorced
> W. Widowed
> X. Separated

Code 4: Handicap

Mx	Mental	x1–x9	Type
Sx	Sensory	x1–x9	Type
Px	Physical	x1–x9	Part of body
Xx	Multiple	x1–x9	Type/body part

Code 5: Citizenship
> US. United States (default)
> UK. United Kingdom
> FR. France
> GE. Germany
> NT. Netherlands
> BG. Belgium
> IT. Italy

Code 6: Employee Category/Status

Category		*Status*	
1x	Regular, full-time	x1	Active
2x	Regular, part-time	x2	Voluntary separation
3x	Temporary, full-time	x3	Involuntary separation
4x	Temporary, part-time	x4	Retired
5x	Seasonal	5x	On leave
6x	Contractor	x6	Disabled
7x	On call	x7	Deceased

In a purchased system, vendors supply most or all of the data base elements, complete with definitions, so the project team needs to address each of these questions in detail only if it is considering in-house development.

Field Type and Size

Programmers may set up an application to accept only certain types of characters as input for a particular field. Some fields are clearly alphabetic (name),

Choosing Data Formats

Systems may allow a human resources department to select from a variety of format options for data such as dates, times, names, dollar amounts, and telephone numbers. Here are a few examples:

Date Format Options for February 19, 1937

Format Name	Format	Example
American	MM/DD/YY	02/19/37
Canadian/European	DD/MM/YY	19/02/37
Military	DD MMM YY	19 Feb 37
Julian	NNN YY	050 37

Name Format Options for Michael Victor Grist

Grist, Michael Victor	Michael V Grist
Grist, M V	M V Grist
Grist, Michael V	Michael Victor Grist

Note: If Grist uses a first initial and his middle name, even more possibilities exist. Some systems also provide space for an employee's familiar or nickname (Mike, Mickey) and former or maiden name.

some are clearly numeric (number of dependents), and some are alphanumeric (street address). Designating the field type for data elements as appropriate helps increase data accuracy and consistency.

For any field designated as numeric, the designer or programmer specifies the format in which characters in that field should appear. Choices include integer, fixed decimal point, floating decimal point, dollars, percent, or date.

Most fields are designed to accept only a certain number of characters. If a system designates a field as a *fixed-length* six-character field, each entry in that field must have exactly that number of characters (six characters, not seven or five). A *variable-length* field will accept any number of characters up to a set maximum. In determining coding and formatting for any field, the project team should consider the most readable form of the data as well as the optimum field length within the system.

Input Method

By reviewing the data elements, the project team determines which elements users will input directly into the HRMS and which ones the software will derive or calculate on the basis of other elements. For example, some systems produce a projected retirement date derived from an employee's birth date. In other cases, making a new entry, such as a salary increase, automatically bumps the previous entry in that field to employee history. The system often derives data elements from data such as base salary, seniority, performance review, and job location.

Certain fields work best as calculated or derived fields, such as age, time in position, and length of service. Vendors usually have certain designations and established formulas for entry in such fields. Either in-house or vendor programmers usually can change these designations and formulas to accommodate the organization's needs.

Some people use the terms *calculated data*, *derived data*, and *computed data* interchangeably, while others attribute a distinct meaning to each term. *Calculated* may imply that authorized users can change the formula, while *derived* may imply that the relationship between certain fields remains constant. Alternately, *calculated* may refer to fields dealing with money and *derived* to numerical fields not related to money. Sometimes *calculated* refers to numeric fields that contain data based on other fields, while *derived* refers to alphabetic fields that contain such data. In any event, the project leader should make sure that all team members, vendors, and consultants agree about what these terms mean in the context of the specific system under consideration.

Coding

For each element, designers must decide the extent to which the system should use codes. Elements such as name are, of course, recorded in literal form; they cannot be abbreviated or expressed symbolically (though designers must decide about how to handle middle names, length of names, and so forth). An element such as sex may be easily coded as M or F. Salaries and dates are already absolutes because they are numeric. But what about educational level, absence type, skills, geographic preference, referral source, and job category—should these use words or codes? The design team should develop a coding standard before entering the first record into the system.

Some data fields can be entered as either mnemonic entries (E ENG) or coded entries (Job Class: EN02). The best choice depends on what users want to do with that data. Most users can easily interpret E ENG as electrical engineering and M ENG as mechanical engineering. But if users want an alphabetic system to differentiate between electrical engineering and electronic engineering, extra characters must be used (ELCTRC ENG versus ELCTRN ENG). A coded system would require fewer characters (EN01 versus EN02), with less potential for error in transcription or data entry.

Moreover, the computer cannot test for a range of E to M. If users want to sort records according to a category, that category should contain standardized choices. Testing for "greater than," "less than," or "within a range of . . ." obviously requires numeric codes.

To permit codification (and, therefore, sorting and selection), categories should have a common stream of choices. First, users must input abbreviations in a consistent fashion. Supervisor is always SUPV, not SUP or SUPER. From a list of codes, the data entry clerk may choose the code that most closely matches the English-language entries provided by an applicant, employee, human resources staff member, or supervisor.

A code-supported system does not mean that everyone who reads an applicant's or employee's computer file must interpret cryptic abbreviations and codes. Some systems pair the coded entry with a standard alphabetic interpretation (E-2: Electrical Engineer) as part of the field both on the screen and in reports. Some systems allow the screen display for each individual's file to show just the code in the appropriate field but provide full text either adjacent to the subject data or, at a prompt, in a window displayed on the screen. When the user does not know the range of choices for a particular field, the system may allow access to authorized code values by using the help function.

Edit and Validation Rules

Modern human resources systems usually contain a powerful set of edit and validation rules. These rules are algorithms that the computers uses to perform various types of logical checks for data accuracy. Based on the results of such actions, the computer decides whether to accept, reject, or flag data as entered. These edit and validation features take over important detail-oriented clerical tasks that humans used to perform, freeing users to review entries for the kinds of errors computers still cannot catch. As described in the material that follows, the major types of edit rules include tests for accuracy, reasonableness, and computational accuracy, as well as relational edits.

The system first checks field length and type. It prevents six characters from being entered in a five-character field. It also blocks alphabetic characters where it expects numbers, such as in a salary field. As mentioned earlier, if the system defines month as an alphabetic data element, it would accept an entry of NOV but reject 11.

If a particular field is designated as a derived field (such as age being derived from date of birth and current date), a system with good edit rules will reject manual entry in that field. Some systems permit the use of override functions, but users should utilize these with care so as not to defeat the benefits of the edit and validation rules.

The system's edit and validation process then checks for legitimate values. It begins by accepting only data within certain ranges. For instance, in a month field, it would accept only numbers 01 to 12. Similarly, the system checks for valid codes. A salary increase type field, for example, may accept only the values M (merit), P (promotion), B (bonus), or D (demotion) as valid.

The HRMS must review each field (or sometimes parts of fields) to ensure accuracy. In a date field, the specification may call for a value of 01 to 12 in the first two positions, 01 to 31 in the next two positions, and a value of not greater than XX90 in the last two positions. However, the system will block an entry of 30 in the middle two positions if the first two positions are 02.

The most sophisticated type of editing is relational. In this process, the system compares data from two separate fields and alerts the user if the entries are outside the expected ranges for the relationship between them. For instance, an employee may have a highest education level code representing high school graduate but an academic major code of nuclear physics. Each code is valid independently, but when the codes appear together, one of them is probably wrong. The system issues a message, then allows the user to correct one or both entries or to override the edit.

Data Sources

Data sources generally influence data organization. Traditionally, HRMS developers needed only employee information provided by employees and human resources staff. With the broadening of the human resources function, the system now collects data on many more subjects. These may include the organization itself, demographics, dependents, applicants, retirees, surveys, external data bases, and other human resources programs. Some of the sources of information for building the HRMS data base include not only applicants, employees, and human resources staff but also insurance carriers, survey firms, payroll service bureaus, government agencies, and test specialists.

Data from Existing Systems

If design of a new system includes plans for inputting data from a manual system or importing data from another computer system, data base design should consider the format and structure of each data element in that system. If the current system includes middle name, should the new system continue that practice or convert each middle name to middle initial? If the current system lists five codes for performance rating, should the new system continue that practice? The advent of a new system presents numerous opportunities for streamlining codes that may have grown obsolete.

Any organization that uses two or more applications may encounter integration and interfacing issues. In an integrated system, a single entry of data should automatically update all affected subsystems and invoke all relevant routines and procedures. For example, when a user enters a salary transaction, that single entry should (1) update the employee file; (2) post the transaction to work history; (3) post it to the general ledger, if applicable; (4) inform the payroll system of the new salary rate to pay; (5) take deductions and process a net paycheck, and so on.

The most common and most complicated interface and integration problems arise between payroll and general human resources functions. An integrated personnel/payroll system can be a tremendous time saver, since data are input only once. All subsystems are given the same information, which reduces the chance that salary totals will not balance. For example, if separate systems are used, the personnel clerk might accidentally enter $553 into the file update cycle and the payroll clerk $535 into the payroll file. HRMS designers should bear in mind, however, that a combined, fully integrated personnel/payroll system means a lot of work—more than an organization may be willing or able to take on all at once. Designers can find as much justification for developing each part of the HRMS separately as for integrating them. The most important advantage of separation is that the payroll or personnel subsystem can be operational sooner than an integrated system. Because payroll applications often involve integration and interfacing issues, this topic is discussed in detail in chapter 20.

Data from Applicants, Employees, and Human Resources

Applicants and employees provide data via forms, interviews, notes, and tests. Data on applicants present a unique challenge because human resources usually needs the information for only a short time. Applicant records are much shorter than employee records, however, because they have no data in areas such as benefits, training, or internal employment history.

Various human resources and payroll functions provide information about employees. This includes job, location, compensation, benefits, and safety incidents. Line managers furnish information on performance reviews, job transfers, and other changes in job status.

To collect data from employees, new hires, human resources staff, and managers, the HRMS often uses special input forms. Human resources establishes and maintains a policy that requires use of such forms to report any new data or changes. Forms that are properly designed and used control data format and content choices, thus increasing input accuracy. Provision of custom systems and adaptations should include input forms for human resources activities. As systems grow and users add more applications, they often develop supplemental forms.

Data from External Sources

The system may import or access data from external sources. For instance, many EEO functions use demographic data from the U.S. Census Bureau, Department of Labor, independent survey firms, regional employers' councils, or professional associations. Some firms subscribe to external data bases to keep abreast of labor laws and safety issues. Such external data may come in on-line, batch, disk, or tape form. The design team should consider how best to import this material electronically, to select needed information from the total amount provided, and to establish routines that standardize this information with internal data definitions, including codes, job groups, or hazardous materials inventories. Because integration and interfacing most often affect payroll, this issue is discussed further in chapter 20.

Data from Other Departments

Most HRMS need some data that come from departments outside human resources. For instance, they may need accounting information, bases for commissions and bonus payments, and pensions information from treasury and finance for high-level succession planning. They may need to extract information from general management and corporate planning. At all stages of data base development, from data element definition through data conversion, the HRMS project team should consult with representatives from every function that affects HRMS data needs or sources.

Data Flow

Defining all the specific data elements and creating an initial data base only gets human resources ready to work. To create a truly functional system, the project team must focus on how data will flow through the system and how users will get the system to do what they want.

Transaction Flow Analysis

Having determined the sources for data in each field, the project team should make sure that entries and changes occur only on an authorized and auditable basis. To do so, they must engage in a process known as transaction flow analysis.

The term *transaction flow* refers to where data come from, how the system manipulates them, and their ultimate output form. In other words, transaction flow is the path a particular status change takes between some triggering event and its recording and reporting via the HRMS. That trigger may be a new

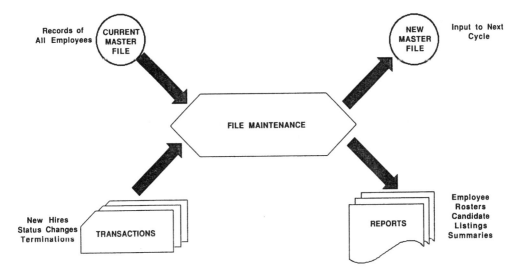

Figure 3–1. Typical HRMS data flow. Depending on the circumstances, the project team may be able to use simple flow diagrams or may need to develop detailed graphics.

hire, salary change, leave of absence, performance review, or any of thousands of events taking place within the human resources context of an organization.

The project team should examine the projected transaction flow of every data element and desired output to make sure that the process includes proper checks and balances. For many data elements, the transaction flow might include the following steps:

- Status-change submission (electronic or paper)
- Approval(s)
- Coding
- Data entry and verification
- Transaction processing (on-line or batch)
- Transaction edit and validation
- Request for output
- Processing (includes sorting and batching)
- Calculation routines as required
- Output formatting
- Output generation (printing and electronic transfer)

The project team can depict the transaction process graphically using flowcharts. These show where the transaction originates, how it progresses through the approval and coding processes to data entry, and how it is processed and output.

At this point, the project team probably also will consider which types of data the system should process at the time of entry (on-line processing) and which it should hold in a pending status for processing at a later time (batch processing). This decision usually depends more on the needs of the human resources functions themselves than on the technical requirements of the system. For instance, the system might process on-line any changes in the salary, job, or organization field, but batch process additions or deletions to records to meet a payroll cycle, such as on the fifteenth and thirtieth of every month. If the system operates on an on-line basis, transaction flow may involve fewer steps and be more streamlined than with batch processing.

In particularly complex, disorganized, or sensitive situations, the human resources department may facilitate the most effective and efficient transaction flow by having the HRMS project team work with a human resources industrial engineering specialist. Such a processional can identify problem areas in information transactions within the organization. The specialist would then suggest improvements in information management techniques, such as increased on-line processing or electronic transfer. Facing transaction flow issues during HRMS design often makes the design process more complex and time-consuming. However, because of their mutual dependence, the joint results of the HRMS design and the industrial engineering consultation usually have a far more positive impact than they would have if tackled separately.

Data security frequently arises as an issue during transaction flow analysis. Because these issues often (though not always) relate more to controlling output than input, they are discussed in this chapter immediately following the sections on screens and reports.

Algorithms, Routines, and Macros

To manipulate data in any way, the user or system must invoke one or more instructions. The typical system contains thousands of sets of instructions. An instruction may include one or more forms of computer logic, such as IF, THEN, ELSE, and GO TO. Of these, one of the most common and useful to understand instructions is the IF/THEN/ELSE string. In its most basic form, it works as follows:

> IF   (data meet a certain condition or conditions)
> THEN (take this action on the data)
> ELSE   (take alternative action)

Programs may contain thousands of such instructions. Programmers combine these basic computer instructions in groups to form sets of instructions, often referred to as algorithms, routines, and macros. The number, complexity, and variety of their arrangement in large measure determine the capabilities of that application. Many of these instructions relate to transaction processing, calculations, screen layout, table maintenance, report generation, and other activities required on a sporadic, periodic, or regular basis.

Algorithms are rules and mathematical calculations that the HRMS uses to manipulate data in particular ways. These calculations may range from simple addition to complex functions that interrelate data from numerous fields. The system has hundreds or even thousands of algorithms. For instance, a payroll module may contain multiple formulas for computation of overtime wages (1.5 x base wage rate for regular overtime, 2.0 x base wage rate for Sundays and holidays, and so forth).

A *routine* tends to be a more complex set of instructions, one that may govern not just calculation but input/output functions. Selecting an option from a menu or submenu actually triggers a routine. Routines trigger activities such as data retrieval, data processing, data storage, and output generation. Some routines use auxiliary functions, such as word processing, graphics, and electronic mail. These functions are discussed in greater detail in chapter 4. The project team should consider the requirements of these programs when evaluating and designing routines.

Sometimes a complicated routine is called a *macro*. A macro usually handles a string of routines, such as the following: On the first of each month, review all employee length of service fields; when this category reaches x months of service, add a certain percentage of benefits coverage. Many programs use macros to implement global changes to a series of records or data strings. For instance, an authorized user could construct a macro that would change all occurrences of NOV (November) in the date field of all records to 11. Programs usually come with some macros built in, such as global search and replace. Many programs now offer users various degrees of latitude in building custom macros.

For in-house systems, designers may simply designate relations and actions, leaving actual formulation to technical experts. Programmers must pay attention to the smallest of these instructions. They must work with users to establish command strings, formulas, and trigger mechanisms for instructions.

Entering Data Updates

To remain current, an HRMS data base must permit fast, logical, and efficient updating by authorized users. The typical organization experiences three to five updates or other changes per employee per year. Sometimes a user needs to update many fields in one record; sometimes he or she needs to change one field in hundreds of records. The system should allow users to do either of these things with the fewest possible commands and keystrokes.

Many HRMS use transaction codes to access and control data updates. Each transaction code, usually consisting of two to four characters, corresponds to a specific human resources-related activity, such as demotion (DEM) or job information change (JIC). Transaction codes function as special macros. In terms of IF/THEN logic, a transaction code may indicate, "If this field is changed for this reason, then these other fields need updating also."

Usually the user selects a field, then chooses a transaction code. The system then displays or highlights the related fields that the user must update to complete the transaction. Alternatively, the user may select a transaction code before indicating a specific field; then the system either presents relevant fields or prompts the user to choose a field. For instance, if the user indicates demotion (DEM), the system may prompt for updates to the following fields:

- Reason for job change
- Effective date of change
- Job code
- Salary decrease amount

If the user fails to provide new, acceptable data for each field affected by the specified action, the system will prompt the user for the required data. The system will accept the change only when the user has updated all the related fields. Packaged systems often allow modification of predesignated transaction codes. Transaction code design for custom systems requires particularly careful, time-consuming work.

Handling Historical Data

When changes are entered into the data base, human resources usually needs to retain a record of the superseded data. The definition for each data element should include instructions to the system about how to handle updates to that field. Some elements (such as date of birth) require no history, so any new entry simply overlays the previous data. Other elements (such as position, location, and employee name) track the employee's history. An update to such a field sends the replaced data to a history segment. The history portion of each employee's record usually has several components, so each field also must be correlated with the particular segment or segments to which its data should flow. A particular human resources application may have several history segments. For instance, applicant and employee tracking may have segments on past applicants, current employee job, current employee status, former employees, and retirees. As shown in figure 3–2, some types of data updates trigger distribution of the outdated data to more than one history segment.

Eventually the system may accumulate more history than human resources would reasonably need on-line. To keep the system working effi-

Action	Description	History Segment		
		Compensation	Position	Status
MKT	Market Adjustment	X		
DEC	Salary Decrease	X		
DEM	Demotion		X	
JOB	Job Change		X	
REV	Job Revaluation		X	
LOA	Leave of Absence			X
INC	Salary Increase	X		
PRM	Promotion	X	X	
REH	Rehire	X	X	X
RLA	Return from Leave of Absence		X	X
ETY	Employee Type Change	X	X	X
TRM	Termination			X
TRF	Employee Transfer		X	

Figure 3–2. Transaction codes and history segments. A transaction that updates fields in an employee record triggers transfer of the replaced data to work history. Some transactions affect more than one record segment. The system should process all affected segments simultaneously. This list shows the transaction codes and the segments that each action affects.

ciently, human resources may include an off-line data archive for outdated historical data. Many HRMS, particularly large systems, perform such off-loading to tape on a batch basis. Once a field has reached a set maximum number of entries in a history segment, it sends its oldest data to a queue to await the next periodic archiving.

Each archived entry contains some unique identifier for the employee (or applicant or retiree) concerned. The design team should consider which data the department needs to maintain for a lifetime and which it needs only for a limited time.

Screens

Output refers to data that are in a form ready for use. Most people think of printed reports as the most common form of output, but many users interact more often with another form of output—screens.

Most HRMS programs use screens and menus to guide users through choices of activities and data. A system uses the computer screen to present information, messages, and options to the user. An even moderately complex system might feature dozens of ways of arraying information and inquiries, each of which is called a screen. For instance, a benefits module might contain an eligibility screen, an enrollment screen, and a premium accounting screen, among others. The screens are linked by a menu or other option procedure.

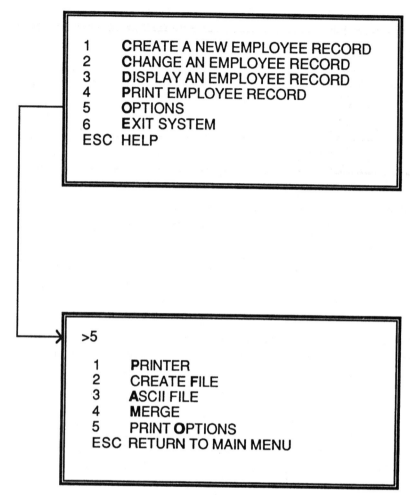

Figure 3–3. Main menu and submenu. In many parts of a menu-driven system, selection of one menu option presents the user with another menu of more specific choices. Sometimes the user must navigate through three or four menus to complete a transaction.

To help maximize the ease, speed, consistency, and accuracy of user access to the data base, an HRMS should feature an attractive screen layout, clearly worded messages, and logical, flexible triggering processes for operations options.

Proper screen layout involves as many (if not more) artistic as technical considerations. Screen designers should understand both the psychology of text layout and graphic design. The layout should strike a conscious balance between the content required and the amount and type of context appropriate for users.

A well-defined system issues on-screen *messages* to users as appropriate. A message may alert the user to a problem in data editing and validation ("Value exceeds input of 00 to 12"), provide a response to the user's processing request ("Printing to printer"), define the computer status ("File not found"), or provide other information that the user should know. System designers can enhance readability by using English-language screen messages. Good messages are straightforward, contain simple words, and direct the user to corrective action where needed.

Menus are a special type of screen—specifically, a method of displaying operations choices for user decision making. The user may see a menu as soon as he or she enters the system and may have to work through a series of menus until he or she reaches the specific record and activity desired. A typical introductory menu screen might look like this:

*A*DD NEW EMPLOYEE RECORD

*C*HANGE/MODIFY EMPLOYEE RECORD

*F*IND EMPLOYEE RECORD

*D*ELETE EMPLOYEE RECORD

PRINT A REPORT

(**ESC**) EXIT

Alternately, the screen may boldface and capitalize the initial letter of each option. To select a command, the user can use the cursor control keys, tab up or down the list, or type the initial letter of the command. When the user makes a choice, such as "Print a report," and hits the Enter key, that choice invokes a routine. The routine executes a master command or a set of commands, known as a macro. The routine may take the user to a submenu with additional choices. "Print a report" may take the user to the menu that lists the standard reports available.

Reports

Personnel reports are the most common end product of the HRMS. In fact, when most people assess system responsiveness, reports are all they see. People are still more comfortable with paper than with electronic reports. Designers need to consider the report needs of each human resources function that will be using the HRMS. They must consider not only in-house reports but

**Attributes of Effective
Information Retrieval Systems**

Whether retrieving information for on-screen display or for a printed report, an HRMS works best if users can quickly get just the information they need. The following features help meet that goal:

- Field and constant comparisons
- Search parameters (equals, not equals, greater than, less than)
- Arithmetic functions (addition, subtraction, multiplication, division)
- Summaries and totals
- Sequence levels
- Variable page formatting
- Table decode/explosion
- Multiple detail lines
- Search on multiple parameters (AND/OR logic)
- IF/THEN/ELSE logic
- Report cataloging and scheduling

also government reporting requirements and communication with employees. The project team should address the following issues for each report:

- Content (including detail or summary information)
- Type (tabular, text, graphics)
- Design (layout, type style, headers, and so forth)
- Frequency (monthly, quarterly, and so forth)
- Means of generation (automatic, as needed; printed, electronic)
- Distribution (means, quantity)

Report Content

The report design process begins with the development of a list of reports that the system should be able to produce. The design team should try to obtain copies of current reports and mock-ups of new ones. Designers must take into account the report requirements of every type of user. Chapters 12 through 21 detail the report requirements for the most important human resources functions. Review of this information can help ensure that the list of reports needed is complete.

In deciding what information each report should contain, the project team should focus on the attributes of quality information, as discussed in chapter 2. Specifically, quality information has these attributes:

- Reliability
- Timeliness
- Comprehensiveness
- Readability
- Significance and relevance

Early in the report design process, the project team must decide which reports should contain detailed information (such as listings by individual employee) and which should contain summary information (figures by group of employees). Many potential buyers are impressed that an HRMS vendor supplies hundreds of report formats with the base system. But most of these standard reports consist of detail listings and numbers; senior managers and executives need reports that the standard package may not include.

HRMS staff can easily assess the comprehensiveness of reports for lower-level professionals, who are primarily interested in detail information. They can measure the contents of a listing against the specific information requests of users. For example, a human resources user might consider the head-count report in figure 3–4 comprehensive if it listed the specific detail requested.

The project team may have more difficulty assessing the comprehensiveness of reports for senior management staff, who are primarily interested in summary-level information. Summary reports (such as figure 3–5) often provide comparisons, trends, exceptions, and so forth—information that management can use to focus decisions and activities.

A report designed for senior management often produces more questions than answers. Consider the matrix report in figure 3–6, which provides head-count totals only. This report gives information on who works where, but it raises questions about trends. A more comprehensive report is provided in figure 3–7. This report has some additional components: current application volume compared with the same time last year, a comparison with the previous month, and bulleted points highlighting key issues and questions. It illustrates the point that reports often require additional context in order to convey information most usefully. To describe a trend or issue properly, a user may need to create a set of two or three reports.

Senior management staff find brief summaries useful because such reports add important insight not visible in the matrix. Providing such material promotes the human resources department's image among senior management as

1989 TOTAL HEADCOUNT AS OF SEPTEMBER 1, 1989

Business Unit	Employee Name	Employee No.	FLSA Code
Applications Software	Blacker, James	569427328	N
Applications Software	Boswell, Steven	422674312	E
Applications Software	Charles, Patricia	569026793	E
Applications Software	Dixon, Timothy	198004532	E
Operations	Hampton, Daniel	369329486	N
Operations	Lowell, Sarah	187241390	N
Operations	Mannery, Kathyrn	555273782	E
Operations	Otello, Charles	427826341	N
•	•	•	•
•	•	•	•

Total **Exempt:** 580
Total **Nonexempt:** 140
Total **Headcount:** 720

Figure 3–4. Sample detail report. This report lists each employee by name and number.

being proactive and responsive. The report in figure 3–7 may still fall short of the mark for comprehensiveness, though, since a single report can present only a limited amount of relevant data effectively; for more information, users may need to work with the computer on an interactive basis. Most, if not all, hard copy reports fall short because once the computer has printed the report, the information it contains is fixed.

1989 TOTAL HEADCOUNT AS OF SEPTEMBER 1, 1989

Business Unit	Exempt	Nonexempt	Total
Applications/Operations	580	140	720
Information Systems	182	269	451
Telecommunications	348	73	421
Company Totals	1110	482	1592

Figure 3–5. Sample summary report. This report on an organization's current head count lists number of employees by business unit.

PERFORMANCE VERSUS INCREASE INTERVAL MATRIX

Performance Level	Months Between Increases														
	<6	6	7	8	9	10	11	12	13	14	15	16	17	18>	
DISTINGUISHED	0	1	8	12	10	12	5	5	3	4	0	1	1	1	63
COMMENDABLE	0	2	15	14	5	4	5	5	5	5	5	1	2	2	70
COMPETENT	0	0	2	10	7	11	5	5	14	16	10	5	5	4	94
ADEQUATE	0	0	0	1	0	10	9	14	16	11	14	9	11	6	101
PROVISIONAL	0	0	0	0	0	2	3	3	8	4	1	5	2	10	38
TOTAL	0	3	25	37	22	39	27	32	46	40	30	21	21	23	366

Figure 3–6. Sample matrix report. In a matrix report or array, data are plotted on a graph in which the horizontal axis represents one variable and the vertical axis represents another. As in the above example, when time is a variable, it is usually on the horizontal axis. In this case, the vertical axis represents performance rating. The data points indicate the relationship between performance rating and time since last salary increase.

Report Type

Reports come in various forms: tabular (rows and columns), text (words), and graphics (charts and graphs). The use of text versus columns versus graphics is a more complex issue than many HRMS planners realize. To determine the most effective approach for each report, the design team should consider a number of variables, including the purpose of the report, the content, and the audience's expectations and preferences.

The difference between the needs of people at lower levels of the organization and those of people at the highest levels can be significant. As readability of information has become increasingly important to users higher up on the organizational ladder, graphics have become an integral part of HRMS and other business applications. Senior managers who cannot ascertain a report's message from glancing at the content will probably not even read the report. Experience indicates that upward of 75 percent of all reports go unused, and many surveys indicate that poor report readability is a key reason for this.

Tabular reports present data in a row-and-column format. Such reports come in two basic forms—detail and summary. As discussed earlier in this chapter, detail reports work best when users need to check specific data, while

APPLICATION VOLUME

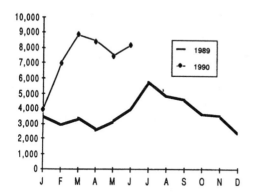

TRENDS/ISSUES:

• TOTAL YTD APPLICATION VOLUME – 43,994

  – LAST YEAR THIS TIME – 19,811

• ALL SITES INCREASED VOLUME IN JUNE
  TOTAL INCREASE – 9.7%

  – 44% OF NORTH TOTAL YTD APP VOLUME
  OCCURRED IN JUNE

CURRENT MONTH DATA:

SITE	THIS MO.	TOTAL Y-T-D
WEST	2,282	10,554
EAST	3,458	23,476
SOUTH	1,939	8,867
NORTH	485	1,100
TOTAL	8,164	43,994

Figure 3–7. Sample combination report. A combination report includes several different report formats. This example includes a graph, a table, and brief text statements. Each presentation form addresses the same topic, but each covers a slightly different aspect. When one format would demonstrate a major point effectively but not cover other points adequately, a combination report may be a good solution.

summary reports provide information about trends. If used to excess, detail listings can result in information overload. Generally, clerks and paraprofessionals need detail reports, and management requires summary reports.

Management also finds *text reports* useful. Some organizations use text reports to provide background, explanations, and clarifications of graphic and tabular material. Text also helps to focus readers' attention on the most important facts or conclusions. This often results in a deeper understanding of the material presented, as well as less confusion and fewer questions. Producing text reports often requires more human effort than producing other types of reports.

Far too few HRMS use graphics to their full capacity. Bar charts, pie charts, graphs, and other computer graphics provide visual and intellectually powerful summaries of information. With just a glance at such a presentation, readers can grasp patterns, trends, comparisons, and variances. Graphics do not allow for presentation of the detailed information required for decision making. Moreover, graphs and charts work only with staff who know how to generate and read information in graphic form.

The relative advantages of several basic types of reports are shown in figure 3–8. Some graphics packages provide the capability to combine several formats. As shown in figure 3–7, a single sheet may include a graph, a tabular summary, and text. Senior managers and executives often prefer this form,

CRITERION	TABLES	GRAPH	COMBINATION
Accuracy	1	3	2
Usefulness/Relevance	3	2	1
Appearance	3	1	1
Gaining/Maintaining attention	3	1	1
Learning information quickly	1	1	3
Understandability	3	2	1
Avoiding information overload	2	1	3
Avoiding visual fatigue	3	1	2
Retention	3	2	1
Problem definition	3	2	1
Correct information	3	2	1
Comparing alternatives	3	2	1

3 = GOOD
2 = BETTER
1 = BEST

Figure 3–8. Comparison of different report formats. To select the best format, designers and users must consider the content, audience, and objective of the specific report. This table shows how well tables, graphs, and combination reports fulfill some common criteria.

but it usually requires more effort to produce. Some readers may wonder whether the various formats repeat information or give additional data. In general, a combination report should be provided only when the audience expects or needs information in multiple formats.

Consider the summary report in figure 3–5. This report begs for a graph, as do most summary reports. But what type of graph—a bar chart, pie chart, or line graph? A few possibilities are shown in figure 3–8. Each of the dozen or more types of graphic presentations is best used to present a certain kind of information.

Bar graphs (figure 3–9) show relationships or comparisons among variables. *Stacked bar graphs* (figure 3–10) show not only relationships or comparisons among sets of data but also the composition of each data set. These should be used to emphasize several totals and the breakdown of their com-

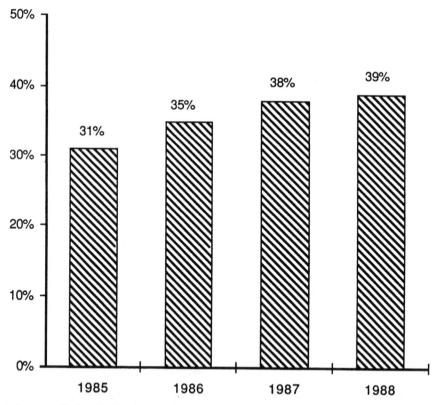

Figure 3–9. Bar/column graph. One of the most widely used business graphs, a bar graph shows relationships or comparisons among variables. It is ideal for comparing values in multiple categories.

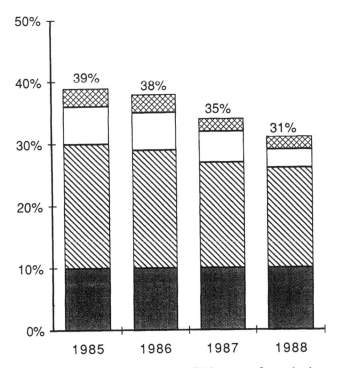

Figure 3–10. Stacked bar/column graph. This type of graph shows relationships or comparisons among variables as well as the composition of several larger values. It can be used to emphasize several totals and their component parts and can effectively show how the parts of a whole change over time.

ponents. Such graphs effectively show how the parts of an entity change over time. *Three-dimensional bar graphs* (figure 3–11) show multiple relationships or comparisons among data sets. This type of graph works well for comparing several types of values for various regions, organizations, departments, or other groupings. Unless designed carefully, this graph can confuse rather than enlighten viewers. This kind of graph often requires considerable sophistication to create and interpret it effectively.

A *pie chart* (figure 3–12) illustrates in what proportions various parts make up a whole. For example, a very general human resources pie chart might illustrate the proportion of employees in each area of an organization. The whole pie would represent 100 percent of employees; each piece of the pie would represent the percentage of employees in a particular area. Many systems can produce pie charts easily, and this is one of the most widely used business graphics.

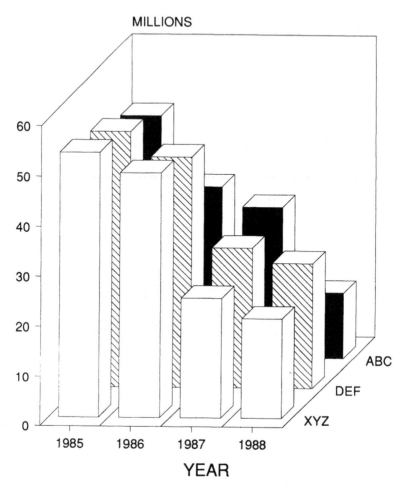

Figure 3–11. Three-dimensional bar graph. This type of graph shows multiple relationships or comparisons among variables. It is ideal for showing comparisons of values collected for a number of categories for several regions, organizations, departments, or other groupings. Unless designed well and used carefully, a three-dimensional graph can be very confusing.

A *line graph* (figure 3–13) shows the differences among variables over time or in relation to some other regularly changing independent variable. Human resources systems often use line graphs to show percentage differences among employee populations. Line graphs work well in illustrating trends. Users can create a line graph by using solid lines to represent past and current trends and dotted lines to project estimates based on those trends and other factors.

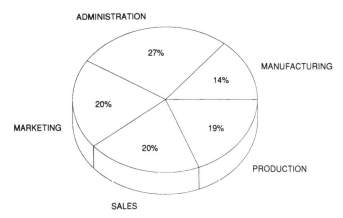

BUSINESS EXPENSES
1989

Figure 3–12. **Pie chart. This widely used business chart shows the way in which various parts make up a whole. The whole is always a complete circle totaling 100 percent. Each part is represented as a slice of the pie, with the size of that slice determined by the percentage of the whole the component represents.**

In an *area graph* (figure 3–14), the area under a horizontal line represents a quantity or volume. This graph often works well to show elapsed time and other cumulative values. Such charts can conceal small changes in data. Area graphs are most effective when no dramatic changes take place from one point to the next.

Other types of graphics used in business include a high/low graph; a combination pie/stacked bar graph; a combination line, area, and/or bar graph; a scatter graph; a dual y-axis graph; a proportion pie chart; a 100 percent bar/column graph; a cumulative bar or line graph; and a paired bar graph. Project team members responsible for report design should have or develop familiarity with a wide variety of graphic options.

Report Design

An effective report uses sorts, breaks, headers, footers, and titles as appropriate. It also uses type styles, markers, and other highlighting schemes for specific purposes.

The project team should establish design styles that pertain to all or most reports. Choices should derive from several factors, including professional understanding of the relationship between graphic design and readability, report

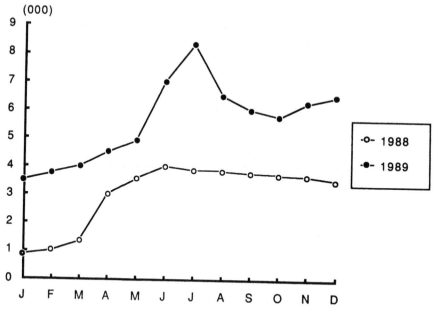

Figure 3–13. Line graph. This graph shows the differences between variables. It can show percentage differences between groups, as well as frequency or distribution of a group. Line graphs are most effective for showing changes in one or more sets of data over time, especially if data change dramatically from period to period.

standards and procedures for the organization, and the specific audience and purpose of each report. The formatting standards should address the following issues:

- Report titles
- Column and row titles
- Section titles
- Type style or font options
- Margins and indentations
- Page breaks
- Headers and footers
- Date and page number location
- Borders or frames

Describing these elements is beyond the scope of this book, but a few general comments may guide the project team in making report formatting decisions that facilitate communication. First, the system should use consis-

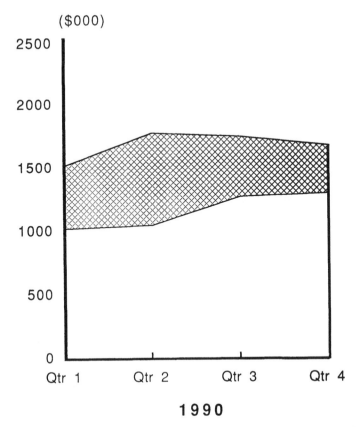

Figure 3–14. Area graph. This is a line graph in which the area under the horizontal line represents a quantity or volume. It works best when illustrating cumulative value over time. Area graphs are most effective when no dramatic changes in data take place from one period to the next. They must be used carefully, as they can conceal small changes in data.

tent formatting for all reports. Particular words used in one report title should have the same meaning in other report titles. Main headings in EEO reports should look the same as main headings in career planning reports. Dates and page numbers should appear in the same place on every page of every report. Every report should have some unique identifier, which may be as simple as name and date. Some organizations assign each report title a number and print that number on the report.

Virtually all the design elements that pertain to reports apply to screens as well. Screen design has some additional features, however. For instance, most organizations now have color monitors. In spite of the attraction of color, report designers should use color primarily to highlight or group items. Color should provide a sort of visual coding or emphasis; it should not be used merely to cover up basic layout problems.

Report Generation and Distribution

The design team should consider how frequently users will need each report. Each human resources function has responsibility for certain reports, updates, and notices. Users within that function ask the system to invoke particular programs or routines. This may occur on a monthly basis or on an ad hoc basis. The user may request that processing take place immediately or on a particular future date. In some sophisticated systems, the HRMS can make certain routines self-scheduling. These operations take place on specific dates without any operator action. For instance, once a month the HRMS may need to send notices to all supervisors on employees overdue for performance reviews. Once a quarter the system may need to generate benefit termination letters to individuals whose coverage for particular elective benefits expires.

The HRMS project team should establish ground rules regarding turnaround times for reports and information access. Information users should take part in establishing these standards and must understand the constraints of the human resources system. Without such standards and understanding, conflicts that impugn the integrity of the HRMS and the quality of its information will inevitably develop.

Taking several steps during the HRMS design process can increase the timeliness of access of information:

- Give users direct access to reporting tools and the data they need to satisfy their own reporting requirements. The advent of more advanced users and the development of reporting and graphics packages that are easy to learn and use have made this approach more feasible.

- Centralize reporting activities with information-retrieval specialists who can develop advanced reports more quickly and efficiently.

- Give users direct access to standard reports and models previously set up by HRMS professionals. Some companies build standard reporting packages and modeling templates for users. The user selects a reporting choice from a menu, then the system displays the information on a screen, routes it to a printer, or does both.

Most reports still take printed form, but systems are producing more and more electronic reports for both internal use and external distribution. The project team should consider when electronic reporting may be preferable to hard copy. Most government agencies can now accept computer-generated reports. Some even accept electronic submissions, though printed reports have some advantages in terms of data control and documentation of submissions. Firms usually support electronic submissions with paper reports anyway.

Too often, a new HRMS comes on-line with better data, better reports, and yet the same old slow distribution system that keeps users from getting information as quickly as they need it. Proper system planning can eliminate this bottleneck.

In traditional office organization, someone produces a report, makes photocopies, and then arranges for interoffice mail distribution to each individual who should receive a copy of the report. Modern office management offers much faster, more cost-effective alternatives. For instance, with distributed printing, a user or central computer orders printers at multiple remote locations to print the report. Readers in those locations receive copies much more quickly. In some circumstances, users receive reports as electronic mail, which is even faster. They may retain the option of ordering a nearby printer to produce a printed copy. Since such options involve particular system and hardware arrangements, the best time to consider the most advantageous distribution scheme is during system planning and design.

Ad Hoc Reports

No matter how many standard reports a system offers, situations arise in which users have a legitimate need for another type of report. If human resources believes that users will need this kind of report on a recurring basis, then it should be added to the array of standard report options. If, however, only a few users might need it, and perhaps not on a recurring basis, then creating a standard report needlessly consumes computer resources.

System designers can overcome this hurdle through the use of screen-based report generation, also called ad hoc report generation. This feature allows the user to fine-tune the information until it provides answers to all the relevant questions. With this capability, users can get the information they need directly and quickly, without having to work through the HRIC. Planners and human resources managers should remember to guard against having ad hoc reporting invoked by users who do not know how to identify the most useful information or most effective method for presenting that information.

In some circumstances, users and organizations may become inappropriately dependent on ad hoc reporting. The ease of learning and using ad hoc reporting may offer an unsuitable substitute for proper planning. Unfortunately, this approach ultimately leaves the human resources department without consistent information and analysis, thus seriously degrading the potential usefulness of the system.

Electronic Output

To the extent that the new HRMS will exchange data with, import data from, or export data to another system, the project team must establish specifications for this interface. Electronic output may take the form of a formal report, an entire data base, or selected updated data. The technical considerations for such decisions are discussed in detail in chapter 20, but the design specifications should cover the following requirements for any interface or integration:

- Purpose of interface
- Specifications of other system
- Direction or directions of information flow
- Common data elements
- Unique data elements
- Data format in other system
- Data volume per interchange
- Frequency of interchange
- Interface medium (modem, disk, tape, or network)

Data Control

Periodically, the media report that a disgruntled employee or overenthusiastic computer hacker has destroyed or damaged large sections of corporate or government data bases. It is impossible to protect an HRMS from such problems totally, but designers can take many steps to ensure that only authorized persons have access to data and only authorized procedures take place.

As part of designing and implementing a system, the project team should identify data security needs, establish data security measures, and design routines that audit the activity and effectiveness of those measures. Many of these steps take place only during the implementation phase, but the design team should establish the general framework for the security procedures.

Legal Aspects of Data Privacy

Based on concerns for personal privacy, the Department of Health, Education, and Welfare conducted a study in 1973 that focused on citizens' concern about their rights to privacy. As a result of the findings, Congress enacted several bills to protect citizens' rights to privacy relative to personal information. These included the Privacy Act, the Family Educational Rights and Privacy Act, the Bank Secrecy Act, the Freedom of Information Act, and many more. Three landmark objectives resulted from these acts:

1. To create a proper balance between what an individual is expected to divulge to a record-keeping organization and what he or she seeks in return
2. To open up record-keeping operations in ways that minimize the extent to which recorded information about individuals is itself a source of unfairness in any decision about them
3. To create and define obligations with respect to the uses and disclosures that will be made of recorded information about an individual

Toward those ends, one of the greatest responsibilities of HRMS design is the protection of the privacy rights of individuals about whom data are stored in the data base. This privacy issue should not be confused with data security. Privacy requirements refer to the rights of all employees as individuals; security refers to the protection of information or resources accessible through computers and the prevention of access to unauthorized users, such as competitors.

Users should collect and store only information that employment and management decisions require. The legal aspects of storing employee information in a computer data base relate principally to defensible information and freedom of information.

The project team must review current personal data systems to determine whether those records contain any information that is prohibited by privacy or affirmative action regulations. The team also must clear up any inaccuracies in data input. These checks can point out inadequacies in the human resource function, such as salaries below minimum wage, overlooked salary and performance reviews, or high turnover for a given class of workers. Staff must determine whether the information is accurate, as these records can be used in legal cases, particularly in employment discrimination suits. The system manager is responsible for making sure that the data base does not contain flawed or inaccurate information that may be detrimental to the employer's defense.

Determining Data Security Needs

Designers must include a framework for system security that limits access to personal data. Human resources managers must establish policies and procedures about data control and retention. Certain data are more sensitive than others and must be more rigorously controlled. Newer data base approaches establish authorization systems through access matrices to control personal data. The lack of literature or consensus on how to manage access to personal data contributes to the problem faced by human resources managers.

Computer Viruses And Worms

In the past few years, creative hackers have developed new types of data security threats—viruses and worms. These unauthorized computer instructions destroy or alter important data, leaving analysts, programmers, and entry clerks to straighten out the chaos. When these phenomena first appeared, systems managers could only hope they would not become victims. Now they can use procedures and programs to protect valuable data from tampering.

A *worm* is a set of coded instructions that deletes data as the it "eats" its way through the system. A *virus* is a set of instructions that replicates itself quickly and endlessly throughout a system. Some viruses destroy the file directory, making it impossible for the system to locate requested files and their records. Of the two, viruses pose the greater threat because they can not only infect entire disks but also invade other systems with which the first system interfaces.

Worms and viruses do not appear out of nowhere. To inflict harm on a system, a user must physically import some code to the system. That code must contain the virus or worm, and the user must run the program that contains that code.

Several firms now offer invader detection programs for microcomputers, midrange computers, or mainframes. Using these on existing programs may isolate invasions that took place before the HRSC began its protection procedures. It also is necessary to check programs on systems with which the HRMS interacts. This may entail working out a joint protection plan with other departments and service bureaus.

Any new software should be run through the detection process before it is loaded into the HRMS. Commercially purchased programs pose a negligible threat. Borrowed programs, shareware, bulletin boards, and networks are the main sources of viruses.

The HRSC should establish and enforce a policy of frequent disk backups. This minimizes downtime if a problem does arise. Backups protect the system from many kinds of problems, so protecting against worms and viruses in this way requires no special effort.

Decisions about access depend on the feasibility of their implementation. Designers should address these issues early in the system development process. HRMS designers or managers must determine who should have access to the system, to what parts of the system, and on what basis. As a partial solution, some organizations develop a privilege matrix. This displays a list of potential users against the functions or applications to which they have access. Users have access to the computer system only for specific purposes. Some can add records, change records, or delete records. Other have access to the system only for browsing or viewing records. Although management may have difficulty accepting the concept, those higher up the ladder should have fewer privileges. Managers should not make any alterations to data because they usually do not document their actions.

What specific personal data do organizations need to collect, and who owns that data? Who has the right to access that information? The answer lies in determining who has the *intended use* of the information. For example, a health plan administrator needs access to information about an employee's dependents to define eligibility for benefits. The design team must determine which data need restricted access, then determine which job classifications have access to which data. Data security is a matter of position held, not of specific individuals. A visual representation of a privilege matrix is given in figure 3–16.

The following types of information most commonly require some level of security:

- EEO data. Restrict access to EEO staffers only. Such information should never appear on information distributed to supervisors or for activities such as performance evaluations, except when seeking verification of data.
- Government security clearance. Restrict access to those staffers working with government security clearance planning and supervision. Each government agency has its own special requirements for maintaining the security of such information, and different types of clearances require different levels of security.
- Executive compensation. Restrict access to compensation analysts special-

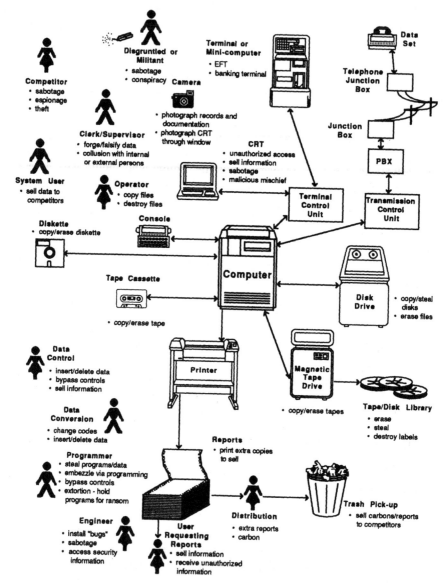

Figure 3–15. Sources of threats to data security. The typical computer system offers numerous points at which individuals may use either physical or electronic means to sabotage or disrupt a firm's data security.

(Source: *Information Center*, Weingarten Publications, Inc. Reprinted with permission.)

DATA SEGMENT	Pos 11462 A. Andrews				Pos 08414 B. Baker				Pos 33718 C. Carlson			
	A	C	D	V	A	C	D	V	A	C	D	V
Employment												
• Applicant Data	X				X							X
• Relocation Data					X	X	X					
• Recruitment Data	X		X									X
Compensation												
• Job Evaluation Data		X	X									
• Performance Data	X											X
• Salary Data	X	X			X	X						X
Training and Development												
• Scheduling Data					X	X						
• Course Data							X					
• Management Data												X

A = ADD
C = CHANGE
D = DELETE
V = VIEW

Figure 3–16. Privilege matrix. This matrix indicates which positions (or individuals) have access to various HRMS data segments. During implementation, this is incorporated into the system's security structure so that access is restricted to staff with need-to-know clearance.

izing in executive compensation or performing duties related to such compensation, such as calculating bonuses, stock options, and so forth.

- Benefits. Among these are data pertaining to medical status and to nonemployees
- Performance reviews.

Limiting Data Access

HRMS designers take various approaches to the practical aspects of data security. In some cases, when data access is limited, the employee file (or other file within the HRMS) will have the affected field blanked out, with a pointer indicating that the data are unavailable for security reasons. The screen may indicate the location of the data, or it may indicate that special clearance is required to access those data. In particular, only certain staff should have the security clearance to invoke the routine that allows changes to be made in those fields. Such actions may require not only a password but also knowledge of a set of procedures that are not self-explanatory.

Access controls and codes play an important role in data security. In many cases, however, designers and managers who are still in the design phase cannot tell who will have intended use. The most acceptable criterion for determining who should have access to personal information is that of a legitimate business need to know. This shifts the burden of proof to the individual seeking access.

Designers must develop access controls, and managers must maintain them after implementation. For example, one company determined that all personal data fell into one of twenty subcategories of classified data. The criterion used to determine access of the data was need to know. Gaining access required a written request that had to be evaluated and approved. Managers evaluated regular access requests based on functional responsibility, organizational level, and scope of authority. They evaluated requests for one-time access based on the nature of the information sought and preset criteria for access.

Some systems place sensitive data in a separate file or program that is accessible only to individuals having certain passwords. In some cases, secure information resides in an entirely separate microcomputer. The security level of data may indicate how data are organized. For instance, certain job classifications or attribute responses automatically trigger unavailability of data on a particular system. Designers can accomplish a similar result while keeping all data on one system, but most companies feel more comfortable keeping the protected data physically separate.

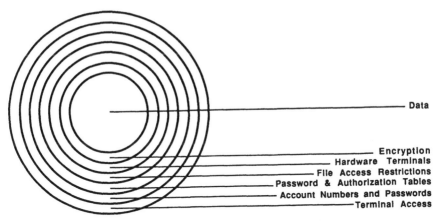

Data

Encryption
Hardware Terminals
File Access Restrictions
Password & Authorization Tables
Account Numbers and Passwords
Terminal Access

Figure 3–17. Layers of security. An effective HRMS has several features designed to safeguard data security. As indicated above, some depend on user or operator actions; others apply to records, files, or terminals.
(Source: *Datamation*, Reed Publishing USA. Reprinted with permission.)

Working with the Implementation Team

The design process is not an end in itself but part of a much larger process. The design work must provide a clearly documented product that others can use in completing their portions of the HRMS development.

HRMS Specifications

The design team should present the specifications for each aspect of system design in a well-organized written report. This report should address the following issues:

- Data base size and content
- Data elements
- Coding structures
- Data base structure
- Tables
- Transaction flow

- Screen designs
- Report designs (type, format, and distribution)
- Data control
- Linkages among various modules

If the organization decides to purchase a system, this information serves as a basis for creating a detailed, useful RFP. To the extent that the organization will be creating or adapting a system, it will use this document to guide programmers and other technical staff in building a system that meets users' needs.

Working with Other Aspects of HRMS Development

When the project team and associated technical staff have completed the HRMS design, their results form the basis for software purchasing, adaptation, and creation. In many cases, the system designers play a key role in software decision making, including whether to purchase a software package, adapt one, or develop custom software.

Several other aspects of HRMS development also require input from the design team. These include the following:

- Vendor selection
- Staff and user training
- Documentation design and production
- Certification and audit procedure development

In some cases, these procedures are included in the design process itself. Other projects define design as pertaining strictly to system performance, with specialists handling these ancillary tasks. In either case, those responsible for training, documentation, and auditing will need to consult with designers to produce a meaningful and complete HRMS. Documentation is discussed in chapter 4; training and auditing are covered in chapter 9.

Glossary

Ad hoc report   A report created by an HRMS user to satisfy a specific reporting need on an as-needed basis.

Algorithm   A procedural or mathematical calculation built into a computer system to compute or manipulate data according to specific rules.

Archive   The process of removing from the data base records not needed on a daily basis and storing them off-line either electronically or by micrographics.

Audit   The process of analyzing data or procedures in the system to see whether the organization's policies are being followed. An audit may report variances to correct immediately or after further review.

Audit trail   The printed documents and computer-maintained records that show the path of transactions through the system.

Batch processing   The procedure by which a computer system accepts transactions, accumulates them, and processes them as part of a group, or batch, of transactions handled at a certain point in a weekly, monthly, or other cycle.

Benefits profile   Output that presents relevant information on an employee's benefits. Among these benefits are group and supplemental life, medical, and dental insurance coverage; long-term and short-term disability and other risk benefits; pension, profit-sharing, and savings plan data; and nonfinancial benefits such as vacations, holidays, and sick leave.

Career profile   Output that records certain events in an employee's career, including skills and experiences, performance appraisals, foreign language fluency, training completed, and potential career paths. Also referred to as *skills profile*.

Coding   The process of using a numeric, alphabetic, or alphanumeric code to represent an element of information. For instance, most systems use M and F to indicate employee sex.

Data element   A named unit of specific information in a data base. The definition of each data element usually specifies data element name, number of characters or integers, and type (alphabetic, numeric, or alphanumeric).

Data security   The protection of information or resources accessible through computers and the control of access only to authorized users. Security has both technical and procedural components.

Demographics   A set of data on a specific population. In employment, the term refers to workers by state, age, income, and education level, as well as information about workers in similar organizations. Some demographic analyses include distribution by race, sex, age, marital status, or other items specific to the issue at hand.

Employee profile   A demographic report on an individual employee that includes a chronology of significant events in that employee's tenure with the organization, such as hire, changes of status, promotions, transfers, salary changes, breaks in service, and termination.

External data base   Information obtained from a source outside the organization's own records or system, such as relevant labor market statistics, health and safety indexes, or labor law citations. May be distributed by an industry association, public agency, or survey firm.

Field   A data element that has a specific location within a record or table; each field is of a designated size and contains very specific data. Also called *data field*. Sometimes used interchangeably with the term *data element*.

File   An electronic collection of records on related subjects. Each record may represent an employee, with a file containing either all current employees or a particular group of employees.

File key   The data element that uniquely identifies a record and classifies it as a member of a category of records within a file. The most common file keys are employee number or social security number for the employee file and job classification code for the job file.

Graphics   Pictures, symbols, or other illustrations generated by a computer. In an HRMS, graphics most often augment text and statistics in management presentations. Usually available as an add-on package rather than as part of a standard HRMS package.

Information   Data that are logically organized, sequenced, and displayed so that users can analyze, interpret, and draw conclusions.

Macro   A string of computer commands or routines that are invoked to trigger a series of data manipulations and other system operations.

Master file   The core data elements for each employee; the data to which most or all human resources applications require access. The master file includes data such as employee name, department, salary, and job classification, as well as demographic data elements that describe individual employees.

Menu   An array of user choices displayed on a screen. The user's choice may trigger one or more system activities or lead to other menus, known as submenus.

Message   A computer-generated statement or choice that appears on the screen to alert the user to a problem, respond to a user request, report on the computer's status, or provide other operating information.

On-line   A term that refers to processing that permits immediate, direct interaction with the data base, including inputs and corrections. Characterized by random transactions, immediate reports (such as a one-time inquiry), and distributed data entry.

Privacy   The rights of employees as individuals to have access to certain data restricted to those having a professional or legal need to know.

Real time   The actual time during which a physical process takes place; generally implies an equivalency to human perception of elapsed time.

Record   A single set of data elements representing one subject. In an HRMS, each record may represent a single employee. A group of records makes up a file.

Routine   A set of computer commands that may include not only mathematical computations but also input/output commands.

Screen   The physical display portion of a computer monitor; the image the user sees on the monitor. The image may include an arrangement of borders, messages, field names, data, icons, and other graphic elements.

Subsystem   A secondary or subordinate small system within a large system.

Table   A set of data organized in columns and rows, with factors identified in the column headings and specific values or conditions provided in the rows descending from those headings. An HRMS usually contains numerous tables listing acceptable codes for certain fields together with their meaning. Other HRMS tables contain data related to jobs, locations, or other conditions.

Transaction code   A macro the user invokes (usually from a list of possible actions) to indicate the type of human resources–related action being taken that will affect an employee's HRMS record. Invoking an action code may trigger the system to expect data updates to specific fields in the employee's record.

Transaction flow   The path data take from the source, through data entry and file maintenance, and to their ultimate output format.

Virus   A computer program designed to invade and disrupt other programs and files. This disruption takes various forms; some viruses fill up systems with meaningless or unwanted data; others destroy the system's file directory, thereby preventing the system from locating requested records.

Worm   An undesired computer program designed to disrupt legitimate programs and files. Once activitated, a worm deletes data in one or many areas of the system.

Discussion Points

1. Describe tasks in HRMS design that in-house staff often accomplish without external resources.

2. Describe tasks in HRMS design that external resources might accomplish best.

3. What are the factors to consider when developing a coding system for employee records?

4. Discuss the components of the human resources data base that the project team must consider before implementing a system.

5. Define the attributes of quality information. Which is the most important aspect and why?

6. What are the differences between on-line and batch processing? For what types of data processing is each most advantageous?

7. What are the most important tools for data security management? Which of these can the HRMS handle internally, and which must the organization handle in other ways?

8. What are the various sources of data? How might they be used in building a data base?

Further Reading

Anderson, Kirk J. "Four Stages of User Maturity." *Journal of Human Resource System Management,* July 1987.

Bassett, Glen A. "EDP Personnel Systems: Do's, Don'ts and How To's." *Personnel,* July/August 1971.

Bena, Bernard G. "What Do We Do with All the Data: Moving from Automation to Analysis in HRIS." *HRSP Review,* Fall 1988.

Ceriello, Vincent R. "A Guide for Building a Human Resource Data System." *Personnel Journal,* September 1978.

Chapman, Robert B. "Securing the HR System: An Introduction." *Computers in Personnel,* Fall 1986.

Fernandez, Eduardo B., Rita C. Summers, and Christopher Wood. *Data Base Security and Integrity.* Reading, MA: Addison-Wesley Publishing Co., 1981.

French, Sue. "Introduction to HR Systems Design." *Computers in Personnel,* Fall 1986.

Harris, Donald. "A Matter of Privacy: Managing Personal Data in Company Computers." *Personnel,* February 1987.

Hoffman, Carl C. "The Potential of Human Resource Data." *Personnel Administrator,* September 1985.

Hoffman, Lance J., ed. *Computers and Privacy in the Next Decade.* New York, Academic Press, 1980.

Martin, M.P. "The Human Connection in System Design: Designing Sytstems for Change." *Journal of Systems Management,* July 1987.

Seamans, Lyman H. "Establishing the Human Resource System Data Base." *Personnel Administrator,* November 1977.

Sharrott, Lawrence. "The Team Approach to Systems Development: You've Got the Advantage." *Computers in Personnel,* Fall 1986.

Simon, Sidney H. "On-Line, Real-Time and Expert System Software Defined." *Personnel Journal,* March 1986.

Southwick, Sarah, and Diane Hatch. "Using Creative Caution in Data Base Management." *Personnel Administrator,* October 1978.

Taylor, J. "Designing a Computerized Personnel Information System: The Benefits of Involving the Users." *Personnel Management,* July 1983.

Westin, Alan F. "The Impact of Computers on Privacy." *Datamation,* December 1979.

Witkin, E. "Developing Requirements for An Applicant Tracking System." *HRSP Review,* Part I, Fall 1988; Part II, Winter 1988.

4
Software for an HRMS

We are entering the information age woefully lacking in information.
—Milton R. Wessel and John L. Kirkley

S oftware refers to computer programs that instruct a computer to perform specific functions. An HRMS incorporates a variety of software
that collects, stores, maintains, retrieves, validates, and outputs data
that pertain to employees, applicants, former employees, and jobs. The software that organizes and manages that data forms the core of the system.

Early systems were used for payroll and other basic operations, such as
compensation and employment history. Less than a decade ago, human resources departments that wanted a comprehensive, adaptable HRMS usually
had to create their own software. Now most departments can find a commercial package that suits the great majority of their needs. Computerization automates more strategic personnel functions, such as job analysis, forecasting,
and performance appraisal. Some modeling systems allow users to pose "what
if" questions in an interactive format in areas such as salary administration
and human resources planning. The rapid growth of human resources software
has irrevocably changed the ways organizations conduct personnel administration. Whether the explosion in available HRMS software has caused or resulted from the growing number and sophistication of HRMS, effective management of human resources in any modern organization of any size requires
an HRMS.

HRMS Software

Software that performs specific functions within human resources is known as
applications software. Applications software handles tasks such as applicant
flow, retiree processing, and payroll accounting. Buyers find no shortage of
good applications software; the challenge is finding the software that best
matches the operating philosophy and needs of a particular human resources
department. Most experts consider applications software the most important
part of any computer system.

Software Attributes for Happy Users

HRMS planners must consider not only technical and functional priorities but also factors that promote user productivity and comfort. These include the following:

- Easy to sign on and establish contact with the software.
- Software uses icons, menus, or both to guide user choices; no need to learn codes and mnemonics
- Software easy to learn and use
- Software guides users through mistakes, process steps, and so forth
- All error messages fully self-explanatory; on-line help provided.
- Data dictionary available on-line
- Software checks syntax, semantics, and integrity
- Software uses windows, scrolling, highlighting, pointers, and other helpful features
- Software offers a tutorial or other self-paced instructional aides
- Software allows for downloading to and uploading from microcomputers
- Software makes effective use of graphics

Vendors generally refer to packaged software as products. HRMS software may address only one function, or it may handle many. The simplest products offer a basic data base with a few functions built in. They may use one of the popular data base management programs that are now extremely popular for business applications. Other HRMS software products have quite specific functions already tailored to human resources. They may come bundled with a complete collection of HRMS software, such as applicant tracking, EEO, benefits, and compensation. Some even come bundled with hardware, utility programs (such as spreadsheets, word processing, and file management), and peripherals.

Some vendors offer products relating to only one human resources function, such as benefits, but offer a choice of several products ranging from basic to sophisticated. Some vendors offer products for only one operating system. Others have several versions of the same product, even coordinating migration paths among such versions.

Selecting and adapting a good set of software allows a human resources department to create a system with the following characteristics:

- Flexible, comprehensive data base management
- Efficient, accurate, and timely data entry
- Rapid retrieval of information on individuals or groups
- Compliance with government regulations
- Generation of standard reports and profiles

In recent years, the growing volume of available software and the emergence of new products have allowed human resources departments to perform these tasks more easily. The ever-increasing external and internal reporting requirements make this even more important.

Some HRMS products are modular—that is; users can implement programs for basic human resources functions at one time, then implement programs for additional functions later. Modular implementation often allows users the greatest degree of comfort, spreads out cost and chaos, minimizes disruption, and allows the new system to be up and running faster than if the department implemented the entire system at once.

Data Base Structure

Data base structure determines how users can access, sort, select, compare, and otherwise manipulate data elements. Of the main types of data base structure—flat, hierarchical, and relational—relational is by far the most prevalent and the most practical in HRMS applications. Flat file structures have a significant limitation: The user can sort only according to a limited set of fields, and the records are much longer, which slows system response time. In setting up separate but related tables or files, the system cannot connect information from one file with information from another file without duplicating at least part of that information in both files.

A diagram of a hierarchical data base looks like a tree, with each set of data having subsets and those subsets in turn having further subsets. Each group of data is completely separate from the others. This type of data base works well in very structured, stable information systems, such as presentation of military organizations—squad within platoon, within company, within battalion, within army corps, and so forth. However, most personnel systems contain too much interrelated and multiuse information to work well in hierarchical data bases. An inverted hierarchical data base has an upside-down arrangement: Several groups of data feed into one set, then a group of sets feeds into a larger set. This type of data base cannot relate information in one set to information in another parallel set. Again, such a structure does not work well for an HRMS.

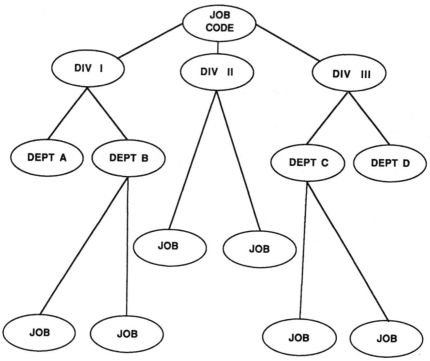

Figure 4–1. Hierarchical data base. A hierarchical data base resembles a tree; each set of data has subsets that, in turn, have subsets, but each subset connects to only one set. To connect data in one group with data in another, a hierarchical data base must duplicate data in the other set.

By comparison, relational data bases can sort on any field, which facilitates not only ad hoc reporting but also overall system flexibility. A relational data base presents its data as a collection of tables. Users can relate information in different files by using a common element, such as employee name or number. For instance, each employee record may contain a job location field. That field links each employee's record to a file on job locations that contains fields such as address and safety hazards. Thus, changing the safety hazard list in the job location file automatically changes the safety hazards linked to each employee at that site without having to access each employee record.

A typical human resources application of a relational data base may connect data on people, job, and salary range. The employee master record might include a field called job classification code. This points to a field in a job file that converts the code to its English-language equivalent—a job title. The job file also contains a salary grade field for each job classification. That field, in

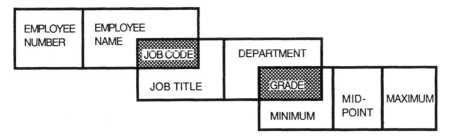

Figure 4–2. Relational data base. Relational data bases allow linking of multiple files and tables by a common field. In this example, the job code field establishes a relationship between an employee's personal record and the job record. The user can access data from both files simultaneously without having to access duplicate data.

turn, points to a field in a salary range table that lists the authorized minimum, midrange, and maximum salary for each corresponding job classification.

In the past few years, Apple Computer, Inc. and other manufacturers have introduced a new type of data base known as hypertext. Hypertext uses a decision tree-type process. Any entry in a file may connect to a pathway of additional related information. As with other Macintosh applications, hypertext has strong graphics and visual design elements. Users can access data paths that look like on-screen file cabinets, file folders, and Rolodex cards. Most hypertext users need to handle massive amounts of related but not necessarily matrix-style information. Such approaches work well for sophisticated users or users with unpredictable information needs. However, vendors have not yet found significant applications for this approach to human resources data base management.

As any system sorts data, it may tie up the entire master data base. The design team should look for a system that not only does this sorting rapidly but also transfers the sorted data into a new file and releases the master data base. This new file, known as a data set, contains only the data elements requested. The system can then manipulate the data set without impeding other users' access to the system.

Data Base Content

Data Elements. Each system comes with a set of data elements, and each element comes with certain characteristics, such as definition, field length, field type (alphabetic, numeric, or alphanumeric), and associated codes. Most systems offer some flexibility about data elements. Often buyers can add and delete elements. Most allow users to change element names, field size, and other characteristics. For instance, most packages have specific date formats but allow authorized users to change them to conform to in-house requirements. Thus, an organization may acquire a system that regularly displays dates as MM/DD/YY (03/11/89) but then converts the format to DD/MMM/YY (11 MAR 89). In older systems, particularly mainframes, the vendor set field length, and users had limited flexibility in making adjustments. In newer systems, users may adjust field length through the dynamic data dictionary. Most systems allow users to designate almost any field as a calculated or derived field. Only the user's imagination and requirements limit the variety of information the system can derive from other data instead of requiring direct entry.

More and more HRMS now use mnemonic coding, which usually maximizes user comfort and accuracy. Even so, HRMS packages use widely differing code tables. The type and complexity of coding for any particular data element depends on the users' needs. For instance, one HRMS may express a data element such as education level in as few as four codes (Less Than High School, High School, Some College, College Degree), which may be expressed as choices 1 through 4. On the other hand, a company with highly technical job classifications may need 40 or more education codes to include every degree type (High School Diploma, Associate of Arts, Bachelor of Science, Master of Business Administration, Doctorate, Postdoctorate, and so forth). With so many choices, using numbers may leave users without sufficient reference points; in such cases, use of two-letter abbreviations may work better.

Files. Packaged systems come with several sets of files ready for the HRMS implementation team to add the organization's own data. Most files are employee files; others are job classification files. Each file has a set of data fields. Some organizations with a large volume of employees may choose to segregate various employee types such as full-time, part-time, temporary, seasonal, and so forth. Others simply add the organization, division, region, or other locator code to the file key so that employees are automatically segregated.

A relational data base system minimizes the amount of duplicate information needed in employee and job files. For instance, when working in an employee's record, the system can automatically display on the screen information from the job classification table that corresponds to that employee's job classification number.

Tables. An HRMS needs dozens, even hundreds, of tables. Vendors provide three basic approaches to tables: canned, structured, and user defined. Completed tables, called canned tables, contain mandated codes, such as EEO codes, that most users will not need to change. Vendors usually provide many more tables that do not contain any data but that have columns and rows corresponding to particular fields. For instance, the wage-rate table may list column names as Wage Rate 1, Wage Rate 2, Wage Rate 3, and so on. It may designate rows as Base Hourly Rate, Overtime Hourly Rate, Holiday Hourly Rate, and so on. The user then provides the actual table data, such as $12.50, $18.75, $25.00, and so on.

Vendors have discovered that users find it easier to build new tables than to modify existing ones. Most programs have facilities for table generation, using a special table maintenance area of the program. To create new tables, authorized technical users obtain data from a human resources functional expert who understands the data and how they should relate to each other. The technical person then creates or adapts the table and routes it back to the human resources functional expert for review and approval.

Every organization should assume it will need a certain number of tables in addition to those the vendor supplies. Creating and adapting tables is part of the adaptation of even a purchased system to work in a specific environment. The project team should evaluate documentation to see the extent to which the vendor gives clear, complete instructions for how to create and adapt tables.

Many programs also allow users to obtain listings of existing tables by working through a series of menus in the table maintenance area. Usually the system can create lists that sort tables according to the human resources functional area to which they pertain.

Data Flow and Control

Effective transaction flow stems primarily from organizational procedures and practices. However, some aspects of software can make this process function more smoothly. For instance, vendors often supply input forms that correspond to their data bases and screens. By using these forms (and adapting them in accordance with modifications made to the system), the department can increase the accuracy and completeness of data entering the system. Purchased HRMS usually come with transaction code schemas already completed. Each time the user enters a transaction of a certain type (such as salary change, job transfer, or layoff), the system prompts for a transaction code. This code indicates the reason for the transaction, such as promotion or performance review. Some systems allow the addition of custom transaction codes together with the required alterations to the data dictionaries and macros that control updating.

As discussed in chapter 3, users control system activities by invoking algorithms, routines, and macros. The typical system already includes hundreds of such formulas; contemporary microcomputer systems allow advanced users to add and edit such procedures. The project team must make sure that the data base will contain all the data such instructions require. They should also check that formulas and routines will be available for any data that depend on calculation or derivation.

In purchasing a system, the project team should expect to spend time early in the implementation phase making some changes in algorithms. Before vendor selection, the team should ask about provisions for changing or adding instructions as appropriate.

Users should not have to specify every available option each time the system is run, so look for automatic defaults. This means that if nothing is specified, the computer automatically assumes that the user wants to use the default value. Most systems come with preset defaults for certain formats and operations. For instance, a sequencing program might be set to sort automatically in ascending order unless told to do otherwise. Or, in the absence of an entered date, the system assumes the current date. Each system allows authorized users to change the values of some of these automatic defaults. It designates which default elements and operations authorized users can change and what choices users have for these defaults. The more flexible these rules, the more human resources can wind up with a system that adapts to the organization rather than the other way around. Microcomputer systems usually have significant flexibility in operations and value choices, as well as in data base adaptability, because they use more modern technology designed to respond to the needs of a wide variety of users. To make such changes in a mainframe system, the vendor must supply the source code, and technicians must modify the program.

Because human resources activities involve such high volumes of data entry and update, the data management package must guard against the considerable potential for data error. For this reason, most systems have procedures for edit and validation of data entry. Adequate edit and validation rules, as well as good on-line inquiry, make the system more accurate and easier to use. User mistakes cause most system malfunctions. As discussed in earlier chapters, edit and validation procedures prevent an operator from entering an obvious mistake—the computer traps it and will not accept it. For example, a salary transaction should not allow posting of an entry to work history if old salary plus salary increase does not equal new salary. It should perform the arithmetic and reject any mistakes. Similarly, the software should trap any zip code entries that have only four digits, include alpha characters, or do not match the state abbreviation. For example, a zip code for a California (CA) address always begins with 9.

One HRMS user learned this lesson the hard way. He bought an integrated system that worked fine until a personnel clerk accidentally entered the wrong month when posting certain transactions. He pressed 7 for July when he meant to press 6 for June. The company had to hire a contract programmer to come in for several weeks to straighten out the ensuing mess. The moral of the story is to make sure the software has adequate safeguards against human error.

Human resources data base users often must move from one record to another to perform their tasks. On-line inquiry allows authorized users to query and display any record contained in the data base and to generate hard copy if needed.

Virtually all HRMS have a variety of data security features. Human resources records involve a significant amount of data to which only certain staff should have access. Data access is a function of job responsibility rather than of a specific individual, so access authorization should depend on position code rather than on the specific user. An HRMS usually has a method by which it recognizes a unique password for each user; it links the password to that individual's employee identification number and thus to that individual's position code. The position code includes codes for data restrictions, which the system then activates whenever that user logs on the system.

Systems should include two different types of restriction—restricted view and restricted edit. Numerous human resources staff members may have legitimate reasons to view a particular data field, such as salary, but only a few authorized individuals may have authorization to change it. Some systems even allow field value security; for instance, the system may allow a particular user to view salary fields for all employees, except those whose salaries equal or exceed $50,000 per year.

Output

Good data input and processing achieves the desired results only when coupled with good screen design, report design, and output distribution. Most systems are *menu* based. At the start of system execution, a main menu outlines the basic options. The user simply enters the number or code or moves the cursor to the appropriate choice. Choosing an option may take the user to a submenu that lists more specific processes from which the user can choose. Self-explanatory menus make navigating around the system easier. The menus and submenus allow users to select activities and data records without having to remember function keys or codes. Some systems allow operators to use menus to move from one file to another or from one human resources application to another. Not all software is sufficiently complex to require menus, but in general, the enterprise should not settle for HRMS software without this feature. Systems that are not menu based seldom have other features that override the disadvantages of working without menus.

Each application has not just one but numerous *screens* of information for each individual. For instance, a benefits module may have screens such as: eligibility enrollment, insurance coverage, vacation/sick leave, and COBRA

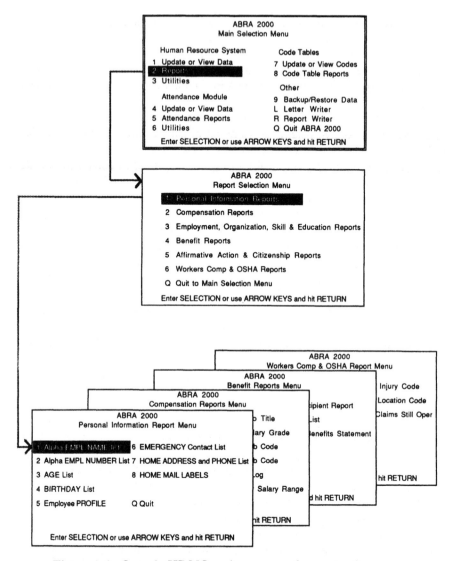

Figure 4–3. Sample HRMS main menu and report submenus.
(Source: AbraCadabra Software. Reprinted with permission.)

transactions. Good systems design screens so that the most common human resources transactions and inquiries require movement among as few screens as possible.

Data base management software contains dozens, usually hundreds, of different *messages* available for display to users. The most common messages are help comments, error messages, status messages, prompts, and menus. For instance, help messages answer user requests for further information about a particular command or other feature. Error messages may pertain to improper command sequences or to conflicts in edit and validation of data. Status messages tell the user what the central processing unit (CPU), printer, or other associated components are doing. Prompts give the operator instructions about what to do next. For instance, some prompts ask for the entry of certain data to complete a particular transaction. Messages should be written in simple, unambiguous English, not in technical jargon. Messages should provide action choices and suggestions wherever appropriate. The greater the specificity and diversity of messages, the more users can correct mistakes and solve problems independent of HRIS staff.

The typical HRMS contains hundreds of *standard reports*. Most of these are detail reports, or the simple compilation of data from individual records. Executives and other analysts need summary reports that provide totals, comparisons, and other analyses based on individual records. To produce most summary reports (as well as some additional detail reports), users generally must rely on their system's *ad hoc report capability*, which allows them to add new reports. Most HRMS include this feature, but they vary considerably in flexibility and ease of use. To define a new report, the analyst first uses a command language to specify headings, descriptions, formats, totals and subtotals, and sequences. Then the analyst specifies which data will be included, such as the field, values, and logic desired. A report generator increases the usefulness of any program and also can extend its life, since it gives users the ability to modify output to meet changing conditions and new requirements.

Operating Systems, Utilities, and General Business Software

Selecting software for an HRMS involves more than finding a system that performs most of the human resources functions well. The system must work with other hardware and software. Many organizations want new software to run on existing hardware, so the new system must be compatible with those machines. An organization also may want its system to interact with additional support software.

Operating Systems

Every computer, large or small, has an operating system. The operating system is the special language the operator and the software use to control computer activities. Operating system selection is generally intertwined with software selection. Each specific version of a software program can run only on one specific operating system, so selection of particular HRMS software determines which type of operating system the applications software can use for those operations.

Increasingly, vendors offer software programs in various versions for different operating systems. However, an HRMS running under one operating system may not have exactly the same features as the "same" program in a version that works under a different operating system. To ensure compatibility and maximum performance, HRMS planners must consider the operating system and application software jointly.

Each model of computer, particularly a microcomputer, is designed to run only one specific operating system (or at most two). The first major wave of microcomputers used DOS (Disk Operating System). This operating system has diversified into newer and more powerful DOS releases to incorporate improvements and enhancements. Most microcomputer systems use some version of DOS.

The newest generation of IBM-compatible microcomputers can use both DOS and a new operating system known as OS/2. OS/2 is designed to facilitate use of larger data systems and more powerful software.

Apple's Macintosh family and Hewlett-Packard computers feature completely different types of operating systems. Users control the operating system (and other programs) by manipulating a mouse pointer, icon, and pull-down menus. Such features produce a level of operating system transparency that works well for many users. Although the Apple Macintosh series and some Hewlett-Packard computers have made inroads in many business environments, very few HRMS applications are available in these operating environments.

UNIX and XENIX, used in microcomputers, minicomputers, and mainframes, are powerful operating systems that facilitate custom programming, telecommunications integration, multiuser operation, and higher-level operations. Only a few vendors offer HRMS applications for the UNIX environment, however, and some experts feel that gaps in protocols and standards development have impeded the acceptance of UNIX in HRMS applications.

Operating systems for mainframe computers come in many different forms. All have different protocols and require particular types of expertise. Although system programmers must have knowledge of the operating system, most application programmers do not need too much experience with it beyond its basic functions.

In computers, the term *architecture* refers to the way in which a machine routes and processes data internally. This level of design is ingrained in machine design and is the basis for the operating system. Only machines with compatible architecture can run compatible operating systems. Some large computer manufacturers have begun promoting a type of system architecture that allows mainframes and microcomputers to trade data and applications using a common processing environment. Systems taking advantage of this link are still limited, but there probably will be significant growth in this area in the near future.

If the HRMS trades data with another department or external system, the project team should find out what operating system the other group uses. Conversion packages translate data from one operating system to another, and outside firms also provide data conversion services. Transfer between different operating systems or programs can work efficiently if it is used for the coordination or consolidation of efforts rather than as an ongoing production process. The project team must examine the options thoroughly. If information exchange takes place only once a year or so, such as to provide data for year-end accounting, translation may be appropriate. If the organization's current microcomputers use DOS, a switch to OS/2 for new IBM-compatible microcomputers may work—if data exchange is periodic rather than ongoing.

System Utility Software

Some simple utility programs perform limited but critical functions in keeping the HRMS working well. Many such programs exist, but most HRMS applications require only a few. Three types to consider follow.

Backup and Restore Utilities. Usually these are part of the operating system. Some software converts these into a more accessible form, written in the same style and menu-command structure as the HRMS software. These can then appear as part of the main menu or are available to authorized staff through submenus.

Data Conversion Programs and Emulators. These programs convert data from user files into other formats for telecommunications and for transfer to other computers or systems. Most packaged software includes some conversion facility. It is important to check whether the packages under consideration can handle the conversions the organization's HRMS will require. If not, the system may need to accommodate special conversion software written for that application or package. With any conversion utility, the project team should check to see whether such software handles output from and input to the HRMS without special coding.

Screen Protection Software. This software automatically turns off the monitor's screen if a given number of seconds have passed without a keystroke. This not only protects the screen from image burn-in but also promotes data security when users leave their workstations without closing sensitive files. This software will not close the file or program or remove the record being displayed but will cause the screen to go blank. A single keystroke will bring back the screen image exactly as it was before.

In general computer environments, the term *utility software* refers to special programs that help the user maintain or interact with the operating system more easily. In human resources applications, *utility software* also refers to the general business software on which users sometimes rely, such as word processing and spreadsheets.

Word Processing Software

Many HRMS packages contain only the most rudimentary word processing software or provide an interface to some of the more popular word processing packages. If an organization does not intend to produce text-intensive, narrative reports with its HRMS, the simple word processing capabilities of the HRMS package might meet its basic requirements, such as form letters. However, the features provided must be compared carefully with those needed or desired. If a gap exists, the project team should explore packaged word processing software that interfaces with the HRMS packages under consideration. Most word processing software can also receive and save files in ASCII for exchange with other programs.

In evaluating such software, the project team should consider the capabilities already discussed for HRMS-related software in general. Several other factors relate specifically to word processing, including the following:

- Mail-merge capabilities
- WYSIWYG ("What you see is what you get"), the extent to which the on-screen image shows how the printed document will look
- Spell-checking features
- Automatic repagination
- Capability to create custom glossary of frequently used text
- Ease of formatting output
- Ease of using column and column-and-row formats
- Ease of moving, inserting, and deleting text
- Ability to access multiple documents simultaneously
- Ease of generating outlines and tables of contents
- Ability to preview full-screen formatting before printing

Graphics Software

Most HRMS reports are tabular, with rows and columns of words and figures. For extensive text or graphics reports, the HRMS package must interface with a word processing or graphics program.

Desktop publishing software and specialized graphics packages allow for easy graphics creation and integration of graphics and text. This facilitates production of newsletters, brochures, presentations, benefits booklets, and reports that include both text and graphics. These capabilities have become popular in business software. Other programs augment laser, impact, and dot matrix printers with a wide variety of font options. Although not every human resources application requires these capabilities, many could benefit from them.

Chapter 3 describes the types of graphic presentations that are most common and useful in HRMS. When considering graphics packages, the project team should evaluate features such as the following:

• Ease of interface with the HRMS package
• Ability to include multiple graphics on a single page
• Variety of print fonts
• Ability to shrink and expand graphic displays
• Insert text and labels as appropriate
• Built-in images and icons (such as maps, coins, or human figures)
• Ability to accept additional images
• Ability to preview output on screen before printing

Telecommunications Software

Teleprocessing is the act of sharing data and files among computers and terminals. To carry out teleprocessing, the HRMS needs software that converts the computer codes into electronic signals ready for transfer over phone lines. The project team must choose telecommunications software that works with the selected HRMS software. Team members also should determine and comply with the hardware requirements and protocols for telecommunications software. Increasingly, firms require files and records to be accessible to users in multiple locations on a simultaneous basis. Telecommunications software is the medium for achieving this.

For internal electronic communication, many firms have implemented electronic mail or voice mail, also known as E-mail or V-mail. These processes allow authorized employees to send messages to other employee workstations. E-mail allows easy proof of transmission and time, inclusion of reports or other data in the message, and routing of identical messages to multiple recipients simultaneously. E-mail users avoid inconveniences such as lost slips of paper, overlooked messages, and unnecessary call-back messages. In most instances, it allows more information security than does paper transmission. In human resources, many firms now use E-mail as part of various employee transactions that do not involve any other data linkage with the HRMS.

Spreadsheets and Other General Business Software

Most human resources departments use general business software such as spreadsheets, accounting packages, data bases, mail-list packages, and planning and scheduling applications. Since all these programs use HRMS data, users appreciate having a central system that interacts with the business software they use. In fact, as will be discussed further in chapter 18, many human resources planning and forecasting applications are special models based on commercial spreadsheet programs.

In selecting a spreadsheet program, the project team should consider the following features in addition to the features already discussed for software in general:

- Types of statistical operation possible
- Ability to set width of individual columns
- Insert, delete, and move columns and rows
- Ability to protect cells from alteration
- Macro commands
- Ability to link spreadsheets with the data base
- Global search and replace
- Flexible page formatting
- Entry of descriptive text

Packaged or Custom Programs?

An organization can acquire software in one of three ways—packaged, custom, or a combination of the two. The decision depends on the needs of the organization, commercial options available, and the organization's resources for HRMS development.

Packaged Software

Packaged, or canned, software products are, by definition, already written and ready for the buyer to install. Vendors design and market packaged software for a wide range of users and an equally wide variety of needs. Most packages include a series of programs and documentation designed and written to perform defined functions. Vendors may offer packages that perform payroll accounting, personnel record keeping, forecasting, benefits administration, or budgeting. Packaged software prices include supporting documentation and basic maintenance agreements. Most vendors provide extended training, maintenance, and customization at additional cost.

Packaged HRMS software offers many advantages. First, because the cost of development is spread among many buyers, canned software costs much less than comparable custom-developed systems. More importantly, a packaged system is ready to run. Potential users can test packaged software before purchase and ask other users about their experiences with it. Because vendors continually field-test their packaged software at customer sites, such systems often run faster and have more options than does custom software.

Despite all these advantages, an organization that relies on commercial packages for all its needs may encounter problems. The company may have difficulty comparing HRMS software vendors scattered across the country. Many excellent vendors are small operators who advertise little, if at all. Potential customers should consider such firms, since some of their products surpass those that are widely advertised. Moreover, some of these products satisfy unique needs, such as pension and profit-sharing reporting, workers' compensation, succession planning, flexible benefits, and the like.

No system will ever match an organization's needs 100 percent, even if users have stated those needs properly. Most experts consider 75 percent a good fit. Using packaged software may require some adjustments of internal procedures. For example, tax accounting may mean one thing to the buyer and quite another to the designers of the tax accounting programs. To use this software properly, a firm may need to change schedules, eliminate procedures, revise forms, alter certain reports, or otherwise modify business practices. "We sell our products the same way they sell hot dogs at the ballpark," admits one vendor's marketing vice president. "If you want them grilled or with rye bread, you have to go somewhere else."

To get the right HRMS software, potential buyers must spend considerable time evaluating different packages. This time and expense raises the real price. Canned packages also have other hidden costs, such as software maintenance. Systems deteriorate over time and become less responsive as new updates conflict with modifications made to earlier versions. In addition, the operating environment may change, and more and different peripheral devices may be needed. Bugs appear long after the HRMS goes into operation. Business, regulatory, and tax conditions change, requiring software updates. Murphy's Law certainly applies here.

Usually buying software really means leasing or licensing the products from the vendor. Alternatively, it could mean accessing an HRMS through time-sharing or service bureaus, though the cost of time-share networks has decreased the viability of this option. In this case, the organization does not own anything and therefore cannot control how the system is modified or enhanced. If the service does meet the basic system requirements, however, a subscribing firm may save a significant amount of money.

Packaged software plays a central role in turnkey systems. A turnkey system is a combination of hardware and software developed for a specific market. Vendors bundle the hardware and software with services and support to make

Turnkey or Turkey?

A turnkey system should arrive ready to begin processing transactions, computing salary increases, forecasting staffing needs, generating EEO and OSHA reports, and doing other useful work. Why, then, do many turnkey systems turn out to be turkeys?

Problem 1. Like an absentee landlord, the absentee system developer may not be immediately available to help if something goes wrong or if something is not completely understood by the user. If the developer is available, it may be difficult for him or her to help, since he or she is probably working on some other job at the time.

Problem 2. The vendor may no longer be in existence when the firm needs help. As a result, the user is left without support, documentation, or repair facilities.

Problem 3. The firm grows, and its needs change. The key still turns, but it no longer satisfies the firm's needs. The system may be expandable, but it may have become expendable. The most important single fact about a minicomputer is that its very presence generates a need for more computing and different types of computing.

The real problem is systems design. A solid computer professional, confronted with a firm's functional and operational needs, methods, plans for expansion, and computing problems, will design, develop, and help implement a system that is sufficiently flexible for the future. He or she will include hardware that can grow and software that can be modified later. He or she will provide good documentation and thoroughly train in-house staff. Vendors that have standard turnkey products should be ready, willing, and able to modify them— or else not recommend them for a firm's human resources application. This is a difficult decision for them even if they are completely honest about it. Thus, it is important that an organization have some computer literacy.

Many of the problems of turnkey systems occur because users depend too heavily on outside support. If a firm can modify programs itself or hire someone to fix the system when the hardware breaks or the software crashes, it is in much better shape.

(Adapted from: Vincent Ceriello, "Minicomputer HR Systems: Turnkey or Turkey?" *Personnel News,* January/February 1988.)

it immediately and directly responsive to special needs. Vendors offer special-ized turnkey systems for many vertical markets, such as banks, contractors, and retailers.

Custom Software

Custom software generally refers to systems that are tailor-made by software vendors or system development firms to solve specific problems for individual clients. A user may turn to custom systems because of difficulty finding the right package. Although this software process is more expensive, some people believe that it is worth the extra cost to have control over the HRMS, not the other way around. Ideally, this process results in software that is exactly what the client wants. Such systems differ from packaged products in much the same way that custom-built homes differ from housing developments.

Some firms with sophisticated computer experience may even build their own HRMS in-house. A firm's HRMS design team may start with a skeleton or framework and customize the HRMS to suit the organization's needs. A skeleton system is a basic collection of data elements, usually from an existing system. The team builds the system around some specific data base manage-ment system (DBMS). Focus, DB/2, Informix, ORACLE, Revelation, and dBase are a few of the more popular DBMS in wide use today. In rare cases, an organization may even try to develop a system from the ground up.

A new and prominent feature of HRMS software is the advent of fourth-generation languages (4GLs). 4GLs are high-productivity languages that facil-itate faster, less technical approaches to system development and modification. Their predecessors, third-generation languages (3GLs), include FORTRAN and COBOL at the mainframe level and BASIC for microcomputers. As shown in figure 4–4, the second generation refers to assembly language, a very technical but versatile type of language that is rarely used for programming. The first generation refers to machine language, the binary communication method into which all languages eventually must be translated in order for the computer to understand them.

Compared with these other types of languages, 4GLs are generally easy to learn and use. Their command protocols more closely resemble English-language statements. Although 4GLs are still quite technical, users can make changes and issue report requests in relatively nontechnical language. A 4GL needs fewer lines of code than a 3GL to perform similar functions.

A 4GL includes a veritable tool kit of system utility and productivity com-ponents, such as DBMS, report generators, screen generators, graphics lan-guages, application generators, and querying of individual records. A dynamic data dictionary allows users to change the definitions of data elements, codes, and edit rules within the system at a level that does not require changes to program code. Thus, when a user changes a data element in the data

GENERATION

1

| MACHINE LANGUAGE |

BINARY   OCTAL

```
0101111110100000000010001000010010001   277200104
0100010000010110000000000010000011100   210160000
0110100000010100000010110100011100110   320120132
0000010000010100000011100011111111001   010120161
```

| ASSEMBLED LANGUAGE |

2

```
LX,M    X8,OLDMAS
LA      A5,GRSPY,X8
MSI     A5,TAXRT
SA      A5,NETPY
CT      A5,GRSPY,=>,050000
```

| COMPILED LANGUAGE |

3

```
NET = GROSS – TAX
TAX = GROSS * TAX_RATE
IF GROSS > 5000 THEN TAX_RATE =.4
ELSE TAX_RATE =.3
```

| NEAR-ENGLISH |

4   Compute Net Pay From Gross Pay and Tax Rate.

Figure 4–4. Four generations of computer languages. As shown in this example, each succeeding generation has moved closer to human speech, becoming easier for users to learn and use.

dictionary, the system applies this change every time that element appears within the HRMS, such as in screens, reports, and data sets.

One of the greatest contributions of 4GLS is higher productivity in developing new computer applications. IS departments often experience increases as high as 5:1 or 10:1 in programmer productivity compared with third-generation compiled languages. Employees at most levels can learn to use the basic feature of 4GLs with much less formal training than 3GLs require. Further, 4GLs can help achieve the desired results sooner, which saves both time and money.

These higher-level languages do have some drawbacks, such as reduced computer speed and higher overhead. In the end, computers convert all infor-

Group for Which Function is Suitable

4GL Function	User Community	Systems Analysts	Computer Programmers
Simple Query Languages	X		
Complex Query and Update Languages		X	X
Report Generators	X	X	
Graphics Languages		X	
Decision-Support Languages	X	X	
Application Generators		X	X
High-Level Programming Languages			X

Figure 4–5. 4GL functions and the groups that use them. 4GLs come with a variety of programming tools; the choices of which tools to look for and which ones to use depend on who will be using the 4GL. These are only some of the possible 4GL functions; many 4GLs come with a wide array of additional technical options.

mation into machine code, or numbers. As a computer language moves farther away from machine code and closer to human speech, the need for translation increases, which reduces machine efficiency. For these reasons, 4GLs require comparatively more computer resources to achieve similar results. As a result, system efficiency may decrease. Given the speed, power, and inherent input/output-bound character of the modern HRMS, however, this generally is not a significant concern.

Security is another issue with such systems. Easy system change increases the chance that an unauthorized individual may affect system structure in a way that is detrimental to operations. Proper planning for 4GL adoption requires implementation of data security limits that compensate for this potential exposure.

Not all 4GLs are the same; developers must investigate the likely candidates before selecting the best 4GL for their needs. Developers should consider several factors in adopting a 4GL for a specific environment. These include integration with existing 3GL-based applications, status of standards and guidelines, availability of training and support, and lack of security. Having chosen and used a 4GL, users should try to stick with this approach if possible. Changing 4GLs in midstream causes many problems and can bring the HRMS to its knees.

An organization that decides to develop its own system should use experienced developers and implementers. These may be internal staff, job-shop personnel, or consultants. They should be able to give advice about what is and is not possible to provide in the system under consideration. Often they can suggest enhancements and additions that will make the HRMS even more productive. In addition, they generally service what they sell, and they will maintain and enhance the software as needed. Finding someone to do custom development can be difficult. Few people have the experience to evaluate whether a given developer is suitably qualified. Experienced analysts and programmers—especially those who know HRMS applications—are in great demand, as are people who can function effectively as consultants. Custom development involves a massive amount of deliberation and decision making. People working on such projects should have good communications skills and should be able to handle changes with grace and responsiveness.

A Combination of Packaged and Custom Software

Some firms combine the lower cost of packaged programs with the more tailored functions of a custom system by using specialists to modify a standard package to meet their particular needs. This combination approach is not easy. First, many vendors do not want to modify packages. Such assignments do not pay as well as starting from scratch, and they present less of a challenge. In addition, some commercially available systems use machine language coding that is difficult, if not impossible, to alter. Because of these difficulties, modified systems are often more cumbersome to run and more costly to maintain than off-the-shelf software. One way out of this dilemma is to have the software developer or vendor who wrote the package make the modifications. This can work if the buyer negotiates a firm contract that establishes cost and specifies a definite completion date.

Make or Buy?

Acquiring an HRMS does have many advantages over creating one in-house. For one thing, unanticipated higher-priority projects can result in delays and staff reassignments. Delays may lead to a breakdown of the consensus on the system's original goals and objectives. Originally, management may have wanted cost-control features, but as time passes they may want program sup-

Make Or Buy Decision Making

If it is important to...	...then consider this option:		
	Make	*Buy*	*Use Consultant*
Conserve internal technical resources	No	Yes	Maybe
Utilize available internal technical and management resources	Yes	No	Maybe
Avoid increasing staff	No	Maybe	Yes
Find out more about other system development options	Maybe	No	Yes
Have system match organization rather than pressure organization to change procedures	Yes	No	Maybe
Be compatible with existing or related system	Yes	No	Maybe
Develop a complex system, serving numerous human resources functions	Maybe	No	Yes
Protect data from external security risks	Yes	Maybe	No
Implement efficiently even if not perfect	No	Yes	Maybe
Assign accountability for HRMS success	Maybe	No	Yes
Have an external service organization provide support and upgrades	No	Yes	Maybe

(Source: Richard A. Kaumeyer, Jr., *Planning and Using Skills Inventory*, Van Nostrand Reinhold, 1979. Reprinted with permission.)

port instead. If the organization cannot afford to make these changes, it is probably better not to try to build an HRMS in-house. To reach a make-or-buy decision, the HRMS project team must consider time, internal resources, cost, scope, and maintenance.

Time and Internal Resources. Consider how long it will take to develop the HRMS. Do the in-house technical resources have the time to invest in the project? How complex and comprehensive will the system be? If the organization decides to develop the HRMS internally, will the project, once started, be managed properly so that it can be brought to a successful conclusion?

In-house development can be time-consuming and can involve personnel directly or indirectly for one to three years. If the organization is sure that it can dedicate the proper resources for at least twelve to eighteen months, it might consider developing the HRMS itself. However, if the project is going to take longer than that or if the resources may not be available, acquiring the HRMS may be a better option.

One alternative is to divide the work load between the technical staff of the firm and a consultant. For example, the contractor may provide the software for file maintenance, while the firm writes the input, edit, and validation programs or the report generator. If the firm is already using a particular DBMS, the contractor might provide the application software—the HRMS itself—while the firm brings the system to operational status under the DBMS.

Unlike vendors, in-house staff traditionally have not been held accountable contractually with performance clauses. Some firms are now contracting with their in-house technical resources for staff, computer time, facilities, and documentation, and they enforce performance terms as they would with an outside vendor.

Costs. If managers decide to acquire the HRMS, will the results outvalue the costs? A firm must compare estimated consultant fees for each option and consider both direct and indirect costs associated with the acquisition options under consideration. Direct and overhead costs relate to current in-house activities. They also include the losses the organization may incur if IS staff are involved in developing or redesigning an existing system and, therefore, are unavailable for other projects. These costs can be direct dollar and time losses or opportunity costs. The organization must determine whether it has qualified resources to undertake HRMS development. Likewise, in-house resources must be evaluated concerning their experience in developing and maintaining an acquired HRMS.

Scope. The scope of the proposed system may influence the advisability of make versus buy. A more complex system may require time and resources beyond what the organization can commit. The following factors tend to determine the complexity of system design:

- Inclusion of numerous human resources functions (A system that serves just applicant tracking and EEO will be easier to make or buy than one that also serves benefits, training, and compensation.)
- Inclusion of certain human resources functions more likely to require custom design (For instance, because planning and forecasting are usually highly individualized, canned packages appeal to a relatively small proportion of this market.)
- Interfacing with other existing systems (either internal or external) and with utility software (such as graphics, word processing, and spreadsheets)
- Unique needs and highly specific human resources practices

The more specialized the application, the more likely it is that the human resources department will need and want to build its own system. In general, if the special requirements affect only a few human resources functions, the HRMS design team may consider buying what it can for most functions, with the source code included, then building modules for the remaining special functions. For example, one company bought a management succession module, integrated it with its master HRMS data base, and modified the module to function as an emergency replacement planning tool rather than for management succession.

Sometimes the technical environment plays a major role in the decision of whether to build or buy a new system. If the firm has a special primary computer language, a customized compiler, or a unique hardware configuration, in-house work may proceed more smoothly than implementing a purchased system.

Maintenance. The project team should consider maintenance issues in deciding whether to make or buy. Such factors include availability of maintenance staff and the need to optimize the performance of the HRMS. The operating philosophy of the IS department also makes a difference. Some departments believe that users should take responsibility for developing system enhancements, whereas others keep this responsibility within technical IS operations.

Which way is best? The debate has raged for years and will continue because no acquired system is ever perfect. Each of the three methods—making, buying, or using a combination—has proved satisfactory for thousands of users. At the same time, each has produced its share of horror stories based on unmet needs, reduced staff morale, and overextended budgets. Over the life of the HRMS, an organization will probably use all three methods.

Many experienced HRMS users suggest that first-time buyers start with a package even if they think they will want custom software eventually. This helps them save money and learn more about computerization before taking on the task of custom system development. Since most buyers do not know which features they really want in an ideal system, those who jump too quickly into custom development spend thousands of dollars prematurely, only to end up with an HRMS that is unresponsive to their needs. Using packaged software teaches users what to look for in a custom system; in that alone, it serves a valuable function. Abandoning a purchased system to develop a new custom system is easier to justify if the canned system is part of a microcomputer-based HRMS costing $5,000 to $10,000. This approach is less justifiable for mainframes costing factors of ten to twenty times more.

If possible, buyers should start with a package that meets at least 75 percent of their stated requirements. To accommodate this new system, the human resources department may need to make minor operational changes in the way it does business. However, a system that requires major shifts defeats the purpose for which the department set out to acquire an HRMS in the first place. If the package contains unacceptable or unusable features, sometimes a minor amount of custom programming can modify these features. If none of these solutions works, or if the organization has an unusual application for which it can find no canned HRMS software, the project team should consider custom system development.

The Process of Software Development

An organization that decides to customize packaged software or develop its own software from basic programs must follow all the procedures described for evaluating packaged software but with an inward view. Additionally, the firm must undertake numerous detailed steps in the software development process that add overhead to the HRMS effort. With purchased systems, the vendor assumes responsibility for most development activity and has both an implementation plan and prior experience. The in-house resources may or may not have a plan and prior experience.

Software development basically uses the HRMS planning and design documents as blueprints for data organization and manipulation. The design team follows each step developed during earlier phases, including the following:

- Design a data base with the capacity to handle the relevant employee populations.
- Label each field and each data element to create a complete data dictionary with complete data element forms for each field.
- Create tables of values that the data fields draw on as appropriate. As necessary, build these as tables of codes. The codes should be consistent and easy to understand, and the tables should include English-language equivalents of the codes.
- Establish data relationships, including all algorithms and routines, to optimize editing and validation of fields.
- Create menus and screens to assist users in navigating through the HRMS.
- Create operator messages that specify action options.
- Build in error-checking routines.
- Build in data security, including audit trails.
- Define standard reports and ad hoc reporting as required.
- Include a tutorial module to assist new users in learning the HRMS capabilities.

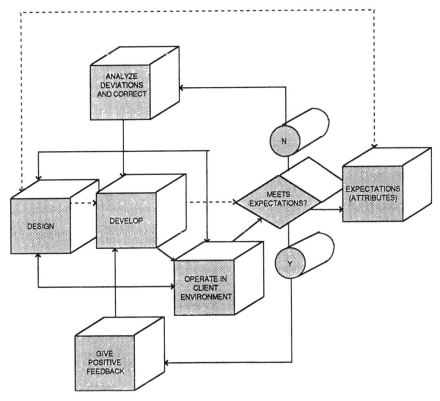

Figure 4–6. Developing quality software. To create effective custom software, developers must have not only advanced technical skills but also the ability to analyze deviations and correct inadequacies. In return, management and users should give developers positive feedback when results do meet expectations.
(Source: *Datamation*, Reed Publishing USA. Reprinted with permission.)

- Provide complete, professional documentation at the technical, user, and administrative levels.

Chapter 3 provides a basic overview of these processes, but the actual system design process for an HRMS is beyond the scope of this book. For information sources dedicated to programming, consult the Further Reading section at the end of this chapter.

Not every customizing story has a happy ending. When a midwestern electronic parts dealer bought a $35,000 minicomputer system two years ago,

Creating Software Documentation

Many HRMS system developers have written documentation, but few have written it well. As with any other field, obtaining good results may require the services of an expert. A firm should use experienced documentation writers to write the documentation for any in-house systems or modifications. Manuals should be available at installation; to meet this objective, developers should include documentation creation as part of the implementation timetable.

If possible, drafts of the documentation should be tested on users and revised based on their feedback. As with documentation for any purchased software products, manuals should cover the entire system as completely as possible and include an index, table of contents, and cross-referencing. Each procedure, screen, and report should be documented, and complete explanations for each error message or condition should be provided. The manual also should document how to link HRMS applications with other programs.

All information should be presented in clear language and in an attractive format. The firm could hire someone with knowledge of graphics and desktop publishing to consult on layout and typefaces. The format should be easy to update. For example, three-ring binders allow for replacement of obsolete material.

he also paid $50,000 to a software company to write special programs and modify the HRMS. After laboriously entering all the personnel information into the computer, this firm discovered that it could not retrieve the information because of deficiencies in the HRMS. The dealer was forced to return to manual record keeping at the height of his busy season to prepare year-end reports. Unfortunately, such horror stories are all too common. Some software houses just do not have enough experience to tackle custom HRMS development. Others routinely bid low to win business, then take shortcuts or back out of agreements. Even qualified firms routinely take months or even years longer than expected. These delays may result from improperly specified user requirements or from the vendor's underestimating the size of the task.

Custom system development demands extremely thorough identification of user requirements. Programmers will write only what their clients specify, and clients must specify parameters that can be translated into concrete, technical actions. Another drawback to custom software is that the client is a

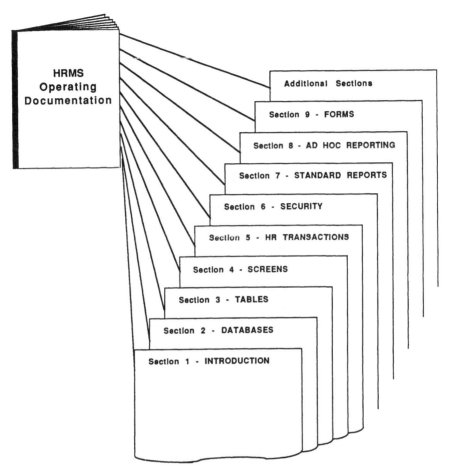

Figure 4–7. A look at effective documentation. Whenever an organization builds a system or modifies a packaged system, it must create documentation that supports all affected system features and functions. Several approaches to the organization of such documentation can work well; one example is shown here.

guinea pig. Few systems are bug-free, especially custom-written ones. Even if custom software developers are competent and the client's needs are clearly defined and properly articulated, the client is on a treadmill. Frustration and expenses build as the potential user waits for the system developer to finish writing the system, testing it, uncovering the bugs, making corrections, and testing the revisions. Very few custom system development assignments are successfully completed for less than $100,000 even for small-scale systems, and fees five to ten times that much are not unusual for large-scale systems.

Glossary

ASCII   American Standard Code for Information Interchange. A set of codes for the symbols used by computers and peripheral devices. Frequently used as formatting for exchanging data between nonidentical systems or programs.

BASIC   Beginner's All-purpose Symbolic Instruction Code. One of the most popular programming languages for users who are not professional programmers.

COBOL   Common Business-Oriented Language. The most widely used business data processing language for commercial applications.

Compiler   A special program that converts instructions written in a programming language into machine language the computer understands.

Custom software   Programs that are tailor-made by in-house IS resources or contract programming firms to solve specific problems in unique situations.

Data dictionary   A logical structure within data base software that contains the identity and characteristics of each data element, including size, type, codes, edit rules, error messages, dependencies, and relationships to other data elements.

Data set   A collection of data gathered from the main data base as a separate file so that a user can manipulate data without having to access the entire data base. A data set may include data on all or some employee records but on only a selection of data fields.

Edit   The inserting, deleting, rearranging, or selection of needed data in a file. Also refers to such actions when they affect character and document reformatting.

Fourth-generation language (4GL)   Any of a group of high-productivity languages that are generally easy to learn and use. A 4GL is closer to English than previous computer languages.

On-line inquiry   The process that allows the user to query or display any file or record contained in the data base.

Packaged software   A series of programs and documentation designed and written to perform a specific function—for example, payroll accounting, mail-list maintenance, forecasting, benefits administration, or labor-cost accounting.

Relational data base   A form of data base organization that presents data as a collection of tables linked together by common data elements. In human resources, the relational data base may connect data on employees, jobs, and salary range using the job classification code as a link.

Report generator   A simplified procedural computer language with English-like instructions designed to allow users to create customized reports without using programmers. Also known as a *report writer*.

Software   One or more programs that allow a computer to perform specific functions, including storing, retrieving, manipulating, and outputting data. Software also may include documentation, an implementation planning guide, and a warranty.

Source code The statements that a programmer writes to create a program or other routine. A compiler program then converts the source code into the machine language, or object code, computers can interpret.

Turnkey A bundled arrangement of system products and services that includes the entire process of planning, designing, coding, installing, and implementing the computer programs and training users. It sometimes includes acquisition and installation of hardware as well.

Validation The process of determining the accuracy and reasonableness of a code or action, usually by checking the entry against relevant code tables.

Discussion Points

1. What is a turnkey system, and what advantages and disadvantages does it have over other types of systems?

2. Compare and contrast the advantages and disadvantages of packaged and customized software.

3. How can a review of software documentation help a buyer to evaluate software?

4. What types of warranty should a software buyer obtain from the vendor?

5. What are menus, and how can they help users?

6. What are the most important criteria to consider in evaluating software?

7. What are various formats for setting up data fields such as employee name, education level, and date of hire?

8. What are the different types of DBMS?

Further Reading

Anderson, Kirk J. "Acquiring a Human Resource Management System." *Employment Relations Today*, Winter 1985–86.

———. "Managing Human Resource Systems." *Human Resource Systems Management Bulletin*, January 1987.

Anderson, Margaret A., and Stephen L. Robin. "Selecting HR Systems Software." *Personnel Administrator*, August 1984.

Barnett, Eugene H. *Programming Time-Share Computers in BASIC*. New York: John Wiley & Sons, 1972.

Ceriello, Vincent R. "Computerizing the Personnel Department: How Do You Pick The Right Software?" *Personnel Journal*, November 1984.

Lancaster, F.W., and E.G. Fayen. *Information Retrieval On-Line*. Los Angeles, CA: Melville Publishing, 1967.

Martin, James, and Carma McClure. "Buying Software off the Rack." *Harvard Business Review*, December 1983.

Meyer, Gary J. *Automating Personnel Operations: The PC's in Personnel Yearbook*. Madison, CT: Business & Legal Reports, 1988.

Pfeilmeier, Frank. "Time-Sharing and Information Systems." *Personnel Journal*, February 1978.

Rosove, Perry E. *Developing Computer-Based Information Systems*. New York: John Wiley & Sons, 1967.

Sammett, Jean E. *Programming Languages: History and Function*. Englewood Cliffs, NJ: Prentice-Hall, 1969.

Schmiedicke, R. J. "Keep it Simple." *Computers in Personnel*, Spring 1987.

Zimmerman, Steven M., Leo M. Conrad, and Stanley M. Zimmerman. *Electronic Spreadsheets and Your IBM PC*. Hasbrouck Heights, NJ: Hayden Book Company, 1984.

Zurakowski, David S., and William G. Harris. "Software Applications in Human Resource Management." *Personnel Administrator*, August 1984.

5

Hardware for an HRMS

> Where a calculator on the ENIAC is equipped with 18,000 vacuum tubes and weighs 30 tons, computers in the future may have only 1,000 vacuum tubes and perhaps weigh only 1½ tons.
> —*Popular Mechanics*, 1949 (as quoted in Christopher Cerf and Victor Navasky, *The Experts Speak*, Pantheon Books, 1984)

W hen people who are unfamiliar with computers hear that their department is to be automated, their first thought may be that the machines will take over, get in the way, inexplicably swallow huge amounts of valuable data, and be a monolithic, ugly, and noisy presence. HRMS planners and developers can avoid confirming those fears by selecting not only the right software but also the right hardware for the situation. The right hardware helps make an HRMS technically accurate, cost-effective, and comfortable to use. To acquire that equipment, planners must select the correct scale of computer system for their needs, determine the types of components their operation requires, and consider several other specific factors.

Micro, Midrange, and Mainframe

Computer experts commonly refer to three basic sizes of computers: microcomputers, midrange computers, and mainframes. No hard and fast rules exist for what size computer a given employee population size requires, but the material that follows offers guidelines for typical uses of the three types in various HRMS environments.

The boundaries between these categories of computers are shifting. Today's powerful microcomputer may be marketed tomorrow as a low-end midrange computer. Microcomputers used to be stand-alone computers, with only the larger systems supporting multiuser environments. Today, not only can users link microcomputers to other microcomputers, but they also can link them to midrange and mainframe computers. An HRMS can be a mix of computer sizes.

Requirements Definition and Computer Scale

The results of a requirements definition form the basis for deciding which size computer a firm needs. A good requirements definition guides planners in selecting both appropriate computer scale and specific manufacturers and models for each piece of hardware.

In many cases, the deciding factor is not the size of a firm but its structure. A firm of two thousand employees located at one site may use a single mid-range computer successfully for all its computer applications, from finance to manufacturing to human resources. Conversely, a firm of only five hundred employees that operates in four states may need several independent micro-computers linked via modems to a central microcomputer that processes only summary information. Often a human resources department or entire organization already has a significant amount of hardware that defines or constricts hardware choices for an HRMS. In such cases, these limitations become part of the initial requirements definition, and hardware is more of a determining than a dependent factor.

Microcomputers

The fastest-growing area of HRMS is microcomputers. In a 1986 survey published in the *Human Resource Systems Management Bulletin,* 79 percent of responding companies indicated that human resources staff use microcomputers. Of those companies that did not already use microcomputers, 28 percent had plans to do so within the year. As shown in figure 5–1, use of mainframes for HRMS declined by almost one-third in only five years, while use of microcomputers increased by a factor of eight.

Microcomputers enjoyed much initial popularity because of their user friendliness, but many professionals now view this term with some disdain. The barriers that mainframe users once faced have disappeared with the current generation of mainframe keyboards and systems that have many of the same advantages as microcomputers. Conversely, microcomputers have become more complex in order to provide more power to users. Even the simplest microcomputers require that users learn certain conventions in order to perform basic tasks. Users need to know both simple conventions, such as finding the on/off switch hidden on the back of the computer, and more complicated ones, such as learning which combinations of buttons and icons find and save files.

Several traditional advantages of microcomputers remain, including user independence and lower cost (in terms of hardware and software purchase, installation, maintenance, and staffing). Because each microcomputer serves fewer individuals and requires less technical knowledge for software adapta-

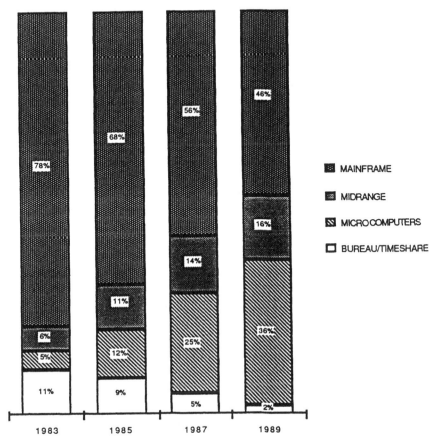

MAINFRAME

MIDRANGE

MICRO COMPUTERS

BUREAU/TIMESHARE

Figure 5–1. The shift to microcomputers. During the 1980s, computer environments to support HRMS have shifted from being primarily or exclusively mainframe to being much more balanced between mainframe and microcomputer. Midrange systems showed only moderate growth during this period.

tion, microcomputer users have more independence than mainframe users in terms of software selection and adaptation, data control, and access to peripherals (such as printers and outside services).

In the past, microcomputers were limited by speed, capacity, and flexibility. The latest microcomputers are faster and have a greater capacity, which allows them to process increasingly larger amounts of data. For these reasons, more and more human resources departments are using microcomputers.

Microcomputers were originally designed to function as independent, single-user computer systems, and most still do. However, the increasing sophistication and variety of networking software have led to the expansion of microcomputers into environments formerly reserved for multiuser midrange systems and mainframe terminal arrangements. Microcomputers meet many types of HRMS needs, including those of stand-alone users, service bureau subscribers, and geographically scattered users.

Stand-alone users typically have from less than 100 to more than 2000 employees. The firm's human resources department handles all its data entry, updating, and processing needs with one computer or a few networked microcomputers. The department does not tie in to payroll.

A firm that contracts with payroll *service bureaus* has correspondingly smaller in-house computing requirements. As with the stand-alone user, a service bureau subscriber may handle all its human resources matters on a few microcomputers, then use modems to perform batch transfer of data from the microcomputers to service bureau mainframes.

Organizations with many *geographically separate sites* may find ongoing linkage to a central mainframe impractical. In such circumstances, they may provide each site with microcomputers and its own copy of the system. Daily business processing takes place independently on the microcomputers. A central mainframe stores the joint data base; periodically, the microcomputer sends data revisions via modem to a central microcomputer programmed to consolidate data and feed it to the mainframe. Overnight downloading allows local report generation. Many HRMS experts predict that this design, often called distributed processing, will emerge as the dominant information architecture within organizations. Telecommunications hardware and standards are discussed in greater detail later in this chapter.

In some setups, microcomputers serve a dual role, functioning as stand-alone computers for small documents and calculations but working as terminals linked to a midrange or mainframe computer for large-scale operations. These linked operations may include exchanging data with the full-size data base, performing complex calculations, or exchanging electronic mail or other telecommunications or printing functions.

Midrange Computers

When microcomputer systems do not have enough capacity, flexibility, or speed and a mainframe is too complex (and expensive), midrange computers are the best alternative. The midrange computer was developed as an alternative to mainframes before microcomputers were developed. They often are promoted as keys to department independence, and some users refer to them as departmental computers. Most midrange computers use the RPG language, though a few can emulate microcomputer operating languages and some use COBOL. A midrange computer may provide for more growth than a microcomputer, but it also requires more on-site technical expertise. Planners also should recognize that few bridges exist between microcomputers and midrange computers.

A midrange computer is designed for multiuser environments. Each operator has a separate monitor and keyboard; cables or telecommunications devices carry information between each workstation and the central computer. By using midrange computers, multiuser systems can avoid some of the networking uncertainties that are still present in microcomputers. This advantage is especially straightforward when the entire network operates on one site, allowing workstation terminals to connect to the midrange computer via direct cables rather than telecommunications. Some communications functions for which a microcomputer system must use software can be fulfilled via hardware on a midrange system, thus reducing complexity and increasing speed.

Mainframe Computers

Mainframes are the largest and fastest computers. Even the smallest mainframe accommodates an almost unlimited number of disk and tape drives. Mainframes are capable of the most sophisticated calculations, including the most complicated quantitative modeling projects.

The prevalence of microcomputers has not eliminated mainframe use. In fact, some surveys indicate that 80 percent of microcomputer users request mainframe access. Over 50 percent of companies responding to the 1986 *Human Resource Systems Management Bulletin* survey said that they downloaded human resources data from mainframes to microcomputers. Of those that did not, 62 percent planned to do so within a year. Fewer companies reported uploading data from microcomputers to mainframes, perhaps because of concerns about data integrity and security. Based on the rate of microcomputer use and integration in business overall, at least 80 to 90 percent probably follow such practices today.

Mainframes are needed in several types of HRMS situations, especially in firms with a relatively large number of employees. First, when all (or most) employees are centrally located, the system that serves them usually must have a large storage capacity. Employers such as colleges and government agencies, as well as manufacturing, health care, and financial facilities, fall into this category.

Second, if other aspects of the firm's activities require mainframe-based operations, using a mainframe for HRMS becomes more attractive. Financial businesses such as insurance and banking firms often use mainframe computers to accommodate their high numbers of policyholders, claims, or depositors. In some cases, HRMS may share a mainframe with operations outside the human resources department; in others, the computers may be separate but share personnel or site accommodations.

Third, firms with an employee population more than about ten thousand usually need mainframe capacity to consolidate data, even if they use microcomputers for data handling at many sites. The mainframe provides data compilation and analysis such as calculations, report generation, modeling, and other planning operations. The decision of whether to consolidate data on a microcomputer or a mainframe often rests on two factors: (1) amount of data to be stored and manipulated, and (2) available software to meet the requirements definition. The more complete the computerization of human resources operations or the greater the integration of HRMS functions with other IS operations throughout the company, the greater is the likelihood that mainframe involvement will increase HRMS effectiveness.

Mainframes need the most sophisticated data processing technical staff for several reasons. Commercially available software is massive, inclusive, and expensive. Packages range from $50,000 to $500,000 and more, yet most still require some degree of customization. Because these programs are written in second- or third-generation languages (such as COBOL), any modification or enhancement requires technical intervention.

In addition, even after implementation, only technicians can operate and maintain mainframes; users have less responsibility but also less independence. Users seeking processing, output, or modifications sometimes must negotiate priorities before getting the service they have requested. Moreover, when the mainframe goes down (is out of service), all human resources applications and users are without a system.

Hardware Components of an HRMS

A computer system is always more than one piece of equipment. Good planning includes specifying in detail each required piece of equipment, not just the major items. Whether a microcomputer or a mainframe, a computer system virtually always includes the following components:

- Electronic storage devices, for storing and trading information among CPUs
- Monitors, for viewing data
- Keyboards, for inputting data and commands
- Printers, for creating drafts and final documents

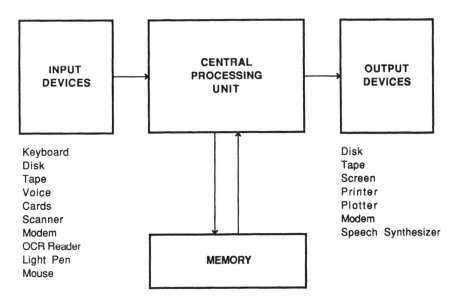

Figure 5–2. Computer input/output devices.

Many HRMS also include auxiliary circuit boards, plotters, scanners, projection devices, micrographics devices, mice, and telecommunications equipment. The complexity, scale, features, and capabilities of the individual components play a determining role in the capabilities of the entire HRMS. Therefore, every component must be selected carefully.

Electronic Storage Devices

Computer data must reside in an electronic medium for retrieval and revision. The most common storage forms are hard disks, floppy disks, and tape. Virtually every computer has more than one storage device to meet different HRMS data storage needs.

Fixed Disk Drive. A fixed disk drive, also called a hard disk, is a disk that is permanently encased in a box. It holds more data and operates much faster than a floppy disk drive. A fixed disk drive is permanently installed in the computer, though external fixed disks also are available for expansion purposes.

With the rapidly falling price of microcomputer disk storage, even the smallest human resources computer system usually has a fixed disk with a capacity of at least 20 megabytes (MB). (A megabyte is one million bytes.) Microcomputer fixed disks are now available in sizes up to 322 MB, and the newest systems can connect two or more of these disks. Midrange and mainframe computers have fixed disks that are proportionally larger in dimension and capacity than those in microcomputers.

Floppy Disk Drive. Systems that have fixed disks still need floppy drives. Floppy drives store and retrieve data on thin plastic disks, the size of which varies depending on the type of equipment used. The earliest and most common floppy disk drives used flexible 5¼-inch or 8-inch disks. In recent years, the developing standard has become hard 3½-inch disks, which are easier to handle and less vulnerable to damage than the larger disks.

Using a floppy disk drive, the user can work with disks containing programs or data from outside sources. He or she can transfer material from the floppy disk to the hard disk or vice versa for use by other computers. Often such a transfer requires routines for converting data to meet the software and operating system conventions of the other computers. Mainframe computers often are linked to microcomputers equipped with floppy disk drives as a way of trading information with these smaller machines.

Tape Drive. Tape drives come in several forms. Microcomputers use cassette tapes primarily as backup storage devices. These "streaming" tape devices can quickly make duplicate copies of all the data on a hard disk. The user can then move the tape or the entire tape device to a fireproof vault or other secure area where the data will be safe from any possible damage. This ensures the integrity of HRMS records in the event of an accident, sabotage, or some other computer problem. Because such security is a basic requirement of any HRMS, most good system specifications include a provision for tape backup. (Chapter 10 discusses backup procedures in detail.)

Mainframes often use tape drives for data storage and retrieval, not just backup. Mainframe tape systems feature large, sealed open-reel tape disks that are approximately twelve inches in diameter and one-half to three-quarter inch wide. These tape systems can store a large amount of data in serial form, which means that records must be queried sequentially. In such systems, the backup tape can be produced in this medium, then stored in a secure environment.

Keyboards

Most microcomputer purchasers use the keyboard that comes with the CPU. This arrangement often works fine, but the design team should consider several factors before accepting that arrangement or selecting an independently manufactured keyboard.

Industry compatibility is important. Most keyboards maintain the letter and number arrangement of a typewriter keyboard, but the placement of the extra keys—ESC (Escape), CTL (Control), ALT (Alternate), the function

Computer Comparisons

Computer Component	*Traditional Equivalent*
Hardware	
Keyboard	Pencil
Screen	Paper
Arrows, cursor	Pointer
Disk drives	File cabinets
Disks	File folders
Random access memory (RAM)	Desktop
Read-only memory (ROM)	Bulletin board
Printer	Typewriter
Modem	Ears and mouth
RS-232 interface	Vocal cords
Tapes	File folders
Software	
Operating system	Secretary
Directory catalog	Index and table of contents
File name	File folder
Format, initialize	Supply clerk
Backup, copy, restore	Photocopy clerk

keys, the numeric keypad, and so forth—is not the same on every keyboard. If users have had previous computer experience, they will be accustomed to one or more of the keyboards used on the most popular microcomputers. Any keyboard that differs from this arrangement will require some adjustment on the part of users. During that transition, errors will be more common and efficiency lower. If other keyboards used in the firm have a particular arrangement and users have to shift back and forth between the systems, it is probably a good idea to select a keyboard like those in the existing system.

If users will be entering and manipulating numeric data, the keyboard should have an integral keypad, in which the keys are arranged like those on a calculator. Function key placement also must be considered. Some keyboards have the function keys in a single horizontal row above the top row of standard keys. Others have a set of two vertical rows on the left side of the keyboard. If the HRMS program style depends heavily on function keys for commands, the horizontal function key arrangement may be more efficient.

Some keyboards have adjustable keystroke resistance and adjustable keystroke sound adjustment. For staff whose primary task is data entry, such features may provide an added degree of comfort and user friendliness. Most operators, however, will adjust to the feel of any keyboard.

Monitors

Monitors have several variable characteristics, including screen size, image technology, color, resolution, and screen adjustments. For most data entry and administrative functions, standard monitors work quite well. Many human resources departments use the monitor made by the CPU manufacturer. Certain applications, however, particularly graphics and desktop publishing, require larger or specialized monitors that are available from monitor manufacturers. Some graphics applications, particularly desktop publishing, benefit from extra-large screen size. Some monitors allow full-page display, which promotes effective and efficient publication preparation by allowing the user to preview an entire page of text for proper format and alignment.

The mechanism by which most computer monitors produce the lighted image on the screen is a light-emitting diode (LED). LEDs are far superior to the liquid crystal diodes (LCDs) usually used in low-end laptop computers and very early microcomputers. Because LCD images are more difficult to read, portable computers and other devices with such monitors should be used only when other equipment cannot fill the need. Some newer portable computers use plasma displays, which offer significantly better visual quality.

Color monitors are generally more pleasant to work with, but they are not needed for most applications (and they cost considerably more than monochrome monitors). In fact, color is actually more difficult to read in word processing applications. Color is necessary for many graphics applications, however, and some HRMS planners like to use color in designing data input screens. Increasingly, color is a necessity.

Monochrome monitors have been available predominantly in amber and green versions, but many new colors have emerged in recent years. Some individuals claim that one color or another is more soothing to the eye, but scientific experiments have not yet confirmed such claims. White-on-black monitors increase eyestrain; black-on-white is easier to read.

One way to improve the monitor image is to use a polarizing screen, which attaches to the front of the monitor. This flat plastic frame cuts down on glare from natural and artificial light and thus increases readability and minimizes eyestrain. Many HRMS include a polarizing screen on every monitor.

An HRMS may be used to produce newsletters, presentation materials, slides, overhead projection materials, brochures, and high-quality reports that include graphs and other figures. Workstations that will be used for such activities may need monitors with high-resolution screens. Normal monitors produce an image using an array of 526 points of light, known as pixels. Graphics screens feature much higher resolution. Professional specialty graphics areas such as animation may use screens featuring more than 300,000 pixels.

Printers

Printing is an inextricable link in the computer process, but a printer is more a mechanical than an electronic device. A printer carries paper through a roller, manipulates a printing head across a page, and applies ink to the page.

A good HRMS requirements definition for printer hardware includes speed, appearance quality, type styles and other printing elements, intensity of use, and software compatibility. The project team must consider what each part of human resources needs, then evaluate the extent to which those needs can be commingled. If cable connections are planned properly, several operations often can share printing resources. One large central laser printer may provide faster, more varied printing results than numerous distributed letter-quality or dot matrix printers. Some firms find that different technologies fill different needs. A small site may need a smaller printer with a communications connection to a large-scale laser printer for longer or more formal documents. Most operations benefit from having more than one printer, not only to meet different needs but also to provide backup when one printer is temporarily out of commission.

There are four main types of printers: laser, impact, thermal-ink, and dot matrix. Until recently, laser printers were very expensive. In the past few years, printer technology for business applications has advanced rapidly, and more and more businesses are using laser printers for everything from letters to documentation to forms generation.

Laser printers operate essentially by taking a picture of the arrayed computer image of each page. They are fast, high quality, and graphically flexible. They print quietly, using a high-resolution dot matrix pattern, typically three hundred by three hundred dots per inch. Laser printers can produce a wide variety of type fonts and can handle both graphics and word processing. Properly produced laser-printed documents look as good as professionally typeset documents. Leading laser printers for microcomputers can print approximately eight to ten pages per minute; those for midrange and mainframe systems have significantly greater output capacity.

Laser printers are significantly more expensive than other types of printers. However, many firms find that the savings in personnel and production time, and the savings in outside graphics and printing services, more than compensate for the higher initial outlay. Laser printers are sheet-fed machines designed for correspondence and reports. They cannot handle wide paper, such as for large spreadsheets, nor can they handle rolls of labels or other continuous-feed arrangements. Such applications require wide-carriage, tractor-fed impact or dot matrix printers.

Many businesses still use impact printers. These printers work something like a typewriter. A wheel with letters rotates, then strikes an individual letter

A good HRMS requirements definition for printer hardware
includes speed, appearance quality, typestyles and other
printing elements, intensity of use, and software
compatibility. Consider what each part of HR needs, and
then evaluate the extent to which those needs can be
commingled. If cable connections are properly planned,
often several operations can share printing resources.
One large central laser printer may provide faster, more
varied printing results than numerous distributed letter
quality or dot ma
different techno.
site may need a :
connection to a :
more formal docur
having more than
needs but to pro\
is temporarily o(

SAMPLE DOT MATRIX
(DRAFT QUALITY)

A good HRMS requirements definition for printer hardware
includes speed, appearance quality, typestyles and other
printing elements, intensity of use, and software
compatibility. Consider what each part of HR needs, and
then evaluate the extent to which those needs can be
commingled. If cable connections are properly planned,
often several operations can share printing resources.
One large central laser printer may provide faster, more
varied printing results than numerous distributed letter
quality or dot
different techr
site may need ε
connection to ε
more formal doc
having more the
needs but to pɪ
is temporarily

SAMPLE DOT MATRIX
(LETTER QUALITY)

A good HRMS requirements definition f
includes speed, appearance quality, t
printing elements, intensity of use,
compatibility. Consider what each pa
then evaluate the extent to which tho
commingled. If cable connections are
often several operations can share pr
One large central laser printer may p
varied printing results than numerous
quality or dot matrix printers. Some
different technologies fill different
site may need a smaller printer, with
connection to a large-scale laser pri
more formal documents. Most operatio
having more than one printer, not onl
needs but to provide essential backup
is temporarily out of commission.

SAMPLE LASER PRINTER

Figure 5–3. Sample printer outputs.

affixed to a stem against a ribbon, which comes in contact with the paper, leaving an imprint. Because this technology is quite noisy, these printers usually need an acoustic hood to reduce noise. Such printers offer many type styles, but users must change the wheel manually during document printing. Supplies and maintenance generally cost less for such printers than for laser printers.

Some manufacturers produce letter-quality printers that use thermal-ink technology. In this approach, an electronically interchangeable font sends an electronic print head a signal to apply heat in a particular letter shape to the printer ribbon; the ink instantly melts onto the paper. This technology produces crisp printing. Because thermal-ink technology is considerably quieter than daisy-wheel printing, it eliminates the need for a hood. Although these printers are much more limited than laser printers, they offer several fonts that can be activated by software commands embedded in report files. Thermal-ink machines may be appropriate for small operations that need high-quality documents but cannot accommodate a wheel-type impact printer plus its hood. Supplies are somewhat more expensive than those for wheel-type impact printers, and speed is in the midrange for letter-quality printers.

Dot matrix is a fast, inexpensive printing technology. Contemporary dot matrix printers often have two modes—draft and correspondence quality. High-resolution dot matrix printers, with twenty-four dots per character, are rapidly replacing dot matrix printers with lower resolution, as well as wheel-type impact and thermal printers. Dot matrix printers have graphics capabilities that impact and thermal-ink printers lack. Many organizations deem the output from high-resolution dot matrix printers acceptable for draft or internal distribution but require that all final and external documents be printed on a letter-quality or laser printer.

An HRMS printing configuration may differ quite a bit from its computer arrangement. For instance, not only may many computers share a single printer, but one computer may access numerous printers. With distributed printing, a headquarters computer could produce a new employee manual, then order printing by laser printers at several remote sites, speeding up distribution and review processes. A firm that only occasionally has heavy printing needs or produces graphics (such as a newsletter or quarterly report) may integrate graphics software for laser printing but contract out the laser printing to a print shop.

Auxiliary Boards

The brain of the computer is the CPU, the main circuit board on which computer operation takes place. Computers also may have auxiliary circuit boards to provide enhanced or additional functions. Special boards can add capability in speed, numeric calculation (via mathematical coprocessors), graphics, communications (via internal modems), and emulation of other operating systems. HRMS planners can use auxiliary boards in planning for growth. Boards can be added in the future as additional capacity or performance features are needed or become available.

Although these boards are installed in the same computer case as the CPU, they are sold as add-ons. Microcomputer technology for these boards is expanding rapidly, and manufacturers are continually offering new features at a lower cost. The project team must pay careful attention to independent performance and reliability reports for any board being considered. Such reports often are featured in computer magazines.

Plotters

Dot matrix printers and laser printers can produce certain types of graphics, but if a firm requires multiple colors or complex graphics representations, it may need to consider buying a plotter. A plotter is a printer with several colored writing "pens" that operate simultaneously based on electronic signals. These have limited HRMS application, except for high-quality graphics produced in-house for reports such as benefits packages.

Scanners

A scanner is a device for transferring information from printed form to computer data. Some scanners transfer printed material; others work with a graphics pointer or mouse to input graphic designs. Scanners often have a high level of data dropout, which means that they work only when much information is available and the accuracy of each specific piece of data is not critical. For this reason, scanners have limited application in human resources departments, except that they do work well for computer-coded responses to attitude surveys. In surveys, individual responses are less important than ease of processing large amounts of data. Often the scanner vendor works with the user to develop custom survey sheets that the scanner can read.

Mice and Other Graphics Pointers

A mouse is a hand-held device that the user moves around a spongy pad to make an arrow or similar image move around on the screen. The user issues commands by pressing buttons on the mouse. If a menu-driven system has incorporated a mouse use into its design, users can use the mouse to select human resources functional activities, records, fields, reports, and other aspects of HRMS operations. Some programs use mouse functions extensively, such as those by Microsoft and those for the Macintosh. Graphics programs usually depend on a mouse. Most such programs are faster to use with a mouse than without, though few (except graphics programs) require a mouse. Few human resources environments will benefit significantly from using a mouse unless users process a significant amount of text or graphics. Any workstation that has a mouse also should have a pad or other special surface for mouse use.

Microform Devices

Some firms transfer out-of-date records to microforms, either microfiche or microfilm. A microfilm device photographically transfers data from a printed form to a micrographic image. Most organizations use this technique only for documents that bear an employee signature or for some other reason should be retained in their original form. Microfiche equipment transfers an array of twenty to forty microfilm images onto a small card for compact storage. A microfiche reader projects an enlarged version of these images so users can access (and sometimes copy) large volumes of microfilmed documents. Some firms have their own equipment for performing microfilm transfers; others use an outside service, particularly if these transfers take place only a few times a year.

Telecommunications Equipment

Mainframe computers come with virtually unlimited multiplexing capability. For many years, this ability to link multiple terminals stood as a major advantage of mainframes. In recent years, the development of computer telecommunications capability has brought many of these features to the microcomputer level. Telecommunications equipment usually provides great efficiency for a human resources department that shares data among several work sites or that gathers data from other sources (such as computerized data sources) on a recurring basis. Such systems vary significantly in complexity. *Netware* refers to a combination of hardware and software that has telecommunications capability.

The simplest telecommunications system consists of a *modem*—a modulator/demodulator device—and associated software that use telephone lines to exchange data between two computers. Users pay telephone-line usage rates while the modem is operating (rates vary depending on the modem's speed of data transmission, known as its baud rate). In the past, a modem was a separate box to which users attached a regular telephone and the computer. Now most users have more compact, faster, more adaptable internal modems. An internal modem is an expansion board installed inside the microcomputer and fitted with a cord that plugs into a phone jack.

Organizations that want to avoid the high cost and security problems associated with using telephone lines for computer communications often consider developing their own *local area network* (LAN). A LAN is composed of dedicated communication lines connecting specific computers and terminals within a confined range. Many systems limit this range to approximately one-half mile. Networks are often organized into groups of destinations, with each group referred to as a node. A node can usually handle up to four workstations. LANs work in real time, facilitating ongoing and frequent communication among staff at different locations.

LANs allow multiple users to share and access files simultaneously. Such networks may integrate mainframes, microcomputers, and workstations that in turn include features such as voice mail, electronic mail, paging systems, and distributed printing. A human resources system needs telecommunications capabilities when the organization contains mutually exclusive, autonomous end users who share data under certain circumstances. The primary issue in telecommunications decisions should be the need to share data rather than simply potential savings in capital costs.

A LAN is particularly appropriate if a firm already has telecommunications experience or if the firm or department decides to use electronic mail. A

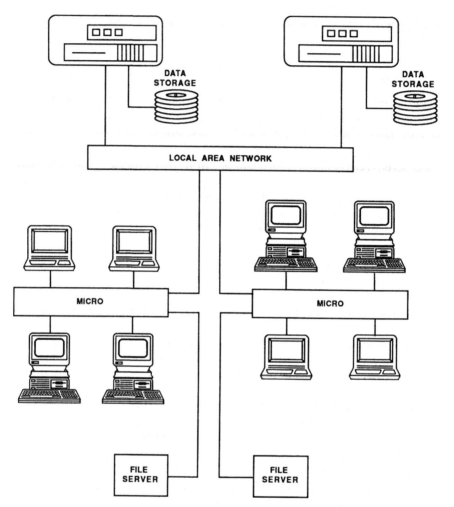

Figure 5–4. A typical LAN configuration.

firm that has a LAN for other purposes (such as sales and marketing) may need to keep that network dedicated to its original purpose. Although human resources would have to establish its own LAN, the organization could conserve resources by using the same telecommunications staff for both LANs.

Whenever possible, a new LAN should match the organization's existing LANs and policies in terms of software standards (and possibly vendor), security requirements (backup, power supplies, and so forth), and maintenance

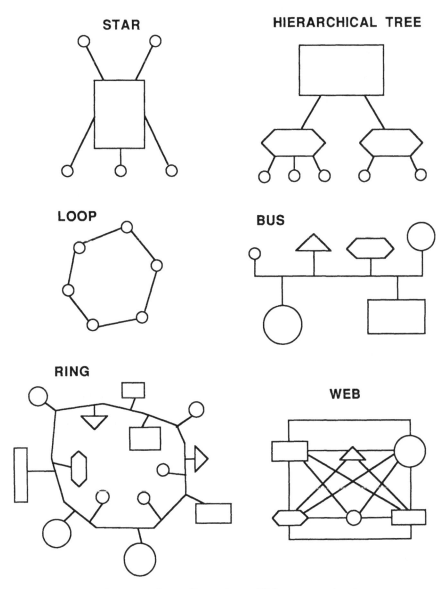

Figure 5–5. Basic network configurations. Telecommunication systems come in many forms. Some telecommunications software works only with particular arrangements of telecommunications hardware.
(Source: From *DATA MANAGEMENT* Magazine. Copyright and reprint permission granted. 1985. Data Processing Management Association. ALL RIGHTS RESERVED.)

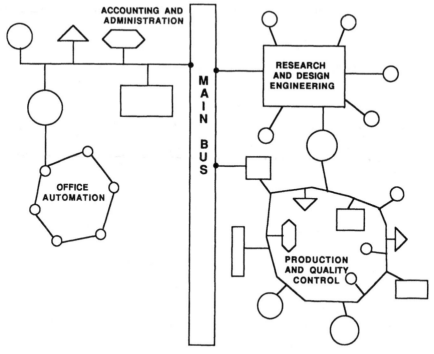

Figure 5–6. Example of a large network with multiple configurations. A large organization may have several types of network arrangements. It may use different network configurations to meet the needs of different departments, then connect these smaller networks to a main network to facilitate interdepartmental data exchange, electronic mail, and so forth.
(Source: From *DATA MANAGEMENT* Magazine. Copyright and reprint permission granted. 1985. Data Processing Management Association. ALL RIGHTS RESERVED.)

procedures. A LAN usually has numerous economic benefits, including the following:

- Software that permits microcomputers to operate in a LAN environment is much less expensive than software for midrange and mainframe computers.

- Network versions of microcomputer software cost less than buying separate copies for dozens of microcomputers.

- Networked users can share the cost of peripherals. These include modems for external communication and high-speed, high-quality printers.

- To work with an associated midrange or mainframe computer, multiple microcomputer users can share a single terminal emulation setup through the LAN rather than using a separate setup for each microcomputer.
- Additional users can enter the system at less cost. A new network station costs less than a new stand-alone microcomputer.

A LAN offers several operational advantages. Most important, it allows multiple users to access and update records simultaneously. Most human resources departments using a LAN increase their speed of transaction processing because more than one person can handle update requests. Upgrades and maintenance also take place more smoothly and quickly because they are done at one site rather than at many locations. Finally, using a LAN allows human resources to operate independently of IS, unlike the situation with a midrange or mainframe computer.

No single accepted standard exists for LANs. Some technologies work well for human resources, and some do not. Microcomputer networking is a rapidly evolving technology. Many vendors are still competing for software and standards domination. In general, HRMS software can be equally useful with any one of a number of possible LAN protocols. Software requirements analysis should include evaluation of which networks the HRMS software vendor's product will support. If human resources is justifying the network, technicians can evaluate requirements and select the best possible network to run personnel applications. If some other application is driving the network, such as computer-assisted design and manufacturing, personnel users may find a severe degradation in performance. Response time may render the system a hindrance rather than an aid.

Establishing a LAN requires a significant investment in both hardware and software, referred to collectively as netware. LANs also require a longer development cycle than stand-alone single-user systems. However, the operating costs for such LANs are often somewhat lower than for an equivalent number of stand-alone microcomputers because many users are sharing the same data base. When LAN requirements are complex, even an HRMS consultant may have to bring in a telecommunications specialist.

Cables and Other Electromechanical Components

Even the simplest microcomputer workstation needs more than one or two wall outlets. Virtually every piece of hardware requires its own electrical outlet. Also count on computer cables, printer cables, telephone lines, and other pieces of electrical "spaghetti." Each workstation should have adequate electrical outlets in combination with surge-protection devices. Even small variations in electrical current can damage data.

When an HRMS Needs
Telecommunications Capability

If the human resources environment includes any of the following, the HRMS hardware plan and budget should include telecommunications equipment:

- The firm has several sites, each of which keeps track of data for its own employees. These data may include applications and hiring decisions, new employee intake, attendance, and performance. Most companies need to gather all data into one central site for analysis of corporate needs, such as payroll, budgeting, EEO compliance, and staff planning.

- Other significant aspects of the organization, particularly management, use telecommunications equipment for communicating between sites or functions.

- Human resources or other related departments subscribe to on-line computer services that provide demographic or employment availability data.

- The human resources department contracts with outside service agencies for performance of particular functions, most commonly payroll and benefits.

To protect against loss of data in case of power failure, some midrange and most mainframe systems include a backup power source that automatically takes over if commercial power fails. This source may be battery or generator powered depending on the size of the computer system and the length of time the system must continue functioning in the event of a commercial power outage. Battery-powered backup systems also are available for microcomputers.

Devices for the Disabled

Computers have facilitated equal opportunity for persons with a wide variety of disabilities. In recent years, much special adaptive equipment has been developed. Firms that have employees who are blind, hearing impaired, or mobility limited or who have other disabilities should investigate this equipment. Providing such equipment when needed helps employers satisfy affirmative action goals and support effective, successful staff performance.

Such equipment includes Braille printers, print readers, talking terminals, voice-activated terminals, and phone lines with telecommunications devices for the deaf (TDD). In some cases, hardware vendors provide adaptations of their own equipment, but for the most part, specialized companies produce this equipment. Often a good resource for manufacturer contacts is a local center for independent living, an occupational therapy program, or another program that works with disabled persons. It is important to involve disabled employees in the selection and arrangement of equipment that meets their needs.

Ergonomics

Office furniture and equipment are not just a matter of aesthetics. The right furniture selection and arrangement reduce job-related stress, including eye-strain, back strain, and psychological discomfort.

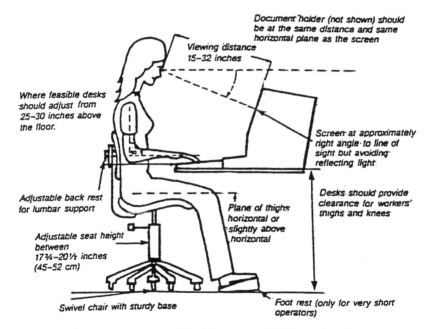

Figure 5–7. **Basic design considerations for a VDT workstation.**
Employers and employees must work together to achieve proper ergonomics at a VDT workstation. Though employers must provide proper equipment and training, each employee is responsible for adjusting equipment to achieve the least strain and most comfort.

The key word in such selection is ergonomics—design that enhances human comfort and effective activity. The project team should consider workstations, desks, and tables that are specially designed to accommodate computer-oriented functions. Each work surface should have a size and shape that can accommodate the computer equipment and also allow staff to perform their noncomputer functions without pushing aside keyboards to do so. Chairs should be at the proper height for the tables and work surfaces.

Reasonable, convenient storage is needed for computer consumables such as paper, labels, ribbons, and disks. Keeping supplies readily accessible encourages users to label files properly and to replace consumables as necessary and appropriate.

Factors in Selecting Hardware

After determining what types of equipment the HRMS requires, the next step is detailing the equipment specifications. To do so, planners must consider software selection, operating system requirements, hardware reliability and service reputation, manufacturers' business stability, hardware expandability, and cost.

Select Software First

Many nonexpert users have a hard time separating software and hardware. The type of software an operation can use is at least partially determined by the hardware selected, so a project team cannot select one without proper consideration of the other. A firm that finds the right software can probably find the hardware to run that software. But a firm that selects the hardware first may discover that certain software is unavailable for that equipment. Therefore, most business enterprises should determine their requirements first, then select specific software, and finally select specific hardware on which to run that software.

The Role of Operating Systems in Hardware Selection

Each computer has a particular operating system that controls and tracks basic computer operations, such as sequencing of activities, location of data, and communication with other equipment. Once human resources knows which computer size and type will be needed for the HRMS, all but the most technical staffers become virtually unaware of the operating system. This special program does its work, allowing users to interface with the software without having to worry about how it translates those commands. However, many software packages are designed to run on only one operating system. Vendors often produce their software in several versions, each of which runs on a different operating system. These software programs are quite different, however, not only technically but also from the user's point of view, with different command structures and screen designs. A project team's selection of software will determine which operating systems the HRMS can use. This leaves the team with a significantly shorter list of manufacturers whose computers might be appropriate.

Hardware Reliability and Service Reputation

A human resources department that installs an HRMS only works until the system crashes, the printer refuses to spit out results, or the modem jumbles data. To avoid such catastrophes, the HRMS must include only the most reliable equipment. Vendors themselves are seldom the best sources of information about reliability. For more impartial views, check computer journals, other users, competing vendors, and potential maintenance providers. The best source may be a consultant who specializes in the size and type of equip-

---

Assessing Hardware Reliability and Service

Here are some questions to consider when evaluating how well a piece of hardware will hold up under use:

- How long has this model been available? Vendors often have a vested interest in keeping more established models working well, so they have qualified service staff and appropriate replacement parts for them.
- What kinds of service have installed units already required? New models have persistent "bugs" more often than established models.
- What volume of work is this unit designed to handle? Buyers who exceed practical limits often cause accelerated repair or replacement rates.
- Has this equipment lived up to expectations? If not, in what ways has it not met those expectations? To find the answers to such questions, talk with other users.
- What would vendors, users, and potential buyers change about this equipment if they could? Has anyone made such modifications? If so, what were the results?

---

ment under consideration. The accompanying sidebar lists the major questions to consider in assessing reliability and service.

Even the most reliable equipment may malfunction. Some problems result simply from ordinary use. Print heads accumulate dust and oil. Fixed disk drives work more slowly and even erratically after retrieving and saving thousands of files hundreds of times. Often human error plays a role. An operator may try to fix a paper jam but accidentally break a tractor spring. Someone tries to hook up a new peripheral but overloads a system's capabilities. A workstation has an inadequate power supply. Whatever the cause, human resources can minimize complications when machines malfunction or need servicing by having specific individuals take responsibility for making frequent, regular backups of data stored on disk and tape drives. Human resources also should make arrangements before implementation for who will take responsibility for computer maintenance. The department may want to keep easily replaced spare parts on-site to speed minor repairs. Larger departments may have spare microcomputers, terminals, or other equipment available to substitute for equipment being repaired or serviced. Human resources may need to develop a policy of work priorities in case of overload of printers, computational capabilities, or terminal access.

Manufacturer's Stability

Most computers use parts available from sources other than the manufacturer. Boards, microprocessors, and plugs all are available even if the computer manufacturer goes out of business. Some of today's best microcomputer bargains are available from small companies that put systems together from a wide variety of parts from around the world.

If a company does go out of business, other service organizations can provide reliable support, replacement parts, and, sometimes, upgrades. Nonetheless, it is important to check the stability of both specific equipment and manufacturers, as well as third-party suppliers. An organization that does decide to buy from a fledgling or unstable company should have an adequate backup plan for parts and maintenance.

Hardware Expandability

HRMS design should consider long-term as well as present and short-term needs. The plan should take into account changes forecast for the human resources department and for the company as a whole. It is not a good idea to select a system that is barely big enough to cover the firm's needs for the next two years. If employment is projected to double in the next five years, hardware choices should be based on the equipment's ability to handle such data expansion.

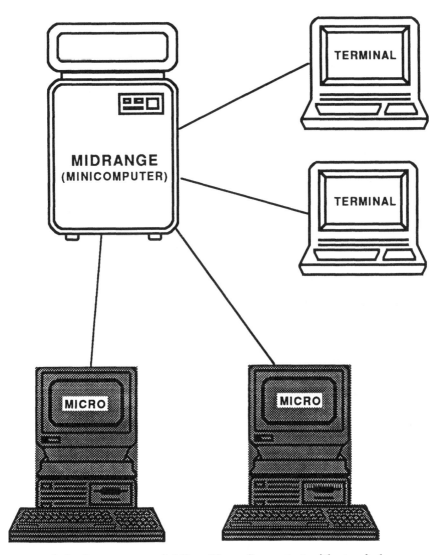

Figure 5–8. System expandability. Many firms start with stand-alone microcomputers, then grow into a larger configuration of networked microcomputers. They may add other microcomputers in a LAN or file-server arrangement, then move to a midrange computer for the file server, with the microcomputers serving as terminals.

A firm that plans significant changes may not be able to stay with the same type of computer. Perhaps a midrange computer will work now but not in the future. In that case, the firm should consider leasing equipment, linking equipment, or buying a low-end but expandable larger computer. Creating and evaluating such alternatives is often the strong suit of an HRMS consultant.

Hardware Cost

Hardware purchase cost usually has an ancillary role in HRMS cost-benefit-value analysis. Many firms decide to buy their entire hardware package from a single vendor or dealer because that vendor has responsibility for making sure all the components work well together. This also provides more financial negotiating advantage.

Vendor and dealer sources for microcomputers may be numerous. Comparison shopping is possible, but the project team also should factor in which sources are more likely to provide the best support and maintenance. To get the best price, planners should check whether their corporate purchasing department already has an arrangement with a computer hardware vendor. Such a source might offer the politically best price, particularly considering warranties, service, common source, security, and local support. Cost comparisons of alternative arrangements should include additional charges such as sales or use tax, supplies, shipping, installation, training, and maintenance costs.

Mainframes have substantially higher environmental costs because they take up more space and require more sophisticated heat dissipation arrangements. Mainframe hardware usually requires specially built or adapted rooms dedicated to the computer. Such space costs are sizable, not only because of square footage requirements but also because of environmental specifications (air cleanliness, cooling requirements, sound barriers, and security). Data storage also requires more space, as do operating personnel. A consultant can help assess these needs and their associated costs.

Glossary

Auxiliary boards   Additional electronic circuit boards installed in a microcomputer to add specific increased capabilities. Special boards can enhance performance, graphics, mathematical calculations, emulation of other operating systems or computers, and color utilization.

Backup   The process of copying a file or files onto another electronic medium in case the original becomes damaged.

Baud   The unit of measure for speed of data transmission. A rate of 300 baud equates to 300 bits per second, or roughly 300 words per minute. High-speed transmission operates at up to 19,200 baud.

Bit   A contraction of *binary digit*, the smallest unit of data recognized by a computer; a single yes/no or on/off condition.

Boot   A shortened version of *bootstrap*, meaning to start up a computer. Booting a microcomputer usually involves just switching on the power, provided the operating system is installed and set to run.

Byte   A string of eight bits. The amount of storage space required to represent a single character (such as a letter, number, or punctuation mark).

CRT   (Cathode ray tube) The tube used to light a monitor display screen; similar to the tube used in a television. The monitor screen used to be referred to as a CRT; now a more generic term—video display terminal (VDT)—has become common, reflecting the use of many screen-lighting technologies besides CRT.

CPU   (Central processing unit) The part of a computer that consists of a core memory component, a calculations component, and an operating control component. The CPU interprets and executes machine instructions.

CPS   (Characters per second) Used to measure the speed of a computer printer.

Cursor   The illuminated or flashing symbol on the computer screen that marks the spot where the user is working.

Disk drive   The mechanical unit that reads and writes data to fixed or floppy disks.

DOS   (Disk operating system) A type of computer operating system. Different computer and software companies offer different versions of DOS.

Dot matrix printer   A printing method in which the printer forms each character by inking an array of dots selected from a matrix. Usually the matrix offers nine or twenty-four dots from which the printer composes the approximate shape of the designated character.

Electronic mail   A telecommunications process in which users can exchange memos, reports, queries, and other information with each other via computers and other devices having monitors. Colloquially referred to as E-mail.

Electronic storage device   Any device used for storing information (data and programs) and providing that information to the CPU. Their main forms are disk drives and tape drives.

Ergonomics   A concept that regards human comfort and effective activity as intrinsic parts of the design and arrangement of furniture, equipment, and other physical aspects of a created environment.

File   A collection of information, such as a program, document, or set of data, that the system stores and retrieves under one name and treats as a logical unit.

File server   The central processor in a network. It provides network management functions such as file and program storage, record locking, security, and backup. It may be connected to one or more centralized high-speed printers. In LANs, the file server is usually a single high-powered microcomputer dedicated to server activities.

Fixed disk   A rigid metal disk coated with a magnetic recording medium, then encased in a box usually installed in the same unit as the CPU. A fixed disk holds from 10 MB to more than 300 MB (approximately 10 million to 300 million bytes). Also referred to as a *hard disk.*

Floppy disk   A flexible plastic disk coated with a magnetic recording medium used to store a limited amount of data or other information. Most microcomputer systems use floppy disks to store programs and data because users can then physically move the disk to another system.

Formatting   The process by which an operating system maps out the sectors on a disk where it will later read and write data. Also refers to preparing a floppy disk for use with a particular operating system.

Hardware   The physical components of a computer system, including the CPU, disk and tape drives, monitor or console, printers, and modems.

Impact printer   A printer that produces fully formed characters by striking the appropriate characters on a printed element.

Input/output (I/O)   The process of entering and retrieving data from a computer system. Every operation to enter, update, calculate, analyze, store, or output data requires I/O activity. The I/O process requires more time per record than the actual computing process.

Input/output device   Any component used to enter data into a computer system or to transfer data to another form or system. For instance, a mouse or a keyboard is an input device; a printer or a plotter is an output device; disk drives, tape drives, and modems are input/output devices.

Keyboard   The primary input device for computers. The layout of a keyboard is similar to that of a typewriter, but it has additional control and function keys, as well as some additional special character keys. The striking of these keys sends signals to the CPU.

Kilobyte (K or KB)   Approximately 1,000 bytes (2^{10}, or 1,024, exactly). Microcomputer memory and floppy disk capacities are often expressed in kilobytes.

Laser printer   A printer that produces images by creating an arrayed electronic image of each page, then projecting a picture of that image directly on paper. Contemporary laser printing can produce graphically complex high-resolution images.

Letter quality   Any of several printing methods whose output looks similar to that of a typewriter or typesetting equipment. Originally only daisy-wheel-type impact printers could produce such results; now several technologies, predominantly laser printing, can do so.

LED   (Light-emitting diode) The light source most commonly used in computer monitors.

LAN   (Local area network) Any multiuser electronically linked system for communicating data in the same format, one-way or interactive, in one building or at many sites.

Mainframe computer The largest type of computer in general business use. Mainframes best serve companies having large employee populations, complex HRMS requirements, and sufficient resources to support their larger space and technical requirements. They usually serve large numbers of users, often in multiple locations.

Megabyte (MB) Approximately one thousand kilobytes or one million bytes.

Microcomputer A microprocessor and related components that form the smallest type of computer system. Originally designed to function as stand-alone single-user systems, they now frequently find uses as terminal emulators and as parts of larger networks.

Microfiche A card containing an array of microfilm images.

Microfilm A very small photographic image of a printed or written document.

Microform A very small photographic image of some printed or written material; specifically, microfilm or microfiche.

Microprocessor A single chip that performs a complex set of functions. In a microcomputer, a microprocessor performs the actual calculations and manipulations of a CPU.

Midrange computer A set of computer components with more storage capacity and speed than microcomputers but less than mainframes. Midrange computers serve multiple users, use both disk and tape storage devices, and usually support networks. Also known as a *minicomputer*.

Modem A modulator/demodulator device that translates the output of a computer into sounds that can be sent over telephone lines to another computer; the modem on the receiving end then translates those sounds back into computer data.

Module A part of the HRMS that performs a specific function. See Subsystem.

Monitor The hardware component that contains the screen on which the user views data, menus, system messages, and commands. *Monitor* is sometimes used interchangeably with the term *video display terminal* (VDT), but they are not identical.

Mouse A small computer peripheral device that, when pushed around on a surface, controls the position of the cursor on the computer screen. An operator may use one or more buttons on the mouse to perform other actions, such as selecting text or commands, without using the keyboard.

Operating system A software program that handles internal computer communication and functions. It also handles communication between the microprocessor and peripheral devices. It controls all operations of reading and writing data to storage devices and allocates space for files.

OCR (Optical character recognition) The technological process by which a scanner can convert printed characters into electronic bytes that represent the characters.

Peripherals Devices external to the CPU that perform input, output, storage, or other functions; may include printers, modems, keyboards, disk drives, and tape storage devices.

Pixel Picture element; a single point of light, the smallest element by which computers construct images. The number of pixels per inch is used as a measure of resolution in monitors and other graphics devices.

Plotter A special printer that can produce multicolor complex graphics on paper by using several "pens" that each receive a separate signal.

RAM (Random access memory) Computer memory to which the system may read and write data or programs. RAM is volatile; turning off the machine completely erases it.

ROM (Read-only memory) Memory protected from any deletions or additions during operation of the system. ROM is nonvolatile; turning off the machine does not affect it.

Record locking A function that presents two users from updating the same record or document at the same time.

Scrolling The process of moving the screen display up, down, right, or left to view another portion of the file or text.

Subsystem A set of components of a larger system. These components share common data definitions, operating mechanisms, policies, and procedures. A subsystem can operate on a stand-alone basis or as a subsidiary to a larger system.

Surge protector A device that smooths out power surges and drops to prevent damage to computers, their resident programs, and files.

System Some array of components that interact to serve a common purpose or application. Because the term has such wide application, its meaning derives from the context in which it appears. A human resources computer system may include hardware, software, users, manual operations, and policies and procedures.

Tape drive An input/output device used with midrange and mainframe computers. It uses large reels of magnetic tape capable of storing much more data than disk drives.

Tape streamer A specialized tape cassette device used for backing up computer data resident on fixed disk drives. Physically removing the cassette and storing it in a secure environment protects the data in case of computer problems.

Terminal An input/output device for a computer system. It usually includes both a keyboard and a monitor; in mainframes these may be a single device or separate units, as with microcomputers.

Terminal emulator A microcomputer used as a mainframe terminal for purposes of communicating with a mainframe system. Some systems allow users to switch the microcomputer from stand-alone to terminal emulation as needed.

Thermal-ink printer A nonimpact printing device that sprays microscopic ink particles onto paper to form characters.

Time-sharing Process of providing multiple users simultaneous access to central computer files. Service bureaus formerly provided this service to a wide range of business users, including human resources departments. Today, only payroll accounting functions use time-sharing.

VDT   See *Video display terminal.*

Video display terminal (VDT)   A mainframe terminal that includes a screen and a keyboard. Most VDTs use CRT technology, though several alternatives also are used. This term is sometimes used interchangeably with the term *monitor,* but they are not identical.

Discussion Points

1. Describe the major functions of at least ten input or output devices.

2. What are the major advantages of microcomputers compared with mid-range and mainframe computers? What are the major limitations of microcomputers?

3. Describe several different types of organizational situations in which a human resources department might use microcomputers to its advantage.

4. What are the major factors to consider in selecting a printer for a human resources environment?

5. Under which circumstances might an HRMS benefit from installing a LAN?

6. Why are ergonomic factors an important consideration in the selection of hardware?

7. What sources should a project team use in assessing hardware reliability and the service reputation of the vendor?

8. What are the primary cost factors in the selection of hardware and peripheral equipment?

Further Reading

Awad, Elias M. *Automatic Data Processing: Principles and Procedures.* Englewood Cliffs, N.J.: Prentice-Hall, 1966.
Becker, Joseph, and Robert M. Hayes. *Information Storage Retrieval: Tools, Elements, Theories.* New York: John Wiley & Sons, 1967.
Briar, Alan, and Ian Robinson. *Computers and the Social Sciences.* New York: Columbia University Press, 1974.
Ceriello, Vincent R. "Microcomputers and Personnel: The Leading Edge." *Human Resources Management Systems Report,* November 1985.
Gruenberger, Fred, and David Babcock. *Computing with Mini Computers.* Los Angeles: Melville Publishing, 1970.
Hellwig, Jessica. *Introduction to Computers and Programming.* New York: Columbia University Press, 1974.

Kent, Allen, Orrin E. Taulbee, Jack Belzer, and Gordon D. Goldstein. *Electronic Handling of Information: Testing and Evaluation.* Washington, DC: Thompson Book Company, 1967.

Kustoff, Marc. "Commit Your Micro to the Company Mainframe." *Computers in HR Management,* September 1989.

McCarthy, E. Jerome, J.A. McCarthy, and Durward Humes. *Integrated Data Processing Systems.* New York: John Wiley & Sons, 1967.

Meyer, Gary J. "What Every Personnel Manager Should Know About Computers." *Personnel Journal,* August 1984.

Optner, Stanford I. *Systems Analysis for Business Management.* Englewood Cliffs, N.J.: Prentice-Hall, 1975.

Szymanski, Robert, Donald Szymanski, Norma Morris, and Donna Pulschen. *Computers and Application Software.* Columbus, OH: Merrill Publishing, 1989.

Turn, Rein. *Computers in the 1980s.* New York: Columbia University Press, 1974.

Weinberg, Gerald. *Rethinking Systems Analysis and Design.* Boston: Little, Brown and Company, 1982.

Part II
HRMS Implementation

You can have it good or fast or cheap. Pick any two.
—Harry S. Truman

Getting a system to look good on paper is a tremendous relief. A plan that coordinates the needs of potential users with related technical and financial constraints serves everyone well—but only momentarily. Many human resources departments put great pressure on HRMS development staff to move forward with a real system as fast as possible. Having learned something about the future system, managers and staff become impatient with the inadequacies of the present system. Maintenance becomes lax as people begin to feel that the replacement system will take care of the problem.

To balance out the need for speed with the need for quality results, the HRMS project leader must move carefully through every step of implementing and managing a new system. These steps include the following:

- Vendor selection
- Contract negotation
- Implementation planning
- Conversion
- Training
- Testing
- Maintenance

These steps require a good set of general management skills in areas such as interpersonal communication, time management, negotiation, and staff motivation. For best results, the persons in charge of each step should have those skills as well as HRMS implementation experience. The more limited this background, the greater is the need to work with a consultant.

Regardless of who provides which aspect of guidance, internal management must work carefully to build support and enthusiasm for the new system before, during, and after it becomes operational. The project leader must present the capabilities of the new system as fully as possible but not promise more than the system will be able to deliver by the end of the acceptance cycle. When the time comes to manipulate data on the HRMS, all the care taken in the planning phase now bears fruit. The successes of system implementation should be publicized and celebrated.

At some point in the life cycle of the HRMS, management may face serious difficulties, some of which may be technical, such as conflicts between system capabilities and user requests, and some financial, such as conflicts between costs and available resources. The HRMS manager can often work out better solutions to these problems by using mediation and compromise than by using confrontation. Sometimes the best HRMS motto is "A good plan is two-thirds of system design" or "Good planning leads to good design; good design makes for smoother HRMS development and implementation."

6
HRMS Vendors

Caveat emptor . . . caveat venditor.

W hen shopping for software, the saying "Let the buyer beware" applies as much to choosing the vendor as to selecting the HRMS software or hardware. In the process of looking for HRMS consultants, software, and systems, members of the project team usually encounter numerous firms willing and anxious to provide software, hardware, or entire system packages. The project manager must pay careful attention to choosing the experienced vendor rather than one who is merely enthusiastic, the reliable vendor rather than one with big promises but no follow-up. Many companies can relate horror stories about having bought from the wrong supplier. These companies bought software or equipment that was inappropriate for their needs because of misrepresentation, miscommunication, or mistakes. In some cases, they did not get the service they required, or the vendor went out of business. The search for an appropriate vendor entails identifying potential vendors, communicating with them clearly and thoroughly, and evaluating their proposals with care.

Identifying Vendors

An HRMS based on a purchased system can be only as successful as the search for the right vendor. For almost twenty years, vendors have offered mainframe, time-share, and service bureau packages. Generally, these packages are expensive and have limited functions and features. Until a few years ago, human resources departments had difficulty even finding a vendor that offered microcomputer products directed specifically at human resources needs. Today, human resources departments face the challenge of finding a vendor that can provide an HRMS that matches their needs.

Types of Vendors

Vendors come in all shapes and sizes: manufacturer's representatives, systems development houses, and value-added resellers (VARs), a catchall term for any firm remarketing someone else's product. VARs may be software brokers, service bureaus, time-share utilities, turnkey vendors, systems development houses, and various hybrids of these types of firms. They also may be software vendors, with sales volumes ranging from several hundred thousand dollars to a hundred million dollars per year.

Bigger does not necessarily mean better. Some better-known applications vendors have excellent reputations, but they may have earned them by selling applications for specific mainframes, not for midrange computers or microcomputers, or for applications for areas other than HRMS, such as finance or production. They actually may have shorter track records in this market than do some smaller, newer, more innovative firms. Despite strong reputations for supporting big corporate clients, small users may find the big vendors maddeningly slow and inflexible. Also, unlike some smaller suppliers, the larger firms have not concentrated on narrow, vertical applications—that is, applications software and equipment packages tailored to specific industries such as health care, insurance, or retail operations. Large firms tend to be compartmentalized, often with resulting miscommunication between sales and support areas.

Some small firms deliver superior software products and services. Others are understaffed, overworked, and, worst of all, undercapitalized. Each year, several go out of business, merge, or are acquired by other firms. Under such circumstances, a company may abandon a product line, leaving customers stranded without support or service.

Some vendors are outstanding professionals. Others are little more than glib salespersons who know virtually nothing about HRMS software from the end user's point of view. In selling hardware, the motto is "Move iron!" If hardware manufacturers also offer software, question what they are *really* selling—machines or solutions? As with all relatively new and growing industries, HRMS software retailing has attracted some fly-by-night operators.

Locating Vendors

Whether a human resources department decides to accept as standard or modify packaged software, the department must first choose among the different HRMS packages available. A company must assess the potential fit between its needs and the functions and features each system offers. Ideally, an organization should acquire software before hardware because the programs an organization requires may run only on certain computers or under specific

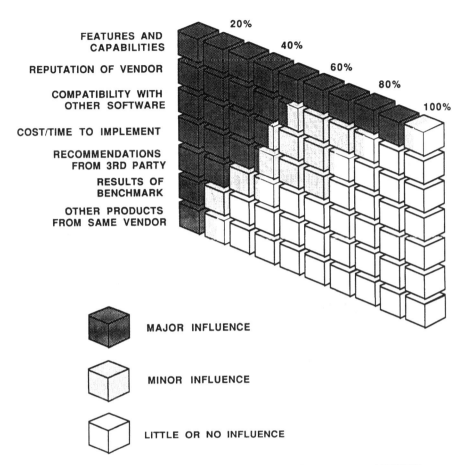

FEATURES AND CAPABILITIES

REPUTATION OF VENDOR

COMPATIBILITY WITH OTHER SOFTWARE

COST/TIME TO IMPLEMENT

RECOMMENDATIONS FROM 3RD PARTY

RESULTS OF BENCHMARK

OTHER PRODUCTS FROM SAME VENDOR

20%
40%
60%
80%
100%

MAJOR INFLUENCE

MINOR INFLUENCE

LITTLE OR NO INFLUENCE

Figure 6–1. Factors affecting HRMS selection. In a survey of HRMS users, the system's features and capabilities had the greatest influence on system selection. Vendor reputation ranked as the second greatest influence.

operating environments. In most cases, however, an organization must find software that works with existing hardware. In a few cases, organizations have purchased computer equipment that has gone unused for lack of compatible software that runs effectively in that specific environment.

No single clearinghouse on quality software exists, but several excellent sources describe special segments of the HRMS market, such as micro-computer-based systems. The following material describes some general areas in which to search. Even after selecting and acquiring HRMS software, the project team may use these sources to locate additional software needed to improve or extend HRMS capability, add new applications, or optimize system performance.

Computer Manufacturers. The firms that build computers usually maintain a list of packages that run on their systems. This is a good place to start, especially when using equipment not supported by many software vendors. Since many vendors support only IBM or IBM-compatible hardware, if a firm is looking for suitable software for Digital Equipment Corporation, Prime, NCR, Hewlett Packard, Wang, Data General, Tandem, Unisys, Honeywell, Apple, or other hardware, it may have to rely on the computer manufacturer for sources of software.

Other Users. Direct competitors do not normally share information, but clients of the vendors may be willing to share their HRMS experiences. Many national and international professional associations have local chapters that meet regularly to share their experiences. Such organizations include the Association of Human Resources Systems Professionals (HRSP) and the Society for Human Resources Management (formerly ASPA). The following organizations also have special-interest groups or task forces dealing with HRMS:

- International Personnel Management Association (IPM)
- American Compensation Association (ACA)
- American Payroll Association (APA)
- Human Resources Planning Society (HRPS)
- American Society for Training and Development (ASTD)

Addresses for these and similar organizations are included in Appendix A.

Trade Associations. The Association of Computer Users (ACU) helps its members find suitable software products but offers little or no help in HRMS. Members can have the ACU search directories for packages that support specific applications not limited to HRMS, but since the ACU does not list nonmembers, its lists are often incomplete. Organizations such as the Association of Computer Programmers and Analysts, the Data Processing Management Association, and the Association for Computing Machinery also may be of nominal assistance. The list of vendor sources in Appendix C offers additional resources.

Human Resources Trade Publications. Personnel and human resources trade publications are plentiful. They regularly print "how to" articles and case histories of successful HRMS installations. Potential clients may ask for assistance from the publisher, the editor, or the company described. Vendors also advertise widely in trade journals and provide reader response cards (and frequently toll-free phone and fax numbers). A list of such publications is included in Appendix B.

Computer and Information Systems Publications. Both the editorial and advertising sections of computer publications are a potential source of contacts. Some of these publications run an annual theme issue on HRMS and include a listing or matrix of vendors, products, prices, and features. Some of the major publications that have published such listings are *Computerworld*, *Business Software Review*, *Datamation*, *Computer Decisions*, *Infosystems*, *Software News*, and *Information Center*.

Human Resources Conferences. Most human resources conferences offer at least one seminar, panel, or speech on the practical uses of computers. Some annual conferences, such as that of the Association of Human Resources Systems Professionals (HRSP), are devoted entirely to HRMS. HRSP has also begun to publish directories of HRMS software products and services. Their listings generally include only the vendors who market at the conference or place advertisements in the directory. The speakers (and attendees) at these affairs are a mix of practitioners, consultants, and vendors. Most of the personnel and computer publications also publish calendars of forthcoming events such as seminars, workshops, conferences, and symposia.

Directories. Hardware and software vendors, professional associations, publications, research groups, and other organizations publish numerous directories. Some list packages; others list consultants and specialists. Most directories cost between $50 and $500. The more expensive ones list other applications as well as HRMS. Some of the modestly priced directories have the best information. They cannot cover all the software options, but they are usually more comprehensive than those that accompany trade journal articles.

Mail Order and Catalogs. The growth in available software has been accompanied by the publication of numerous software catalogs and direct-mail marketing of software. Although direct mail and catalogs often offer more competitive prices than direct sales, they have far too many limitations to make their use appropriate for most HRMS situations. For instance, catalogs include very little information about the software offerings; potential customers should know what software they want before consulting the catalogs for price information. In addition, catalogs offer no installation or maintenance support, no customization or source code, and usually no opportunity to preview the software. Mail-order purchase usually works well in only a few situations, such as small, no-growth operations; users needing little or no help; "power" users operating well above the level of other users in their organization; and applications that are unlikely to require significant modification.

Consultants. Organizations that have trouble developing an appropriate list of possible vendors may consider retaining a consultant for this task. If the consultant can find a package that fits the organization's needs and saves the expense of custom development, the fees for the consultant's services will be more than covered. Some firms consider this an effective insurance policy, since creating a more effective, efficient decision-making process usually more than offsets the consultant's fees.

As chapter 7 indicates, there are many specialist HRMS consultants. That chapter suggests how to locate and evaluate consultants. Consultants know the products of many vendors, have seen many different systems in operation, and have heard product raves and horror stories. But beware! Some consulting firms sell software or have financial connections with a particular vendor. A firm must make sure that a consultant will provide independent and objective advice, so it must require the potential consultants to disclose any relationships they have with vendors. Conversely, some consultants and vendors have adversarial relationships. A consultant may let those attitudes affect the list of vendors the consultant recommends. Other vendors that are aware of the situation may then refuse to participate in a deal.

Doing Preliminary Vendor Screening

Most contacts with prospective vendors begin with a few preliminary phone calls or meetings to confirm that the vendors have the potential to provide what the HRMS project team needs. Because there are more and more vendors, many firms narrow their search with a list of the criteria any potential vendor must meet.

Before undertaking a formal vendor evaluation process, a firm must consider the quality of interactions with each vendor. Personal integrity has significant value in client-vendor relationships, so it is important to pay attention to the quality of professional behavior. Sometimes firms eliminate certain vendors simply by evaluating their selling approach. A firm should be wary of a vendor that begins with glowing stories about the magical capabilities of the software. No single software product can solve every problem. No one can suggest proper solutions before knowing what the customer hopes to achieve. Vendors reveal their value by the extent to which they solve problems.

The HRMS project team also can do a preliminary check of a vendor's financial stability. Potential clients need not run financial checks on the largest

Vendor Marketing Language

What Vendors Say	What They Mean
"You trust me, don't you?"	I'm counting on our relationship.
"You can believe in our technical expertise."	Take us at face value; don't probe.
"We can solve your problem now."	I'm counting on your impatience.
"This is our best price."	We have little incentive to lower the price.
"Our package will fit your situation."	We'll use creative packaging.
"Buy now before the price increases."	This is a good deal (for us).
"Try it; you'll like it."	I'm hoping to create a dependence.
"How can you refuse something for nothing?"	We will have to give up too much if negotiations continue.

vendors, but they can obtain a Dun and Bradstreet report for almost any firm. A few firms are listed on a stock exchange, publish annual reports, and issue a 10-K disclosure statement available through a subscription data base such as Dow Jones News/Retrieval, The Source/CompuServe, or Prodigy or through a stockbroker. Ask smaller firms to provide a current financial statement.

When the team is satisfied with the prospective vendor's approach and financial status, members should proceed to the tough questions. Many firms use a checklist as a preliminary test to narrow the field before asking vendors to submit bids. They talk with potential vendors' current and former clients only after determining finalists in the selection process. The following paragraphs suggest some questions to ask in relation to possible vendors.

1. *How long has the vendor been in business?* Potential clients should find a vendor who is likely to remain in business. One need not disqualify a firm just because it is new, but such a firm must fulfill all the other requirements. The client should investigate what the newly established vendor did before selling HRMS products and services. Someone with extensive experience in the human resources or IS field may have the necessary functional or technical expertise or at least know where to obtain it.

2. *Is the vendor experienced in the client's business?* Few firms have the

time or resources to develop products and services for every kind of business, but buying from a specialist increases the chances of getting the right package.

3. *How many HRMS applications has the vendor already installed?* The client should ask the vendor to provide names, contacts, and telephone numbers of firms for which it has provided comparable applications. Asking for this list encourages vendors to minimize exaggeration because they know the potential client can check out their claims. This list also provides the basis for checking references later, after narrowing the list of potential vendors.

4. *Does the vendor provide a firm guarantee?* Most vendors claim to provide a full guarantee, but some merely pass along inadequate hardware and software warranties from manufacturers. The more reputable firms offer their own warranties for all components. When paying retail prices, the customer should expect a strong guarantee. Later, when contracts are under discussion, the human resources project manager can make the guarantee a major negotiating point.

5. *Does the vendor provide implementation support?* Implementation means more than delivering software and plugging it in. What about software installation? Can the vendor help convert data from the existing system to the new HRMS? Can the vendor supervise any necessary changes to the basic package, interfaces, report generators, DBMS, and so on? The vendor should be willing to modify the package as needed. In this case, the HRMS project team should ensure that the vendor's firm is financially stable and has a good track record of implementing modifications. Many vendors farm out changes in the basic package to implementation specialists who are organizationally independent of, but closely aligned with, the vendors whose products they support. For mainframe systems, the vendor should provide the needed source code or make the necessary changes. This protects the client if the vendor goes out of business or stops supporting a particular version of the HRMS.

6. *Does the vendor offer training?* Training means more than handing employees a manual. Can the vendor train clerical operators? Can it train clients and their employees to train others? Can the vendor train management to get the most from the HRMS? When and where does the vendor hold classes?

An organization can add other questions that pertain to its unique circumstances. The project team should check the validity of vendor statements about experience and reliability carefully. It should not rely only on answers to one or two key questions. Firms should carry out this crucial screening process no matter who the vendor is. HRMS evaluators should not be swayed by a vendor's size or degree of specialization or by the resources of its parent company. A vendor that fails critical parts of the checklist probably cannot deliver the needed services. No vendor will meet all criteria perfectly, so some firms rank vendors in order of their ability to meet requirements.

Communicating with Vendors

After performing the preliminary vendor screening, the project team prepares the more formal aspects of the vendor selection process. These steps are request for information (RFI), request for proposal (RFP), and vendor evaluation. These written procedures help ensure that each vendor understands the project requirements and bases its bid on this understanding of the project.

Request for Information

Many firms perform formal prescreening prior to distributing their RFP by sending a preliminary letter to vendors asking for an expression of interest. This letter is referred to as a request for information or interest (RFI). The RFI describes the project in one or two pages, then requests that potential vendors provide an expression of interest and a list of their qualifications. An example of an RFI letter is presented in the accompanying sidebar. Some firms perform this step by phone. Throughout this process, the potential client finds out whether the vendor is prepared to submit a formal written proposal and bid. The RFI response also provides the name of a primary contact to whom the project team should send the RFP.

Sample RFI Letter

This is an actual letter used in a vendor evaluation project to solicit interest in a client's HRMS project.

To: Prospective Bidders

From: VRC Consulting Group

Subject: Human Resources Management System Project

The XYZ Manufacturing Company has retained our organization as a consultant to assist in the process of choosing alternatives for the development and implementation of an automated human resources management system (HRMS).

VRC and XYZ have completed the user requirements definition, and we are currently in the feasibility study phase. This phase will, among other things, address the best course of action for XYZ. There is no preconceived view as to whether XYZ will make or buy its ultimate system, modify what it has, or do anything at all. The decision will rest in large part on whether any vendor can adequately support XYZ's unique computer configuration: IBM 3031, MVS operating system, 3278 terminals, VSAM/CICS, Easytrieve.

The project steering committee, comprising senior management, representatives of human resources information systems, finance, and the consultant, intend to solicit bids from interested and qualified vendors for the design and implementation of the HRMS. These bids may be in several parts, addressing time, cost, and scope of activity as follows:

- System design and development through programming specifications and
- Software development, system implementation, and acceptance testing or
- Development and implementation of packaged software to include installation and acceptance testing

In other words, XYZ reserves the right to award a contract for either part separately and independently or both parts contiguously or make no award at all. The successful bidder for the first part is not guaranteed a continuance for the second part.

It should be emphasized that HRMS development activity will not begin before May 1, 1991. It also should be noted and clearly understood that all contact with XYZ on the HRMS project will be through the consultant. The vendor may choose to bid on either or both parts of the project separately but will be permitted to alter the bid for the second part. Some of the factors that we intend to evaluate on the vendors who are invited to bid are presented on the attached. Feel free to call if you require clarification. Under no circumstances should you contact anyone at XYZ until authorized to do so.

We expect to be interviewing vendors either at our office or at XYZ headquarters. If your firm is interested in bidding and will abide by the ground rules, please contact me by telephone as soon as possible to discuss this project further and make an appointment to present your HRMS capabilities. If we have not heard from you by March 19, 1991 we will assume you have no interest in bidding on this project.

Request for Proposal

The RFP describes in detail the customer's ideal computer system in terms of requirements and asks each qualified vendor to submit a bid. A typical RFP has several sections, discussed in detail in the material that follows. The RFP process does not guarantee that the firm will obtain the perfect system, but it does ensure that the customer will find the option that fits those requirements as closely as possible.

The mainframe and midrange HRMS marketplace commonly uses the RFP as a buying tool, but firms with smaller HRMS requirements that intend to acquire microcomputer-based systems also can use it. Organizations that plan to spend more than $50,000 for software and related services probably should use this method. Vendors often cannot justify spending the resources to prepare a proper RFP for less expensive systems. In such cases, the HRMS project team may need to research vendor literature, complete questionnaires via telephone or fax, or use a consultant.

Whether a client buys an expensive system or an inexpensive one, developing an RFP tailored to the organization's individual needs is worth the time it takes. This process brings together all the elements of the system acquisition process in a compact document. In fact, putting this document together need not require much time, as the planning and design processes have already compiled most of the background information required. Some organizations hire a consultant to develop and write their RFP, but most can do a great deal on their own. If the project team needs help, a consultant can review the draft and make recommendations.

Sometimes HRMS project team members need a reason to use such a formal process for a buying decision. Here are a few reasons why an RFP can contribute significantly to successful HRMS selection:

- The RFP defines the user's goals and requirements. The process of completing the worksheet crystallizes these goals and requirements. For that reason alone, it is worth the time and effort, even if no vendor ever sees it.
- The RFP simplifies the decision-making process. Numerous combinations of hardware, software, and services exist. With the RFP as a benchmark, the project team can compare each system being considered.
- The RFP saves time and facilitates comparisons of vendor responses. The organization provides the same information to competing vendors, eliminates repetitive interviews, and should expect to receive consistent responses in a consistent format.
- The RFP reduces the potential for errors. In preparing an RFP, the or-

194

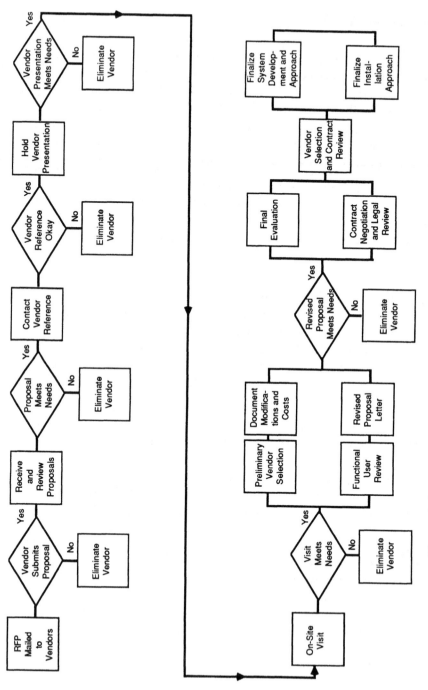

Figure 6–2. The vendor selection process.
(Source: Towers, Perrin, Forster & Crosby. Reprinted with permission.)

ganization has less chance of overlooking important factors. If it turns out that the project team has overlooked a major point, the more ethical vendors probably will volunteer the required information, particularly if doing so makes their proposals look more attractive.

The RFP reduces the chances for disagreements. The vendor understands what the human resources department expects. Some firms incorporate portions of the RFP into the final contract. For example, the vendor should have no objection to including the RFP questionnaire as an exhibit in the contract. If the vendor does object, the client and the vendor should try to achieve a consensus on this issue before signing the contract.

Components of an RFP

The HRMS project team may not need to prepare a complicated RFP, but its work must be comprehensive. Many HRMS RFPs use a five-part format:

1. Introduction, including business profile and statement of objectives
2. Proposal instructions
3. Functional requirements
4. Vendor requirements
5. RFP administrative information

Introduction. The introduction should provide an overall understanding of the organization, the required HRMS, and the environment in which it must operate. The introduction should begin by describing the purpose of the RFP itself. This portion should explain that the organization requires an HRMS but has made no decision concerning a vendor. The RFP is not an offer to contract but represents a definition of specific HRMS requirements and an invitation to recipients to submit a proposal addressing these requirements.

The introduction should profile the potential client and its human resources department. The client describes the organization's business or service—the industry, number of locations, number of employees, primary products or services, and other relevant information. As appropriate, the RFP should describe the roles and responsibilities of each human resources function, as well as the emerging issues and future direction of each function. It should provide an overview of why the human resources department is looking for a new system. This discussion may summarize the kinds of functions and features the new system should provide that the current one cannot. It may describe the steps performed in defining requirements, such as interviews, surveys, and operational audits.

The introductory section should specify briefly the technical environment in which the new system must perform, including hardware the firm plans to continue using, systems with which the new HRMS must interface or integrate, size of the data base, and number of transactions expected.

Proposal Instructions. This section is usually brief but concrete. It should state clearly that the potential client may reject and return any proposals not conforming to the instructions in the RFP. Proposals should be concise, clear, and complete, and they should conform with the prescribed format.

Bidders should propose only currently available capabilities. If a proposal reflects capabilities not currently available, the bidder should clearly note these capabilities and the date on which they will be released.

The instructions might list required content for the transmittal letter to accompany the RFP, but the organization should expect that vendors will use this letter as a marketing vehicle to highlight the areas of their proposals that put them in the best light. The instructions also should outline the expected proposal to be submitted by each bidding vendor as follows:

- Introduction (vendor credentials, location, and contact person)
- Functional requirements (responses to the requirements specified in the functional requirements section of the RFP; sometimes on the forms provided in the RFP)
- Vendor requirements (responses to the requirements specified in the vendor requirements section of the RFP)
- Proposal costs (packaged software costs, cost of each software modification, hardware costs, implementation costs, training costs, maintenance costs, payment terms, and sample contract)
- Appendix (includes complete user documentation, other system documentation, standard reports, data dictionaries, samples of source code, vendor financial information, samples of training course materials, résumés or staff profiles, and screen formats)

Functional Requirements. This is the largest part of the RFP and describes what the system must do. This material covers general and detailed requirements in each functional area of human resources affected by the proposed HRMS. Some RFPs list each line-item requirement and ask vendors to comment on their ability to meet these requirements. However, this approach sometimes leaves evaluators without sufficient quantitative measures to use in comparing proposal responses.

With increasing frequency, firms are using a self-scoring system that re-

Sample RFP Self-Scoring Instructions

Although most of these questions are stated in a "yes/no" format, strict "yes" or "no" answers are unacceptable. Answer each question with a "yes" or "no" *and* a detailed explanation.

For "yes" answers, you must explain how your *unmodified, currently deliverable system* fulfills the requirement. This explanation should include the appropriate data elements, the part(s) of your system involved, and specifically how the requirement is handled by your system.

For "no" answers, where your current system does not completely meet the requirement, you must specify the level of effort and cost associated with modifying your system to meet the requirement and specifically what must be done to the system to operate as asked.

The following scale should be used for the requirements in this RFP:

0 =	Meets the requirements without modification.
1 to 2 =	Can meet the requirements with *minor* software modification. Minor is defined as requiring 1 through 4 person-days of effort. Code 1 through 2 days as 1; code 3 through 4 days as 2.
3 to 4 =	Can meet the requirement with *moderate* software modification. Moderate is defined as requiring 5 through 9 person-days of effort. Code 5 through 7 days as 3; code 8 through 9 days as 4.
5 to 6 =	Can meet the requirement with *major* software modification. Major is defined as requiring 10 through 20 person-days of effort. Code 10 through 15 days as 5; code 16 through 20 as 6.
7 to 9 =	Does not meet requirement without *extensive* system redesign or restructuring. Extensive is defined as requiring more than 20 person-days of effort. Code 20 through 29 days as 7; code 30 through 39 days as 8; code 40 days or more as 9.
N/A =	Stated requirement asked for a list of data, tables, reports, or other information that did not warrant yes/no answer and description of the system's capabilities.

Use the space provided for your answer. If you cannot fully respond in the allotted space, use a separate sheet of paper for each requirements section. List the number and question, then provide your answer.

Proposers must indicate *both* the person-hours and the cost the proposer will charge for the modification(s) on the form found in the appendix to this RFP. The form corresponds exactly to the following questions with two exceptions: general requirements and technical system requirements. You are not required to complete a separate form for these requirements.

After each question has been answered, transfer the number from the above scale (0 to 9) to the summary in the appendix and indicate the costs involved in modifying your system.

---

quires bidders to rank the degree to which their proposed systems meet each requirement. A sample set of scoring instructions is presented in the accompanying sidebar. Most RFPs instruct bidders to write their answers directly on the RFP and provide space after each question to allow bidders to make clarifying comments. Because the RFP is a request for extensive information, there should be plenty of room for the vendor to provide it. Some sections call for a narrative response to questions pertaining to issues such as security, data base management, and interfaces. Vendors should be instructed to elaborate on their answers even when the question implies a simple yes or no answer: for example, "Does your product provide security at the field value level?" Obviously, if the capability exists, the vendor should describe it in full.

General requirements usually cover a wide array of issues, including but not limited to on-line and batch capabilities, real-time processing, archiving and history creation, table maintenance, menus, edit and validation rules, help functions, retroactive transactions, pending transactions (those with future effective dates), standard and ad hoc reports, system access, and audit trails. Each firm must develop its own list based on its requirements definition.

The functional requirements section contains a separate description and set of questions for each human resources function or application in the proposed HRMS. The firm should include a paragraph or more about each of the various roles and responsibilities of that function, including regulatory requirements, interface requirements, history requirements, future needs, and any special data or reporting needs. The questions should cover every item included in the requirements definition for this function, as well as additional information gathered during data base design.

Finally, the functional requirements section covers the technical environment, the hardware configuration, and other system requirements in which the proposed HRMS must operate. This includes questions pertaining to data structures, data modeling, data dictionaries, on-line and/or batch operating environments, languages and special utilities used, and interfaces. Any requirements for support of new hardware should be listed. The vendor should be asked to describe the equipment configuration its new HRMS would require and compare it with the existing configuration. Potential vendors also should list and price components individually or at least provide cost estimates.

Vendor Requirements. This section often appears in question form, with space for bidders to provide their answers about product name, version, release level, and history. In this section, the vendor should include a list of references of other clients whose needs have been similar to those described in the RFP. Many firms request a complete customer list.

This section inquires about standard and optional training, conversion, acceptance testing processes, implementation support, and procedures for fixing bugs. It also should ask about hot line support and about forums for exchange of information among clients (known as user groups).

RFP Administrative Information. This section provides the administrative terms and conditions bidders need to consider when reviewing and responding to the RFP. It usually addresses the following issues:

- Nondisclosure of the RFP itself; an agreement between the vendor and the potential client that neither will disclose the RFP to unauthorized parties
- Schedule for the proposal process, vendor selection, and implementation, including the deadline for submitting the proposal and bid. (Three to four weeks from the date of the RFP mailing usually provides sufficient response time.)
- Policy on further inquiries regarding the RFP, including name, address, and phone number of designated contact person (sometimes the consultant)
- Proposal submission requirements, including deadline, address, and number of proposal copies
- Required affirmations, such as EEO policy, small or minority business status, and lack of possible conflicts of interest
- Time, place, and purpose of any bidders' conference, including agenda and list of invited bidders

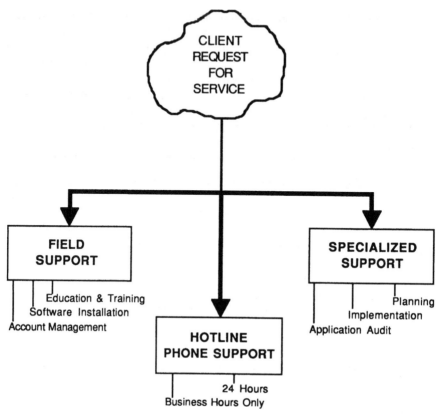

Figure 6–3. Types of client support. To compare vendors fairly and to make sure HRMS users get the kind of support they need, a firm must ask detailed questions about each kind of client support a vendor offers.
(Source: ASK Computer Systems. Reprinted with permission.)

- Requirements for demonstration of proposed system at a time and place convenient to both client and vendor

- Provision for consideration of alternate proposals (Most firms ask bidders to propose a system that comes as close as possible to the one described in the RFP. The firm may state that it also will consider viable alternatives if the bidder forwards information about them separately. The vendor should suggest alternatives if none of the available options meets specific needs. Only as a last resort should the organization consider custom HRMS development, a very expensive and time-consuming process. Probably some commercially available packages will accommodate 75 percent of the user's needs.)

- Request for itemization of products, services, and requirements not specifically mentioned in the RFP but necessary to provide the functional capabilities the bidder's proposal describes (Each implied requirement should indicate the cost basis under which the bidder would provide it—fixed fee, time and materials, retainer, or some combination.)
- Request for bidders to quote prices in specific terms, itemizing prices for software, modifications, training, maintenance, and other support services (The potential client understands that the vendor will guarantee prices only at the time of a signed contract and that the contract may expire in 30, 60, or 90 days.)
- Request for bidders to agree to append to the contract any sales literature or other information provided either in the response to the RFP or during the initial presentations, since these are representations of the package's capabilities
- Request for vendors' standard contracts or license agreements, noting that final contracts and guarantees are to be mutually negotiated (This should eliminate any vendor determined to stick to its standard contract at any cost. As chapter 8 details, the organization should not sign a standard contract before negotiating for modifications and other postsales services.)
- Agreement that all costs associated with proposal development and submission and with system demonstration, visits, and other such efforts by bidders prior to signing a contract are the responsibility of bidders
- Agreement that withdrawal and return or disposal of proposals of the unsuccessful bidders is a joint responsibility of the vendor and the client

Finally, the RFP may include as appendixes any relevant human resources policies and procedures, affirmative action plans, company brochures, preliminary data bases, organizational charts, samples of current reports, and relevant internal memoranda.

Distributing the RFP

Ideally, a soliciting organization should send the RFP to about three vendors of any one type. Types may include custom-software developers, service bureaus, or software vendors that support specific technologies. Sometimes the HRMS project team settles on a mix of these types, with four or five viable choices. In reality, an organization has a wide choice of available vendors, but after the preliminary screening process, the number of viable bidders drops sharply. Because sending the RFP to unqualified or uninterested vendors wastes time, it is wise to obtain bids only from qualified and responsive vendors.

Each prospective vendor should receive two copies of the RFP, one to return and one for its own records (though many retype it anyway). Because the project team may modify or clarify the RFP as a result of vendors' queries, the original or master copy should be available so that any inquiries or requests for classification from the vendors can be resolved. Developing an RFP and responding to it take time and effort on the part of both the vendor and the HRMS project team, but this effort increases the likelihood that the eventual contract will protect the interests of the client and the vendor.

Evaluating Vendors

If only a few vendors respond to the RFP, the human resources department might view this as an additional screening process. For example, some vendors will not participate in an RFP process because they know they will probably lose in open competition. Vendors that realize they cannot meet the described system requirements probably will not return the RFP.

Organizations in remote areas and those that want inexpensive software may have trouble convincing vendors to complete an RFP. They may effectively substitute a structured questionnaire administered in one or several teleconferences, but they probably will have difficulty getting detailed responses. They should persevere until at least two vendors have responded to all the requirements of the RFP.

Evaluating RFP Responses

Once the project team has received the expected RFP responses, the evaluation and selection process begins. Ultimately, the key to selecting packaged software lies in asking the right questions. Many firms use an evaluation worksheet, which assigns points to each response by a vendor. The weighting of responses depends on the importance of that feature or function to the organization.

Vendor selection often involves compromises. HRMS vendors offer strengths in different areas. One vendor's excellent applicant tracking system may include a mediocre job requisition tracking feature that does not, for example, check for duplicate entries. Another excels in benefits administration but processes financial data very inefficiently. Sometimes the need for certain functions or features necessitates accepting a package with limitations in other areas. In many cases, modifications can correct these problems; when they cannot, the project team leader should keep the HRMS project team and the human resources community focused on the strengths rather than the deficiencies of the alternative.

Worksheet For Evaluating
HRMS Products and Services

Most HRMS project teams use a comprehensive worksheet to evaluate vendor responses to the formal RFP. The project team also may want to use a worksheet at several other points, such as during preliminary vendor evaluation or evaluation of product demonstrations.

	Vendor 1	*Vendor 2*	*Vendor 3*
Documentation			
Overview			
Instruction section			
Technical section			
Index			
Troubleshooting guide			
Uses English, not jargon			
Software			
Support of human resources functions			
Modularity			
Subsystem integration			
Ease of modifying			
Data base management			
On-line inquiry			
Rapid sorting and retrieval			
Error trapping			
Edit and validation features			
Flexible defaults			
Menu driven			
Screen layout			
English-language operator messages			
Report generation			
Compatibility with existing hardware/ software			
Support Services			
Training			
Implementation			
Maintenance			
Newsletter			
User group			
Costs			
Basic HRMS			
Additional modules			
Modifications			
Implementation			
Maintenance			

	Vendor 1	Vendor 2	Vendor 3
Warranty			
Money-back guarantee			
Replace defective storage media			
Fix bugs during warranty period			
Updates available at no cost			
Runs on existing hardware			
Local service and support			
Hot line for questions			

Many packaged systems carry only implied guarantees that they will do what the advertisements imply. Price or reputation does not necessarily ensure that the organization will get the best HRMS. Some of the best software on the market is reasonably priced, while some high-priced packages are second-rate. Relying on name brands provides no assurances either.

By carefully considering functions, features, and costs of the vendors' proposals, decision makers can eliminate the less responsive HRMS packages. This "de-selection" process results in identifying the vendor whose package best fits the organization's needs. Best does not mean that the system is technically the most advanced but that the package most closely fits the user's requirements. Best for one firm may not be best for another.

The HRMS project team has primary responsibility for vendor evaluation, often in conjunction with a qualified HRMS consultant. Experience is critical at this point. Top management may play a role in the final selection. The entire evaluation process usually takes two to three months, including site visits, reference checking, RFP evaluation, telephone conferences, and numerous follow-up meetings. It may take considerably longer if the system includes a broad scope, multiple products, multiple vendors, technology migration plans, changing business conditions, or other complicating factors.

Evaluating Product Demonstrations

Firms must avoid judging software externally—from the outside in. Far too many firms are enticed by the packaging, believe advertising claims literally, or put faith in brief demonstrations in which the sales representative runs the show. To ensure acquisition of a responsive system, the HRMS project team must evaluate alternatives internally—from the inside out. Since testing every part of the HRMS is impractical, however, the HRMS project team should examine only the most viable candidates in detail. After reviewing and evaluating the written RFP responses, the project team should arrange for detailed demonstrations of the finalists' products.

The potential client should test the software in a working environment.

Ideally, the HRMS project team should install it on the computer that will run the production system. If that is not practical, the team should evaluate the software as a complete system in a parallel environment. Mainframe vendors prefer to demonstrate at their own site, to avoid technical difficulties that may arise in a remote demonstration. Most midrange computer and microcomputer demonstrations also take place at the vendor's site. Holding the demonstration away from the organization's site eliminates unwanted distractions and interruptions. In this way, the HRMS project team can control who participates in the demonstration evaluation.

Most vendor presentations, including the product demonstrations, take one to two days, depending on the complexity of the system, the number of separate or specialized presentations, and the needs of the project team. The HRMS project manager and human resources management will decide ahead of time who will represent the organization at the vendor's demonstration. Participants should include both technical and functional experts.

Most vendors orchestrate their demonstrations carefully. They emphasize the functions their systems perform well and may avoid or gloss over the systems' shortcomings. The potential client has somewhat different priorities than the vendor. To make sure that the demonstration responds to those issues, the HRMS project team should assist in developing an agenda and arrive at the demonstration with a list of questions and issues the members would like to discuss.

Designated project members should take as assertive a stance as necessary to raise key points at appropriate times. Because demonstrations take place in a rather compressed time frame, the team should focus on examining the major elements rather than every minor detail. Many potential clients find consultants quite helpful in identifying key issues and making sure the vendors address the organization's agenda. The consultant often drafts the agenda and helps orchestrate the vendors' presentations and demonstrations.

As discussed in chapters 2 and 3, different systems work best for different types of users. The project team should know the extent to which neophytes or technical experts will be using the system and keep these workers' needs in mind during the demonstration.

The demonstration should clarify how the various human resources functions would interact under the new system. If the department is considering implementing the system in phases, the team should ask to see an installation that includes only the modules planned for the first phase. If the team must hurry to implement the full HRMS before users can substitute the new system for the old one, it may overlook critical functions. These shortcomings will reduce system credibility among users.

Required integration and interfacing capabilities should be tested as much as possible. The team should try to arrange to have transactions from the demonstration read and transferred to the existing system and vice versa, then perform an audit trail and evaluate the results of these interactions. The team also should consider the ease of making modifications. Members should test the process of changing formats for reports and screens and try to adjust automatic default values to reflect the organization's preferred policies and procedures. Are these changes easy to make? Does the system have many options, or does it allow only one way of performing critical functions?

The demonstration should include tests of the systems edit and validation features. Many HRMS evaluators make a crucial mistake when they test an HRMS: They run it only with good data. The system should be tested with bad data such as February 30 or sex code T. Team members should hit incorrect function keys to try to make the system crash. They should create error conditions, such as pressing conflicting function keys or asking for nonexistent files, then see how the system recovers.

Audit trails are another important part of the evaluation process. Authorized users should be able to trace HRMS transactions that contain input errors. For example, the system should identify all human resources–related postings to the general ledger with codes identifying the subsidiary account from which it came, the date of the transaction, and the operator who entered it.

The team should consider how the system organizes and arranges screen information. In virtually every case, menu-driven HRMS programs work best because they guide the user through the system navigation process. When examining potential systems, members should move among menus to evaluate the ease of handling common data transactions, such as adding, updating, and deleting data.

The system should allow easy on-line inquiry. The team should try to gain access to various employee records by using just social security number, employee number, or part of the employee's surname.

The vendor's documentation on standard reports should be reviewed ahead of time. What constitutes a standard report from the vendor's point of view may not work well for some users, so the team should look at report format, content, and comprehensiveness. No matter how many reports the vendor provides, its packaged systems rarely offer all the report formats an organization wants or needs, so team members can use the demonstration to try out the system's ad hoc report generation options. They can create several custom report formats with various levels of complexity. Report generation should allow users to create customized reports easily and successfully without technical intervention. Everyone who will eventually need such reports should review these samples.

The system's provisions for data security also should be examined. Vendors often can provide additional written information on these features. The team should test how well the system handles data restrictions at the field-value level. For instance, it can create a parameter that limits a user to viewing

Evaluating HRMS Documentation

HRMS software evaluation should include a thorough examination of the documentation. A comprehensive set of technical and functional manuals may mean that the rest of the package also is of high quality (though this is not necessarily so). Conversely, if the manuals are not current, cross-referenced, and comprehensive, potential clients should take a harder look at the package and may wish to eliminate it from further consideration. No matter how good the software may be, poor documentation keeps users from accessing its capabilities effectively. Good documentation usually has four parts:

1. Overview. Explains the product and its available options. This section should contain a summary. Without a summary, a manual can be more confusing than helpful.

2. Instruction section. Presents a step-by-step guide through the system for entering, updating, and deleting transactions, forms, records, or data with sample screens, files, reports, and program links.

3. Technical section. The source code and program logic should be described so that technicians can modify program logic, add user-defined routines, and optimize programs for specific needs. The manuals should have instructions for linking the program with other programs, both vendor supplied and user developed.

4. Index. Should be cross-referenced and should include a list of error conditions, error messages, recovery procedures, a troubleshooting guide, and a comprehensive data dictionary or data element table.

Some manuals are written for users, others for programmers. User-oriented manuals should have as little technical jargon as possible. The overview should be easy to understand and use. The instruction material should be logical and have sufficient detail. The technical sections are directed to more advanced users and technical support staff. The ideal manual allows any user to understand the system without needing constant explanations from the vendor. In this regard, good documentation is in the vendor's best interest as well.

To get a better view of a manual's clarity, look at the treatment of error conditions and help documentation. Some manuals do not even contain these; others explain what the symbols mean but may give no clue as to how to correct the errors. The documentation must explain how to get back on track after diagnosing and correcting operations errors.

---

only salaries less than $50,000 per year. Technical staff should try to find ways around password protection and protected fields. The proposed system should accommodate the type of privilege matrix for data access that the human resources department requires.

Checking References

Once finalists have emerged from the evaluation process, firms to whom those vendors have sold software should be contacted. Any HRMS package vendor that has a good track record will readily supply a user list and specific references. The decision-making process should include factors such as other clients' satisfaction and vendor responses to user problems. The project team should ask these clients comprehensive questions about the functionality of the system, the implementation process, the quality of training provided, overall performance, post-implementation enhancements, service after the sale, types of modifications made, and how the vendor resolves problems.

Can users readily obtain information from others in their industry or geographic area? Periodic seminars and annual conferences are useful, but they are not, in themselves, the best forum for exchange. They often are designed primarily to be sales and business development meetings highlighted by announcements of new enhancements or strategic directions.

Once the HRMS project team and human resources management have selected a final candidate, contract negotiations begin. Often, however, the installation of the new HRMS has taken place and implementation is well under way before contract negotiations are completed.

Glossary

Access level A term used in data security design to refer to the limits within which a user may view data in a particular file, record segment, or field. If the value of the data in a field is outside set parameters, the system will not allow the user access to those data.

Functional requirements The main portion of an HRMS RFP; this material covers the general and specific requirements in each of the functional areas of human resources affected by the proposed system.

RFI (Request for information) A document that solicits an expression of interest from prospective vendors to determine which ones shall receive the RFP. Usually an RFI takes the form of a letter, but sometimes it is a short version of the RFP.

RFP (Request for proposal) A document that solicits potential vendors or consultants to submit proposals and bids for proposed work. Using an RFP helps elicit consistent complete responses.

Service bureau A firm that contracts to perform certain operations on its own computer system. Clients usually provide raw data (timekeeping and base salary or wage information); the service bureau processes the data (gross-to-net calculations), then returns finished results (payroll checks, tax returns, and data ready for transfer to the general ledger). Many HRMS must interface with service bureaus, particularly payroll-related services.

VAR (Value added reseller) A vendor that packages and sells some combination of computer products originally manufactured by other firms. Typically a VAR may bundle services with software to offer a package aimed at a particular vertical market.

Vendor A firm offering something for sale. In the context of an HRMS, it usually refers to a firm offering human resources applications software products and services. It also may refer to firms offering hardware, training, and other computer-related products and services.

Vertical market A group of users having specific computer needs. To meet those needs, vendors may package a collection of computer system components such as the CPU, terminals, applications software, communications software, graphics, training, and implementation services. Vendors market a variety of HRMS packages for human resources departments in specific types of organizations such as banking institutions, medical firms, and colleges.

Discussion Points

1. Under what circumstances might a small vendor give better service than a larger one?
2. What are the advantages and disadvantages of using large vendors?
3. How should a human resources department begin its search for a vendor?
4. What information should an HRMS project team learn about a vendor before deciding to do business with it?
5. What is an RFI? What is an RFP? When should an HRMS project team use them?
6. What are the advantages of using an RFP?

7. What procedures might an HRMS project team use in developing effective vendor evaluation criteria?

8. How should a potential client check vendors' references?

Further Reading

Anderson, Kirk J. "Acquiring a Human Resource Management System." *Employment Relations Today,* Winter 1985/86.

Buss, Martin D.J. "How to Rank Computer Projects." *Harvard Business Review,* January/February 1983.

Cancro, Frank. "The User/Vendor Relationship." *The Review,* Spring 1990.

Ceriello, Vincent R. "Computerizing the Personnel Department: How Do You Choose a Vendor?, *Personnel Journal,* December 1984.

———. "Acquiring Human Resources Software." *Personnel News,* September/October 1987.

———. "HRMS: One More Time: Build It or Buy It." *Personnel News,* September 1989.

Kalow, Samuel J. "Getting Started: What Is a DBMS?" *Computers in Personnel,* Fall 1986.

LaVan, Helen, Nicholas J. Mathys, and Gary Nogal. "Issues in Purchasing and Implementing HRIS Software." *Personnel Administrator,* August 1984.

Plantamura, Lisa M. "Choosing an HRIS Vendor." *Personnel Administrator,* November 1985.

———. "Basic Training for a New HRIS." *HRSP Review,* Fall 1987.

Spirig, John E., and Joe Pasqualetto. "Software: Buy It Right." *Personnel Journal,* June 1988.

Stix, Gary. "User vs Vendor: To Sue or Settle." *Computer Decisions,* October 1985.

Walker, Alfred J. "How to Evaluate a Prepackaged Personnel System." *Personnel,* May/June 1979.

7

Use of Consultants in an HRMS

Today's consultant sells *value*, not time—his/her contributions are a function of product and service—experience is still what the client buys.

—Dr. Anthony J. Tasca

As the HRMS software marketplace expands and becomes increasingly confusing, many first-time buyers look for consulting help. Even experienced HRMS practitioners now find that they need consultants for at least part of the project. Consultants can provide objectivity, sort out functional and technical requirements, and assist with selection of the most appropriate system for automating personnel records. Experienced consultants can cut through the vendors' advertising claims, help to negotiate and acquire the system, and oversee its implementation. A qualified consultant can lead companies out of the chaos of automating and managing personnel records. On the other hand, an inexperienced or unresponsive consultant may prove to be a poor investment, committing the client to an expensive and time-consuming process that fails to meet the stated objectives. Worse yet, the consultant may steer the client to a totally inappropriate solution.

What Constitutes the Right HRMS Consultant?

The term *HRMS consultant* refers to any professional who offers human resources and IS advice to clients for a fee. The explosion in the number of firms and individuals offering HRMS consulting services demonstrates not only the growth in computerized human resources applications but also the recognition that different circumstances benefit from different types of consultants. The best consultant for a small manufacturing company may not be the best one for an international banking firm. A start-up company with evolving personnel policies and procedures has very different needs from a more established firm. Each organization must carry out its own process of consultant selection and not rely solely on the experiences of a competitor or an organization for which human resources staff worked in the past.

Generally speaking, consultants have the most positive impact when their knowledge and experience exceed those of the firm's internal resources. Firms may have many good reasons to use consultants, but in some cases, use of consultants is ill-advised. If managers do not know how to choose the right HRMS package, how can they be expected to select the right HRMS consultant? First, they must define their requirements and goals. Then they must deal with a host of other problems. Inexperienced users sometimes face these issues:

- They cannot find a consultant they can afford.
- They engage an unqualified consultant.
- They fail to get proper references.
- They use a consultant the wrong way.
- They do not define the terms of engagement.
- They do not get value for their money.

Human resources management and others involved in consultant selection can increase their chances of selecting an HRMS consultant who can help them develop an effective, efficient, responsive system by following these steps:

- Determine the extent and availability of relevant in-house knowledge and skill. (A firm with experienced internal resources may not need a consultant.)
- Determine whether the HRMS project needs or could benefit from the services of a consultant.
- Decide which type of consultant the organization should seek.
- Establish criteria for consultant selection.
- Contact several likely HRMS consultants and hold preliminary discussions with them.
- Submit an RFP to finalist consultants if the scope of the engagement warrants. Ask them to submit bids based on this RFP.
- Evaluate consultants' proposals, references, and backgrounds to select the one who is most appropriate for the HRMS project.
- Negotiate a contract with the consultant selected if the project scope warrants.

When to Use a Consultant

Some firms engage a consultant for the entire HRMS automation process, from planning through implementation. In this case, the consultant plays an advisory role, and the firm does most of the work. This can be a high-cost option, but the result probably will be a quality job. To save money, some firms hire a consultant to help with just a portion of the vendor evaluation and selection process. The HRMS project team does the rest, using internal resources guided by the consultant. Even if funds are limited, using a consultant may make sense when an organization has one of the following needs:

- Specialized experience, skill, or other expertise
- Independent, unbiased, and objective opinions
- Someone to help deal with political or organizational problems
- Limited internal staff must remain available for other projects
- Specialized staff training

Of these, the need for specialized expertise or experience most commonly spurs human resources departments to use consultants. Although HRMS planners should learn as much as possible about their systems, certain special skills may be outside their range of expertise. The department should consider using a consultant when the need for skills, talents, and experience are not part of the capabilities resident within the firm.

Retaining a consultant may be helpful when a firm is planning a conversion from an old manual system or partially automated system to a brand new HRMS. Big corporations can afford in-house experts and specialists for installation, staff training, and so on, but smaller firms may be better off letting an experienced outsider handle these one-time tasks.

When to Consider a Consultant

Consultant's knowledge and experience exceeds that of internal resources

Consultant keeps current with and can apply state-of-the-art concepts

Project has limited funding, which may dissolve if not promptly or properly used

Project has an unrealistic time frame or schedule

Limited availability of qualified internal resources

Application must have special functions or features not normally part of vendor's packages

Project is at a standstill because of analysis paralysis

Consultant can achieve better, faster, or cheaper end result

Consultants should be familiar with a wide variety of HRMS products and services. Based on experience prior clients and with a large number of vendors, as well as detailed knowledge of the available packages, the consultant can point the organization toward vendors whose software best meets its important criteria. HRMS consultants can help determine the extent to which packages can be integrated or interfaced successfully with existing or planned applications. Some consultants, who are actually implementation specialists, customize commercial packages for individual firms.

Many consultants offer expertise in using computers to achieve greater productivity and efficiency. Some specialize in compliance with regulations related to human resources. Some offer special programs to train staff on new systems. In many cases, businesses of all sizes lack the expertise to perform strategic planning and find long-range planning difficult. A qualified consultant can perform such tasks and help the organization set long-range goals, translate its strategic goals into tactics, and guide the process of developing functional specifications.

An HRMS consultant also can be invaluable during contract negotiations with the software vendor. An experienced HRMS consultant knows what questions to ask vendors and how to handle the delicate give-and-take of the negotiation process. The consultant thus serves as an expert who represents and protects the firm's interests.

When a firm has limited in-house resources or must devote those resources to other programs, the consultant provides an effective surrogate. A firm that plans to hire or develop a full-time HRMS coordinator and wants to find exactly the right person might consider using a consultant to fill in and buy time for the organization to fine-tune its requirements. Having the consultant serve in an active capacity as an immediately productive contributor whom the firm can disengage when necessary more than justifies the consultant's fees.

The HRMS consultant also can serve in a mediating role. In many corporations, natural adversarial relationships often exist among the human resources, payroll, and IS staffs. In such circumstances, a consultant can provide needed objectivity. Even smaller firms can benefit from the fresh perspective of an outsider, someone not entangled in personality conflicts or bureaucracy.

Types of Consultants

Some organizations need a consultant to serve as project leader, with significant organizational and political ability. Some need technical expertise or additional staff resources. Some need a complete educational process, particularly if the HRMS will replace a manual or outgrown system. Others have no budget or a very tight financial situation and cannot justify consulting services. The best consultant for a particular project depends on skills and resources available within the organization, the type of expertise the organization wants to transfer to its staff through the HRMS development process, and whether the organization wants the consultant to make contributions oriented toward the theoretical or the practical.

Before shopping for an HRMS consultant, the firm must consider the type of consultant needed—operational versus advisory, process versus functional, academic versus commercial. An operational consultant's main concern is executing the task rather than teaching clients how to perform the work and manage the system. An operational consultant actually performs the necessary work. A firm that hires an operational consultant often becomes dependent on this type of consultant because he or she acts as an extension of the client's staff. The advisory consultant informs and supports in-house management but enables management to make the decisions, learning as they go. The advisory role should not create a dependence on the part of the client.

The process consultant is often a generalist or planner who provides useful guidance in organizing the project or intervening in conflict resolution but leaves operating details for in-house staff. In contrast, the functional consultant is familiar with the practical aspects of HRMS planning, development, and implementation and can extrapolate those skills to other phases or projects. Academic consultants have a place in situations in which theory or context is as important as practice or content. Finally, commercial consultants should have hands-on experience, possibly industry specific. Most HRMS users need this knowledge base; they particularly need an HRMS consultant whose expertise relates to the organization's unique situation.

Among consulting firms, bigger does not necessarily mean better. In the HRMS arena, sometimes a small firm of dedicated, qualified consultants can run circles around larger firms. Also, smaller clients often get lost in the practices of large consulting firms, where building a working relationship with individuals may be more difficult. Big firms may send out partners or senior principals to sell the assignment, then give the job to junior people who lack relevant experience. When considering hiring a big firm, the HRMS project team should find out exactly who will be doing the work. They will be living with this individual for a long time.

A firm should avoid accepting "free" consulting help from vendors or service bureaus. Saving money may be tempting, but no self-respecting vendor could possibly recommend a competing brand even if it really fits the client's needs better. Furthermore, vendors are probably not familiar with all the products on the market. If a vendor really wants to help, ask if it will accept a consulting assignment that terminates prior to the vendor selection process. A vendor's true business is software, not consulting.

How to Find a Consultant

Some decision makers look in the Yellow Pages for a consultant. Some wait for a consultant to hear about the firm's needs. These are ineffective methods of locating a qualified consultant. Some firms network at seminars, conferences, and professional society meetings. Some get referrals from their clients, other consultants, or colleagues. Some advertise for a specialized consultant. Different sources tend to lead to consultants with different strengths.

Sources for HRMS Consultants

Several groups supply consultants to HRMS software system users. Each group tends to bring certain advantages and disadvantages to HRMS consulting work. The most likely sources include the following:

- General management consultants
- Accounting firms
- IS, or technical, consultants
- College and university professors
- Specialized HRMS consultants

General Management Consultants. General management consultants may be excellent advisors if they speak the language of the firm's business and have professional experience in the field of human resources and HRMS. They should approach automation of human resources from the correct perspective—as a way to enhance business objectives.

These consultants also have a negative side. Many so-called management consultants have only recently added the words *computer expert* to their résumés, without having significant IS experience. They may, in fact, assign the project to a team of fresh MBA graduates who have some computer knowledge but little, if any, HRMS application experience. Compounding the problem, general management consultants are usually very expensive. To avoid such problems, look for specific HRMS experience and check billing rates.

Accounting Firms. Many accounting firms have well-established consulting divisions, but they may be interested in a long-term relationship with vendors rather than with HRMS users. This tendency may stem from a new strategic relationship that has surfaced in the past few years. Vendors often have sought the assistance of consultants who implement HRMS. Obviously, consultants find that promoting these vendors is in their own best interests. Therefore, some accounting firms have formal or informal subcontractor relationships with one or more vendors. Sometimes this works well for all parties—consultant, vendor, and user. If accounting firms sell software or have clients that, they cannot be objective consultants and advise clients on the best HRMS products and services. Lack of objectivity seriously limits the usefulness of any adviser. To add to the precarious nature of this choice of HRMS consultant, accounting firms may end up auditing the system they once recommended.

To avoid this problem, companies should not use the same firm that audits its financial status. At the very least, the accounting firm's consultants should clarify from the start that any recommendations for their own software or software provided by the vendors they support would be a breach of faith and a violation of the consulting agreement. This could present a problem if both the human resources department and the consultant eventually determine that a particular vendor's software is the most appropriate for the circumstances. Potential consultants should disclose the vendors with which they have worked in the past or with which they contemplate entering into formal relationships. This presents human resources decision makers with relevant information on which to base their choice of a consultant.

IS Consultants. Another category of HRMS consultant is the IS, or technical, expert. These people often are former programmers or analysts who have set up their own businesses. IS consultants generally have strong technical skills but tend to be weak in the all-important area of human resources knowledge and experience. If IS consultants are selected in tandem with human resources consultants, they can make a powerful team. Ideally, HRMS advisers should understand the technology and the business of human resources management generally and specifically. If the HRMS project team can find these skills and experiences in one consultant, it is even better.

College and University Professors. HRMS users constrained by a tight budget may find academicians helpful. Professors often offer top-notch consulting services, particularly process skills, at very reasonable rates because consulting is not a full-time job for them. Contracting with an academician may prove worthwhile as long as he or she has some relevant experience in the real world of HRMS, even if that experience comes only from case-study teaching. Academicians usually have some commercial experience as well, and they also have access to students who can perform low-cost research in support of the HRMS project.

Specialized HRMS Consultants. Over the past 10 to 15 years, many consultants have begun to specialize in HRMS. They may handle HRMS planning, design, evaluation, and/or implementation. Prior to 1970, only a handful of HRMS specialists were not employed by a vendor or major accounting firm. Today, literally hundreds of HRMS consultants offer independent services. In considering specialized HRMS consultants, a firm must differentiate between implementation specialists and HRMS planners, between technicians and human resources functional experts. These specialists often have a small staff of professionals with little backup and can easily become overextended. On the other hand, they can take on a few complex projects and perform them very well. Potential clients should investigate the track record of such consultants thoroughly, including their use of subcontractors to augment their own staffs.

Locating Consultants

The best way to find a qualified consultant is through personal referrals. Members of the various trade associations have an edge in this area, since they have local contacts. These individuals often can provide contacts and information useful in making an informed choice. Many of the sources of HRMS vendors mentioned in chapter 6 also provide good leads on HRMS consultants.

Conferences and exhibitions can be good sources of information. HRMS conferences, workshops, and seminars; computer software exhibits; and vendor fairs (not limited to HRMS) are held throughout the year in most major cities; many of the speakers are consultants. By scouting these gatherings, potential clients can size up several prospects at once. They may meet other participants who have already used a particular consultant and can provide valuable insight about the services they received.

Additionally, several consultant organizations provide free referrals or offer a directory of consultants. These organizations are listed in Appendix D.

Evaluating Potential Consultants

The HRMS project team should screen potential consultants concerning experience, areas of expertise, availability, rates, and personal compatibility. As finalists emerge, the team should prepare an RFP for distribution to potential consultants. This RFP should have a structure and format similar to those for vendors. It should include the following sections:

- Introduction (information on the firm, the required services, and the major goals and objectives of the study)
- Proposal instructions
- Scope and deliverables of the consulting assignment (with space for consultant responses)
- Consultant qualifications
- RFP administration

The RFP should describe and differentiate consultant and client responsibilities as specifically as possible. This allows the consultant to develop a proposal that covers exactly what the client wants included. It also helps the consultant develop worthwhile estimates of overall fees and expenses.

The contract should specify which aspects of the HRMS project in-house staff will handle and which the consultant should provide. Specific responsibilities will differ from project to project. A qualified consultant may be asked to handle complete project management or just one phase of HRMS planning, design, or acquisition—for example, vendor evaluation. In general, because of their specialized experience, HRMS consultants often handle the following tasks more efficiently and with better results than do in-house staff:

- Supervise HRMS design, particularly the creation of data base structure and relationships
- Evaluate appropriateness of the firm's current HRMS
- Identify appropriate vendor software packages
- Prepare (or review) the RFP to vendors
- Verify the competence of vendors under consideration
- Recommend selection of the best available system
- Advise on negotiation of vendor contract terms and conditions
- Supervise implementation, particularly conversion from an existing to a new system

Selecting the right consultant depends on both quantitative and qualitative factors. In developing the RFP for a prospective consultant and in evaluating consultants' proposals, project managers should consider the following factors:

- Technical and human resources knowledge. An effective HRMS consultant must understand computer systems and human resources issues and practices. The consultant's approach to HRMS and whether it fits the specific project must be evaluated.
- Experience with similar projects. Some consultants offer planning services only; others offer a combination of implementation services as part of their total package. Some concentrate only on payroll systems, some only on human resources systems; others work on all aspects of an HRMS. A firm should select a consultant whose technical expertise, experience, and services match the needs of this specific project.
- Effective communication skills. The human resources staff and management should feel that the consultant hears what they say, speaks clearly in ways they can understand, and communicates well both orally and in writing with those who will be involved in the project.
- Independence. An HRMS consultant must have no ties to any particular vendor. This is, of course, unlikely if the consultant has a relationship with a vendor. This can occur when the consultant specializes in implementing the systems offered by a particular vendor. In such situations, the consultant has a vested interest in which vendor's system a client selects. At the very least, the client should require that potential HRMS consultants disclose any financial or other working relationships with vendors before contracting for consultant services.

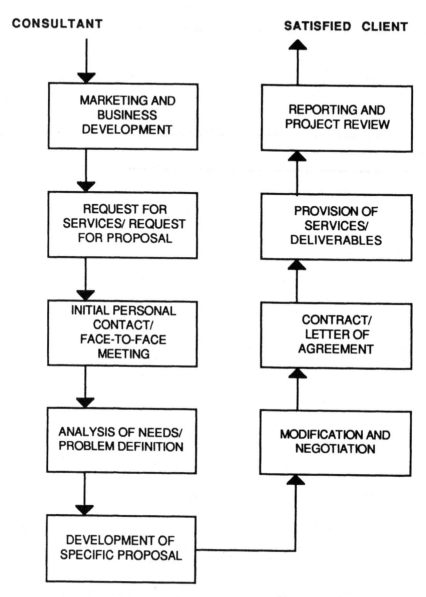

Figure 7–1. The consulting process. By following these steps, the client and the consultant can move into progressively closer agreement about the scope of the HRMS project, needed consultant services, and satisfactory delivery of those services.

(Source: Shenson, Howard L., *How to Select and Manage Consultants*, Lexington Books, 1990. Reprinted with permission.)

- Sufficient staff resources. The client must make sure that the consultant has staff who are experienced in HRMS planning and development. New MBAs or IS graduates may work well as HRMS project team members, but experienced people should oversee the project.

- Accessibility. In today's electronic world, the location of a consultant's offices has relatively little significance; accessibility is more a matter of operating style than geography. A firm must make sure that the consultant has room for this project on his or her schedule. Specifically, the project team should discuss the scope of the project and the pace with which it will proceed. The team and consultant also should agree on the level of on-site presence expected of the consultant and the types of remote support the consultant will provide during and after the actual consulting.

- Good references. References from management, technical, and functional people at other firms for which the consultant has performed comparable HRMS planning are important. When considering a technical consultant, HRMS project team members should check with IS staff at that firm; in the case of a functional expert, they should talk with human resources staff. Whenever appropriate, members should check with peers of the consultant as well, especially if they are not competing for the contract.

  If the consultant's name did not come through a personal referral, extra care must be taken to check references. The team should determine not only how others assessed the consultant's performance but also what products and services the consultant recommended. If a disproportionate share of clients has the same make or model, this consultant may be biased or ill-informed. It is important to remember that setting up a consulting firm is easy and does not require certification.

- Affordability. Consultants tend to charge more than most firms consider reasonable, but a firm should consider the benefit of cost avoidance when using consultants in place of in-house staff. Staff can continue to be productive in other areas; consultants provide their own support services, and they do not receive benefits.

  Cost and value may sometimes correlate in terms of consultants' fees, but high hourly rates do not necessarily guarantee value. A potential client must gather as much data as possible about hourly or daily rates, as well as total project fees and expenses. Chapter 8 contains information about some arrangements that may reduce the financial burden and risk.

During the evaluation process, consultants should be interviewed as though they were applying for a permanent in-house position. The project team should make assessments and recommendations on the basis of functional experience, technical expertise, and how well the consultants respond to particular stated requirements. Ultimately, price may prove to be less important than good communication skills.

The HRMS Consultant as an Investment

If a firm learns only one thing about hiring an HRMS consultant, it will probably come to realize that these services do not come cheap. In selecting an HRMS consultant, the firm should look carefully at costs but also at value received.

Demand for combined human resources and IS expertise continues to increase dramatically. As a result, HRMS consultants command substantial fees. This can get expensive. Fees can easily range from $1,000 to $1,500 per day (plus expenses) for mid-level consultants and $1,500 to $2,500 per day or more for top experts. Some independents may charge as little as $500 to $600 per day but can do so only if they have very low overhead (with just one or two people operating out of modest quarters). In HRMS consulting, as with so many things in life, you get what you pay for.

Typically, a firm will require four to six days of a consultant's time for even the most fundamental HRMS planning services. Including expenses, a firm may spend upward of $10,000 for advice on which HRMS product to buy and for help planning the development and implementation of the system. Firms can easily spend many times that amount if the job involves a complex system, customized documentation, legal compliance, management intervention, or system modifications. One rule of thumb suggests that companies with more than 5,000 employees and a human resources staff of about 40 to 50 can expect to pay for 20 to 30 days of consulting time to obtain a comprehensive requirements definition and functional specifications. This works out to approximately $25,000 to $40,000, including expenses. Companies with less than 1,000 employees (and 5 to 10 human resources staff) will pay about $8,000 to $10,000 for the same services. Thus, a $250,000 investment in a mainframe system for a firm of 2,000 employees may easily justify a $20,000 to $30,000 consulting engagement; a $20,000 microcomputer-based system for a 500-person firm could cost as little as $5,000.

A lot depends on choices among mainframe, midrange, and microcomputer platforms; system scope; whether the firm wants to automate personnel records with or without payroll; availability of in-house staff; management commitment; and many other variables. Consulting fees start to look more reasonable when compared with the cost of management's time and the potential cost of acquiring the wrong package. Some firms consider the involvement of an experienced HRMS consultant insurance against major system development and acquisition deficiencies.

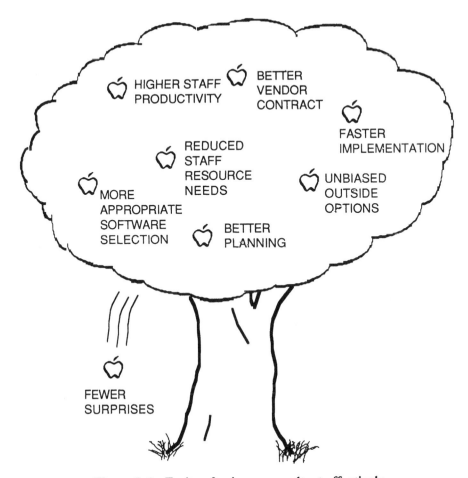

Figure 7–2. Fruits of using a consultant effectively.

Getting the Most out of an HRMS Consultant

Having selected a consultant, the HRMS project manager will help to make many in-house decisions that will help to keep costs down and maximize the consultant's contribution to the HRMS development and implementation process.

Doing Consulting Work in Phases

Large projects could be divided into smaller ones, perhaps by reserving the go-ahead decision for the next step pending results of an earlier one. With this approach, the project manager may back out at any time and keep track of costs as they develop.

Involving Human Resources and IS

Internal human resources and IS staffs shoud be informed about the purpose and scope of the consultant's work. Key managers should be asked to interview the final candidates so that they can make their own compatibility judgments. Employees and managers should share appropriate information and work as closely with the consultant as possible so they can benefit from the consultant's skills and expertise, and vice versa.

Doing Background Work In-House

The consultant should not learn on the client's time. The firm is not paying consulting rates for inexperienced staff to learn as they go, other than becoming familiar with the client's background and culture. For example, if the consultant's staff are evaluating possible HRMS packages, the firm should make sure they have access to current information. If the consultant is providing information that can be learned from sales literature or from other firms, the client is wasting valuable time and money.

The firm also should not pay someone $100 to $200 or more per hour to do basic research—that is, to ask the same questions or do the same work that the firm can do itself unless time or the availability of resources dictates otherwise. The client should do the homework, then retain the HRMS consultant to validate the results.

Continuing to Take Responsibility

HRMS consultants should be used for the right reasons. A firm cannot expect them to come in and wave a magic wand. To maintain cost-effectiveness, HRMS planners and potential users should use HRMS consultants as a "voice of experience" and for overall guidance with a view to learning to live with and use the system themselves.

The poorest results occur when management tries to delegate decision-making responsibilities to consultants. In matters of significance and commitment of the firm's resources, in-house people must make the final decisions. Good consultants teach clients how to do without them. Clients must dedicate themselves to learning enough to make the services provided truly value added after the consultant has left.

Amidst the large and growing market for HRMS consulting, many qualified HRMS consultants are offering their services. Some of them are experienced and competent and have good track records. Others lack one or more of these traits. By taking an organized and thoughtful approach to consultant selection and use, the HRMS project team can work with a consultant whose contributions add to the ultimate success of the project.

Glossary

Advisory consultant   One who guides or trains in-house staff in how to execute certain tasks, perform analyses independently, and provide interpretation of results; the advisory consultant aims to become expendable.

Consultant   In terms of HRMS, a consultant is a person paid for professional, technical, functional, and administrative advice on the application of IS to human resources.

Operational consultant   A hands-on resource who gets involved in the problem and may even be assigned to solve it directly, often without assistance from the firm's staff.

Process consultant   A generalist and planner who is comfortable in any industry, environment, or size firm. This type of consultant emphasizes the process of getting things done, not the specific content or methodology.

Technical consultant   A specialist with an in-depth knowledge of a particular technology platform, application area, or industry group.

Discussion Points

1. When should a firm use a consultant? When should a firm not use a consultant?

2. What are the various types of consultants? What are some of the essential differences among them?

3. Under what circumstances can a process consultant be more effective than other types?

4. What kinds of questions should the HRMS project team address to a consultant's prior clients when checking references?

5. What criteria or factors should human resources managers use in evaluating a consultant?

6. What should a firm expect from a relationship with a consultant? What should the firm expect to contribute to the relationship?

7. What are the advantages and disadvantages of using a small consulting firm?

8. What are the most effective ways to locate qualified HRMS consultants?

Further Reading

Brady, Joseph. "Guidelines for Using Management Consultants." *P&IM Review*, November 1985.

Ceriello, Vincent R. "Computerizing the Personnel Department: Do You Need A Consultant?" *Personnel Journal*, October 1984.

Charles, Susan. "When Choosing a Consultant, Common Sense Is Key." *The Business Journal*, August 1983.

Datapro Research Corp. "How to Get Your Money's Worth with Consultants." *Feature Report 70F-050-01*, January 1972.

Epner, Steven A. "Getting the Most out of Your Computer Consultants." *ICP Interface—Small Business Management*, Summer 1981.

Fersko-Weiss, Henry. "Managing Your Computer Consultant." *Personal Computing*, January 1986.

Forest, Robert B. "Time Is All Consultants Have." *Infosystems*, April 1982.

Gallessich, June. *The Professional Practice of Consultation*. San Francisco, CA: Jossey-Bass Inc., 1982.

Holtz, Herman. *Choosing and Using a Consultant*. New York: John Wiley & Sons, 1989.

Kelly, Robert E. "How to Choose a Consultant." *Inc.*, March 1987.

Laska, Richard M. "Should a Consultant Be Your Guide Through EDP Country?" *Computer Decisions*, January 1971.

Lundin, Stephen. "The Case for the Independent Consultant." *Training/HRD*, January 1982.

Martin, Josh. "Taking the Risk out of Choosing Consultants." *Computer Decisions*, April 1981.

Millman, Gregory J. "Taking the Con out of Consultants." *Business Month*, February 1990.

Murdoch, S.J. "How to Use a Management Consultant." *Journal of the Academy of Management*, September 1980.

Raine, Ronald V. "Selecting the Consultant: Useful Guidelines on Choosing the Right Outside Firm." *Personnel Administrator*, December 1980.

Rosenberg, Norma V. "How to Hire, Work with and Manage a Consultant." *The Office*, July 1987.

"SBR Consultants Directory." *Small Business Reports*, Winter/Spring 1987.

Shenson, Howard L. *How to Select, Manage and Compensate Consultants*. Woodland Hills, CA: H. L. Shenson Publishing Co., 1984.

———. *Bibliography on Consulting*. Woodland Hills, CA: H. L. Shenson Publishing Co., 1986.

Soderquist, Al. "The Software Evaluation Consultant: Friend or Foe?" *Salt 'n' Pepper*, Culpepper and Associates, July 1981.

Turner, Arthur N. "Consulting Is More Than Giving Advice." *Harvard Business Review*, September/October 1982.

Ucko, Thomas. "So You Want to Hire a Consultant." *Personnel News*, July/August 1987.

———. *Selecting and Working with Consultants - a Guide for Clients*. Los Altos, CA. Crisp Publications, 1990.

Wood, Robert C. "When You Need Experts to Help with Your Staff." *Inc.*, February 1983.

8
Contracts and Warranties for an HRMS

The man who in the view of gain thinks of righteousness and who does not forget an old agreement however far back it extends—such a man may be reckoned a complete man.
—Confucius

The first thing we do, let's kill all the lawyers.
—William Shakespeare, *Henry VI*

Shakespeare may have had a point, but he would indeed have been a fool to suggest carrying out business transactions today without competent legal help. A successful HRMS needs a solid contract between vendor and client. A contract gives all parties concerned a road map for tracing responsibilities. Without a good contract, even the most well-intentioned vendors and clients can end up at each other's throat when something goes wrong. Moreover, the contract process itself often helps clarify expectations, limits, and potential problems before they arise. Confucius may have had it right.

Understanding Contracts

HRMS projects usually require one or more contracts. Most projects involve at least a contract with the software vendor; many others also include (or should include) contracts with consultants, trainers, contract programmers, technical writers, and other outside services. The terms of these contracts materially affect the outcome of the project. By studying the factors that influence HRMS contracts, the HRMS project team can avoid common pitfalls and build contractual relationships that work for all parties. The material that follows refers most often to contracts with software vendors, but much of the information applies to any HRMS-related product or service agreement. After a general discussion of contracts, the chapter covers contracts with vendors and other suppliers, as well warranties of various types.

The Role of Contracts

A contract clarifies responsibilities and limits for individuals or entities involved in a business relationship. The ideal HRMS contract contains the information the HRMS project team learned from evaluating the RFP responses. This includes material that relates to requirements for software, implementation, hardware, service, and support. It anticipates future problems and defines remedies. The firm may ultimately decide to do business with a vendor even if it does not get everything on its wish list; at least it will be doing business with its eyes open.

Discussing contracts does not presume that disagreements will end up in court. If the parties must go to court, nobody wins. The client has already lost the battle, since even a favorable judgment three or four years down the road would probably not lead to recovery of all true costs and lost business opportunities. The HRMS community quickly learns of the litigation, and the vendor's integrity may be irrevocably tarnished.

In any contractual relationship, some rules apply:

- The contract cannot encompass all eventualities, but it should cover the major risks involved and clearly set forth the intentions of both parties.
- The contract should be written, executed, and filed. The parties involved develop contractual agreements to provide for successful HRMS operation. If the parties must consult and constantly reinterpret the contract, the project is probably in trouble.
- Do-it-yourself contracts invite disaster. Most firms should use legal counsel in developing and negotiating contracts because of the high value of the software purchase and the even higher cost of failure.

Tips for Successful Negotiating

The contract negotiating team usually contains one or more members of the HRMS project team. A typical team might include the project team manager; representatives from the technical, functional, legal, purchasing/procurement, and financial areas; and the consultant, if one is involved. Members should consider all risks and objectives involved from their own perspectives.

Sometimes the HRMS project or negotiating team may wish to develop a rough contract even before the distribution of the vendor RFP. This document may help shape the RFP and vendor selection criteria. It also helps counter the temptation to use the vendor's standard contract as the basis for beginning negotiations, since the HRMS project team then has a much more specific document with which to work.

Contract negotiations should begin even before the firm has decided to acquire the products and services of a particular vendor. Trying to negotiate after signing a purchase order or after hinting to the vendor that it has the inside track usually weakens the client's position. Once a vendor thinks it has the sale, the client's leverage evaporates. To have any impact, the client must negotiate early and often. Although formal negotiations generally take place late in the process, informal give-and-take starts the first time someone from the firm speaks with the vendor's sales representative. Most first-time HRMS clients do not know what to ask for, what is at stake, or what leverage they have.

To get the best terms and prices, the negotiating team must keep potential vendors competing until the last minute. Maintaining multivendor competition helps the potential purchaser receive the most attractive deal in two ways. First, vendors may offer a lower price, hoping to look more attractive. Second, issues may arise during discussions with various vendors that would not arise if the team dealt with only one vendor. Comparing vendor comments may spur the team to discuss and resolve such issues before signing the contract. Such interchanges increase the thoroughness and accuracy of the eventual contract.

Negotiating an HRMS vendor contract usually takes more than one meeting. To maintain control, the team should arrange to hold negotiations at the organization's site rather than the vendor's. The firm's negotiating team often benefits from meeting as a group before and after negotiating sessions with the vendor. At these meetings, the team can establish an agenda for future negotiating sessions, as well as discuss parameters for the issues on that agenda. It is important that the vendor sends to each negotiating session someone with the authority to make decisions and negotiate agreements. It is equally important that those who represent the firm can commit the organization.

Negotiations should deal with overall issues before working through details. It is a good idea to start with the organization's rough draft of a contract, if one exists, rather than the vendor's standard contract. If an uncomfortable issue arises, it should be dealt with promptly or at least decided what information each side needs to gather in order to address it. Handling abstract challenges at this stage involves less pain than handling real ones during implementation or later.

The contract should contain as many of the provisions on which the firm's negotiating team has decided as possible. The team should not expect to get everything it wants, however. It should ask for as much protection as possible but be willing to make trade-offs.

Standard Contracts versus Custom Contracts

As discussed in chapter 6, most vendors have a standard contract or license agreement that they consider ideal. They would like all their customers to execute this standard document because it gives the vendor maximum protection. Standard contracts contain a fine-print disclaimer called the entirety or

PROFESSIONAL SERVICES AGREEMENT

Client _____

Address _____

_____

City _____ State _____ Zip _____

XYZ agrees to perform for Client the services described in Attachment A hereto and incorporated herein by reference. Client agrees to pay XYZ the compensation provided in the attached schedules.

Executed as of the dates set forth below by the authorized representatives of Licensee and XYZ.

CLIENT: _____   ACCEPTED BY:
                                             XYZ CORPORATION

LICENSE AGREEMENT

Licensee _____

Address _____

_____

City _____ State _____ Zip _____

XYZ grants to Licensee, and Licensee accepts from XYZ, a perpetual, non-exclusive, non-transferable license to the software programs listed below (herein "Licensed Program(s)") and related materials, documentation and information furnished by XYZ (herein "Licensed Materials" and collectively with the Licensed Program(s) as the "Product(s)").

LICENSED PROGRAM(S)/DOCUMENTATION   FEE

_____   _____

This agreement, including the terms and conditions set forth on the reverse side, constitute the entire agreement between the parties and sets forth all obligations of the parties with respect to the License and use of the Product(s) licensed hereunder.
Executed as of the dates set forth below by the authorized representatives of Licensee and XYZ.

CLIENT: _____   ACCEPTED BY:
                                             XYZ CORPORATION

By (Officer) _____   By _____

Title _____   Title _____

Date _____   Date _____

Figure 8–1. Standard vendor contracts. Vendors often offer a separate contract for software (license agreement) and for custom services such as development, installation, training, and maintenance (professional services agreement). The standard contract includes numerous legal clauses about terms and conditions, sometimes printed on the reverse side of the agreement. Clients who work with a vendor's standard agreement should consider an addendum that modifies these clauses as appropriate.
(Source: Tesseract Corporation. Reprinted with permission.)

merger clause. This states that the vendor is bound only by what is in writing in the contract.

The HRMS project team may have some contract provisions in mind from the outset, but members should assume that what you see is what you get. Terms not specified in writing do not exist and are not enforceable. Some clients insist that vendors deal only with terms and conditions they are willing to put on paper.

For example, a sales representative may promise that the organization's clerks can produce all month-end summaries in less than one day. By requesting that the vendor put this and other performance issues in writing, the client can determine whether the vendor is making a reasonable claim. Although the vendor may indicate that its product has certain high-level capabilities, these features may not conform to the requirements of the human resources department. The department and the vendor may have two very different ideas about the function of position control. Discussing and negotiating such points usually bring the parties to a document that defines what position control is or can be. Thus, the final contract bears a decreasing resemblance to the vendor's standard contract.

Rather than sign a standard contract, the firm usually should counter with its own version of an ideal contract. From this point, client and vendor can negotiate a mutually agreeable contract. (As noted in chapter 6, the RFP should ask vendors to submit their standard contracts with their proposals.)

General Clauses for HRMS Contracts

Contracts have both general and specific clauses. General clauses deal with the overall business relationship; specific clauses cover the objectives, responsibilities, and limits of the actual project. A few examples of general clauses to include in software package or development contracts follow. Not all these issues apply to every contract. The HRMS negotiating team may include some and add others. Participants must tailor each contract to the specific users and vendor (or other service provider) involved.

1. *Arbitration.* The contract must be enforceable by law or by arbitration. In hardware contracts, arbitration is almost always the preferred method of dispute resolution. The cost and delays involved in litigation give the larger hardware vendors an enormous advantage over the customer. Arbitration settles disputes quickly and shifts the advantage to the smaller organization with fewer resources. Similarly, if the software vendor is smaller than the client, arbitration may not work to the vendor's advantage.

The following is an example of an arbitration clause:

> Any dispute under this agreement shall be submitted to binding arbitration in the City of XXXXXXX under the rules then prevailing of the

American Arbitration Association. Judgment upon any award made in such arbitration may be entered and enforced in any court of competent jurisdiction.

2. *Force majeure* (causes beyond the reasonable control of either party). The contract should include a definition to prevent the use of unacceptable excuses for failure to deliver. For example:

Neither party shall be responsible for delays or failures in performance resulting from acts beyond the control of such party. Such acts shall include, but not be limited to, acts of God, strikes, lockouts, riots, acts of war, epidemics, government regulations superimposed after the fact, fire, communication line failures, power failures, earthquakes, or other disasters.

3. *Confidentiality.* To protect the client from breaches of confidence, the vendor and appropriate vendor personnel should sign a nondisclosure agreement or include a clause in the contract as follows:

Each party acknowledges that all material and information which has or will come into the possession or knowledge of each in connection with this contract or the performance hereof, consists of confidential and proprietary data, whose disclosure to or use by third parties will be damaging. Both parties, therefore, agree to hold such material and information in strictest confidence, not to make use thereof other than for the performance of this contract, to release it only to employees requiring such information, and not to release or disclose it to any other party. Each party agrees not to release such information or material to any employee who has not signed a written agreement expressly binding himself not to use or disclose it.

Other clauses that the firm's negotiators might include as part of the general section of a software contract include the following:

- All amendments shall be in writing.
- Consent to a contractual breach does not waive the rights of the consenter in case of future breaches.
- The client's liability is limited.

Software Contracts

Software acquisition for the HRMS is a substantial investment. This risk requires an effective contractual relationship between client and vendor. Software leasing or development usually poses a greater challenge than contracting for consulting services or hardware.

At present, most organizations spend more money on hardware than on software. Much of that is capital acquisition, contained and depreciated within the organization. In the 1990s, however, the software package market will probably exceed $50 billion. If equivalent growth is maintained in outside purchases of software, the total value of software purchases will continue to eclipse the value of hardware purchases. The cost of software probably has passed that of hardware permanently.

Special Circumstances

With the increasing investment in software, organizations must have as watertight a contract as possible. Software contracts differ in several respects from those for other goods and services. Most importantly, software contracts usually do not refer to the actual purchase of software but rather to its licensing, with rights to use a certain number of copies at a certain number of locations. Negotiators should, therefore, keep the following points in mind:

- Defining clearly the functions of software requires more effort and precision than defining the functions of hardware.
- Defining the operating characteristics of software requires more effort and precision than defining the operating characteristics of hardware.
- Software vendors may not have assets and resources as substantial those of hardware manufacturers.
- Software acquisition has certain unique risks about which the average contract lawyer may know little. The principal risks to consider when buying software include the following:

  Nonperformance. The package may fail to meet the organization's specifications, schedule, or budget. If the software package does not work or requires too much time to modify, implement, or operate, the organization may find its overhead or resources overburdened.

  Vendor solvency. Software companies are often undercapitalized, and many are quite small. The HRMS negotiators should make sure that such organizations can perform, since legal action against them in case of nonperformance would yield no useful result. Protection for the client may include measures such as requiring placement of the vendor's source code in "escrow" in the event the vendor closes down operations.

  Infringement. A software package, even a tailored application, may not have a clear title belonging to the vendor. Thus, a third party may assert claims against the client that must be defended, especially if the vendor did not own part or all of the program code being used. Sometimes this occurs in relationships with value-added resellers.

Progress payments. Software development contracts almost always require progress payments, in return for which the client receives nothing immediately tangible. This type of arrangement poses some risk, as the vendor (particularly a small firm) may dissolve (or be acquired) without first delivering the product. It is in the client's best interests to put as little money down as possible.

Product quality. Internal standards for software product quality generally do not exist, so clients and vendors have difficulty setting standards for externally developed software. Even if the two parties can agree on standards, they may have difficulty interpreting at what point the software meets the standards. When standards do exist, they should be reflected in the appropriate clauses of the contract.

Excessive resource usage. Most software contracts call for the client to supply some resources, such as computer time or data entry. The vendor may use far more of these resources than the client envisaged, perhaps because of underestimating the scope of system development.

Staff qualifications. Some vendors may not assign employees to the client's HRMS project on a full-time basis or may elect to transfer them to other projects without the client's permission. The client has much less control over the vendor's employees than it has over its own. Because the people assigned to the project are important, the contract should reference them by name or by experience. For example:

Personnel assigned by the vendor to the performance of the work required by this contract shall meet the following minimum standards: (1) education: x years after secondary school; (2) IS training: x months/years; (3) IS or human resources work experience: x months/years; (4) service with vendor: x months/years; (5) HRMS applications experience: x months/years.

Principal Clauses

In addition to general contract provisions, software contracts must define the deliverable product and performance expectations. The contract also must cover installation facilities and support, financial terms, other business specifics, and warranties. The principal clauses in a contract for purchase or perpetual license of a specific software package may include some of the issues discussed in the material that follows. A longer list of suggested contract provisions is presented in the accompanying sidebar.

Suggested Contract Provisions

Attachment of functional specifications

Attachment of hardware configuration (if applicable)

Attachment of proposal and sales material

List of systems software required

Reliance on vendor expertise

Vendor review of user documents

Responsibility for development

Phases and tasks for development

Right to cancel at phase ends

Percentage completion by phase

Equipment and resource requirements

Performance and operating characteristics

Rights to enhancements

Price and payment terms

Price protection for current prices

Price protection for future hardware

Price protection for software enhancements

Software maintenance

Installation responsibility and costs

Risk of loss at all stages

Pass-on of price reductions or discounts

Delivery of software

Delivery deferral rights

Delay impact

Client site access

Installation timing

License to use vendor software

Acceptance tests for software

Acceptance of deliverables

Acceptance test failure actions

Warranty of original development and system conformity

User and vendor confidentiality

Bankruptcy of vendor

Termination rights

Nonsale to user's competition

Staff quantity and qualifications

Project manager assignment and right to change

Staff execution of nondisclosure

Compliance with client security

Vendor financial statements

Staff access on business termination

User right to modify software

User access to source code

Contents of documentation and standards

Vendor status as independent contractor

Time records and progress reports

Right to reproduce documentation

Right to use the system anywhere, any way

Right to provide consulting services to others

Constraints on vendor use of user's resources

No subcontracting without consent

Indemnities and inclusion of costs

Data conversion specifications/assistance

Trade-in credit for upgrades

Training content, location, and supplies provided by vendor

Continuing training availability

Right to use software in other locations

Payment terms and conditions

Response time for software maintenance

Nonhire of vendor's staff

- Specifications. The client can make sure that the system meets the specifications by attaching to the contract the vendor's sales material (including the completed proposal) used to sell the package:

  Exhibit A attached hereto describes the major features and functions of the package to be delivered hereunder.

- Run-time performance. A benchmark, or a level of volume, that gives operating time that can be verified on the user's configuration should be included:

  The run-time and other performance characteristics of the software package licensed hereunder are warranted by the vendor as follows: On a daily basis per unit of volume (records, transactions), the package will require xx minutes to run; on a monthly basis per unit of volume, the package will require xx minutes to run.

- Corrections. As appropriate, the vendor should state in writing that it will handle all warranty and support problems, even if the vendor will be delivering the system using software and utilities from several different sources. It is important to consider how fast the organization will need the vendor to respond in case of system problems. Certain minor problems may not require as rapid a response as major ones. To the extent that the organization requires a rapid response, the firm's negotiators may need to insist on a quantifiable speed and thoroughness of response. To ensure that the vendor makes all corrections available to technical staff quickly, the contract might state the following:

  During the time of this license (for a period of x years or months after installation), the vendor will correct all errors found by the user, any other user, or the vendor. Such corrections shall be made within x hours after their discovery, and shall be at no cost to the user.

- Schedule and deliverables. The principal challenge in a software acquisition relationship is ensuring that the organization gets value for its money.

To do so, a contract establishes performance tasks and associated deliverables. A clause covering phases and deliverables might read as follows:

> The tasks to be performed hereunder are set forth in Schedule A attached hereto. This schedule also sets forth the products to be delivered at the conclusion of each task. Finally, Schedule A sets forth a reasonable percentage of completion represented by the satisfactory completion of acceptance of each task.
>
> The percentage of completion established for each task should be determined so that, in the event of business termination or contract cancellation, the client can elect to have the remaining tasks completed by another organization for an amount not to exceed the remaining funds unpaid to the original vendor.

- Documentation. The contract should specify what documentation is to be delivered with the software package:

> The vendor will furnish the user with the following documentation as part of the package to be delivered hereunder, which shall be in a form and substance at least equal to comparable materials generally in use in the industry.

- Source code availability. The firm should secure the right to obtain the source code for possible modification either after expiration of maintenance or after vendor business termination. Access to the source code allows the firm to conduct its own maintenance, make modifications, and otherwise control its own destiny should the vendor not perform these services.

- Periodic progress reports. The client should require the vendor to supply written progress reports and oral presentations to management at intervals throughout the term of the business relationship. This clause applies more if the vendor has a continuing, long-term relationship with the client for training and implementation support. Otherwise, the vendor-client relationship ends shortly after delivery of the software.

- Acceptance by phase. Acceptance of the package by the client involves meeting specifications, run-time performance, documentation acceptance, and so on. The acceptance clause should refer to all of these. The client can accept each phase separately, using a test at the completion of each phase. Various kinds of testing are described in chapter 9. The contract might refer to the following testing:

> Upon notification to user of the completion of each stage described in Schedule A and of delivery of the products attendant to such stage, the user shall, within xx days, perform the following acceptance tests, at the

user site, upon the configuration described above to determine whether: (1) the products meet the specifications and standards described in this contract and (2) they perform repetitively on a variety of data without failure. Upon completion of the last stage described, these tests shall be performed as to the entirety of the products and also to determine whether the HRMS meets the generalized specifications defined in the RFP and operates with internal consistency.

- If the project plan includes implementation of certain modules at one time and others later, the negotiating team must guard against committing the organization to paying for the licensing of the first set of modules after they pass testing, since the team does not yet know whether those modules will work successfully with modules installed subsequently. A firm might consider an agreement that allows the withholding of part of the payment for the first group until the latter group passes acceptance testing.

- Right to cancel at each phase. The client should have the right to cancel at each phase of the project:

  The client may, at its option, elect to cancel the contract at any time, by notice to vendor, upon completion of any stage described in Schedule A above. In such event, the client will pay to the vendor the amount due by virtue of completion of the products therefore delivered, and if such cancellation is not based upon any claim of vendor default, such payment shall include any sums withheld pursuant to above.

- Right to rescind during warranty. As long as the vendor provides a warranty period, the client should have the right to rescind the contract, paying only for use of the package on a lease basis.

- Guarantee of ownership. To prevent infringement, clear title should be warranted. The client needs to know that the vendor has the power and authority to sell and service the software.

- Business termination rights. If the vendor goes out of business, the client should become an owner of the package:

  In the event that vendor shall, for any reason, cease to conduct business, this license shall automatically and without notice be converted into a perpetual license and shall thereafter be free of any cost.

- Right of access to staff upon business termination. If the vendor goes out of business, the client's only recourse (besides not paying the fees) may be to hire specialists who are knowledgeable in the application area. This may include people who were involved in the development of the system and are now out of work.

- Price and payments. The client should set forth the exact purchase price, when payments are due, and that the client is liable only for charges stated in the agreement. The contract should cover any potential charges for rental, supplies, service agreements, site preparation, and training. Some vendors mention such charges only after the client makes a commitment to the system itself. Progress payments should be tied to acceptance of specific project phases. Vendors have an incentive to keep clients happy. If the vendor receives the final payment only after the client accepts the completed, tested system, it is putting some money on the line as well. Under most circumstances, the client should not pay more than 60 to 80 percent before final acceptance.

- Delivery dates. The client should have the right to a refund of deposit or lease payments in full if the vendor fails to meet the deadlines. The firm shoud watch out for the fine print: Some agreements contain nonrefundable restocking charges or security deposits, but these usually occur only with microcomputer-based systems that have a separate system software license.

Contracting for Other HRMS Services

A contract is essential when agreeing to any significant service or product that will be part of the HRMS. This includes HRMS consulting, training, implementation services, and maintenance. It also includes contracts for software developers and technicians. More human resources departments contract for consulting services than for the other separate services, so the following material uses the consultant as an example of the service provider, but most of the discussion applies to other service providers as well.

Negotiating with the Consultant

In almost every case, the client should have a written agreement with any service provider. Unless the consultant or other provider's references have been carefully checked, the project is very small, or the firm has used this consultant previously, a handshake agreement is not sufficient. In some cases, scope or circumstances eliminate the need for a formal contract.

The contract or agreement should identify the roles and responsibilities of both parties—consultant and client. Sometimes these responsibilities are fluid, but the contract should articulate them to provide as much concrete information as possible. Among other things, the agreement should guarantee the services of senior consultants experienced with all aspects of HRMS planning, development, and implementation.

Rules for Negotiating Contracts

Before starting, draft a list of the issues, including price and features.

Start high—do not be shy about asking for concessions right from the start.

Do not make the first concession. More often than not, the loser concedes first.

Never accept the first offer; the other party is probably willing to make additional concessions.

Never give a concession without getting one; this contributes to the sense of satisfaction the other party derives.

If the other party makes an unreasonably high demand, do not make a counter offer; insist on a reduction of the demand first.

Concessions do not have to be matched in kind; a concession now can lead to another concession later in the negotiating process.

Keep track of the kinds of concessions the firm's negotiators have made; this list can provide leverage in another part of the negotiations,

State that concessions are tentative, based on reaching an overall mutually satisfactory agreement, including price.

The contract should specifically state the time, cost, and scope of the assignment. This contract usually incorporates material developed as part of the RFP process, such as schedules, deadlines, objectives, and evaluation criteria.

Financial Options in Service Contracts

The financial aspect of a service contract may take several different forms. Which approach most benefits the HRMS client and which benefits the service provider depends on the circumstances. In general, the lower the risk to the client is, the higher the rate or initial cost.

The classic and simplest contract is the *fixed-price contract*. Both parties must agree on the amount to be paid for services rendered. The contractor/

consultant assumes the risk that actual time and material costs might exceed that price; to compensate for that risk, the contractor usually charges more than the time-and-materials estimates. The client gains the security of a fixed fee in exchange for a slightly higher cost. Some fixed-price contracts contain an incentive clause, in which the contractor receives increased compensation if the work meets or exceeds certain quality or delivery standards. Fixed-price contracts work best when both consultant and client can predict the scope and complexity of work and the HRMS project team can thus justify to management the funds involved.

Some would argue that any consultant's estimate reduces to the simple formula of x days times y rate plus out-of-pocket expenses. Such calculations may have validity in any contract, but they are the backbone of a *time-and-materials contract*. In this arrangement, the client agrees to pay certain hourly or daily rates for labor the consultant provides on the project, as well as reimburse authorized, direct expenses. Some consultants call these arrangements a *fees-and-expenses contract*. This contract may list fees or per diem rates for just one individual or may include different rates for different kinds of work, such as consulting, training, and installation. Consultants often offer their responses to HRMS RFPs as time-and-materials bids.

A time-and-materials contract usually states the amount of time the service provider estimates the project will require. If the project requires fewer hours, the client pays less; if it requires more hours, the client pays more. Such contracts often limit the maximum total the client will be charged, referred to as a not-to-exceed figure.

Some consultant arrangements work best when the parties use a *retainer contract*. The consultant guarantees the client a fixed number of days per month in return for a lower rate over a set time period. This applies when the project duration exceeds six months and the firm needs to guarantee that the HRMS consultant or other service provider will remain on the project throughout that period.

Consulting fees are negotiable, but consultants do not have much room to negotiate, since their services are a function of time and time has value. In a seller's market, HRMS consultants usually get close to what they quote. Only offering concessions, such as doing without a final written report or reducing the scope of the project, may reduce the overall cost of the contract. As a minimum, the client should require written progress reports and regular project review meetings.

The HRMS project team should know what kinds of contract arrangements its own internal management will consider before beginning such discussions with consultants and service providers. Negotiations should address the financial basis for calculating charges. Some consultants work only on a time-and-materials basis; other prefer retainer arrangements. Any advantage or disadvantage in using the particular type of arrangement the consultant

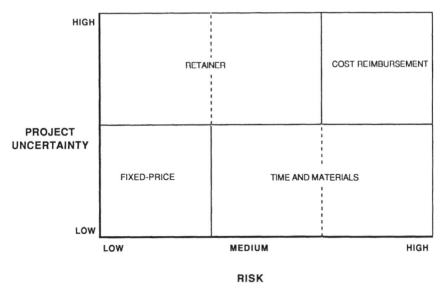

Figure 8–2. Factors in choosing a financial arrangement for consulting services. Two major factors influence the appropriateness (and likelihood) of agreeing on a particular type of financial arrangement. If an organization has a low-risk project, it should use a retainer or fixed-price contract. For projects involving higher risk, a firm should use time-and-materials contracts. A cost-reimbursement contract poses a greater risk, but it is appropriate if a project has a high level of uncertainty in scope, design, or time frame.

usually prefers depends on the scope of the project and the need to promote a longer-term relationship, perhaps beyond the HRMS project. For example, a qualified consultant who is a human resources generalist first and an HRMS specialist second can assist the organization in many other areas, such as compensation and benefits analysis, employment and training programs, and strategic planning.

Warranties

A warranty is a form of contract that a vendor provides with equipment or services. The warranty provides some protection to the client in the event of certain types of problems or defects. Warranties are important because most systems contain defects that show up long after installation. The warranty is generally separate from the contract or license agreement for the software itself and applies only to off-the-shelf packages. In some rare instances, it also can apply to custom products, or adaptations of packages.

The word *warranty* means many things to many people, so any warranty deserves careful inspection before the client agrees to purchase goods or services. Most vendors claim to provide a full guarantee, but some merely pass along what may be inadequate manufacturers' hardware and software warranties. The more reputable vendors offer their own warranties for all components. When paying retail prices, the client should expect a strong guarantee. The guarantee can be a major negotiating point in contract discussions.

Adequate HRMS software warranties are often hard to define, so the HRMS project team should regard a full, money-back guarantee as a valuable concession. Following are some of the minimal provisions for an adequate software warranty:

- The vendor agrees to replace defective disks or tapes on which their software is shipped.

- The vendor guarantees to fix any bugs that occur within a given time period.

- The vendor will make updates and revisions available at nominal or no cost.

- The vendor states in writing that the HRMS software will run in the client's computing environment. The statement should be more specific than just saying it runs in any MS-DOS environment or on any computer that supports a COBOL compiler. Clients should ensure that the warranty refers to the particular version of the package they are acquiring.

- The vendor warrants that the software conforms to the vendor's own specifications for performance criteria, such as run time, response time, and maximum downtime.

Most warranties exclude consequential damages. That means that even if the system makes so many mistakes that it damages the productivity or revenue-generating potential of the client, the vendor will only replace or repair the system, not cover any business losses. The negotiating team can try to eliminate this clause or at least soften its impact if the firm desires.

Glossary

Cost-reimbursement contract   A contract in which the client agrees to pay the service provider an hourly or daily rate for labor provided and to reimburse the provider for authorized direct expenses. Unlike a time-and-materials contract, a cost-reimbursement contract does not contain a not-to-exceed ceiling.

Entirety or merger clause   A clause stating that the vendor is bound only by what is in writing in the contract. No verbal or other representations apply.

Fixed-price contract   A contract in which the client agrees to pay the service provider a set amount for services rendered regardless of the actual time and expenses required.

General clause   A contract clause that pertains to the overall business relationship between the parties.

Retainer contract   A contract in which the service provider guarantees the client a fixed number of days of services per month in return for a lower daily rate over a set time period. For example, three days for $3,000 for six months.

Time-and-materials contract   A contract in which the client agrees to pay the service provider certain hourly or daily rates for services rendered, as well as reimbursement for certain direct expenses. This contract usually includes a maximum charge ceiling. Also called a *fees-and-expenses contract*.

Warranty   A contract that protects the client in the event of certain types of problems, defects, or deficiencies in the product or service provided.

Discussion Points

1. In relation to a software contract, comment on the expression "What you see is what you get."
2. What are some rules that should apply to any contractual relationship?
3. What makes software contracts different from other kinds of contracts?
4. What are the principal risks to avoid when buying software?
5. Who should draft the contract between vendor and client? Why?
6. What are some clauses that should be included in a contract for purchase or license of a software package?
7. What factors should the project team consider in the financial arrangement with an HRMS consultant?
8. What are some differences between contracts for software packages and contracts for software development?

Further Reading

Auer, Joseph, and Charles Edison Harris. "Popular Vendor Ploys." In *Computer Contract Negotiations*, edited by Charles Edison Harris. New York: Van Nostrand Reinhold, 1981.

Brandon, Dick H., and Sidney Segelstein. *Data Processing Contracts: Structure, Contents and Negotiation*. New York: Van Nostrand Reinhold, 1976.

Cunningham, Sheila. "100 Things You Need to Know Before Buying Software." *ICP Interface*, Spring 1981.

Deutsch, Dennis S. "How to Avoid the Pitfalls of Computer Contracts." *Inc.*, June 1981.

Frantzreb, Richard. *Microcomputers in Human Resource Management: A Directory of Software*. Roseville, CA: Advanced Personnel Systems, 1988.

Gallagher, Michael. "Before You Sign the HRIS Contract." *Personnel Journal*, November 1989.

Goldfinger, Edward. "A Manager's Guide to Computer Software." *Inc.*, June 1981.

Hallett, Jeffrey J. "Computers and the HR Professional." *Personnel Administrator*, July 1986.

Harris, Charles Edison. *Major Equipment Prodcurement*. New York: Van Nostrand Reinhold, 1983.

———. "Negotiating Software Contracts." *Datamation*, July 1985.

Harris, Charles Edison, ed. *Computer Contract Negotiations*. New York: Van Nostrand Reinhold, 1981.

Johnson, Everett C., et al. *Management, Control and Audit of Advanced EDP Systems*. American Institute of Certified Public Accountants, 1977.

Leavitt, Don. "Multiple Influences Interact in Selection of an HRMS." *Software News*, March 1983.

Meyer, Gary. *Automated Personnel Operations: The Human Resource Manager's Guide to Computerization*. Madison, CT: Bureau of Law and Business, 1984.

O'Brien, Paul R. "Software Selection: It's Not a Game!" *ICP Interface*, Winter 1983.

Rimbert, Suzanne B. "Negotiating a Contract for Computer Software and Related Services." *Personnel Administrator*, April 1981.

Szmadzinski, Joseph R. "Software Contracts: A Customer's Perspective." *ICP Interface*, Summer 1982.

9
HRMS Implementation

A really great talent finds its happiness in execution.
—Johann Wolfgang von Goethe

HRMS implementation refers to the process of bringing the HRMS from a design state to an operational state. This task is frequently complex, lengthy, and expensive. Implementing a mainframe HRMS can take a year or two and cost three to five times as much as the software itself. A microcomputer-based HRMS takes less time to implement (although numerous instances have involved implementation cycles lasting six to twelve months or longer) but has the same relative cost picture.

During implementation, HRMS staff may ask corporate administrators, computer specialists, human resources staff, and many others to accept temporary inconvenience, learn some new techniques, and shift responsibilities. But change can be stressful. Lack of good planning and project management during system introduction can result in unnecessarily high levels of stress. This stress can negatively affect users' views of the HRMS, no matter how well it operates technically.

Implementation demands good management skills, technical and functional knowledge, and continuous communication with everyone involved in the HRMS. Good management begins with considering every step in implementation and the staffing required for proper implementation. The implementation phase usually includes a number of overlapping processes:

- Implementation planning
- Policy and procedure development
- Project team training
- Installation
- Modification
- Interfaces
- Conversion
- User training
- Controlled testing
- Parallel testing

Keys to Successful Implementation

The client and vendor each must take steps to ensure project success. This chart identifies some of the major contributions each can make toward that goal.

	Client	Vendor
Management commitment and support	X	X
Quality training		X
Installation of working product		X
Realistic time frame for planning and control	X	X
Good vendor support (short term/long term)		X
Competent staff (managerial/analytical/technical)	X	X
Timely communication	X	X
Strong communication to users	X	
Working hardware/software environment	X	

Whether the human resources department implements all modules of the HRMS at once or in stages, many of these implementation steps may occur concurrently.

Implementation Planning

First applications typically suffer from being either overdeveloped or incomplete. Overdevelopment is usually a symptom of other problems, such as Parkinson's Law or misdirection. Lack of completion occurs when firms underestimate the need for proper planning and scheduling. As with most major projects, HRMS implementation needs a plan that identifies project goals, sets timetables, assigns responsibilities, allocates resources, and establishes monitoring mechanisms to keep the project on track. Depending on project complexity, as well as on individual company and manager preferences, planning and management tools may include Gantt charts, CPM, PERT, and project management software. Most implementation planning steps are the same as those for any management project. The guidelines that follow address the particular nature of HRMS implementation.

Prioritizing

HRMS implementation planning must integrate two types of priorities: the goals of the human resources department and the primary targets of the IS department for system development in the future. In many cases, human re-

Sample Implementation Checklist

	Task	Responsibility*
1	Copy vendor-supplied system tape to backup reel.	IS
2	Compile and catalog all programs. Resolve compile errors, if any.	IS
3	Make only the minimum programming changes necessary to enable the vendor's test streams to run.	IS
4	Run vendor-supplied test data.	IS
5	Review results; contact vendor on any questionable items. Save this run as a benchmark for future reference.	IS, HR
6	Review input and output forms design; place printing order.	HR
7	Prepare user test data reflecting samples of live data conditions.	HR
8	Make any necessary program modifications to the system or feeder subsystems.	IS
9	Rewrite job-stream programming to meet installation standards and the user's desired method of operation.	IS
10	Conduct a test of the modified system under realistic operating conditins.	IS, HR
11	Review the results of the systems test for adequacy and performance.	IS, HR
12	Train accounting and data processing personnel.	IS, HR
13	Load or convert data base files	IS, HR
14	Establish new procedures and working methods	HR
15	Begin a parallel or controlled changeover to the new system, with close review for any errors that might be detected in the live environment.	IS, HR

*IS = information systems; HR = human resources.

sources can set an implementation schedule only with the cooperation and participation of IS management, often through negotiation and compromise. For instance, human resources management may recognize the need for a computer-based system, and IS may support computerization of human resources data management throughout the organization. However, human resources may have as a specific goal the implementation of a performance measurement system or a flexible benefits program. Although the human resources department may wish to support these systems independently, these new projects will have a major impact on the HRMS because they and the HRMS share a lot of common data. IS may have other high-priority business applications to make operational during the same period. For example, management often considers a new customer billing system or inventory control system a higher

INCREASES STABILITY	DECREASES STABILITY
CURRENT SYSTEM	
HRMS is automated	HRMS is manual
HRMS needs are constant	HRMS needs fluctuate
TYPE OF APPLICATION	
Processing system	Management information system
Straightforward design and development	Complex design and development
User community is within one functional area	User community crosses functional boundaries
Project is small (less than one year)	Project is large (over one year)
USER BASE	
Experienced in their functional area	Inexperienced in their functional area
Experienced in information systems	Inexperienced in information systems
HRSC/IS	
Experienced in application area (HR)	Inexperienced in application area (HR)
Experienced in implementation activities	Inexperienced in implementation activities

Figure 9–1. Factors influencing the implementation environment.

priority than the HRMS. To get IS support and participation in module integration, human resources must keep other IS priorities in mind as well.

HRMS planning also must take into account restrictions on staff and technical resources availability imposed by noncomputer priorities, as well as how such outside priorities may influence data and procedures that affect the

HRMS. Members of the HRMS project team must work with their counterparts and managers in IS and other functions to reconcile potential priority conflicts.

To establish implementation priorities, the HRMS project manager should give department or functional heads opportunities to explain their perspectives on how and when to integrate their functions into the new HRMS. Conflicts usually arise about which part of the system the HRMS project team should implement first. Such conflicts occur particularly when payroll is part of the HRMS. Once management has decided on a plan, everyone should know that a complete (but flexible) implementation plan exists; every function or unit should understand the rationale for its place in that plan.

The HRMS project team should develop the implementation plan before finalizing any equipment or software purchases or introducing even one piece of the new HRMS. Some priority plans implement the most important applications first. Others bring up a relatively easy module first to score a demonstrable quick win, then proceed with the list of priorities. Still others choose the prototyping route (discussed later in this chapter), a process of developing applications by starting with a rough version of the system, then refining it through a series of iterations.

Some organizations with sufficient expert functional and technical staff might be able to implement a complete HRMS in an "all at once" approach. However, due to the enormity of HRMS implementation and its demand on resources, many organizations choose to phase in the new system. Other advantages to phased implementation include less interruption of human resources and IS operations, more financial flexibility in terms of the investment in hardware and software development, greater opportunity to gather corporate and interdepartmental support for later phases, and a broader HRMS knowledge base among human resources staff.

Implementation Schedules

In HRMS implementation, as with most projects, scheduling is a critical component in planning and development and, ultimately, in management success. Only by developing, monitoring, and maintaining an accurate schedule can managers control costs and resources effectively.

The schedule should include estimated start dates, end dates, and elapsed time or duration of each implementation task or activity. These figures should be correlated with staffing requirements for each activity. The team should then estimate time requirements based on the experience of staff, vendor, and consultant with similar projects. Delivery dates and the schedule of deliverables from outside sources should be double-checked. Draft copies of the schedule should be sent to all HRMS project team members and management staff, and their input should be solicited before dates are finalized. Every

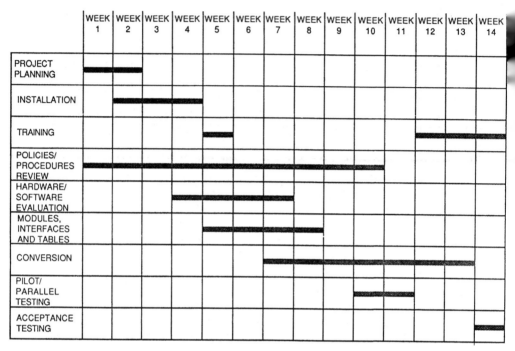

	WEEK 1	WEEK 2	WEEK 3	WEEK 4	WEEK 5	WEEK 6	WEEK 7	WEEK 8	WEEK 9	WEEK 10	WEEK 11	WEEK 12	WEEK 13	WEEK 14
PROJECT PLANNING	████													
INSTALLATION		████████												
TRAINING					██								████████	
POLICIES/ PROCEDURES REVIEW	████████████████████████████████													
HARDWARE/ SOFTWARE EVALUATION				████████										
MODULES, INTERFACES AND TABLES					████████████████									
CONVERSION						████████████████████████████								
PILOT/ PARALLEL TESTING											████████			
ACCEPTANCE TESTING														██

Figure 9–2. Implementation Gantt chart. Implementation of a system of even moderate complexity may require several months. Performing a thorough policies and procedures review and converting data from the old system to the new require considerable time, but these steps help easily ensure that the new HRMS works in harmony with, rather than in opposition to, the overall human resources organization.

member of the HRMS implementation team should have the opportunity to participate in the development of the schedule.

Inevitably, schedules change during the course of an HRMS project. Perhaps the delivery of a new computer or peripheral is delayed. Software developers often run behind schedule in delivering new releases. Unexpected problems with other computer applications of equal or greater importance take an unexpectedly large share of IS staff time. If time estimates change, the schedule should be updated accordingly.

Staffing for Implementation

During the HRMS planning and design stages, the principal people involved are the human resources staff and the project manager or consultant. During

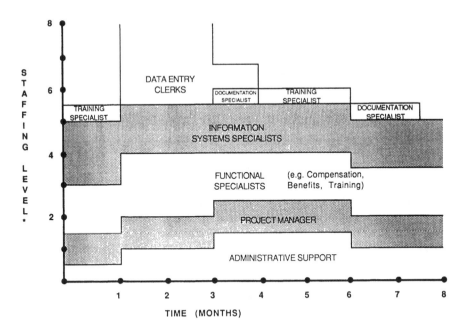

* FULL-TIME EQUIVALENT

Figure 9–3. Implementation staffing plan. This plan displays the project's staffing needs over time. It depicts the amount of work each specialty should plan to provide during various periods throughout implementation. An HRMS project requires different types of staff to accomplish various project objectives. For instance, a project may need more than one IS specialist during modification but only part-time IS involvement later on.

implementation, the number of people involved in the new HRMS increases dramatically. Virtually the entire human resources staff plays some role; outside departments such as IS and facilities also take part. Several specialists who were not involved earlier may participate as part of the implementation team. Brief descriptions of some of these new members and their roles follows.

HRMS Manager. Sometime during or immediately following implementation, management responsibility of the new system shifts from the HRMS project manager to the actual HRMS manager, sometimes called the human resources systems center (HRSC) manager. The HRMS manager supervises and assumes responsibility for the ongoing system, staff, and user relations. The individual who has served as HRMS project manager may or may not be the best system manager. Someone skilled and challenged by project planning, development, and implementation may not wish to serve as administrator of a comparatively steady-state system. As discussed further in chapter 11, the HRMS manager needs effective skills in three main areas: human resources operations, computer systems, and organization management.

One person or group should have general oversight responsibility for the entire HRMS implementation process. This responsibility usually rests with the HRMS manager. The project implementation plan should include benchmarks and dates for shifting responsibility from the HRMS project manager to the HRMS manager.

Implementation Specialist. In certain situations, a consultant who is an implementation specialist provides important planning, administrative, and technical guidance. An implementation specialist may be part of the vendor's staff or an experienced consultant.

IS Auditor. This function is not generally part of the implementation team. The IS auditor reviews the operations of the HRMS from a reliability standpoint to ensure that the system performs as expected, processes transactions consistently, and calculates valid totals.

Training Coordinator. Because user training takes place at various points during implementation, the HRMS implementation team should include at least one member of the training function. This person coordinates all aspects of training team members, management, and users. Responsibilities include training program design, staffing, scheduling, facilities, and materials.

Establishing the HRSC

No matter how well the HRMS project team may have performed up to this point, the implementation phase marks the time for a new crew to come on board—the ongoing staff who will maintain and manage the HRMS and deal with the user community. The project team may include numerous individuals who specialize in system design and development but lack the interest or expertise to handle ongoing user interactions, modifications, and routine maintenance issues. The well-planned project takes into account the differences between the project team and the ongoing staff; of course, having some staff overlap usually makes for a smoother transition. Implementation planning should include particular time periods for the future ongoing staff to learn from the HRMS project team, to take on increasing responsibility, and finally to acknowledge the contributions of the project team.

Some organizations refer to this staff as the human resources systems cen-

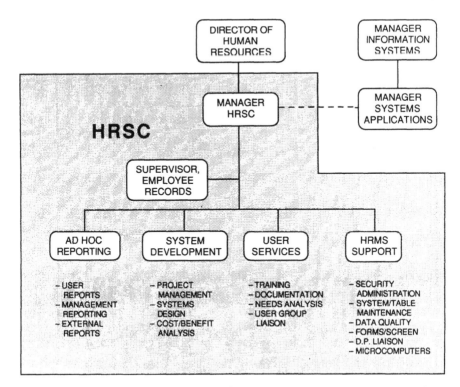

Figure 9–4. Typical HRSC organization. Some components of the HRSC involve significant contact with users, providing training, documentation, and reports. One component often handles financial and management issues; another handles technical maintenance. In a small organization, each component may require only one staff person. In a large organization, each may have a dozen or more.

ter (HRSC). This group, under the direction of the HRMS (or HRSC) manager, supervises maintenance, user services, technical quality control, system development projects, vendor and consultant relations, and ad hoc reporting. The HRSC may perform some of the clerical tasks formerly assigned to data processing operations, but it tends to concentrate on tasks that nontechnical staff cannot perform, such as systems analysis and programming. Infrequently, the HRSC performs only a liaison role with contractors who have been engaged to do the work.

During implementation, the HRMS manager should complete HRSC staffing and make sure that every member of the HRSC staff receives appropriate training on the new system.

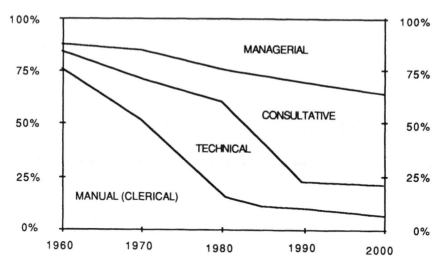

Figure 9–5. Evolution of HRSC staff skills requirements. Several decades
ago, the human resources system provided primarily clerical
assistance with data entry and standard reports. Since that
time, users have become more knowledgeable and
independent, and systems have become more powerful and
flexible. In response, the HRSC needs fewer clerical staff
and a greater ability to provide guidance in complex projects
and facilitate users' more diverse needs and expectations.

Policy and Procedure Revisions

Every automation project affects company and department policies and procedures for both computer-related and manual operations. The HRMS is no
exception. The HRMS project needs to reconcile the new system with existing
human resources and IS policies and procedures so that all computer operations and manual activities work toward common goals rather than at cross-
purposes.

Human Resources Policies and Procedures

A new automated system will undoubtedly have a great impact on manual
procedures and policies within the human resources department. For one
thing, the computer cannot deal with ambiguity. The HRMS cannot easily
address policies enforced on a case-by-case basis. If the human resources department does not unify the bases for automated and manual procedures, it
may experience conflicts, inaccurate data, and missed deadlines. The HRMS

project team can take the first step in resolving potential discrepancies by identifying the areas needing review and possible revision.

Work Flow and Timing. Manual processes must be addressed, streamlined, and revised so they blend into the automated system. Timing considerations such as deadlines for entering payroll and human resources data and for report runs should be included.

Bottlenecks. The flow of work, paper, and timing issues must be reviewed to identify potential bottlenecks. To ensure a smoothly functioning system, solutions for these problems should be worked out before going on-line.

Transaction Flow. HRMS project team members should address, revise, and reach agreement on issues that affect who must act on, approve, or receive data between initial receipt and final output. This includes items such as input forms, authorization signatures, and report routing.

Human Resources Rules. Many times a new system causes the human resources department or corporate management to reexamine procedures used in crediting, penalizing, or organizing employees. Other times, the system must adapt to existing human resources rules, particularly if they stem from government regulatory requirements. For example, if company policy allows for time off with pay but only for employees who have achieved a certain service record, are at a certain level, or are within a given operation, the HRMS must include specification of these rules (within the guidelines or mandates of applicable labor laws).

System Rigidity. A new HRMS may force increased rigidity on manual processes. For example, taking clerical work home Thursday night to turn in first thing Friday morning when it was due at the close of the previous workday may no longer be acceptable if it holds up an HRMS production run. Users must understand that some of the flexibility in the familiar manual processes may evaporate with the new HRMS.

The HRMS project team also should develop and execute a plan to reconcile the manual and automated systems. In some cases, the manual system will change to conform with the new HRMS; in others, staff attitudes and operations flexibility may suggest that the automated system must be adapted to fit the manual system.

Computer-Related Procedures and Policies

Operating instructions for the HRMS must reflect the organization's processing and work-flow requirements. The types of issues addressed include the following.

Data Entry Policies and Procedures. What is the process for entering data? Will data entry be centralized in the HRSC, or will users enter data on-line? What are the specific responsibilities of users who enter their own data?

Timing Considerations. When will the HRMS generate monthly reports? By what date and time must staff complete all data entry and validation in order to include that data in the processing run? When will the payroll be run? What is the pay cycle—Sunday through Saturday; Monday through Sunday; first of the month through the fifteenth and the sixteenth through the end of the month; pay periods ending on the tenth and twenty-fifth; or any of several other arrangements?

Data Updates. Can anyone update information at any time or only at certain times? Is some information available for update at any time but other data available for update only by individuals in certain positions at certain times? To what extent will computer production control limit data updates, and to what extent will written policy dictate?

A human resources department using a networked system may want to schedule master file updates for particular times of the day or week. This allows users to know that they are receiving the most current information, as well as eliminate conflict within the network if one user's updated data and another user's request for that data occur simultaneously.

User Access. Strict adherence to a comprehensive HRMS policy can minimize many of the risks associated with unauthorized access to sensitive employee and human resources information. Such a policy deters inappropriate use, reassures individuals, and helps protect the organization in case of legal action related to allegations of invasion of privacy.

The core of the policy is user access. Which users should have access to which portions of the HRMS data base and on what basis? What type of access will they have (read only, add/change/delete)? What means will control this access? What is the procedure for requesting and changing passwords? Who controls passwords? Such considerations often take on additional significance and complexity if some users have microcomputers linked to a mainframe data base.

Because many aspects of privacy policy affect system design, many of the risks and techniques associated with data privacy and control have already been discussed in chapter 3. For instance, the design phase often includes creation of a chart of user access according to position code. This chart, sometimes called a privilege, or grant, matrix, serves as a guide for technical staff in establishing access limits during system design and modifications.

Security Administration. Security policy extends far beyond user access. It also includes preventing sabotage, accidental data damage or loss, unauthorized distribution to outside agents, and computer viruses and worms. The

HRMS project team must determine what constitutes a breach of security, what measures to take to minimize each such risk, and how to respond if a security breach occurs or is suspected.

Data Backup. The HRMS should include policies on backup of data and program files. Timely and methodical backup does not necessarily prevent system damage, but it does help speed recovery, minimizing the cost of natural or human errors. An effective backup policy might mandate the following:

- Daily backup of data base changes
- Weekly backup of the complete system
- Monthly backup of the complete system for long-term storage

The project team also should address backup of documentation (including user guides), working prototypes, system specifications, and user-developed programs. Many organizations mandate off-site or fire-safe storage of backup copies.

Disaster Recovery Planning. Even with the best planning and procedures, a computer system may experience significant loss—whether through a natural disaster such as an earthquake or through human action such as user sabotage. If such an event occurs, the HRMS should be ready to restore a fully functional system with a reliable data base as quickly as possible. To do so, the HRMS project team should develop a disaster recovery plan before the system ever becomes operational. The plan may address aspects such as alternate power sources, backup equipment, installing backup copies of the operating system and applications software, reformatting storage media, restoring backup data bases, and system checks and safeguards. The plan should assign tasks and responsibilities to specific functions within both human resources and IS, as well as sometimes to the vendor.

Installation

Installation is not a synonym for implementation; installation refers to implementation's technical core—hooking up the hardware (if required) and loading the software into the hardware. Implementation includes installation, but it also encompasses record and file conversion, system modifications, training, and testing.

Hardware Installation

From an HRMS standpoint, hardware installation is a much simpler operation than the software installation that follows. Technicians must, however, install the new terminals, microcomputers, printers, and other components carefully so that equipment foul-ups do not slow down software installation. Some firms arrange for either the hardware or software vendor to perform this installation independently, but generally the client is involved. In-house staff may perform at least some of the preliminary and administrative functions of hardware installation. In any event, the implementation team or specialist should ensure that the installation process includes the following steps.

Site Preparation. For a mainframe operation, site preparation frequently requires months, particularly if the site has not had a mainframe computer before. The HRMS project manager must demand completion of all construction and remodeling in rooms that will house computers before permitting hardware delivery. Unfinished site preparation could mean potential electrical problems, mechanical problems, and water or dust contamination. Technicians should make sure that all cooling and air-circulation systems are operational. They should complete any needed electrical rewiring and additional ceiling or floor channels. They should have all electrical and phone cabling in place ready for use so the implementation team can test the HRMS as soon as possible after delivery.

Delivery. The HRMS project manager should coordinate all delivery dates and confirm delivery arrangements in writing. He or she should take special care to conform to every aspect of company policy about the delivery of capital equipment, including access by installation staff, acceptance of delivered equipment, damage checks, serial number and warranty registration, insurance, payment terms, and installation date records.

Installation. Technical specialists should ensure proper placement and leveling of each piece of equipment. Installers should connect all cables, including not only electrical supply and telecommunications links but also computer cables and printer cables delivered with the hardware, to test their capacity and interdependence. Telecommunications systems may require specialized outside installation. The HRMS project team should double-check that all necessary connections are in place before installing software; otherwise, the team may have difficulty identifying whether problems with the new HRMS are caused by hardware, software, the network, or a combination of these things.

Software Installation

If human resources purchases the HRMS from an outside vendor, the vendor's representatives usually install the software with assistance from the firm's technical staff. Depending on the hardware configuration, the expertise of the installation staff, and the number of programs or modules being installed, the

Software Package Implementation Myths

The project does not require a detailed implementation plan.

The vendor will provide sufficient support.

The software is delivered error-free.

IS must take responsibility for the project.

Junior-level people can handle implementation.

Users do not need training from the vendor.

The vendor does not need to test the system.

The project does not require acceptance testing.

process may take two days to two months but usually can be accomplished in a week.

Software installation includes the following steps:

- Install the operating system (if not continuing to use the same operating system as on existing computers). The hardware manufacturer furnishes instructions on how to perform this installation or performs it. Installation involves loading onto the computer's resident memory via disk a set of computer operations and instructions that tell the computer how and where to accept, read, and store data files.
- Make a backup copy of the application programs from the original medium furnished by the vendor or developer. The copy should be in the same medium as the original. System staff should keep the original in a secure area, safe from dust, moisture, temperature extremes, fire damage, and sabotage.
- Install the application programs in the CPU of the computer in which they will reside. As with operating system installation, this activity involves copying certain files from the backup copy of the software to the resident memory of the computer.
- Perform initial acceptance testing to demonstrate operational compatibility of the HRMS and the hardware. In all but off-the-shelf packages, IS staff and the vendor usually perform this testing jointly. The initial test commonly involves moving through various system screens, commands, and functions with an absolute minimum of data. The vendor usually supplies data for this initial test to ascertain that the HRMS is running prop-

erly. System implementation also usually involves levels of acceptance testing with the client's data. The general principles of such testing are discussed later in this chapter.

Once the HRMS implementation team confirms successful installation, technical staff (and vendor, if appropriate) can proceed with modifications, interfaces, and conversion.

Modifications and Interfaces

Some users can simply install and run an off-the-shelf software package, but most human resources departments must make at least some modifications to the system after installation. Some of this takes place during the system design phase, but most occurs after the new system is installed.

Modifications

Custom and packaged HRMS tend to require different types of modifications during implementation. Custom system implementation involves correcting mistakes and other inadvertent deficiencies. Packaged system implementation involves making changes and enhancements to bring the system closer to user needs.

Custom systems, by definition, already include the data elements, data relationships, codes, tables, edit and validation rules, screens, and reports that correspond with the requirements definition and specifications. Because such a system has not received the extensive testing and use that a packaged program has endured, however, implementation modifications often consist primarily of correcting design mistakes and unintentional errors, or bugs. The term *bug* refers to a problem that occurs as a result of incorrectly written program code; sometimes the term refers to the code itself. Such modifications usually involve system design and programming by technical staff.

An organization that has selected a packaged HRMS can expect to modify even the best system by about 20 to 30 percent to correspond to the requirements definition or specifications. These modifications may be as small as adding a byte to an existing data element or adding a field to a screen using a screen painter, or they can be as large as restructuring an entire file or providing a unique interface.

Sometimes the vendor performs some or all of these modifications before delivery. The appropriateness of performing these modifications in-house depends on several factors, including staff skills, experience, and availability; project budget; type of programming language used; and type and extent of modifications required.

Caveat

"The management question, therefore, is not whether to build a pilot system and throw it away. You will do that. The only question is whether to plan in advance to build a throwaway, or to promise to deliver a throwaway to the customers. Seen this way, the answer is much clearer. Delivering that throwaway to the customer buys time, but it does so only at the cost of agony for the user, distraction for the builders while they do the redesign, and a bad reputation for the product that the best redesign will find hard to live down. Hence plan to throw one away, you will anyhow."

—Fred Brooks, *The Mythical Man Month*

The development cycle of a modification is an abbreviated version of the system development cycle, since the project team has already defined and documented requirements. The steps in the modification cycle are as follows:

- Design
- Specification
- Coding
- Testing
- Documentation
- Implementation

Some situations do not require exactly this series of steps. If the problem stems from a programming error, the technical staff can make corrections without design revisions or user involvement. If an internally developed HRMS requires modifications because of misinterpreted user specifications, the modification cycle begins with a meeting between the user and the analyst to review the design, determine the nature of the discrepancy, and specify needed changes. This information forms the basis for a reworked design, specification, or both; the rest of the steps in the modification cycle follow.

The HRMS project team should avoid redoing the requirements definition whenever possible, since such activity wastes time and money and generally takes place too late to effect change anyway. The team should reexamine the requirements definition only if modifications are required as part of a later implementation phase that comes a long time after the initial requirements determination. In this case, the project team would do well to revalidate the original requirements document with the users affected. An operational audit (discussed in chapter 10) may serve this process well.

Perhaps the most common and potentially most time-consuming task (depending on the HRMS design) is revising and loading tables. Two types of changes are most common—content changes and format revisions. Content changes most commonly arise when a firm needs to load organization-specific codes and values. Format changes should occur only if tables do not properly or completely support organization requirements. Vendor-supplied software generally compromises tables and, therefore, should permit the addition of data fields or attributes specific to the client.

Many HRMS staff find writing and revising documentation their biggest chore in modification. Avoiding or paying too little attention to this step saves time and money in the short run but can cause long-term headaches. Poor documentation not only confuses users and technicians, but it also makes maintenance a nightmare. For more information on writing documentation, see chapters 3 and 4.

Once the HRMS software is installed, data base administrators and computer specialists, as well as human resources managers, will make many suggestions about how to improve, refine, and maximize the new system. The project team must be prepared to control modification activity, or it will spend an inordinate amount of time and resources on these changes. Some organizations try to satisfy user needs immediately by developing and implementing all "good ideas" about modifications and interfaces. Others wisely freeze all but essential changes for a specified time following the advent of system operational status. Users generally accept the system as delivered (provisionally), with modifications that are the responsibility of the vendor noted and accumulated during a three- to six-month trial period.

Prototyping

Several techniques frequently play important roles in modifications of packaged HRMS. Fourth-generation languages (4GLs), described in chapter 4, facilitate the adaptation of software by qualified users. Selection of a 4GL-based system increases the likelihood that in-house technical staff can modify data elements, screens, and reports during initial implementation rather than forcing users to begin with a less appropriate version of the system. Some technical staff use 4GL tools and related techniques to prototype changes to a packaged system.

Prototyping is an iterative system development methodology that results in a working model of a system. Through prototyping, staff can quickly develop a new module or other enhancement, allow users to work with this prototype, and then fine-tune or otherwise revise the enhancement based on user feedback. Prototyping can increase productivity by giving users a quick means

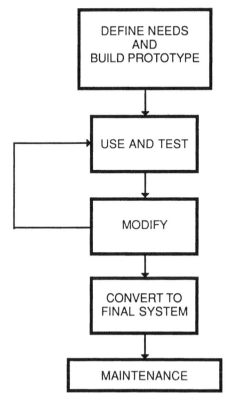

Figure 9–6. The prototyping cycle. Prototyping is basically an iterative process in which developers and users keep trying incremental or partial modifications until they achieve acceptable or desired results. This allows users to work with the system even though it is not yet complete. It also can give users more input in system design.

of developing an application and obtaining useful business information. Prototyping produces a series of approximations that approach the desired goal; in contrast, formal system development techniques work more methodically to produce a finished product. The development of modules that are more flexible and maintainable than hard-coded systems increases staff productivity. Rather than rewriting the program code, HRSC staff can use prototyping to create not only a trial module or subsystem but also a final version.

In certain circumstances, prototyping works particularly well compared with other approaches. For instance, firms may attempt it if users require system modifications, but only if users and technicians communicate well. In that case, the application itself becomes a direct communication medium rather than having to rely on more abstract verbal descriptions. Prototyping allows technical staff to provide a more rapid response to user requests. It also works if the system has users with considerable computer skills who are willing and able to spearhead system modifications that stem from specific user needs. Even human resources departments that do not use prototyping as a modification tool during implementation often adopt that approach for enhancements and maintenance later in the system's life cycle.

Interfaces with Other Systems

Although requirements definitions have already identified and designed HRMS interfaces to other systems, detailed specification and programming of these interfaces takes place only during or after the implementation phase. The most common interfaces include the following:

- Personnel to payroll
- Payroll to general ledger
- Personnel (or payroll) to benefits
- Personnel (or payroll) to cost accounting

Because most interfaces involve payroll, a more detailed discussion of the issues involved in interfaces is covered in chapter 20. The interface development cycle resembles the development cycle for the overall system: requirements definition, design, coding, and implementation. To develop workable interfaces, the HRMS project team must specify the following:

- What data will users pass between the systems?
- In what direction(s) will the data flow?
- How does each subsystem define the data?
- What is the format of the records and files?
- On what media do the data reside?
- What labeling and naming conventions does each system have?
- What code values does each system have?

Programmers often do not have to create the entire interface. In some cases, they just have to make some refinements or identify recommended procedures for transfer of data between files. Some application packages come with utilities that interface with the packages of other major vendors. Most of these utilities offer several different structures or paths for the transaction flow, however, so technical staff must try each option with a data sample. They can then decide which options provide the optimal solution for the particular systems and needs involved.

Data Conversion

Before the new system can become operational, it must contain the current, complete HRMS data base (or whatever portion applies if the system pertains to a specific human resources function). To accomplish this, technical staff must transfer those data from the old system to the new one. Converting data from one system into a format that is readable by another system can be lengthy and difficult. Conversion often involves both automated data transfer and manual data entry. To carry out the conversion process, the HRMS project team should create a detailed conversion plan that includes the following steps:

- Determine which data to carry forward and the sources of these data.
- "Clean" the data in the current system before transferring them to the new HRMS.
- Specify and write automated conversion programs.
- Develop manual data input and collection procedures.
- Review and test conversion results.
- Run parallel production cycles for a limited time.

Time and staffing requirements for successful conversion depend on the condition and availability of data as well as the size of the organization and the application. The earlier stages of the conversion process may begin even before implementation starts, but actual conversion to the new HRMS should occur after completion of the controlled test (discussed later in this chapter).

Compared with manual transfer, an automated conversion can result in better-quality data, take less time, and save the organization money. The HRMS project team may take either of two approaches to automated conversion: (1) master file to master file transfer or (2) use a program to generate transactions from the old system(s) to be input directly into the new HRMS (known as populating the new data base). The advantage of the second approach is that it allows staff to pass data through the edit and validation components of the new HRMS. This helps trap errors and ensures "clean" data. This approach may require staff to sift through printouts of data transaction errors and reload data manually, but this procedure is preferable to contaminating the new data base with erroneous data.

Inputting data from employee questionnaires, load sheets, or other non-automated media can seem tedious, but this process is more an industrial engineering or methods and procedures activity than a computer systems problem. Approaching the task from this perspective with regard to use of temporary staff, assignment of tasks, assembly-line operations, and so forth will make HRMS development faster, more accurate, and less nerve-racking.

Training

The best HRMS in the world will work only if users know how to make it work. Human resources management can foster that knowledge by providing explicit training and ongoing support as part of the HRMS. In fact, training human resources staff is probably the most important step in the implementation process.

In the software and systems areas, many organizations have treated training as the stepchild of the development process. Lately, however, experienced system planners have put the word *human* back into human resources. HRMS people are becoming increasingly aware that project planning must include adequate training of users in how to deal with the new HRMS.

Training Plan

The HRMS training coordinator should work with a group of project team members or other members of the training function to prepare a training plan. An effective plan will do the following:

- Identify specific kinds of users requiring training
- Estimate the number of users of each type
- List the specific information and skills each group needs to acquire
- Decide on training media for each type of user
- Identify trainers (internal or external)
- Schedule training sessions
- Plan development of training materials

The project plan should allocate dedicated staff and time specifically for training. Every individual who will interact with the HRMS will require some training, but different types of users require different types of training:

- HRMS project team members and trainers must receive thorough, early training in virtually every aspect of the system. They must prepare to answer the questions of the other users.

- Technical support staff need to know the operational and program linkages to install, implement, and maintain the new system.

- Human resources managers and analysts require a more detailed understanding of the system's capabilities as they apply to their respective functions. They need to be familiar with the range of reports available from the system and procedures for making changes. They should know how to manipulate data to produce reports, such as spreadsheets, graphs, and matrices.

Considering Training?

Thinking about training? Here are some points to keep in mind.

Training makes people learn faster. A good training course involves hands-on training that accelerates learning and enhances retention.

Training saves money. The faster your staff learns your systems, the sooner the return on your investment.

Ask to see training materials. For insight about the scope and depth of the course examine the materials.

Not just experts but teachers. No matter how much expertise an instructor has, it's meaningless if he or she doesn't understand the process of education—what it takes to facilitate learning, enhance retention, and so forth.

Will they customize a course? You may find a course that comes close to what you're looking for, but isn't quite right. Check to see if a company will tailor its courses to fit your needs.

Do they provide "front-end" analysis? Are they willing to sit down with you to figure out the current education level of your staff, help you establish your education goals, and create a plan?

How responsive are they? Do they return your phone calls or send things when they say they will? These can be early indicators of just how responsive they'll be *after* you sign them up.

Look for experience, expertise, and commitment—not just size. Small companies are often more flexible in their preparation of custom course material, and generally have more control over the selection of instructors. Don't focus on size alone.

Choose a company for the long term. This makes economic sense. Most companies offer training packages with volume discounts, so you get more value for your training dollar when you work with the same company.

Check references. Ask for a list of references. This is the best way to check the quality of a company's training.

(Source: John Teasley, "Common Sense Commandments," *Information Center,* March 1990.)

SEMINAR NAME	CLASS CODE & TITLE		DAYS	TUs
INSIGHT	INIP	Implementation Planning	3.0	7
HR-1	HR1	HR-1 Workshop	1.0	3
Personnel Workshop	PSW	Personnel Workshop	4.0	13
System Architecture	SAPS	Personnel System Architecture	1.5	4
	SAPR	Payroll System Architecture	2.0	5
	SAOA	ATS & PCS Overview	.5	1
Hands On Payroll Workshop	PR350	Hands On Payroll Workshop (VSAM & DB2 workshops)	4.0	15
Advanced Payroll	PR250	Payroll Configuration, Calculation & Customization	4.0	13
ASAP for Programmers	IR281	ASAP Information Retrieval Workshop	2.5	7
	IR282	ASAP System Maintenance	.5	2
ASAP for Users	IR381	ASAP Information Retrieval Workshop	3.0	9
Online Screen Applications (CICS)	PI225	OLAG (Online Screen Application Generator) Data Base, Batch, and Online Modifications Personnel (Release 9.1 and later)	3.0	10
CSP / DB2 for Integral Product	PI230	Data Base, Batch, and Online Modifications	3.0	12
Generic CSP / DB2	DB2C	DB2 Concepts and Facilities	1.0	2
	DB2A	DB2 Application Programming	3.0	7
	CSP	CSP Application Development and SQL	3.0	7
	QMF	Query Management Facilities	1.0	2

* *Indicates 1:00 pm start time. All other classes start at 9:00 am.*

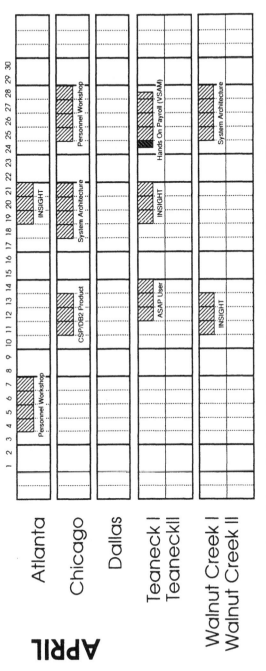

Figure 9–7. Sample vendor training schedule. A large organization might have its own similar schedule. The schedule includes several levels of classes in several locations, with repeats of some classes. Most HRMS courses require more than one day.
(Source: Integral Systems. Reprinted with permission.)

- Senior managers need to be aware of the system's general capabilities and should have a basic understanding of what the system can and cannot do.
- System users have a wide variety of training needs, depending on their job responsibilities. System users need to know how to navigate through the menus and screens. Most functional users must understand how to input and retrieve data; some need to know how to maintain tables. Some users need to know how to request standard reports and others how to create ad hoc reports. To meet these needs, the training plan should provide different types of training according to individual and group needs and skill-level requirements.

The training schedule should offer courses for each major type of user. Some of this training will take place before the system becomes operational. Team members and trainers may, therefore, need to receive more off-site, simulation and hands-on training so they can be ready to demonstrate, debug, and train on the new HRMS as soon as technical staff (or the vendor) completes installation. Many human resources departments mandate that employees complete training before being assigned a password that allows them to access the system.

A public relations campaign for the system also promotes user confidence and enthusiasm when users begin their training and start to use the system. This campaign can include articles in employee newsletters, posters, and handouts.

Another portion of this campaign can aim to increase the support of line managers and other supervisors for their subordinates' participation in HRMS training. Some managers may balk at letting their subordinates leave their regular assignments to attend orientation sessions, but before long those employees will be back at work, conversant with the new system and able to produce more efficient, consistent, and complete results.

Team Training

As implementation gets under way, HRMS project team members may be like the men in the story of the blind men and the elephant: Each member knows a lot about one piece but not enough about the rest of the system to be able to form an accurate picture of the whole.

Specific training of project team members at this point will give them a better understanding of the system, which in turn will help them judge how to do their work so that it integrates with that of other human resources staff. Such training greatly reduces errors, misunderstanding, and wasted time. Vendor classes can provide some training, but custom-designed team training also should include review of HRMS documentation for both users and technical staff, system walk-throughs, site visits, processing schedules, system testing, relationships among new modules, how to design screens and reports, and specific responsibility for answering questions.

When a firm is in doubt about whom to include in these early activities, it should err on the side of including more rather than fewer staff members. Such training allows the emerging HRSC staff to build expertise on the HRMS. The HRSC staff can then assert themselves as internal consultants.

User Training

Training of users must begin before the system becomes operational. Depending on organization staffing, human resources department staff will probably need the two types of training discussed below.

Education on Computing Fundamentals and User Responsibilities. This segment is popularly dubbed Computer Literacy 101. Topics may include introduction to computer and software terms, concepts, and equipment; benefits of the HRMS; basic user responsibilities (including accident and damage prevention); security procedures; and orientation to resources such as manuals, IS services, and reporting packages.

Training Specific to the HRMS. This training segment emphasizes how to use the system for better performance. A sound approach starts by providing an overview of the HRMS and how it will affect human resources operations. The program then details the specifics of operating the system. This information includes procedures for logging on and off, main menus and submenus, screen formats, data entry, edit and validation rules, error messages, report generation, printing, interfaces, and other activities specific to individual human resources functions.

Most organizations underestimate the amount of training required to orient employees to work with the new HRMS. Inputting data is generally a new discipline for most personnel clerks and requires special training. Improper transcription leads to inaccurate reports. To maximize data accuracy, system reliability, and user confidence, each course should cover what to do if questions or problems arise. Among their resources are help screens, written support, and HRSC staff.

Trainers

For organizations that acquire an HRMS from a vendor, the best initial source of training is the vendor or other external resources that specialize in that vendor's products. Depending on organization size, HRMS budget, and vendor capabilities, most user training can come directly from the vendor. Clients should be wary of vendors that have small or remote training facilities, are already overextended in their training operations, do not have local support, and cannot provide on-site training. The client should examine the ratio of users to staff in training classes, as well as the qualifications and experience of the trainers. If possible, the client should observe other classes offered by the vendor before making decisions about training sources and check with other clients for evaluations of training and trainers.

Rather than have the vendor train all HRMS users, some firms contract to have the vendor educate key human resources staff, who in turn train the remaining users and HRSC staff. This may work well if the initial group emerges as capable, qualified HRMS specialists who are able and willing to train others. The obvious drawback of this approach is that many of those trainers may lack previous HRMS experience. It does, however, allow the evolving HRSC to establish itself as the internal expert and develop a rapport with the human resources user community. The HRSC should position itself early on as a clearinghouse for professional HRMS services and support within the organization. HRMS training provides an excellent boost to this image.

If the department builds a custom HRMS, initial training is the responsibility of the developers, whether those developers are in-house resources or consultants. Depending on their expertise in training, these developers may provide all the training or, more likely, train in-house, computer-literate trainers, who in turn will train human resources users. If HRSC or other in-house staff provide training, they should begin with pilot training sessions to give themselves and others familiar with the HRMS an opportunity to refine their presentations.

Training Media

Lectures, videotapes, slides, tutorials, and hands-on experience are all appropriate training approaches. Which are most effective at achieving the objectives of the specific training?

Studies prove that a hands-on approach greatly enhances learning. In the case of the HRMS, this approach may be some form of computer-based training (CBT). CBT serves a valuable role because HRMS user training must contain a reasonable amount of hands-on experience. However, trainers should make personal assistance available as required. People do not learn about computer systems from computers alone; they also need human interaction.

First-time computer users particularly need this interaction. Group training with an instructor often meets this need. Once users begin to feel comfortable with the idea of working with a computer, they are ready for CBT.

Regardless of the principal training media used, they should include printed materials such as concept summaries, sample screens, sample source documents, preprinted forms, report samples, flowcharts, and lists of common commands. Trainers and HRSC staff should prepare these materials. Qualities of successful training materials include completeness, organization, clarity, cross-referencing, indexing, prompts, and help functions.

Trainers must make sure materials are clear, concise, and comprehensive. They can prepare printed material in packets ahead of time and distribute them prior to the session. All materials should include a date or version number. If printed material is extensive, a loose-leaf format can facilitate updating.

Training Process

Selecting the right time and place for training is as critical to its success as is selecting the appropriate content. This scheduling should allow time for presentations, hands-on work, and a forum for answering questions, as well as time for integrating the training schedule into the daily routine. Group meetings should follow general procedures, including participant name tags, coffee and stretch breaks, beginning the session with a summary of what will follow, and pertinent interaction.

In many ways, the most important part of any training program is not what trainers present but what trainees ask. Trainees should be told from the outset that they will have an opportunity to ask questions that may arise either in formal training sessions or when they return to their normal work assignments.

Evaluating Training

To make sure future training is as responsive as possible, present training should be evaluated. At the end of each training session, students should be given an opportunity to complete an evaluation form. Particularly in pilot training sessions, trainers should note which topics prompted the most questions or misinterpretations. As appropriate, training plans should be refined and presentations revised to include clearer instruction.

A training session evaluation form should include questions that explore the extent to which participants found the session interesting, valuable, and relevant to their jobs. Trainees also should evaluate the material, pace, and individual trainers.

Similarly, it is a good idea to solicit evaluations from the supervisors of employees who have undergone training. Did the employees learn what they needed to know to perform their functions with the new HRMS? Do the supervisors feel that they themselves have gained appropriate knowledge about these functions?

Finally, input from in-house and external offices, divisions, or regions that receive the output of the individuals who have received the training can be valuable. Is material complete and accurate? Do problems appear in certain types of operations with significant frequency?

The HRSC staff can use this information to refine and revise the training program as necessary. Depending on the desired improvement, staff may consider adjusting the type of information covered, priorities of various topics, hands-on activities, different media, and ongoing support.

Acceptance Testing

The HRMS project team must complete performance testing before making a final payment to the vendor or developer and before releasing technical staff to other assignments. The team should develop a testing scheme that involves two levels of testing—controlled testing (which uses sample data) and parallel testing (which uses the actual data base and compares results with those produced by the old system). The team should identify appropriate staff to run each set of tests and check the results.

Controlled Testing

After the completion of HRMS installation, initial modifications, and interfaces, but before the actual data conversion takes place, the team should test the new HRMS with controlled data. This process basically involves the following steps:

- Entering user-developed data into the new system
- Generating output (reports, screens, and error messages)
- Comparing the output to predetermined results

A Cynic's View of the Phases of a Project

1. Enthusiasm
2. Disillusionment
3. Panic
4. Search for the guilty
5. Punishment of the innocent
6. Praise and honors for the nonparticipants

This procedure should reveal any bugs in the system. If it uncovers any problems, technical staff (or the vendor) should correct these before implementation proceeds. The project team should repeat the controlled testing until the test results reveal no major problems. These results validate the storage and processing functions of the system.

Controlled testing involves a series of tests. First, HRSC staff should test separate programs within the HRMS to ensure their reliability—that is, that they achieve the same end result each time. Then the staff should test each module separately to validate the modules—that is, that they process transactions accurately. Finally, the staff should test the entire HRMS to ensure that all the pieces work together.

The second phase of controlled testing involves entering intentionally incorrect data through the edit and validation process. This test validates that the system traps errors instead of entering them into the data base.

Users should take some responsibility for designing, developing, and implementing the controlled tests. This accomplishes several objectives besides validating the system. First, the users have an opportunity to practice what they have learned in training and thus become more comfortable using the system. Second, the test reassures users that the HRMS functions correctly. The credibility of the new system is very important at this stage.

Parallel Testing

After successful controlled testing, data conversion takes place. One last step remains—the final test the HRMS must pass before "going live." This is called a parallel test. After conversion is complete, the new HRMS data base contains live data. Running parallel involves processing the same set of data in both the old and the new systems to generate output for comparison purposes. When the two systems produce the same results consistently, parallel testing can end. Parallel testing generates a higher confidence level in both the processing and the output of the new HRMS.

Many users have the misconception that parallel testing means that the two systems must operate concurrently. Concurrent testing is not necessary, as long as the two systems process the same data using the same sets of input and output parameters. Some operations schedule nonconcurrent testing during off-hours, when staff can halt live data entry and system consolidation operations. In fact, because a parallel test should duplicate the output of the old system, staff can actually run the test on the new HRMS as many times as are necessary to prove the reliability and validity of the new system. If payroll is involved, staff should run a parallel test specifically to ensure that data are processed in the required format and on time.

Conducting a parallel test requires a lot of careful planning. The key steps to a successful parallel operation are as follows:

- Arrange for enough staff to operate, support, and test both systems for at least one production cycle, possibly more.
- Compress the test to validate month-end, quarter-end, and year-end cycles.
- Identify the specific fields, reports, and totals to be compared.
- Develop a manual scheme or automated routine to reconcile the results of the two production runs.
- Make plans to fine-tune the flow of input to and output from the new HRMS.
- Establish benchmarks that the new HRMS must meet in order to be accepted.

No hard and fast rules apply about the length of time a system should run parallel. In fact, some organizations do not run parallel tests at all. One simple rule of thumb is that parallel testing should continue until users, HRSC staff, and management are comfortable with and confident about the new HRMS. The easiest way to establish consensus about parallel testing is to establish benchmarks before testing begins—that is, to agree on critical success factors or other measures that will indicate the HRMS has been accepted.

User Support

As the system becomes operational, effective user support demands two types of awareness: The HRSC must understand users, and users must know of the HRSC.

Knowing User Skills

Users may need guidance in exploring a new system's basic functions and features. As an HRMS grows and becomes more mature, it continues to attract new users as continuing or technically sophisticated users gain important experience. As the number and sophistication of users expand, so do their maintenance needs. By being aware of the maturity levels of users, HRSC staff can provide the training, tools, and computer capabilities that best suit them. Users fall into several levels of maturity: novices, practitioners, experts, and trailblazers (figure 9–8).

- *Novices* interact with the HRMS at the transaction or simple query level. They may not be total beginners in human resources, but they are gen-

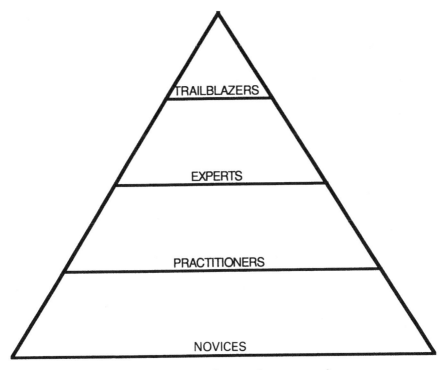

Figure 9–8. Four phases of user maturity.

erally new to computers and HRMS applications. To the extent that novices primarily perform input transactions, they rely heavily on menus, prompts, and edits. Their queries usually involve simply locating a single employee record.

- *Practitioners* are human resources staff who can proceed independently with standard input and can use summary reports with only occasional reference to detail listings and paper backup. Interaction with the HRMS occurs not only at the transaction level but also at the report level. These people know how and when to request and schedule reports and may initiate ad hoc queries.

- *Experts* are the key users of the HRMS. In general terms, they understand complex human resources and IS issues, so they can use data and available software tools with limited assistance from the HRSC. Experts may use ad hoc query tools to solve problems proactively. They also may specify and control service requests.

- *Trailblazers* are human resources staff who use ad hoc retrieval tools, conduct their own development projects, stretch the limits of the HRMS, and discover creative ways of using human resources data. Their focus is both analytical and business oriented. Trailblazers make the most productive use of the HRMS by leveraging its data with non–human resources data and other systems.

By staying in touch with levels of user maturity, the HRSC can make appropriate training and support decisions regarding both the original system and enhancements. For instance, novices need more step-by-step instruction, more reassurance, and easy access to immediate support. CBT is more appropriate for and works best with experts and practitioners. Without refreshers and attempts to have human resources users expand their capabilities in the HRMS arena, use of the system soon peaks, experts and trailblazers lose interest, and the return on the HRMS investment may level off prematurely.

The HRSC staff should expect to handle an extraordinary number of inquiries in the first few weeks and months following implementation. Some questions will be disturbing because they point out problems not discovered during design or implementation. Other questions will be merely annoying, as users tend to ask questions that have been answered in documentation or training already provided. HRSC staff should bear in mind that users will accept the system at different rates. The HRSC must help users not only work with the system but also become comfortable with it.

Informing Users About the HRSC

Soon after human resources and other users leave the training program, they will probably begin using the new HRMS. Particularly in the early weeks, people are bound to make mistakes, misinterpret instructions, and encounter confusing situations. Getting staff through these first daunting encounters often makes the difference between whether they resent or embrace the new system. The key to staff confidence is setting up ongoing support ahead of time and making sure people know how to get help when they need it.

The HRMS manager should make sure that everyone who works with the system knows what to do if a problem arises. Employees should know how to use documentation properly and how and when to use available on-line help. Every workstation should have a written description of problem-solving resources. Overall, users need to know whom to contact if they have a problem. Additional strategies and techniques for developing a positive, effective relationship between users and the HRSC are discussed in chapter 11.

Glossary

Acceptance testing A set of data and system tests performed on a new computer system to validate the storage, processing, and output functions of the system. Acceptance testing usually involves two forms of testing—controlled and parallel.

Controlled testing   A set of data manipulation tests performed on a new computer system to make sure the system performs as specified. This process includes tests of representative commands, operations, and edit and validation routines. These tests are performed on a sample data set rather than on the complete data base.

Conversion   The process of transferring data from an old system into a format that a new system can read. Conversion often involves both automated data transfer and manual data entry. Conversion may involve custom programming to accommodate the data format and arrangement needs of the new system.

Disaster recovery plan   A plan for coping with a significant loss of computer data or capability that may occur because of a natural disaster or human action.

Expert   A user with extensive computer and HRMS experience who can utilize a wide array of data and software tools with little technical assistance. Experts may perform complex, interdisciplinary data analyses using the system's full capabilities and are capable of leading HRMS projects.

Installation   The part of the implementation process that includes physically connecting the hardware (if applicable) and loading the software into the computer's CPU.

IS auditor   This function has responsibility for ensuring that the system operates as specified, particularly with respect to control totals, record counts, and transaction volumes.

Modification   A change made to software after its installation. Modifications during the implementation phase may include correction of programming errors and refinement of system functions through programming enhancements.

Novice   A user who has no or little previous computer or HRMS experience but may have considerable human resources experience. A novice primarily performs input transactions and simple queries and uses standard reports.

Parallel testing   A set of data manipulation tests used to validate that a new computer system handles data as accurately as the old system it is replacing. During parallel testing, both systems use the actual HRMS data base and perform identical functions; evaluators then compare the results from both systems.

Practitioner   A user with limited computer and HRMS expertise who can usually handle standard and ad hoc reporting tasks independently. A practitioner may request and schedule reports and even construct special queries.

Procedures manual   An instructional document written to aid staff in performing tasks. Sometimes the document covers the specific manual activities within a computer-based operation.

Prototype   A working system developed quickly and inexpensively to evaluate alternatives.

Prototyping   In computer terms, a specialized development modeling technique used to create working (sometimes trial) versions of system alternatives. Uses powerful applications software development tools, such as 4GLs.

Team training Training given to HRMS project team members and HRSC staff about the system. Performing such training before the system becomes operational allows team members to establish their role as HRMS resources for other users.

Trailblazer A user with advanced computer and HRMS experience who can use existing system functions and features to produce new results. Trailblazers may conduct their own development projects using the most advanced software tools available. They generally work best alone.

Discussion Points

1. Describe the main steps in HRMS implementation.
2. In what ways might the human resources department and IS have different priorities that affect HRMS implementation?
3. What steps are involved in software installation?
4. Under what circumstances may prototyping be more appropriate than traditional system implementation methodologies?
5. What are the major goals in HRMS training?
6. What different types of users need training? In what ways should their training differ?
7. Why is establishment of an HRSC integral to the implementation process?
8. Describe the objectives and activities of the various types of system testing and how they differ from each other.

Further Reading

Anderson, Kirk J. "Controlling Human Resource Costs: The Role of HR Systems." *Human Resource Systems Management Bulletin*, September 1987.
Bernstein, Amy. "Shortcut to System Design." *Business Computer Systems*, June 1985.
Burns, Peggy. "Seizing the Information Center Opportunity." *Infosystems*, August 1984.
Coch, L., and J.R.P. French, Jr. "Overcoming Resistance to Change." *Human Relations*, Volume 1, 1948.
DeMarco, Tom. *Structured Analysis and Systems Specification.* Englewood Cliffs, NJ: Prentice-Hall, 1979.
Dickie, R. James. "Implementation Demands a Personal Approach." *Datamation*, February 1984.
Eason, Emily. "Implementing HRIS: What Now?, Part I" HRSP Update, Fall/Winter 1989.
———. "Implementing HRIS: What Now?, Part II" *HRSP Update*, Spring/Summer 1990.

Enderle, A. "For the Record: Personal Software." *Personal Computing*, December 1983.

Fay, C.H. "Educating Old and New HR Managers." *Computers in Personnel*, Summer 1988.

Harrison, Ralph. "Prototyping and the Systems Development Lifecycle." *Journal of Systems Management*, August 1985.

Head, Robert. "Information Resource Center: A New Force in End-User Computing." *Journal of Systems Management*, February 1985.

Horsfield, Debra. "Homegrown Documentation." *Computers in Personnel*, Summer 1987.

Howard, G.S., and G.J. Weinroth. "Users, Complaints: Information System Problems from the User's Perspective." *Journal of Systems Management*, May 1987.

Kutnick, Paul. "Information Center Success Hinges on 10 Important Axioms." *Data Management*, November 1985.

Morse, Jane, and Laurence Chait. "In Info Center, the User Always Comes First." *Data Management*, February 1984.

Nikkel, Deborah. "HRIS Implementation: A Systematic Approach." *Personnel*, February 1985.

O'Dell, Peter. "Design: Do-It-Yourself Systems." *Computer Decisions*, May 1985.

Pasquelletto, Joe. "Creating an Effective HRIC: Beyond Data Management." *HRSP Review*, Spring 1987.

Personal Privacy in an Information Society: The Report of the Privacy Protection Study Commission. Washington: U.S. Government Printing Office, 1977.

Petruzzelli, Vito G. "The Info Center: A Powerful Tool For Modern Times." *Data Management*, February 1984.

Walker, Alfred J. *HRIS Development: A Project Team Guide to Building an Effective Personnel Information System*. New York: Von Nostrand Reinhold, 1982.

Witkin, Elliot. "Training for Computer Literacy." *HRSP Review*, Spring 1988.

10

Maintaining and Enhancing an HRMS

> It is the machines that make life complicated, at the same time they impose on it a high tempo.
> —Carl Lotus Becker

Maintenance requests flow into the HRSC even before the HRMS becomes operational. Bugs, new modules, and major enhancements all bring their own proponents, costs, and other considerations. To keep up with expanding user needs, the changing business climate, and government regulations, a responsive HRMS must undergo periodic evaluation and evolution. By planning and evaluating maintenance options, the HRSC can maximize the life expectancy of the HRMS. Lack of proper maintenance diminishes the system's useful life considerably. Guidelines for successful maintenance have as much impact on the success of the HRMS as do guidelines for development. Maintenance guidelines cover recognizing when system modification is necessary, what kinds of modifications to make, and how to execute modifications smoothly.

Defining Maintenance

In an HRMS, maintenance refers primarily to software maintenance rather than hardware maintenance. (Hardware maintenance is more straightforward and often takes place under contract with the equipment vendor or an outside maintenance organization. This is discussed in chapter 5.) Even software maintenance means different things to different people. Some of these meanings follow:

- Technical changes that do not alter HRMS functions and features
- Correcting bugs in programs or data
- Altering data definitions (field sizes, types, and codes)
- Modifying a system already in production
- Fine-tuning a system so that it will run faster
- Major enhancements such as the addition of new modules

The following broad definition encompasses most of these changes: Maintenance refers to any changes made to the HRMS after the system becomes operational and has been accepted by users.

Types of Maintenance

In the book *Software Maintenance Management*, Lientz and Swanson identify three categories of maintenance—corrective, adaptive, and perfective.

Corrective maintenance refers to fixing problems that prevent the system from working the way designers and users intended it to work. These bugs may stem from incorrect design (such as may occur from an improper or incomplete requirements definition), development (such as poor coding), or implementation. In the postoperational state, bugs are mistakes that did not appear in system testing performed during implementation. As shown in figure 10–2, more than half of all bugs result from a poor definition of requirements. Most corrective maintenance takes place relatively early in the HRMS development cycle, while the system is still growing and users are learning to use it in the real world of human resources and corporate needs.

Adaptive maintenance refers to modifications to the HRMS in response to changes in technology, government regulations, or external forces, such as fixes or new system releases from the vendor. Adaptive maintenance may add

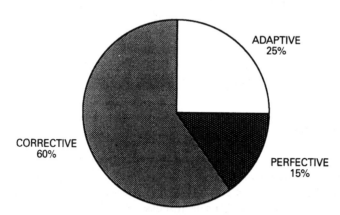

Figure 10–1. Types of maintenance. In a well-planned system, corrective maintenance can require a smaller proportion of maintenance resources than adaptive and perfective work. In such situations, maintenance helps the system meet an increasing number of human resources needs as the HRMS grows and matures.
(Source: Bennett P. Lientz and E. Burton Swansen, *Software Maintenance Management*, Addison-Wesley, 1980. Reprinted with permission.)

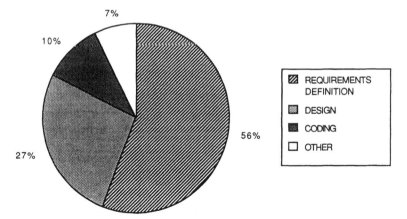

7%

10%

27%

56%

- ▨ REQUIREMENTS DEFINITION
- ▦ DESIGN
- ■ CODING
- ☐ OTHER

Figure 10–2. Sources of problems requiring corrective maintenance. In a typical system, more than half of all the bugs result from a poor definition of requirements. (Source: Tom DeMarco, *Structured Analysis and System Specification,* **Yourdon Press, 1979. Reprinted with permission.)**

entirely new functions to the system or fine-tune existing capabilities and performance criteria. Examples include increasing the size of the zip code field from five to nine characters, changing certain calculations and reports to meet new government regulations, and replacing dedicated terminals with microcomputers. Ideally, adaptive maintenance should not begin until after completion of corrective maintenance. Practically, corrective maintenance is an ongoing process.

Perfective maintenance refers to modifying the system to respond to changes and requests from users and technicians. Users react to what they see in the HRMS and how it works. This reaction generates ideas for improvements or additional functions. Often this maintenance aims to optimize performance. Perfective maintenance includes activities such as adding a new file, adding a new screen or report, and modifying schedules for distributed printing of reports during facility expansion.

Perfective maintenance may take place periodically throughout the HRMS life cycle, but the HRSC should treat it as subordinate to corrective and adaptive maintenance. While the system is still growing, perfective maintenance may include activities that are part of the original long-term HRMS development plan, such as module acquisition and subsystem consolidation. In a mature system, the HRSC accomplishes these tasks as users become more expert with the system and integrate new tools and techniques into HRMS work. They begin to envision and desire improvements, which they ask for as maintenance requests. Eventually, significant increases in the frequency and cost of perfective maintenance, coupled with a decreased capacity for problem solving, may signal that the HRMS has outlived its usefulness.

Approaches to Improvement

Studies indicate that about 60 percent of maintenance requests are for corrective changes, 25 percent for adaptive, and 15 percent for perfective. With either adaptive or perfective maintenance, the HRSC may address a need for HRMS improvement in one of several ways:

- Enhance the existing HRMS. This involves implementing software changes that make the system work better without adding new programs or human resources functions. Examples of common enhancements include improving system response time, changing field size, converting from batch to on-line processing, and adding more sophisticated interfaces such as mainframe-to-micro downloading or distributed processing.
- Add a module. In some cases, the easiest, fastest, and best solution is a software package that adds a new human resources function. Such modules might add features such as succession planning, self-insurance analysis, flexible benefits, or advanced graphics capabilities. This form of maintenance is really an extension of the original implementation process, adding functions perhaps originally included in the HRMS master design but scheduled for inclusion after completion of the original implementation.
- Implement systems developed or acquired by users. Users may create improvements through use of a 4GL, or they may deal directly with vendors to acquire software revisions that operate independently of the HRMS. This option obviously requires good communication between the HRSC and users.

Keys to Successful Maintenance

To control the escalating costs of maintenance, the HRSC must take a proactive approach to managing maintenance activities. The HRMS needs a maintenance strategy. That strategy should include planning for maintenance throughout the life of the HRMS from system acquisition to eventual replacement.

Maintainability

The most cost-effective, least painful approach to minimizing maintenance yet maximizing system performance and life span is to create an HRMS that re-

Minimizing the Disruption
of Maintenance

The following steps can help minimize the disruptions that maintenance activities cause ongoing HRMS and human resources operations:

- Use a scheduled rather than an on-demand approach to maintenance scheduling.
- Give all affected staffs—human resources, IS, and HRSC—plenty of notice of maintenance activities.
- Schedule the maintenance for less busv periods, when other staff are less likely to contend for available resources.
- Provide the clearest possible documentation and training concerning the changes to all users and technicians affected by them.

---

quires as little maintenance as possible and is easy to modify when maintenance becomes necessary. This is easier said than done. A maintainable HRMS has the following characteristics:

- Is easy to understand
- Operates reliably
- Operates efficiently
- Has good documentation
- Is easy to test
- Is easy to modify
- Is programmed in structured and modular code
- Incorporates 4GL and data base management technology

In-House Systems. Here are some suggestions on how an in-house HRMS development team can build in maintainability:

- Design the HRMS with the aforementioned characteristics of maintainability in mind. Set maintenance objectives and guidelines.
- Involve maintenance staff during design to consult on maintainable features and how to build them into the HRMS.
- Keep a development log. Include HRMS development pathways, decision-making strategies, rationales for specific designs, errors uncovered, and actions taken to correct errors. Maintenance staff may work more effectively if they review this log periodically.

- Provide thorough, concise, and understandable HRMS documentation. The documentation format should provide for easy documentation modification. (For more information on documentation, see chapter 4.)
- Involve maintenance staff during all testing procedures. Solicit evaluation of the completed system from a maintenance perspective. Before declaring the HRMS acceptable, the project team should get approval from the maintenance staff.

Vendor Systems. Purchasing an HRMS from a vendor presents different maintenance challenges. The project team has much less flexibility to build in maintainability because the vendor has developed a generic system. When purchasing an HRMS from a vendor, the following steps help ensure system maintainability:

- Set specific measurable maintenance criteria and benchmarks and build these into the RFP and vendor evaluation.
- Have the vendor specifically address in what ways this HRMS is built to ease future maintenance. Questions to ask include the following:

  In what language is the HRMS written? Is it structured? Modular?

  What kind of data base architecture does the HRMS use?

  Are user exits built into the HRMS to facilitate attaching company-developed modules to it?

  How many tables must staff maintain? To which data calculations does each relate?

  Are standard reports hard coded, or are they developed using a report generator?

- Based on the answers to such questions, investigate the development of this HRMS—its design, language, structure, modularity, and other technical aspects that affect maintenance.
- Evaluate the vendor's maintenance program. This includes how the vendor decides on enhancement priorities, how the technical staff implement these enhancements, the frequency of updates, and the cost of enhancements.
- Using maintenance benchmarks (to be discussed later in this chapter), estimate and affix a cost to any improvements required to bring the package in line with the maintenance requirements. Add to these costs the purchase price and implementation estimates to determine actual costs for this package.
- Make maintenance a contract issue by specifying what maintenance service the department expects and at what price.

Maintenance Policies and Procedures

To run smoothly, a maintenance management system needs consistent policies and procedures with which all relevant users are familiar. Organizations should try to involve not only maintenance staff but also the rest of the HRSC, IS, and human resources staff in the formation of those policies. Here are some issues to consider.

Maintenance Request and Acceptance Process. The HRSC should establish and publicize a detailed maintenance request and acceptance process. Most HRSC provide users with *maintenance or service request forms.* These forms usually include the requested change, cost center or budget authorizing the work, staff assigned to perform the work, chargebacks, other systems or modules affected, critical impact, and expected completion date.

Maintenance procedures should spell out clearly who has responsibility and accountability for specifying, reviewing, and evaluating proposed projects, as well as decisions about which projects to support. Such responsibility can rest with a manager of systems maintenance (usually part of the IS function) or with a maintenance committee or group that meets on a periodic basis and includes representatives from affected human resources functions, the HRSC, and IS. The HRSC should encourage users who initiate significant maintenance requests to make complete presentations and participate fully in group decisions.

Maintenance policies must identify the criteria that the HRSC will use to prioritize and evaluate maintenance requests including cost-benefit-value analysis requirements, standards for performance and compatibility, impact on production systems, and other relevant factors. The evaluation process itself is discussed later in this chapter in the section "Accomplishing Maintenance."

Upon approval of the request, the affected user (manager) and the HRSC complete and authorize a *maintenance contract* similar in content to the service request form. It includes scope of work, responsibilities of each party, and schedule.

Scheduling Considerations. Maintenance policy may dictate the frequency with which the HRSC will perform maintenance or cycles in which it may occur. It may indicate periods within the business year when the HRSC should avoid performing maintenance in order to minimize interference with normal operations. It also may indicate a time limit by which the HRSC should address and resolve a request.

Service Agreements. Many IS groups base many of their maintenance activities on service agreements. A service agreement is an arrangement, or contract, between the user community (human resources management, representing human resources users) and the HRSC that defines the responsibilities of each party. An agreement may include the following issues:

- Performance objectives
- Performance standards
- Tools for tracking and measuring performance
- System for reporting on performance

Standards for the HRSC may include the following:

- Accuracy level of standard reports
- Delivery schedules for HRSC reports
- Turnaround times by request type
- Quality of performance

Standards for users may include the following:

- Accuracy and timing of input
- Lead time for special requests
- Completeness of specifications for requests
- Maintenance of tables
- Security and access control

Service agreements are of the greatest value in the period immediately following start-up because they can help the HRMS get off on the right foot before inefficient or unproductive patterns become ingrained. Annual adjustments can reflect environmental, developmental, and financial changes. Service agreements also may reference departmental chargebacks.

A properly administered service agreement benefits both users and systems staff because it does the following:

- Promotes better services, with improved timing, results, and accuracy
- Fosters more realistic expectations
- Helps track and predict user demands
- Establishes agreement on priorities
- Aids production scheduling
- Establishes total performance over time
- Provides management with summary information

The degree of compliance with the service agreement offers a valuable perspective on how successfully the maintenance apparatus is performing. Compliance can be a performance measurement tool for the HRSC and the HRMS.

Logs. Every HRMS should keep complete and adequate maintenance and service logs. Such logs list every maintenance request, activity, problem, and resolution. A log page form solicits information such as the following:

- Request date
- Request summary
- Start and completion dates
- Staff assigned to maintenance item
- Activities performed
- Hours required to complete maintenance
- Effect on operations during maintenance
- Effect on system after completion
- Effect on human resources after completion

Maintenance logs allow future generations of HRSC staff to learn from earlier triumphs and failures, to analyze trends, and to understand the details of the HRMS. Such logs can provide hints about system health. As a system begins to decline, the number of maintenance requests will increase, types of maintenance requests will shift, mean time to make changes will increase, and number of staff and other cost considerations will increase.

Chargebacks. Many HRSCs use chargebacks as part of the maintenance system. Charging back maintenance costs to users provides numerous benefits, including the following:

- Users become more aware of maintenance costs.
- Management recognizes the value of maintenance.
- The HRSC controls unnecessary requests.
- Users tend to be more serious about their priorities.

Audits. Audits of HRMS performance help the HRSC staff and users discover which aspects of an HRMS need maintenance, as well as which are working satisfactorily. Such audits are discussed in detail later in this chapter. Several features of audits relate to HRMS maintenance policies:

- As appropriate, they should include participation by maintenance staff.
- Maintenance staff responsibilities include a review audit of reports to develop plans for appropriate HRMS improvements that maintenance could provide.
- These audits should include specific review of maintenance activities. If they do not, the HRSC should include in its policies and procedures a special maintenance audit mechanism that calls for periodic audits.

A Maintenance Control Philosophy

Even before the HRMS becomes operational, the HRSC must make a strategic decision about who controls and will be responsible for HRMS maintenance. Essentially, four types of control options exist—rigid, flexible, phased, and user.

Rigid Control. This strategy implies an inflexible HRMS with no discretionary changes allowed. Vendors of packaged systems used to impose this strategy. Now that sophisticated tools for making modifications have become more available, however, vendors seldom find it practical to offer a rigid system that users cannot modify. When rigid controls are practical and desirable, this type of arrangement may permit users to implement table modifications, data base modifications, and routines that trigger user exits. However, all program code changes come from the vendor or other service provider. Modifying core system code against vendor instructions may lead to problems elsewhere in the system. Vendors warn that such tampering may invalidate the maintenance contract and render the HRMS incapable of accepting vendor-supplied changes. Before entering into contracts with vendors, the HRMS project manager should check maintenance and enhancement control provisions carefully. The manager should make sure that the agreement does not conflict with what users can accept.

Flexible Control. This strategy supports the view that the HRMS will be flexible and adaptable to support the human resources community for as long as possible. The HRSC determines and administers criteria for evaluating most maintenance requests. This approach often works well, but the HRSC must establish return on investment (ROI) criteria to keep demands for maintenance at a reasonable level. As with rigid control, flexible control can create problems when maintaining a vendor-supplied system, particularly because once staff make changes to one system version, they also may have to work them into newer versions.

Phased Control. This strategy integrates the two previous approaches. Initially, control may be rigid and the HRSC may restrict virtually all enhancements. As users gain experience with the HRMS, however, control may relax.

User Control. This strategy recognizes the user community as the consumer and allows users to help determine maintenance approaches. It may even include making users accountable for part of the maintenance load. This approach works best in organizations that have an experienced user community, a professional information center (discussed in chapter 11), and a full array of maintenance tools. These tools should include data base technology, 4GLs, data dictionaries, and screen editors. The HRSC still must serve as control

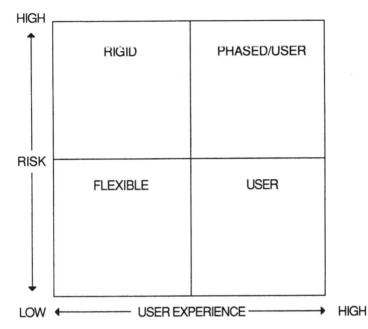

Figure 10–3. Factors in selecting a maintenance control scheme. HRMS management should decide how much system control users have and how much the HRSC and vendor have. To do so, they must consider the experience level of users and the risk level they are willing to accept. For instance, rigid control keeps inexperienced users from impeding the system, but it may limit system usefulness.

point for maintenance activities and standards, to ensure that projects do not conflict with the needs of other users or affect the system negatively.

The appropriate forms of control for various user circumstances are shown in figure 10–3. Depending on which strategy the HRSC selects, maintenance management may range from loading vendor-supplied software containing only changes to establishing an organization charged with responsibility for a full range of maintenance activities. By consciously establishing a control philosophy, the HRSC can better appropriate, schedule, and use needed resources for maintenance. These resources include the following:

- Maintenance tools and techniques
- Standards for HRMS components
- Adequate maintenance budget
- Staff assignments for maintenance responsibilities

- Maintenance policies and procedures
- Maintenance evaluation mechanisms

Useful Tools for Maintainability

Tools for maintainability are of several types: technical tools to help keep maintenance flexible and fast and organizational processes and techniques to help HRSC staff and users understand the system and each other. The greater the extent to which the HRMS and HRSC staff use such tools, the more cost-efficient and effective service the system can provide.

Fourth-Generation Languages. 4GLs, described in more detail in chapters 9 and 22, are English-like programming languages. Many organizations that choose systems written in a 4GL do so precisely because they can use its features to improve the maintenance performance of HRMS staff and users. 4GLs increase the ease with which users can create their own enhancements, thus providing more options for answering maintenance requests.

4GL report and prototype development takes place more quickly and at less cost than changing or adding a routine in one of the procedural 3GL languages such as COBOL, FORTRAN, or BASIC. Additionally, use of a 4GL reduces the danger of contaminating core HRMS data. So great is the contribution of 4GLs to system maintainability that those integrated into system design can promote the growth of the system and extend its useful life.

Data Dictionaries. Data dictionaries, discussed in chapter 4, allow maintenance staff to make changes in field definitions easily, completely, and quickly, without the need for complete system review. They work particularly well in systems that also use a 4GL philosophy. In fact, a data dictionary is generally a major component of a 4GL.

Local Area Networks. A LAN improves the HRMS maintenance process in several ways. First, it gives staff greater flexibility about the computer assigned to perform maintenance, which minimizes interference with ongoing, routine human resources work. With a network, the addition of new workstations involves less hardware and software expense than in a stand-alone environment. A LAN also eases the process of transferring corrections, enhancements, and new modules to all affected computers in the system. Indirectly, a LAN aids maintenance by making consistent the data that the HRMS maintains.

Decision Support Systems. Decision support systems (DSS) are interactive, special-purpose applications designed to help users perform management analyses to aid the decision-making process. DSS increase both user and HRMS productivity by tailoring a subset of the HRMS without changing core code and by providing management decision support to users in a more timely and cost-effective manner. Mature HRMS users may use prototyping to create DSS. This powerful technology will continue to evolve, especially with the increased use of 4GLs. DSS are discussed further in chapter 22.

Early Development of the HRSC. Building an HRSC foundation early in the acquisition or development process allows the HRSC staff to grow with the HRMS. Ensuring that the people responsible for the HRMS throughout its life cycle are involved in acquisition minimizes the temptation to cut corners now and let someone else solve the problems later on. This early HRSC involvement often pays long-term dividends to human resources by minimizing system maintenance and gaining credibility and acceptance for the HRMS.

Standards for HRMS Components

For the HRMS to continue functioning effectively as long as possible once modifications are required, HRSC staff and users must maintain the compatibility and quality of both hardware and software components. To do so, the HRSC must have standards to which all modifications must conform. Often IS issues standards, and HRMS standards merely follow suit. Common examples of issues involving standards are listed in the sidebar. Certainly the HRSC and IS must follow these standards when performing modifications and other maintenance on the HRMS or related systems. To get users to comply with these standards, the HRSC can use either a participative approach or a mandate. The HRSC might encourage compliance by making one or more of the following offers:

- Fund the project. Having the HRSC offer to fund the project works well if the HRSC has staff and budget and the project will provide an adequate ROI.
- Offer HRSC support staff. The HRSC can supply qualified staff on an irregular or loan basis to provide consulting and guidance during modifications.
- Provide a hot line service. If the HRSC has limited staff and money, it may offer a phone-in service for queries about the acquisition and implementation effort.
- Provide maintenance support. For systems that meet HRSC standards, the HRSC can offer maintenance support after the initial development effort.

Common Standards Issues

Software

- Data base
- Word processing
- Graphics
- Spreadsheets
- Telecommunications
- Operating systems
- Security

Hardware

- Computers
- Printers
- Plotters
- Telecommunications
- Disk drives
- Mice
- Security

Data Attributes

- Field names
- Fields lengths
- Field types
- Field descriptions
- Codes

Alternatively, the HRSC (or the human resources department) could force the issue by developing a policy that all human resources computer-related projects must meet HRSC standards or that the HRSC will support and maintain only those human resources applications that conform to these standards.

The Maintenance Budget

Effective maintenance needs effective funding. The HRSC and the human resources department must begin budgeting for maintenance by regarding the HRMS as an asset rather than a liability. Many organizations list software systems on the balance sheet as an asset and, therefore, should treat the HRMS as one. In this context, it is easier for management to view maintenance not merely as an expense to minimize but as an opportunity to protect and enhance assets.

An organization will direct the largest proportion of its IS budget toward maintaining operational systems. Of the overall cost of building and operating a system, maintenance generally consumes over 50 percent of resources during the useful life of the HRMS. Some studies place maintenance costs as high as 80 percent.

In the case of an HRMS, maintenance accounts for about two-thirds of system life-cycle costs. The maintenance burden for an HRMS is potentially higher than for other systems for several reasons:

- The human resources department and its system requirements are dynamic. Constant change is the rule rather than the exception. Government regulations often dictate a large proportion of these changes.

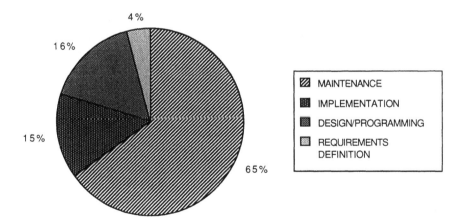

Figure 10–4. **Sources of life-cycle costs. Most system planners and department managers worry more about the expense of planning and implementing a new system than about maintenance. In a typical HRMS, however, maintenance may consume approximately two-thirds of total costs, much more than any of the earlier phases.**

YEAR	HRMS PLANNING	HRMS SOFTWARE	HRMS IMPLEMENTATION	ACTUAL HRMS MAINTENANCE COSTS	BUDGETED FOR HRMS MAINTENANCE	SURPLUS/ SHORTFALL
01	$150,000	$150,000				
02			$225,000			
03			$225,000			
04				$40,000	$100,000	$60,000
05				$60,000	$110,000	$50,000
06				$110,000	$121,000	$11,000
07				$210,000	$133,000	($77,000)
08				$335,000	$146,000	($189,000)
09				$485,000	$161,000	($324,000)
10				$660,000	$177,000	($483,000)
11				$1,100,000	$195,000	($905,000)
	$150,000	$150,000	$450,000	$3,000,000	$1,143,000	($1,857,000)

ASSUMPTIONS:

(1) The HRMS is mainframe-based, written in COBOL

(2) Costs for project planning were at least that of software cost, implementation at least three times software costs, and maintenance costs totaling 80 percent of all lifecycle cost of the HRMS

(3) In addition to vendor maintenance contracts, the HRMS was being changed internally

(4) Staff serviced all or most maintenance requests by changing the HRMS

(5) Management established a fixed budget for maintenance, with adjustments for inflation only

(6) The HRMS has an eight-year useful life

Figure 10–5. Budgeting for lifetime maintenance. As a system attains maturity, maintenance costs rise. If the department continues to use the system after it has exceeded its useful life, the resulting sharp increase in maintenance costs usually results in serious shortfalls in the HRMS budget.
(Source: Computerworld, CW Publishing, Inc. Reprinted with permission.)

- The traditional lack of IS resources for human resources applications leads to compromises in application design and documentation. These compromises, in turn, make maintenance more difficult.

- The lack of IS support leads to a larger backlog of maintenance requests for human resources applications.

- Increased use of microcomputers by human resources imposes additional strains because of the consequent need to maintain hardware and software that are independent of, and sometimes incompatible with, the main system.

In many cases, HRMS management discovers partway through a system's life cycle that insufficient funds have been budgeted to handle HRMS maintenance. In the example shown in figure 10–5, maintenance costs for a standard HRMS are projected over an eight-year period. Assuming a yearly maintenance budget of $100,000, adjusted only for inflation (10 percent per year), maintenance demands soon outstrip available resources. The chart assumes that the HRMS is being altered internally. Vendor-supplied maintenance, enhancements, and new releases also occur periodically. As an HRMS ages, maintenance becomes more costly. The increase stems from the gradual deterioration of the system and its documentation. The system no longer supports users' requirements, which have been constantly changing. Finally, modifications deviate further and further from the original design signaling that the HRMS may be entering its decline stage and will need to be replaced.

Maintenance Staff

Although some need for development staff continues in the period after implementation as the system acquires new modules, maintenance and support soon become the key issues. At this point, the HRSC needs more maintenance staff. Maintenance programmers should be at least as experienced as system developers; they need to understand the big picture of how all the programs work together. The maintenance group should have sufficient experience to grasp the impact of the proposed changes, make the changes without negatively affecting other programs, and learn how to test the updated HRMS and

---

Characteristics of Good Maintainers

Experienced. Exposed to a variety of applications and programming environments.

Flexible. Adapt to difficult or changing styles of coding, user requests, and priorities.

Self-motivated. Initiate and complete work independently after receiving an assignment.

Responsible. Reliably perform assigned tasks in a dependable, timely manner.

Disciplined. Consistent in the performance of duties and disinclined to try haphazard approaches.

Analytical. Apply well-thought-out analyses to problems.

Thorough. Address even the smallest detail to ensure that all aspects of the problem are understood and nothing remains untested.

---

validate the modifications. Perhaps more important, the maintenance department must realize that its job is difficult, important, and often thankless.

In an unfortunate paradox, many management and technical people assign more prestige to development than to maintenance, thus straining the supply and quality of proper maintenance support. Developers and maintenance staff have quite different characteristics. Developers are creative and are frustrated by "editing" someone else's work. Maintainers may or may not lack creativity, but they are willing to adapt to others' methods. The ideal maintainer is profiled in the accompanying sidebar.

When Is Maintenance Needed?

Ideas for HRMS modifications can come from any department. Rather than respond to each request or suggestion in an isolated context, HRSC staff should periodically coordinate all input from users or IS. Sources of input may include evaluations, service requests, user surveys, audits, analyses of changing business and government situations, and technological improvements. HRSC staff can then examine all these suggestions for patterns and conflicts. With this information, implementation of an adequate maintenance decision-making process can take place.

Evaluations

Once the system is operational, the HRMS project team should give everyone a chance to critique the new HRMS. The team should not hesitate to get feedback from anyone involved with the system. The ongoing HRSC staff can keep such communication going even after the initial training period.

In-house Evaluations. The team should solicit evaluations from several functional groups or subgroups of in-house staff—users, human resources functional managers, technical staff, and corporate users of HRMS-generated reports.

One of the most reliable tools for an in-house evaluation is a *forced-choice questionnaire*. Human resources staff who use the HRMS should receive this questionnaire. Department managers, IS staff, and other users who interact with the HRMS on a recurring basis also should be asked to complete the questionnaire. Managers as well as those who do data entry and analyses should participate. These users often provide the most useful feedback.

To make the questionnaire more easily coded, each question should have specific choices. In some cases, multiple choice works well. In others, the questionnaire may provide a range of responses, such as a range from 1 to 5 or lowest to highest in terms of relative agreement or disagreement with a particular statement. Questions should cover the following areas:

- Type of interaction user has with HRMS (data entry, report generation, programming, and so on)
- Human resources function with which user has the most contact (employment, compensation, benefits, and so forth)
- Specific features. For each feature, satisfaction level (poor, adequate, excellent).
- Desired enhancements. For each feature, choose level of importance (unimportant to critical).
- Critical success factors (CSFs) established in planning phase (level of achievement attained and possible measures for each CSF)

Some HRSC staff use *situational analysis* as an in-house evaluative tool. This approach presents a historical or hypothetical scenario to users, then asks them to evaluate the extent to which the existing HRMS could cope with the situation. Different human resources functional groups might work with different scenarios. Scenarios might feature situations such as the following:

- EEO evaluation: If an EEO audit finds employment testing invalidity that could lead to charges of discrimination, could the firm gather and analyze data to demonstrate that discrimination has not occurred (if it indeed has not)?
- Succession planning evaluation: A plant manager becomes disabled. Does the HRMS help identify potential candidates? To what extent could the system help the firm find an appropriate in-house replacement?
- Benefits analysis evaluation: To what extent does the system assist benefits managers in determining the most attractive benefits package for a population predominantly under 40 years of age?

Any evaluation tool needs both developmental and analytical support from a source less attached to the HRMS than the project team. This source could be human resources managers not involved in HRMS development, a special panel not synonymous with the HRMS project team, or an outside consultant experienced in evaluation techniques.

During the evaluation process, people with functional or staff responsibilities (such as marketing, finance, or recruiting) often share ideas with people who have technical responsibilities (applications development, operations, or data base administration). Functional specialists may know what they want to do but not how to do it. Technical people should know what is possible but perhaps not what is important to users. By bringing the perspectives of these two groups together, not only does in-house evaluation increase user understanding of the HRMS, but it also encourages an interdisciplinary approach to HRMS activities and a better overall result.

In addition to problems, users often identify functions that the system has not been designed to provide. The problems may signal a need for corrective maintenance or user-directed enhancements. The HRSC staff should treat functionality improvement requests as perfective maintenance options and manage them accordingly.

Evaluations by a Consultant. Because most users see only a small part of the HRMS, their maintenance ideas tend to be more tactical than strategic. A consultant, viewing the overall system, can make recommendations about strategy. An HRSC that uses a consultant during the implementation process should make sure the consultant's contract includes built-in evaluation components, such as a final report, a final presentation, or both. The contract may specify that the final report include topics such as a maintainability evaluation and recommendations for future enhancements.

A final meeting after completion of system implementation, and perhaps after completion of the in-house evaluation, should be scheduled. Those attending the meeting should discuss which aspects of the project went well and why. They also should discuss processes that did not go as well as expected and how to avert such problems in the future. Most important, the system's future needs and a recommended timetable for such enhancements or changes should be discussed.

Long after completion of implementation, complicated or potentially costly maintenance options may arise on which a consultant may be able to provide valuable insight. In such cases, the HRSC should consider using HRMS consultants who have already worked with the organization. In any event, it is important to select a consultant who is familiar with the industry in which the organization operates. Selection of the consultant should be based on the criteria discussed in chapter 7.

Service Requests

Maintenance or service request forms, if they are part of the maintenance management system, are an ongoing source of maintenance suggestions. As discussed earlier, every human resources staff member, as well as others who work with HRMS data, reports, or hardware, should understand and have easy access to this process.

Soon after implementation of an HRMS that serves basic human resources functions, some staff and line business planners will quickly recognize the added value of computerized career development, succession planning, and job evaluation; they may push the HRSC to expand the data base and provide more decision support capabilities. The HRSC should be responsive to such requests but without overextending its resources. It must never compromise its basic mission of establishing and maintaining the availability and integrity of the data it controls.

User Surveys

Periodic user surveys help promote closer ties between the HRSC and the user communities, which in turn help ensure open communication and trust. Surveys can cover topics such as HRMS issues, strengths, and weaknesses; user satisfaction with the HRMS and HRSC; and changing human resources needs. To obtain useful responses, the survey should include objective benchmarks that help define acceptable and unacceptable levels of satisfaction for specific functional features of the HRMS.

Formal or semiformal user groups, comprising human resources decision makers and chaired by HRSC staff, provide input on system performance that complements and helps the HRSC interpret broad user surveys. Monitoring human resources newsletters also provides valuable insight into developing needs and problems.

Audits

An audit is an organized check of the functions and performance of a system. HRMS should undergo several different types of audits. An HRMS audit evaluates system performance over time in relation to established HRMS standards. HRSC maintenance activities may include three types of HRMS audits: a postimplementation audit, an indicator analysis, and an annual audit. HRMS review also may form part of an overall human resources or electronic data processing (EDP) audit.

Each type of audit provides maintenance-related information. An audit accomplishes several objectives:

- Provides information about how well the system is meeting its specified goals
- Identifies corrective and enhancement maintenance needed; helps HRSC staff pinpoint specific weak points in a general area in which users or technicians have had difficulty
- Evaluates HRMS and HRSC staff performance objectively
- Provides HRSC management with objective data to deal with organizational and IS management

---

Sample Audit Questions

Are individual users or human resources functions responsible for their own data?

Does the HRSC charge back the cost of functions it performs for users?

Have noninformational duties such as data entry been removed from the HRSC?

Does HRSC management receive all the information, at the same time, that other human resources managers do?

Does the HRSC have meaningful input into strategic and annual planning cycles?

Do HRSC staff rotate to other human resources jobs as easily as do compensation, benefits, or employment staff?

Are project priorities established according to published policies?

Are development, enhancement, and other systems decisions based on objective criteria?

Does the HRSC offer business solutions rather than technical excuses?

Are HRSC staff compensated as human resources professionals or according to a separate salary schedule?

- Demonstrates to management, users, and IS that the HRSC is accepting responsibility for HRMS problems and solutions

The team for such audits should include HRSC staff, IS staff, users, and possibly a consultant or vendor representative. By performing and participating in audits, HRSC staff are taking a major step toward HRMS acceptance in the organization's overall business community.

Building an effective audit process begins before implementation. The requirements definition and specifications should include features that build auditability into the system. Features include thorough security and access provisions; well-defined table maintenance procedures; adequate edit and validation rules; and transaction files that track time and operator of each data entry, change, and deletion. During planning and implementation, the HRMS project team should develop audit policies and procedures. Planning should identify when each type of audit should take place and which tasks it will include.

An audit usually includes the following steps:

1. Agree on key factors and evaluation criteria.
2. Solicit input from management and functional users on system performance.
3. Run sample tests and review resulting data, tables, reports, and data dictionaries.
4. Compare results with established criteria.
5. Prepare an audit report and an action plan. Note achievements and deficiencies, include recommendations for correcting any deficiencies, and assign accountability for these actions.
6. Distribute the audit report and action plan, soliciting feedback. Presentations and meetings provide opportunities for users to give their responses.
7. Review the action plan based on responses to the report and plan.
8. Authorize maintenance on the basis of audit results.

Evaluation criteria for an HRMS audit, particularly during the early portion of a system's life cycle, usually address the extent to which the system achieves anticipated benefits, such as CSFs or other specifications established during planning and design phases. Criteria include the following:

- Data accuracy and integrity
- Response times
- Error rates in data entry and on reports
- Information availability
- Security and access levels
- Paperwork flow
- Report responsiveness and accuracy
- Documentation completeness and clarity

As much as possible, the HRSC should quantify these criteria, establishing benchmarks that the system should meet. If the system undergoes maintenance that alters its capabilities, the staff should adjust benchmarks accordingly.

Once planners or HRSC staff establish key evaluation criteria or benchmarks, they must determine the measures of system success: How many new-hire transactions should an operator process every hour? What level of data accuracy does the department require? Planners must develop a preliminary measure for each key item prior to system implementation, although they can amend these measures later.

Technical activities that help assess these factors typically include the following:

- Production of standard and ad hoc reports
- Measurement of system performance at various transaction volume levels (throughput rate, turnaround time, and error rate)
- Review of data dictionary for completeness and accuracy
- Comparison of system components and operations to organizational IS standards
- Review of transaction processing

Post-implementation Audit. The post-implementation audit, also referred to as a postmortem audit, is designed to evaluate the completed HRMS development activity. This early analysis can help refine the HRMS and HRSC before staff waste significant effort. Postmortem audits often identify needed improvements in technical areas and in areas such as documentation and team building. The results of this initial audit form the basis for future system audits.

Everyone pays lip service to the concept of the post-mortem or post-implementation audit, but, few development efforts actually include such audits, except when managers or technicians engage in self-protective behavior to justify system shortcomings. People fail to analyze past performance for several reasons: They prefer to get on with new work rather than rehash old activities, they have other priorities that take precedence over audits, and they do not plan time and resources for the audit task.

To ensure that everyone plans to cooperate with the post-implementation audit, the HRMS project manager should make sure that team members, IS staff, vendors, consultants, functional users, and management staff know that an audit will take place prior to certifying the system as fully operational. Particularly for the post-implementation audit, both HRSC and IS staff play important roles. In fact, each department should keep its own audit notes and records until system acceptance.

Annual Audit. Most systems should have a regular HRMS audit on a semiannual or annual basis. These periodic audits identify maintenance needs and early signs of problems, and they are a valuable first step in keeping the HRMS in line with user needs.

Both annual audits and indicator analysis use a combination of human resources, HRMS, and IS staff. During the annual audits, the HRSC manager should target key individuals in all three areas and educate them in audit techniques and responses. When indicator analysis must take place, the pace of the work and response required is too rapid to allow audit beginners to take significant responsibility.

The audit process requires some extra effort from human resources, HRSC, and IS staff, but most departments find this more acceptable than a reorganization of sporadic and unfocused system planning and evaluation. The resulting measurements and action plans portray HRSC as a potential partner in the overall business area, a dramatic departure from its current image as a technical nonparticipant in both human resources and the organization at large.

Indicator Analysis. As discussed earlier, sound management practice indicates that the HRSC should have a list of objective performance indicators with which to evaluate the HRMS. The HRSC should monitor these indicators on an ongoing basis for signs that the system may need maintenance. A performance level that indicates that a problem may be developing is called a leading indicator; one that indicates that a problem has probably developed is called a

---

Leading and Lagging Indicators

Here are a few examples of situations that indicate that a system is functioning under stress—out of balance with user needs and perhaps its own specifications. Any of these occurrences signals the need for maintenance.

Leading

- System maintenance time increases.
- HRMS downtime increases.
- Vendor enhancements decrease.
- Pirate systems proliferate.

Lagging

- HRMS EDP audit performance declines.
- User survey results are unfavorable.
- Cost/benefit analysis results are unfavorable.
- Data quality is rated below standard.

INDICATOR	PERFORMANCE STANDARD	FIRST LEVEL	SECOND LEVEL	CRITICAL
OnLine Response Time	3 seconds	5 seconds	10 seconds	12 seconds
System Cost/Employee	$5/month	$7/month	$10/month	$12/month
Average Service Request Age	30 days	44 days	60 days	90 days
Maintenance Cost: Total Budget	50%	55%	70%	80%
User Satisfaction Survey (5-point Scale)	3.0	2.8	2.4	2.0
Outside Timesharing Costs	$750/month	$1000/month	$3000/month	$5000/month
New Hire to Database, Elapsed Time	1.0 days	1.5 days	2.5 days	5.0 days
"Standard" Ad Hoc Turnaround	< 1.0 day	1.0 day	1.5 days	2.0 days
"ROI" Required	1.0	2.0	5.0	8.0

Figure 10–6. System performance indicators. Some HRSCs use a multilevel indicator scale. A simple scale might include performance standards, several levels of warning, and a critical or failure level. The HRSC and IC agree on what types of action each warning level may trigger. Critical levels demand immediate attention.
(Source: *Information Center,* Weingarten Publications, Inc. Reprinted with permission.)

lagging indicator. Leading indicators identify a trend, while lagging indicators confirm it. Some leading and lagging HRMS indicators are listed in the accompanying sidebar. Some HRSCs use a quantified, multilevel indicator scale, as shown in figure 10–6. Such systems help staff differentiate between minor and major problems.

The appearance of such an indicator triggers a more thorough examination of the system. This examination is often called a trip-wire audit because it stems from some particular event rather than from a prescheduled plan to perform an audit.

Such audits are designed to spot the early signs of system decline. They differ from other HRMS audits in that they are confined to specific areas of concern. For instance, one analysis may look only at reasons for unacceptably slow responses to requests for ad hoc reports. Certain indicator alerts, such as those identifying problems with data accuracy, signal more pervasive trouble and may trigger a fairly wide-ranging evaluation.

Human Resources Audit. The HRSC manager should leverage the annual HRMS audit process by combining it, whenever possible, with overall human resources audits and organization-wide EDP audits. Both activities are becoming more common in well-managed organizations. Most enlightened human resources departments regularly audit specific functions, such as compensation, benefits, and training, to see that they are responsive to their clients. Part of this responsiveness stems from HRMS performance in areas such as accuracy and timeliness of personnel records and reports.

Human resources audits are similar to HRMS audits in that they evaluate performance against a set of benchmarks. In the modern organization, the human resources audit covers areas that affect or are affected by the HRMS, such as job evaluation, human resources goals, work flow, and policies and procedures. HRSC participation in the human resources audit boosts the group's image within human resources, adds legitimacy to HRMS efforts, and helps ensure that the entire department views human resources issues from a systems perspective. The human resources audit can help identify HRMS maintenance needs in several ways:

- It identifies the level of information support required and obtained by human resources staff.
- It identifies problems and opportunities that may require changes or additional support from the HRMS.
- It highlights human resources goals and strategies that may benefit from HRMS support.
- It pinpoints areas in which non-HRMS changes are appropriate, thereby minimizing the need for modifications of the HRMS.

EDP/IS Audit. This type of audit concentrates on testing how the automated IS deals with factors such as security, changes to the data base, system performance (such as response time), and other technical areas. An EDP/IS audit normally covers technical issues rather than functional needs. However, a problem identified in the timekeeping data entry process, for example, may affect the payroll process. The EDP/IS audit can be part of the HRMS audit or a separate study initiated by corporate EDP/IS or conducted by third-party auditors.

Although computer technology has evolved significantly in the past decade, the types of activities that take place during an EDP/IS audit have remained essentially the same. The tasks performed depend on system complexity, the willingness of EDP/IS audit management to take a proactive role, and the relationship between the EDP/IS and user communities. Audit tasks usually include some, but not all, of those listed in the accompanying sidebar.

Typical EDP/IS Audit Tasks

No single EDP/IS audit will include all the following tasks. The HRSC and EDP/IS should agree on which tasks are most appropriate for the situation, since many are unrelated to the HRMS.

- Normal financial audits related to the operation of the system
- Traditional postimplementation reviews, such as review of controls in an installed application
- Computer installation review (simple review of security and operation procedures; nonpolicy, nonmanagement review)
- Operational audit of EDP/IS department (review of efficiency, effectiveness, adherence to policy, and so forth, of EDP/IS departments; may include EDP management)
- System feasibility studies (participation in or review of hardware/software purchase or make decisions)
- System design control (reviews of controls in a proposed EDP/IS system)
- Project control review of timeliness, cost, and so forth, in an ongoing EDP/IS project
- Use of an audit software package
- Consult with other auditors on use of audit software
- Writing computer programs for auditor usage
- EDP consultant or team member responsible for EDP/IS for non-EDP/IS audit staff
- Design of generalized audit software
- Traditional testing of installed system
- Acceptance testing of new EDP/IS system before installation of system
- Supervise or sign-off on EDP/IS system
- Supervise other EDP/IS auditors
- Conduct training of auditors in EDP/IS topics
- Use of ITF (integrated test facility) approach
- Use of COMBI (COBOL missed branch indicator) or other analyzer of tests

- Use of DBMS (data base management system) as audit tool
- Review of EDP/IS adherence to recent legislation, such as privacy legislation

(Source: Charles R. Litecky and John E. McEnroe, "Job Definitions of Bank EDP Auditors," Magazine of Bank Administration, April 1980.)

Business and Government Changes

HRMS management must stay in close contact with human resources and senior management and remain attuned to internal and external forces that may affect how well the HRMS serves the needs of the firm. Within an organization, a dramatic shift in number of employees, number of facilities, types of insurance or pension benefits, or shifting awareness of workplace health and safety exposures may require revision of the data base or reports or even the addition of new modules.

Changes outside the organization also affect the functionality of the HRMS. The most important external change affecting the HRMS is when government agencies alter their reporting requirements. (The ill-fated and widely publicized Section 89 regulations are an example. Section 89 aimed to increase benefits equity between lower-compensated and higher-compensated employees, but its data analysis and reporting requirements proved so complex that businesses could not comply, and the program was significantly curtailed.) Other factors also arise, such as the onset or outcome of discrimination lawsuits, health and safety liability litigation, a rapid rise in corporate competition, or a shifting economic climate.

New Developments in the HRMS Field

HRMS managers must stay in touch with emerging trends in HRMS-related products, services, and project-management techniques. The best sources of such information are human resources and HRMS journals, networking, and professional conferences. The appendixes at the end of this book list publications and organizations that can help provide such support.

One other way to stay in touch is to consult periodically with a specialist, particularly one who has worked with the firm and its HRMS and therefore knows the system's relevant capabilities, long-range goals, and challenges. A small-scale, relatively inexpensive consultation often can accomplish much if management plans the agenda and participants carefully. An intensive day of meetings and discussions attended by the key players and possibly one or two interviews with high-level managers can pay enormous dividends and capitalize on the consultants' experience. The HRSC should not waste time educating consultants unless it intends to extend the engagement.

Accomplishing Maintenance

Revising a system that involves a significant number of people and a large amount of data can be complicated, involve financial and other risks, and have either marvelous or disastrous consequences for the organization. Although modifications usually are not as traumatic as introducing an entirely new HRMS, successful modifications involve procedures that should be just as carefully designed as those used in the initial system introduction.

As illustrated in figure 10–7, the major steps in performing HRMS maintenance are as follows:

1. Understand the goals and objectives of the HRMS.
2. Evaluate the potential changes.
3. Design the approved changes.
4. Implement these changes.
5. Evaluate maintenance performance.

Understanding the HRMS

The initial step of understanding system goals and objectives usually goes smoothly if maintenance staff have been working on the HRMS for some time. However, the HRSC must take special care with this step in the transition period between implementation and comfortably established routine operations. The HRSC manager should make sure that newly assigned technical staff, consultants, and vendors understand the system as a whole before they begin to work on specific modules or segments.

To coordinate results, the human resources department or the entire organization must standardize hardware, software, and application development tools. Such steps ease system integration and increase the longevity of new applications. The HRSC staff should pay particular attention to promoting this understanding among users who will play decision-making roles in developing or acquiring maintenance enhancement or modules.

As human resources departments become more computer literate, more IS operations are sanctioning users' developing their own modifications. Policy should establish which members of the HRSC or IC will handle user-directed inquiries and enhancements. The HRSC must provide clear opportunities and pathways for training in user development tools and mandate that users who wish to create modifications and new applications attend relevant training sessions, as well as participate in project review processes for any developments.

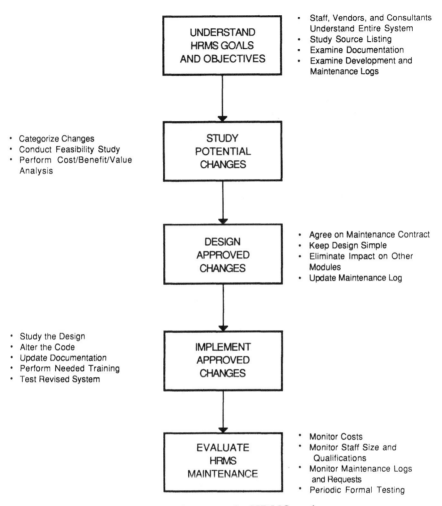

Figure 10–7. Major steps in HRMS maintenance.

Evaluating Potential Changes

To encourage user trust and participation, the HRSC should not ignore user demands for new applications or more support for current ones but try to accommodate them as much as possible. The HRSC should make every effort to respond to maintenance requests in a timely manner. HRSC management cannot and should not grant every request. A system of chargebacks and initial screenings of maintenance requests helps regulate such requests to more reasonable levels by actually billing users for services requested and performed.

As discussed earlier, the HRSC, working with departmental and functional management, should establish criteria for prioritizing requests.

Categorizing Changes. Technical staff should not approach maintenance on a piecemeal basis. For best results, staff should begin every maintenance cycle by collecting all the suggested changes gleaned from evaluations, audits, surveys, business and government changes, professional sources, and related material. The staff then should organize these changes into categories, either by human resources function or by type of technical change required. For example, some changes will optimize the way the HRMS runs; others will fix bugs caused by improper data entry or procedures; and still others will call for an entirely new design and development effort.

Conducting a Feasibility Study. Based on this categorization, staff can develop a conceptual design (or several designs) for carrying out these revisions. Perhaps adding certain types of reports will benefit several departments, but it also will require more storage capacity or different printing requirements. Options may include the following:

- Development by the HRSC, consultants, vendors, or user resources
- Development via 4GLs, prototyping, or both, with or without final transfer to other high-level languages
- Integrating subsystems into the main system
- Altering nonautomated procedures (such as changes in staffing or methodology)
- Replacement of the entire HRMS with a new system
- Maintaining the status quo

The feasibility study should include objectives and CSFs for the maintenance project. It should conclude by comparing options and making recommendations. The feasibility study should include the following for each option:

- Functional design: content and format (data, screens, and reports)
- Technical design: the specifications coding programmers require, such as information on table look-ups, screen revisions, calculations, data relationships, and report generation
- Staffing: who performs the maintenance (HRSC, vendors, consultants, users, or some combination)
- Schedule and timetable: maintenance scheduling following either the on-demand approach or a scheduled approach (The scheduled approach involves grouping maintenance activities, performing several in a specific

period of time, and then waiting until the next scheduled release data to perform further maintenance. This approach has several advantages. Among them are keeping users informed about whether they are using the current HRMS, allowing maintenance staff to contact key users just before beginning work on the batch to find out whether any other changes are required, and reducing duplication of effort.)

- Training and documentation components: revisions that change user interaction with the system; these require updating of both user and technical documentation, as well as some retraining of users
- Cost-benefit-value analysis

Performing a Cost-Benefit-Value Analysis. As the financial portion of the feasibility study, the staff should do a cost-benefit-value analysis for each option. They should consider the extent to which such a revision is consistent with the long-range goals of both the firm and the human resources department. Together with the issues already mentioned in chapter 2 in regard to this type of analysis, the maintenance version should include user and technical expert views on the value of the new or revised function or feature. It also should address the status of the function or feature in terms of technical development. For instance, does it represent leading-edge technology, or is it standard procedure for an expanding HRMS? In addition, this analysis should address the time value of performing this maintenance.

Designing Approved Changes

Based on the cost-benefit-value analysis and the rest of the feasibility study, human resources decision makers and the HRSC team can decide which maintenance options to address. The decision process should lead to the development of a maintenance contract between the user and the HRSC to have as clear an understanding as possible of what is required. The HRSC team can then proceed to develop the programming sequences, including pathways, gateways, tables, and so forth. Staff also design revisions of related manual procedures, documentation, and existing and additional training.

The HRSC should publicize its maintenance efforts. Specifically, the staff should publish maintenance release dates, together with descriptions of the changes they will make. Timely maintenance maximizes the effectiveness of the HRMS and its users and minimizes disruption of ongoing HRMS operations.

Implementing Changes. Implementation of maintenance changes basically follows the same steps as those described in chapter 9. In most regards, modification implementation is simpler and quicker than implementation of the initial system. However, integration has relatively more importance because modifications must work with the ongoing system. Technical staff must test modifications rigorously to ensure that they do not inadvertently cause erroneous processing in any other segment of the system. Testing usually involves both function and integration. This step may include checks of many features, such as security, data portability, and data consistency.

Evaluating Maintenance Operations. Evaluating maintenance may take place on both an ongoing and a periodic basis. On a frequent, ongoing basis, HRSC management should consider how well the HRSC is handling maintenance operations. The following factors deserve monitoring: direct and indirect costs, timeliness, documentation revisions, maintenance staff number and qualifications, number and types of users, and maintenance logs.

More formal periodic evaluation of a maintenance system involves comparing results with a set of goals and quantifiable benchmarks, as well as perhaps using trend analysis to identify negative or positive trends. A checklist of factors to consider in such evaluations is included in the accompanying sidebar. In most cases, information about these factors emerges as part of HRMS and human resources audits, user surveys about maintenance, and maintenance logs.

When Maintenance Is Not Enough

Good management helps extend the productive years of an HRMS to its maximum capacity. However, as with any technical creation, every HRMS eventually outlives its usefulness. Many staff members and managers may have difficulty recognizing and acknowledging this state. The health of the HRSC, and indeed the health of the entire human resources department (and possibly the entire organization), depend on accepting this concept and acting to move beyond the decline stage and into the start-up and growth stages of a new system.

Why Systems Decline

Given enough time, all systems decline. Business needs evolve, new technology emerges, the system has experienced a certain level of change from its original form, and human resources finds that the wonder system of five years ago has become an albatross. If the system has functioned well during its lifetime, no one should point fingers or be disappointed when the HRMS begins a perceptible decline. If such behavior occurs, staff, users, and management will spend more time finding fault and attaching blame than extracting from the HRMS everything it is capable of doing in its old age.

Maintenance Evaluation Checklist

Number and Type of Maintenance Requests

What is the number of HRSC maintenance requests?

_____ Corrective
_____ Adaptive
_____ Perfective

What is the number of maintenance requests for each module?

_____ Corrective
_____ Adaptive
_____ Perfective

Timeliness of Maintenance Requests

How much time are staff spending on maintenance?

_____ Corrective
_____ Adaptive
_____ Perfective

How much time are they spending on the following?

_____ Understanding the HRMS
_____ Designing the change
_____ Making the change
_____ Validating the change

_____ Are maintenance schedules being met?
_____ How long does it take to fix the average failure?
_____ How much time does the HRMS sit inoperative?

HRMS Quality

_____ How many total corrective changes have been made to the HRMS?
_____ How old is the HRMS?
_____ Is the documentation current?
_____ What is the mean time between failures?
_____ What is the accuracy rate of transaction?

How much time and money is being spent on maintenance?

_____ Corrective
_____ Adaptive
_____ Perfective
_____ What are the transaction costs?
_____ What is the failure rate?

Causes of Premature HRMS Decline

Requirements defined improperly

Poor HRMS design

Poor coding

Changes in corporate IS standards

Poor documentation of the HRMS

Dramatic increase in transaction volumes

Changes in human resources organization structure (mergers, divestitures, and so forth)

Human resources user needs change

HRMS not data base driven

HRMS uses old technology (batch processes, tab cards, and so forth)

Vendor goes out of business

Sometimes systems decline prematurely. This can result from poor design, poor maintenance, or unusual or significant changes in outside factors or business conditions. Premature decline has numerous causes, some of which are listed in the accompanying sidebar.

How to Know When Maintenance Is Not Enough

Many tools give HRSC managers information about system performance, such as audits, logs, and user and consultant evaluations. This information allows managers to compare system performance to preset standards or benchmarks. By performing such analysis, HRSC staff can quantitatively differentiate declining systems from thriving ones.

Over time, managers may notice that maintenance resources—both time and dollars—have been increasing. Maintenance requests increase in number, with users increasingly agitating for external system add-ons. Maintenance activities provide less dramatic productivity improvements. Such trends may indicate overall system decline. Managers should look at the overall trend in maintenance to assess the state of the system.

What to Do with a Declining System

Decline does not mean the same thing as failure or defeat, but many managers and technical people do not want to be associated with a system that is regarded as declining. Too often, people ignore the signs or cover them up with quick fixes.

In addition, few HRSC or IS staffs have experience managing HRMS decline effectively. Moreover, because this stage is so uncomfortable, neither consultants nor human resources professionals have written about or researched this subject significantly. Unfortunately, many HRSC managers feel very isolated in the analysis and decision-making processes associated with declining systems.

An appropriate first step is to summarize the accomplishments of the present system. Taking this long view may allow HRSC staff to reestablish among themselves an overall positive attitude toward the system. Armed with this information, they can discuss with the firm's management the possibility of a new HRMS while promoting the conviction that the current system was prudent investment that has paid off well.

A cost-benefit-value analysis that compares the current system with a new system often provides background that is helpful in such discussions. Human resources management staff face several possible replacement strategies:

- Do not replace; let the HRMS collapse (as it inevitably will).
- Replace modules as they reach decline.
- Replace the entire system once it reaches decline.
- Replace parts of the system as cost-benefit-value analysis indicates.
- Replace the entire system as cost-benefit-value analysis indicates.
- Replace the system before decline begins, but diagnose the problems early.

During the decline and replacement process, the HRSC may need to take temporary steps to cope with expanding and changing human resources needs. Such options include expanded use of microcomputers, use of expendable systems (discussed in detail in chapter 22), use of unauthorized, user-developed or user-acquired systems, and time-sharing (which has lost favor, largely because of microcomputers).

New system planning takes a considerable amount of time, often up to two years. During that time, human resources computing needs will continue and grow, so the HRSC should continue to maintain the old system to some extent during some portion of that planning period.

During the bridge to the new system, the HRSC may become dichotomous, supporting both system efforts. Formalizing job assignments, finances, and policies and procedures helps avoid conflict and confusion. During development of the new system, users become impatient; they have difficulty waiting for the promised big improvements. IS staff also need special attention; they may be skeptical and should, therefore, become familiar with the rationale and plans for the new system as early in the process as possible.

Glossary

Adaptive maintenance Modifications of the HRMS made in response to changes in technology, government regulations, or external forces. Adaptive maintenance may add entirely new functions to the system or may fine-tune existing capabilities and performance criteria.

Audit An organized check and validation of the functions and performance of a system. An HRMS audit evaluates HRMS performance over time in relation to established HRMS standards.

Benchmark Objective criteria that help define acceptable and unacceptable levels of satisfaction for specific functions and features of the HRMS. Failure to meet benchmark criteria may trigger a system audit to analyze and correct the problem.

Corporate information center A support function that assists users who work with independent and interdepartmental computing needs. Assists management-level users to be comfortable with microcomputers and workstations.

Corrective maintenance Alterations designed to fix problems that prevent the system from working the way designers and users intended. Problems may stem from errors in design, development, or implementation and may be corrected programmatically, with training, or through changes in documentation.

Indicator analysis An investigation of system performance triggered by the appearance of specific performance indicators signaling that the system may need maintenance.

Lagging indicator An objective performance indicator signaling that the HRMS probably has already developed a problem. Its appearance may trigger an indicator analysis; maintenance often follows.

Leading indicator An objective performance indicator signaling that the HRMS probably will develop a problem if maintenance is not performed. Its appearance may trigger an indicator analysis; maintenance often follows.

Maintenance Planning, programming, documentation, training, and other activities designed to keep a computer system in line with its specifications and continuing to meet the needs of its users. Maintenance related to software may range from debugging programs to developing new modules.

Perfective maintenance Modifying a computer system in response to changes and requests from users and technicians with the aim of optimizing performance by improving or adding to the functions the system can perform.

Post-implementation audit The process of systematically evaluating system performance after implementation. An audit involves following particular procedures, analyzing results, and soliciting or accepting feedback from users. The results of this audit become the basis for further maintenance activities.

Discussion Points

1. What are the three types of maintenance? How do they differ from each other?
2. In what ways do decisions made during system acquisition or development influence system maintainability?
3. What techniques can an HRSC use to maintain compatibility between the HRMS and user enhancements?
4. What are the three types of HRMS audit? What types of issues might each be most likely to monitor effectively?
5. In what ways does implementation of enhancements usually differ from implementation of the main HRMS?
6. What steps might an HRMS manager take in evaluating system maintenance activities?
7. What are the major indicators of system decline? To what extent can HRSC actions mitigate their effect, at least temporarily?
8. What steps should the HRSC manager take when system decline is suspected or acknowledged?

Further Reading

Allen, Brandt. "An Unmanaged Computer System Can Stop You Dead." *Harvard Business Review*, December 1982.

Couger, J. Daniel, and Mel A. Colter. *Maintenance Programming: Improved Productivity Through Motivation.* Englewood Cliffs, NJ: Prentice-Hall, 1985.

De Marco, Tom. *Structured Analysis and System Specification.* New York: Yourdon Press, 1979.

Eason, T.S., and E.D. Eason. "HRIS Documentation: A Road Map to Application and Maintenance." *Computers in Personnel*, Fall 1988.

Fitz-enz, Jac. *How to Measure Human Resources Management.* New York: McGraw-Hill, 1984.

Glass, Robert L. "Help, My Software Maintenance is Out of Control!" *Computerworld*, February 1990.

Hartsfield, William E. *HRS Audit: How to Evaluate Your Personnel Policies and Practices.* Madison, CT: Business & Legal Reports, 1990.

Hobuss, Jim. "Service Level Agreements." *Information Center*, January 1990.

Horsfield, Debra. "Satisfying Corporate Customers." *Computers in Personnel,* Fall 1987.

Johnson, Maryfran. "Drowning in a Sea of Code." *Computerworld,* January 1990.

Lasden, Martin. "Decision Support Systems: Mission Accomplished?" *Computer Decisions,* April 1987.

Lientz, Bennett P., and E. Burton Swanson. *Software Maintenance Management.* Reading, MA: Addison-Wesley, 1980.

Martin, James and C. McClure. *Software Maintenance: The Problem and Its Solutions.* Englewood Cliffs: Prentice-Hall, 1983.

Mathys, Nicholas, Helen La Van, and G. Nogal. "Issues in Purchasing and Implementing HRIS Software." *Personnel Administrator,* August 1984.

National Bureau of Standards. *Guidelines on Software Maintenance.* Washington: U.S. Department of Commerce, 1984.

———. *Software Maintenance Management.* Washington: U.S. Department of Commerce, 1985.

———. *The Executive Guide to Software Maintenance.* Washington: U.S. Department of Commerce, 1985.

Need, Loretta G. "The Importance of Being Audited." *Computers in Personnel,* Spring 1988.

Parikh, Garish. "Software Maintenance Strategies for Success." *Data Management,* March 1985.

———. *Handbook of Software Maintenance.* New York: John Wiley & Sons, 1986.

Perry, William. "A Plan of Action for Software Maintenance." *Data Management,* March 1985.

Perry, William E. "Quality Through Documentation." *Computerworld,* February 1990.

Spencer, L.M. Jr. *Calculating Human Resource Costs and Benefits.* New York: John Wiley & Sons, 1986.

"Third-Party Maintenance Provides a Cost-effective Alternative." *Data Management,* February 1985.

Winter, Charles R. "Improving Productivity and User Satisfaction Depends on Structured Systems." *Data Management,* November 1984.

Yourdon, Edward. *Techniques of Program Structure and Design.* Englewood Cliffs, NJ: Prentice-Hall, 1975.

11
Managing an HRMS

> No one remembers the juggler if he is successful, but have him drop
> something and watch heads turn.
> —Richard E. Byrd

Because an HRMS is an interdisciplinary activity, the HRMS manager
can play an extremely powerful role. This person has more freedom to
act and more linkage to other people than managers in most other
functions. The HRMS manager must interact with many different professionals, many of whom may interact with each other much less than the HRMS
manager does. The HRMS manager can learn a great deal about how the entire
organization functions—its strategic needs, problems with the outside world,
power sources, human knowledge banks, and competent individuals.

The manager cannot just sit behind a desk, writing plans and directing
the activities of others. He or she must personally interact with many people,
going from department to department, workstation to workstation. Only in
the very largest organizations does the HRMS manager have subordinate staff
who handle these interactions. The job of HRMS management is to facilitate
constructive interaction within the HRMS and between the HRMS and many
other organizational units. Managing the HRMS involves relationships with
the following:

- HRMS project team
- HRSC staff
- Users (both human resources users and others)
- Other departments (such as finance and IS)
- Management
- Employees
- Government agencies
- Consultants and vendors

The performance of the HRMS manager is critical in determining whether
the HRMS will be a success or a failure. Systems with poor management often
develop infighting, low morale, performance problems, underutilization, un-
derfunding, and premature obsolescence. An effective manager can inspire

efficient, effective problem solving among staff, mutual support and respect between the HRSC and the other organizations it affects, and a system with a maximum cost-effective life span.

The Evolving Role of the HRMS Manager

Regardless of the size or maturity of the system, the goals of the HRMS manager parallel those of the HRMS as a whole. Sound performance as an HRMS manager rests on recognizing certain goals of the HRSC and the system itself, including the following:

- To develop and maintain systems that support human resources and contribute to overall corporate management success
- To ensure delivery of maximum benefits from the HRMS, at the lowest possible cost, through the application of accepted human resources and IS tools and techniques
- To balance the needs of users with the needs of IS and to obtain clear direction for prioritizing, developing, and operating the HRMS
- To gain acceptance among corporate, human resources, and IS management as an integral part of the overall structure and as an asset to the entire organization

Qualities of an Effective HRMS Manager

The HRMS manager handles more administrative than technical responsibilities. Unlike the supervision of implementation, HRMS management does not require specialized computer systems knowledge. A manager who needs computer expertise can consult with HRMS maintenance and HRIC staff or with IS staff.

Someone with a background as an industrial engineer, a biochemist, or a psychologist may do the job well if he or she also has the right mix of business and communication skills. Briefly, an effective HRMS manager needs the following skills and experience:

- *Goal setting.* Establish goals based on CSFs or other well-established business procedures. Make those goals clear to supervisors and staff.
- *Communication.* Good communication skills are so basic to successful management that a few of particular importance to HRMS managers are included in the accompanying sidebar.

Effective Communication Skills
for Management

Many resources can teach good communication skills. Among these are informal discussions with supervisors, in-house seminars, career development programs, college extension courses, and relevant reading (see "Futher Reading" at the end of this chapter). Even sources that are not necessarily management oriented, such as Toastmasters, stress management training, and personal therapy, can provide helpful insight. Here are some skills management should possess:

- Listen well. An effective manager asks for clarification when confused. To make sure that he or she understands someone clearly, a manager may want to restate the other person's point: "So you're saying that . . . ."

- Emphasize "I" statements rather than "you" statements. For instance, instead of saying, "You need to make requests like that in writing," the manager might say, "I can act more responsively on requests if I get them in writing."

- Choose the right time to discuss sticky issues. The manager may set up a mutually convenient time, away from the heat of the moment, to try to resolve problems with a subordinate or another manager.

- Ask for and give performance feedback. An effective manager gives subordinates specific praise when they perform well. Constructive criticism also has a place, if it includes suggestions on how to improve performance. A manager also may try to ascertain what others think of his or her performance. This feedback may come from performance reviews, questionnaires, or meetings.

- Maintain professional relationships. No matter how upset a manager is, he or she should not raise his or her voice, use inappropriate language, threaten, or become insulting.

- *Planning.* HRSC planning includes staffing, budgeting, facilities, equipment, and project prioritizing. Many of the most useful planning approaches and techniques for HRMS development and maintenance are described in more detail in chapters 2 and 10.

- *Organization.* Organizational skills are particularly important in an interdisciplinary field such as HRMS management. Management must tailor procedures specifically to particular situations. Moreover, many of the individuals whom HRSC decisions affect directly do not work under the supervision of the HRSC manager; some may not only report to separate functions or departments but also hold relatively high positions in the organization.

Often the manager must delegate organizing responsibilities, such as software development planning, coding, testing, project monitoring, request tracking, and auditing. Staff who have these responsibilities should recognize that organizing this material is part of their job assignments. Filing protocols for software development, coding, error checking, and test results must be established. The manager also must ensure proper organization of all vendor and in-house system documentation and other communications, especially material for distribution among users.

- *Negotiation.* With so many functions and departments to serve, HRSC management involves an almost nonstop give-and-take process of compromises and consensus.

- *Delegation and supervision.* The first step in delegating is determining what to delegate and to whom. The HRMS manager should delegate clearly, making sure staff members understand the criteria for satisfactory performance. Successful delegation includes accepting that the results may be different from what the HRMS manager would have done.

- *Team building, intervention, and group dynamics.* The effective HRSC manager uses these skills to make the entire HRSC work as a unit and as a vehicle to develop effective user groups.

- *Willingness to learn.* HRMS management is complicated and multidisciplinary. A manager loses no professional status by acknowledging that he or she needs to learn more about certain areas to maximize job performance.

The HRMS manager should have a broad knowledge of human resources but often lacks familiarity with specific, technical operations. In large organizations, the right HRMS manager may have elegant business management skills but very little human resources knowledge and may not even come from the corporate world. This type of manager can do a fine job by consulting with human resources experts within the department.

Finding and Developing an HRMS Manager

Many organizations that are new to HRMS express surprise that the project team leader is not necessarily the best choice for HRMS manager. If the HRMS simply replaces an existing system, the existing manager often makes the transition to managing the new system as it becomes operational. However, development of an organization's first system may require finding a new HRMS manager.

Rarely does a person with the creative skills needed to lead HRMS development readily switch to an operational or maintenance mentality. Someone with expertise in system planning, feasibility studies, and researching vendors is not necessarily a whiz at handling the details necessary for running the system itself. Too often, however, a project team leader develops a proprietary feeling about controlling the system and moves into the HRMS management slot despite his or her lack of appropriate business management skills. In such situations, outside consultants often are needed to solve problems that develop from poor management.

Organizations can take steps to get the best possible HRMS manager. First, they must recognize that the positions of project team leader and system manager are two different jobs. Neither position is necessarily subordinate to the other—for example, the HRMS manager might be subordinate during development but shift to a leading role following installation.

Second, organizations must define the system manager position, creating a complete job description and background requirements. More often than not, this is a new position and the organization has few other comparable positions. External surveys may help in this process.

Third, organizations must make designating and preparing someone for the manager's role part of the project team's goal. They should conduct an internal search and selection procedure first and then an external search if necessary. Usually this involves freeing someone from his or her human resources duties to manage, perhaps someone already on the project team but not necessarily.

Fourth, as the project team identifies potential managers, the manager should coordinate their project team assignments to help them develop and refine the management skills and technical background appropriate to manage the ongoing system properly.

In some organizations, the HRMS manager may report to the director of the human resources department, but if that manager does not want another direct report, the HRMS manager may report to the head of the human resources area that has the most contact with the HRMS, such as employment, compensation, or benefits.

The job of HRMS manager does not remain steady throughout the life of the system. Some responsibilities remain—such as coordinating interactions with outside agencies, vendors, and user groups and facilitating staff training—but the challenges and needs of the system change over time. As the HRMS evolves, the HRSC may use different tactics, tools, and techniques. Recognizing the HRMS's life-cycle stage provides much guidance about appropriate management priorities.

Managing a Start-up System

During most of the start-up phase, the project team leader, rather than the HRMS manager, often leads system development. The transition usually takes place after the HRMS installation, when the system can provide some production in the form of reports and analyses. Although start-up management has many technical components, software and hardware do not provide all the answers. Many of the tools and techniques for this stage are business based, including cost-benefit-value analysis, RFPs, scheduling via Gantt charts, and using CSFs. All of these are discussed in more detail in other chapters. A project team manager or HRMS manager who is unfamiliar with these tools and techniques should talk with peers or colleagues about the applicability of such tools to the HRMS planning and start-up process. He or she can use these techniques to develop a project plan that identifies major tasks, milestones, time lines, responsibilities, and project staffing needs. To avoid overextending resources, the manager should divide the project into manageable parts.

The manager should never allow technical needs to overshadow the process of getting input from all relevant individuals and keeping them informed about the progress of the system. The more people are informed, the more they can support the system, begin to identify with it, and become ready to participate in implementation and operation activities when the time comes.

During requirements definition and design, the manager talks with many types of users, from corporate managers to human resources data entry staff. When conflicts arise, the HRMS manager or project team leader should ask for information that helps explain the opposing points of view. When compromises are needed, the manager should explain the rationale for these compromises to those who will be affected. To maximize system success in the long run, the manager must base design decisions on the specific organization—not only on its human resources needs but also on the technical experience and expertise of future users, the extent of consistent behavior in the department, and the existing relationship between human resources and IS, as well as between top management and other functions.

Staffing decisions for the project team, implementation, and other start-up activities often present a dilemma. The manager must select appropriate staff for meeting the immediate goals but also promote staff continuity between start-up and operation. He or she also should pay careful attention to advancing the skills of staff from their project team roles to implementation roles and from implementation roles to HRSC roles. It is important to provide or facilitate technical and management training where appropriate. Additional tips for "growing" staff are given later in this chapter. Some individuals will want to continue in a purely developmental or technical role. Management

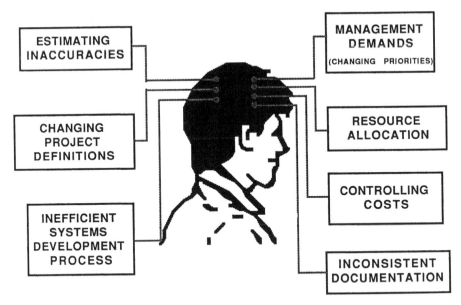

Figure 11–1. Problems that pressure the project manager. During
planning, design, and start-up, the project manager faces
pressure from many sources. The manager must make sure
not only that staff find a solution to each problem but that
these separate solutions work together to optimize overall
results.

should not try to fit the square technical resource peg into the round user-support hole.

The HRMS manager usually has become involved by the time implementation begins. He or she should begin by reviewing the project team's log which details the team's decisions, design changes, philosophies, assumptions, pitfalls, successes, and solutions to problems. As needed, the incoming manager may review and revise standards for development of human resources software and acquisition of hardware.

The HRMS manager should make sure that the staff complete every implementation step thoroughly, especially training and testing. Right after implementation, a lot of energy goes into improving the system. This phase requires careful attention to coordinating the efforts of everyone concerned. Sometimes, though not always, six people all working on one project yield better results (or happier users) than each person working on a separate issue. The manager must take an active role in assigning priorities and specific responsibilities for technical activities. Staff members should be creative; the

HRSC manager must walk a fine line between encouraging technical staff's problem-solving inclinations and giving license for actions that conflict with system priorities.

Managing a Growing System

Once the project team has installed and tested the new system, the HRSC emerges as an active interface between users and the system. Management of the growing HRMS and HRSC structures includes complete staffing assignments, communications links, organization charts, reporting mechanisms, and the adoption of more sophisticated maintenance tools and techniques.

During this period of growth, staffing needs shift as technical demands moderate and communication skills become central to interaction with users and external agencies aiming for additional data and improved reports. The HRMS manager must develop or import staff to meet these emerging needs. Even the most attractive and best run HRSC experiences staff turnover. Written documentation and procedures allow replacement staff to come up to speed more quickly.

The HRMS manager must supervise system maintenance in a well-organized manner, keeping track of every request and response. The manager must direct the revision of HRMS policies, procedures, record keeping, and data analysis so that everyone—managers, staff, and users—knows what to expect.

The manager should seek out user involvement by soliciting suggestions for new systems and support and for criteria for evaluating requests. He or she also should keep management informed about usage levels and demands made on the HRMS and HRSC. If the HRSC budget is constraining legitimate user needs, the HRMS manager may need to negotiate with management for increased resources and consider trade-offs.

In conjunction with IS technical staff, the manager should develop a consolidation strategy that identifies the basis on which other systems can interface or integrate with the HRMS. It is important to promote the HRSC as the control point for HRMS management—both technically and in terms of policies and procedures.

Amidst struggling with new modules and small improvements, the manager must facilitate the decision about whether to continue and grow (adding more modules over time) or to prepare to accept the system as is. No system meets every need perfectly, but eventually an HRMS may become as complicated as it needs to be.

Managing a Mature System

When maintenance demands increase tremendously and become the main consumer of HRSC resources, the system has achieved maturity. The overall management goals during maturity are to keep use and productivity at their peaks and to counter the increased maintenance burden with more effective productivity tools and techniques. The HRMS manager probably spends more time on the administrative aspects of running the system, since a mature system runs well.

In this stage, the more expert user begins taking a creative role in system evolution. The HRMS manager must establish a system for approving, reviewing, and otherwise monitoring changes to the system. By providing users with development tools as needed and training them in the proper use of those tools, the HRMS manager frees HRSC staff to work on interdisciplinary issues that would otherwise have to wait. The HRSC manager should ensure that the IC, user groups, newsletters, and other activities that maximize the applicability of the system are established, well run, and appropriately staffed.

Managing a Declining System

The HRSC manager has responsibility for monitoring the health of the system and calling attention to its status and needs. Audits and surveys (discussed in

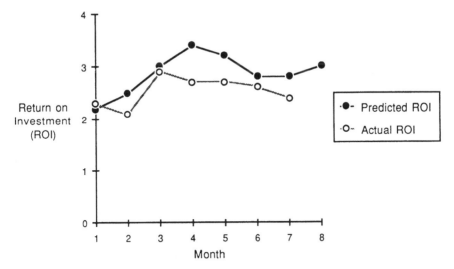

Figure 11–4. **Graphic display of performance data. Using the same data as in figure 11–3, this graph provides a picture of the trend in ROI. Projections are overly optimistic. The trend of actual month-to-month performance is far more useful. Although actual performance declined in the later months, it remained higher than at the beginning. This may not signal a decline but merely a short-term downturn.**

chapter 10) suggest but seldom identify precisely system malfunction. The most useful monitoring tools for pinpointing decline are indicator analyses and evaluation of ROI or assets.

With indicator analysis, the HRSC manager compares quantifiable measures of HRMS and HRSC performance with preestablished standards. The manager may define system decline not necessarily as a lessening of output or efficiency but as a failure to meet standards. Measures may include average backlog of service requests, mean time between HRMS failures, average time to run a standard or ad hoc report, and so forth. A more illustrative list of indicators is given in chapter 10. Some HRSC managers convert performance data to graphic form, as shown in figure 11–3.

ROI analysis is a standard business principal that also applies to HRMS vendor and software evaluation. The investment variable includes the cost of people, budget, facilities, and equipment. The return on that investment is

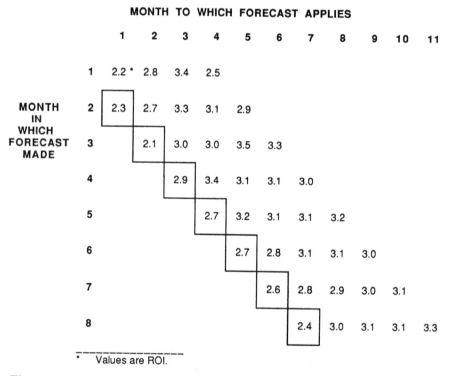

* Values are ROI.

Figure 11–3. Predicted versus actual ROI. For every month, actual ROI is less than predicted ROI. At first glance, these data may lead to the observation that the system is not living up to expectations and must, therefore, have significant problems.

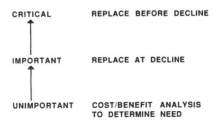

WHEN TO REPLACE DEPENDS ON
HOW IMPORTANT THE HRMS,
SUBSYSTEM OR MODULE IS . . .

CRITICAL   REPLACE BEFORE DECLINE

IMPORTANT   REPLACE AT DECLINE

UNIMPORTANT COST/BENEFIT ANALYSIS
TO DETERMINE NEED

AND A VARIETY OF "POLITICAL" ISSUES

Figure 11–2. When to replace a system. When to replace an automated system depends on the importance of the HRMS in the activities of the entire enterprise or the human resources department. Managers also must consider numerous political and financial factors.

often intangible but real nonetheless. Some managers include ROI as one component of indicator analysis. They also may use ROI to evaluate potential maintenance projects, such as new modules or enhancements.

When audits, surveys, indicator analysis, or ROI evaluation indicate a system in decline, the HRSC manager must decide what action to take. Alternatives include patching the existing system together to buy time, accelerating the decline by pulling the plug on the system, or planning to develop or acquire a new system. Essentially, the HRSC manager must decide whether to bring in a new system or redefine his or her job in terms of the declining capabilities of the existing system. The HRSC manager may decide to ignore the problem or leave, thus accelerating system decline. Much depends on the character of the HRSC manager (developer or technician, conservative or risk-taker) and the organization's culture.

If the manager decides to begin work on a replacement system, the HRSC is put in a dichotomous position, becoming both caretaker of the old system and project team for the new one. The HRSC manager must decide on the relative importance of these two functions and assign staff and resources accordingly. In establishing a project team, the manager begins the HRMS cycle again—plan, design, implement, and maintain. Many firms assign staff members responsibilities in both arenas, but keeping these activities separate usually works better. This is, of course, easier said than done, since the HRSC generally has scarce resources.

Actual management of a declining system has three components: planning for the phase-out of existing operations, allocating reduced staffing and support to users during transition to the new HRMS, and halting operation of the current system. As shown in the accompanying sidebar, establishing some strategies and tactics for evaluating and shifting from the old system to the new one minimizes user dissatisfaction with human resources and the HRSC.

Full Circle: Declining System to New Start-up System

The following steps can help an HRSC manager meet user needs throughout a period of system decline and replacement with a new system.

1. Identify benchmark indicators, as addressed in chapter 10. As soon as a system reaches maturity, the HRSC should specify eight to ten key indicators that it believes presage system decline. For each indicator, HRSC should establish a first-level warning, second-level warning, and critical values. HRSC management also should obtain IS and user agreement on these indicators.

2. Monitor benchmarks. Measure and report on the indicators periodically. The HRSC should annotate its reports, including recommended revisions.

3. Initiate action. Immediately upon confirmation of system decline, the HRSC should initiate an ROI-based screening of active and proposed projects. The staff should undertake only those projects that meet ROI standards. Management may then decide to establish or accelerate project team development of a replacement system. This development follows the same process as for the start-up of the initial system: Plan, design, and implement.

4. Inform users. The HRSC may consider publishing a monthly or quarterly analysis of declining indicators and staff hours shifted as a result of the ROI analysis. At the same time, indicate the status of new system development.

5. Publish timetables. Timetables inform users, IS, and others

when to expect support for service requests to be phased out and implementation of the new system to begin.

6. Accept requests for transfer of services. The HRSC transfers applications from the old system to the new, beginning with requests having critical levels of payback and moving down the priority levels. HRSC staff should publicize the criteria they are using to prioritize these transfers.

7. Reduce service according to a prepublished and agreed-upon schedule. In turn, the HRSC will transfer applications to the new system according to the schedule.

8. Cease production on the old system. At this point, the HRSC uses and maintains only the new start-up system.

Managing HRMS Staff

From the beginning, the HRSC manager shapes the staff. The behavior and attitudes of the HRSC manager set a tone for that staff and for how the rest of the organization views the HRSC and the HRMS. A manager with a positive outlook (if tempered by reasonable action) inspires others to look on the bright side. A manager who values an environment in which people enjoy their co-workers attracts others with similar values. A manager who acts according to principles of professional, ethical behavior and who aims to perform quality work inspires others to interact in that manner as well. Such standards contribute directly to an HRMS, and to an overall working environment, about which people feel the greatest job and personal satisfaction.

Establishing the HRSC Staff

The process of establishing the HRSC staff starts quite early in the system planning process. Even before system development begins, the requirements analysis and feasibility study should determine how many people of what type to use for developing, and then running, the system. These documents should point to both strengths and deficiencies of available staff.

The HRMS staff must contain a balance of individuals with computer expertise and those with human resources backgrounds. Often the manager has few choices; people are lining up internally, or human resources management assigns individuals to the HRMS. Sometimes such situations necessitate taking on people who are not otherwise qualified for the work at hand. The HRMS manager may ask other supervisors to take partial or total responsibility for the assignment of other people; supervisors then tell those people what

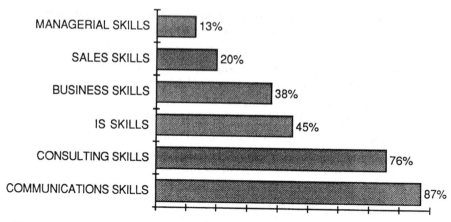

Figure 11–5. Skills required for IC staff. Surveyed human resources professionals ranked the skills that IC staff should possess. They overwhelmingly selected communication and consulting skills over technical, business, and sales skills. (Source: Science Research Associates, a division of the Macmillan/McGraw-Hill School Publishing Company, a joint venture partnership owned equally by New York publisher McGraw-Hill and New York publisher Macmillan, Inc.)

to do. Often the human resources department manager, or even corporate management, becomes involved in resolving conflicts about how much time people should spend on the HRMS compared with their other duties.

The size of the HRSC operation plays a significant role in the type of person best suited for HRSC staffing. In some firms, the HRMS manager supervises only a single clerical support person and perhaps one technical person. Because each person has multiple responsibilities, each must be able to work independently without much imposed structure, enjoy handling multiple tasks, and be flexible. In the largest firms, the HRMS management team alone may number in the dozens. In such settings, team members welcome the stricter definitions of responsibility and may feel motivated by the corresponding clearer opportunities for career development.

An organization that has acquired a system must depend on the vendor to know program applications and technology better than internal staff ever will. For internal assistance, HRMS must enlist IS people. An organization that has developed or modified a system in-house will have more people with acquired system knowledge. Mainframe systems require significant technical background. Microcomputer-based systems (especially those that include 4GLs) permit HRSC staffing increasingly independent of technical background. The HRMS usually needs both kinds of expertise: Human resources people can learn more about computers but not enough to do complex coding; technicians are scientists who are generally uninterested in becoming very involved with an art or social science such as human resources.

Growing HRSC Staff

HRSC staff growth usually begins with the transition from primarily development staff to staff dedicated to enhancement and maintenance work. Although some development projects, such as adding new modules, continue, this soon tapers off, leaving maintenance and support as the key issues. This change in responsibility requires a change in the HRSC skills mix.

The HRMS manager should strive to maintain a significant level of continuity between project team staff and HRSC staff. To do so, goals, CSFs, staff assignments, compensation structures, resource allocation, and training and development plans aimed at maintaining a core group of people must be developed.

Maintenance programmers should by now be more senior than developers; these people need to understand the big picture and how all the programs and modules work together. Staff building is more complex because the skills and knowledge required are interdisciplinary, split between technical and functional backgrounds.

One of the most powerful tools in reallocating staff successfully throughout the system's life cycle is offering professional growth opportunities. A rapidly growing field such as HRMS offers many opportunities to learn; in fact, staff must continue to learn just to keep up with their peers within and outside the organization. Three successful techniques for cultivating this growth to the advantage of the HRSC are fostering cross-training, networking, and supervisory support.

The process of growing staff members involves presenting different levels of experience to individuals as they become ready to grow. To promote cross-training or develop expertise, new staff should be asked to do background research. This could include vendor contacts to gather sales literature, periodicals summaries and synthesis to get a feel for the latest thinking, interviews with users, and focus groups. These efforts should contribute to future decisions, but the activities themselves are low risk. If the research results are not perfect, someone else can fine-tune the material or suggest further work by the staffer. The next phase of cross-training involves assigning simple activities, such as participating in solving a particular problem or developing a new report. This person should be assigned to deal with the most patient, clearest communicators. Finally, as the person becomes senior in his or her field, the person can be assigned to deal with more powerful, high-risk users.

Managers also can encourage staff career growth by facilitating exposure to other people who are working on computers in human resources applications. This may take place at conferences, professional organization chapter meetings, HRMS and related courses, and even internal seminars. Networking sometimes becomes a two-edged sword, since HRMS staff then find out if other companies or departments are looking to hire new staff, potentially inspiring some turnover. In a well-run organization, however, the benefits outweigh the potential risks.

Through networking, staff learn how their peers in other firms do their jobs—what kinds of skills, approaches, processes, and technical specialists they use. They find out how other people get things done on time, on budget, and with success. Vendors' user groups provide very specific information about particular systems. Staff learn how other users of the same system have applied it to particular situations, how they have maximized its capabilities, minimized its limitations, coped with problems, and integrated it with other computer options. With any of these peer interactions, staff gain knowledge, get ideas they look forward to applying in their own positions, and feel they are getting low-stress, off-site, high-quality time. Perhaps most important, they come to identify themselves more strongly as members of the HRSC and the HRMS community, not just the human resources department.

As with any supervisory position, the HRSC manager should communicate with individual staff members frequently. He or she should give positive feedback at times other than performance review, give negative feedback in private, with suggestions and agreement on what went wrong and how to improve, and do periodic self-evaluation in terms of providing for staff development needs. Such activities may serve as part of the manager's own performance review.

A manager who tries to keep everybody happy as system needs shift eventually makes no one happy. Instead, the effective manager tries to grasp each person's or the group's real needs, burning issues, and sensitive points. If the HRSC can incorporate these forces and maintain its overall goal, fine; if not, the manager should expect HRSC staff turnover.

Some turnover usually occurs as the system matures. The manager should not necessarily interpret as a failure the fact that someone who was great on the project team a year or two ago is taking another position outside the organization because the established HRMS cannot meet his or her career goals. Some people are more suited to system development; the HRMS manager should recognize this and treat it as a positive experience. When the time for replacement system planning arrives several years down the road, the manager may remember this person and find in him or her a pretrained candidate for a position on the new project.

Often the emerging HRSC needs not only a different kind of professional staff but also more staff. As the HRSC becomes larger and more comprehensive, and as users become more involved with the system and demand more sophisticated support, HRSC capacity must increase correspondingly. In some cases, a more productive method of providing support will suffice, but often

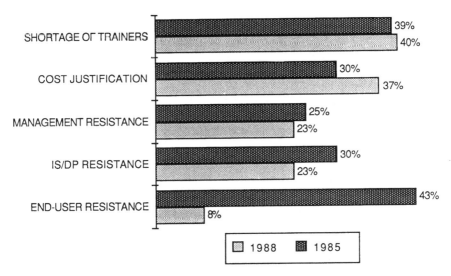

Figure 11–6. Major obstacles to ICs. Comparison surveys in 1985 and 1988 show that resistance to ICs has decreased considerably. Cost remains the major hurdle that ICs must overcome.
(Source: Science Research Associates, a division of the Macmillan/McGraw-Hill School Publishing Company, a joint venture partnership owned equally by New York publisher McGraw-Hill and New York publisher Macmillan, Inc.)

an HRSC really does need more staff. Additional demands on training, maintenance, and advisory services may indeed require more staff with a broader base of skills and knowledge.

HRSC staff should understand that the charter of the HRSC will change over time. As the HRMS matures, top management may adopt an *information resources management (IRM)* concept, which holds that information belongs to the organization as a whole, not just to a single department. As this occurs, the HRSC may need to shift again, this time to a smaller, more business-oriented staff with a mission of integrating human resources data with corporate data bases. The HRSC relinquishes its traditional role as human resources' technical expert and dismantles the barriers that have separated it from the rest of the human resources organization. The HRMS manager must concentrate on smooth information transfer as well as on training and retraining staff for new responsibilities.

When it is time for system replacement, the HRMS manager must reassign staff so the HRSC can simultaneously care for the old system and implement its replacement. He or she also should cushion staff members who have come to identify with the present system. The manager must instill in staff members the knowledge that the system performed well but emphasize that the organization now needs to develop a new system, possibly because of technological improvements and organizational evolution, in which they also can share.

Managing User Relations

As discussed earlier, HRMS users include not only a wide variety of managers, administrators, and clerical staff within the human resources department, but often counterparts in other departments that handle their own personnel-like functions, such as sales and engineering. The HRMS manager has several responsibilities toward users: to create and maintain an HRMS that best meets the needs of users within budgetary and other resource constraints, to promote full use of the HRMS, and to respond to changes in management and user expectations. Specifics include good documentation, training, IC or other ongoing support, software and hardware maintenance, and problem resolution.

Promoting User Involvement

The most successful HRMS projects involve users from the beginning. As detailed in chapter 2, the first steps are to inform users that the project team is planning to develop an HRMS and solicit their input in the design process. The manager should use inquiry methods—questionnaires, surveys, interviews, and checklists—that are appropriate to the users' sophistication and availability and ensure that the inquiry process includes users from a wide variety of backgrounds. The effective manager selects interviewers carefully, making sure that they have experience or at least training in interviewing skills such as accuracy, asking nonleading questions, and good listening.

Whenever possible, the strengths and limits of the user community should be taken into account when designing the system. HRMS consultants often recommend avoiding computerizing functions that the department cannot handle manually. The HRMS project manager or HRSC manager should give users feedback about what kinds of procedures and policies they must develop to be ready for computerization.

The manager may study the results of user surveys during planning phases and periodic evaluations to assess how forthright users are about their experiences with the system. If user surveys provide useful information, they should be continued. If users hesitate to provide realistic assessments and suggestions, the manager may choose to rely more on quantitative measures of actual system use and maintenance requests.

Whenever users provide input, the HRMS should keep them informed of later developments so they know that their efforts did not fall into some bottomless pit of bureaucratic red tape. The HRSC may even publish a newsletter and maintain wide distribution throughout the life of the HRMS.

Users, particularly human resources functional heads, must agree to provide what the HRMS project team and HRSC need from them in order to design a successful system. Among these needs are:

- Accurate, appropriate data
- Individuals who understand the data
- Individuals who understand how to use data and support analytical functions
- Individuals willing to learn new ways of doing things

The HRMS manager has major responsibility for creating affinity between human resources users and HRSC staff. This affinity starts with users having realistic expectations of the system. The project team should not oversell the HRMS before it comes on-line. Rather than billing it as a speed enhancer, the team can stress the consistency of format, freedom from some drudgery, increased automatic data checking, and other, more attainable and realistic attributes. Many potential users, particularly clerical staff, fear that a computer system will result in unemployment. Fears may subside as users learn about the upcoming roles they will play and the training they will receive. They will benefit from hearing about other companies that have made such automation shifts successfully without layoffs but with increased job satisfaction.

All users should receive sufficient information about the patience and new responsibilities they will have to acquire to work with a computerized system. The manager should not allow the complexity of the HRMS to surprise users. He or she should assure them that the system has layers of accessibility and that they can take this learning one step at a time, with many layers used only by experts.

Getting Users Started

Orienting users to a new system involves understanding not just the practical aspects of change but the psychology of change as well. An effective manager makes sure that all HRSC staff are sensitive to the fact that people resist change, even when they know it is inevitable. Getting people to let go of something they have known and been comfortable with for a long time can be difficult, whether it is an old car, old clothes, or old ways of doing their job. Introducing change incrementally rather than all at one generally causes less stress and resistance.

User relations during this period should take account of the qualities of the specific change involved. A manual-to-automated change creates different challenges than an automated-to-automated change or a mainframe-to-micro-computer change. Sometimes what appears to be a single change often involves several distinct components. For instance, a large oil company moved from a centralized Honeywell environment to a distributed IBM environment; simultaneously, the company reorganized to give one central unit responsibility for all computer-related processes. This company's change had three variables—a hardware shift, an organization shift from centralized to decentralized, and a responsibility shift. Once the manager has identified the particular aspects of the transition that cause the most stress, he or she can concentrate staff resources on working through this difficulty with users.

Rather than engage in empire building, HRSC management should look for ways to include end users in its projects, first in support roles, then as task or project leaders. The HRSC must make sure that participating users have both the guidance and the tools they need to succeed in systems work. Management should shield them from the more technically oriented aspects of project development.

To maximize appropriate user participation, it is important to provide personalized and, where appropriate, computer-based training (CBT) for users. Training is an often overlooked but critical component in ensuring that users

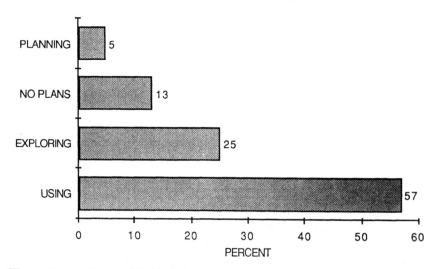

Figure 11–7. Use of CBT in ICs. According to a 1985 survey, more than half of the ICs surveyed used computer-based training. Only 13 percent had no plans to use this technique in the future.
(Source: Science Research Associates, a division of the Macmillan/McGraw-Hill School Publishing Company, a joint venture partnership owned equally by New York publisher McGraw-Hill and New York publisher Macmillan, Inc.)

participate in and feel comfortable with the new HRMS. The HRSC should not charge back this training to users' organizations unless circumstances dictate otherwise. The HRSC can offer resources in support of a user-led development activity, provided it meets HRSC standards.

Once the system and HRSC staff have survived the exhausting process of implementation, departmental management often pays less attention to the HRMS, wanting only to reap the benefits of this investment. This is the time to work with users, familiarize them with ongoing support, form them into groups, have regular communication, and expand training sessions.

Establishing an IC

Some HRSCs coordinate their user services via a group known as the *human resources information center (HRIC)*. The HRIC may handle training, user hot lines or other on-call support, assistance with use of report and screen creation tools, decision support systems (discussed in chapter 22), 4GLs and prototyping (discussed in chapter 10), and other advanced user techniques. ICs may use tutorials, checklists, and computer-based and other forms of training to prepare users to query data bases, write reports, develop special-purpose ap-

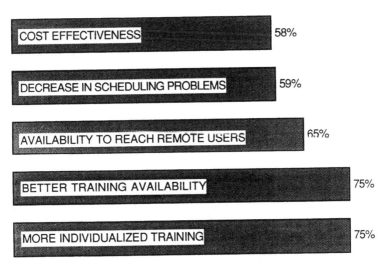

COST EFFECTIVENESS	58%
DECREASE IN SCHEDULING PROBLEMS	59%
AVAILABILITY TO REACH REMOTE USERS	65%
BETTER TRAINING AVAILABILITY	75%
MORE INDIVIDUALIZED TRAINING	75%

Figure 11–8. Why ICs value CBT. IC professionals who responded to a 1985 survey overwhelmingly valued CBT because of the advantages it offers.
(Source: Science Research Associates, a division of the Macmillan/McGraw-Hill School Publishing Company, a joint venture partnership owned equally by New York publisher McGraw-Hill and New York publisher Macmillan, Inc.)

plications, implement decision support systems, and handle their own business computing needs. The main role of the IC is to bridge the communication gap between users and the technical community. In an organization with an IC, users know where to go for solutions to problems, and they can exercise more control over conflicting maintenance priorities.

If an organization provides user services in several other departments as well, such as finance, management, or production, then a central, unified IC may be more efficient. Sometimes a departmental IC (such as the HRIC) supports users on a specific system (such as the HRMS), while a corporate IC supports users who are working with independent or interdepartmental computing needs. For instance, management-level users often use microcomputers with packaged programs or systems they have customized. The corporate IC often helps users in one department, such as finance, learn how to access and analyze data from other departmental systems, such as the HRMS.

Independent management and administrative users who work with a corporate IC may find reasons to develop interdependent ties with applications or data bases in other systems. The corporate IC facilitates such information exchange, often with mutually beneficial results. Such efforts add value to the work of formerly independent applications.

In most cases, the IC reduces maintenance by helping users do their own computing. In so doing, the IC helps shift maintenance responsibility from HRMS or IC staff to users. Even when users approach the IC with complex requests, having an IC to coordinate these needs can facilitate maintenance. In such cases, the corporate IC learns the new software, hardware arrangements, interfaces, modifications, and reports that would help accomplish these nonstandard user requests. The IC can then translate this knowledge into efficient, effective training and maintenance that meet user needs directly.

Developing a User Community or Communities

Even before implementation, the HRMS project team and HRSC staff can do more than identify which individuals and positions will be using the system. They can group these users according to their functional or technical needs and their sophistication levels. They can then establish particular communication approaches for each identified user community. In a large organization, each user community may have its own HRSC contact person, training sessions, and even regular meetings to share ideas, questions, and feedback. Building strong, informed, involved user communities helps the HRSC ensure that maintenance resources meet user needs.

To bring users together as a community, the HRSC must convince them that the users own the system. Although people often think that the HRSC owns the system, this is usually a false perception because most HRMS project teams try to design the new system as a resource for all other departments and users. An HRSC manager can find many ways to reach users and have them accept ownership of the system. Effective approaches include user groups, newsletters, and surveys.

User Groups. Users are more comfortable dealing with new information when they are formed into groups. User groups can provide a level of comfort that facilitates learning and system utilization. Such groups also help the HRSC keep in touch with users' developing needs and abilities.

Users may talk about wanting a group, but they normally do not start groups on their own. The manager can use intervention and team-building approaches to overcome user resistance to the new system. Users can meet in an off-site session or in a series of on-site meetings to discuss what they want from the system. What have they received so far? In what ways is the system deficient? The HRSC manager should tell them about developmental, maintenance, and training agendas for the coming year. Once encouraged, users will probably bombard the HRSC manager and staff with complaints and questions. It is important that HRSC staff understand that they will hear complaints much more often than they will hear praise, since both management and users expect a smoothly functioning HRMS at all times.

Off-site meetings, though initially more costly, often build group identification, rapport, and clear communication more effectively. If possible, managers should budget for an off-site user group meeting during the first year following initial system implementation. This tactic can provide an excellent forum for hearing good and bad comments about the new HRMS in a setting that is away from the inevitable interruptions of the workplace. It also eliminates a sense of territoriality among participants.

Newsletters. User newsletters foster both the user groups and the feeling of user ownership. The HRSC may create a user-oriented HRMS newsletter and distribute it widely. Financial and staff resources, the distribution network, and circulation size will determine whether the newsletter has a simple or elaborate format. Bimonthly or quarterly publication usually is sufficient.

Regular features might include the HRSC manager's report, new features, new reports, user profiles, a user question-and-answer segment, and announcements from the vendor, if applicable. The newsletter also may contain articles in which individuals go on record about benefits and values received from the system. Such demonstrations show other users that they, too, can own a part of the system. The HRSC may approach organizational managers to write or be interviewed about benefits received, particularly on a management topic. Even if the HRSC writes the article based on an interview, once that manager sees her or his own name in print, the manager tends to be more supportive of the system.

Surveys. The HRSC should study the results of user questionnaires and other survey instruments used during periodic system audits and evaluations. This includes assessing user perceptions of the system. If user surveys provide useful information, the HRSC should continue them. If users do not provide realistic assessments and suggestions, management needs to determine what causes this reticence and correct the situation. Sometimes user groups can contribute significantly to this process. Meanwhile, the HRSC will rely more heavily on quantitative measures of actual system use and maintenance requests.

Giving Users What They Need

By designing the system properly from the start, the HRSC can meet most users' needs with standard reports and procedures. Staff can package standard reports for management use, as well as reports and analyses for other applications. They should make sure that all appropriate users know what the HRSC offers or know how to find out.

The HRMS works best when it includes an ad hoc reporting capability, since this facility can help users get what they need when they need it while minimizing system maintenance projects. As much as possible, users should receive training from HRSC staff in preparing ad hoc reports. The HRSC should develop or mandate standards for factors such as algorithms, naming data elements, and report formats. These processes can use both the HRMS vendor and IS retrieval capabilities. To maximize users' learning about how to perform these processes, the HRSC may wish to provide as much consultation as possible without charge but charge back to the requesting department ad hoc reporting requested by users capable of doing their own. Since ad hoc reports often become periodic reports, the HRSC should save users' ad hoc report shells and reuse and share them with other users whenever possible.

With any system, users sometimes want what the system cannot yet provide. For these cases, the HRSC should make maintenance or service request forms available. This approach, described in more detail in chapter 10, is one of the most powerful negotiating tools between the HRSC and HRMS users.

If the HRSC receives all corporate or human resources requests in writing, the staff will be more likely to develop a plan, gather any additional information, estimate resource requirements, and prioritize each request relative to other requests before they begin to work on it. In turn, users receive written responses to their requests, indicating resources needed, a timetable, and reasons for any changes in scope or timing. If the user does not accept these changes or limitations, human resources management may become involved in negotiations. This process can improve the timeliness and technical appropriateness of maintenance projects, and everyone can share the same information and understanding of how and why HRSC management makes decisions on service requests.

The written service request provides a good basis for resource allocation decisions. If HRSC management, or human resources or corporate management, believes that dedicating certain time and financial resources to a particular issue conflicts with other HRMS priorities, the service contract can include corresponding adjustments in scope of work. By coordinating the time and cost estimates from all service requests, the HRMS manager acquires support materials to justify either realignment of conflicting priorities (among users) or allocation of additional resources (from management).

Historically, other areas of human resources have hesitated to accept the HRSC as a professional partner because of its inability to provide useful information to the human resources community in a timely manner. When data recipients must invest additional effort to reformat or extract their information, they discount the value of the data received. The HRSC needs to search out and identify individual decision makers and community interests to determine the nature and extent of strategic needs beyond merely operational issues.

Eventually, technical members of the HRSC staff must be willing to compromise system efficiency to provide the information that users want in the correct form. They must accept the need for temporary data manipulation to arrive at the format users will accept. They can then use this input to create a set of standard reports for management's use. Staff should query more expert users early and often to identify and update needs, since these individuals use and benefit from the system more than do other staff.

Managing HRSC Relations with Other Departments

The HRSC may have ongoing contact with other departments such as IS, finance, industrial engineering (called methods and procedures analysis in banks and insurance companies), and facilities. In terms of these departments, the HRMS manager has a threefold job: (1) to help the rest of the organization identify and agree on the needs the HRMS will meet; (2) to make sure that the HRMS meets those needs; and (3) to make sure that the HRSC staff receive adequate support to do their work successfully.

Managing the image of the HRMS among other departments often involves managing expectations and planning much more than it does technical knowledge. HRSC actions that foster a desirable image among other departments include the following:

- Keeping commitments once made
- Being responsive to requests, comments, and other communications
- Actively maintaining contact through tools such as newsletters, bulletins, staff profiles, and vendor press releases

The HRSC manager should strive to get other departments involved in decision making on projects they want the HRSC to handle. For example, if another department wants a new application developed, the HRSC can investigate and draft several options, then ask the requesting department for guidance regarding which direction to pursue. The HRSC should structure options they themselves can accept. Participating in problem solving makes the other department a partner in the process.

An experienced HRSC manager expects that when people from various departments interact vis-à-vis a single system, they may have different agendas. In negotiations, participants should discuss these agendas openly, and each should describe the compromises his or her group is willing to make. Sometimes just these questions help the HRSC make decisions without formal conflict resolution or other intervention techniques. Regardless of what consensus participants eventually reach, the HRMS should remain under the control of users rather than technical staff.

The HRSC manager should arrange to hold such meetings and discussions on HRSC turf if possible. Not only will HRMS management have additional support materials readily at hand, but participants will see more clearly that solutions must fit in with the rest of human resources and the HRMS.

The HRMS and IS

Human resources, through the fledgling HRMS project team, usually initiates contact with IS technicians, ideally in the earliest HRMS planning phase. The planning phase poses many challenges in an HRMS-IS relationship, but implementation is even more difficult. Implementation will underscore unclear communications, conflicts in priorities, and mistakes made at any level. Once the system becomes operational, the relationship with IS usually proceeds on a more even keel. When the system inevitably declines, the HRMS manager can reasonably expect less IS support for the HRMS.

IS may begin by furnishing a standards manual or other straightforward, apparently inflexible, feedback. Human resources and IS can proceed from this point by getting to know each other better. Each human resources and HRMS representative should try to establish rapport and build relationships with IS staff. Management should encourage professional relationships between HRMS staff and IS, including mutual respect and courteous conduct. To help promote such relationships, the groups may consider joint social functions whenever appropriate to celebrate the successful implementation of new HRMS enhancements.

Staff should strive to learn about the other group's area of expertise. They can learn how to respond in ways that help both work together better, share background information, and help the others become better informed without shoving information down their throats. Sometimes this involves simply forwarding relevant information in the form of periodicals, articles, or seminar brochures. People respond well to receiving material that shows someone else is thinking of their perspective.

Here are some additional aspects of a good relationship between HRMS staff and IS:

- Respect the standards and rules IS has established for system applications.
- Earn respect for the HRMS (which is more eclectic and has more functional areas).
- Be willing to admit lack of knowledge. No single person can know all human resources functional areas. A person may know compensation but not benefits, for example.
- Do not expect technicians to be experts in all technical areas. For instance, a COBOL programmer may not know much about microcomputers or 4GLs.
- Use HRMS technical staff as a language bridge to IS whenever appropriate.

The HRMS and Finance

The HRSC and the finance department have a twofold relationship. First, they are partner operations, sharing information about fiscally important aspects of human resources management. This information covers areas such as payroll, taxation, benefit costs, and labor-cost accounting. In this regard, the HRSC should include finance staff in user activities, such as training, meetings, newsletters, surveys, and audits. Clear communication links should exist between the HRSC technical staff and the finance staff or IS staff most knowledgeable about finance's other computer applications. Management should help finance understand that HRMS data are owned by other human resources functions and not by the HRSC and that the HRSC facilitates the collection, manipulation, and presentation of these data.

Second, the HRSC has a responsibility to finance in terms of HRSC budget and expenditures. Often this reporting occurs via overall human resources management. As with any department doing financial reporting, HRSC administration must submit all necessary requests and reports on time and with complete documentation. An effective manager provides background information (such as industry comparisons and ROI justifications) and requests for funding, especially if finance has little experience with budgeting for HRMS applications. HRSC and finance also should follow up with personal meetings whenever appropriate.

Managing Management

Only by having management support can the HRMS continue to function and improve service to users. Many HRMS managers feel that the most important issue in their relationship with corporate staff is managing the expectations of management.

Selling the HRMS

The manager (and the project leader) should never oversell the HRMS. Each project or enhancement has salient arguments for adoption. These include cost savings or avoidance, lawsuit avoidance, more timely and accurate data, more timely and better service to management, and a better-managed, more proactive human resources department. Selling the system (or improvements) to management goes beyond the budget to making sure management knows that the organization will derive some ROI and other ongoing benefits and values from it.

In successful dialogues, the HRMS manager acknowledges what management needs from HRMS:

- Timely, organized, accurate, logical information
- Data arrayed to present the information needed for decision support
- Conclusions from the HRMS when solicited

Having make sure that the HRMS will provide what management needs, the HRSC manager must receive in return management's ongoing commitment to provide support for the system. To do so, the HRSC manager should communicate the level of commitment management must make to build and maintain a successful HRMS in terms of money, time, resources, appropriate staffing, productive tools, and willingness to learn and change.

Fostering a System That Earns Management Support

Assuming that the system provides accurate data that management expects, HRSC staff must make sure those data are available in a timely fashion. They also should respond promptly to any management communication, in writing

Acting as an Internal Consultant

Many HRSC managers have discovered the value of thinking of themselves as internal consultants. As an inside consultant, a system manager provides advice and assistance rather than actually doing the work.

People hire consultants to provide answers when something goes wrong or might go wrong or to suggest a new direction. To become known as an internal consultant, a manager needs to develop a reputation as someone who can either provide or research the answer to problems and challenges.

An internal consultant must keep particularly well informed about developments in the field of HRMS and in human resources overall. Conferences, professional societies, and specialized education can help provide this knowledge. Resources are listed at the end of this book.

Being considered an internal consultant has some disadvantages in certain circumstances. In times of financial difficulties, many organizations forgo consultant services as part of a belt-tightening policy. In such cases, department or corporate management may see an internal staff member as expendable if that person is apparently functioning as a consultant rather than in an executive or line-management capacity. The HRSC manager may overcome this potential liability by retaining some hands-on responsibilities and providing regular, thorough documentation of HRSC management accomplishments.

whenever possible, to create a trail of alternatives and decisions, as well as to reinforce the feeling of being in touch.

Management, like users in other departments, should receive news of all HRMS successes and improvements, as well as positive feedback from users. For example, the HRSC should send copies of favorable audit reports to management, along with a cover letter pointing out the highlights.

The HRMS manager should take a proactive, independent stance, anticipating the needs of the system and of management. Such projects might include a compilation of human resources report formats, including ad hoc options. A proposal for graphics options, including storyboards to facilitate presentation, gives management something concrete to support the investment. More thorough procedural documentation helps ensure the reality and the impression of a well-organized, efficient operation.

Resolving Conflicting Priorities and Perceptions

An effective HRMS manager acknowledges the political reality that management holds ultimate power over the HRMS. In assigning priorities to HRMS work, the manager must ascertain management's highest priorities and apply tools and resources accordingly whenever possible. If management places a strong emphasis on staying out of trouble with government agencies, the HRSC may need to help management understand that the HRMS must apply more resources and attention to this area than to functions such as benefits or compensation.

If a conflict develops between management requests and other priorities or what the HRMS can currently provide, the HRMS manager must point out the conflict and develop alternative solutions. For instance, if management needs several new reports, alternatives might include HRMS creation of the reports, use of existing reports, or user development of reports using ad hoc or 4GL tools.

Management may not perceive some of the capabilities and limitations of staff. For instance, if management expects higher levels of ad hoc creation of reports than is currently taking place, the HRMS manager may suggest additional training, migration of HRMS staff into user functional areas, or use of HRMS staff instead of users to create the new reports. If the desired applications are overextending user skills, however, the HRMS manager will need to explain the situation to management, then suggest putting more training budget and time into getting users up to speed. The manager may want to point out how the HRSC staff or other available resources can help fill the gap.

When conflicts arise between HRMS requests and management's willingness to allocate additional resources, HRSC staff may find several techniques useful. They may compare the organization's situation with that of comparable firms, suggest phased goals, get input from people in other departments, or ask to borrow resources from other human resources projects to accomplish the additional goals.

Keeping the Management Committee Active

During the planning phase, a management steering committee meets regularly to develop policies and review the feasibility of the proposed HRMS. The committee should continue to meet during implementation to resolve issues as they arise. Usually this committee meets periodically with the HRMS project team or with the HRMS manager.

Once the system becomes operational, many management committees disband. Because these individuals understand the HRMS better than do other managers outside human resources, they can perform a valuable liaison function. Although the committee is certainly less active than it was during the early phases, it should meet about every six months. Some organizations hold management committee meetings as part of a semiannual audit process.

Corporate management input is a standard component in the audit process, so an ongoing committee serves as an established conduit for this communication. The committee can suggest issues that need attention and give feedback on HRMS activities, achievements, and needs. Members of this committee offer management's perspective on HRMS priorities, such as which modules to undertake, integration with the corporate data base, and planning for system replacement.

Committee members also may feel a greater sense of ownership than do other members of corporate management. Thus, they can understand the HRMS perspective on emerging issues and campaign on behalf of HRMS interests as necessary. Corporate management benefits by maintaining a more thorough awareness of HRMS activities.

The HRMS manager should assume responsibility for keeping this committee responsive and contributing to the HRMS. The manager should schedule and facilitate meetings, as well as help justify continuance of the committee to management. Unless the committee decides otherwise, the HRMS manager must take responsibility for disseminating management committee meeting results to all interested parties as appropriate. Often these results are distributed not only to committee members but also to other managers.

Managing HRSC Relations with Other Groups

The HRMS manager's responsibility for good relations does not end with the human resources department and top management. Interactions take place with employees, external agencies, vendors, and consultants. In whatever arena the HRMS exercises influence, an effective manager makes certain that others perceive the system and HRSC staff as competent and responsive.

The HRMS and the General Employee Population

The corporate culture of the organization determines the extent to which the HRSC maintains direct contact and communication with the overall employee population. Some banks, for example, view computer systems as tools for production, improving productivity, or providing management decision-making information. In this context, they do not communicate the introduction of a new system to all employees. More open companies, such as computer manufacturers, often make a special point of reporting system changes in employee newsletters. Whatever the philosophy, the more HRMS changes affect users, the more employees need information about the changes and how they will experience them in their daily routines.

This communication should stress how the system will benefit employees, such as through more flexible benefits, more accurate career development and tracking, or affirmative action support. Employees also should know their role in the implementation phase of an HRMS project. Perhaps employees will need to review their employee files for accuracy and complete data forms for the new data base. When employees know in advance what they will be required to do, the data verification and collection task proceeds more easily.

The HRMS and External Agencies

External agencies with which HRMS must deal include employment firms, federal and state departments of labor, workers' compensation commissions, insurance carriers, other benefits providers, labor unions, banks, and payroll processing services. A few tips on how to ensure good relations follow:

- Make sure HRMS staff understand protocol for interacting with outside agencies. Establish and clarify for all staff exactly which individuals have the authority to provide information or make comments to outside agencies, whether via phone, fax, or written communication.

- Limit access to the HRMS. Remember that the main responsibility of the HRSC is to support internal users. Only pay as much attention to external agencies and individuals as these internal duties permit. Unless otherwise directed by management, staff should give external agencies what they require but nothing more.

- Be responsive. Submit reports on time and answer letters promptly, even if the response simply states that more information is forthcoming. The HRMS should furnish reports that meet the content and format criteria required or preferred by outside agencies. For example, the Equal Employment Opportunity Commission (EEOC) has set standards for some reports. Taking such factors into consideration during initial design avoids problems later.

- Make sure external agencies understand that the HRSC is only the custodian of the data in the HRMS. If an agency has problems with interpreting data, the human resources function that is responsible should probably handle the inquiry.

- Most interactions between the HRSC and outside agencies are procedural in nature. With a properly designed and implemented system, completeness and accuracy of data are correct from the HRSC perspective; problem resolution and interpretation rest with the functional area.

The HRSC and Outside Experts

The HRSC may need to use vendors and consultants on an occasional basis for further maintenance of the system or to help resolve planning issues or particular problems. The HRSC manager needs to keep in frequent contact with the vendor, know what enhancements are imminent or planned, and possibly assign a technical person to monitor this and report significant developments. If the system needs additional service from the vendor, the HRSC manager takes responsibility for procuring it. The manager establishes objectives, negotiates a contract, provides liaison and resources, facilitates cooperation with vendors or consultants, and receives and reviews final reports.

In terms of consultant relations, the HRSC manager should use a consultant who has the appropriate knowledge and experience required and who also works well with the HRSC staff members who are involved. A technically competent but arrogant, abrasive, or uncommunicative consultant seldom makes an overall positive contribution to the system. The manager should make sure that both the consultant and in-house staff focus on goal-oriented activities rather than social interchange or extraneous (though technically interesting) topics. Consultants cost money, and the manager has the ultimate responsibility for making a wise investment.

Glossary

Decline stage   The final stage in a system's life cycle in which the HRMS becomes a growing problem because regulatory, technological, or organizational changes have caused the system to outlive its usefulness. During decline, maintenance increases, users become dissatisfied, and staff have difficulty justifying further investment in enhancements.

Growth stage   The stage in a system's life cycle after acquisition and development during which the system consolidates user needs and gains the greatest user acceptance. The key growth area is the user community, which now comes to depend on the HRMS. In a well-run organization, the system experiences increasing productivity and more requests for support services during this phase.

HRIC   See *Human resources information center.*

Human resources information center (HRIC)   A function within the HRSC that coordinates user services. The HRIC may handle training, user hot lines or other on-call support, and assistance with advanced user techniques.

IC   (Information center) Department or function that responds to service requests for computer system repairs, audits, modifications, and training. IC staff have high levels of software knowledge, skills and experience, and tools and techniques at their disposal.

IRM   (Information resources management) The concept that information belongs to the organization as a whole, not just to a single department. IRM assumes extensive and complex interfaces and integration among computer systems and data within an organization. Sometimes referred to as information warehousing.

Maturity stage   The stage in a system's life cycle during which growth ceases and the system stabilizes. This is the period of highest ROI. The HRMS shows continued improvements in the productivity and effectiveness of users and management.

ROI   (Return on investment) A financial term used to indicate the net margin or profit of a particular activity or project. In this case, ROI is a subjective measure of how well an HRMS returns to management the investment in it in the form of tangible and intangible values.

Start-up stage   The beginning stage in a system's life cycle during which the organization plans and develops a new system to replace an existing automated or manual one. This stage encompasses requirements definition, feasibility analysis, and acquisition or development of software.

User community   All the users of a system. Alternatively, one of a number of groups of users, in which each group has its own functional and technical needs as well as different sophistication levels.

Discussion Points

1. In what ways do the desired qualities of an HRMS project team leader differ from those of a manager of an ongoing HRMS?

2. What are the four phases in the life cycle of a computer system? What signals the transition between one phase and the next?

3. How does managing a growing system differ from managing a declining one?

4. What are the major ways of prolonging the maturity stage of an HRMS?

5. What actions should an HRMS manager take to "grow" an effective, stable HRSC staff?

6. What kinds of interactions are the HRSC and IS likely to have during the various stages in the system's life cycle?

7. What are the roles and responsibilities of management after system implementation?

8. Under what circumstances does HRSC staff interact with representatives of external agencies?

Further Reading

Arthur, Diane. *Managing Human Resources in Small and Mid-Sized Companies.* New York: AMACOM, 1987.

Block, Robert. *The Politics of Projects.* New York: Yourdon Press, 1983.

Callahan, John. "Need for the Systems Generalist." *Journal of Systems Management,* January 1985.

Chen, Richard. "The Trained-User as a Systems Analyst." Journal of Systems Management, July 1985.

Corney, William J. "Human Information Processing Limitations and the Systems Manager." *Journal of Systems Management,* March 1985.

Crouse, Roger L. "An IC Approach to Productivity." *Infosystems,* February 1986.

DeMarco, Tom, and Tony Lister. *Peopleware: Productive Projects and Teams.* New York: Dorset House, 1987.

Dorfmann, Joan. "Making the Most of User Groups." *Infosystems,* March 1985.

Fay, C. H. "Educating Old and New HR Managers." *Computers in Personnel,* 4, 1988.

Fleix, Robert G. and William L. Harrison. "Project Management Considerations for Distributed Processing Applications." *MIS Quarterly,* September 1984.

Goldmacher, Edward S. "HRIS Project Management and Ownership." *Personnel Administrator,* January 1986.

Gordon, Dr. Thomas. *Leader Effectiveness Training: The No-Lose Way to Release the Productive Potential of People.* New York: Bantam Books, 1977.

Leote, Dennis M. "Evaluating the Need for Software Modification." *Personnel Journal,* July 1987.

Mann, Leonard. "The Need for Business Analysts." *Journal of Systems Management,* February 1985.

Need, Loretta G. "The Importance of Being Audited." *Computers in Personnel,* Spring 1988.

Newman, Michael. "User Involvement: Does It Exist, Is It Enough?" *Journal of Systems Management,* May 1984.

Nicholas, John M. "User Involvement: What Kind, How Much, and When?" *Journal of Systems Management,* March 1985.

O'Connell, Sandra E. "A New Position in the Department." *HRManagement,* March 1990.

Serlin, Omri. "Departmental Computing: A Choice of Strategies." *Datamation,* May 1985.

Simon, Sidney H. "Accountability and Control of Human Resource Information." *Personnel Administrator,* July 1985.

Wescott, Russ. "Client Satisfaction: The Yardstick for Measuring MIS Success." *Journal of Information Systems Management,* Fall 1985.

Part III
HRMS Applications

> Computers and information systems are not synonymous. A computer is nothing more than mechanical leverage for implementing information systems.
>
> —Milt Bryce

The typical firm collects and tracks hundreds, if not thousands, of data elements on each employee (not to mention applications, terminees, and retirees). Most organizations either cannot afford to or choose not to automate all possible employee-related data. Moreover, though some software vendors offer products that deal with a wide range of human resources issues, others handle just specific applications. The more diverse the data the system will handle, the more modification the HRMS ultimately requires and the more attention the planning team must pay to the process of data organization and management.

Each human resources function has its own place in the HRMS, with a specific allocation of data segments reserved for its needs. Often the HRSC function may have at its disposal specific software and decision-support tools that provide the data base management and analysis that a particular human resources function requires. These include report writers, spreadsheet programs, and statistical analysis packages. Staff and financial limitations may force HRMS planners to exclude some human resources functions or specific modules at first, but they will eventually establish a time line and set of criteria for inclusion of additional modules at some future time if needed. Many human resources departments start with a basic employee records application to meet the tracking and reporting needs of employment, equal employment opportunity/affirmative action (EEO/AA), and perhaps some fundamental benefits and compensation administration. Training and development and parts of human resources planning also are frequently among the initial HRMS functions developed. Other modules may then be integrated with the core system, particularly if the function is part of the human resources department, such as health and safety, time and attendance, and workers' compensation. Sometimes these applications operate independently, borrowing data for specific uses. Sometimes they add new information to the master data base and require unique sceens and reports.

The chapters that follow are designed to help HRMS planners and managers of human resources functions make informed decisions about which functions to include in the HRMS. These decisions encompass system planning, development, selection, modification, enhancement, implementation, and utilization. Of course, each human resources department subdivides its functions uniquely depending on priorities and internal organization. The typical human resources functions described here represent just a few of the possible ways to organize human resources data. As guides for HRMS development, planners and developers should consider the structure of their users' departments and the constraints of hardware, software, and maintenance resources.

No HRMS will ever have the exact configuration of data elements, screens, and reports described in the following chapters. The applications in these chapters present some typical alternatives, but most systems permit extremely wide latitude in adding data fields, creating code tables, and generating screens and reports. The terms and arrangements used here should serve as a starting point rather than rigid definitions in constructing an HRMS.

12

Applicant and Employment Management

People are the common denominator of progress.
—John Kenneth Galbraith

A pplicant and employment management is one of the most important uses of computers for personnel. Many HRMS emphasize applicant-tracking modules quite heavily, even to the exclusion of a main record-keeping system, at least at first. The biggest reason for this is that most firms process a much larger volume of applicants than of employees. At the same time, applicant records are not very large (because they have no history), and they age rapidly. With computerized applicant and employment management, an organization can more effectively handle EEO issues and recruitment in today's labor market.

The Role of Applicant and Employment Management

The main users of an applicant and employment management module are human resources staff fulfilling the employment function—recruiting, screening, and facilitating the hiring of persons needed to meet staffing goals. Additional users include other human resources functions and organizational management.

This type of HRMS module may follow only applicants, or it also may include new hires, current employees, terminated employees, and retired employees. It may track not only individuals but also jobs, both filled and open, including job requisitions. The system may go beyond applicant and employee demographics to include EEO categories (ethnicity, gender, handicap, and age), skills and qualifications, and job applied for or held.

The operation of the employment function directly affects the rest of the organization. To the extent that employment does its job well, the rest of the organization has the best possible people with whom to work. Here are some

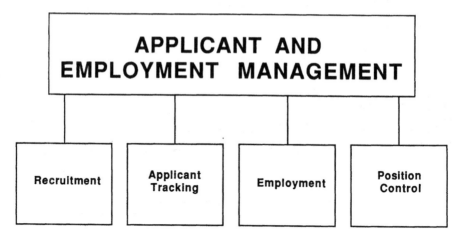

Figure 12–1. Principal roles of the applicant and employment management function.

examples of how an HRMS applicant and employment management module can help increase productivity in comparison to manual tracking:

- Save money. Computer searches are more efficient than file searches, computerized letter writing is more efficient than manual creation, and automatic data sorting and calculation are more efficient than manual processes.

- Foster more efficient, productive recruiting. With computerized data, recruiters can analyze past performance to determine the location and media strategies that produce the greatest number of applicants who are offered and accept positions (and who become successful employees.)

- Coordinate placement activities of recruiters working on the same or overlapping projects. Employment may have several recruiters working to fill related positions, particularly if an organization is looking for a significant number of new employees simultaneously (such as in the case of a plant or new branch expansion).

- Screen applicants faster and more consistently. In a supply-side labor market, an organization may receive upward of fifty applicants for a typical job opening. A series of selection algorithms can perform screening that would otherwise require additional employee resources. Moreover, when a new position opens, the system can screen applications already on file. If this screening yields a sufficient number of qualified applicants, recruiters may save the time and expense of placing ads and engaging in other external recruiting activities.

- Contribute to faster, more appropriate hiring decisions. Other departments may experience heightened productivity because they have the correct new staff in needed positions with less elapsed time between opening the requisition and filling the position.
- Create more complete, consistent, and professional-looking communications with applicants and new hires.
- Keep job-posting lists current, thus fostering the goodwill of employees and human resources staff. Maintaining an accurate list also increases the percentage of relevant inquiries by reducing the number of applications for closed positions or from unqualified individuals. (Only about 25 percent of firms have a job-posting system.)
- Increase ease of compliance with EEO requirements. This includes not only completing reports for government agencies but also developing plans for meeting goals and timetables and otherwise furthering compliance with and promotion of EEO-appropriate hiring processes. This is detailed in chapter 13.
- Provide a self-monitoring and evaluation process for employment functions. Using this module, human resources can track and analyze performance by individual, time period, elapsed time, process used, or other criteria. Such information can help human resources staff and management build a professional, effective service department.

A system that tracks employees as well as applicants also will do the following:

- Provide all basic data about employees in one consolidated master file. This data base can serve as a solid, well-organized foundation for the rest of the HRMS.
- Enhance management understanding of employee use and costs. Information from this data base can contribute to management planning on employee movement, transfers, promotions, and career training and development.
- Automatically monitor salary and wage costs by cost or profit center.

Data Requirements and Sources

An organization may require a substantial amount of data on every applicant and employee. In fact, relevant data elements are so numerous that this chapter cannot discuss each element or report. Rather, it mentions the most salient features and typical and useful applications. Data in the applicant and em-

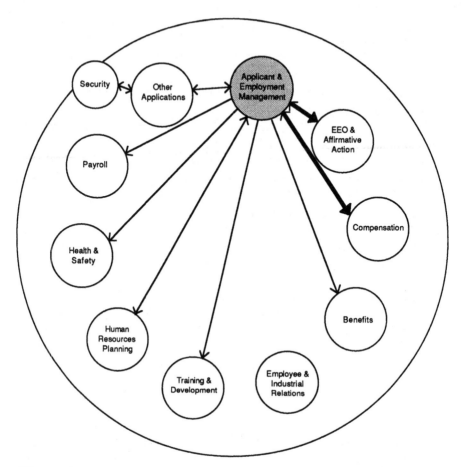

Figure 12–2. Information flow between applicant and employment management and other human resources functions.

ployment management module fall into three categories: applicants, employees (who usually begin as applicants), and jobs.

Applicant Data

The applicant management module should ask for only the educational and skills data the firm needs. One danger of an applicant and employment management program is gathering information just because it exists. It is important to begin by determining what the organization really intends to do with the data. (This is discussed in greater detail in chapter 3.) Consider a company that employs nine thousand blue-collar workers, five hundred managers who have some college education, and one hundred executives whose positions require college degrees. Most positions require simple education information, such as number of years of education completed. In these cases, the applicant tracking program monitors college, major, and degree only for certain job categories.

Sources. On the applicant side, the system almost never has any preexisting data unless the applicant is a former employee. In most circumstances, an application form provides the initial data on an applicant. The applicant completes this form, and a recruiter or data entry person codifies and enters the information. Data entry usually takes place on a batch basis depending on volume and processing schedules. For ease, consistency, and completeness of data entry, fields in the application and on the computer screen should appear in the same order and have corresponding wording.

Recruiters and others in personnel add other data to the applicant's file during the employment process. For each applicant contact, the recruiter fills out an interview summary. If the recruiter has a computer at her or his desk, she or he can enter the information into the computer. In most cases, however, the recruiter fills out these summary forms, and data entry inputs the information.

Requirements. The application includes not only standard demographics, such as full name and address and home and work telephone numbers, but also numerous other data elements, such as the following:

- Position(s) for which applying.
- Application date.
- Salary requested.
- Education. An organization may require basic education data or very detailed information depending on the position for which the applicant is applying. A simple procedure inquires only about number of years of education completed. A more complex form may ask for highest educational level, major field of study or discipline, highest degree obtained, and school/college/university attended. (Grade point average is less frequently used because its meaning varies with the specific school attended.) When a particular position requires detailed course information, the recruiter or interviewer usually asks for a paper copy of a transcript but does not enter this information into the system.
- Job skills. If the firm regularly requires certain skills—such as typing, operating heavy machinery, or familiarity with certain programming languages—codifying such skills facilitates retrieval of applicants suitable for particular positions.

- Employment history. This section covers traditional résumé job history information. The application should ask for positions in reverse chronological order, with the most recent or current position first. For each job, the application can probe for employment start date, employment end date, position title, employer name, and location. The application can allow space for descriptive material about position activities and responsibilities. These may be full sentences, phrases, or keywords. Some human resources departments enter this descriptive information onto the HRMS; others simply keep it as part of the backup file for review during the application and interview process.

- Credentials and licenses. These are appropriate or necessary for certain positions, such as nurses, drivers, teachers, and accountants. The form should include the expiration date.

- Geographic preferences. This list also may indicate limitations or exclusions—that is, locations where the applicant will not accept employment. These are usually coded multiple choice.

- Referral source. This field contains choices such as advertisement, agency, campus recruiter, or current employee. The application could probe for the specific name of the newspaper, job fair, or employee referral source. Such information, if codified, can help the employment function identify the most effective recruitment approaches for successful applicants or for qualified applicants corresponding to certain EEO goals.

- References. The application may probe for several employment references, including name, title, address, and phone number. The screen also may include a field for the reviewer to note whether the references have been contacted and the results obtained.

Some fields in the applicant file get filled in as the application process proceeds. These include the following:

- Demographics. These classifications include sex, ethnicity, age, handicap status, and other information of a personal nature. The applicant may be asked to volunteer such information but, in most cases, does not need to provide it. Because regulations may require organizations to collect such data, recruiters and others involved in the selection process often must gather it through visual observation. The recruiter or interviewer collects this information and notes it on the interview sheet or on a supplemental form, then the data entry person enters it into the record.

- Interview notes. The applicant file often contains basic interview information, such as interview date, interviewer, and recommendation. Such information helps track applicant status and recruiter activity. The interviewer's notes and comments usually remain in the applicant's paper file

Coding Applicant Sources

Most applicant and employment management functions track the source through which each applicant learns of a firm or an available position. By coding these responses, they can use the system to determine which sources provide the largest number of qualified or successful applicants. Such coding may be numeric, or, as in the following example, mnemonic.

WI   Walk-in
UR   Unsolicited résumé
RR   Employee referral—relative
RN   Employee referral—non-relative
EA   Employment agency
EM   Employment agency—minority
BR   Business referral
FE   Former employee
CS   College and university—student placement
CA   College and university—alumni/alumnae placement
ES   Executive search firms
AD   Advertisement
PS   Professional societies
FA   Job fairs/career days

because they are generally useful only to the few people making hiring decisions.

- Rejected offer information. Human resources and the organization should try to find out why applicants reject offers. What did the applicant find unacceptable—salary, hours, location? The interviewer or human resources recruiter should have explicit responsibility for inquiring about this issue when an applicant rejects an offer. Those involved must bear in mind that people generally hesitate to mention uncomplimentary reasons. Such information may contribute to word-processed correspondence encouraging desirable applicants to contact the organization again in the future.

- Applicant status. Each applicant's record indicates which steps in the employment process have been completed. These steps may appear as a checklist that is available for entry and review as appropriate. Possible steps to include are listed in the accompanying chart. Some of the steps may be required only for certain jobs, but the complete list can be in-

372

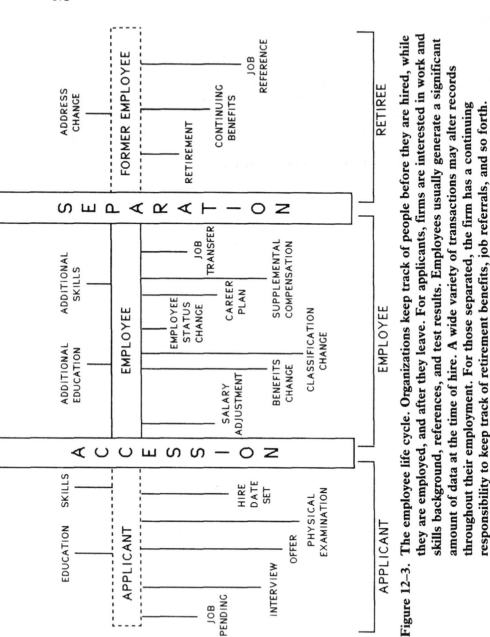

Figure 12-3. The employee life cycle. Organizations keep track of people before they are hired, while they are employed, and after they leave. For applicants, firms are interested in work and skills background, references, and test results. Employees usually generate a significant amount of data at the time of hire. A wide variety of transactions may alter records throughout their employment. For those separated, the firm has a continuing responsibility to keep track of retirement benefits, job referrals, and so forth.

Steps in the Application
and Interview Process

For each applicant, the file may include a list of standard steps, such as those noted here. As the applicant or staff completes a step, a notation in the file can appear as a check mark, coded multiple-choice response, or date as appropriate. The options or steps may include the following:

01   Résumé received

02   Application offered

03   Application completed

10   Interview(s) scheduled (and dates)

11   Interview(s) held (and dates)

12   References checked

13   Educational background checked

14   Other qualifications checked

20   Testing scheduled (and dates)

21   Testing completed

30   Recommendation made

31   Hiring decision made

32   Offer made

33   Offer accepted or rejected

40   Agreement signed

41   Disposition (when rejected)

42   Start-date scheduled

43   Supplemental data collected

cluded for each applicant, with unneeded steps marked not applicable (N/A) as appropriate.

• Comments. Many people believe that comment fields are what you complete when you have not covered all the bases. Any element that forms the basis for sorting or comparisons in reports needs a unique data field rather

374

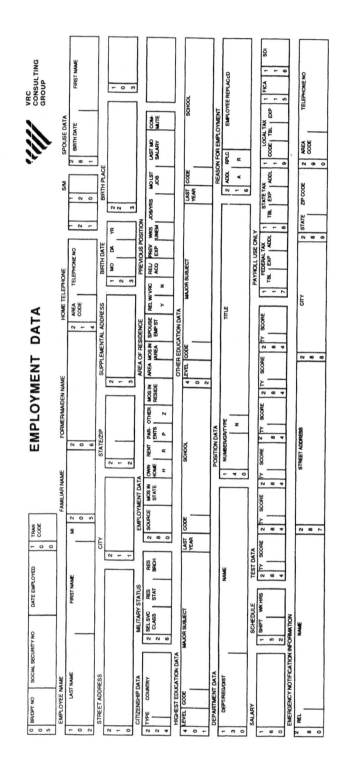

AUTOMATIC PAYROLL
DEPOSIT AUTHORIZATION

I hereby authorize VRC Consulting Group to pay all net sums of money due or to become due to me as an employee, by depositing the same to my checking account indicated below:

Checking Account No.

EMPLOYEE'S SIGNATURE

AUTHORIZED SIGNATURE   DATE

Form **W-4**

Department of the Treasury
Internal Revenue Service

Employee's Withholding Allowance Certificate

▶ For Privacy Act and Paperwork Reduction Act Notice, see reverse.

1 Type or print your first name and middle initial	Last name	2 Your social security number

Home address (number and street or rural route)

City or town, state, and ZIP code

3 Marital Status

☐ Single ☐ Married

☐ Married, but withhold at higher Single rate.

Note: *If married, but legally separated, or spouse is a nonresident alien, check the Single box.*

4 Total number of allowances you are claiming (from line G above or from the Worksheets on back if they apply) . . | 4 |

5 Additional amount, if any, you want deducted from each pay . . . . | 5 | $ |

6 I claim exemption from withholding and I certify that I meet **ALL** of the following conditions for exemption:

• Last year I had a right to a refund of **ALL** Federal income tax withheld because I had **NO** tax liability; **AND**
• This year I expect a refund of **ALL** Federal income tax withheld because I expect to have **NO** tax liability; **AND**
• This year if my income exceeds $500 and includes nonwage income, another person cannot claim me as a dependent.

If you meet all of the above conditions, enter the year effective and "EXEMPT" here ▶ | 6 | 19

7 Are you a full-time student? (**Note:** *Full-time students are not automatically exempt.*) . . . . | 7 | ☐ Yes ☐ No

Under penalties of perjury, I certify that I am entitled to the number of withholding allowances claimed on this certificate or entitled to claim exempt status.

Employee's signature ▶ _____ Date ▶ _____, 198___

8 Employer's name and address (**Employer:** Complete 8 and 10 only if sending to IRS)	9 Office code (optional)	10 Employer identification number

Figure 12–4. Employment data form and W4. At the time of hire, some firms have each employee complete a form similar to this one. The hiring authority (recruiter or supervisor) fills in some of the elements, such as department, position, salary, and test scores. Note that this form integrates the tax withholding certificate. (Instructions for this certificate are on the reverse side of the employment data form.) Combining these forms helps human resources obtain required data in a timely fashion.

than narrative entry in a comment field. Some systems do capture comment fields for information, such as interviewer notes. In such cases, each comment can begin with a keyword or code so that the user may ask to see only comments of a particular type.

Employee Data

Sources. Information in an employee's record combines some of the information gathered during the employment process with the following:

- Information provided by the employee upon starting employment
- Information provided by the hiring authority or recruiter at the time of hire
- Manual files accumulated over time
- Other automated systems, such as shop floor control, labor distribution, or the payroll system
- Supervisor's reports, which include performance reviews and forms regarding terminations, firings, leaves, transfers, and other changes in personnel status

The employment staff (or supervisor) responsible for each employee should make sure that the employee provides all necessary information.

Elements. The information provided by these additional sources includes the following:

- Employee number. Most organizations use the employee's social security number for his or her identification. The exceptions are usually companies that are still using an older, internally developed system. Back in the days of keypunch cards, companies needed a number no longer than four or five digits, because space was limited to 80 columns. Space considerations do not apply to today's systems, but some companies hesitate to shift to social security numbers because of the effort involved in converting to a new numbering system.
- Social Security Number. Every organization must maintain this number for tax purposes, even if it is not used as the employee number.
- Employee category. This field indicates the basis on which the individual is involved with the organization. The options may include full-time, part-time, temporary, contractor, or special status.
- Employee status. This field indicates activity status. The options may include active, voluntarily separated (resigned), involuntarily separated (terminated), medical or other types of leave, retired, deceased, or laid off.

The employee category and status fields are very basic and useful sorting fields. By assigning a code to each choice within these fields, the computer can provide a specific list or tally of employees of a particular type. For instance, perhaps in the category field, full-time equals 1, part-time equals 2, and temporary equals 3; in the status field, active equals 1, retired equals 2, and medical leave equals 3. Asking for a tally of all 1–1 employees would yield the total number of full-time, active employees; asking for all 1–3 employees would yield a list of all full-time employees currently on medical leave.

- Hire date. The original date of employment may differ from the benefits eligibility date, tenure date, seniority date, and reinstatement date.

- Job family/job/position. Terminology referring to how jobs are classified or coded is often quite confusing, as it differs considerably among vendors and businesses. For the purposes of this book, *job family* refers to a general grouping of work assignments according to overall skills or activities involved; *job* or *job classification* refers to a more specific work assignment, such as executive secretary; and *position* refers to each slot for someone in that job, such as secretary for the accounting department, secretary for the marketing department, or secretary to the vice president for finance. Different jobs within the same job family may be at different levels, or grades.

In some systems, data may not be entered in the position field; rather, it may result from other information provided, such as job and department. In many systems, each position has a unique identifier. The title may include type of work and area of specialization or location.

Additionally, all firms required to do EEO reporting must assign each specific job to one of twelve EEO occupational categories. EEO/AA staff usually make this assignment, though some organizations have job evaluation staff within compensation handle this responsibility. The field titled EEO occupational category is often an attribute of the job classification table. EEO occupational categories seldom correspond to the ways in which an organization needs to categorize its employees for recruiting, salary administration, or other purposes, so firms use their own job classification system for all but EEO reports.

- Title. Title describes the job functions performed, such as programmer/analyst or sales representative. It also may refer to rank or level of authorization. For instance, a bank may have several hundred persons with the official title of vice president, each of whom has unique responsibilities, with some vice presidents reporting to other vice presidents.

- Job grade. A large organization, or one with many levels of management or a collective bargaining agreement, may have strict job grades, or levels, that determine pay and eligibility for certain jobs. Generally, job classification determines grade, which is another attribute included in the job classification table, thus requiring no separately entered data.

- Pay type. Some organizations have all employees on the same pay basis (hourly); some use weekly and monthly salaries and hourly wage rates. Some have complicating factors, such as partial or full commission, profit sharing, hardship pay, or annual bonuses. If the system includes a payroll module, the system already includes information on all pay types. Whether or not payroll is a separate system, management and compensation administration will benefit from being able to tally and track numbers of employees in various pay types by location, job, and status category.

- Salary/rate of pay. This is usually base pay, independent of incentives, bonuses, shift allowances, and overtime. It is usually expressed as a dollar amount with a suffix, referred to as the pay basis (hourly, weekly, monthly), which indicates frequency.

- Citizenship status. Federal law mandates that employers verify that employees have a legal right to work in the United States—be a U.S. citizen, have permanent resident status, or have a work permit. In this field, an employment staff member notes that status has been checked. Recent legislation requires employers to verify the citizenship or alien status of all employees. The rules are very simple. Employers must submit a federal I-9 form for all new employees, stating that citizenship status has been verified. Keeping this information in each employee's record helps the firm meet federal requirements efficiently.

- Security clearance. An organization that requires government security clearances needs a well-organized system for tracking the clearance level of each employee, whether or not all employees do security-level work. Organizations working with government agencies such as the Department of Defense or the Nuclear Regulatory Commission must report these data when asked to do so. Management also requires this information when planning staff assignments for projects that require clearance and when applying for higher levels of clearance. As discussed in chapter 21, security clearance data sometimes reside in an independent system rather than in the main HRMS.

- Bonding. Fewer organizations are going through the process of bonding individual employees because bonding has become time-consuming and often is enforced inconsistently (particularly with employees who have not had a long U.S. work history). Instead, a bonding agency indemnifies an entire firm (such as a bank) and has thirty days to accept or investigate any individual employee.

- Internal job history. The HRMS usually tracks the chronology of significant events in the career of each employee. Depending on the firm's needs, this group of fields might include job, organization (department, division, region), title, transaction effective date, and salary or wage rate. The system uses effective dates to track breaks in service, such as leaves of absence, layoffs, and rehires, and to compute time in position, seniority, or basis of reinstatement. When new information replaces current work history data, the old information automatically becomes stacked as past historical data. Managing history is discussed in more detail in chapter 3.

- Site/location. This information may include one or more fields: physical work location, floor, lab unit, mail stop, or level at which the employee works. This information facilitates communication, space planning, and occupational safety and health monitoring.

- Supervisor. These fields include the immediate supervisor's name, title, phone number, and location. Sometimes employment must enter this information, but most systems use an organization code table to tie each position with the corresponding supervisor. This table lists each organization unit with a unique identifying number and identifies which other units the supervisor heads; thus, it can keep track of the employees in each unit. For instance, if employment staff enter organization code 1120 (marketing) and location 24 (Houston), the system could generate the name of the supervisor automatically.

- Seniority. Seniority is not normally entered into an employee's record. It is a calculated field based on dates. In fact, an employee's file may have more than one relevant date on which to calculate seniority: original employment date (an actual point in time) and adjusted service date (which takes into account the effects of layoffs, recalls, other breaks in service, and prior part-time work). Sometimes union rules dictate particular formulas for calculating seniority. The HRMS may need to track four different kinds of seniority—within the company, division, and department and for the specific job. Many organizations that have predominantly exempt employees use the term *service* to refer to this field. In this book, the terms *seniority* and *service* are usually used interchangeably.

  The algorithms for calculating seniority usually exist within payroll or in a separate time and attendance module rather than in employment management. When seniority data are needed for reports for the employment function, the system usually retrieves the information from that module.

  Seniority plays a significant role in promotional patterns and in employee and labor relations. From an applicant's point of view, seniority applies only if the person is reapplying and is therefore already eligible for certain benefits.

- Emergency contacts. The file should provide name, day (or work) phone number, evening (or home) phone number, and relationship to employee for a person to be contacted in case of an emergency. The prevalence of two-income families means that organizations should have alternate contacts (with complete information) and must keep that information current. Because this information often changes over time, companies should periodically generate lists of emergency contact information and distribute them to employees, who must update the lists as necessary.

Job Requisition Data

The applicant and employment module often tracks not only applicants and employees but also positions available within the organization. Most firms have some type of job requisition process. Those that do generally include its data-handling requirements in an HRMS.

Sources. To enter a job requisition into the system, employment works with supervisors or managers in other departments to complete the job requisition form; most job requirements originate from the source department or unit. A data entry person then enters the relevant information into the system.

Requirements. Job requisition processes vary widely, but most usually require the following data:

- Requisition number. This number identifies and tracks each requisition (because an expanding organization may simultaneously have multiple position openings for certain jobs, such as secretaries). The requisition number may indicate when the requisition was opened, which allows tracking the length of time required to fill each requisition.
- Requisition type. This field indicates whether the requisition is for an addition (to fill a new position) or a replacement (to fill an existing position vacated by an incumbent).
- Job category. Like the employee category, this field indicates the time basis for the job to be filled. Options may include full-time, part-time, temporary, seasonal, or contractor.
- Position/job classification/job title. Use the code and title as described in the preceding section on employee data.
- Organization. This field indicates the department, project, or function to whose budget this position applies. It is sometimes linked automatically to department or cost center via position.
- Date job requisition authorized. This also may include date filled, date closed, or date withdrawn.

- Experience requirements. This field lists skills or experience and numbers of years required (such as "Operating room supervision, 3 years" or "Expert systems programming, 5 years"). Codifying this information permits users to sequence candidates by level of skills or experience.
- Education requirements. This field may indicate the required number of years of schooling, the degree required, and the major field of study. Codifying this information facilitates easy access.
- Certification/license requirements. This applies particularly to professions that require licensure or certification, such as teachers, nurses, and certified public accountants. Expiration date, renewal data, and/or date rejected are included. If an employer or field of specialization allows, the renewal date may be several months later than the expiration date, to allow employees a grace period.
- Department. Depending on the organization's structure, the requisition may indicate department, division, region, unit, or some other organizational subset.
- Site. This is the physical facility or location at which the employee will work.
- Job grade. This usually also determines compensation range, which the requisition will list.
- Start date. This may be "Immediate" or a specific future date.
- Hiring authority. This includes name, title, phone number, and location. The person with the hiring authority is usually also the supervisor of the unit with the open position, though in a large firm, they may be different people. Some systems establish an organization code table that includes this information as attributes of the department or division.
- Requisition status. This list contains some of the same data as the applicant status list discussed earlier in this chapter, but it tracks the status of a specific job requisition rather than a specific applicant.

The employment management module may provide a standard checklist of employment procedures, which the recruiter then customizes to reflect the circumstances of each requisition. The actual steps usually depend more on the position than on the organization as a whole. Secretaries need typing tests; executives do not. The organization may require five interviews to hire an executive but only one or two for a file clerk. Most systems provide a list of all possible steps; the individual recruiter or interviewer then enters N/A for steps not needed and fills in other activities as they occur (or may add additional steps for specialized positions). If an organization needs individuals with high-demand skills, recruiters may choose to waive some of the steps. For instance, some clients faced with high demand may hire first, then do educational and employment verification later, so as to avoid losing a promising candidate because of delays in making and accepting offers.

The list also may include information such as dates of advertisements, dates of responses to ads, testing required, interviewers and interview date, disposition of applicants, offers made, and offer accepted. This allows employment to monitor operational performance. When the system receives data that an offer has been accepted and a start date set, it indicates that requisition as filled.

- Job requisition status. This field indicates current status, such as authorized, open, applications being accepted, interviewing, closed, withdrawn, offer pending, contract submitted, or position filled.
- Date filled. The actual date the open position was filled.

Reporting Requirements

Because the applicant and employment management module contains so many different data fields, its information can form the basis for a wide variety of reports. Many of these reports are for internal employment function use, but other groups also use reports created by this module. Users include human resources management, company or organization management, supervisors in other departments, employees themselves, and outside agencies interested in job placement or EEO (also discussed in the next chapter).

Job Requisition Reports

Job Posting List. The job posting list itemizes a firm's open job requisitions for the purpose of posting them in a central place where incumbent employees can see them and bid on open positions in which they are interested. This list usually includes job requisition number, job title, department, location, salary, skill or experience requirements, start date, and requisition status. This list is sequenced by date requisition open or by job classification and sometimes by location.

Employment staff and employees are the most frequent users of this list. When firms post this list for employees interested in internal transfers and promotions, human resources makes it accessible to everyone and updates it frequently. In certain circumstances, human resources may distribute this list externally, such as to no-fee, community-oriented job-finding resources such as college placement offices, government agencies, and nonprofit groups. Such actions may even increase EEO responsiveness. To meet those needs, employment staff must keep this list complete, accurate, and timely.

Job Requisitions by Site. This report lists all open job requisitions at a particular job location. Managers and staff are more likely to request this report when sites are distant from headquarters.

Job Requisitions by Qualifications. This report lists all open job requisitions that require a particular set of skills or experience.

Job Requisition Summary Report. Management may find useful a summary of job requisitions by department, location or quarter. This report could list job category, salary range, number of job requisitions opened and number filled, and so forth. This report helps management evaluate department turnover, staff budget, staffing planning, vacancies, and so forth.

Job Requisition Status Report. This report lists the status of each job requisition for which a specific recruiter has responsibility. It could include data such as job requisition number, job title, and status (open/closed, withdrawn, filled/unfilled.)

Applicant Tracking Reports

Applicant Log. An applicant log is basically a date-stamping procedure that counts and dates each individual applicant. A clerk who serves as a central funnel (such as in the lobby of a large organization) records each application form given to someone walking in. Similarly, a clerk in the recruiting area receives and logs all résumés received as a result of college recruitment or unsolicited correspondence. The log indicates not only the name, date of application, position applied for, and demographics for each applicant, but also, in the case of walk-in candidates, visual observations pertinent to EEO, such as age, race, sex, and handicap status. EEO (discussed at length in chapter 13) may require such reports if the organization has any history of systemic discrimination against any applicant population.

Each firm should carefully define what constitutes an applicant. Certainly, compliance with the spirit of EEO obligates a firm to make such definitions clear. Moreover, lack of a standard policy can lead to excessive or inconsistent paperwork, computer use, and unwanted scrutiny by the EEOC.

In some organizations, if a designated representative takes an action to generate an application and the applicant responds with activity demonstrating some interest, that respondent is, by definition, considered an applicant. Someone who sends in an unsolicited résumé is not necessarily an applicant, but someone who sends in a résumé in response to a newspaper advertisement may be. If the unsolicited résumé prompts a letter or call from the firm asking that the individual come in for an interview, that person becomes an applicant.

Someone who asks for an application at the front desk, receives one, and completes it is an applicant. Walk-ins and write-ins are generally not applicants.

Applicant Flow Report. An applicant flow report gives employment a picture of which applicants are at particular stages in the employment process. The purpose of this type of report is to provide information on the status of applicant and application processing. The report may list actions (such as testing and interviews scheduled or conducted) and decisions (applicant rejected, offer made, offer rejected).

By sorting applicants either by the specific position for which they applied or by the time period during which they applied, human resources can analyze factors such as number of applicants who applied for a particular position, their EEO status, and their source. These lists can include all applicants or just new hires during a particular period. For instance, a report could show the number of applicants for a specific requisition who have completed each step in the employment process.

Applicant and Employee Source Report. An applicant and employee source report is a special version of applicant tracking. By tracking how applicants and new hires learned of the position (or the organization), human resources can analyze employment costs and allocate resources to assess the cost-effectiveness of various sources and to identify the most appropriate candidates and employees. Sources include newspaper ads, trade journals, job fairs, college placement services, agency referrals, and current employees.

Some modules track not only the category of source but also the specific source. For instance, having identified which university and college placement offices are the most effective sources, recruiters can adjust their travel schedules accordingly. If certain newspapers are attracting primarily unqualified candidates, employment can drop those publications. With applicant and employee source reporting in place, human resources can test various forms of advertising and applicant promotion, such as comparing small ads versus large ads, trying radio spots, or comparing specialized versus general personnel agencies.

These reports also can track sources of applicants based on race/ethnicity, sex, age, or handicapped status. This type of report is the basis for EEO reports on protected classes. This information also can help an organization establish and adjust recruiting plans to meet EEO goals and timetables. If certain newspapers bring in a high proportion of qualified candidates having relevant EEO characteristics, the organization could choose to place a greater proportion of its recruitment advertising with this publication.

Applicant Tracking and Job Tracking Reports. Perhaps the aspect of this module that recruiters value most highly is the ability to match available jobs with qualified individuals. This can take several forms:

Applicant Disposition Codes

Some firms track reasons why they reject an applicant; others do not. Those that do generally use a set of codes such as the following:

- 01 Hired
- 10 Qualified, no opening
- 11 Referred to department for interview
- 12 Failed test(s)
- 13 Did not report for test(s)
- 14 Did not appear for scheduled interview
- 15 Physical or other job-related handicap
- 16 Failed physical examination
- 17 Misrepresentation on application
- 18 Inadequate work references
- 19 Lacks bona fide occupational qualification (BFOQ)
- 20 Conviction for dishonesty, breach of trust, or other reason
- 21 Alien without proper documents
- 22 Underage (18)/overage (65)
- 23 Relatives employed here
- 30 Compensation offer not acceptable
- 31 Applicant refused offer
- 32 Cannot work required hours
- 33 Withdrew application
- 34 Unable to contact
- 40 No openings
- 41 Other, unknown disposition

SOURCE		OPERATOR / LABORER	SECTY / CLERICAL	TECH / PROFESSIONAL	SALES / MARKETING	TOTAL
WALK IN	Number	12	5	2	3	22
	%	55	23	9	14	
LOCAL NEWS AD	Number	2	3	9	2	16
	%	13	18	56	13	
REG/NATL NEWS AD	Number	1	0	1	9	11
	%	9	0	9	82	
EMPLOYEE REFERRAL	Number	1	3	4	6	14
	%	7	21	28	43	
JOB FAIR	Number	0	1	3	4	8
	%	0	12	38	50	
EMPLOYMENT AGENCY	Number	1	1	2	2	6
	%	17	17	33	33	
EXECUTIVE SEARCH	Number	0	0	0	4	4
	%	0	0	0	100	
OTHER SOURCE	Number	2	1	0	1	4
	%	50	25	0	25	
TOTAL		19	14	21	31	85

Figure 12–5. Applicant source report. The applicant and employment
management function can use this type of report to learn
which applicant sources bring in which types of applicants.
Different sources work most effectively for different job
families.

- Selection process status report. This report lists activity that has taken place against a specific job requisition, such as number of candidates interviewed and number of offers. Information for this report comes from that gathered as part of the job requisition management process.

- Applicants for specific jobs. Human resources often needs a current list of available, qualified candidates for each opening. Recruiters use this list themselves and also distribute it to interviewers and other participants in the hiring process outside human resources.

- Applicant qualification summary. This report lists all applicants who meet specific criteria (such as skills, experience, location, or salary), whether or not they have applied for a particular job. This type of report is helpful in high-demand labor markets or when the recruiter wants to include promising candidates who submitted unsolicited résumés or applications at some time in the past. When the volume of applicants is low or the position is in a demand-side market, recruiters may need to screen each application or résumé. In a high-volume, supply-side market, the HRMS can perform preliminary screening according to criteria the recruiter may select. A company required to meet mandated EEO goals and timetables may instruct the system to include for review only applicants in certain EEO categories who also meet basic criteria.

- Employee qualification summary. This report lists all current employees with certain qualifications. This is essentially a skills inventory listing, which is discussed in detail in chapter 17.

Applicant Profile. During the interview and hiring process, employment staff, interviewers, prospective supervisors, and others need to take a careful look at a particular applicant's file. An HRMS can furnish this information in the form of a report known as an applicant profile.

For most professional positions, applicants submit résumés. For many line or clerical functions, however, the job application serves as the sole written source of applicant information. In either case, much of this information may be transferred to the HRMS. From such data, employment staff can create several types of profile reports, depending on the organization's needs. A report on an individual can display data in either graphic or résumé form. Graphs may come in several versions:

- Personal data, including demographics such as EEO data

- Qualifications data, including education, training, experience, skills, licenses, and certificates

- Interview data, including interviewer, routing, comments, dates, offer content, and disposition

Some systems use a computer-generated résumé to standardize the content and format of résumés distributed to interviewers, potential supervisors, and other reviewers. By using such forms instead of the applicant's original material, human resources can mask irrelevant fields, such as EEO data, yet retain this information for other analyses.

Staff also can use an inquiry-by-name capability to call up the file of a particular candidate. This listing may be alphabetic, by assigned number, or by date. Some programs can do a phonetic search for names. This allows the user to locate any applicant or employee currently in the system by using an approximation of the last name.

Applicant Communications

For legal reasons, as well as good business and professional practice, the hiring process requires a substantial amount of written communication between the firm and a prospective employee. Human resources must tailor specific letters and other documents to individual applicants. By integrating word processing and mail-merge capabilities, the applicant and employment management module can create complete, accurate, and professional-looking documents.

The first document is usually a follow-up letter to acknowledge receipt of an application. This letter helps keep an applicant from accepting another offer before human resources can complete the applicant-screening process. Employment should send a letter as a record of the activity even if a staff member acknowledges the application by phone.

Most organizations will reject many more applicants than they hire. The ratio could be 50:1 or higher. An organization may want to send a message to some rejected applicants (but not to others) that offers hope of future employment. Thus, the module should include several different types of response letters. Each should have a particular code or name recruiters can use to indicate which letter to send. For instance, response letter A may go out to those answering advertisements or other recruiting activities. Letter B may go out to individuals who send in unsolicited résumés that do not correspond to the organization's immediate needs. Letter C may go to individuals in high-demand fields whose applications will receive consideration. Letter D may confirm an appointment for an upcoming interview.

Other communications to applicants during the hiring process include offers, contracts, and benefits letters, as well as rejection notices to applicants no longer being considered. Because the applicant or employee's file already contains all the information needed for an individualized letter, the word processing function can create these letters without requiring additional customization. For instance, once an applicant accepts a verbal offer and confirms a start date, the appropriate information is entered so the system can generate a confirming letter that contains these details.

Finally, many organizations give every new hire a package of background and welcoming materials as part of its orientation process. This package usually provides information about the firm and its policies and procedures. It may include parking stall assignment, a security badge, cafeteria hours, social activities, grievance procedures, and educational opportunities. The package also includes a schedule of medical, dental, and life insurance and other benefits.

The organization may update this information periodically as company policies and situations change. By computerizing the issuance of the orientation package and noting in the employee's file that it was issued, the company can document that employees have received the information they need.

New-Hire Forms and Reports

New-Hire Forms. Every firm has many documents for new employees to complete and sign. These may include emergency contact information, tax-withholding forms, benefits-enrollment forms and certificates, nondisclosure agreements, patent agreements, corporate credit cards, and a corporate phone card. A new-hire package within the applicant and employment management system can provide not only the actual forms for the employee to fill out but also a checklist of required forms and information.

A sophisticated system can tailor this collection of forms and the checklist to the individual employee and position. For instance, a new employee hired for a position that requires certificates or licenses would automatically receive in the packet a request to bring in a specific type of license or credential for the supervisor to review. The master checklist would indicate that the supervisor must submit confirmation that such action has taken place.

Any company needs additional information from a new hire that was not acquired in the application and employment process. Most companies give new hires a questionnaire to complete. Some HRMS provide a printed new-hire form that contains all the relevant information gathered about an employee during the application, interview, and offer process (such as name, social security number, address, EEO data, job title, location, pay type, and salary). The form asks for additional information, which may include birth date, felony convictions, and citizenship status. Usually the employee completes, signs, and returns the form.

Some organizations believe that the amount of data that transfers from an applicant file to an employee file is too small to warrant developing the capacity for automatic transfer. In such systems, the person doing the hiring has a data entry clerk complete a load sheet, transcribing from the applicant profile and other needed reports whatever data the applicant will need as an employee.

The new employee should review, correct, complete, and sign the new-hire form. A data entry person then enters all the new and corrected information from this form.

The employee usually receives numerous other forms to complete, along with instructions about how to submit them. A computer-generated checklist allows employment to monitor the status of these submissions (distributed to employee, not applicable, pending, or received).

As the employee turns in each form, employment checks the information for reasonableness and completeness, updates the master checklist, and then makes sure each form reaches the proper internal function, such as benefits or payroll. If documents are not forthcoming after some time has passed, employment can use the master checklist to send a reminder notice to the employee or supervisor about which forms are still missing. Some sophisticated systems generate these reminder forms automatically.

One benefit of using the HRMS to issue new-hire documents is that the system can then track documents, information, and other material issued to the newly hired employee. Such items might include credit cards, vehicles, equipment, keys, and security passes. Part of the applicant and employment management module can list which equipment an employee has checked out (such as microcomputers) either on-site or off-site. This tracking helps the firm monitor and ensure appropriate usage of its resources.

New-Hire Report. All human resources functions need notification of new hires. A new-hire report lists name, job title, department, site, supervisor, and start date of each new employee. Reports sent to compensation and benefits also may include salary or pay type.

This listing may go to several human resources functions, including internal placement, employee relations, EEO, benefits (for enrollment monitoring and planning), compensation (to monitor that salary is within the authorized range), training (to plan courses and schedules), and payroll.

Employee Referral Bonus Report. When trying to hire employees with skills that are in high demand, some companies have instituted employee referral bonus programs. In such a program, an employee whom an applicant mentions on the initial application as the source of information about the available position receives a bonus if that applicant is offered and accepts a position with the firm. This process usually can use the same load sheet as is used for any payroll change. In many systems, employment completes a form identifying the employee receiving the bonus, then fills in the blanks for the following:

- Type of payment. This is usually designated as L (for lump sum) or P (for periodic payments). In some cases, the referred employee must work for the firm three to six months before the bonus is payable.

- Amount. Employment calculates the amount, which is either a percentage of the new employee's salary or a set sum.

The authorization path for this bonus depends on who makes decisions about the bonus program and on the related cost accounting. If cost of hire is the responsibility of the new employee's department, the department manager approves the bonus payment. If the employment function is responsible for the cost of hiring, it approves the payment. After approval, the referring employee may receive a system-generated notice that he or she is eligible to receive a bonus. This notice usually includes name of new employee, position of new employee, and bonus amount. To keep informed about the bonus program, corporate management may request a periodic list of new hires and their positions, including employees who have made successful referrals and the dollar amount of bonuses awarded.

Employment Management Reports

Employee Profile. This profile, in the form of a report or screen, provides a one-page summary of a particular employee. Both the human resources and supervisory functions use it to provide a display of the employment status of the employee. This report includes basic information such as hire date, job classification, department, salary, pay type, employee category and status, and supervisor. It also includes historical information, such as past positions in the organization, breaks in service, pay changes and effective dates of changes, reasons for changes, performance review dates, and ratings. Employment may provide this profile to employees who want to review their performance review file, as well as to supervisors considering disciplinary action (firing or probation) or a transfer of this employee to their area.

Employee History. Corporate managers may wish to create a historical profile of specific employees within the organization. The system may profile individuals or the population as an entire organization or by selected job categories, departments or facilities, EEO categories, or status and category codes. It can produce a current profile or a profile as of a particular date. Such reports, particularly if graphically displayed, can help management monitor trends, correct imbalances, and plan for the future.

License and Credential Reports. The licensing and credential date in the system should include required renewal and expiration dates. The module can then generate renewal reminders to the affected employee, his or her supervisor, and/or human resources staff several weeks or months before expiration to ensure that employees keep all necessary licenses and credentials current.

EMPLOYEE PROFILE

EC/S   PROFILE DATE

102 EMPLOYEE NAME

205 FAMILIAR NAME   206 FORMER NAME

100 TRAN CODE   TRANSACTION MESSAGE   DATE   EMPLOYEE CATEGORY/STATUS

SOCIAL SECURITY NO.   EFFECTIVE DATE MO DAY YR

201 STREET ADDRESS   211 CITY   214 HOME TELEPHONE   152 SHIFT   WK HRS

123 BIRTH DATE   223 BIRTHPLACE   104 DATE EMPLOYED   DATE FT/PT/PRIME   120 SEX/MARITAL   226 MILITARY CL RS   281 SPOUSE'S DATA BL BIRTH DATE   FIRST NAME   282 EMP ST   213 SUPPLEMENTAL ADDRESS

BRANCH/DEPARTMENT NAME   REGION NAME   COUNTY   EDUCATION LEVEL   MAJOR SUBJECT   YEAR   SCHOOL

140 POSITION GRADE   TYPE E-NTR   POSITION TITLE   OFFICER TITLE   160 SALARY DATA TYPE AMOUNT   SALARY   ANNUAL SALARY   150 PERF RATING

393

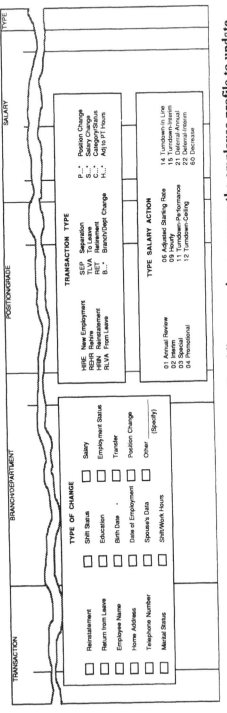

Figure 12–6. Employee profile. Human resources staff and line supervisors may use the employee profile to update an employee's job history. The user enters a transaction code, a brief description of the transaction, and a transaction effective date. As shown in the list of transaction codes, changes may include return from leave status, promotion, or transfer, among others. This update automatically stacks preceding information in the history section of the employee's record.

The supervisor usually does not need to see the actual certificate. Some modules generate two reminders and a final notice that the employee's eligibility to perform certain work has been suspended pending a renewal document.

Internal Reports

The employment function can use the applicant and employment management module to provide self-monitoring reports as well.

Employment Activity Reports. Some systems can generate reports that focus on how many people pass through particular employment activities. Such reports may cover requisition activity and aging, requisition inventory (open, filled, or withdrawn), total number of applicants, and number of applicants meeting qualifications for certain requisitions or those obtained by certain recruiters. For instance, the employment function in a rapidly expanding electronics firm found that even though its hiring activity was accelerating, it was not gaining much ground because the total volume of requisitions was growing almost as fast as the rate of hiring. Employment staff realized that they had to become more efficient or add more staff.

Most applicant and employment management modules produce many types of employment activity reports, but one of the most common is the *authorized versus actual report*. This report lists all unfilled positions, including authorized but unfilled (open requisitions), authorized and filled (new hires), and unauthorized and unfilled (pending requisitions not yet approved). Each entry may list job title, job classification, job family, employee (if filled), department, supervisor, location, and salary. Other data may be included, such as addition/replacement indicator, dates, and cost center.

The applicant and employment management module can sort requisitions many ways, such as by location, cost center, division, or date. The module also can sort open requisitions as well as employees. It can generate a list of all employees in a particular job family and their salaries—for instance, a list of all secretaries and what each is being paid.

Recruiter Reports. Recruiter reports help human resources management track the work of individual recruiters. Such reports contain assignment listings and the number of assignments, contacts, interviews, offers, and hires by each individual recruiter during a particular month, quarter, or year. For each recruiter, a report may calculate the average number of days required to fill positions. Users may find this report much easier to interpret if it presents data graphically as well as in written or tabular form.

College Recruitment Scheduling Reports. Recruiters need to inform college placement offices about schedules for interviews and about job descriptions or

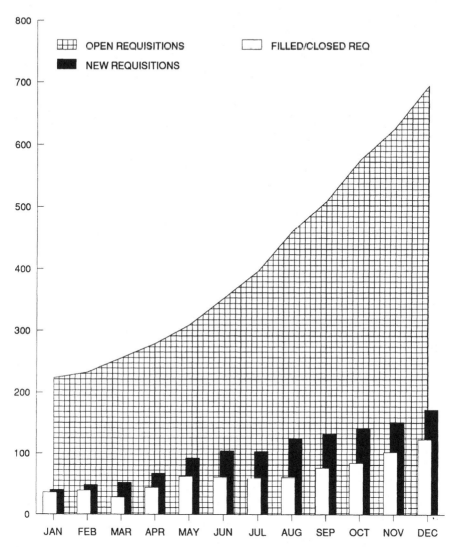

Figure 12–7. Tracking requisition activity. As shown in this graph, the applicant and employment management function discovered that even though it had been filling an increasing number of requisitions, it was still falling behind in its inventory of open requisitions. The function had two choices: increase productivity or increase staff.

qualifications for which they will be interviewing. The module can contain a separate data base of college placement officers. The file for each college would include college name, placement office, address, contact person(s), and telephone number. Recruiters can use this information with a mail-merge function. They can send letters that request information about recruiting opportunities and college schedules. Based on this information, recruiters put together their travel schedule, then perform a mail merge to send a letter to each college with the date(s) the recruiter(s) will be on campus.

Position Control

Position control involves identifying the types of jobs done in an organization, how many people perform each job (incumbents of specific positions), and at what levels or ranges of pay. Position control sometimes includes determining the rate at which the organization will need people to fill these jobs. In this book, this part of the process is covered in chapter 18.

Each *job* has certain features, definitions, characteristics, other requirements, classifications (EEO occupational category, workers' compensation code, job grade), and seniority rules. Tallying all the jobs permits the monitoring of authorized count and filled count. A job may have multiple incumbents, single incumbents, or no incumbent, as in the case of unfilled positions. Each *position* has certain additional characteristics, such as location, department, and scheduled hours. By defining each job and each position, computerized position control can help an organization define its internal structure and establish criteria for job requisition approval. More importantly, it can help the organization develop realistic budgets and control salary costs.

Some vendors include up to thirty kinds of position control reports in their applicant and employment management module or in an independent position control module. For instance, a position inventory lists all filled and available positions. Position costing lists the current salary range or salary for each position within a particular job. Position budget variance lists all filled positions with a salary outside the range established for that job. Some reports can provide total costs for all listed positions, for all currently filled positions, or for all authorized but unfilled positions. A system that incorporates position control can use this information to create job requisition files and documentation, prepare job postings, and monitor performance against budget, since the computer already contains information about job requirements, location, supervisor, and salary range.

Including position control in an HRMS involves the addition of a type of process that, practically speaking, human resources cannot do manually. Human resources often concentrates computerization priorities on activities that replace manual operations so that limited resources meet department needs.

Partly for this reason, only relatively few HRMS currently include position control.

Position control is most prevalent in the public sector, where budgets and authorized head counts are tightly controlled. A state or community college might have a certain number of authorized faculty positions in each academic area and a certain number of each type of administrative position. In the private sector, managers who have a staffing need may more easily justify an addition to staff. Even in the private sector, however, a large firm can use position control to help resolve anomalies in organizational structure and create more fiscally responsible operations.

Special Circumstances

Human resources must provide reports to external agencies and internal groups based on data gathered via the applicant and employment management module. When planning data collection and reporting capabilities for this module, system designers should consider the role of these groups in the activities of the organization.

Outplacement Programs

Some companies make provisions to help workers who are being laid off find new employment. The applicant and employment management module can help maximize the efficiency and cost-effectiveness of this assistance, which is often called outplacement services. By providing visible, concrete aid, human resources can help reduce some of the tension and bad feelings that usually arise during layoff situations.

With this module, human resources can furnish each affected employee with a current, customized, professional-looking résumé. Human resources can match outside employers that have positions available with workers who have appropriate skills and interests. Human resources can monitor the status of affected employees by tracking résumés prepared, interviews scheduled, new positions accepted, and offers rejected.

Interface with EEO Reporting

The data in this module form the basis for EEO reporting requirements, as discussed at length in chapter 13. By integrating the two modules, the HRMS can help the organization monitor potential compliance problems on a continuous basis to identify trouble spots and take corrective action. Moreover, by demonstrating that the company tracks such data and uses the information to refine a fair and quality-oriented hiring process, human resources can help promote a good working relationship between the organization and various government agencies, as well as with minority communities, special-interest groups, and employees.

Interface with Benefits Planning

Benefits costs are high and will continue to increase. The HRMS can help contain these costs. The applicant and employment management module is the source of much of the data that the benefits function needs in order to establish the benefits package for each employee and to develop adequate and cost-effective benefits planning for the entire organization. This information includes hire date, job classification, department, age, marital status, number and age of dependents, location, and salary.

With this information, benefits can review retirement planning options (by evaluating the age distribution among employees), calculate costs of various dependent coverage options, and correlate benefits packages with cost-of-living patterns in various geographic areas. Such actions can contribute significantly to employee satisfaction and to organization stability. The HRSC, therefore, justifies its own contribution to the organization by responding to the data needs of the benefits function, particularly in the area of cost containment.

Interface with Payroll

Payroll first learns of a new hire via information transmitted from the employment function. This may come as a personnel action notice or other form that provides basic information about the new employee. If the payroll system is integrated with the HRMS, this notice can list just employee name, number, and pay rate, since payroll staff can access and review all additional data directly from the HRMS. If payroll data are separate from the HRMS, the applicant and employment management module should provide more information and develop an interface between the intake process (employment) and the payroll process.

The Computerized Interview

Several software vendors now offer programs that allow the computer to pre-screen applicants. The applicant completes an application form, and the information from the form is entered into the computer, as with most systems. The applicant then sits at a microcomputer or terminal and responds to a series of forced-choice questions that elicit additional information. Technical staff can customize both the application and the computer questions for particular job families. The questions for clerical support positions naturally differ from those for technical assembly positions. Management positions probably do not include a computerized interview at all.

Some studies have encountered little or no resistance to using computers in this context and have found that applicants are more honest and relaxed with computers than with human interviewers. The computer evaluates and summarizes the applicant's responses, then prints the summary for the applicant. It also prints a summary for the interviewer and points out any contradictions, missing information, or particular points about which the interviewer should inquire.

Archiving Applicant and Employment Management Data

Applicant records can pile up in the data base of even small but growing organizations. Without a plan for dealing with this overload of data, a system can soon exhaust its storage capacity. Because the applicant and employment management module contains so many records that are needed for only a short time, development of this module must include appropriate policies and procedures for retention and purging of records.

Different retention criteria apply to applicants, current employees, and various types of terminated employees depending on their status (retired, deceased, on leave, vested, and so forth). The organization's affirmative action priorities and skills needs also affect the decision of which records to archive or purge.

The purpose of purging is to eliminate obsolete information and to maintain adequate capacity by allocating space only for information that users need on a regular or reasonable basis. Purging usually does not involve deleting data but rather transferring unneeded historical data from on-line files to an off-line storage medium. Purging usually takes place on a regular, periodic basis.

A sophisticated HRMS may purge automatically. The computer may purge every applicant record with a disposition more than ninety days old. It may even make exceptions for applicants in certain high-demand job categories or with certain hard-to-locate skills or experience. Because supply and demand conditions can change dramatically, however, most departments purge manually.

Purging is a much more common feature of applicant tracking than of employee tracking. Most of the information in an applicant file does not pertain to the rest of the system; much of it does not even roll over into the employee file if the applicant is hired. The information needed during the application process is not needed in the employee file, so it can be transferred to a file for off-line storage and eventual purging as appropriate.

Organizations may segment applicant files by type or into categories such as clerical, technical, administrative, and executive. Management may instruct the HRSC to purge all rejected applicants in certain categories if openings in such areas arise infrequently, the labor market provides a plentiful supply of such candidates, or the organization has a reasonable contingency plan for staffing needs, such as agencies or special retraining facilities. If, however, the company receives an unsolicited application from a well-qualified individual but has no opening at the time, employment may place the individual's credentials and qualifications in the data base. If an appropriate position becomes available within a reasonable time, a report request for applicants by qualification retrieves the candidate's file.

The system should store records of former employees in off-line archives rather than destroy such data. Sometimes an applicant is also a former employee. In such cases, former employee records provide valuable background information, such as demographics, prior performance and salary history, and reason for termination. Organizations should keep track of separated employees for at least two years. Some federal and state laws stipulate retention periods for certain types of records.

Glossary

Applicant The definition of *applicant* varies among organizations, but one definition would be an individual who responds to a solicitation (ad, posting, or referral) or who receives an application form or some other response from the organization.

Applicant flow The movement or status of applicants with regard to the specific steps in an organization's employment process, including source, contact, interviews, tests, reference checking, offer, and decision to hire or reject.

Applicant log A procedure that tracks the number and EEO characteristics of applicants. For each applicant, the log includes application date, position applied for, and visual observations of race, sex, and handicaps.

Applicant tracking The process of collecting relevant data about job applications, matching applicants with available positions, monitoring their status in the hiring process, and disseminating this information to individuals involved in hiring.

Employee category The basis on which the individual is employed by the organization. Options may include full-time, part-time, temporary, contractor, or special status.

Employee number A unique number that identifies a particular employee. Increasingly, though not always, the employee's social security number serves as his or her employee number.

Employee status The working status of an individual within the organization. Options may include active, retired, deceased, voluntarily separated (resigned), involuntarily separated (terminated), on medical leave, or on other type of leave.

Job classification A subdivision of job family, referring to types of work with specific common responsibilities and skill requirements. Examples include secretary, production supervisor, analyst, forklift driver, and custodian.

Job family General type of job within an organization, such as clerk, teller, or engineer; the broadest type of job categorization.

Job grade The attribute of a job that indicates the relative worth of the work to the organization. Grades are usually numeric, with higher numbers indicating higher relative worth (grade 7 is higher than grade 5). Pay level or compensation range generally correlates with grade, though ranges for adjacent grades may overlap. Some organizations may use one job grade scale for jobs in collective bargaining units and another for executive jobs.

Job posting A list of current job openings, with information such as status (open/closed), location, department, grade or pay level, and perhaps a short job description.

Job requisition An authorization to solicit and interview applicants for an open position in the organization.

Outplacement The process of assisting employees targeted for layoff to find employment with other organizations. Outplacement also may include psychological testing, family counseling, and other services.

Position A specific set of duties and responsibilities performed by a single employee. Each position has a unique identifier and is filled by just one individual. For instance, an organization may have many jobs called secretary, but it has only one position of secretary to the vice president of marketing.

Position control The process of identifying the types of jobs done in an organization, how many people perform each type of work (incumbents of specific positions), and at what rate of pay. Components of position control often include requisition tracking, budget status, skills inventory, job evaluation, and position authorization control.

Discussion Points

1. Why is applicant and employment management often one of the first modules implemented in a new system?

2. In what ways can automated applicant and employment management contribute to more efficient, productive recruiting?

3. What are the differences in job family, job, and position? Give several examples of these relationships.

4. In what ways do privacy and freedom-of-information laws affect the kinds of data an HRMS might contain about an applicant?

5. What are some of the likely uses for an applicant and employee source report?

6. Under what circumstances would a human resources department consider using the HRMS as part of a position control process?

7. What are several different ways in which a firm may define the term *applicant?*

8. What kinds of data acquired in an applicant's record during the hiring process are *not* likely to be needed if that person is hired? What should human resources do with such data?

Further Reading

Armandi, Barry R. "A National On-Line Personnel System." *Personnel*, May 1986.

Carlisle, Linda K. "Working with Employees to Develop an Automated Personnel System." *Personnel Administrator*, September 1984.

Casper, Raymond E. "On-Line Recruitment." *Personnel Journal*, April 1985.

Craig, Jeffrey L. "GE's Electronic Corporate Ladder." *Datamation*, April 1986.

Enderle, R.C. "HRIS Models for Staffing." *Personnel Journal*, 1987.

Ference, T.P. "Can Personnel Selection Be Computerized?" *Personnel*, November 1968.

Grant, David. "Automating the Selection Procedure." *Personnel Management*, July 1986.

Heiken, Barbara E., and James W. Randell, Jr. "Customizing Software for Human Resources." *Personnel Administrator*, August 1984.

Herren, Laura M. "The Right Recruitment Technology for the 1990's." *Personnel Administrator*, April 1989.

Kreider, Paul. *The Interviewing Handbook*, San Anselmo, CA: KCE Publishing, 1981.

Luck-Nunke, Bonnie. "Selecting a Computer System in the Employment Function." *Personnel Administrator*, September 1984.

———. "Easing Your Company into the Computer Age." *Personnel Administrator*, June 1988.

Meyer, Gary J. "Application Sphere of Operations Needs Modernizing?" *HR/PC*, August 1986.

Profant, Lawrence M., and Catherine L. Yancy. "Database Management Systems for Developing Personnel Applications: A Comparison." *HR/PC*, January 1986.

Richards-Carpenter, Colin. "The Recruitment Process." *Personnel Management*, March 1986.

Verdin, Joanne, and J.R. Lapointe. "Measurements II: Case Study of a Decision Evaluation Cost Model Using HR Data." *HRSP Review*, Winter 1987.

Willis, Rod. "Recruitment: Playing the Database Game." *Personnel*, May 1990.

Witkin, Elliot. "Developing Requirements for an Applicant Tracking System." *HRSP Review*, Fall 1988.

———. "Developing Requirements for an Applicant Tracking System, Part II." *HRSP Review*, Winter 1988.

13
EEO and Affirmative Action

Make (your employers) understand that you are in their services as workers, not as women.

—Susan B. Anthony

The contemporary human resources department pays significant attention to equal employment opportunity (EEO) and affirmative action programs (AAPs). The goal of these programs is to monitor and promote progress toward achieving equal access to employment and promotional opportunities in the workplace. Much of the development and effect of EEO regulations has depended on societal perceptions of discrimination and the role of government. These goals, and the means used to achieve them, have their roots in government regulations going back to the Civil Rights act of 1964.

Compared with the 1960s, many more firms and human resources professionals now recognize the value of EEO. In some cases, goodwill, ethics, and a belief in the bottom-line benefits of equal employment and promotional opportunity provide sufficient motivation. For many organizations, however, government enforcement remains the critical factor in motivating the monitoring and improvement of EEO. These regulations require significant record keeping and statistical analysis. More and more companies are using computer applications to meet these requirements.

Definition and Role of EEO Reporting

In the early days of EEO, employers merely counted the numbers of applicants and employees in racial and gender categories. EEO was part of a function called personnel record keeping. In 1970 and 1971, stronger legislation mandated annual reports to the federal Equal Employment Opportunity Commission (EEOC). In response, many human resources departments created a separate EEO/AA function or made it part of whatever group seemed most affected by issues of race and sex discrimination.

Companies that began automating their human resources data found EEO/AA among the easiest functions to computerize. First, most EEO/AA data come from other human resources functions; EEO/AA requires little unique information or separate data gathering and entry. Second, the most basic EEO/

The Development of
EEO and Affirmative Action

In many ways, EEO and affirmative action mirror society's concept of the rights and responsibilities of the employer toward the community and the individual. Traditionally, businesses just tried to find a person to fill a job slot. Society generally felt that the decision about whom a company hired and why was up to the employer. Most jobs went to men, who were presumed to be the breadwinners; women stayed home and raised families. During wars, women took over many types of jobs that only men had held previously, such as bank teller, insurance claims processor, and some forms of sales. After the war, men experienced some difficulty in getting those jobs back, mostly because women were willing to work for less pay. During the labor surpluses of the postwar periods, employers often considered factors such as race, age, ethnicity, gender, and marital status in hiring and promotion decisions. With the advent of civil rights and social reform, however, a consciousness about discrimination in the workplace arose in the 1960s.

In 1963, the Equal Pay Act required most employers to provide equal pay for men and women performing similar work. Soon after, arguably the single most important employment-related legislation to result from the shift in consciousness became law—Title VII of the Civil Rights Act of 1964. Title VII prohibits discrimination because of race, color, sex, religion, or national original in any term, condition, or privilege of employment. Although this act discussed affirmative action, it functioned more as a set of guidelines than a law, so few firms took its message seriously. Some firms kept track of numbers of applicants and employees of various ethnic groups but did not do anything about whatever these numbers demonstrated.

In 1965, Executive Order 11246 began to make EEO goals more concrete by codifying the practice of affirmative action for private employers contracting with the federal government. Five years later, Executive Order 4 carried these reforms one step further, creating the federal Equal Employment Opportunity Commission (EEOC). These orders, together with later amendments to Executive Order 11246, mandated procedures for reporting and monitoring compliance with EEO requirements; they also established sanctions for noncompliance. EEO finally had some teeth.

In the past twenty years, companies have learned about EEO requirements and how to comply with them. Many organizations now have human resources staff and overall management who belong to a generation that has grown up with the concepts of civil rights and equal opportunity. Ostensibly, cases of discrimination have become fewer as companies have created policies in compliance with the goals of EEO and as the conservative federal administration of the 1980s and early 1990s has devoted comparatively fewer resources to social reform and, therefore, to EEO compliance. Nonetheless, government regulations still mandate reporting and compliance. Cases of discrimination are still alleged and still occur. In many instances, they are very subtle. Tracking, analysis, and reporting of EEO and affirmative action data will remain important human resources responsibilities for the foreseeable future.

AA data (ethnicity and gender) tend not to change; the one variable is occupational category. An EEO/AA module involves adding some standard formulas and reporting tools to this simple set of data. Therefore, this module is fairly easy to implement and often appears early in HRMS development.

Who Is Covered by EEO/AA?

The ease of EEO/AA automation, coupled with stringent government surveillance and compliance enforcement throughout the 1970s and into the 1980s, motivated many human resources departments to implement computerization. Firms with voluntary AAPs also included in their EEO/AA module the work force analysis and reports for monitoring AAP activities. Human resources must support EEO compliance and AAPs in similar but not identical ways. Most EEO/AA modules can provide analyses and reports for both tasks.

The two main agencies that oversee EEO/AA issues are the EEOC and the Office of Federal Contract Compliance Programs (OFCCP). The EEOC provides educational and technical assistance to ensure equality of opportunity. It also investigates, conciliates, and litigates discrimination complaints. The OFCCP, which is part of the U.S. Department of Labor, audits federal contractors, which are required to be equal opportunity employers and to have an AAP that promotes employment equity.

In general, EEO regulations require that every employer with fifteen or more employees must keep records on the sex and race/ethnicity of employees by occupational category. Employers with more than a certain number of employees (usually fifty or one hundred depending on circumstances) or that participate in federal contracts must file annual reports. The EEOC and OFCCP have established a joint reporting committee that oversees compliance with reporting guidelines.

Employers discriminate on the basis of many different factors, but the most common, significant, observable, and socially unacceptable instances usually occur with regard to ethnicity and gender. Federal laws prohibit employment discrimination based on race, color, sex, religion, national origin, age, or handicap. Standard EEO/AA functions monitor race and sex. A system also may track other factors, such as age, handicapped status, or work restriction because of religious beliefs. However, firms usually report on such issues only if an individual or set of circumstances points out a potential problem.

Defining EEO

Among human resources professionals, the term *equal employment opportunity* generally refers to the process of monitoring and reporting the number of applicants and employees in each reportable protected class. Each position belongs to a particular occupational category identified by the EEOC, such as professional, technical, managerial, or craft worker. Most organizations file an annual report that lists the number of employees in each occupational category by sex and race/ethnicity. As with tax returns, most companies file the reports and receive no further response from the recipient agency. Only if statistical analysis, random selection, or a complaint prompts an audit do government authorities investigate how an organization functions.

If an audit occurs, then the EEOC, OFCCP, or other agency may request additional information, thus expanding the report responsibilities of the EEO/AA function within human resources. If the agency determines that an organization is not in compliance with federal laws or regulations, the audit report may note which actions (or inactions) may be contributing to this noncompliance.

Although the federal agency involved may recommend corrective action, the affected organization can design its own remedial programs and activities. The organization then proposes these programs to the agency auditors. If a company is grossly out of compliance and does not take sufficient steps to correct the problems, the EEOC can bring suit in federal court. If the judge finds discrimination, a court ruling may dictate the exact details of how to achieve compliance. In some cases, rulings have not only directed an organization to set up a trust fund for minority development projects but also selected trustees and established guidelines for operation of the trust fund.

Defining Affirmative Actions Programs

The term *affirmative action program* (AAP) refers to an organization's goals, timetables, and actions designed to reduce employment discrimination against members of protected classes and to promote their employment opportunities. *Goals* describe staffing objectives for specific protected classes and job classifications. The goals may include the number of members of protected classes the organization aims to reach through employee recruitment, hiring, promotion, placement, or development. *Timetables* refer to the schedules by which the organization aims to achieve those staffing changes.

Firms establish AAPs for various reasons. Most companies doing business with the federal government must implement a written AAP and so must their subcontractors. Some organizations, particularly large firms, establish such functions voluntarily. An organization found to be not in compliance with regulations usually develops an AAP for correcting the discovered deficiency.

Most AAPs center on actions in which the human resources department has some responsibility, such as recruiting, training, medical care, education and career advancement opportunities, child care, parental leave, and other supportive services. AAPs involve tracking and reporting additional data in these affected areas. Such modifications are usually fairly easy to implement. They require only that the EEO/AA module include some extra formulas and report formats so that human resources can produce reports on program status, goals, and timetables. In most cases, even a module with extensive AAP functions is a comparatively simple subsystem of the HRMS.

The EEO/AA Function

EEO/AA issues often affect human resources functions such as employment, compensation, and employee relations. EEO/AA programs often have the most effect when human resources establishes a separate EEO/AA function. This avoids placing other human resources functions in the difficult (if not impossible) position of monitoring their own actions for discrimination.

To fulfill its responsibilities, the EEO/AA unit may perform a wide range of services:

- Provides timely EEO reports that meet regulatory requirements
- Works with line management to develop appropriate goals and timetables as required
- Develops, implements, and monitors internal AAPs to achieve those goals
- Develops, disseminates, and revises EEO/AA policies and procedures
- Receives, tracks, and facilitates resolution of discrimination complaints
- Provides timely internal EEO-AA progress reports and assessments
- Interprets, with the assistance of legal counsel, new developments in EEO/AA issues
- Supports legal actions relating to EEO/AA issues, including interrogatories

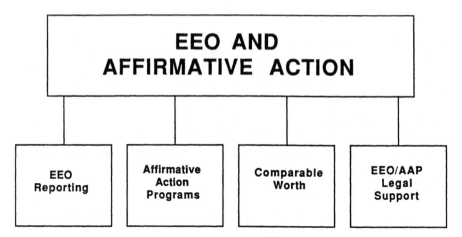

Figure 13–1. Principal roles of the EEO/AA function.

Some of these responsibilities, such as monitoring and report responsibilities, involve the HRMS centrally. Others, such as supporting legal actions, may place additional demands on the system. Some, such as policy development and complaint resolution, primarily involve management decision making or interpersonal communication skills.

Advantages of Computerized EEO/AA Reporting

Human resources departments have found many advantages to computerizing their EEO/AA reporting. Manual procedures can handle the computational requirements of the standard EEO reports, but automated procedures do so in a more accurate, less tedious fashion. Moreover, many EEO/AA reports involve significant statistical analyses. Determining the statistical significance of trends, ratios, and changes requires sophisticated methods. Computers can do these analyses faster and more reliably than can humans, and computers virtually eliminate computational errors.

Data accumulation requires similar levels of effort whether data are entered via typewriter or computer terminal. Creating additional outputs (such as new reports) involves less work with a computer than with a manual system. With data more available and accessible, an organization can respond more promptly and completely to EEO/AA requests during audits, thus earning the goodwill of auditors.

At no time do EEO/AA reports focus on any individual; instead, they list numbers and characteristics related to EEO/AA and employment. Only when an individual files a complaint does the investigating agency look at the characteristics of individuals. As discussed in chapter 3, system designers should use appropriate security to protect information about each individual's ethnicity, age, and handicapped status, as well as other information related to fair hiring, employment, and promotion practices.

Finally, computerization allows better and faster modeling, including in-house simulations. To create and monitor goals and timetables, EEO/AA modules often test assumptions, compare alternatives, and create fact-based scenarios. Computer-generated modeling facilitates appropriate decision making because it is based more on complete information than on guesswork.

Data Requirements and Sources

The EEO/AA module receives virtually all its data from other human resources functions, particularly if the HRMS also supports those functions. The major human resources groups that provide such data are employment, payroll, compensation, training, and employee relations.

The EEO/AA function does not return data for use by other human resources functions. Rather, it produces statistical analyses and reports that go to external agencies, various human resources functions, management, and departments involved in EEO/AA activities or needing assistance with EEO/AA compliance.

Existing Manual Files in the Employment Function

When companies first started gathering EEO/AA data, supervisors periodically walked around with clipboards, noting the race, national origin, and gender of each employee. Since then, organizations that file EEO reports manually have maintained this information in paper files. At the time of computerization, organizations often get most, if not all, of the needed information from these records. Many firms use this information to create lists of employees and EEO/AA data by unit. The organization then distributes such lists to supervisors for review. Supervisors need not gather additional data, just correct inaccuracies. Each employee also may receive an individual profile to review, correct or complete, sign, and return on a voluntary basis. This process helps establish and maintain accurate EEO/AA data.

Employment Data

The applicant and employment management module forms the link between the HRMS and the employment and EEO/AA functions. The following employment sources provide data that the EEO/AA module uses.

Applicant Flow Log. Staff who have direct contact with applicants, such as the front desk, employment reception, and recruiters, may maintain an appli-

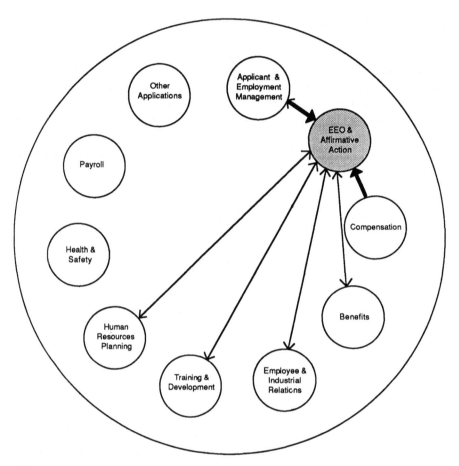

Figure 13–2. Information flow between EEO/AA and other human resources functions.

cant log. In the log, they may note visual observations of the ethnicity, sex, age range, and handicapped status of each applicant, as well as location and date of application.

Applications. Employment or data entry clerks enter information from each application into the applicant data base. Individual résumés may offer additional material. Applications provide geographic data, skills and experience, education level, job sought, and applicant source (where employee learned of the opening or the organization). The application may have a separate section in which a staff member notes observed race, national origin, gender, or handicapped data. The EEOC recommends that EEO-related data be kept separate

Who Is Handicapped
and What Does it Mean?

U.S. law states that "the term 'individual with handicaps' means . . . any person who (i) has a physical or mental impairment which substantially limits one or more of such person's major life activities, (ii) has a record of such an impairment, or (iii) is regarded as having such an impairment."

Handling HRMS requirements for handicapped status requires an understanding of the issues involved. A handicap for one job is not necessarily a handicap for another. A paraplegic could not be a firefighter, but he or she could be a computer programmer. For this reason, EEO/AA staff must define handicapped programs in terms of job content.

Although some handicaps are self-evident, workers often must self-identify relevant handicaps. For example, if certain work situations are unsafe during the first trimester of pregnancy, a woman must alert her supervisor if she becomes pregnant, since the supervisor cannot visually identify pregnancy in this period.

The employee's file should include a handicap field with a status code that identifies the type of handicap. The HRMS should protect this information from unauthorized access. Some systems use a two-character field that interfaces with a table of codes for disabilities such as blindness, deafness, paralysis, mental impairment, neurological disorder (cerebral palsy or seizures), and hemophilia.

The most relevant aspect of affirmative action for the handicapped is often reasonable accommodation. This concept includes workplace features such as special parking, accessibility (ramps, elevators, and doorways), rest rooms, table heights, adaptive equipment, and counseling programs. For the HRSC, the major requirements are follows:

- To create and maintain a clear, usable set of codes
- To develop reports on applicant and employment status of handicapped persons as needed
- To provide documentation of reasonable accommodation in the organization's affirmative action reports

from the (applicant or) employee's basic personnel file or other records available to those responsible for personnel decisions. Nonetheless, some firms do collect these visually observed EEO-related data on the application form in a space marked "for office use only." If needed, EEO/AA staff may retrieve non-time-sensitive data about former applicants from off-line storage media, such as microfiche.

Race/Ethnicity Information Form. Some firms give each applicant a supplementary form that requests race/ethnicity data. This form does not require the applicant's name or other individual identification. Use of this self-identification tool eliminates ethnic misidentification that may occur with visually observed data. Because some individuals may decline to fill out such forms, this process often provides unreliable results.

Employment Process Records. These are part of each applicant's records. They include information such as interviewers, interviewers' recommendations, hiring decision, and reasons for decision.

Employee File. The new-hire process produces additional information for each employee file, such as job classification, salary, department, employment source, employee category (full-time, part-time, temporary, or seasonal), employee status (active, on leave, or on furlough), hire date, and citizenship status.

Job History Information. An employee's job history may enter the HRMS via several different sources, such as employment, employee relations, and line management. This history includes positions held, supervisors, salary changes, performance ratings, transfers, promotions, terminations, leaves, and effective dates.

Organization Chart. Organization charts identify the name of each position in the organization and its hierarchical and geographic relationship to other positions. Sometimes employment creates these charts; more often a planning and forecasting function handles this responsibility. EEO/AA reporting does not directly involve these organization charts, but EEO/AA staff may use an internal organization chart to build a table that connects individual job titles with corresponding EEO job categories. EEO/AA also uses the internal organization chart when tracking possible patterns of discrimination within units or departments.

Geographic Recruiting Area Boundaries. EEO/AA may need information not found within the applicant and employment management module but that is still within the employment function. For instance, when comparing ethnic composition of the employee population with that of the surrounding community, EEO/AA may need information about how the employment function interacts with that community. To determine the current geographic recruiting area boundaries, EEO/AA staff must analyze the reach of current recruitment resources used by employment staff. This may include the circulation of newspapers in which the firm advertises, colleges at which it recruits, and agencies that refer applicants.

EEO/AA Function Data

EEO Occupational Categories. The federal government has created twelve employment categories (several of which do not apply to the average business enterprise). EEO/AA must use these categories in filing standard EEO reports. The job evaluation function must assign every job to one of these categories; the EEOC reports allow no exceptions. These categories are as follows:

1. Professional
2. Managers and administrators
3. Sales workers
4. Clerical
5. Craftsmen
6. Operatives, except transport
7. Transport equipment operatives
8. Laborers, except farm
9. Farmers and farm managers
10. Farm laborers
11. Service workers, except private household
12. Private household workers

Organizations usually make their own decisions about how to convert internal job titles to EEO occupational categories. In case of a field audit, the government may ask for more information to support these decisions.

Because the EEO categories have such broad definitions, firms generally find them difficult to use for internal planning. Conversely, the more subgroups an organization uses to identify its employees, the more likely it is to spot patterns of discrimination.

AAP Records. Some AAPs involve services or activities that are not necessarily part of the HRMS, such as career development seminars or counseling referrals. EEO/AA must track participation in these activities, including race/ethnicity, gender, participation dates, and type of participation. Sometimes AAPs include particular benefits handled by the benefits function, such as child care or parental leave. In such cases, the benefits module includes tracking and reporting functions for these activities; EEO/AA then uses data from that module.

Test Data

Most EEO/AA functions do not take responsibility for tracking and analyzing test data. However, such information may become significant when the function is trying to determine reasons for hiring and promotion patterns. Tests for selection (usually done by the employment function) include proficiency tests, skills tests, and aptitude tests. By the 1980s, most firms had begun to use only employment tests generally viewed as nondiscriminatory. A thorough testing and EEO/AA review process must determine whether the skills or aptitudes the standardized tests measure are actually job related.

Testing for promotion (usually done by a separate function called training and development) takes many different forms. These include in/out basket exercises, assessment centers, visual observation, and peer reviews. Federal guidelines restrict testing for higher level jobs to users that promote a majority of the employees who remain with them to the higher level job within a reasonable period of time. In reviewing and analyzing tests for selection or promotion, EEO/AA may need individual testing records and evaluations of the testing instruments.

Testing Records. These records include the number of employees or applicants tested and each one's name, protected class, and educational background; tests scheduled or given; test dates; and test scores. If a test has codable responses, a sophisticated program can match variations in answers to the protected class of persons taking the test. Although the test developer usually performs this type of analysis, EEO/AA should make sure the developer can provide this information if needed for compliance reviews.

Testing Evaluations. Larger firms often have at least one test specialist or psychometrist on staff who is qualified to evaluate the validity of the tests. Other firms use professional test-scoring firms or consultants. These specialists perform professional analyses of the relevance of each question or of the test protocol itself. These analyses may come in the form of codable responses by subject experts on a question-by-question basis. Firms are more likely to do thorough analysis if they are socially responsible or need certain competency testing and promotion policies as part of collective bargaining agreements.

EEO in the Twenty-First Century

1. If equally qualified candidates applied for a job, one a robot and another a human being, which one would you choose?
2. If a "disabled" person uses a prosthetic device that is actually superior to the human counterpart, should your firm count this person as disabled under EEO law?
3. As robotic devices decline in price, can employers use the argument of "business necessity" to defend against the adverse impact of robots?
4. Should the selection criteria for intelligent robots simply be "does it work"?
5. If a manufacturing facility completely automates its operations with robots, should those robots count when determining whether the site has enough employees to fall under EEO provisions?
6. Should intelligent robots be considered "employees" and "persons" under the EEO laws?
7. If EEO regulations should stipulate that employers must consider robots "persons," should employers count robots as 3/5, 1/2, or 2/1 of human beings?
8. To what extent do robots pose a threat to currently "protected groups"?
9. What should EEO functions consider as the "relevant labor market" for robots?
10. If robots impact the socioeconomic status of humans, should EEO regulations then consider human beings a "protected class?"

Data from Other Human Resources Functions

EEO/AA often requires data from the compensation and benefits functions to evaluate comparable worth, affirmative action, and related issues. Employee relations also may play a role in such analyses.

Wage and Salary Scales. EEO/AA staff need wage and salary scales when working on issues related to equal pay and comparable worth. EEO/AA staff can use wages and salaries of individuals (coded to protect confidentiality) to examine whether pay disparity is a function of seniority, tenure, education, or other objective, job-relevant variables or is really discriminatory.

Flexible Benefits. An AAP report may need data on who uses certain benefits established or maintained to aid AAP goals. These include child care, parental leave, tuition reimbursement, and special training programs. Again, data need not include names or individual identification, just the ethnicity, gender, and job class of participating individuals.

Seniority and Other Employee Relations Data. Employee relations tracks disciplinary actions, performance, and seniority information. As discussed in chapter 12, a firm may need to track several types of seniority. For instance, each individual may have seniority within the organization, department, position, and location. Employee relations occasionally handles some information discussed under the employment function, such as job history.

External Data Bases

To monitor the thoroughness of a firm's efforts to avoid discrimination, EEO/AA sometimes needs information about the community that surrounds the organization. This requires the acquisition and use of external data bases.

Census Data. The U.S. Census divides the country into discrete areas, each of which is known as a standard metropolitan statistical area (SMSA). The census includes the location and the gender and ethnic distribution of the population within each area. The 12 occupation groups in the census data correspond generally to the EEOC categories. This information figures prominently in the determination of an organization's relevant labor market (discussed later in this chapter). An organization can purchase SMSA data for just the geographic areas in which it operates. SMSA data are in the public domain and are available via telecommunications or printed reports.

Occupational Data. Several private consulting and research firms offer data based on census figures but arrayed in more detail. One service maintains an index of 23,000 occupation titles grouped into 426 occupational job groups. Using such data allows an employer to match the firm's own skill and educational needs with those of the relevant labor market. For instance, there are almost fifty subheadings under the general heading of clerical workers, including cashiers, bookkeepers, typists, mail carriers, telephone operators, and bank tellers. Because each subcategory may involve different skills, this finer detail facilitates a more accurate analysis of actual availability of qualified individuals.

External Wage and Salary Rates. Several private organizations and state and federal labor departments publish surveys of prevailing wage and salary rates. These surveys cover a wide variety of jobs, which are differentiated by geographic location. These are useful but do not replace salary surveys. They often support analysis of comparable worth issues and litigation defense.

Labor Law. EEO/AA practitioners need ready access to comprehensive, current information about many aspects of labor law. Several dial-up data bases provide such material. A more detailed description of some of them is provided in Appendix E. EEO/AA staff use this narrative information primarily as a reference tool.

Reporting Requirements

A major portion of the EEO/AA module is report creation. Staff must produce reports for several reasons:

- To meet filing requirements for various federal agencies
- To meet internal report requirements regarding AAP goals, timetables, and achievements
- To investigate formal and informal complaints
- To support or respond to legal actions
- To respond to government field audits

Even firms without an AAP may need to generate a variety of internal reports. For instance, an EEO/AA coordinator may generate a particular report as a way to evaluate the validity of an employee's complaint or comment, to share information with a line manager, or to suggest ways of resolving a problem.

Current federal regulations require annual EEO filings. Most firms also do their AAP reports annually. Human resources departments often schedule AAP reports for several months before EEO filing deadlines. Not only does this distribute production pressure, but if the AAP report reveals any problems, the firm has several months to take corrective action before compiling the EEO report.

The Report Generation Process

Generally speaking, EEO/AA reports use the same process to convert raw data to a finished report:

1. The specific report routine lists which data to collect from files on the entire population.

2. The routine builds summary files of data. At this point, the routine separates the names of individuals from their attributes, and the computer tallies how many individuals meet each criterion being examined. This summary file is transitory; it exists within the system only until the report has been created.

3. The report-generation routine may prompt the user to provide additional parameters or limits, such as number of years to reach goals or estimates of future employment trends.

4. The module already contains certain analytical parameters, such as formulas, determinants of statistical significance, and tables of job classifications. The routine applies these parameters to the summary files to perform analyses and produce the requested report.

Most firms submit required reports in printed form. The joint reporting committee for the EEOC and OFCCP allows computer printouts for EEO-1 reports for subsidiary establishments but requires a consolidated report on the entire organization on an actual EEO-1 form. They accept certain other types of reports on electronic media such as disks or tape. Firms considering such submissions must be careful not to submit more data than are necessary, as such information may give government auditors grounds for further investigation.

EEO Reports

In general, organizations that have one hundred or more employees (or fifty employees and $50,000 or more in federal government contract awards) must file with the EEOC. However, the pertinent employee population size varies depending on the type of organization. The EEOC also has different forms for various types of organizations. Employers doing business at more than one establishment must file several reports: one covering the principal or headquarters office, a separate report for each establishment employing fifty or more persons, and a consolidated report.

Firms doing business with the federal government also must file other EEO-type reports with the OFCCP. Firms that have defense contracts must file yet another type of report with the Department of Defense. Each of these agencies has its own set of required reports. All accept computer-printed submissions that meet certain format standards. Adapting these reports from standard EEO/AA reports is fairly easy. In fact, vendors' EEO/AA packages often include report forms for these non-EEOC reports.

EEOC filing requirements may include one or more from a series of reports, dubbed EEO-1 through EEO-9. Most EEO/AA packages include these as standard reports. EEO-1, for private sector organizations, is the most common report. Others are for apprenticeship programs, nonprofit organizations such as churches, and schools and other educational institutions. If the EEOC has questions based on one of these reports, the agency may ask a firm to submit supplemental reports about salary levels or definitions of job categories.

Introduction to Other EEO/AA Reports

Some situations require more information than the government's standard reports provide. For these, EEO/AA often prepares a series of additional reports. The individual reports may have various titles depending on the software developer and the terminology favored by the human resources department, but their creation and presentation usually require that issues be addressed in a particular order:

1. Describe the organization's *work force* by job categories and classifications (not by individual employee).
2. Evaluate the *adverse impact* of various employment variables on representation of protected classes in that work force.
3. Determine the *availability* of qualified individuals in protected classes.
4. Evaluate the organization's *utilization* of qualified individuals in protected classes.
5. Describe *goals and timetables* for EEO/AA actions.
6. *Self-monitor* EEO/AA activities.

Common forms of these reports are described in the material that follows. An organization often develops variations of these reports to meets its own needs.

Work Force Analysis

Work force analysis reports review the structure of the organization's current work force. The EEO/AA function uses these reports internally, to assess the sex or racial/ethnic distribution in the organization's employee population. This information can aid in planning transfers, promotions, training, and other actions that promote employment equity.

A work force analysis report may include employees in just a few specific jobs, such as those within a particular department. One report may list positions (rather than incumbents) by location; another may list positions by job classification, regardless of location. Work force analysis requires accurate po-

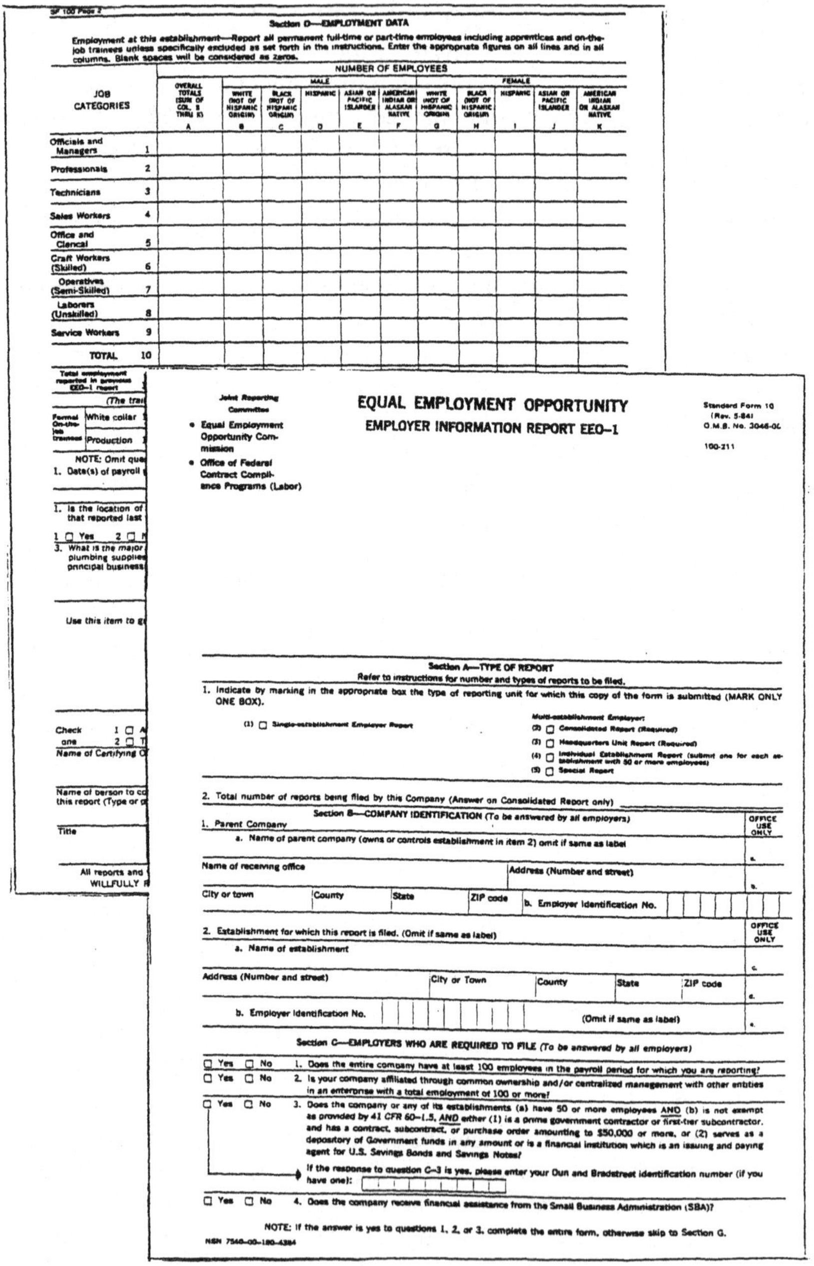

SF 100 Page 2

Section D—EMPLOYMENT DATA

Employment at this establishment—Report all permanent full-time or part-time employees including apprentices and on-the-job trainees unless specifically excluded as set forth in the instructions. Enter the appropriate figures on all lines and in all columns. Blank spaces will be considered as zeros.

JOB CATEGORIES		OVERALL TOTALS (SUM OF COL. B THRU K) A	MALE: WHITE (NOT OF HISPANIC ORIGIN) B	MALE: BLACK (NOT OF HISPANIC ORIGIN) C	MALE: HISPANIC D	MALE: ASIAN OR PACIFIC ISLANDER E	MALE: AMERICAN INDIAN OR ALASKAN NATIVE F	FEMALE: WHITE (NOT OF HISPANIC ORIGIN) G	FEMALE: BLACK (NOT OF HISPANIC ORIGIN) H	FEMALE: HISPANIC I	FEMALE: ASIAN OR PACIFIC ISLANDER J	FEMALE: AMERICAN INDIAN OR ALASKAN NATIVE K
Officials and Managers	1											
Professionals	2											
Technicians	3											
Sales Workers	4											
Office and Clerical	5											
Craft Workers (Skilled)	6											
Operatives (Semi-Skilled)	7											
Laborers (Unskilled)	8											
Service Workers	9											
TOTAL	10											
Total employment reported in previous EEO-1 report												

(The trai

Formal On-the-job trainees: White collar; Production

NOTE: Omit que

1. Date(s) of payroll

1. Is the location of that reported last

1 ☐ Yes 2 ☐ N

3. What is the major plumbing supplies principal business

Use this item to g

Check one 1 ☐ A 2 ☐ T

Name of Certifying C

Name of person to co this report (Type or p

Title

All reports and WILLFULLY F

Joint Reporting Committee

- Equal Employment Opportunity Commission
- Office of Federal Contract Compliance Programs (Labor)

EQUAL EMPLOYMENT OPPORTUNITY

EMPLOYER INFORMATION REPORT EEO-1

Standard Form 100 (Rev. 5-84) O.M.B. No. 3046-0007

100-211

Section A—TYPE OF REPORT

Refer to instructions for number and types of reports to be filed.

1. Indicate by marking in the appropriate box the type of reporting unit for which this copy of the form is submitted (MARK ONLY ONE BOX).

(1) ☐ Single-establishment Employer Report

Multi-establishment Employer:
(2) ☐ Consolidated Report (Required)
(3) ☐ Headquarters Unit Report (Required)
(4) ☐ Individual Establishment Report (submit one for each establishment with 50 or more employees)
(5) ☐ Special Report

2. Total number of reports being filed by this Company (Answer on Consolidated Report only)

Section B—COMPANY IDENTIFICATION (To be answered by all employers)

OFFICE USE ONLY

1. Parent Company
a. Name of parent company (owns or controls establishment in item 2) omit if same as label

Name of receiving office | Address (Number and street)

City or town | County | State | ZIP code | b. Employer Identification No.

2. Establishment for which this report is filed. (Omit if same as label)
a. Name of establishment

Address (Number and street) | City or Town | County | State | ZIP code

b. Employer Identification No. (Omit if same as label)

Section C—EMPLOYERS WHO ARE REQUIRED TO FILE (To be answered by all employers)

☐ Yes ☐ No 1. Does the entire company have at least 100 employees in the payroll period for which you are reporting?

☐ Yes ☐ No 2. Is your company affiliated through common ownership and/or centralized management with other entities in an enterprise with a total employment of 100 or more?

☐ Yes ☐ No 3. Does the company or any of its establishments (a) have 50 or more employees AND (b) is not exempt as provided by 41 CFR 60–1.5, AND either (1) is a prime government contractor or first-tier subcontractor, and has a contract, subcontract, or purchase order amounting to $50,000 or more, or (2) serves as a depository of Government funds in any amount or is a financial institution which is an issuing and paying agent for U.S. Savings Bonds and Savings Notes?

If the response to question C–3 is yes, please enter your Dun and Bradstreet identification number (if you have one):

☐ Yes ☐ No 4. Does the company receive financial assistance from the Small Business Administration (SBA)?

NOTE: If the answer is yes to questions 1, 2, or 3, complete the entire form, otherwise skip to Section G.

NSN 7540-00-180-4384

Figure 13–3. EEO-1 report. The EEOC requires this report of organizations having more than 50 employees. The completed form should provide a tally of all employees by race and sex within prescribed job categories. This report is normally submitted annually.

sition descriptions, a quantifiable job-evaluation system, and wage and salary scales.

Work Force Analysis Report. For each job, a work force analysis report lists title, pay grade, and total number of employees in each protected class. This report typically has twelve to sixteen columns of data in summary form. It lists position and job title rather than the name of the employee holding that position. The EEO/AA module can generate a report that lists the number of positions in each job, the supervisor for each position, and the number of employees of each protected class in each type of job.

Employee Report. This report lists active employees by employee category. It uses the employee status code to exclude contractors, employees on leave, those hired but not started, those on temporary layoff, and so forth.

Census/Job Category Report. This report matches EEO job categories to the organization's own job titles. EEOC or OFCCP audits sometimes request this report; management may use it to evaluate the relevance of other reports. This report generally does not require additional computation; it is usually just a printout of a table. In some systems, the computer accesses this table on an ongoing basis. For example, when a data entry clerk enters the job title in an employee record, the computer searches the table and inserts the corresponding EEO category in the appropriate field.

Adverse Impact Analysis

Adverse impact exists if a hiring, promotion, or other employment decision works to the disadvantage of members of a protected class. Adverse impact may occur even if an employer does not intend discrimination. For instance, an employer may require that employees have five years of service with the firm before becoming eligible for promotion to management. If the firm actively began seeking to hire women and minorities only a few years previously, this policy discriminates against those protected classes.

Employers with one hundred or more employees are required to assess adverse impact annually. Several types of reports evaluate possible bias in the hiring and promotion process.

Selection Process Impact Report. This report uses statistics on applicant qualifications, testing, interviewer actions, and other selection processes to determine whether any aspect of these procedures adversely impacts the selection of applicants who are members of a protected class.

Interviewer Impact Report. This report, also called a rater reliability report, identifies interviewers who give ratings inconsistent with those of other interviewers. Often an individual complaint triggers such a report.

Report ID: PER025
As Of Date: 06/19/89

PeopleSoft HRMS
WORK FORCE ANALYSIS

Page No. 2
Run Date 07/05/89
Run Time 10:23:31

Job Title	Job Group / Pay Grade	Total Employees	Total Minorities	MALE						FEMALE					
				Total	White	Black	Hisp.	Asian	Am.Ind	Total	White	Black	Hisp.	Asian	Am.Ind
Department: 1050301 Walnut Creek Branch															
Branch Mgr	005	1	1	0	0	0	0	0	0	1	0	1	0	0	0
TOTAL		1	1	0	0	0	0	0	0	1	0	1	0	0	0
% OF TOTAL		100.00	100.00	0.00	0.00	0.00	0.00	0.00	0.00	100.00	0.00	100.00	0.00	0.00	0.00
Department: 1050303 Lafayette Branch															
Branch Mgr	005	1	0	1	1	0	0	0	0	0	0	0	0	0	0
TOTAL		1	0	1	1	0	0	0	0	0	0	0	0	0	0
% OF TOTAL		100.00	0.00	100.00	100.00	0.00	0.00	0.00	0.00	0.00	0.00	0.00	0.00	0.00	0.00
Department: 107 Operations Administration															
SVP & Div Mgr-Operations	007	2	0	0	0	0	0	0	0	2	2	0	0	0	0
Sr Secretary	003	1	0	0	0	0	0	0	0	1	1	0	0	0	0
TOTAL		3	0	0	0	0	0	0	0	3	3	0	0	0	0
% OF TOTAL		100.00	0.00	0.00	0.00	0.00	0.00	0.00	0.00	100.00	100.00	0.00	0.00	0.00	0.00
Department: 10701 Computer Services															
AVP & Mgr-Computer Svcs	005	1	0	1	1	0	0	0	0	0	0	0	0	0	0
TOTAL		1	0	1	1	0	0	0	0	0	0	0	0	0	0
% OF TOTAL		100.00	0.00	100.00	100.00	0.00	0.00	0.00	0.00	0.00	0.00	0.00	0.00	0.00	0.00
Department: 10703 Item Processing															
AVP & Mgr-Item Processing	005	1	0	0	0	0	0	0	0	1	1	0	0	0	0
Clerk II	001	2	0	0	0	0	0	0	0	2	2	0	0	0	0
TOTAL		3	0	0	0	0	0	0	0	3	3	0	0	0	0
% OF TOTAL		100.00	0.00	0.00	0.00	0.00	0.00	0.00	0.00	100.00	100.00	0.00	0.00	0.00	0.00
FINAL TOTAL		24	7	8	6	1	0	0	1	16	11	3	2	0	0
% OF TOTAL		100.00	29.17	33.33	25.00	4.17	0.00	0.00	4.17	66.67	45.83	12.50	8.33	0.00	0.00

Figure 13–4. Typical work force analysis report. This report shows the number of staff by job title and by department. It is used as part of the process of analyzing patterns of discrimination. (Source: PeopleSoft, Inc., Walnut Creek, CA.)

EEO CATEGORY	INTERNAL CATEGORY
Officials and Managers	Executive Plant manager Department manager Superintendent Regional manager
Professional	Accountant Architect Editor Attorney Registered nurse
Technician	Computer programmer Designer Drafter Licensed nurse
Sales	Sales representative Real estate agent Sales clerk
Office and Clerical	Secretary Billing clerk Messenger
Crafts (Skilled)	Electrician Engraver Mechanic
Operatives (Semiskilled)	Apprentice mechanic Service station attendant Chauffeur
Laborers (Unskilled)	Longshoreman Car washer
Service Workers	Hospital attendants Elevator operator Guard

Figure 13–5. Job category report. This report correlates EEO occupational categories with the internal job categories that a firm might use for its own organizational purposes. The HRMS may link these two data fields by placing each as a field in the job classification table.

Statistical Cutoff Score Analysis. This routine evaluates the effect of using cutoff scores for various test ratings. It determines how much adverse impact each possible cutoff may have on test-related decisions about any protected class of test participants.

Testing/Scoring Impact Report. This report presents analysis of the job relevance of tests and scores. Organizations may use this report on a periodic basis as part of an ongoing effort to ensure reliable and valid testing. EEO/AA modules often can perform many types of test and score evaluations.

Report ID: AAP003   ADVERSE IMPACT REPORT   Page No. 1

For the period 01/01/89 through 12/31/89   Run Date 2/10/90

Actions	White Males	<------------ETHNIC GROUP------------> White	Black	Hisp.	Asian	Am. Ind.	<----SEX----> Male	Female	Total
Total Applicants	2	4	1	0	1	0	3	3	6
Total Offers	2	2	1	0	1	0	3	1	4
% Total	100.00	50.00	100.00	0.00	100.00	0.00	100.00	33.33	66.67
% Impact		50.00 *	100.00	0.00	100.00	0.00	100.00	33.33 *	66.67 *
Total Hired	1	1	0	0	0	0	1	0	1
% Total	50.00	25.00	0.00	0.00	0.00	0.00	33.33	0.00	16.67
% Impact		50.00 *	0.00	0.00	0.00	0.00	66.67 *	0.00	33.33 *

An * (if any) denotes this group is below the 4/5ths measurement.

Figure 13–6. Sample adverse impact report. An adverse impact report helps determine whether specific actions by the employer are influenced by ethnicity, sex, or other EEO/AA-related issues. This report compares employment offers and hiring decisions concerning white males with those concerning members of ethnic minorities and data concerning males with those concerning females.
(Source: PeopleSoft, Inc., Walnut Creek, CA.)

Interview or Review Board Scheduling. This report assigns individual applicants or employees to specific interviewers and schedules times for testing and interviews. This computerized process eliminates bias in assignments. Firms may use this report if an audit or complaint questions the objectivity of these procedures.

Availability Analysis Reports

Availability analysis determines the number of employees in protected classes who are qualified for certain jobs. Most EEO/AA modules can produce many types of availability analysis—for the entire organization, for any specific affirmative action issue, or for any job group. This analysis can measure internal availability (employees) or external availability (applicants).

One type of availability report identifies the number of members of protected classes in feeder groups. Feeder groups are positions from which individuals have traditionally progressed to more senior positions. For instance, one report might ask for the number of employees in protected classes available for each job group mentioned in a specific AAP, such as senior nurses.

Labor Market Verification Report. An employer filing an EEO/AA report with the government must state the relevant labor market used for its availability analysis. These reports help auditors and EEO/AA staff analyze the extent to which the labor market from which the employer is drawing is relevant for the specific job categories, locations, education levels, skill levels, and wages.

A firm may choose a central city, an SMSA, a county, or a state as the relevant labor market for a specific job category (or for the entire firm). This choice depends on factors such as the nature of the firm's business, the nature of the job, and the demographics of the surrounding area. For instance, for a maintenance person, the geographic area may need to be only the size of a single SMSA because the skill requirements are relatively low and, therefore, candidate availability relatively high. A management position, however, may need to include several SMSAs or even an entire state in the relevant labor market because the qualified labor pool is smaller and someone applying for this position may be more willing and able to relocate if offered the job.

Defining an organization's relevant labor markets often involves much work, but once this information is gathered it needs only occasional revision. Government auditors may ask for a variety of labor market analyses. Basically, these reports consider the size of the organization, the demographics of the surrounding SMSA or other geographic area, and the types of labor the organization requires. Depending on the results of this analysis, the government may suggest or order (or a firm may voluntarily decide) that enlarging or otherwise changing the recruitment scope will provide a more relevant labor force.

Internal Availability Report. By examining historical records of promotions, this analysis can give likely sources for promotions of members of protected classes. For instance, secretaries may become administrative assistants, drivers may become loading dock supervisors, and lending officers may become loan reviewers. This analysis may use not only employee job histories but also preference surveys that ask people holding particular jobs about their short-term and long-term career goals.

Utilization Analysis Reports

Utilization analysis compares the number of members of protected classes who actually hold certain jobs with the number expected based on availability. Generally, work force analysis and availability analysis must precede utilization analysis. Utilization reports also can compare actual and expected patterns of promotions, transfers, terminations, and so forth.

Most standard vendor packages and most organizations have the report print out the data, with no warning flags. The EEO/AA coordinator then spots underutilization by looking at the data in the report. This human analysis approach usually works best if the organization is under duress to resolve EEO/AA problems and if staff are not overloaded with other cases.

Some HRMS have utilization reports that can flag statistical variances. To provide this, EEO/AA packages need capabilities for statistical and discriminant analysis functions. Such flags help an organization that has had problems in the past. They also work well for employers with a large employee base, established EEO/AA activity, and staff specialists. The flag identifies any job group in which underutilization exists and calculates the extent of underutilization by standard deviations. In this way, the user can see which job groups need more EEO/AA attention and which have the most critical need. If staff (or an audit) identify particular EEO/AA trouble spots, utilization analysis can provide more detail.

Goals and Timetables Reports

Based on the results of utilization analysis, EEO/AA staff and human resources management can work to develop goals and timetables to correct identified inequities. In fact, some EEO/AA modules can automatically move shortfalls identified in a utilization analysis into the firm's goals and timetables report. Goals and timetables pertain to the hiring and promoting of qualified members of protected classes for jobs in which they are underutilized. Management usually sets the priorities and tone, but EEO/AA staff must make sure that goals and timetables are achievable, enforceable, and meaningful.

Goals are usually statistical and quantitative. A goal may simply compare the previous year with the current or upcoming year, with projections for improvement. A quantitative goal for a bank may be "To have twenty-five women vice presidents within five years." A firm with a disparate number of male employees may start with a qualitative goal, such as "To develop a work force environment conducive to presenting appropriate opportunities to female employees." Serious progress in EEO/AA programs obviously takes longer than a year. Timetables are usually for five years, sometimes with phases.

Whether quantitative or qualitative, a goal also requires concrete strategies. Such strategies might include recruitment at colleges having a high proportion of female students, on-site child care, more conveniently located women's facilities, and additional training opportunities for individuals in certain types of jobs. The goals and timetables report often itemizes supporting strategies.

An advanced EEO/AA module may contain two major functions that help staff create goals and timetable reports. These are ad hoc reporting and work force forecasting.

Ad Hoc Goals and Timetables Reports. Goals and timetables reports are not so much statistical reports as narrative declarations. The module may include a report outline and some standard paragraphs, with room for customization for each report. With a powerful ad hoc report writer, EEO/AA staff can more easily prepare reports and make it easier for report users to compare current goals and timetables with past ones.

No single report structure works best for all organizations. Some companies use main headings to identify each EEO/AA issue by protected class. Others discuss subjects by location. Companies may have five or six separate goals and timetables, with tactics and strategies for achieving each goal within its timetable. Staff often present these plans in a specific and steplike fashion. Some firms combine goals and timetables with AAP reports, but most keep these separate. A sample outline is shown in the accompanying sidebar.

Work Force Forecasts. Forecasting helps EEO/AA staff and management evaluate the feasibility of achieving specific goals within an assigned timetable. Staff also can model alternative strategies to determine which actions would be most effective.

Such routines can feature an infinite variety of forecasts. Topics may include training options, hiring needs, or effects of various promotional patterns. To create forecasts, a module may prompt the user to provide certain variables, including number of years in plan period, expected staff growth rate, expected attrition rate, and expected training program retention rate. The user can examine the significance and results of varying these figures by asking for a series of forecasts, each time varying one or more of the user-defined limits.

For instance, perhaps a large advertising firm wants women to occupy half its account representative positions within the next two years, even though men currently hold most of those positions. A projection might indicate that, in the next two years, five such positions would likely come from growth and four from turnover. To achieve the 50 percent goal, the firm would have to fill almost all these positions with women. This could create a situation of reverse discrimination against men. Therefore, the simple goal of 50 percent women within two years may need to be revised, perhaps to include other job categories or to refer to a rate of placement rather than a fixed percentage of job holders.

Some sophisticated modules can give the user data that help assign reasonable values to the independent variables in these forecasts. Availability analysis, utilization analysis, and other functions can provide numerical values or percentages of change in past periods.

A few years ago, modeling required more computer capacity than all but the largest organizations could manage. The growth of computer power and speed in the business world, as well as the refinement of relevant application packages, has increased the ease with which organizations can perform computer modeling in-house. Some EEO/AA modules have facilities that include forecasting and modeling. Forecasting often is part of a separate HRMS module referred to as planning and forecasting. Some organizations achieve useful

428

Goals and Timetables:
A Sample Report Outline

A. Introduction
  1. Overall philosophy of firm's EEO/AA program
  2. Assignment of responsibilities for policy development and administration
  3. Purpose of report
  4. Time period covered in report
B. Women in engineering
  1. Analysis of current situation
  2. Goals
  3. Timetables
  4. Strategies and tactics
C. Women in management
  1. Analysis of current situation
  2. Goals
  3. Timetables
  4. Strategies and tactics
D. Minorities in sales
  1. Analysis of current situation
  2. Goals
  3. Timetables
  4. Strategies and tactics
E. Minorities in management
  1. Analysis of current situation
  2. Goals
  3. Timetables
  4. Strategies and tactics

---

results with standard forecasting or spreadsheet programs (even microcomputer programs). Many firms do not need forecasting programs specially designed for human resources applications.

Self-Monitoring Report

Almost all organizations with AAPs have a procedure for evaluating their effectiveness. A self-monitoring report may simply note the number of employees in a particular program by protected class, dates of participation, job grade at time of participation, current job grade, and movement between and within

TITANIC WIDGET COMPANY

TRAINING SUMMARY REPORT

NUMBER OF EMPLOYEES

TRAINING DESCRIPTION	TOTAL EMPL	MALE					FEMALE				
		WHITE	BLACK	HISPANIC	ASIAN/PAC ISL	AMER IND	WHITE	BLACK	HISPANIC	ASIAN/PAC ISL	AMER IND
ACCOUNTING PRINCIPLES	5	0	0	1	1	0	2	1	1	0	0
ADVANCED MAGNUM CLASS	22	4	1	1	0	0	12	1	2	1	0
ASTRONOMY I	1	0	1	0	0	0	0	0	0	0	0
BASKET WEAVING I	12	3	0	0	0	0	7	2	0	0	0
BEGINNING TENNIS	5	1	0	0	0	0	3	0	1	1	0
CHINESE COOKING	10	3	0	1	0	0	5	1	0	0	0
CREATIVE LITERATURE	2	0	0	0	0	0	2	0	0	0	0
INTRODUCTION TO COMPUTERS	5	1	0	0	0	0	4	0	0	0	0
MUSIC APPRECIATION	5	0	0	0	1	0	4	0	0	0	0
PHOTOGRAPHY II	1	0	0	0	0	0	0	1	0	0	0
PUBLIC SPEAKING I	11	1	0	0	1	0	8	0	0	1	0
REAL ESTATE INVESTMENTS	18	1	1	0	0	0	12	1	2	1	0
STRUCTURED PROGRAMMING	1	0	0	0	0	0	1	0	0	0	0
TRANSCENDENTAL MEDITATION	3	0	0	1	0	0	1	1	0	0	0
TOTAL	101	14	3	4	2	0	61	8	6	3	0

Figure 13–7. Sample affirmative action self-monitoring report. Human resources can use a self-monitoring report to evaluate the extent to which minorities and other affected classes have access to or participate in opportunities for training or advancement. This report analyzes the extent of participation in various training programs.

functions. It may compare current statistics with those of a previous date. The report may compare goals and timetables for a specific program with the actual activities and achievements of that program.

Special Circumstances

EEO/AA staff frequently must provide additional documentation for special activities. Sometimes existing report capabilities can provide the right data in the required form. Other times new reporting requirements use an ad hoc report writer or require additional programming.

Compliance Audits

Just as with tax returns, the EEOC and OFCCP computers have built-in algorithms for checking ratios and other figures reported on annual filings. An organization whose statistics fall outside the formula may be subject to an EEO audit. Individual complaints or random surveillance also may trigger an audit of a particular organization.

Once an audit begins, the audit team asks specific questions and requires specific data and reports to support statements that the organization made in EEO filings or other correspondence. A compliance audit is usually very specific. It may deal with certain types of positions, just one location, or just one issue. The government is aware of how expensive audits can be to both the company and taxpayers, so auditors keep questions as focused as possible. Sometimes, however, an investigation that begins with a particular individual expands into a much wider area, such as a work group, an entire unit, or a class of employees (all women or all Hispanics, for example).

To handle an audit as well as possible, the EEO/AA manager should personally handle all communication with the government agency involved or designate a specific person to assume this responsibility. EEO/AA should discern the nature of the audit by trying to discover what triggered it and what the audit team sees as its central questions. Perhaps a simple solution is available. Maybe some statistics are wrong or the complaint has come from an employee or employees already involved in other employer-employee issues.

It is important to prepare as much data as possible and give auditors exactly the information they ask for and in the form they specify. EEO/AA staff probably will need to develop new reports to defend the firm's position. For example, demonstrating the relevance of certain educational requirements for particular job categories might require correlating educational background, performance ratings, and promotions. If data are not available (such as information about the work force of five years ago), EEO/AA must explain why data are not available and present information that is reasonably accurate.

Legal Actions

The organization's legal department (or its outside law firm) handles most of the work involved in an EEO-related lawsuit or complaint. The role of legal counsel is to be supportive of the EEO/AA function. Communication between EEO/AA staff and legal staff usually takes place on a case basis and can flow more freely than when EEO auditors are involved. The legal staff will ask EEO/AA to provide and interpret data. With the possible exception of extremely sophisticated EEO/AA systems, responses to such requests will almost certainly require creation of new types of reports.

Comparable Worth

Many discrimination charges stem from allegations of unequal pay for similar work. This issue is called comparable worth. At its simplest, comparable worth means that employees performing tasks of similar value to the employer should receive similar pay, allowing for differences in the length of time in position, years of service, promotion schedule, leadership responsibilities, and the like. When an employee complaint compares specific employees or classes of employees, the burden of proof is on the firm to demonstrate the objectivity of its job evaluation scheme.

Comparable worth issues usually involve considerable coordination among various human resources functions, especially EEO/AA and compensation. Because the central issue in such cases is usually compensation, responsibility often rests with the compensation function. Comparable worth analysis often requires EEO reports. For instance, such cases almost always involve utilization analyses that measure the number of members of various protected classes in particular job classifications.

Glossary

AAP (Affirmative action program) An employer's program to promote equal access to employment opportunities for all qualified individuals. Depending on the circumstances, an AAP may address issues of race, ethnicity, sex, age, handicapped status, and religious belief. A program may seek to correct imbalances or eliminate discrimination in hiring, employment, or promotional practices.

Accommodation   To make reasonable allowances in working conditions to facilitate access to facilities by persons in protected classes, such as physically disabled persons. Also refers to employer accommodation for employees' religious practices regarding work schedules.

Adverse impact   The result of a hiring, promotion, or other employment action that leads to a substantial difference in selection rates that work to the disadvantage of members of a particular race, ethnic group, sex, age-group, or religion.

Availability analysis   Statistical analysis to determine the representation of qualified individuals in protected classes within the relevant labor market for a particular employer.

Comparable worth   The doctrine that firms should provide equal pay for jobs of substantially equal value to the employer.

EEO   (Equal employment opportunity) Federal regulations that require employers to provide equal access to all aspects of employment, inluding hiring, retention, development, and promotion, regardless of ethnicity, gender, age, religion, national original, or handicapped status.

EEOC   (Equal Employment Opportunity Commission) The federal agency charged with monitoring and ensuring compliance with Title VII of the Civil Rights Act of 1964 and subsequent legislation. Most states and some localities also have EEO agencies.

Equal Pay Act   The Equal Pay Act of 1963, an amendment to the Fair Labor Standards Act, says that men and women should receive equal pay for work requiring the same skills, effort, and responsibility. To ensure compliance, employers need data to analyze pay and job content by sex.

Goals and timetables   The objectives and schedules for each program within an employer's overall AAP. Each goal may relate to a separate group, such as women or blacks.

OFCCP   (Office of Federal Contract Compliance Programs) The agency within the U.S. Department of Labor that monitors compliance with the regulatory requirement that all firms doing business with the federal government have an AAP.

Protected class   Persons having a particular characteristic identified by legislation or statistical analysis as being at risk for unequal access to employment opportunities. Race, ethnic origin, and sex are the characteristics most commonly considered to identify a protected class. Sometimes the term may refer to age, religion, national origin, or handicapped status.

Relevant labor market   The geographic area from which an employer should attract and draw applicants and employees. The relevant labor market may be the SMSA, state, region, entire country, or other geographic division. An employer should use the civilian labor force demographics of this area as a yardstick for measuring the extent to which the firm has achieved equal employment opportunity.

Selection procedure   A standardized procedure used by an organization to assess a candidate for employment. The procedure may include particular schedules, actions, communication to candidates (verbal or written), and other steps.

SMSA   (Standard metropolitan statistical area) A unit of demographic division within the United States as defined by the U.S. Census Bureau. Employers frequently use SMSAs to establish their relevant labor market in work force analyses.

Title VII   Part of the Civil Rights act of 1964, amended in 1972, that prohibits discrimination on the basis of race, color, sex, religion, or national origin. With later executive orders, this statute requires employers that have more than one hundred employees to file annual EEO reports with the EEOC.

Utilization analysis   A statistical examination of an employer's available employee and applicant pool to determine the correspondence between availability of qualified individuals belonging to protected classes and their participation in that employer's work force.

Work force analysis   A statistical report on an internal employee population to show the extent to which members of protected classes are present in various job groups in that work force.

Discussion Points

1. Why do many human resources departments include an EEO/AA module in their HRMS? Why might they not include this module?

2. What steps might an HRSC take to make sure that its own staffing and operations conform to affirmative action standards?

3. How do EEO data and reporting requirements differ from those of AAPs?

4. What data fields might the EEO/AA function use in exploring a comparable worth issue?

5. What are the relationships among work force analysis, availability analysis, and utilization analysis? What overlapping data might they use?

6. How does the EEO/AA function interact with employment, compensation, benefits, training?

7. What steps can the EEO/AA function take to minimize an organization's likelihood of becoming the target of EEO/AA complaints?

8. How can EEO/AA staff best contribute to clear communication with EEOC and OFCCP representatives?

Further Reading

Aaron, H.J., and C.M. Lougy. *The Comparable Worth Controversy.* Washinton, D Brookings Institution, 1986.

Aldrich, M., and R. Buchele. *The Economics of Comparable Worth.* Cambridge, MA: Ballinger, 1986.

Allard, Henry S., and Greg Jarboe. "Removing Barriers in the Electronic Workplace." *Personnel Administrator,* February 1986.

Awad, Elias M. "Using Computers as an EEO Compliance Tool." *Data Management,* February 1982.

Bell C.S. "Comparable Worth: How Do We Know It Will Work?" *Monthly Labor Review,* 108, 1984.

Bryson, Mory. "On the Firing Line: The Case of 'Ace Investigator.'" *Personnel News,* May/June 1988.

Ceriello, Vincent R. "Concerning Compliance—Prepare or Defend?" *Journal of Systems Management,* April 1979.

DeForrest, S. "How Can Comparable Worth Be Achieved?" *Personnel,* 1984.

Equal Employment Opportunity Commission. "Affirmative Action Guidelines." *Federal Register,* January 1979.

———. *Affirmative Action in the 1980s: Dismantling the Process of Discrimination.* Washington, D.C.: U.S. Government Printing Office, November 1981.

Flast, Robert H. "Taking the Guesswork Out of Affirmative Action Planning." *Personnel Journal,* February 1977.

Grauer, R.T. "An Automated Approach to Affirmative Action." *Personnel,* September/October 1976.

Grider, D., and M. Shurden. "The Gathering Storm of Comparable Worth." *Business Horizons,* July/August 1987.

Hudis, Paula. "Other Affirmative Action Applications." *Computers in Personnel,* Winter 1989.

Hutner, F.C. *Equal Pay for Comparable Worth: The Working Woman's Issue of the Eighties.* New York: Praeger, 1986.

Jongeward, D., and D. Scott. *Affirmative Action for Women: A Practical Guide.* Reading, MA: Addison-Wesley, 1973.

Lasden, Martin. "Federal Monkey on Your Back?" *Computer Decisions,* September 1982.

Ledvinka, J., and R.L. Laforge. "A Staffing Model for Affirmative Action Planning." *Human Resource Planning,* 1, 1978.

Livernash, E.R. *Comparable Worth: Issues and Alternatives.* Washington: Equal Employment Advisory Council, 1980.

Lorber, L.A., et al. *Sex and Salary: A Legal and Personnel Analysis of Comparable Worth.* Alexandria, VA: ASPA Foundation, 1985.

Marshall, R., and B. Paulin. "The Employment and Earnings of Women: The Comparable Worth Debate." In *Comparable Worth: Issues for the 80s.* Washington: U.S. Commission on Civil Rights, 2 Volumes, 1984.

Milkovich, G., and F. Krzytofiak. "Simulation and Affirmative Action Planning." *Human Resource Planning,* 2, 1979.

Remick, H. *Comparable Worth and Wage Discrimination.* Philadelphia: Temple University Press. 1984.

Sape, G. "Coping with Comparable Worth." *Harvard Business Review,* 63: 1985.

Twomey, D.P., *A Concise Guide to Employment Law EEO & OSHA.* Cincinnati: South-Western, 1990.

14
Compensation

You get what you pay for.

—Gabriel Beck

C ompensation administration sets standards for and monitors all direct financial remuneration for employee work. This includes both exempt (salaried) workers and nonexempt (hourly or salaried) workers, as well as commissions for sales employees. The compensation function faces its biggest challenge in determining the standards for compensation for each job. With appropriate information, the department can match an incumbent to specific compensation rates more easily. Compensation tracks the amount each individual is entitled to receive, then payroll takes responsibility for the amount each individual actually receives.

A properly staffed and supported compensation function can help an organization control costs, increase productivity, and keep pace with competitors in attracting and retaining appropriate employees. Such resources also help a firm work more harmoniously with unions (or avoid unionization) and comply with EEO/AA goals and timetables.

Compensation in an HRMS

Compensation provides the core information that human resources needs to fulfill its mission—information about jobs. Jobs are the foundation of human resources work, not people. Only by understanding the content and value of a particular job can human resources select, support, and evaluate an individual for that position. For such reasons, management will almost always include job evaluation and other core compensation activities in the HRMS.

In general, management more readily supports the development of modules that hold significant promise of administering or using financial resources efficiently. Because compensation involves money directly, human resources systems almost always have compensation modules. Planning and implementing a compensation module requires more compensation skills than computer skills. Developing a system design for wage and salary tables requires less

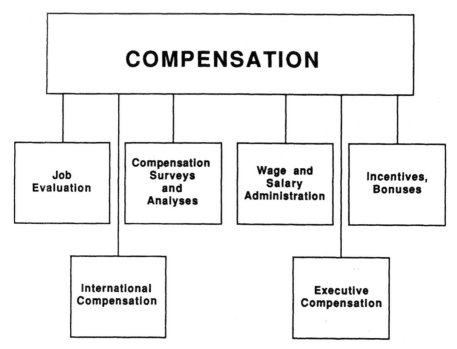

Figure 14–1. **Principal roles of the compensation function.**

expertise than does determining the best values to assign to each field in such tables.

Roles of Compensation

Compensation staff have a wide range of responsibilities. The following paragraphs give a general overview of those assignments.

Job Evaluation. In job evaluation, compensation determines the responsibilities of each job and its corresponding value to the organization. Some human resources departments refer to these responsibilities as job content. The job evaluation process entails providing both written job descriptions and quantified analysis. Based on weighted factors, points or levels, compensation establishes for each job a grade, salary range, and eligibility status for various forms of compensation. Compensation also uses the job evaluation to establish performance review criteria for each job.

Surveys and Analysis. Compensation follows the policies dictated by management about how to allocate compensation dollars, but it often sets up mechanisms for studying alternatives, providing reports on existing practices and alternative scenarios. As a resource for establishing competitive and effective compensation rates, compensation also may use salary surveys to monitor compensation structures or pay levels at competing organizations. In various forms, compensation performs research to help management establish, review, and revise compensation policies.

Wage and Salary Administration. Keeping track of approved wage and salary schedules for each job is compensation's major responsibility. Compensation staff provide guidelines for supervisors and managers to use in processing compensation transactions. They also may develop and monitor schemes to monitor departmental costs and productivity.

Incentives, Bonuses, and Stock Options. Compensation administers and supports policies regarding proper cash incentives needed to reward superior performance. Generally, line operation or staff support units, such as sales and marketing, are responsible for granting such incentives. As required, compensation may analyze the cost of various incentive distribution schemes.

Comparable Worth. EEO/AA performs most of the activities involving comparable worth, but compensation provides the reports that compare the various features of certain jobs, including salary ranges, point factors, performance criteria, and job grade. Much of this information comes from the job evaluation process. If inequities are discovered among comparable jobs, compensation must reevaluate job classifications, adjust point factors, and revise compensation structures to prevent discrimination.

International Compensation. Companies with more than a handful of employees based outside the organization's home country may have a compensation specialist who is responsible for the details of international compensation. This includes compensation of expatriates and third-country nationals and possibly administration of home leave policies. A large company may administer international compensation through several domestic offices. For example, New York may handle Europe and Africa; San Francisco may handle Pacific Rim countries; and Atlanta may handle Latin America.

Executive Compensation. An organization may assign a specialist to deal with executive compensation, since this activity often involves special forms of salary and bonus administration, such as deferred compensation and other long-term incentives. It also often includes additional forms of compensation, such as country club memberships, financial counseling, and stock options. As discussed in chapter 3, the HRMS may need more restrictive security for executive compensation data than for general wage and salary administration.

Advantages of Computerization

The compensation function must perform some of its analytical work manually, particularly in the areas of job evaluation and performance appraisal. A computerized system can, however, carry out a considerable amount of the required quantitative analysis and computations faster and more accurately. This includes the process of salary adjustment. Because compensation calculations involve dollar amounts, any improvement in speed and accuracy improves organizational productivity and reduces potential sources of error.

Computerization also increases timeliness, consistency, and flexibility in other compensation tasks. These include internal surveys of compensation by variables (for example, time in position or years since degree), simulation of the effects of merit salary policies, salary administration controls and limits, and preparation of data for outside salary surveys.

Data Requirements and Sources

Compensation enters pay and performance information into employee records and retrieves such information from them. This function also focuses a large percentage of HRMS efforts on data that reside elsewhere in the system. Compensation usually takes significant responsibility for the job classification table, which lists attributes of specific jobs (including compensation types and ranges for those jobs). Additionally, this function maintains separate tables for salary, wage, and commission scales.

Compensation also gets information from modules maintained by other human resources functions. For instance, basic data on individuals come from employment, and seniority and performance review information comes from employee relations. In turn, EEO, employee relations, and, eventually, payroll base a significant portion of their work on the tables compensation creates within the HRMS.

Job Evaluation

To compensate employees, an organization must place a value on the work associated with each job. That process, referred to as job evaluation, is the function from which all other compensation activities flow. In job evaluation, compensation staff determine the attributes of each job and then assign a value and ranking to that job. These attributes may include mental effort, skill, physical effort, responsibility, and working conditions.

Job evaluation considers each job without regard to the individual or group holding that job. The process involves collecting information about job content, creating a description of each job, assigning points or some other

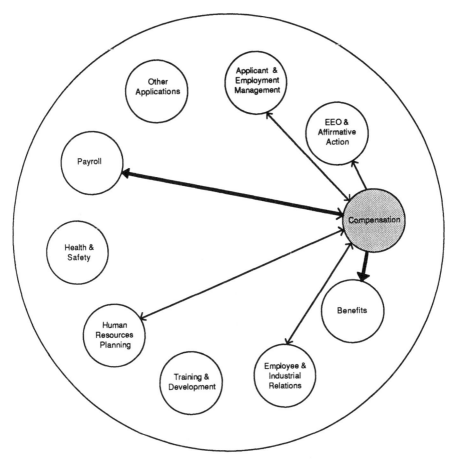

Figure 14–2. Information flow between compensation and other human resources functions.

quantitative measure to each attribute, and assigning a grade or ranking to the job. These results are usually the single biggest factor in setting compensation levels and become the basis for determining performance appraisal criteria.

Job Content Data. Job content data include knowledge requirements (education, skills, experience, and credentials), responsibilities (level of required effort, equipment operation, supervision, and time management), and working conditions. Compensation uses a variety of methods to gather information about each job under evaluation. This process usually starts with coded questionnaires that are filled out by supervisors or individual employees in each job. Through surveys, compensation staff may compare notes with their counterparts in other organizations. Evaluators often believe that such processes provide all the relevant information about low-level and mid-level paraprofessional jobs. The higher the job level, however, the more the evaluator may encounter unfamiliar technical, functional, or administrative components. In these circumstances, compensation uses market pricing to assess the relative worth of the job in comparison with the market.

To the extent staff can code information from interviews or questionnaires, compensation may use the computer to perform quantitative analysis on this input. Since much of the analysis is qualitative and somewhat subjective, only the quantitative results of the analysis become part of the system.

Written Job Descriptions. With much effort, compensation evaluates survey responses for completeness, accuracy, and consistency. Based on that analysis, compensation develops a profile that describes each job. This material is sometimes made part of the HRMS compensation module as text-processed files. Printed records of these files become the master job description directory for human resources.

Points and Job Grades. Compensation consultants and professionals have developed several point-factor systems for quantifying job value. Some systems group individual attributes into several general categories, such as mental effort, skill, and responsibility. Categories in another system might be know-how, problem-solving, and accountability. The total points become the basis for the job grade, and the grade becomes the basis for establishing the salary or wage range.

Compensation enters the point values into the job classification table. The number of points may automatically trigger assignment of a particular job grade. Job grade is a coded representation of the ranked value of a particular job. An organization may have grades for all jobs or only for those up to a certain managerial level. These higher, ungraded jobs may be rated according to a ranking scheme or have a special designation in the job grade field, or they may not be listed in the field at all.

Productivity Indexes. As an adjunct to job evaluation, some organizations use productivity measures. This process establishes criteria on which supervisors can determine productivity for each job classification. In some firms, supervisors and managers examine productivity on an individual basis as part of performance reviews. Other companies determine productivity only on work units, departments, or divisions. The productivity indexes can be units produced, customer inquiries handled, sales volume achieved, or any other specific, relevant, and quantifiable activity that has a realistic target or goal. Firms sometimes use productivity evaluations to determine the compensation structure that provides the proper motivation.

Realities of Computer-Assisted
Job Evaluation

A human resources department with computerized compensation certainly uses its system to record the results of its job evaluation process, usually in some form of points or grades. Compensation packages are now available that involve the computer more in the evaluation process.

Computer-assisted job evaluation starts just as with a conventional process—with a poll of employees, supervisors, and peers concerning the skills, responsibilities, effort, and work conditions for the specific jobs being evaluated. Computerized schemes give participants a finite set of possible responses about the importance and value of each potential job component.

A poll may ask respondents to select whether attribute A is more important than attribute B, then ask whether B is more important than C, and so forth. Often these choices are in the form of lists that start with action verbs. For instance, in evaluating a bank lending officer, respondents may have to decide whether it is more important that a bank lending officer "Make a good loan" or "Manage the lending process," then decide whether it is more important that a bank lending officer "Make a good loan" or "Complete paperwork on time."

A program may begin with a set of manually evaluated benchmark jobs to determine weighting factors for each criterion. It then uses the forced-ranking responses in the questionnaires as the basis for a quantified analysis that assigns point values to the attributes required for each job being evaluated. Finally, the system may use these point values to assign salary ranges to each job.

Computer-assisted job evaluation is still somewhat esoteric, though several vendors do offer such programs. Several actions can help make such programs work effectively and be acceptable to employees and compensation staff. Management outside compensation should be involved in identifying and evaluating benchmark jobs. Automatic computer checking for data discrepancies should be established, and data changes should be made only by compensation specialists. Finally, as with a manual system, employees should have access to a process for appealing job evaluation results.

DIVISION: ABC MANUFACTURING

04/90

•••••••••••••••••
JOB EVALUATION DETAIL
•••••••••••••••••

JOB CODE	TITLE	INCUMBENT	KNOW HOW SLOT	KNOW HOW POINTS	PROBLEM SOLVING SLOT	PROBLEM SOLVING %	PROBLEM SOLVING POINTS	ACCT SLOT	ACCT POINTS	TOTAL POINTS	PROFILE	EVAL DATE	BNMK DESIG
239642	PUBLIC RELA OFF	CLARK, J.	F32	460	F4	50	230	F2C	200	890	52-26-22	03/90	8
459732	DIR, ADVERTISING	HILLSON, M.	F32	528	F4	57	304	F4S	400	1232	43-25-32	10/89	9
786432	EMPL RELA SUPV	JACOBS, S.	E33	400	E4	50	200	F3S	304	904	44-22-34	08/89	8
171342	SALES MANAGER	JEFFRIES, P.	F23	400	E4	59	200	E3P	264	864	46-23-31	09/89	7
149632	ASST TO CASHIER A	TONER, R.	F32	460	E4	43	200	E5R	200	860	54-23-23	08/89	9
237462	ADMIN ASST	SPRAGUE, A.	E32	400	E4	50	200	E5R	200	800	50-25-25	08/89	9
176435	INTL SVCS ADMIN	CAMPBELL, J.	F33	460	E4	50	230	E3P	304	994	46-23-31	03/90	8
237934	TAX ATTORNEY	SHUSTER, H.	F22	400	E4	50	200	F3C	230	830	48-24-28	10/89	7

Figure 14-3. Job evaluation detail. Human resources uses this report to display the job evaluation points assigned to specific jobs. The total number of points determines the compensation level for that particular job and may be used to calculate a salary range.

Job Evaluation Updates. Designing and implementing a job evaluation scheme involves such intense effort that most companies stay with the same plan as long as possible, often longer than the plan remains useful to the organization. Compensation professionals recommend reviewing the overall appropriateness of the entire job evaluation scheme every few years. Usually a human resources department will undergo a complete overhaul of this process if there are indications that the methodology used is no longer right for the department's needs. Sometimes a change becomes necessary when an organization becomes involved in entirely different sets of jobs due to mergers and acquisitions, a new manufacturing process, or a new product line.

Even a well-designed system needs periodic record updating to account for jobs that have been created, deleted, changed, or combined. In such reviews, compensation staff evaluate only the affected jobs. After they complete this analysis, they must update the HRMS tables to include the revised values.

Job Classification Table

In most organizations, the job classification coding scheme is the heart of the HRMS. Job classification tables include the major attributes of each job, regardless of the individual or group performing that job. Keeping the job classification scheme accurate is one of compensation's basic responsibilities. A firm with 10,000 employees may have 1,000 or more jobs; defining each of these jobs requires massive amounts of data, which are referred to as attributes. For each job classification, a typical entry in the table contains a field or fields for the following attributes:

- Job classification (unique identifying number)
- Job title (using standard abbreviations where appropriate)
- Job grade, level, or step (linked to salary-range tables)
- Wage steps (automatic increases overtime)
- Fair Labor Standards Act (FLSA) status (indicates exempt or nonexempt status for determining eligibility for overtime)
- Frequency of performance review (if this varies within the organization)

Other human resources functions provide additional information on other job attributes. For instance, EEO/AA assigns EEO occupational category; employee relations may enter bargaining unit information for unionized jobs; benefits uses fields to indicate eligibility for various benefits; safety and health may include fields for toxic substance exposure; and employment may issue a job code for supervisors.

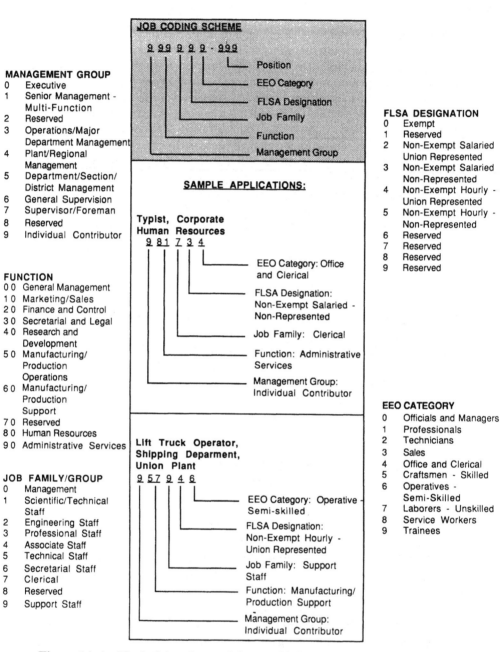

MANAGEMENT GROUP
0   Executive
1   Senior Management - Multi-Function
2   Reserved
3   Operations/Major Department Management
4   Plant/Regional Management
5   Department/Section/ District Management
6   General Supervision
7   Supervisor/Foreman
8   Reserved
9   Individual Contributor

FUNCTION
00 General Management
10 Marketing/Sales
20 Finance and Control
30 Secretarial and Legal
40 Research and Development
50 Manufacturing/ Production Operations
60 Manufacturing/ Production Support
70 Reserved
80 Human Resources
90 Administrative Services

JOB FAMILY/GROUP
0   Management
1   Scientific/Technical Staff
2   Engineering Staff
3   Professional Staff
4   Associate Staff
5   Technical Staff
6   Secretarial Staff
7   Clerical
8   Reserved
9   Support Staff

JOB CODING SCHEME

9 99 9 9 9 - 999

Position
EEO Category
FLSA Designation
Job Family
Function
Management Group

SAMPLE APPLICATIONS:

Typist, Corporate Human Resources
9 81 7 3 4

EEO Category: Office and Clerical
FLSA Designation: Non-Exempt Salaried - Non-Represented
Job Family: Clerical
Function: Administrative Services
Management Group: Individual Contributor

Lift Truck Operator, Shipping Deparment, Union Plant
9 57 9 4 6

EEO Category: Operative - Semi-skilled
FLSA Designation: Non-Exempt Hourly - Union Represented
Job Family: Support Staff
Function: Manufacturing/ Production Support
Management Group: Individual Contributor

FLSA DESIGNATION
0   Exempt
1   Reserved
2   Non-Exempt Salaried Union Represented
3   Non-Exempt Salaried Non-Represented
4   Non-Exempt Hourly - Union Represented
5   Non-Exempt Hourly - Non-Represented
6   Reserved
7   Reserved
8   Reserved
9   Reserved

EEO CATEGORY
0   Officials and Managers
1   Professionals
2   Technicians
3   Sales
4   Office and Clerical
5   Craftsmen - Skilled
6   Operatives - Semi-Skilled
7   Laborers - Unskilled
8   Service Workers
9   Trainees

Figure 14–4. Maximizing the usefulness of job classification codes. Some firms use numerical sequencing for job identification, but developing meaningful codes in which each digit signifies some attribute of a job allows users to access job information more easily. This sample shows a system of hierarchical job classification coding for a public utility.

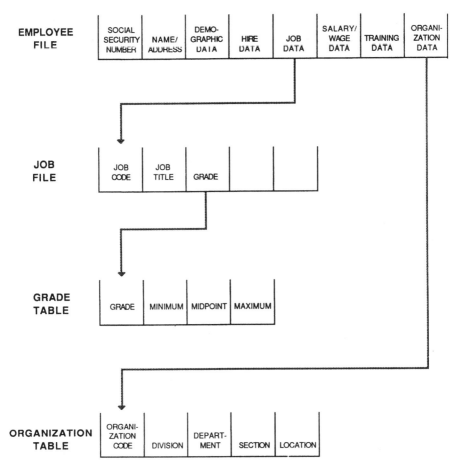

Figure 14 5. Information flow between the job classification table and other data bases in an HRMS. Data flows among employee, job, and organization files or tables in an HRMS. Linking these files eliminates the need to repeat common fields. For example, the employee file contains the job classification code. This code links that file to the job classification code file or table, which contains job title, grade, and other job attributes.

Employee Files

Compensation must enter data into and retrieve information from individual employees' files. It uses the following information about individuals most often: job classification, present rate of pay, pay history, time in job, performance rating, date of last performance review, and seniority.

Job Classification Code. This field links each individual's record to information about his or her job in the job classification table. Employment (or the personnel records function) enters a position code for a new, transferred, or promoted individual. This code links to a specific job classification code. Many systems perform this link via a separate table that includes just job classification codes and corresponding position codes. Often there are multiple position codes for a single job.

Present Salary or Wage Rate. This field displays the salary or wage rate of each employee. Compensation does not normally originate transactions involving salary changes for individuals; it simply handles them. Compensation enters this information based on forms completed by supervisors or employment staff, whoever makes the decisions about hiring, promotion, and salary changes. Compensation checks to make sure supervisors have completed all the required items on the compensation change form. Among these items are approval signatures, employee name, transaction type and effective date, increase type, amount or percent of change, and performance rating.

Special Forms of Compensation. The job classification table may include associated fields indicating whether each salaried job is eligible for special forms of cash compensation, such as shift differentials, hardship pay, or housing allowances. These fields may indicate dollar amounts, may list the special compensation as a percentage of the regular salary, or may link to a table that lists special compensation in relation to job grade.

Work History. A career or work history segment tracks information about previous jobs held, function or organization, salary or wage rate, and breaks in service, such as leaves, layoffs, and furloughs. Compensation uses this information when considering patterns of increase and exceptional cases. Line managers may use it when contemplating possible future pay increases.

Performance Rating. When supervisors conduct periodic performance reviews of employees, the summary result is often a single number or letter indicating performance. Typical rankings may range from 1 (poor) to 5 (outstanding) or from A to E. Some firms use one-part rating schemes; others have separate indicators for various factors. Compensation may work on setting up performance evaluation criteria, but employee relations monitors the reviews. Employee relations or the supervisor enters the performance rating into the HRMS. In organizations with pay-for-performance schemes, compensation uses performance ratings to analyze whether salary changes conform to policy.

Seniority. Seniority is usually a calculated field based on dates entered by employment, employee relations, payroll, or whatever function tracks atten-

TITANIC WIDGET COMPANY
SALARY GRADE CODES REPORT

CODE	MIN PAY RATE	MID PAY RATE	MAX PAY RATE	PER	PERCENT RANGE SPREAD
EM10	0.00	583.33	1166.66	M	0.00
EM11	1160.00	1395.00	1624.00	M	40.00
EM12	1450.00	1740.00	2030.00	M	40.00
EM13	1600.00	2000.00	2400.00	M	50.00
EM14	1775.00	2225.00	2675.00	M	50.70
EM15	1950.00	2437.50	2925.00	M	50.00
EM16	2150.00	2687.50	3225.00	M	50.00
EM17	2325.00	2962.50	3600.00	M	54.84
EM18	2550.00	3250.00	3950.00	M	54.90
EM19	2800.00	3575.00	4350.00	M	55.36
EM20	3100.00	3950.00	4800.00	M	54.84
EM21	3325.00	4325.00	5325.00	M	60.15
EM22	3650.00	4750.00	5850.00	M	60.27
EM23	4025.00	5237.50	6450.00	M	60.25
EM24	4425.00	5752.50	7080.00	M	60.00
EM25	5325.00	6922.50	8520.00	M	60.00
NH10	3.00	3.75	4.50	H	50.00
NH11	3.50	4.13	4.75	H	35.71
NH12	4.00	4.75	5.50	H	37.50
NH13	4.50	5.38	6.25	H	38.39
NH14	5.00	6.00	7.00	H	40.00
NH15	5.50	6.50	7.50	H	36.36
NH16	6.25	7.38	8.50	H	36.00
NH17	7.00	8.25	9.50	H	35.71
NH18	7.75	9.50	10.75	H	38.71
NH19	9.00	10.75	12.50	H	38.89
NM10	1000.00	1333.34	1666.67	M	50.00
NM11	1120.00	1400.00	1680.00	M	50.00
NM12	1220.00	1525.00	1830.00	M	50.00
NM13	1330.00	1662.50	1995.00	M	50.00
NM14	1450.00	1812.50	2175.00	M	50.00
NM15	1500.00	1960.00	2340.00	M	48.10
NM16	1725.00	2154.17	2583.33	M	49.76
NM17	1880.00	2348.33	2816.66	M	49.82
NM18	2045.00	2555.83	3066.66	M	49.96
NM19	2250.00	2812.50	3375.00	M	50.00

Code Count: 36

Figure 14–6. Sample salary and wage table. This table expresses the approved salary and wage ranges (pay rates) for each grade. It is generally linked to the job classification table, which is linked to employee files to facilitate compensation administration and the calculation of compa-ratios.
(Source: AbraCadabra Software. Reprinted with permission.)

dance. It may be several fields, such as seniority by job, unit, department, and location. Some firms use the terms *time in position* for exempt employees and *seniority* for nonexempt employees, especially if a collective bargaining agreement includes such rules.

Salary Tables

Salary range may be a separate field in the job classification table. Alternatively, job grade may link each job classification record to a corresponding record in a separate set of salary and wage tables.

An organization usually sets salary scales for each class of exempt employees. Each job classification has a salary range, typically expressed as minimum, midpoint, and maximum rates. Some firms establish policies about the proportion of employees who should have salaries within a specific quartile or quintile of a salary range. Some companies permit occasional out-of-range conditions in which an employee's salary is above or below the range specified for his or her job.

Salary Schedules. Almost every firm uses surveys to find out how its pay levels compare with other firms. External surveys compare and contrast pay policies and practices at similar firms. This allows firms to compete in the market, correct inequities, and attract, retain, and motivate the type of individuals who can help the enterprise meet its goals.

Companies have many ways of obtaining this information. They may perform surveys themselves, hire consultants to do so, obtain survey results from vendors or professional organizations, examine public information such as proxy statements, or even join with competitors to perform joint surveys. Only the biggest companies can afford to develop their own surveys, host meetings to discuss the results, participate in common industry groups, and process the data.

Some professional societies specialize in analyzing pay schedules. Numerous consulting organizations develop and market extensive compensation surveys. A subscribing firm can specify the kinds of comparisons it wants in terms of location, job classifications, and other variables. These surveys often are available on-line, and subscribers may choose which data selections to receive. A representative sampling of these services is included in Appendix D.

International Compensation. International compensation often involves a set of special forms of compensation. These may include home leave travel pay, hardship pay, special duty pay, car allowance, and servant reimbursement. A firm having more than a few employees stationed in foreign countries may assign a particular compensation specialist to handle international compensation. This specialist may create computerized tables of international compen-

SURVEY COMPARISON

		TWC INFORMATION				
JOB CODE	JOB TITLE	NUMBER EMPLOYEES	MINIMUM ($)	MID-POINT ($)	MAXIMUM ($)	AVG PAID ($)
2345	CONTROL ADMINISTRATOR	17	1519	1693	1867	1640
4356	ACCOUNTANT	13	1519	1693	1867	1629
1224	PROPERTY ENGINEER	22	1519	1693	1867	1638
6572	ESTIMATE COORDINATOR	4	1519	1693	1867	1641
3245	PROGRAMMER/ANALYST	25	1519	1693	1867	1692
4445	PLANT PRODUCTION MANAGER	1	1519	1693	1867	1607
TOTAL IN GRADE		12	82			

	SURVEY INFORMATION					
JOB TITLE	NUMBER EMPLOYEES	AVERAGE MINIMUM ($)	AVERAGE MID-POINT ($)	AVERAGE MAXIMUM ($)	AVERAGE PAID VS ($)	TWC SURVEY (%)
CONTROL ADMINISTRATOR	361	1454	1603	1753	1575	11.30
ACCOUNTANT	31	1449	1589	1730	1558	12.72
PROPERTY ENGINEER	230	1446	1591	1736	1566	12.72
ESTIMATE COORDINATOR	287	1483	1676	1847	1635	0.94
PROGRAMMER/ANALYST	54	1629	1824	2020	1762	0.10
PLANT PRODUCTION MANAGER	47	1390	1509	1628	1531	14.31
	1010					

Figure 14–7. Salary survey by job. This report combines an internal salary range table (top) with data from an external salary survey (bottom) to compare the organization's salary practices with those of other firms. The variance between TWC average salaries for specific positions is shown as a percentage on the far right side of the lower report.

MATURITY CURVE SURVEY ANALYSIS

YEARS SINCE B.S.	B.S. NON SUPERVISORY				M.S. NON SUPERVISORY			
	NUMBER EMPL	MEAN SALARY	SURVEY MEAN SALARY	DIFF VS SURVEY	NUMBER EMPL	MEAN SALARY	SURVEY MEAN SALARY	DIFF VS SURVEY
0	2	1800	1882	-4.56	0	0	2100	
1	9	1950	1912	1.95	0	0	2093	
2	7	2250	1994	11.38	2	2000	2149	-7.45
3	14	1971	2072	-5.12	5	2010	2164	-7.66
4	18	2078	2142	-3.08	9	2017	2207	-9.42
5	15	1970	2192	-11.27	15	2103	2264	-7.66
6	16	2244	2240	0.18	5	2110	2313	-9.62
7	19	2218	2304	-3.88	21	2217	2380	-7.32
8	9	2272	2375	-4.53	8	2213	2443	-10.39
9	9	2350	2453	-4.38	20	2370	2495	-5.27
10	14	2321	2481	-6.89	17	2409	2568	-6.60
11	18	2422	2515	-3.84	24	2489	2610	-4.86
12	12	2542	2612	-2.75	25	2462	2714	-10.24
13	6	2767	2685	2.96	11	2486	2754	-10.78
14	10	2550	2759	-8.20	20	2620	2847	-8.66
15	16	2469	2758	-11.71	18	2694	2942	-9.21
16	11	2586	2809	-8.62	16	2775	2960	-6.67
17	14	2940	2846	-2.97	13	2781	2982	-7.23
18			2940				3093	
19								
20	72	2818	2988	-6.03	76	3005	3168	-5.42
TOTAL	291	2659	2777	-4.46	303	2764	2929	-5.98

Figure 14–8. Maturity curve analysis. In this type of report, employees are grouped according to the number of years since they received a bachelor's degree. It compares the salaries of internal and external groups, then computes the difference between them. This figure and figure 14–7 show different ways of identifying salary discrepancies.

sation options that are linked to an employee's file via a special field or flag. Deciding how to organize this information depends in part on whether these factors are unique to international employees or also pertain to domestic employees.

Data Security Needs of Executive Compensation. Many aspects of executive compensation are discretionary, so data usually involve higher levels of security. Some human resources departments may keep their demographic information on executives in the main HRMS and specific compensation data in a separate microcomputer-based system. To mimic this arrangement within a single large computer, mainframe HRMS vendors offer special executive compensation modules, which can have special security provisions. In either arrangement, if a job grade is above a particular level, screens may show blanked-out fields for certain compensation-related information.

Wage Scales

A wage table contains wage scales for each job grade or job classification. Each scale gives the specific wage rate or steps based on seniority, tenure, time in position, and so forth. The job classification table usually links to the wage table via the job grade or job code. The proper linkage depends on factors such as organizational diversity, bargaining unit agreements, and market conditions. Wage rates are established through union contracts, organizational policy, or government regulation, as in the case of the minimum wage.

Special wage rates for overtime, holidays, weekends, off-site jobs, hazardous duty, and the like usually do not require separate tables. These rates usually bear some arithmetic relationship to base wage rates. For this reason, the job classification table often includes a separate field for each category of special wage rates; each field contains either the percentage by which to multiply the base wage rate or the flat amount to add to it to obtain the special rate.

In some circumstances, employees may spend time at several assignments. Each of these tasks may have a separate wage scale, particularly in unionized industries. In such cases, an effective compensation module would include a labor-cost distribution system that allows for coding how many hours an employee spent doing which job. This involves linking an individual employee's record with more than one job classification. Hours worked in any specific job classification are paid at the wage rates for that job classification code.

Commission Tables

Commission structures come in many forms. They range from straightforward ($40 per widget sold) to complicated ($40 each for the first 50 widgets; $45 for widgets 51 through 100; $50 for every widget over 100; plus $20 for every thingamajig). Some include commission caps—that is, limits on the amount of commission an individual can receive. Some companies use one commission structure for everyone eligible for commissions; others have multiple commission structures (for example, separate rates for sales managers, telemarketers, and field sales).

A compensation module may not require a separate commission table if the structure is simple. In such cases, the commission field in the job classification table can give a simple set of percentages. The employee is eligible to receive a percentage of the dollar amount of sales. The job classification table can even accommodate a set of percentages in which the commission percentage changes depending on dollar volume.

For complex commission structures, the most efficient arrangement may be a separate commission table. The module then links this table to the job classification table via the job code or special commission code.

Sales management and top executives set commission structures; compensation merely administers them. The human resources department often becomes involved in helping develop and analyze alternative plans. To do so, compensation needs not only its own records but also those of sales and payroll, including sales figures (by individual, division, and organization) and total periodic cash compensation to each person receiving commissions. Compensation staff usually can use standard business planning software when analyzing commission structure alternatives.

Other Compensation Data

When an organization offers other types of compensation, each type generally requires a separate table. The information may require only a separate field in the job classification table, or it may be tied to data already included in the system.

Cost-of-Living Adjustments. Some organizations give their employees a periodic cost-of-living adjustment (COLA) in an attempt to help offset the effects of inflation. A COLA may result from either a collective bargaining agreement or from organizational policy. COLAs are usually annual; in union situations, they may take place automatically. To implement a COLA process on an HRMS, the computer recalculates all salary and wage tables using a set rate of increase.

Equity Participation. Equity participation may take many forms, including stock options, long-term bonuses, restricted stock purchases, or management stock purchases. Most companies offer such forms of compensation only to senior executives. As with other forms of special compensation, a flag in the job classification code table can indicate eligibility. Options that include company stock often require additional monitoring. For instance, in the case of stock options, compensation records in each eligible employee's file the date the individual received the option, the option price, and the number of shares. If only a small percentage of the employee population is eligible for stock, a company may keep all stock option information in a separate (perhaps manual) system.

Special Allowances. The job classification table often includes fields for cash allowances for special job classes. Depending on the type of firm, such items may include clothing, uniforms, safety shoes, safety glasses, meals, travel, or mileage. These fields may indicate dollar amounts, percentages, or eligibility codes. Including special allowances in the job classification table allows compensation to calculate the firm's potential obligation in each category.

Reporting Requirements

Vendors use many different terms to label compensation reports, but these products usually can be categorized according to the compensation area they describe:

- Administration
- Transaction processing
- Policy variances
- Planning

Virtually all compensation reports are for internal purposes. The only external reports are survey exchanges with other organizations and information required for EEO/AA legal reports and procedures. Some of the more typical reports that support the compensation function are described in this section. Depending on an organization's size and circumstances, it may need other reports as well.

Compensation Administration

Compensation administration reports describe the current compensation program—how jobs are evaluated, rating schemes, and compensation tables.

Job Evaluation Detail. This report lists the points accorded to each job for to each measured category of attribute. It usually provides evaluation date, job title and, where appropriate, current incumbent. With this report, compensation staff can review (and allow others to review) the quantitative basis for specific compensation assignments.

Job Evaluation Summary. This report provides synopsized information about evaluation points on an aggregate basis for a group of jobs, such as by department, division, or job classification. This report may list average pay for each job category by location.

Compensation Tables. The compensation module can print out any of the tables the department develops, including salary ranges, hourly wage rates, commission structures, and special compensation tables.

Transaction Processing

Job Tabulation. This report provides number of incumbents, job evaluation data, total annual salary, median compa-ratio (defined below), and other compensation information for each job classification. Staff members use this report to monitor transaction activity by department, job classification, or both.

Wage and Salary Detail Reports. Compensation may prepare wage or salary reports on a particular group of individuals within a department or job family. Reports may include only current data or wage and salary history as well. Background information includes name, social security number, hire date, job title, job classification code, and department. Compensation can then analyze apparent compensation disparities by looking at performance ratings, seniority, location, experience, and skills. In addition, this report usually includes the following information:

- Salary of incumbent
- Salary range for job
- Bonus eligibiity
- Performance rating
- Position in range (Also called range penetration, this index indicates where an incumbent's salary lies along the salary range for a specific job. It is expressed as a percent of the distance from the minimum to the maximum salary in the range. For example, a job may have a minimum of $15,000, a midpoint of $20,000, and a maximum of $25,000. A salary of $20,000 would have a position in range of 50 percent; a salary of $22,500 would have a position in range of 75 percent.)
- Compa-ratio (Expresses basically the same information as position in range but in a different way: salary divided by midpoint of range. For the preceding example of the incumbent receiving a salary of $20,000, the compa-ratio is 20,000/20,000, which equals 1.00, more commonly expressed as a compa-ratio of 100. If a normal compa-ratio range is 80 to 120, the report flags any salary that deviates from this policy.)
- Other statistical relationships such as deciles, quartiles, or quintiles

Wage and Salary Summary. This report provides compensation information on groups of employees, such as by department, division, or job classification. For each job, the report provides the total salary for the group, total bonuses, mean salary, and median compa-ratio (or other ratio). It may list the average increase by percentage or by dollar amount. It also may list the number of incumbents whose salaries are below, within, and above the salary range. Compensation and management use this report to evaluate pay distribution within a unit and among units.

Focal Review. Periodically (usually at the beginning of the year or budget cycle) managers may review the current and projected compensation for all the

DIVISION: ABC MANUFACTURING

****
SALARY ADMINISTRATION SUMMARY
****

04/03/90

JOB CODE TITLE	NUMBER EMPL	TOTAL SALARY TOTAL MIDPOINT	COMPA-RATIO	AVG INCR %	BELOW RANGE	WITHIN RANGE	ABOVE RANGE	TOTAL BONUS PAID	PERFORMANCE DISTRIBUTION					
									PROV	ADQT	COMP	COMM	DIST	NR
487623 FINAN ANAL	24	28,000 30,000	96	100 8.7	2	21	1	1235	2	3	2	12	5	1
127894 BUYER	8	8,000 7,800	102	88 7.9	0	8	0	----	0	1	2	3	2	0
127875 MATL CTL CLERK	15	13,500 13,865	97	78 8.2	2	13	0	----	1	2	10	1	1	0
562891 ENGR SPEC	18	27,000 26,550	102	136 9.1	1	15	2	5876	0	3	2	9	2	2
562875 LAB TECH	25	24,625 26,550	96	92 8.3	3	21	1	----	2	2	16	1	3	0

Figure 14–9. Salary administration summary. Human resources uses this type of report to show patterns and trends of compensation practices for groups of jobs within a specific division or department.

employees they supervise. To aid in this focal review process, compensation provides a focal review report, which lists employees eligible for wage or salary increases based on performance review and service. It includes job grade, salary range, position in range, and effective date of increase. This effective date may be some future date within the calendar or fiscal year or budget cycle. Most companies also include information on the amount of increase compensation policy dictates for each incumbent. Such planning allows firms to plan their total exposure to salary and wage increases during that time period. Managers can then consider planned increases for each employee in the context of an entire budget or department and adjust planned increases accordingly.

Salary Increases Granted. Most compensation functions regularly use salary increase reports. For each individual whose salary or wage has changed since a particular date, this report lists old and new compensation amounts, along with the amount and percentage of the increase, the compa-ratio, and the performance level. The report may be by individual, unit, grade, location, entire organization, or other variable. Compensation usually distributes this report to managers who are responsible for those individuals or units or to management involved in compensation tracking and monitoring issues. With this distribution, compensation can make sure that salary transactions have been done correctly, that out-of-range situations are addressed, and that compensation funds are being distributed equitably.

Some modules can track different types of pay increases. In these cases, the salary increase report can give the percentage and dollar amount of raises in various categories, such as merit, COLA, seniority, and promotion. This information becomes part of each individual's work history.

Months between Salary Increases. This report lists how many incumbents at each performance rating level have had salary increases by month to track the length of time between increases. Alternatively, this report may list the number of incumbents and months since salary change by job grade. Either form of this report allows management to identify and analyze variances.

Salary Reports for External Surveys. Salary surveys usually do not require information on all employees. In fact, they are usually quite specific about which types of jobs are included. If such reports are exchanged on a routine basis, compensation can create specific reports that select the needed information automatically. For benchmark jobs, this report might list salary range, average salary of incumbents, and amount of total compensation.

Compensation Options Report. Staff may need to create reports on the status of special features such as hazardous duty pay, stock options, or clothing allowances. The report might list number of employees eligible (by department or location), number of employees exercising the option, current compensation obligation (cost) for the options exercised, and change in option activity compared with the previous date.

Compensation Policy Variance Reports

Compensation Out of Range. As supervisors submit compensation changes for processing, many systems can check which changes fall within the standard compensation range for that job classification. A sophisticated system automatically takes into account factors that may mitigate out-of-range decisions. Such factors include performance rating, time since last increase, length of service, and job in range.

Compensation periodically issues an out-of-range report that lists all variances. With this report, management can note which specific salary or wage changes are out of the normal range for that job. Compensation usually includes salary or wage history reports for each affected individual. With this information, management and the supervisors who awarded those increases can discuss necessary adjustments or the justification for each out-of-range decision.

Comparable Worth Reports. Comparable worth means that employees receive equal pay for work of equal value. Compensation may perform comparable worth analyses based on job evaluations or on each of several factors, such as ethnicity, gender, age, or handicapped status. Comparable worth most commonly involves investigating how an organization values certain jobs predominantly held by women that may be comparable to ones traditionally held by men.

When effective EEO analysis requires that particular jobs be subject to comparable worth scrutiny, compensation usually produces and interprets these reports. For each position included, a comparable worth report may list EEO occupational category, job classification, and salary ranges. For each incumbent, it may include gender, age, race/ethnicity, annual salary, comparatio, performance rating, seniority, and date and amount of compensation increases. Reports also may include unit or department totals and averages for salaries, increases, position in range, and other factors.

Analysis of these issues may begin by examining whether jobs deemed of comparable value in the job evaluation scheme have equal compensation structures. If compensation is not equal, the compensation function may revise wage and salary rates for various job classifications. In more complex situations, comparable worth analysis may involve evaluation of knowledge, skill, and ability levels required for each relevant job. If job evaluation has assigned points to these qualifications, compensation can include these in the computerized aspect of comparable worth analysis. In such cases, compensation may need to provide special reports that detail job evaluation processes and results, including weighting of evaluation factors and point systems.

Overdue Salary Increases. Compensation's responsibilities include monitoring which employees have not received scheduled or expected salary increases. This report lists all employees whose last salary (or wage) increase occurred before a certain date. It includes information such as current salary, compa-ratio, and time in position. Some systems may consider performance ratings, thus listing only individuals who have had no salary increase within a pre-scribed period and who also have a performance rating at or above a certain level. Some systems can plot the distribution of such increases graphically, as shown in the accompanying figure. These reports and graphs allow compensation staff to identify which individual histories require further investigation.

Unevaluated Jobs. This report lists all jobs needing new or revised job evaluations or job classification analysis. The basis for this material is the log of requisitions for new jobs submitted by employment, as well as reports by line supervisors and managers. This information also may come from college recruiting, employee/labor relations, or external sources that monitor labor market statistics.

This report includes all jobs that have been added since the last job evaluation, as well as those that have undergone significant revision. Job evaluation specialists use this report to plan career development, deployment and distribution, and analysis of questionnaires and other information-gathering tools. This report also may list all jobs that have been eliminated so that compensation can remove them from job classification codes and archive the outdated information off-line.

Planning Reports

Compensation often plays a role in estimating the costs and results of certain management decisions in areas such as financial planning, union contract negotiations, layoff and expansion plans, and revision of salary and wage scales. Even an organization that runs smoothly must consider the influence of changes in tax laws, regulations, union trends, inflation, and the cost-of-living. Firms involved in new product development, expanding markets, or volatile employment environments should undertake more frequent and complicated planning activities.

Salary and Wage Increase Plan. Compensation's most important planning function is to develop scenarios for possible compensation rates, including the estimated costs and effects of such alternatives. The goals of these plans are to

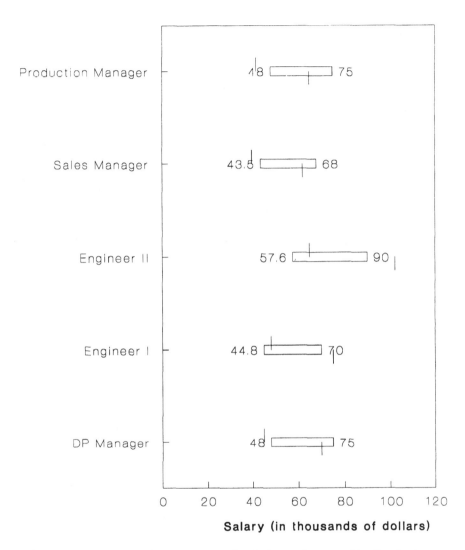

Figure 14–10. **Presenting compensation information graphically. As in other human resources areas, compensation can use graphics to help information recipients understand issues clearly. In this example, the closed rectangles represent authorized salary ranges for the indicated jobs (for example, production manager = $48,000 to $75,000); the vertical lines represent the minimum and maximum salaries of incumbents. Managers can use this chart to evaluate compensation policies or the compensation of specific individuals.**

attract and retain the most qualified individuals as employees. Compensation must work with employment to include turnover and transfer rates, so alternatives can factor in estimates of the number of employees at various points within each salary range.

Most modeling in compensation, as with many other human resources functions, can use existing tools, such as Lotus 123, SuperCalc, or Excel. Organizations seldom require modeling programs specifically developed for compensation applications. A typical plan might consider compensation obligations for each of several jobs levels. For instance, one system may use job grades 1–5, 6–10, 11–15, and 16 and above; another may use 100–200 points, 201–400 points, and 401 points and above.

The type of information included depends on the types of changes the organization is contemplating. An impending layoff might require a plan based on forecasts of seniority levels within each job grade. A growing shortage of engineers might encourage a high-technology firm to plan significant salary increases for such employees to achieve the desired retention rates. Any planned increase in pay structures can result in increased benefit costs, for benefit values are tied to compensation. In this case, modeling may need to include benefits variables as well.

Compensation also uses models to determine appropriate pay-for-performance schemes, which also called merit salary budgeting. Reports can illustrate how various distributions of performance levels affect the economics of such schemes.

Distribution of Salary Increase Funds. This report looks at annual budgeted salary increases, usually by division or unit rather than by individual employee. Using current salary as a base, the report takes into account the current compa-ratio (and perhaps performance evaluations) and then produces the budgeted salary increase, yielding an average rate of increase for each division. With forecasting tools, compensation planners can adjust variables until the dollar increase corresponds with the approved financial plan or allowances.

Salary Planning Worksheet. The path for salary increases depends on the degree of centralization or decentralization in the organization. In some organizations, salary is determined strictly by formula, factoring in seniority, experience, and performance. In others, particularly with professional-level jobs or in smaller firms, salary increases are discretionary, being based on performance, position in range, and the external employment market.

Compensation elicits salary information from supervisors to forecast the organization's salary commitments. On a periodic basis, usually annually, each supervisor receives a salary planning worksheet for his or her unit. The report lists name, identification, title, salary history, and seniority of each individual in the unit. The supervisor fills in the date and the amount and type of the

463

DIVISION: ABC MANUFACTURING

```
********************
SALARY PLANNING WORKSHEET
********************
```

04/03/90

		ANNUAL SALARY	COMPA-RATIO	PERF EVAL	PROMO EVAL	LAST INCR	% INCR	TYPE INCR	EFF DATE	SALARY PLANS				
NAME										TYPE	AMT INCR	% INC	NEW SALARY	EFF DATE
EVANSTON	T J	43500	102	3	NOXX	1750	8.4	M	05-89	A	2500	5.7	46000	5/1
ABEL	F K	29600	115	4	I2AD	1500	8.3	M	04-89	M	2000	- - -	31600	4/1
JOSEPHSON	G G	20500	103	1	T2AD	1000	10.5	P	02-89	D	- - - -	- - -	20500	- -
CHRISTENSON	W T	19500	98	3	FIFN	900	10.5	M	09-89	M	2000	9.8	21500	8/1
YOUNGER	L O	18600	88	2	NOXX	900	11.7	M	09-89	D	- - - -	- - -	18600	- -
WILLIAMS	M J	18500	93	3	I2AD	750	10.1	M	06-89	C	2000	10.3	20500	6/1
SWANSON	O E	18400	101	3	T2AD	780	10.2	P	08-89	M	1600	8.7	20000	5/1

Figure 14–11. Salary planning worksheet. This worksheet is an example of a "turnaround" process. The system generates a list of employees eligible for review. The supervisor enters the amount and percent of any salary increase and the effective date. The form, once approved, can be forwarded to data entry who update employee information, then route the form to payroll.

projected salary increase. The supervisor signs the form and returns it to compensation. With this information, compensation can compute projected compa-ratios and plan salary costs for the upcoming period.

Salary Increase Practices Report. This report compares the information that each supervisor provided on the salary planning worksheet with actual salary increases awarded to each incumbent. For both planned and actual increases, the report lists dollar amount, date, type, and percentage of increase. The report may list these amounts by unit as well as by individual.

Special Circumstances

Compensation staff need special skills when interacting with other functions. Here are some tips for promoting successful working relationships.

```
• • • • • • • • • • • • • • • • • • • • • • • • • •
    SALARY INCREASE PRACTICES REPORT
• • • • • • • • • • • • • • • • • • • • • • • • • •
```

12/31/89

DIVISION: MANUFACTURING

NAME	TITLE	PLANNED INCREASE	DATE	TYPE	%	ACTUAL INCREASE	DATE	TYPE	%
HOPKINS, GERALD	ACCOUNTING CLK	$187	07/89	M	8.7	$199	09/89	M	9.3
CAMPBELL, MARYANN	FINANCIAL ANAL	$208	10/89	M	9.0	$240	07/89	P	12.0
SPRAGUE, ROBERT	SECRETARY II	$172	07/89	M	8.7	NOT PROCESSED			
JENKS, JONATHAN	ENGR. R&D	$211	10/89	P	7.9	$111	07/89	P	7.9
HOLLAND, RICHARD	ENGR. SPEC.	$235	08/89	M	8.3	$135	05/89	M	8.3

TOTALS	$14,874	$15,755
NO. INCREASES	134	137
AVERAGE INCREASE	$203	$207
AVERAGE PERCENT	8.0%	9.4%

DIVISION: ENGINEERING

NAME	TITLE	PLANNED INCREASE	DATE	TYPE	%	ACTUAL INCREASE	DATE	TYPE	%
WOLLIVER, GERALD	MARKETING ANAL	$209	08/89	M	8.5	NOT PROCESSED			
JEFFERIES, JENNIFER	CASHIER	$165	08/89	M	7.8	$175	06/89	P	8.7
TONER, ROBERT	MGR. ACCOUNTING	$220	09/89	M	8.2	$240	09/89	M	9.5
JACOBS, MARYANN	PROGRAMMER	$205	07/79	P	8.7	$205	09/89	M	8.7

TOTALS	$18,009	$14,775
NO. INCREASES	207	197
AVERAGE INCREASE	$200	$207
AVERAGE PERCENT	8.3%	9.0%

Figure 14–12. Salary increase practices report. This report provides detailed information about salary actions planned and taken with regard to specific employees.

Working with Payroll

Compensation and payroll interact on a frequent, ongoing basis. Compensation's job is to administer and monitor policies; payroll's job is to process what is authorized. In such close quarters, one function may step on the other's toes, straining the relationship.

Defining Compensation's Role. To avoid conflict, the role of each function should be defined as clearly as possible. If payroll is not a part of human resources, some companies have payroll handle all the numeric work, with compensation monitoring the process of salary administration transactions. When payroll is a part of human resources, its job is more likely to be integrated with human resources operations but is usually defined as making sure each employee gets paid the approved amount. In either case, compensation should recognize its policymaking role; its staff must monitor compensation levels and productivity, informing management when variances occur.

Establishing Timely Information Delivery. Often the biggest problem between compensation and payroll is late delivery of data. Sometimes this situation stems from poor organizational structure, excessive bureaucracy, or inadequate work flow. In some cases, compensation permits and relies regularly on retroactive pay, manual pay, and adjustments after the fact. Such deviations generally cause extra work, which payroll resents.

To avoid this problem, compensation should have consistent policies and procedures that respect the processing cycles of the payroll unit. Policies on timeliness should be established so that compensation management can work with payroll management to enforce deadlines and procedures.

Establishing Procedures for Exceptions. Compensation and payroll also need to establish procedures for exceptions to the normal processes. In some cases, manual check processing is the only way to avoid penalizing an employee whose check would otherwise be late. Payroll should recognize that granting exceptions avoids bad feelings between employees and payroll that could even be brought before the state labor commission.

Working with EEO/AA

Occasionally, circumstances may suggest that achieving affirmative action and equal employment opportunity requires changes in compensation. If compensation has difficulty adjusting to these changes, tension can develop with EEO/AA. For instance, certain forms of compensation might help attract women to some jobs traditionally held by men. Such compensation might include allowance for taxi fare for late-night workers or allowance for phone contact with child-care providers.

When EEO/AA staff suggest adding certain forms of compensation to particular job classifications, they must provide the overall justification for these changes. Compensation should acknowledge that the organization accrues long-term benefits when it attracts a wide array of qualified applicants and employees.

Working with Employee Relations

In unionized environments, contracts mandate almost all the wage rules. The bargaining process for such contracts usually takes place through a function variously known as employee relations, industrial relations, union relations, or labor relations. Some organizations have this unit administer all aspects of wage-related compensation, from job evaluation and classification to wage tables and compensation planning. A separate salaried compensation unit would handle such tasks for exempt employees.

If compensation is separate from industrial relations, the two functions must work together on many issues, such as union negotiations, compensation planning, performance appraisals, productivity evaluations, disciplinary hearings, and other labor disputes. Because most disputes between employee and employer are directly or indirectly a function of pay, compensation clearly has an important role in the adjudication of these issues.

Glossary

COLA   See *Cost-of-living adjustment.*

Compa-ratio   The ratio of an individual's rate of compensation to the midpoint of the salary or wage range for the job held by that individual. For instance, if an individual earns $20,000 annually in a job whose salary range is $15,000 to $25,000, then the compa-ratio for that position would be 1.00, more commonly expressed as a compa-ratio of 100.

Compensation   All forms of monetary payment for which the employee is eligible or which the employee receives. Includes not only salary or wages but also commissions, bonuses, profit sharing, allowances, and increased rates of pay because of special circumstances (such as overtime or hardship).

Cost-of-living adjustment (COLA)   An adjustment to pay or benefits based on changes in the government-issued consumer price index.

Exempt   Refers to employees not subject to the overtime and minimum-wage provisions of the Fair Labor Standards Act. Applies to bona fide managers and administrators who are salaried and/or commissioned.

Fair Labor Standards Act (FLSA)   The basic federal wage and hours act covering firms in interstate commerce. The act and its amendments require payment of the minimum wage and overtime pay to employees who are not exempt. They also require retention of pay and hours data for two years for Department of Labor inspection.

FLSA   See *Fair Labor Standards Act.*

Focal review   A process by which management considers current compensation and planned compensation increases for a group of employees, such as a unit or department.

Job evaluation   The process of determining the responsibilities of each job, quantifying those factors, and thereby determining the value of each job to the organization. Job evaluation forms the basis for job grades, compensation rates, and performance review criteria.

Merit budgeting   A compensation strategy that determines increases in salary or wages for individual employees on the basis of performance rating, time in position, range penetration, and other factors. Also called *pay for performance.*

Nonexempt   Refers to employees subject to the overtime and minimum-wage provisions of the Fair Labor Standards Act. Usually includes all hourly and salaried workers who are not managerial, professional, or administrative.

Pay   All forms of monetary earnings actually earned or received by an employee. Many people use the term *pay* informally to refer solely to wages and salary, but it also includes commissions, bonuses, profit sharing, and payments for special circumstances, such as hardship, overtime, or severance pay.

Pay basis   The time period to which the stated amount of compensation applies. Pay basis is most commonly hourly, weekly, biweekly, semimonthly, monthly, or annual.

Performance rating   The ranking on a scale that indicates the level of satisfactory performance achieved by an employee. Typical schemes may range from 1 (poor) to 5 (outstanding) or from A to E.

Position in range   An index that indicates penetration in a salary range, expressed as a quartile or quintile. For instance, if a job has a salary range of $15,000 to $25,000, a salary of $22,500 would lie in the third quartile and have a position in range of 3.

Salary   Fixed compensation paid regularly (as by the week, month, or year). Most often applies to officers, managers, and professionals whose contributions are not measured by production standards.

Wage   Compensation for labor or services, often according to a contract on an hourly, daily, or piecework basis. Most often applies to technical, craft, or service workers and those under collective bargaining agreements whose work involves production, manufacturing, or support.

Discussion Points

1. What other human resources functions besides compensation typically use the salary and wage information that compensation maintains in the HRMS?
2. From what sources might an organization gather data useful in maintaining appropriate salary scales? Discuss a few circumstances under which specific sources might yield the most useful information.
3. After establishment of an automated compensation system, what factors typically cause compensation staff to review and update records periodically?
4. In what ways do compensation activities flow from the job evaluation process?
5. What roles do job evaluation data play in a performance review?
6. If a system produces a report that lists individuals whose compensation is out of range, what additional data might it include to maximize the usefulness of that report?
7. What compensation data should a system archive when changes take place? In what ways might such data be useful at a later time?
8. What actions can compensation take in regard to the HRMS to help promote comparable worth?

Further Reading

Bartol, Kathryn M. "Making Compensation Pay." *Computers in Personnel*, Winter 1987.

Belcher, D.W., and T.J. Atchison. *Compensation Administration*. Englewood Cliffs, NJ: Prentice-Hall, 1987.

Berger, Lance A. "Using the Computer to Support Job Evaluation Decision-Making." *Journal of Compensation & Benefits*, July/August 1986.

Buford, J.A., Jr., B.B. Burkhalter, and J.N. Wilmoth. "Auditing the Compensation Function for Sex-Based Salary Differences: Some Needed Refinements." *Compensation and Benefits Review*, 1983.

Burgess, L.R. *Wage and Salary Administration: Pay and Benefits*. Columbus, OH: Merrill Publishing, 1984.

Burkhalter, B.B., et al. "Auditing the Compensation Function for Race- and Sex-Based Salary Differences: Further Needed Refinements." *Compensation and Benefits Review*, 18, 1986.

Finch, James D. "Computerized Retrieval of Pay Survey Data." *Personnel Administrator*, July 1985.

―――. "Personnel Computing: Computers Help Link Performance to Pay." *Personnel Journal*, October 1988.

Finkelstein, James A., and Christopher H. Hatch. "Job Evaluation: New Technology, New Role for HR Managers." *Personnel*, January 1987.

Hills, F.S. "Comparable Worth: Implications for Compensation Managers." *Compensation and Benefits Review*, Volume 14, 1982.

Howe, William. "Manage Salaries with a Goal-Seeking Spreadsheet." *Business Software*, August 1987.

Hutsell, William R., and Stephen L. Quisenberry. "The Computer as a Tool: Forecasting Salary Costs." *Personnel Journal*, June 1981.

Kanin-Lovers, Jill. "Automated Evaluations Can Help but Can't Decide Compensation." *Computers in Personnel*, Spring 1987.

Liswood, Aaron S. *Human Resource Information: A Micro Computer Approach.* Cupertino, CA: Potentials Group, 1984.

Mahoney, T.A., B. Rosen, and S. Rynes. "Where Do Compensation Specialists Stand on Comparable Worth?" *Compensation and Benefits Review*, Volume 16, 1984.

Meyer, H.H. "The Pay-for-Performance Dilemma." *Organizational Dynamics*, Winter 1975.

Milkovich, G.T., and J.M. Newman. *Compensation.* Planto, TX: Business Publications, 1987.

Naughton, Hugh V. "Integrated Support for Salary Administration." *Personnel*, August 1986.

Patten, Thomas H., Jr. *Fair Pay.* San Francisco: Jossey-Bass, 1988.

Pay, Rex G. "Computerized Pay Planning in a Competitive Market." *Personnel*, August 1987.

Polsky, Walter L., and Loretta D. Foxman. "Computerized Job Evaluation Plans." *Personnel Journal*, May 1987.

Russ, Henry L., Jr. "Using Personal Computers to Increase the Productivity of Compensation Specialists." *Personnel*, May/June 1984.

Sibson, R.E. *Compensation.* New York: AmaCom, 1981.

Spirig, John E. "Compensation: The Up-Front Issues of Payroll and HRIS Interface." *Personnel Journal*, October 1987.

Stevenson, S. Price, Jr. "Adapting Decision Aid Software for Human Resource Needs: Job Evaluation." *HR/PC*, April 1986.

Strayer, Jacqueline F. "A High-Tech Approach to Compensation Communications." *Personnel*, October 1985.

Wallace, M.I., and C.H. Fay. *Compensation Theory and Practice.* Boston: PWS-KENT, 1988.

15
Benefits

I advise you to go on living solely to enrage those who are paying
your annuities. It is the only pleasure I have left.

—Voltaire

Benefits play an important role in the attitudes of employees toward the
organizations for which they work. An attractive benefits package
helps attract and retain worthwhile employees. Moreover, health and
welfare benefits that help employees maintain attendance and productivity aid
the organization. What employees used to call fringe benefits can no longer be
considered a fringe. Today, the so-called hidden paycheck adds 30 to 50 percent to direct payroll costs, making benefits issues central to human resources
management.

The Role of Benefits in Human Resources

The benefits function both resembles and differs from compensation. Compensation and benefits are the areas of greatest human resources expense in
most firms. Like compensation, benefits helps an organization decide how to
allocate internal financial resources. Benefits also must evaluate outside resources, such as insurance carriers, claims processors, actuaries, and other
benefits providers and administrative services. Moreover, although government agencies seldom become involved in the methodology of compensation,
they maintain a sharp interest in benefits. This has resulted in the enactment
of a complex body of laws and guidelines.

As with compensation, the primary role of benefits is to help attract and
retain desirable employees. The more closely an organization's benefits package matches the needs and lifestyles of potential employees, the greater its
hiring and retention advantage. To achieve this goal, benefits staff perform
many tasks:

- Survey employee demographics that influence benefits choices and costs
- Develop, evaluate, and select benefits plans that meet the organization's
  objectives

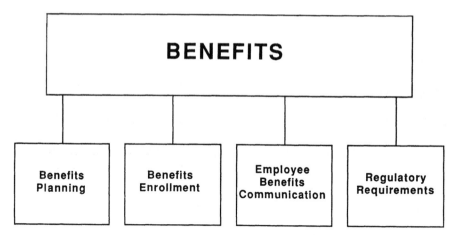

Figure 15–1. Principal roles of the benefits function.

- Determine eligibility for benefit plans
- Track coverage for each individual, including employees, dependents, retirees, and former employees
- Facilitate employee understanding of available benefits
- Maintain communication with carriers; make or authorize payments to providers of benefits.
- Monitor and submit timely reports on changes in employee benefits coverage
- Monitor developments in the benefits industry, especially new legal requirements

Types of Benefits

Every firm has its own list of benefits, and every year new benefits choices emerge. The benefits discussed in this chapter are only examples of the most common ones.

Each benefit has its own data requirements. Because many of these requirements depend on the type of benefit, HRMS designers can clarify their tasks by classifying benefits according to type: time benefits, risk benefits, and security benefits.

Time benefits include sick leave, vacation entitlement, paid time off, jury duty, military leave, parental leave (maternity leave, paternity leave, adoption leave), leave without pay, bereavement leave, relocation leave, and sabbaticals.

Risk benefits are various forms of insurance that help employees and their families in case of injury, illness, or death. These include health insurance, life insurance, long-term and short-term disability insurance, accidental death and dismemberment insurance, and travel accident insurance. Workers' compensation may be considered a type of insurance, and benefits may administer it. Because it relates to job safety, however, the occupational health and safety function may handle its administration. Certainly, the two units often interact on this issue. In this book, workers' compensation is covered in chapter 19.

Security benefits are thrift and savings programs, credit union loans, pension plans, and other retirement-oriented programs. They also include planning services such as estate planning, income tax preparation, and executive financial planning. Employees often consider credit unions to be a security benefit. Because of the personal nature of credit union loans or loans directly from the organization, the human resources department may track such loans. However, this operation may function as a separate administrative unit because it is basically a bank or savings and loan institution.

Pensions and other retirement plans are definitely security benefits, but the heavy fiduciary responsibilities they involve often lead management to place their administration in a separate, financially specialized function such as the treasurer's office or a completely autonomous retirement benefits administration function. In this book, retirement benefits are covered in chapter 21. Consultants and actuaries often perform much of this complex management task. Even in such cases, the human resources department usually serves as liaison, especially for employee communications.

Advantages and Limitations of Computerization

The single biggest advantage of including a benefits module in an HRMS is its contribution to managing the financial aspects of benefits. Computerization allows more accurate, detailed monitoring of expenses and obligations, so benefits staff can achieve more effective cost containment. For instance, more accurate demographics promote more accurate quotes by insurance carriers. More precise actuarial data can reduce pension costs. More timely premium collection via payroll deductions reduces insurance expense.

The benefits function involves a massive amount of paperwork and record keeping. Any company that wants to keep abreast of these demands must automate at least the clerical and administrative activities of benefits. Each employee periodically receives a benefits statement, which is generated more easily by the HRMS than by manual means. Computerization speeds up posting of employee status changes and benefits changes. This timeliness heightens employee satisfaction because employees receive more accurate and timely coverage. Employers benefit by being billed only for benefits available to qualified individuals.

Flexible Benefits in the HRMS

Flexible benefits is a rapidly growing approach to benefits coverage. According to a national poll, employees who have some choices of benefits express more satisfaction with their jobs, salaries, and benefits than do employees not given choices. With a flexible benefits plan, the employer allows employees to choose the benefits that they feel best fit their lifestyles.

Many organizations automatically provide benefits that they feel are necessary to meet legal and social obligations. These may include a minimum level of health, life, and accidental death and dismemberment insurance. A flexible benefits plan then allows each employee a certain number of credits for additional benefits selections. For each possible choice, the information lists the number of credits required, the benefit coverage, and the employee contribution, if any. Some plans even allow employees to choose cash compensation in lieu of additional benefits.

When planning a new HRMS, a contemporary human resources department should consider the role of flexible benefits in its long-term benefits

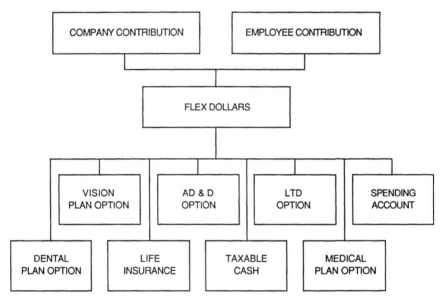

Figure 15–2. Typical flexible benefits plan. Combining employer and employee contributions yields the number of flex dollars available to an individual employee. The employee may distribute those among various benefit options; unused flex dollars remain in a spending account.
(Source: Genesys Software Systems, Inc. Reprinted with permission.)

strategy. Adding flexible benefits to an existing benefits system is as complex as adding a completely new module. Vendors may offer flexible benefits as an optional module at considerable cost, but the flexible benefits software they offer provides only generic treatment and may need extensive customization.

A firm that has an existing benefits module may be able to introduce the flexible benefits system in stages. In these circumstances, some human resources departments introduce only the credits approach, with no additional deductions or contributions allowed. Such adaptations may allow a firm to continue to use an existing benefits program much longer than would otherwise be possible.

Here are some ways in which selecting a flexible benefits plan affects the design and implementation of a benefits module:

- Each record requires more fields to indicate all the benefits status information. Each benefit may require an extra field for credits or coverage options.
- Enrollment status definitely requires its own indicator field. For many benefits, enrollment no longer occurs automatically as a result of employment or job classification.
- Benefits entitlement and contribution algorithms must include credits as a factor. Relating contribution dollars to coverage amount is no longer straightforward.
- Validation and error checking must be provided for credits selection. For instance, the module should flag records whenever the number of benefits credits in an individual's record exceeds the allowed maximum.
- Payroll needs a clear definition of benefits deductions. With flexible benefits, these amounts may vary considerably, so staff must constantly monitor designations of these amounts according to specific policies and procedures, supported by complex algorithms.
- The module must be able to accommodate future expansion. In almost every case, once an organization has introduced flexible benefits successfully, both the benefits function and employees promote additional benefits choices.

Data Requirements and Sources

Traditionally, the benefits function develops and administers almost all the data it uses. The employment function may facilitate collection of some initial benefits data because new employees usually make benefits selections at the time of hire. Benefits usually processes all subsequent changes, such as those

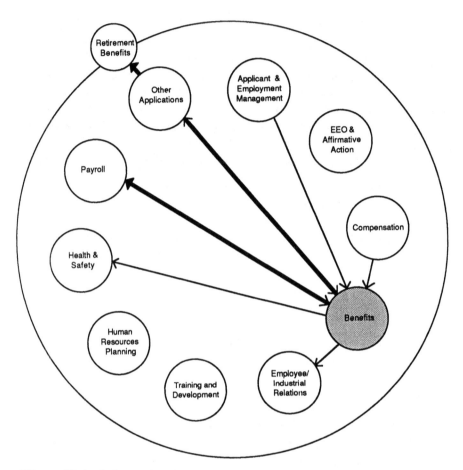

Figure 15–3. Information flow between benefits and other human resources functions.

resulting from open enrollment, changes in employment status, or changes in dependents. In fact, except for demographics, benefits uses only a small amount of information from other functions. Salary information comes from employment or compensation. Breaks in service and credited service are based on data from payroll or employee relations.

Government reporting requirements have become increasingly influential in benefits data tracking and reporting. At the beginning of the 1990s, employers were grappling with a new round of Internal Revenue Service (IRS) regulations that require quite sophisticated and detailed demographic and benefits distribution analysis for almost all employers. Although lawmakers have postponed or suspended certain time-consuming and complex regulations, other data-intensive requirements may surface in the next few years. HRMS managers can prepare for such developments by maximizing system flexibility.

Basic Benefits Data

Benefits uses similar types of data for virtually every type of benefit. The module may allow entry of information that is part of the procedures for administering benefits and performing related calculations either directly or via tables. Data unique to individual employees are maintained in the master record.

Benefits Calculation Data. The calculation of benefits follows certain rules. The system follows these rules, or algorithms, when updating records. For each benefit, the routine requires information that is often maintained in table form. Such information includes the following:

- Eligibility criteria. If eligibility is not automatic with employment, benefits calculation must begin with this consideration. This process may contain a series of IF/THEN statements. These may relate to job grade, union designation, age, service, or other factors in the individual record. Eligibility for some types of benefits may be automatic. Of the data mentioned, few are unique to benefits; all have multifunction purposes and originate in other functions, even external benefits providers.

- Eligibility date. The algorithm calculates eligibility date based on some specific date-sensitive field in the individual record. For instance, the module may calculate the eligibility date as the first of the month following the date of employment or 90 days after hire date.

- Eligibility hours. Federal law mandates that if a firm offers retirement benefits, it must offer them to employees who work more than a certain number of hours in a year (usually 1000 hours, or half-time). Therefore, the system must track days or hours worked. Eligibility calculations also must consider the rules for crediting hours used for various time benefits (such as vacation and sick leave) and for other breaks in service (such as leaves and furloughs).

- Eligibility earnings. Different types of benefits use different earnings in their calculations. This field shows which earnings to use in the algorithm for calculating benefits. Choices include base salary, benefits salary (base plus certain other categories of earnings), earnings year to date, and premium or incentive pay.

- When to calculate. Some vendors refer to this as the calculation frequency. This may indicate the first of the month, the first of the quarter, or some other cycle related to payroll processing. The procedures may include cal-

```
03/15/89                    YOUR COMPANY NAME, INC.
                            BENEFIT PLANS (INSURANCE)


     CODE: MEDICAL                 DESCRIPTION: Major Medical Plan

                            AMOUNT OR FORMULA

              Coverage: 0
      Employee premium: 95.51
     Dependent premium: 175.93
 Employee contribution: (B_EPREMIUM + B_DPREMIUM) / 2
  Employee contrib. per: M

                            ELIGIBILITY CRITERIA

       Employee status:              blank = all status codes
    (S)alary or (H)ourly:            blank = both salary and hourly
           Minimum age: 0.00         0 = mininum age
  Minimum days employed:   0         0 = no minimum days employed
  Minimum hours per day: 0.00        0 = no minimum hours per day
        Other criteria:
 Automatically add this benefit for eligible employees (Y/N): Y

 - - - - - - - - - - - - - - - - - - - - - - - - - - - - - - - -


     CODE: SUPP LIFE               DESCRIPTION: Supplemental Life

                            AMOUNT OR FORMULA

              Coverage: AN1000() * 3
      Employee premium: B_COVERAGE * .00018
     Dependent premium: 0
 Employee contribution: B_EPREMIUM / 2
  Employee contrib. per: M

                            ELIGIBILITY CRITERIA

       Employee status:              blank = all status codes
    (S)alary or (H)ourly:            blank = both salary and hourly
           Minimum age: 0.00         0 = mininum age
  Minimum days employed:   0         0 = no minimum days employed
  Minimum hours per day: 0.00        0 = no minimum hours per day
        Other criteria:
 Automatically add this benefit for eligible employees (Y/N): N
```

Figure 15–4. Benefits plan calculation data. Benefits plan tables give information about each specific plan. These sample tables show code, description, coverage, costs, and eligibility criteria for two specific plans—dental and life insurance. A typical HRMS module may have such data for dozens of plans.
(Source: AbraCadabra Software. Reprinted with permission.)

culation frequencies for several figures, such as eligibility, contribution, credited service, and benefit value.

- Calculation formulas. These formulas establish the relationships among all the factors that influence calculation of eligibility, current benefits, future benefits, and contributions. Each formula includes factors such as employee or employer contribution, flexible spending account, service, and coverage. For most firms, the increasing complexity of this area is adding to the cost of processing benefits in the HRMS.

Standard Benefits Data in Individual Records. For each benefit, the system maintains the following information in the employee's record:

- Eligibility. This yes/no/conditional field indicates whether an individual is eligible for a particular benefit. The term conditional would apply if for some reason eligibility was pending based on some other factor.
- Eligibility date. This field indicates the specific date on which the employee will become eligible for the benefit, unless policy mandates that eligibility is the date of hire.
- Enrollment status. This field indicates the individual's involvement in the plan and may include enrolled, withdrawn, pending, nonelected, refused, or conditional.
- Participation. If the type of benefit includes several options, the record will include type selected. For instance, health plan choices may include major medical alone, hospitalization alone, or a variety of health maintenance organizations (HMOs) or preferred provider organizations (PPOs).
- Coverage. This field indicates who is included in the individual's coverage. It may include employee, sponse, dependents, or a combination of these individuals.
- Level of benefit. This field indicates the level of benefit to which the employee is entitled or that the employee receives, such as maximum health insurance coverage, face value of life insurance, or retirement benefit value. This may be a calculated field based on points assigned, salary, employee contributions, or some combination of these and other factors.
- Defined benefits. This is used instead of level of benefit if a plan provides the employee or beneficiary a specific monthly (or annual) benefit determined by a formula.
- Employee contribution. This contribution may be either an actual dollar amount with a maximum limit or a percentage of base salary converted to a dollar amount.
- Employer contribution. Some organizations base this contribution on a percentage of the employee's base salary; others use a fixed dollar amount. In most cases, the system can calculate this field from other data.

- Defined contribution. This is used as an alternative to defined benefits to establish the limit of the employer's contribution to the plan.
- Credits assigned. This field applies to a flexible benefits system. Its value often derives from a table that contains the coverage or limits of the specific plan.
- Benefit salary. Benefit salary may differ from actual salary if annual salary includes additional amounts for hardship, work schedule, or other special circumstances. Sales representatives may have a relatively low fixed salary because they receive most of their compensation through commissions. In such cases, management may assign a special benefit salary amount as a more reasonable basis for computing benefits.
- Garnishment. In some cases, the human resources department will need to track benefit plan garnishment. The U.S. Supreme Court has held that garnishment of a welfare benefit is not forbidden. HRMS designers should consider whether the capacity of the proposed HRMS to track employee contributions and defined benefits provides sufficient facilities to comply with and track government orders that affect benefits.

Data on Former Employees. Benefits administration often requires that information on former employees remain in the data base for years after their separation or retirement from the company. Individuals currently receiving or who will become eligible for benefits must remain in the system, as must former employees or their dependents who are eligible for continued benefits.

A federal law mandates continued benefits coverage for former employees and their dependents. The Consolidated Omnibus Budget Reconciliation Act (COBRA) of 1986 requires most employers to offer continuation of health insurance for employees and dependents who are no longer eligible for regular coverage because of employment termination, retirement, divorce, or other reasons. If elected, such coverage must continue for eighteen to thirty-six months depending on the specific circumstances. The covered individual is responsible for premium payments. Therefore, COBRA administration must contain a billing provision, which the HRMS usually can handle.

The record will include a benefits expiration date if the affected individual is eligible for extended benefits for only a specified time (as in the case of COBRA). To assist in monitoring the billing and collection process, the individual record also should have a field that indicates whether benefits relate to COBRA, retirement, or some other eligibility variable besides current employment.

Time Benefits

Time benefits include sick leave, vacation, paid time off, holidays, personal time, bereavement leave, jury duty leave, military leave, parental leave, and

The Status Screen

The Status Screen is where you:

-- Assign benefit plans to employees.

-- Set up the employee's Start Date for benefit accrual.

-- Initialize and view the Carryover Hours from previous years.

-- View year-to-date totals for benefits accrued, taken and available.

To reach the Status Screen:

-- From the **Main Selection Menu**, select <u>**Attendance Module - Update or View Data**</u>.

-- (F)ind an employee.

```
------------------------ ABRA 2000 - Status Screen ------------------------

  Functions:  Find  Correct  Accrue   Next  Previous  Quit
  Screens:    Transaction
              Enter first letter of selection or use arrow keys and hit return
--------------------------------------------------------------------------
  EMP#: 1                                         START DATE: 02/14/72
  NAME: Adams, Donald W                          MONTHS WORKED:  196.67

                          VACATION   ILLNESS   PERSONAL    AS OF
              PLAN ID:    VAC-STD    ILL-STD   PER-STD     DATE

  YEAR-END ELIGIBILITY:    160.00     80.00     80.00     12/31/88

      CARRYOVER HOURS: (+)  40.00    199.00      0.00     12/31/87
   YTD HOURS ACCRUED: (+)   80.00     40.00     40.00     07/01/88
      YTD HOURS TAKEN: (-)  32.00     32.00      3.00
 YTD HOURS AVAILABLE: (=)   88.00    207.00     37.00     07/01/88

      LOA YTD HOURS TAKEN:   0.00             LAST CLOSE:  12/31/87
    OTHER YTD HOURS TAKEN:   2.00
```

The data items that are underlined on the previous screen will be highlighted in reverse video on your screen. These are the items which you must initially define for each employee. All other items are calculated by ABRA 2000.

The items which can be <u>directly</u> changed on the Status Screen are:

Figure 15–5. Time benefits status screen. This report shows eligibility for vacation, sick leave, and other paid time off as a basis for monitoring conformance with company policy and accrual rates.
(Source: AbraCadabra Software. Reprinted with permission.)

personal leave without pay. The benefits module tracks and reports time benefits according to the rules established for each. For some time benefits, the annual entitlement depends on service, hours actually worked, job grade, or some combination of these factors. Benefits may establish accrual formulas in the job classification table. The formula may be ⅚ of a vacation day accrued for every month worked (10 days per year) for service of 5 years or less, 1.25 vacation days per month for service over 5 years (15 days per year), and so forth.

For other types of time benefits, each employee receives a certain number of eligible days on a calendar basis (such as a certain number of holiday or sick days per year) or on an incident basis (a fixed number of parental leave days per new child). For each employee, the computer automatically tracks time accrued and time used in each category.

Some organizations permit carryover of some types of time benefits from one benefit year to another. This may apply to vacation, sick leave, or paid time off. A sophisticated benefits module should track carryovers, transfer unused time from the current benefit field to a supplemental field, and automatically apply carryover limits. It also may subtract hours used from the carryover field before subtracting any from the current benefit field and automatically generate notices when employees approach carryover time limits.

Other fields may track the dollar value of certain time benefits, such as vacation, holiday, and sick leave. This may be calculated when needed. Benefits uses this information when preparing employee benefits statements. Payroll may use this information when processing final checks for terminated and retired employees and when tracking the dollar value of time benefits used. Unions frequently require tracking of total compensation, including nonfinancial benefits.

Information on attendance and timekeeping required for monitoring time benefits comes to the system via whichever function handles attendance. In many firms, particularly those with significant numbers of nonexempt employees, payroll handles timekeeping, but responsibility for the origin of the information rests with line management. Payroll checks the data, then enters it into the system to enable payroll to calculate gross-to-net pay. The system automatically updates information on each time benefit (number of sick days, vacation days, and so forth). The benefits program periodically flags problem situations, such as more sick days used than allowed. Benefits then reports such variances to line management, employee relations, or both for resolution.

Risk Benefits

Risk benefits include health, life, disability, and travel accident insurance. For each employee, the firm must track eligibility for and election of the various types of insurance. All risk benefits require basically the same information in the employee record:

- Application pending notes that the application has been given to the employee and is in process
- Application received; notes that the application has been received and is being considered
- Eligibility status. pending, confirmed, denied, or withdrawn
- Date of eligibility decision
- Effective date of coverage
- Participating dependents; includes name, relationship, and birth date for each dependent
- Employee contribution; for self or for dependent coverage
- Coinsurance status: if employee receives coverage through another policy, such as spouse's employment or Medicare, lists provider, policy number, dates, and other relevant data

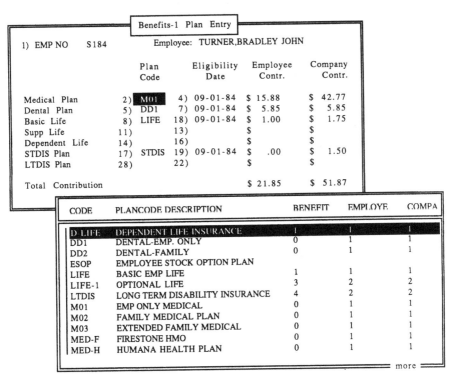

Figure 15–6. Typical benefits module screen. This screen shows coverage and costs for risk benefits for a specific employee. It also includes background information such as plan, eligibility, and employee/employer contributions.
(Source: Spectrum Human resource Systems. Reprinted with permission.)

Health Insurance. Health insurance is no longer one size fits all. More and more firms are offering employees a choice of basic health care options. Traditional medical insurance allows choice of health care providers but also has deductibles and coverage limits. HMOs and PPOs offer some restrictions but lower overall out-of-pocket costs. Many firms also offer supplemental health care coverage, such as dental, vision, travel accident, and prescription drug insurance. Each plan requires a separate set of fields, even though they may have data elements in common, since coverage and premium amounts are subject to frequent change.

Life and Accident Insurance. A benefits package may provide employees with group term life insurance, supplemental term life insurance (individual purchase of additional term life insurance), accidental death and dismemberment insurance, long-term disability insurance, and travel life insurance. For each type of life and accident insurance, the employee's record should include level of coverage, maximum eligible coverage, and beneficiaries. Maximum eligible coverage refers to the maximum amount of insurance for which the employee is eligible. For some types of coverage, this figure may be the same for all employees. For others, such as life insurance, the module may calculate maximum coverage on the basis of annual salary or job grade.

Security Benefits

The most important security benefits are pension plans and other retirement benefits. These are discussed separately in chapter 21. Other security benefits, such as planning services and employee loans, require much less HRMS involvement.

Some firms offer estate planning, financial planning, and income tax preparation, mostly as executive benefits. The IRS treats such services as noncash income, taxing employees who receive these benefits. In response, many firms have shifted the circumstances or terms under which they offer these services. Organizations that do provide such services must track employee eligibility and participation. To do so, they generally use fields in the benefits module. Data and programs used for the actual planning services virtually always reside on an independent system, since such data are highly personal and do not pertain to the individual's status as an employee. This stand-alone system may import some data from the HRMS, such as age, service, compensation history, or retirement contributions.

In a similar fashion, loan administration usually takes place on a separate system set up to function in a banking or savings and loan capacity. The HRMS may do some tracking of employee loans, both to comply with government requirements for monitoring benefits and to ensure that terminated employees fulfill their loan obligations or convert their loans to conventional rates

Dependent Care:
A Special Type of Benefit

Dependent care is a special type of benefit. It usually refers to child care, whether on-site, company run, or reimbursed. As an increasing percentage of the work force strives to support aging dependent parents, a few leading-edge companies have begun including elder care as an elective dependent care benefit. Some organizations may regard dependent care as a risk benefit—reducing the risk that a dependent is not well cared for—but it really is a special type of benefit.

The HRMS tracks cost-related information on dependent care benefits, such as which employees have elected dependent care, the number of benefits credits assigned, the amount of coverage (which may relate to age and number of dependents) for which they are eligible, and the amount of reimbursement. The HRMS may not include actual administration of the dependent care program, beyond names of dependents enrolled in program, locations, and so forth.

as required at time of termination. The HRMS may include a set of fields on loan benefits such as the following:

- Eligibility
- Participation status (no participation, applied, credit approved, loan received, loan repaid)
- Type of loan (home mortgage, home equity, auto, other)
- Initial loan balance
- Loan term (in months)
- Discount rate, if any (some organizations offer interest discounts to qualified employees)

Benefits Statement

The benefits function periodically issues an individual benefits statement to each employee or plan participant. This statement aims to communicate the benefits the employee is receiving and the value of this "hidden paycheck." To generate this statement via the HRMS, the module needs several types of information, often organized into two files. The first contains the rules the system uses to assemble and print an employee benefits statement. The second contains narrative text about each benefit option and its status.

Reporting Requirements

Benefits staff use internal reports to plan the array of benefits available to employees, to track the cost of these benefits, and to analyze individual benefit situations. They also use reports to communicate with government agencies and benefits providers.

Benefits Status Reports

Most benefits packages provide a wide variety of reports to monitor and maintain employee benefits status. Typically they sort data by fields such as plan, employee, provider, or date.

Eligibility and Enrollment Reports. The most basic version of this report lists individuals eligible for or enrolled in a particular benefit plan. The report may contain enrollment status, enrollment date, employee and dependent coverage, employee contributions, employer contributions, credited service, and breaks in service. The report may tally contributions on the basis of a particular pay period, calendar year to date, or fiscal year to date. For benefits in which employees have coverage choices, as often occurs with health insurance, the report lists plan type selected. Benefits uses this information when preparing premium adjustments, performing periodic enrollment verification, and evaluating costs of benefits to the organization.

Sometimes vendors and designers can structure the HRMS to schedule benefits changes automatically. Code responses or dates outside particular ranges in certain fields may trigger these changes.

One form of eligibility report may list all individuals approaching eligibility for a particular benefit. For instance, a firm might offer a retirement plan in which only employees with at least one year's service can participate. The report will include date of eligibility or expected change. Other reports may list employees scheduled for benefit cancellation or change. These reports can indicate reason for change, which may include a dependent reaching the age limit for coverage or a change in employee category or status.

A summary eligibility and enrollment report can list information about all benefits, such as the number of employees eligible compared with the number who have applied and the number of current participants. This information helps the benefits function evaluate the popularity of particular benefits among employees.

Benefits Statement Audit Report. Benefits prepares this report before distributing the employee benefits statements. This audit report, sequenced by employee or date, describes key variables such as contributions to date, contribution in current year, age, service, projected retirement date, defined benefit, or defined contribution. Staff can review this report for out-of-range conditions and other possible errors. In this way, they can ensure the correctness of demographics, coverage, and projected information before producing individual benefits statements.

Vacation, Sick Leave, and Holiday Status Reports. Benefits often requires these reports in several forms. Lists by department or location help identify patterns of time benefit usage. Listing time benefits by employee allows supervisors to identify out-of-range conditions, plan vacation schedules, and help staff plan appropriate use of accrued time benefits. For each time benefit, these reports often include eligible hours, hours used year to date, hours used career to date, hours carried forward, and expiration of carryover of benefits.

Benefits Utilization Report. This report tracks how many employees have exercised specific benefits options. This type of report has particular significance in flexible benefits systems.

Retirement Plan Status Report. If an organization has external actuaries audit its retirement plans, the benefits function must furnish demographic and financial information to those consultants. The amount and type of data included vary widely depending on plan and actuarial services required.

Employee Communications

The communications component of benefits is as important as the accounting component. Employees appreciate and use only those benefits that they understand and believe have value to them. Most large companies provide introductory written communications and annual individualized reports. Many firms arrange group presentations about new benefits or new plans. Some organizations also provide benefits counseling, which may include preretirement counseling.

Summary Plan Description. Whenever an organization hires a new employee or implements a new benefits plan, the benefits staff must distribute a benefits plan description to affected employees. Nearly all plans must meet certain U.S. Department of Labor requirements. The plan is basically a text-processed document. Human resources may establish and follow a summary outline within the HRMS that conforms to these Department of Labor requirements. Linking this capability to desktop publishing software can facilitate production of a high-quality booklet or other publication for distribution to employees.

Benefits Selection Form. A firm that offers benefits choices may have each employee fill out a benefits selection form. Employees receive these forms as part of their initial enrollment package and during periodic open enrollment periods. For each benefit plan choice, the form provides a summary description, employee cost (if any), benefit coverage, and flexible benefits credits applied.

Computerization eases the production of individualized forms. Each computer-printed benefits selection form can include the employee's name and other demographic data, current coverage, and number of benefits credits available. The form lists only those choices available to that particular employee. For instance, health care choices may depend on geographic location. Term life insurance and accidental death and dismemberment insurance options may have a specific value depending on compensation level.

Benefits Selection Confirmation. This notice confirms a particular employee's selection of benefits. The form may give the name and phone number of the appropriate person to contact for further information or corrections. Based on the employee's location or department, the report also may list the benefits representative assigned to that plan. The program may automatically include warnings as appropriate, such as "No health coverage selected" or "Additional unassigned benefits credits available."

Benefits Confirmation Notices. Making decisions about benefits participation requires several internal checks and perhaps reviews by carriers and other outside entities. Once the benefits function approves, denies, or terminates coverage, the system generates an acknowledgment to the affected employee.

This report-writing routine often uses the merge function to integrate a standard form with information from an individual record. For each benefit plan, the approval letter may list effective date, amount of coverage, employee contribution per pay period, claims procedures, and so forth. Denial and termination letters include the benefit, reason for denial or termination, dates, and appeal procedures or person to contact for further information.

Some systems create these types of letters automatically on a periodic basis. For instance, a module that includes dependent birth dates could generate a letter to each employee who has a child whose upcoming birthday would make him or her ineligible for continuing dependent health benefits. Another routine could automatically send terminated employees notices of end dates for benefits not extended under COBRA.

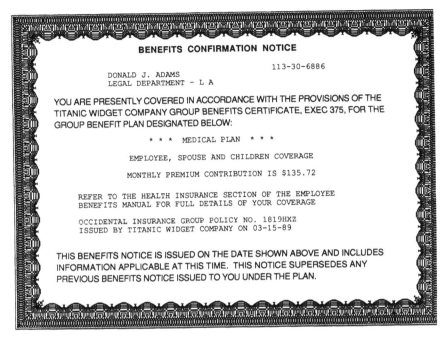

BENEFITS CONFIRMATION NOTICE

113-30-6886

DONALD J. ADAMS
LEGAL DEPARTMENT - L A

YOU ARE PRESENTLY COVERED IN ACCORDANCE WITH THE PROVISIONS OF THE
TITANIC WIDGET COMPANY GROUP BENEFITS CERTIFICATE, EXEC 375, FOR THE
GROUP BENEFIT PLAN DESIGNATED BELOW:

* * * MEDICAL PLAN * * *

EMPLOYEE, SPOUSE AND CHILDREN COVERAGE

MONTHLY PREMIUM CONTRIBUTION IS $135.72

REFER TO THE HEALTH INSURANCE SECTION OF THE EMPLOYEE
BENEFITS MANUAL FOR FULL DETAILS OF YOUR COVERAGE

OCCIDENTAL INSURANCE GROUP POLICY NO. 1819HXZ
ISSUED BY TITANIC WIDGET COMPANY ON 03-15-89

THIS BENEFITS NOTICE IS ISSUED ON THE DATE SHOWN ABOVE AND INCLUDES
INFORMATION APPLICABLE AT THIS TIME. THIS NOTICE SUPERSEDES ANY
PREVIOUS BENEFITS NOTICE ISSUED TO YOU UNDER THE PLAN.

Figure 15–7. Benefits confirmation notice. Sometimes a confirmation or acknowledgment provides complete coverage information, including deductibles, limits, contact person, and exclusions. Other times, as in this case, the notice refers the employee to the benefits manual for details.

Employee Benefits Statement. As mentioned earlier, this report serves two purposes: to keep each individual well informed about his or her benefits coverage and to increase employee awareness and appreciation of benefits provided. Many firms issue individual benefits reports annually. Some issue them only on demand, at least for certain benefits. The benefits statement merges text about plan provisions and coverage with information from the employee's record. The report describes each benefit and lists eligibility status, participation status, employee contribution, flexible benefits credits applied, current coverage, deductibles, beneficiaries, and dependent coverage for each benefit.

Employee Benefits Profile. This report provides information on an as-needed basis. Benefits may request such a report in response to an employee (or retiree) inquiry about accrued vacation. In termination cases, individuals may need to know about their accrued time benefits and security benefits. The report may list current benefit status, coverage, value, and expiration date.

YOUR BENEFITS STATEMENT

HEALTH INSURANCE

The annual premium for health insurance is $_____ and you pay $_____ The Company pays $_____ providing comprehensive coverage for you and your dependents.

To purchase comparable coverage privately you would pay approximately $_____

LIFE INSURANCE

The amount of your group life insurance is $_____ with a double indemnity provision that will provide up to an additional $_____ in the event of accidental death or dismemberment.

Your designated beneficiary is _____

Your dependent life insurance coverage is $_____

Including accidental death benefits, you have $_____ total family coverage.

When you travel on Company business, you have additional travel accident insurance of $_____

Comparable insurance purchased privately would cost you approximately $_____ per year.

YOUR BENEFITS VALUE

If you purchased comparable benefits privately, the cost would be about $_____

For all of the above benefits your portion of the annual expense is $_____

The difference when added to your base salary would bring your total annual compensation to the equivalent of $_____

DISABILITY INSURANCE

SICKNESS BENEFITS You were paid $_____ for _____ sickness benefit days taken last year.

LONG TERM DISABILITY In the event of extended disability, you are guaranteed at least $_____ per month based on your current salary. This amount includes one-half of your social security disability benefit. Comparable private coverage would cost you about $_____ per year.

UNEMPLOYMENT COMPENSATION DISABILITY INSURANCE (UCD) Your premium is 1% of the first $7,400 of annual salary. Based on your current salary, you can receive up to $_____ per week for 52 weeks.

WORKERS' COMPENSATION In the event of a job related injury or illness you are automatically insured by the Company. Based on your current salary, you can receive up to $_____ per week while you are disabled.

RETIREMENT PLAN

Your normal retirement date is _____ when you will be eligible for an annual income of _____ % of average earnings for your five highest consecutive years less an amount equal to _____ % of your social security benefit. In addition, you will have up to $5,000 in life insurance coverage. If you had privately purchased this retirement annuity, beginning with the year of your original date of employment, you would have had to make a premium payment of $_____ last year.

FAMILY ESTATE PLAN

Your participation in this plan will begin in _____   Status as of _____

FAMILY ESTATE PLAN BENEFICIARY _____

SERVICE UNITS + SALARY UNITS = TOTAL UNITS × VALUE OF UNIT $_____ = BALANCE OF ACCOUNT FROM PREVIOUS YEAR _____ SHARES _____ CASH $_____

CURRENT YEAR DIVIDENDS

FUNDS AVAILABLE FOR INVESTMENT $_____ CASH $_____ CREDITS FOR YEAR _____

NUMBER OF SHARES PURCHASED × PRICE PER SHARE $_____ = COST OF SHARES PURCHASED $_____ CASH $_____

SHARES PURCHASED FOR YOUR ACCOUNT DURING YEAR

MARKET VALUE OF TOTAL SHARES ON ACCOUNT AS OF YEAR'S END $_____   PRESENT BALANCE IN ACCOUNT _____ SHARES _____ CASH $_____

Figure 15–8. Benefits statement. This report is a communication to an individual employee to inform him or her about the value of benefits the employer provides. It is written in a narrative style so the employee can understand it easily. This statement also underscores the value of these benefits to the employee by pointing out how much he or she would have to pay to obtain comparable coverage independently and adding the net benefit value to his or her base salary to determine total annual compensation.

491

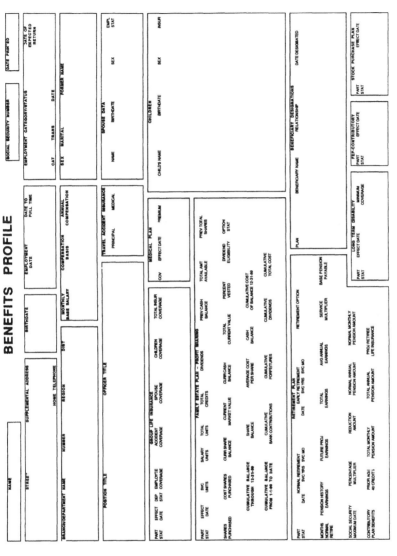

Figure 15–9. Employee benefits profile. This profile is for internal human resources department use. It includes detailed information about each type of benefit, including effective date, coverage, premiums, covered dependents and beneficiaries, and retirement and profit-sharing information.

Employee Benefits History Report. This report describes an individual's history of participation in one or more of an organization's benefits plans.

COBRA Billing. Because COBRA participants pay for their own benefits coverage, the former employer must handle the entire billing and accounting process for converted coverage. Many firms rely heavily on the HRMS to ease these heavy record-keeping and reporting duties. Reports to individuals include invoices, summary statements, notices of benefits and fee changes, and acknowledgments.

Provider Communication

Benefits staff often must provide insurance carriers and other benefits providers with information from the benefits data base.

Census Summaries. Benefits providers and consultants often need demographic information about the employee population. A census summary report may provide tabulations of employees according to age, gender, marital status, service, location, or other factors. Benefits planners and providers need this information to develop actuarial projections about future costs and coverage needs.

Coverage List. This report lists all individuals covered under a particular plan. Depending on the type of benefit, this report may include level of coverage, dependents, employee contributions, age, service, and other related information.

Requests for Coverage. This report lists employees for whom coverage is requested. Benefits usually processes these requests on an individual basis as new employees are hired, but in the case of open enrollment, the benefits function may process a large number of requests at one time.

Changes in Coverage. On a periodic basis, usually monthly or quarterly, benefits sends insurance carriers a list of all individuals removed from the plan and all changes in coverage for continuing participants. These changes may occur because of salary adjustments, change of job or location, change in union membership status, breaks in service, or any other status change that affects the premium paid to the provider.

Requests for Proposal. When soliciting proposals for coverage by outside carriers, benefits prepares a complete package of materials that includes a description of the organization, a profile of employee population, the type of coverage desired, and the time frame for submission of bids. Some of this material is

```
                    Titanic Widget Company
            B I L L I N G     S T A T E M E N T


TO:
    Donna N Christian
    566 Villa Casa Ct
    Saratoga, CA  95020


        INSURANCE COVERAGE FOR PERIOD 01/01/90 THRU 12/31/90


                                        Employee  Dependent    Total
                              Expire    Monthly    Monthly    Monthly
   Plan                        Date    Coverage   Premium    Premium   Premium
   ========================== ======== ========   =======    =======   =======
   Dental Plan                05/01/92              22.59      11.78     34.37
   Major Medical Plan         05/01/92              97.42     179.45    276.87
                                                                       --------
       PLEASE REMIT PAYMENT FOR THIS AMOUNT                             311.24
```

Figure 15–10. **Typical COBRA billing statement. Under federal guidelines for extending benefits to employees who have terminated, COBRA requires employers to bill ex-employees at their home address for contributions to benefits plans in which the individual elects to continue participating.**
(Source: AbraCadabra Software. Reprinted with permission.)

text, and some involves demographic and statistical information derived from the HRMS data base.

RFPs most often pertain to insurance provider options, but they can apply to other external service providers, such as child-care facilities, financial managers, actuaries, and claims processors.

Benefits Planning

Benefits planners face the challenge of constructing an array of benefits that best meets the lifestyle needs of employees within the fiscal limits of the organization. As benefits cost accounting becomes more important and choices proliferate, more firms have outside specialists perform the complex aspects of planning. Consultants and carriers have the data base and large computing resources required for determining the benefits needs and choices of particular populations, but even when these resources handle benefits planning, benefits may still have to provide demographic and administrative information.

Benefits Plan. Benefits plans help management evaluate the cost of changes in benefits availability, employee staffing, demographics, and organizational structure and size. Periodic evaluation of benefits options also allows management to allocate benefit dollars effectively. Depending on the type of benefit under consideration, a report may list the number of employees using and expected to use each benefit, demographics, employee and employer contributions, projected retirement dates, and participating dependents. By adjusting variables, benefits can create numerous "what if" projections.

Flexible Spending Account. Benefits planners use various scenarios to determine the number of credits to assign each choice in a flexible benefits plan. The general basis is the cost to the organization of providing each benefit. Such projections are beyond the capability of the typical HRMS.

This complexity has led to a growth in service among the benefits providers themselves. The major insurance companies, actuaries, and benefits administration firms are spending considerable time and energy developing projections and monitoring demographics. Some even provide computer systems for administration of flexible benefits plans. Under these circumstances, the provider absorbs the risks associated with the unpredictability of employee choices with a flexible benefits plan; the overall risk is distributed among all the organizations that pay fees for that provider's benefit services. In helping employees plan flexible spending accounts, the system can specify requirements, maximums, or minimums for some choices to limit employee risk.

Future Benefit Costs Reports. The Financial Accounting Standards Board (FASB) has proposed that companies treat as a current annual expense the firm's expected costs of postretirement medical and life insurance benefits. A firm's benefits function must furnish accountants with reports of its current employee base, expected retirement dates, and planned postretirement benefits.

Government Reporting

COBRA Reports. COBRA regulations do not mandate particular reports, but in the event of litigation or other complaints relating to continuation of benefits, employers must be prepared to document their policies and practices with regard to COBRA requirements. This documentation may include the following:

- Text description of COBRA policy and procedures, including description of computer systems. Although the text is word processed and not part of the benefits software, the module should include routines that support the COBRA requirements.
- Statistical analysis of COBRA participation among eligible employees. These may be standard or custom reports.
- Individual benefits history, including post-termination participation, for individuals involved in the dispute. The employee benefits history report should include provisions for noting terminations and other breaks in service.

Employee Retirement Income Security Act Reports. The U.S. Department of Labor, the IRS, and the federal Pension Benefit Guaranty Corporation (PBGC) jointly administer the Employee Retirement Income Security Act (ERISA) of 1974. ERISA and the related regulations that have followed it contain the guidelines retirement plans must follow to qualify for tax-deferred status. Many of these regulations pertain to virtually all employee benefits plans (except government plans and certain plans of nonprofit organizations). ERISA regulations cover disclosure, federal reporting, and fiduciary standards for employee benefit plans. All affected employers must file certain reports with these agencies. Because of the need for scrupulous accuracy, most companies need computerization to fulfill these record-keeping and reporting requirements. Many use consultants to check their compliance with ERISA mandates, while still assuming responsibility for the actual data.

As discussed under employee communication, whenever an organization subject to ERISA distributes a new summary plan description to its employees, it also must submit a copy to the Department of Labor. Additionally, every year affected firms must submit a group of reports known as the 5500 series. The most common forms are as follows:

- Form 5500, Annual Return/Report of Employee Benefit Plan (for any plan with more than 100 participants), which includes statistical data on each plan

- Form 5500, Schedule A, which contains insurance information
- Form 5500, Schedule B, which contains actuarial information
- Form 5500, Schedule SSA, an annual registration statement that identifies individual participants who have deferred vested benefits

Section 89 and Benefits Discrimination. Section 89 of the Internal Revenue Code of the Tax Reform Act of 1986 (commonly referred to as TEFRA) promised to have significant implications for benefits analysis and report requirements. Briefly, Section 89 promoted nondiscriminatory access to benefits coverage for employees regardless of their rank within a company. Toward that end, these regulations proposed to require subject firms to evaluate each benefit option periodically to determine the percentage of employees eligible for and covered by the option. Subject employers would have to perform up to six statistical tests for each benefit plan variation offered, potentially totaling hundreds or thousands of calculations. If the tests revealed discrimination, employees receiving that benefit would have to pay taxes on it.

Because of Section 89's daunting record-keeping and analytical requirements, employers lobbied to prevent the implementation of these provisions. As a result, postponement, revision, and repeal of some of the provisions have been the subject of much congressional debate and action. For practical purposes, Section 89 is dead.

Nonetheless, the basic lesson of Section 89 holds: The federal government may require increased monitoring and analytical testing of some types of benefits plans. Therefore, employers should prepare to use their HRMS to help analyze the equity of eligibility and participation in their employee benefits plans. As new regulations arise, the HRSC and benefits functions should consider whether an internal system upgrade would meet those needs or whether they should use external consultants or vendors to perform such work.

Special Circumstances

As with any other aspect of human resources, coordination with other units and outside agencies requires professional attention and acceptance of responsibility. In the case of HRMS benefits data, staff must stress accuracy and attention to detail. Errors such as recording an incorrect beneficiary, wrong address, or improper amount may have a significant negative effect on the lives of employees.

Working with Payroll

Payroll and benefits exchange a significant amount of information. These interactions are probably the strongest argument for integrating payroll and human resources into a single computer system. For instance, in an integrated system, a change in benefits coverage can automatically change the figures the payroll module uses to calculate deductions and accompanying statements. Interaction with payroll involves two major areas: deductions for employee contributions and tracking of employee attendance.

Payroll Deductions. To pay for required contributions, employees must agree to have the employer withhold part of their pay for premium payments or investment. This applies most commonly to health insurance (particularly for dependent coverage) and retirement plans but sometimes pertains to other benefits as well.

For payroll to process checks correctly, benefits must have timely and accurate information in each employee's record. Benefits should coordinate with payroll the schedule of calculations that determine employee contributions. All calculations for the period immediately past should be ready in the individual employee file when payroll begins its processing. As discussed in chapter 3, some systems include automatic invocation of routines for calculation of employee contributions at certain calendar points or intervals.

Arriving at an accurate paycheck requires a separate calculation for every benefit that involves employee contributions. These are the responsibility of benefits. Payroll merely deducts the authorized employee contribution from gross pay and credits the contribution to the appropriate fund and to the employee's file.

Tracking Attendance. Payroll may administer employee attendance records, particularly in organizations that have unions or other hourly workers. Days and hours worked pertain to time benefits, such as sick days and vacations. This information also affects seniority, breaks in service, and other factors that affect many types of benefits. Payroll should establish a schedule for entering these data and provide benefits with relevant information about this schedule. Error checking on attendance information may be handled by those responsible for timekeeping or by the employee relations function. Benefits should resolve any questions or deviations before the records go to payroll. The same recommendations apply if employee relations or a separate time and attendance function handles attendance. Managing time and attendance data is discussed further in chapter 21.

International Benefits

Organizations operating internationally must cope with a complicated set of benefits tasks. Some differences relate to laws; others relate to environmental conditions. For instance, some countries have varying levels of state-provided health care programs. Employees eligible for such programs may need different health coverage than those working in countries without government health coverage. In some cases, certain benefits provide partial compensation for hardships. For instance, a firm may want to provide employees working in certain countries with complete coverage for all inoculations. Employees in remote areas may need medical evacuation insurance, which covers the inordinately high cost of chartering air transportation in cases of serious illness or injury.

Tax laws and retirement fund regulations are completely different in different countries. This usually necessitates having a separate set of retirement benefits for employees who are nationals of another country or for other reasons pay taxes there. Firms often need to consult with experts in these countries to determine the best investment, banking, and benefits plan options in such circumstances.

Glossary

Actuarial data   Information that estimates the future likelihood of covered individuals becoming eligible for benefits collection and at what level. Insurance underwriting, retirement planning, and other benefits analysis frequently require such data.

Benefits salary   Individual salary amount on which benefits are computed. May differ from annual salary or wages.

COBRA   See *Consolidated Omnibus Budget Reconciliation Act*.

Consolidated Omnibus Budget Reconciliation Act (COBRA)   This 1986 law covering employers of twenty or more employees that offer group health plans requires access to continuing coverage, at the worker's expense, for eighteen to thirty-six months after the worker leaves the company.

Defined benefits   Benefits plans that base the entitlement on earnings and length of service rather than on the amount the employee has contributed to the plan.

Defined contribution   Benefits plans that base the entitlement on the value of the contributions made by the employee and employer.

Employee Retirement Income Security Act (ERISA)   A 1974 act setting forth federal guidelines that most employee benefit plans must follow to qualify for tax-deferred status. Covers funding arrangements, fiduciary responsibilities, and other standards and requires reports to the Department of Labor, IRS, and Pension Benefit Guaranty Corporation.

ERISA   See *Employee Retirement Income Security Act.*

5500 reports   A group of reports on benefits plans that must be submitted to the Department of Labor, the IRS, and the Pension Benefit Guaranty corporation.

Flexible benefits   A flexible benefits plan allows employees to choose the benefits that fit best with their lifestyle, age, family circumstances, and service. Also called *cafeteria plan.*

Health maintenance organization (HMO)   A form of health insurance in which participants pay little or no deductible for medical care; coverage usually includes preventive care. Participants must select from a list of approved health care providers.

HMO   See *Health maintenance organization.*

Medicare   Title XVIII of the Social Security Act, added in 1965; a two-part medical insurance program for people aged 65 or older and certain disabled people. Part A is for basic hospital care and part B for supplemental services, physicians, drugs, and outpatient services.

PPO   See *Preferred provider organization.*

Preferred provider organization (PPO)   Similar to an HMO, except that a PPO concentrates more on the provider than on institutions per se.

Risk benefits   Various forms of insurance that help employees and their families in case of injury, illness, or death. This includes health, life, disability, accidental death and dismemberment, and travel insurance.

Section 89   Part of the Internal Revenue Code of the Tax Reform Act of 1986 regarding benefit plans. In order for such plans to qualify as untaxed benefits, the employer must perform particular statistical tests to check that employees receive nondiscriminatory benefits coverage under those plans regardless of their rank in the company. Because of these demanding analytical requirements, congress postponed implementation of Section 89.

Security benefits   Pension plans and other retirement plans, as well as certain financial planning and loan services.

Time benefits   Paid and unpaid authorized time off from work for a variety of reasons. The most common forms are sick pay and vacation, though firms usually have many other types as well.

Discussion Points

1.   Give examples of each of the three types of benefits.
2.   What are the major advantages of computerizing the benefits function?

3. In what ways does benefits resemble compensation? In terms of the HRMS, what are the most important differences?

4. In what ways does having a flexible benefits plan affect the content and structure of the benefits module in the HRMS?

5. What kinds of files and records would an HRMS need to access in order to produce a fairly complete individual benefits statement?

6. Why should the HRMS be able to produce accurate individual benefits reports on demand?

7. What kinds of circumstances might trigger the system to issue a notice of benefits status change concerning an individual employee?

8. What kinds of demographic and statistical information from the HRMS might accompany an RFP sent to potential benefits carriers?

Further Reading

Baily, Phillips B. "Using Personal Computers for Administering Defined Contribution Plans." *HRSP Review*, Fourth Quarter 1985.

Brewer, Thomas. "Human Factors: The Key to Successfully Automating the Benefits Function." *Topics in Total Compensation*. Greenvale, NY: Panel Publishers, Fall 1987.

"Charting Flexible Benefits in an Uncertain Future." *Employee Benefit Plan Review*, April 1986.

"Computers for Employees and Their Benefits." *Employee Benefit Plan Review*, July 1985.

Deverman, Jerome N. "Computer Applications for Employee Benefit Plans." *Pension World*, March 1982.

DiBlase, Donna. "Interactive Benefit System Tool of the Times." *Business Insurance*, May 1986.

Finlayson, Robert A. "Software Untangles Flex Plan Knots." *Business Insurance*, May 1986.

"Flexible Compensation Goal: Meet Diverse Needs." *Employee Benefit Plan Review*, May 1987.

Grant, Dale B. "Total Compensation Plan Design." *Compensation & Benefits Management*, Spring 1986.

Gilchrist, Glen J. "A Menu for the Benefits Feast." *Computers in Personnel*, Spring 1987.

Green, Michael E. "Making HRMS Fit Cobra." *Software News*, January 1987.

Halpern, Barbara. "Employer Goals Reached through Flexible Benefits." *Employee Benefit Plan Review*, April 1986.

Heiring, George W. "Over the Electronic Rainbow." In *Computer Applications for Employee Benefit Plans*, edited by June M. Lehman. Brookfield, WI: International Foundation for Employee Benefit Plans, 1986.

Hoff, Roger A. "The Impact of Cafeteria Benefits on the Human Resource Information System." *Personnel Journal*, April 1983.

Keith, Donna. "The Systems Guide to Section 89." *Computers in HR Management*, September 1989.

Lehman, June M., ed. *Computer Applications for Employee Benefit Plans.* Brookfield, WI: International Foundation for Employee Benefit Plans, 1986.

Lewis, Dickson W. "Benefits Communication: Findings of a Survey." *Employee Benefits Journal*, September 1989.

McCaffrey, R.M. *Employee Benefits Programs: A Total Compensation Perspective.* Boston: PWS-Kent, 1988.

Perham, John C. "Benefits by Computer." *Dun's Business Month*, June 1986.

Pflaum, Marvin B. "Put a PC to Work for You: Interactive Projections of Savings and Retirement Plan Benefits." *Employee Benefits Journal*, September 1989.

Reynolds, John D. *Employee Benefits Report.* New York: Warren, Gorham, & Lamont, January 1986.

Rutherglen, G. "Sexual Equality in Fringe Benefit Plans." *Virginia Law Review*, Volume 65, 1979.

Salibury, Dallas L. "The Corporate Stake in Employee Benefits." *Enterprise*, August 1983.

Simon, Sidney H. "Benefits Administration That Complies with COBRA." *Personnel Journal*, March 1987.

Strayer, Jacqueline F. "A High-Tech Approach to Compensation Communications." *Personnel*, October 1985.

Taplin, Polly T. "What's in Store for Flexible Benefits." *Employee Benefit Plan Review*, June 1987.

Tetz, Frank F. "Integration as the Key to Successful Benefit Plan Administration." In *Computer Applications for Employee Benefit Plans*, edited by June M. Lehman. Brookfield, WI: International Foundation for Employee Benefit Plans, 1986.

Tolson, Richard. "Development of a Microbased Employee Benefits Information System." *Topics in Total Compensation*, Fall 1987.

Trisler, Stewart. "Personal Computers—A Boon to Benefits Planners." *Employment Relations Today*, Winter 1984/85.

"Using PCs to Administer Group Benefits." *Benefits News Analysis*, February 1986.

Valentino, James, and Pamela Keeler. "A Computer-Based Interactive System Works." *Compensation & Benefits Management*, Spring 1986.

16

Employee and Industrial Relations

> In order that people may be happy in their work, three things are needed: They must be fit for it. They must not do too much of it. And they must have a sense of success in it.
>
> —John Ruskin

The employee and industrial relations function provides services and support to facilitate communication among management, employees, and labor unions. It also assists individual employees with special needs. This function sometimes seems like a catchall operation within human resources. Employee relations staff may handle or monitor diverse functions such as attendance and absenteeism, EEO/AA, performance reviews, and career counseling. In this book, some of these issues are covered in other application chapters because in most human resources departments, they are independent functions.

The roles and even the name of this function depend in large part on an organization's activities, structure, and culture. Some call this function industrial relations, union relations, labor relations, or staff relations. In other organizations, employee relations refers to services for largely salaried, white-collar employees. Industrial relations usually appears in organizations that have unionized hourly employees who perform work under a collective bargaining agreement. Industrial relations handles negotiations and interactions between management and labor. If industrial relations deals with hourly workers, a separate function, often called employee relations, addresses corresponding issues with salaried workers. For simplicity, this chapter uses the single term *employee relations* to refer to either or both functions. The term *industrial relations* refers specifically to responsibilities related to union issues.

The HRMS in Employee and Industrial Relations

Although employee and industrial relations staff may access the HRMS frequently, they seldom have a module dedicated to their use. This is because employee and industrial relations plays a largely reactive, though sometimes preventive, role. Their actions usually result from complaints or requests from employees or their supervisors. These inquiries range from personal and financial to job or supervisor related. Most of these issues deal with existing HRMS data.

Role of Employee Relations

The goal of employee relations in its most generic sense is to provide a supportive work environment for employees. Employee relations representatives serve as intermediaries and guides through the complexities of employee services. For this reason, employee relations may have a higher profile among the general employee population than do other human resources functions. In fact, its charter is usually to consider employees rather than management as clients but still function within established company policy.

An employee relations representative is often a human resources generalist responsible for a specific site or work group within the organization. Employee relations staff become involved in specific situations at the request of individual employees, supervisors, or managers. These staffers strive to facilitate resolution of issues that may involve almost any human resources function. Employee relations also has direct responsibility for sensitive issues in which personal judgment and management decision making overlap. These may include performance review administration; problems involving attendance or absenteeism; pay and work rules issues; union relations; and employee assistance programs (EAPs) for issues such as substance abuse, financial troubles, and domestic problems. For specific individuals or positions, they also may interact with the employment function in resolving staffing and internal placement issues. They may work with employment or training on new employee orientation or with compensation and benefits to address pay-related concerns.

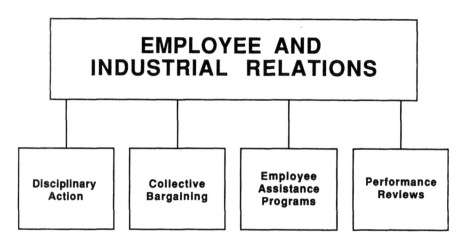

Figure 16–1. Principal roles of the employee and industrial relations function.

Computers in Employee Relations

An individual who has a question or issue about compensation, benefits, career planning, training, retirement, grievances, or performance reviews may meet with the local employee relations representative. A responsive employee relations function can help solve employee problems quickly and shield the rest of human resources from these problems. Some human resources professionals estimate that qualified employee relations staff can solve or refer about 75 percent of all employee-initiated issues. To do so, the employee relations representative needs access to a broad spectrum of personal and job-related information in the individual's HRMS record. Employee relations can best accomplish its goals when this function has the ability to access virtually all the modules within the HRMS.

An HRMS offers more comprehensive, timely information on individuals than does a manual system. Employee relations staff usually have access to individual data only for employees or groups for whom they are responsible. Linking up with the HRMS gives employee relations access to more accurate demographics on the employee population as a whole. This aids the staff in evaluating issues relating to discrimination, performance, supervisory bias, career development, and other complaints.

Limits of Computers in Employee and Industrial Relations

Employee relations seldom has its own module within the HRMS. A few packages have emerged for EAPs, but most simply track events, interactions or referrals by type, then monitor follow-up activity. None can perform analyses or provide actual assistance. Some vendors offer labor relations packages that track grievances, violations of work rules, issue resolution, and related matters.

Employee relations usually has little involvement in the design and development of the HRMS except for suggestions of certain demographic data that should be included. Design involves reserving in certain modules fields for tracking time-sensitive data and results of mediation or intervention processes. Examples include overdue performance reviews, EAP referrals, medical exams, job-related testing, and supervisory orientation.

Some aspects of employee relations require significant data security because they deal with highly personal data and, therefore, the privacy rights of employees. This particularly affects EAPs that handle matters such as substance abuse, personal finances, and family problems. This information also may affect some disciplinary processes. For this reason, an organization may choose to maintain this information in manual records to avoid potential security problems. Whether employee relations obtains relevant information from the HRMS or from manual records, staff must use careful security measures and control of access to protect individual rights. This information is

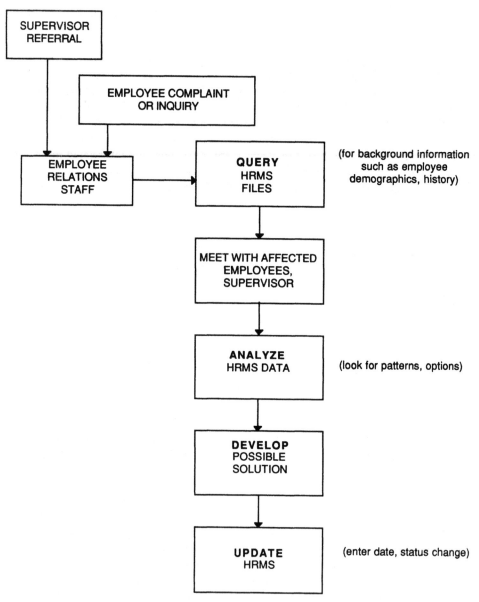

Figure 16–2. **Using an HRMS to resolve employee relations problems.**
Many aspects of problem solving are interpersonal, but an
automated system can increase the speed, thoroughness,
and accuracy of this process. The boldfaced areas in the
figure indicate the steps at which employee relations can use
the system to retrieve and update relevant data.

made available to other internal and external representatives on a need-to-know basis.

Data Requirements and Sources

Employee relations initiates or creates very little data. For the most part, it uses data from other human resources functions. The data it develops and enters are somewhat less quantitative in nature than those of other functions. The main entries concern data related to individual employee action; they typically involve recording dates and results of interviews, incidents, counseling sessions, disputes, physical exams, attendance problems, warnings, grievances, accidents, and follow-up actions. Some of these data are discussed in chapter 19.

Data from Other Human Resources Functions

Employee relations works with individual employee records that include an employee's work history, skills and experience, service, and performance. To do so, employee relations must retrieve employee and career profile information developed by other human resources functions, particularly employment, EEO/AA, compensation, benefits, safety and training.

Employee relations also must consider hire and job history records, including promotions, transfers, salary changes, leaves, layoffs, and terminations. This information may originate with the line manager or enter the HRMS via various human resources functions.

Time and Attendance Data

Employee relations staff do not usually input time and attendance records but mediate when problems arise in this area. Line management is responsible for time and attendance data, and payroll uses these data as a basis for paycheck processing. As discussed in chapter 21, however, some organizations have administrative functions that maintain these data. The function that tracks time and attendance also flags time-related incidents that may require further investigation or problem resolution. Typical incidents include excessive absences, tardiness, and unauthorized overtime. Individuals or supervisors may request employee relations' involvement in dispute resolution. Such disputes may pertain to sick days in excess of the authorized limit, unauthorized overtime hours, disagreements about leave without pay, unused vacation time, and scores of other problems that may arise in the work environment.

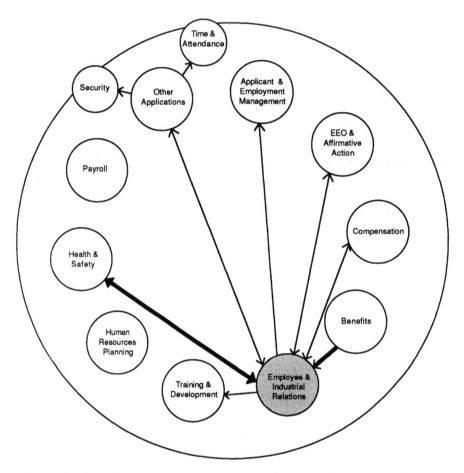

Figure 16–3. Information flow between employee and industrial relations and other human resources functions.

Performance Reviews

Line managers evaluate employees for scheduled performance reviews, but employee relations often plays a monitoring role in this process. They may conduct or attend performance review sessions involving problem employees or those facing disciplinary action or termination. They may use the HRMS to track dates for upcoming and overdue reviews, then generate appropriate listings or reminders to managers. Often the supervisor (or a clerk) receives completed documents and inputs the appraisal information. Occasionally employee relations or the HRIC inputs these data.

Employee relations mediates performance review disputes between supervisors and employees. To do so, the employee relations representative may use historical performance and compensation data. If the employee relations representative negotiates a change in performance evaluation, eligibility for training programs, or other variables the HRMS maintains, employee relations enters that information. In most cases, this does not require additional fields specifically designated for employee relations. Instead, employee relations simply adjusts information in fields maintained by other human resources functions, then issues an acknowledgement to the originator of the data.

EAPs

The EAP has traditionally been a trouble unit—that is, it handles issues initiated by employees. In recent years, it has taken a broader stance. It still assists with personal problems, financial problems, legal problems, substance abuse, and other issues in employees' lives that do not directly affect their employment status but may affect their productivity. More and more organizations now offer diagnostic as well as remedial counseling, particularly through referrals. Some firms help with child-care placement, advice on real estate loans, relocations, and community orientation for new and transferred employees. In the absence of a company credit union, some firms make small loans to employees and may cosign bank loans.

To protect the privacy of employees in these sensitive areas, some organizations choose to avoid computerization altogether by maintaining these rec-

ABRA 2000 - Events Screen

Functions: Find List Add Correct Remove Next Previous Quit
Screens: Main Job History Benefits Dependents Skills Events
Enter first letter of selection or use arrow keys and hit return

Last-name, First-name M — EMP#: 999999999

#	EVENT CODE	EFF.DATE	DESCRIPTION	NEXT DUE	COMMENTS
1	BONUS	12/23/87	Christmas Bonus - $250	/ /	
2	BONUS	12/23/86	Christmas Bonus - $100	/ /	
3	INJURY	10/02/83	Slipped, broke ankle	/ /	Work related
4	LICENSE	06/01/87	CPA License	06/01/88	Must Renew Annually
5	LICENSE	09/01/85	Driver's License	09/01/90	
6	MEMBERSHIP	01/01/87	CPA's of America	01/01/88	
7	TRAINING	02/15/84	How to Prepare Bus. Plan	/ /	AMA course
8	TRAINING	12/15/86	CPR Training	12/15/91	First Aid
9	________	__/__/__	____________________	__/__/__	______________

Figure 16–4. Typical events screen. Employee relations can track and review events that are the relevant to employee performance, needs, and well-being.
(Source: AbraCadabra Software. Reprinted with permission.)

ords manually. Others use the HRMS to track demographics and use of the EAP. They may omit employee identification but create a file that lists date, location, reason for EAP involvement, and referral or other type of assistance provided. To ensure consistency and to permit reliable analyses of such information, the HRMS usually includes codes for types of EAP assistance provided.

Disciplinary and Other Employee Relations Actions

Most organizations occasionally face situations that require some form of disciplinary action. In the case of repeated absenteeism or tardiness, an employee may face a probationary period requiring stricter check-in and check-out procedures. An employee who repeatedly violates certain work rules may face probation or temporary reassignment away from potentially dangerous machinery. Employee relations often plays a role in negotiating and monitoring such procedures; then the employee relations representative enters into the individual employee's record the date of disciplinary action, reason for disciplinary action, recommended action, and action taken. Actions can be coded from tables, as shown in figure 16–5. To avoid possible allegations of wrongful termination, many organizations use nondescript reasons for disciplinary action. The system also tracks dates for review or termination of disciplinary cases; this serves as a built-in monitoring vehicle for time-dependent actions.

In many cases, dispute resolution does not involve disciplinary action. Perhaps a supervisor agrees to perform another performance review in ninety days or the employee is scheduled for remedial training. To monitor whether such activities actually take place, employee relations enters notations and date reminders in the individual's file.

Terminations

Employee relations is generally involved in layoffs and involuntary and voluntary terminations. The process of deciding who will receive layoff notices begins with management, who develop layoff criteria. Sometimes employee relations works with union representatives on criteria such as seniority, job group, location, or certification level. They may then use the HRMS to create an appropriately sequenced list of employees targeted for layoff.

Employee relations does not decide who will be laid off, but it may participate in the distribution of layoff notices and counseling of affected employees. Employee relations may hold group and individual meetings to discuss benefits eligibility, severance pay, and outplacement. In these meetings, employee relations uses HRMS data extensively but seldom needs to enter any new data. In cases of layoffs and furloughs, employee relations may take the responsibility for recalling employees as needed.

REASONS FOR DISCIPLINARY ACTION

CODE   REASON

Code	Reason
01	Absenteeism
02	Late Arrival
03	Early Departure
04	Violation of Work Rule
05	Insubordination
06	Action Dangerous to Self or Others
07	Possession of Prohibited Substance
08	Working Under Influence of Prohibited Substance
09	Illegal Activity on Premises
10	Violation of Security Regulations
11	Failure to Report
12	Improper Notice
99	Other

CODE   TYPE OF ACTION

Code	Type of Action
10	Transfer to Different Work Unit
20	Transfer to Different Work Assignment
3X	Counseling Sessions (X = number of sessions)
4X	Time Off Without Pay (X = number of days off)
5X	Time Off With Pay (X = number of days off)
6X	Referred (X = referral channel)
70	Ineligible for Rehire
99	Other

Figure 16–5. Sample disciplinary action tables. These sample listings of disciplinary action codes are not complete. Each organization must construct its own table to correspond with its own policies, procedures, and circumstances.

Most organizations arrange for exit interviews of departing employees. Through such interviews, employee relations helps management understand the employees' opinions about the organization's strengths and weaknesses. In some cases, the applicant and employment management function handles this process. Employee relations may administer the entire process or just conduct exit interviews. This may depend on the proximity of the employee relations function to the affected employee or employee group. If the HRMS has information on company property checked out to departing employees, employee relations can make sure the employee returns all keys, credit cards, passes, tools, calculators, computers, and other company property.

Based on the exit interview, employee relations enters the following data into the HRMS:

- Interviewer's name (or initials or code)
- Date of termination
- Date of exit interview
- Company property recovered (Yes/No, with checklist)
- Eligibility for rehire (Yes/No/Conditional)
- Reason for leaving (coded)
- Comments, often by both interviewer and interviewee, especially if comments can readily be coded.

Industrial Relations Issues

The basic role of industrial relations is to resolve employee disputes by serving as an intermediary between management and employees. Industrial relations also administers and assists in the negotiation of collective bargaining agreements. This responsibility includes carrying out changes mandated by new agreements as well as handling grievance procedures and other forms of dispute resolution. For instance, if the collective bargaining agreement includes new wage-rate tables, industrial relations works with compensation to make those changes in the appropriate tables in the HRMS. Industrial relations then notifies payroll, line management, and other affected parties of those changes. As required to comply with labor agreements, industrial relations supervises changes in work rules, assignment of job titles, and procedures for calculating seniority.

Because of the rules that accompany collective bargaining agreements, industrial relations may handle more quantifiable data than employee relations. These data include wage-step increases, seniority, scheduled work hours, shift assignment, and work rules. Industrial relations usually is responsible for tracking and investigating contract-related issues, such as disciplinary action, work rules violations, and grievances. In a computerized system, the industrial relations portion of the affected employee's record might include data such as the following:

- Date of incident
- Type of incident (coded from a table of possible violations)

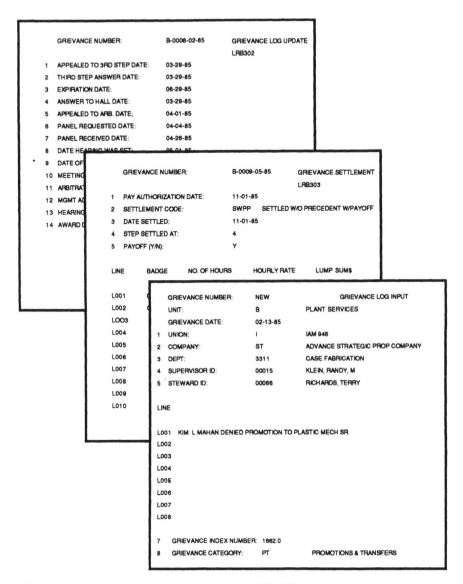

Figure 16–6. Grievance tracking with an HRMS. In this example, the first screen is used to input a new grievance into the system. The system then assigns the grievance an identifying number. The second screen is for updating the log on a specific grievance (note the unique number for this grievance). The third screen is for entering settlement information.
(Source: Solid Logic, 1986. Reprinted with permission.)

- Comments
- Dates of conferences
- Disciplinary (or other) action taken
- Date of review or follow-up
- Involvement of supervisors and shop stewards

Safety-related data in the employee's record usually come from the health and safety function but also may result from direct reporting of isolated job-related incidents.

Industrial relations may reserve a field in the job classification table to indicate which jobs are covered by the collective bargaining agreement. If the organization deals with more than one union, the code can indicate which agreement covers that specific job. The HRMS can use these codes to tally the number of employees or positions affected by each agreement.

Most organizations deal with no more than one or two unions, but some large, diverse manufacturing and transportation enterprises may have forty or more separate union contracts. In such cases, industrial relations may track these contracts via computer, usually a stand-alone system. For each contract, the system may track effective date, expiration date, job classifications affected, location, and union. It also will list the number of affected employees or positions as a calculated field based on HRMS data. If the contract-tracking system has no interface with the HRMS, industrial relations staff enter the data directly.

In preparation for and during contract negotiations, industrial relations representatives may need to provide the negotiation team with massive amounts of data. Employee demographics often become very important in contract negotiations. Negotiators may need projections on the effects of different wage-rate increases or benefits on total payroll obligations. They may need to know which employees have been involved in disciplinary action. They may request a list of employees in descending order of seniority. To meet such wide-ranging report requirements, industrial relations may need to access virtually the entire HRMS data base.

If management and labor have an adversarial relationship, industrial relations has a more difficult negotiating job and needs more data, analyses, and reports from the HRMS. This may require a sophisticated and highly flexible system. As unpredictable situations arise, the HRMS must be able to develop a wide variety of ad hoc reports. In more cooperative situations, the union and industrial relations will take care of minor problems without referring to much data, thus reducing the demand on the system. This is yet another example of the need for flexibility in HRMS design to accommodate change.

Reporting Requirements

Many employee relations professionals would probably love to help improve worker satisfaction and productivity through long-range planning and proactive programs. In truth, most organizations spend almost all their time reacting to specific problems and questions. Reflecting this emphasis, most employee relations reports list specific problems rather than analyzing or forecasting organizational trends. Forecasting these trends requires keeping track of new labor laws, federal and state guidelines, and changing company policies.

More than most other human resources functions, employee relations usually needs the system to produce time-dependent reports. This feature automatically creates a calendar of events from information in various date fields carried in employee records. Many employee relations actions result in the direct entry or projection of dates for future review, such as performance reviews, disciplinary actions, training programs, and negotiating schedules. The system may produce daily or weekly tickler reports, such as that shown in figure 16–7. Each representative receives a calendar report that lists upcoming tasks related to the units (clients) for whom he or she is directly responsible. Employee relations then uses these reports to check on the status of previously agreed-upon actions.

Time and Attendance Reports

Most systems produce individual attendance reports only on an exception basis. On a regular basis (semimonthly, monthly, or quarterly), the system may furnish employee relations with a listing of individuals whose absenteeism exceeds permissible levels. For each listed individual, this report may note the following:

- Employee name
- Other employee demographics
- Employee category (such as full-time, part-time, or temporary)
- Employee status (such as active or on leave)
- Regular hours
- Overtime hours
- Day(s) of the week absent
- Length of absence
- Reason for each absence (usually coded)

Employee relations, payroll, or a time and attendance function distributes these reports to the responsible line managers. The line manager then takes

HUMAN RESOURCE
ACTION PLAN

LONG RANGE REMINDERS   DIVISION 001

ACTION DATE	SOC SEC NUMBER	LAST NAME	TYPE OF ACTION REQUIRED	--ACTION TO BE TAKEN-- COMMENTS/BENEFIT CODES	ACTION TAKEN	DATE OF ACTION
05-15-90	001-00-7654	REYNOLDS	REMINDER COMMENT	OPENING IN ADMIN SECTION	- - - - - - - - - -	- - / - - / - -
05-20-90	142-93-8654	ABEL	REMINDER COMMENT	ASSIGN TO H-SERV TEAM	- - - - - - - - - -	- - / - - / - -
06-15-90	152-64-0926	FUHRMAN	REMINDER COMMENT	CHG BENEFIT CODE ON RCD	- - - - - - - - - -	- - / - - / - -

TOTAL NUMBER OF REMINDERS = 3

06-01-90	164-42-8975	MARDEROSIAN	SALARY REVIEW DATE		- - - - - - - - - -	- - / - - / - -
06-04-90	008-90-0087	CROUTHAMEL	SALARY REVIEW DATE		- - - - - - - - - -	- - / - - / - -
06-05-90	112-56-9834	NEFF	SALARY REVIEW DATE		- - - - - - - - - -	- - / - - / - -
06-10-90	001-78-4332	DOYLE	SALARY REVIEW DATE		- - - - - - - - - -	- - / - - / - -
06-15-90	908-01-8723	MOWRY	SALARY REVIEW DATE		- - - - - - - - - -	- - / - - / - -

TOTAL NUMBER OF REMINDERS = 5

06-03-90	115-32-9854	HENRY	PHYSICAL EXAM		- - - - - - - - - -	- - / - - / - -
06-05-90	165-82-1950	SHERLOCK	PHYSICAL EXAM		- - - - - - - - - -	- - / - - / - -
06-15-90	123-45-9632	ROGASCH	PHYSICAL EXAM		- - - - - - - - - -	- - / - - / - -

TOTAL NUMBER OF REMINDERS = 3

05-16-90	280-42-0826	HARRISON	BENEFIT ELIGIBILITY BENEFIT CODE - 25		- - - - - - - - - -	- - / - - / - -

TOTAL NUMBER OF REMINDERS = 1

Figure 16–7. Employee relations reminders. This type of report alerts a manager or an employee relations or industrial relations representative to upcoming actions. The form also provides space to note action taken. At appropriate intervals, the annotated form can be submitted to data entry to update system records.

responsibility for resolving the situation with the employee as needed. An individual with an attendance problem may receive a warning notice.

Summary attendance reports help management and employee relations analyze current patterns of absenteeism or tardiness in a unit or department. The employee relations representative may use the information to develop analyses as part of a proposal to improve these patterns through changes in shift hours, work distribution, work conditions, or scheduling.

Performance Reports

Employee relations usually monitors performance reports on an exception basis. For instance, the staff may request a list of overdue performance reports by unit and distribute this list to line managers. This report reminds managers to submit performance reviews that were due on a particular date. In cases involving individual patterns of performance, an employee relations representative may request a performance review history report to evaluate the situation.

Employee relations may become involved if employees or managers feel that performance appraisals are overly lenient or strict. In such cases, employee relations uses the HRMS to produce a performance distribution report for a particular unit. This distribution compares the percentage of performance ratings expected in any particular range versus a performance distribution curve with actual figures. For instance, among 20 employees, an organization might expect no more than 5 outstanding performers, no more than 10 in the competent or adequate range, and no more than 5 in the marginal range. If the performance levels do not fit the distribution pattern, employee relations works with the supervisor or manager to identify reasons for disparities and agree upon remedial action needed.

EAP Reports

From an administrative standpoint, management must track the caseload and referrals or other types of assistance the EAP provides. These reports do not include names of users, but they may include dates, reasons, and type(s) of assistance provided. Depending on the degree to which the organization can maintain privacy, these reports might include certain employee demographics, such as department or unit, job classification, sex, or race/ethnicity. For purposes of analysis, they also may include personal characteristics such as age, service, education level, or time in position. EAPs may use these reports to communicate to employees that the employer provides a valuable service, as well as to justify program expense to management.

Disciplinary Reports

In some organizations, policies mandate creation of a special notice whenever managers or others take disciplinary action. The HRMS may produce a report that lists employee name, supervisor, date of action, reasons for action, type of action, and date of review or termination of disciplinary action. Disciplinary reports usually are distributed to the affected individual and the line manager

DIVISION: ABC MANUFACTURING

12/01/89

```
* * * * * * * * * * * * * * * * * * * * * *
    OVERDUE PERFORMANCE REVIEW LISTING
* * * * * * * * * * * * * * * * * * * * * *
```

NAME	JOB CODE	PERF	PERF DATE	ANNUAL SALARY	COMPA-RATIO	SEX	RACE
HOPKINS, G. E.	234896	E	11/89	$12,000	98	F	W
CAMPBELL, M. A.	458234	SP	09/89	$14,250	102	F	W
KARAMAN, J. C.	458235	SP	06/89	$9,825	94	M	B
HOSHIDA, R. T.	684239	S	06/89	$18,265	104	F	A
SCHRECT, T. O.	125649	S	12/89	$15,125	97	M	W
GENTRY, H. G.	125648	E	10/89	$19,625	99	M	W
RODRIGUEZ, R. G.	237148	E	01/89	$8,970	101	F	H
TORAYA, G. H.	237146	SP	09/89	$8,700	103	F	A

Figure 16–8. Overdue performance review listing. Employee relations uses this type of report as a basis for investigating possible problems with performance review frequency.

for confirmation unless union rules dictate further distribution. In serious cases, the employee relations function may handle notices of warning, probation, suspension, or discharge. Some systems can provide these as word-processed forms, with a few fields inserted for employee name, report date, effective date, site, and details on the incident or action that precipitated the notice.

If employee relations date-stamps all disciplinary decisions, it can monitor all disciplinary actions within a particular time period for a specific unit or employee. The employee relations representative then uses this list to review the status of each disciplinary action and affected employee. Alternatively, the system could produce a disciplinary history report listing employee name, location, unit, supervisor, job classification, job grade, sex, and race/ethnicity.

Termination Reports

Projected Terminations Report. The HRMS may provide employee relations with a regular report listing upcoming terminations. Employee relations uses this report to schedule exit interviews and monitor responses. The report may list employee name, position, job classification, job grade, supervisor, effective date, and type of termination (such as layoff, leave, involuntary termination, or voluntary termination).

Voluntary Terminations Analysis Report. Employee relations may analyze the results of exit interviews to determine why employees choose to leave the firm and where they go. The HRMS can assist in this analysis to the extent that responses are coded or otherwise quantifiable. Interviewees often report reasons for leaving more honestly if they are interviewed off-site after termination instead of on-site while still working for the organization. Employee relations can use this report to develop plans for controlling unwanted turnover.

Employee Layoff Reports. Employee relations can use HRMS files to develop a list of employees who correspond to layoff criteria. After approval and finalization, employee relations enters into each record the type of termination (layoff), the effective date, and perhaps the recall date.

Layoff Notices. Employee relations may use a mail-merge word-processing program to generate layoff notices for distribution to affected employees. Employee relations also may produce subset reports of the entire layoff list according to section or department for distribution to those supervisors and managers.

Industrial Relations Reports

Management often requires a wide variety of human resources analyses and other reports as part of union negotiations. To facilitate negotiations, industrial relations should have considerable skill at developing ad hoc reports quickly on data maintained by the HRMS. Many firms now use computers as a tool throughout negotiations to produce scenarios of various proposals under consideration. They may even have a microcomputer present at the negotiation table to access a wide variety of data for real-time decision making. For example, industrial relations may need to generate a summary of employees who meet certain criteria or demonstrate to the union the actual wage rates of a particular class of employees.

Negotiators may require salary and wage-rate tables, attendance summary reports, benefits costs and participation, work force utilization reports, and retirement projections. These tools also may include sophisticated time-series reports, simulation models, and forecasts. Standard reports may meet the needs of negotiators, but sometimes negotiators require information that human resources maintains in the system but in a slightly different format or structure. For instance, they may request a wage-rate table report that includes not only current rates but also the historical progression of wage increases, steps, and levels. In another case, the HRMS may provide basic seniority lists for the entire organization or division, but negotiators may require an ad hoc report listing seniority according to sex, race/ethnicity, or union status.

Sometimes the union needs access to certain data on its members, either individually or in summary form, to prepare for or use in contract negotiations, dispute resolution, or planning. Most of these reports are similar to those management uses for negotiations. In an enlightened (nonadversarial) relationship, management provides authorized union representatives with the reports they know the union needs and can use properly. Management cannot, however, allow the union unlimited access to HRMS data—especially data that are personal, confidential, or not relevant to negotiation of the collective bargaining agreement. The following information provides a brief description of other types of reports industrial relations staff often request.

Negotiating Schedules. If an organization has a single master union agreement, it may not need the HRMS to generate a schedule unless milestone events precede expiration of the contract. A large or diverse corporation may have forty or more contracts. As mentioned earlier, they may track contract information on the HRMS or a separate system. If so, industrial relations can produce a schedule of contracts sorted by expiration date, worker type, location, or another relevant field. Industrial relations staff can use this schedule to plan their work load and integrate negotiation strategies.

Incident and Attendance Summary Reports. Industrial relations sometimes needs summary reports of union issues that staff track or monitor. These may include attendance problems, grievances, work-rule violations, and disciplinary actions. These reports usually list name, incident, date, resolution, and other workplace or personal demographics. Some of these are coded for consistency and to facilitate analysis. For grievances and mediation processes, industrial relations staff may need individual employee reports that summarize incidents and related information. These reports resemble disciplinary reports (discussed earlier in this chapter) except that the resolutions they describe depend less on management discretion and more on certain rules and procedures.

Financial Reports. Industrial relations must work closely with compensation and benefits to generate reports needed during negotiations about the financial aspects of agreements, such as wage rates, market-rate analyses, surveys, benefits packages, and retirement plans. Other reports may project the cost of increasing time-related benefits such as sick leave and vacation.

Special Circumstances

Supporting the Legal Department

Because of doctrines such as employment at will and other developments in labor law, employee relations frequently must support the organization's legal department. One case might involve a lawsuit for wrongful termination or discrimination. Another might involve a state labor commission hearing on a plant closure or on insufficient notice to laid-off individuals. In these individual labor issues, employee relations representatives often must provide ad hoc reports to document the employer's position.

Relationship with Health and Safety

In manufacturing settings, and often in office settings as well, employee and industrial relations may have more contact with health and safety than with other mainstream human resources functions. They often exchange information and cooperate with each other, especially when the two areas have a clearly defined division of effort. In many organizations, employees violate health and safety regulations more often than any other type of work rule. Moreover, some of these violations may lead to workers' compensation cases involving internal or external medical and legal records. In these cases, the employee and industrial relations function often works closely with health and safety or

Employee Climate Surveys

Attitude and climate surveys often come under the jurisdiction of employee relations, but many companies use outside contractors to handle survey development, production, and tabulation. Only very large firms can afford to dedicate qualified resources to this process or can stagger surveys on specific population groups. Employee relations can use the HRMS to make certain that the surveyed population includes a representative sampling of job families, job groups, and demographic groupings. Employee relations also can use employee listings as a basis for scheduling and tabulating responses. Statistical analyses of attitude and climate surveys range from simple cross-tabulations to sophisticated multiple regressions and discriminant functions analysis.

with whatever group handles workers' compensation and health and safety matters.

Glossary

Bargaining unit The local branch of the union authorized to negotiate with employees on behalf of a particular group of workers.

Collective bargaining The process of negotiation between management and the labor union regarding conditions of employment, job assignments, seniority, job security, work rules, compensation, safety, and retirement. The contract that results from such negotiations is referred to as a collective bargaining agreement.

EAP See *Employee assistance program*.

Employee assistance program (EAP) The employee relations function that provides employees with counseling, support, and referrals on issues that relate to not only their job performance but also their personal life. Such issues may include substance abuse, personal finance, family matters, legal problems, child-care placement, relocation, and community orientation.

Employee relations The human resources function that provides services and support to facilitate communication between employer and employees and assists individual employees with special needs. A firm that has an industrial relations function to handle relations with hourly workers often has an employee relations function to deal with salaried workers.

Grievance   A formal complaint that an employee in the bargaining unit files with the shop steward, designated industrial relations representative, or both. A grievance usually deals with alleged mistreatment or misinterpretation of, or failure to abide by, provisions of the collective bargaining agreement.

Industrial relations   The human resources function that handles negotiations and interactions between management and labor, particularly in a unionized environment, though not exclusively so. The terms *industrial relations* and *employee relations* are sometimes used interchangeably.

Labor commission   A state agency that monitors and mediates employment-related disputes. The labor commission usually has jurisdiction over issues such as contract compliance, back-pay disputes, wage and hour rules, and interpretation of labor laws affecting employees and contractors.

Work rules   Provisions in a collective bargaining agreement that stipulate the roles and responsibilities of workers and supervisors. Work rules usually pertain to issues of safety, productivity, dress code, length of work periods, and work assignments.

Discussion Points

1. What are the primary differences between employee relations and industrial relations?
2. How does the employee and industrial relations function interact with other human resources functions?
3. Under what circumstances would employee and industrial relations deal with agencies outside the firm?
4. What are the main functions of an EAP?
5. In what ways can employee and industrial relations use the HRMS to minimize employee problems with layoffs and terminations?
6. What kinds of data does employee and industrial relations add to the HRMS in support of the EAP?
7. In what ways might relations between union and management affect the HRMS needs of the employee and industrial relations function?
8. What responsibilities of the employee and industrial relations function involve little or no computer interaction?

Further Reading

Amico, Anthony M. "Critical Human Resource Issues of the 1980s." *Human Resource Planning*, Vol. 6, No. 2, 1983.

Anderson, Kirk J. "Information Databases on HR Software: One Way to Keep Up." *Human Resource Management Systems Report,* June 1985.

Angel, John, and Alastair Evans. "Data Protection and the Subject of Access." *Personnel Management,* October 1987.

Anthony, William P. "Get to Know Your Employees: The Human Resource Information System." *Personnel Journal,* April 1977.

Benson, Philip G. "Personal Privacy and The Personnel Record." *Personnel Journal,* July 1987.

Cannon, Ted, Jerry Debenham, and Gerald Smith. "Developing a Computer-Assisted Evaluation System." *Personnel Administrator,* September 1983.

DiMonaco, Janis S., and Dan DiMonaco. "The Systems Approach to Managing Mental Health and Chemical Dependency: Synergism at Work." *Employee Benefits Journal,* March 1989.

Fensholt, Carol. "Labor Scheduling: New Software Enhances Savings & Service." *Supermarket Business,* May 1988.

Fitz-enz, Jac. "Quantifying the Human Resources Function." *Personnel,* March/April 1980.

Fraser, Niall M., and Keith W. Hipel. "Computer Assistance in Labor Management Negotiations." *Interface,* April 1981.

Guinn, K. "Performance Management: Not Just an Annual Appraisal." *Personnel,* August 1987.

Hall, L., and D. Torrington. "The Use and Lack of Use of Computers in Personnel." *Personnel Review,* Volume 1, No. 4 1986.

Hall, T.E. How to Estimate Employee Turnover Costs." *Personnel,* July/August 1981.

Henriques, Vico E. "Where Does the Employee Fit in Office Integration?" *The Office,* January 1986.

Horsfield, Debra. "Satisfying Corporate Customers." *Computers in Personnel,* Winter 1987.

"IBM's Guidelines to Employee Privacy." *Harvard Business Review,* September/October 1976.

Jackson, Michael T. "The Personnel File: What and Whose?" *Personnel Administrator,* 1977.

Jones, Allison L. "New Outlook for Outplacement." *Human Resource Systems Management Bulletin,* November 1986.

Kahn, Steven C. "Employee Access to Personnel Records." *Employment Relations Today,* Winter 1985.

Kelleher, Joanne. "Human Factors." *Business Computer Systems,* August 1985.

LaVan, Helen, and Nicholas J. Mathys. "Manufacturer's HRIS's Ignore Union Negotiations." *Computers in Personnel,* Winter 1988.

Linder, Jane C. "Computers, Corporate Culture, and Change." *Personnel Journal,* September 1985.

Martindale, Loren D. "Automating the Analysis of Employee Turnover." *Personnel,* January 1988.

Meyer, Herbert E. "Personnel Directors Are the New Corporate Heroes." *Fortune,* February 1976.

Michaels, C.E., and P.E. Specter. "Cause of Employee Turnover." *Journal of Applied Psychology,* 67, 1982.

Moody, H. Gerald. "Out-of-Touch Telecommuters." *Computers in Personnel*, Fall 1987.

Niemark, Jill. "Psych-out Software: New Computer Programs Offer Advice on How to Clinch a Deal or Fire a Troublemaker." *Savvy*, January 1985.

Privacy Protection Study Commission. *Personal Privacy in an Information Society.* Washington: U.S. Government Printing Office, 1977.

Schmidt, F.L., J.E. Hunter, and K. Pearlman. "Assessing the Economic Impact of Personnel Programs on Workforce Productivity." *Personnel Psychology*, 35, 1982.

Searles, J.R. "Top Three/Bottom Three: A Personnel Evaluation Technique." *Personnel Administrator*, January 1975.

Shifrin, Carole A. "Eastern (Airlines) Computer Systems Reduces Maintenance Layovers." *Aviation Week*, October 1985.

Zarley, Craig A. "PCs Doing Duty as Tools in Firms' Wellness Programs." *PC Week*, December 1986.

Zuboff, S. "New Worlds of Computer-Mediated Work." *Harvard Business Review*, 60 No. 5, 1982.

17
Training and Development

Genius will live and thrive without training, but it does not less reward the watering pot and pruning knife.

—Margaret Fuller

Training and Development in an HRMS

Training, like compensation, has employee retention as its primary mission. Training's strategic contributions to this goal include new employee orientation, diagnosis and correction of skills problems, remedial training, and sometimes long-term career development.

Human resources usually adds training to the HRMS after major functions such as employment, compensation, and benefits have defined and implemented their needs. Training becomes a part of the system when managers see that the HRMS can increase the efficiency of managing the training needs of a large number of employees. As training costs continue to increase, management has begun devoting more attention to this human resources area. In some enlightened firms, company policy prescribes as much as eighty hours (or ten days) of training and development per year, which gives training policy almost equal weight with time-off policy.

The most common training application is tracking course participants, trainers, dates, and results. Other training and development activities interact with the HRMS and may have their own specialized subsystems or modules. In fact, training often winds up with several separate and mutually exclusive programs, each designed to meet a portion of its information management requirements. Ease of integration into the HRMS often becomes an even more important consideration in system design.

Role of Training and Development

The specific objectives of a training function depend on the organization's environment, culture, and approach to training and development. For instance, employees in some firms need significant outside education. Many jobs

Figure 17–1. Principal roles of the training and development function.

require specialized college and university degrees or certificates, such as those in electronics, investment banking, and nursing. Other firms may require skills not usually covered in external educational settings, such as real estate lending, insurance underwriting, and financial planning. These firms may rely more on internal training, especially when their operations are unique. For instance, telephone companies train employees on their own equipment, thereby providing more specialization than outside course work could cover. A broad overview of the most common training activities is presented in the material that follows.

Planning for Training. Training's most basic responsibility is to determine the organization's training needs. Which jobs require training? What skills must this training include? Which types of training work best for each job—vestibule, formal, or on-the-job?

Eligibility Determination. Training must determine which individuals are eligible for or require specific training. They may identify target groups, job families, or individuals on the basis of job classification, service, time in position, or education.

Training Administration. The training function must decide who will provide the training—training staff, line management, or external resources. This function then manages registration, attendance, venues, materials, staff assignments, and reporting of training performance results.

Training Courses and Presentations. Training and development develops and presents internal training. Staff from these functions develop course curricula, materials, and testing. Training may take place on several levels:

- New-employee orientation covers work rules, company policies, benefits, and possibly specific skill requirements and employer expectations.
- Skills training covers practical matters, such as how to perform particular operations, operate new equipment, or analyze a financial statement.
- Supervisory training emphasizes interpersonal skills, communication, time management, and the responsibilities of supervision.
- Management training or management development includes decision-making and analytical techniques such as problem solving, oral and written presentation skills, human interaction, and consultative skills.

Training Assessment and Evaluation. Training may evaluate the courses directly or work with line management to do so. On a subjective basis or by observation, training and line management also may evaluate subsequent performance improvement among employees who receive training.

External Training and Education. Training monitors participation in outside course work for which the firm provides tuition, material reimbursement, or both. Training staff pay attention to the costs and benefits of such courses.

Career Development Programs. Employees who appear to have promotability and a long-term future with the organization may receive special training and counseling to prepare them for future opportunities and responsibilities.

Skills Inventory. Training may develop a complete registry of the skills, experience, and goals of the organization's employee population. Training staff often do this in conjunction with the planning and forecasting function or the management development function. The assignment of this responsibility depends on whether the skills inventory focuses on recruiting, career development, or management succession.

Advantages and Limitations of Computerization

The number of software programs that handle training applications has tripled in the past few years. Although most vendors originally provided programs only for mainframe applications, many options for training functions are now available for microcomputer users. By 1986, almost half of all U.S. organizations with more than fifty employees used computers in their training activities. However, most used them solely for simple tasks such as course scheduling and preparation of rosters. Firms that have adopted computer applications have found several advantages:

- Easier scheduling and tracking of courses and participants
- Better matching of employees with appropriate training
- Easier generation of individual employee training history
- More accurate information retrieval on participants when evaluating training

Some aspects of training and development, particularly planning and counseling, do not lend themselves to computerization. In these areas, software acts as a supportive rather than a dominant force. The counseling and creative roles of the skilled professional remain primary.

Data Requirements and Sources

The training module uses a great deal of information already entered into employee records by employment, EEO/AA, and health and safety. In turn, training adds information on participation in training and development courses and programs. Training also creates and maintains tables and data bases on training events.

Training Planning Data

New training needs sometimes evolve from changes in the organization's business direction or large-scale shifts in the work force. They may stem from a need to improve employee performance and productivity, employee job satisfaction, or affirmative action. They often emerge in response to requests from department managers. To develop specific training plans, the training function must access data about former, current, and potential training participants.

Most training functions tend to focus on training delivery—the implementation and execution of the training course or program. The human resources planning function may provide the quantitative analysis required for identifying training needs via HRMS data. Training staff may do some identification of target groups or otherwise work with human resources planning or management development on such projects. If the planning function does not have sufficient resources to handle queries, training staff may use the HRMS to access historical and current data.

Staff may query HRMS files to determine who received certain types of training, their performance improvement (if any), specific courses they com-

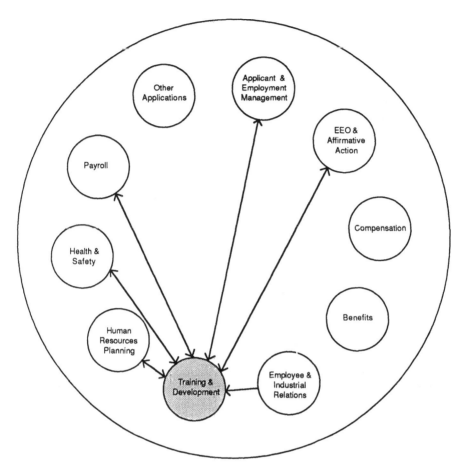

Figure 17–2. Information flow between training and development and other human resources functions.

pleted, and when and where they took such training. This information helps determine the most effective course offerings, schedules, training media, sponsors, and instructors. Training staff also may access HRMS data about employment candidates and new hires. They can then compare new-employee skill levels with job requirements to determine what skills training or on-the-job experience should provide.

If management plans new facilities and other changes in work requirements, training needs lists of affected individuals. For instance, if management wants all offices to adopt a new word processing program, training can query the HRMS to estimate the number of secretaries, word processing specialists, editors, and writers who will require training, when, and at which sites.

Training Applications and Eligibility Data

Participation in training courses or programs is often limited. Employees may complete a training application and submit it to their line manager or directly to training. Training then tracks applications, eligibility, and participation. The education and training profile segment of an individual employee record may contain fields that pertain specifically to training programs. This may list training course, date of application, and status (approved, postponed, waiting list, or denied), as well as prior training, training sponsor, and completion date.

The training function must develop eligibility criteria for training or development activities. Training staff and line management work together to identify target groups for each type of training. They usually use some combination of quantitative information such as job classification, job grade, service, and time in position. In some circumstances, they may use affirmative action criteria to select eligible employees. If training staff enter course application data into the system, the HRMS should be able to evaluate and determine the eligibility of individual applicants for a particular program.

Training Administration Data

Training staff spend considerable time managing training courses and programs. They often have an independent training-event data base, sometimes referred to as the course and program table. This separate table is contained within the HRMS and used primarily by training staff to track course scheduling, location, instructors, and registration. This data base may include records of the actual training courses, including participation, performance, and test results. Most programs automatically flag conflicts in scheduling or location, and sophisticated programs can suggest alternative schedules to resolve conflicts. Training scheduling programs work equally well for conference and meeting management. The training function may track participation in on-the-job training, including dates, assignments, and results.

Training also enters certain information in the employee's record. This includes dates of training, type of training, reason for training, location, reimbursement of costs (if relevant), and training results. The training module

---

Training Module Organization

Each of the following categories indicates data that training and development may maintain in the HRMS. These categories may contain multiple data fields that are often coded for consistency.

Employee Training Profile
    Training applicant (basic employee information)
    Applicant disposition (acceptance/rejection)
    Training events attended or scheduled (course code)
    Test results (course results; self-assessment; pre-tests and post-tests)

Course/Program Table
    Course or program code
    Course or program name/number
    Sponsor
    Instructor
    Dates started and completed
    Location
    Prerequisites
    Attendance
    Course results (or other results)

External Course/Program Table
    Institution
    Course or program name/number
    Instructor
    Dates/hours
    Location
    Prerequisites
    Results
    Cost
    Amount reimbursed

Training Cost Accounting
    Drect costs
    Instructor internal wage/salary hours/rates
    Participant internal wage/salary hours/rates
    Internal location costs

Skills Inventory
    Skill code
    Skill name
    Years of experience
    Dates of experience
    Fluency (for foreign languages)
    Source of skill
    Goals and aspirations
    Career interests
    Licenses and certificates

CONTROL	COURSE CODE	COURSE NAME
CRS	A10	MANAGER ORIENTATION CONFERENCE
CRS	A11	LEADERSHIP PROGRAM
CRS	A14	INTRODUCTION TO MANAGEMENT
CRS	A15	SELLING IDEAS TO MANAGEMENT
CRS	A18	EFFECTIVE SUPERVISION
CRS	A51	OPERATIONS WORKSHOP I
CRS	A59	MODERN MANAGEMENT
CRS	A82	PRINCIPLES OF ACCOUNTING
CRS	B20	EFFECTIVE COMMUNICATIONS
CRS	B23	EXECUTIVE SPEECH
CRS	B27	EFFECTIVE WRITING
CRS	B61	MARKETING SEMINAR
CRS	B63	ORIENTATION OF NEW EMPLOYEES
CRS	B67	EXECUTIVE TRAINING PROGRAM
CRS	B89	MANAGEMENT SKILLS CONFERENCE
CRS	E27	REAL ESTATE SEMINAR
CRS	E65	INTRO TO TELEPROCESSING
CRS	G42	PROJECT ORGANIZATION

Figure 17–3. Training courses table. Human resources staff can use a table of all courses and programs—internal and external—to standardize the names of generic programs and facilitate system inquiry.

usually has tables of codes for many of these fields, such as type of training, reason for training, training objective, and sponsor.

Many administrative programs include auxiliary tables. A program with a built-in calendar of holidays and weekends can flag training events scheduled for days other than regular, workdays. Some programs allow users to build special tables of information about training facilities and equipment. For each training room, the table might include capacity, equipment, location, and contact person.

Most organizations absorb training expenses as a cost of doing business. Relatively few companies use cost accounting to charge back for training except as a means of determining future budgets. Cost accounting has, however, become more common in the past few years, as it helps training managers justify approaches that may have higher initial instructor or sponsor costs but increase productivity among participants, resulting in lower net costs.

Several vendors offer software specifically designed to track training costs. With these programs, training staff can budget for individual courses. Training costing includes not only direct costs but also participants' prorated salary costs, costs of benefits, and overhead. It may involve calculating performance indexes such as cost per seat, cost per class, and cost per student hour. With such features, training can create more detailed cost accounting than general accounting programs allow.

Training Assessment and Evaluation Data

Training assessment has two basic forms, direct and indirect. With direct assessment of training, evaluators address the content and activities of the training event itself, often with an emphasis on the specific trainer or course involved. Training staff may collect response data from several sources, including program participants, training supervisors, line managers, and trainers. The system may track how many employees use each training resource, such as lectures, courses, individual counseling, and resource libraries.

Indirect training assessment involves looking at the job performance of individuals who have participated in specific courses and programs. From employee records, training or line managers can access performance review, job transfers and promotions, turnover, and changes in pay. Trainers may administer specific tests to collect additional data for this evaluation. These tests may be manual, written, verbal, operational, or computerized. Some firms administer pretests and post-tests; some test only after the training; some test not only before and immediately after but also six months to a year after. Some also perform subjective assessment by peers or supervisors.

The training function records date of test, test score, and license or certification granted for each employee. In some cases, training staff also may record answers to individual questions, either through direct computer administration of the test, scanning devices, or manual entry of responses.

External Training and Education Data

Training staff who are responsible for external training and education often develop a data base of eligible institutions and courses. This may include institution name, course location, course name, course number, instructor, course dates, course hours, prerequisites, and cost.

Employee training files sometimes include fields or codes that apply specifically to external institutions. For instance, a sponsor field may include codes for internal departments and external organizations. Reimbursement tracking may relate to salary, service, or an annual allotment depending on company policy. One firm might track reimbursement year to date, while a more complex system might list reimbursement eligibility as a calculated field based on service or other variables in the employee's record. A module also might include fields for date of reimbursement application, reimbursement amount requested, reimbursement amount granted, and date of reimbursement approval. Sometimes the module may include algorithms to approve or disapprove reimbursements. These algorithms may include factors such as grade attained, units achieved within a prescribed time period, or an imposed dollar limit. If reimbursement for which the employee has applied exceeds eligible amounts, the module may issue warning flags so that training or employee relations staff can review the employee's record and consider a possible exception to policy or notify the employee of the reason for denial.

Career Development Data

Some career development modules use the existing HRMS employee data base but add very little to it. Career development counselors refer to existing demographic data, performance history, skills inventory, and promotability indexes. Most career development software originated as products for students and guidance counselors, although several business-oriented versions are now available.

Career Self-Assessment Worksheets. Some software includes a self-assessment worksheet on interests, accomplishments, work-related values, and job satisfaction. This helps the user develop a personal set of career goals and priorities for those goals.

Standard Career Assessment Tests. Some trainers use standard career assessment testing profiles and inventories. Several vendors now make tests available on disk, so employees can take the test at a terminal. Alternatively, an optical scanning device can convert paper-and-pencil tests for computerized scoring and reporting. Test results often become part of the individual's training and development profile; supervisors and career development staff may use these figures when assessing promotability and potential.

Tracking Career Development Costs. Some organizations track the cost of career development activities in a manner similar to training cost accounting. They may include fields such as direct salary, days off (with and without pay), and travel or living costs.

Skills Inventory Data

A skills inventory provides a complete listing of the skills, experience, interests, and aspirations of an organization's employees. In the 1960s, many organizations based their decision to computerize personnel information on their internal need for a skills inventory, as there was a demand for qualified employees. As the economy shifted to a supply-side mode in terms of employment, skills inventories faded in popularity.

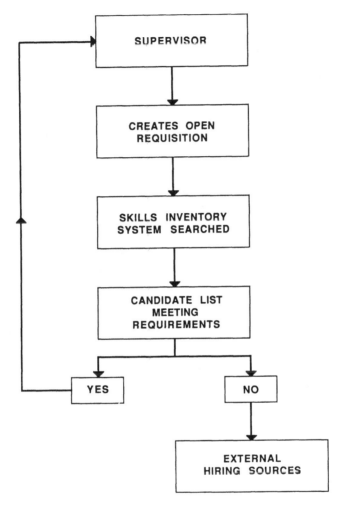

Figure 17–4. **Role of a skills inventory in the internal search process. Once a replacement or new position has been authorized, the supervisor or manager approves the creation of a requisition. The system searches the skills inventory to generate a list of potential candidates. If none is found or deemed qualified, applicant and employment management may use external sources.**
(Source: Kaumeyer, Richard A., *Planning and Using Skills Inventory Systems*, Van Nostrand Reinhold, 1979. Reprinted with permission.)

Skills inventories have recently begun a partial resurgence, particularly when coupled with projective activities or remedial and diagnostic activities. Some companies have adopted skills inventories as a more objective means of identifying employees qualified for internal promotions and transfers.

A skills inventory includes the skills that correspond to present job responsibilities as well as other attributes that the organization may not have utilized yet. A comprehensive skills inventory can help management and human resources staff plan for expansion or reorganization, career development,

---

Issues in Developing Skills Inventories

What data should the skills inventory include?

What information-retrieval capabilities should it have?

In what ways can human resources and line managers use a skills inventory?

Do the prospective uses justify the costs?

Will managers be concerned about retaining their best people if skills are broadly advertised?

Who should have access to skills inventory data and under what conditions?

What procedures should human resources use to verify skills claimed by employees?

How should human resources or managers introduce the skills inventory to employees and managers?

What factors should training take into account in designing forms?

What are some of the internal and external options for developing or acquiring skills inventory software?

What maintenance and updating procedures will this application require? Who should have those responsibilities?

Is an on-line system feasible or desirable?

How should training gather information about managerial-level skills that are hard to define and document?

---

succession planning, and other training and development needs. In fact, many firms have their human resources planning function, rather than training and development, handle the skills inventory.

As an HRMS application, skills inventories work best within a well-established HRMS. Many vendors offer specialized skills inventory software. To compile and analyze the skills inventory, human resources staff develop a special set of vocabulary, forms, and tables. To the extent that the skills inventory information is limited to just one part of the employee population, such as managerial, professional, or technical staff, the data base may be separate from employee master records.

To build a skills inventory, staff must first develop a large vocabulary of skills terms that relate specifically to the tasks and activities of the enterprise. These are generally job-related terms. For instance, a computer hardware developer may need twenty-five terms for hardware engineers but only a few medical terms to describe the health and safety administration unit. Alternatively, a hospital needs hundreds of terms related to medical technology and nursing but fewer computer-related terms. Training (or planning) staff often work with subject-matter experts in each department to develop such lists. Vendors offer software that assists in matching people to positions but none for vocabulary development or selection decisions. Once finalized, the vocabulary is coded to permit the creation of hierarchies. The skills inventory also contains coded fields of qualifiers for each entry, such as years of experience, most recent year of experience, level or intensity, and fluency (for foreign languages).

Training and HRMS design staff then develop a coding structure for these terms and create input forms and procedures. Forms and profiles to depict skills come in many different styles. The training function itself may create these forms or get them from the skills inventory software vendor. Training or employee relations distributes a skills inventory questionnaire to each employee or administers the questionnaire in group sessions. The questionnaire solicits information on skills and experiences, memberships and distinctions, foreign language fluency, licenses and certificates, geographic preferences, and prior work experience. Certain portions of the skills inventory questionnaire may address goals and aspirations, targeted job objectives, and so forth. As with career development questionnaires, a training professional or line manager may counsel the employee on how to complete the appropriate forms.

The self-reporting process involved in collecting skills inventory data may present data validity challenges. Employees may exaggerate the truth, offer subtle or gross fabrications, or fail to complete the questionnaire. The firm can do little about this unless it wishes to validate each individual response. Other data sources for verification may exist, such as employee records, position descriptions, or performance reports. To optimize validity, employees should update the skills inventory annually. Human resources must remember that employees will maintain their interest in participating only if they believe that they have benefited from past inventory surveys, such as receiving additional training, new or expanded responsibilities, increased compensation, or a clear plan of career progression.

Reporting Requirements

The career or skills profile of an individual is the most prevalent report, but most training and development functions produce a wide variety of both detail and summary reports, primarily for use by training staff.

Training and Development Planning Reports

Employee Population Reports. In planning, training staff often use summary reports developed for employment and other functions. For instance, training may need a tally of employees by job grade, job category, FLSA status (exempt or nonexempt), or service. These reports help training and development plan the number and types of courses required.

Training Activity Reports. Planners often use reports that summarize training activities. For a particular period, a report may list internal courses, external courses, participants, course hours, paid time, and dates. Many of these reports are already generated for training administration or cost accounting.

Status and Eligibility Reports

Applications Summary Report. Training staff may use a report of applications to evaluate the popularity of particular courses and to aid in planning future courses. This report typically lists course name, date, and location; number of applicants; eligible applicants; applicants accepted; applicants on waiting list; and applicants rejected. The report may list current number of applicants, year-to-date totals, or other cumulative figures. Some programs can list number of applicants according to certain parameters, such as department, job classification, or service.

Eligibility Report. This report is similar to the application summary report but lists the numbers of employees eligible for a particular course or program.

Notifications. With many programs, training staff can direct the system to send notifications to course participants. These notices may discuss training and development applications, eligibility/noneligibility, acceptance/rejection, participation schedules, and so forth. This notification process often ties in automatically with the enrollee list, sending a certain type of letter to those who are eligible and another to those who are not.

Waiting Lists. If certain programs are popular, the HRMS can create and periodically print waiting lists for classes on demand.

Training Administration Reports

Training administration reports are usually the most numerous reports produced by a training module. They combine data from the employee master files with data from the training data base on participants, locations, dates, and the like.

Training and Course Schedules. Flexible programs can produce schedules according to time, day, instructor, location, sponsor or other variables. Program coordinators may send these schedules to employees, supervisors, and training staff.

Course Enrollment Lists. Enrollee and participant lists may include information on department, job classification, service, and location. They also may provide enrollment figures on course load per instructor.

Course Participation and Results Reports. Depending on the type of course, this report may list grade, certification, readiness for more advanced training, readiness for promotion, or other evaluation. The report usually goes to the instructor (for confirmation), with individual reports going to the participant and his or her supervisor. For internal department use, training may require a report of results by course or by instructor.

Eligible Courses and Institutions Report. Some organizations publish a catalog of external courses and institutions that offer instruction relevant to their employees. Depending on the contents of the data base, the system may be able to build a course list by course location, institution, area of specialization, and date.

Reimbursement Summaries. As necessary, the HRMS can generate reimbursement notices to individuals who participate in external courses, though this is generally done from the payroll system. This notice may list reimbursement amount, courses approved, date of approval, and date of reimbursement. Alternatively, the notice may serve as authorization from training for the individual to submit a reimbursement request to payroll. Payroll then matches the individual's submission with a similar notice sent directly from training to payroll.

Training Accounting Reports. These reports may provide cost accounting for a specific course or general accounting for the entire roster of courses. Generally, they would follow the standard accounting and budgeting report formats of the organization's financial management system. To track training costs, however, a training expenses report might list number of participants, external expenses, internal expenses (by type), instructor hours, and participant hours/cost. A performance measurement report may list calculated figures, such as cost per seat, cost per class, and cost per student hour. Cost-accounting reports also may deal with budgeted versus actual expenses or hours, expenses within a particular time period, and year-to-date expenses.

Training Assessment and Evaluation Reports

Some organizations and training departments assume that their training programs are successful unless they receive information to the contrary in the form of participant evaluations. Others take a more aggressive approach, using the data in the HRMS to look for clues about which training yields the best results. System designers should tailor the list of reports to the types of evaluative measures the organization uses.

Training Event Participation and Evaluation Reports. These reports list number of participants in various training activities and may include quantifiable responses to post-training surveys. The reports may compare results based on types of activities, locations, instructors, internal and external sources, or other criteria. These criteria come from attributes contained in the tables of courses, allowing the computer to generate tabular reports, including statistical analysis.

Participant Testing and Performance Reports. These reports use participants' performance reviews, changes in job status, or test scores to measure the effectiveness of specific courses. The reports often use summary data rather than including names of participants. For instance, a performance review analysis might list number of participants with a performance rating increase of less than one point, number with an increase between one and two points, and number with increases over two points. Some reports might list results of pretests and post-tests, either for employees or according to other variables, such as department, trainer, supervisor, or length of service.

Training can apply these techniques to assessment of external training and trainers. These tools help monitor the effectiveness of the investment in training and determine whether the external resource provides sufficient value for the expenses incurred.

Future Testing Schedules. In some cases, training needs to track required testing for employees who have participated in training events. Training staff also may track qualifications testing for future job openings and certification testing for operation of certain machinery. To handle this tracking automatically, the HRMS must contain fields for date of last test or date of future test, as well as algorithms for calculating testing deadlines. Depending on the circumstances, these fields may include date of certificate expiration or date of course completion. The computer can periodically generate a calendar of upcoming testing deadlines that lists employee name and other demographics, date of last test/certification/training, date of next test, and type of testing required. Training and other human resources functions use this report to monitor certification for positions that require licenses or further testing.

If the system allows entry of responses to individual questions in pretests and post-tests, some sophisticated systems can analyze which types of information participants already knew before training, which they acquired during training, and which they did not learn. Training staff also can evaluate particular instructors and courses, as well as develop appropriate improvements in training.

Career Development Reports

Training History Report. Training staff and line supervisors often use training reports when evaluating an individual's preparedness for a particular training or job opportunity. This type of report lists basic employee information plus course name, sponsor (internal or external), and date of program. Depending on the course, the report may list results, such as grade or certification.

Career Development Plan. Based on career assessment tests, performance reviews, skills inventories, and personal interviews, training staff may create a career development plan for an individual. Besides department, job title, and length of service, it may list information such as current strengths, projected training and development needs, and current training and development needs. It also may list target positions, complete with job code, title, and perhaps some quantified evaluation of the individual's readiness for or likelihood of success in that position.

Some of this information may come directly from computerized tests, but training staff may enter additional notes and suggestions from their own observations and experience. The report may include space for comments, as well as review of past career development accomplishments. Based on employee interviews, it may include comments on career goals and aspirations.

Career Profile. Similar to an individual résumé or skills inventory, this report lists the education, skills, and experience of a particular employee. It helps individuals and their supervisors identify the most effective training and de-

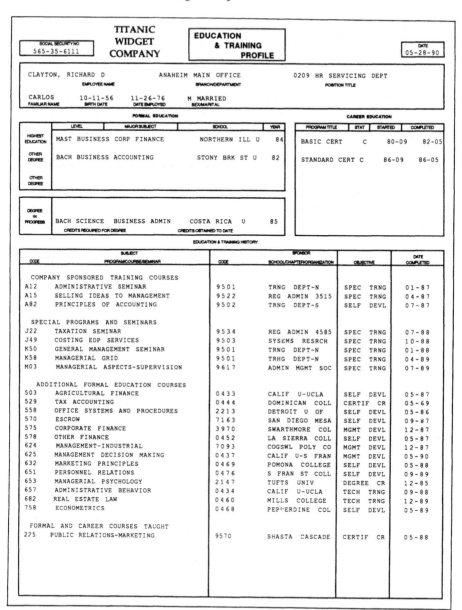

Figure 17–5. Typical education and training profile. Some training and development functions print training reports, career profiles, and other individual profiles on special forms. An education and training profile may list events chronologically, by subject, or as in this case, by training sponsor.

TITANIC WIDGET COMPANY
CAREER PROFILE

RAYMOND	C.	JOHNSON	PROFILE DATE 06-11-89	COST CENTER 69-69	TYPE X	SOCIAL SECURITY NO. 113-30-6886
FIRST NAME	INITIAL	LAST NAME				

ADDRESS	STATE, ZIP CODE	DATE OF BIRTH	SEX/MAR
320 DEANZA LANE, LOS ALTOS	CA 94022	08-30-59	M MARRIED

REGION/SUBSIDIARY	DIVISION	DEPARTMENT		STATE	GRADE	JOB NO.	STATUS
WEST COAST	WIDGET	SALES		CA	SPEC	88	A

WORK EXPERIENCE, PROFESSIONAL LICENSES, GEOGRAPHICAL PREFERENCES, FOREIGN LANGUAGES

CATEGORY	DESCRIPTION	YEARS COMMENT	LAST YEAR	COMMENT	SKILL CODE
ENGRG/SCIENTIFIC/TECH	MATH & STATISTICS, GENERAL	00	89		AA100
	ALGEBRA	02	89		AA200
	GEOMETRY	02	88		AA400
	RETAIL ACCOUNTS	10	89		EB100
	RETAIL GROCERY	10	89		EB105
	RETAIL VARIETY, INDEPENDENT	04	89		EB120
	RETAIL VARIETY, CHAIN	03	89		EB125
	RETAIL DISCOUNT	07	89		EB130
	DIRECT ACCOUNTS	10	89		EB200
	DIRECT GROCERY ACCOUNTS	07	89		EB205
	DIRECT VARIETY ACCOUNTS	03	89		EB215
	SERVICE DISTRIBUTORS	03	89		EB225
	INSTITUTION SALES	06	89		EB260
	HOUSEHOLD PRODUCTS	07	89		EB305
	GROCERY PRODUCTS	07	89		EB310
	NON-WIDGET PRODUCTS SALES	03	83		EB410
	SALES ADMINISTRATION, GENERAL	10	89	FIRST SPECIALTY	EC100
	SALES ADMINISTRATION, GENERAL	71			EC100
	SALES PLANNING	10	89	SECOND SPECIALTY	EC105
	SALES FORCE ADMINISTRATION	10	89	FIRST PREFERENCE	EC110
ADMIN AND STAFF AREAS	PUBLIC RELATIONS, GENERAL	03	83		GB300
	CONSUMER RELATIONS	03	83		GB315
	CONVENTION PLANNING	03	83		GB330
	PRESS RELATIONS	03	83	THIRD SPECIALTY	GB335
	EMPLOYEE COMMUNICATION	05	89		GC135
	TRAINING & DEVELOPMENT	07	89	SECOND PREFERENCE	GC260
MANAGEMENT EXPERIENCE	AREA MANAGER	06	89		MA105
	FIRST LEVEL SUPERVISOR	10	89	THIRD PREFERENCE	MA125
OTHER WORK EXPERIENCE	INSURANCE -SALES/INVESTIGATION	01	60		NE140
FOREIGN RESIDENCE/PREFERENCES	EUROPE, GENERAL	85		CONSIDER ASSIGNMT	SA100
	LATIN AMERICA, GENERAL	85		CONSIDER ASSIGNMT	SA300
FOREIGN LANGUAGES	FRENCH	93		READ/WRITE	WL180

PREVIOUS EMPLOYMENT HISTORY DATA

NAME OF COMPANY	DATES EMPLOYED FROM	TO	JOB TITLE/PRIMARY DUTIES
MOLSON BREWERIES	09-80	06-83	SALES,SUPV,SALES,PROM,ADM
WESTERN LIFE AS	12-79	09-80	SALES,SUPV,TRAINING
CANADIAN PACIFIC	09-77	12-79	CLERICAL, SECURITY,INVESTIG
HENRY JAMES ASSOC	09-44	09-49	SALES CLERK

TRAINING DATA

COURSE TITLE/SUBJECT/SCHOOL	YEAR
CIVIL CRIMINAL INVEST	76
APPLIED SCIENCE	74
MODERN BUS ALEX	71

OTHER ACTIVITIES
MEMBER OF ATHLETIC AND SOCIAL ORGANIZATIONS CLUB ACTIVITIES, CHARITY
DRIVES, HOBBIES: COOKING, PHOTOGRAPHY, TRAVELING

MILITARY RESERVE STATUS

MILITARY CLASSIFICATION	RESERVE CLASSIFICATION	RESERVE BRANCH
NOT ELIG		
RESERVE RANK	RESERVE UNIT NAME	RES COMP / OBG DATE

Figure 17–6. Typical career profile. Information for the career profile comes primarily from the skills inventory but also from training records and employment history.

velopment opportunities for them. Managers use this profile when considering promotions and other career decisions. Much of its content comes from the HRMS, but some is entered into the system manually. Sometimes this profile includes several other reports, such as the training profile or career development plan.

Potential Candidates Report. A potential candidates report typically lists the numbers and names of employees who meet certain criteria related to career development potential. These may include performance rating, promotability index, and willingness to relocate to a particular location. Training, supervisors, management, or employee relations may use this report when assessing promotion patterns and opportunities. Training sometimes integrates these reports with skills inventory reports, which select employees by skills and experience.

Career Development Cost Report. If an organization tracks career development costs, training staff may need to report the costs of providing a certain level of training or an advanced degree program. This report may be a summary report, showing trends, or a full report on costs of career development for a particular employee.

Skills Frequency Reports

Once completed, skills inventories can serve a wide variety of human resources needs. Because the skills inventory data base holds so much personal information, skills inventory reports allow significant flexibility in identifying criteria for including employees in a list or tabulation. Individual skills inventory reports are similar to career profiles, but reports on the overall population can furnish valuable data not available through other means.

Often programs can sort not only by employee but also by level of experience. With a skills frequency report, the user can ask the system to list all employees whose skills profile includes a certain combination of skills and experience. The user creates a set of IF/THEN and AND/OR criteria. For instance, a firm planning an expansion into the Pacific Rim might ask for all employees who have experience in international sales *or* marketing *and* who speak an Asian language *or* have lived in Asia. A company that wants to standardize its word processing programs may want to know how many employees use particular programs, how often, and with what fluency.

One report might list all employees who speak, write, or read a particular foreign language according to a self-assessment of fluency. Another might list all employees in division A who indicated they would consider promotion to division B. Another could summarize the number of person-years of experience in various systems applications. The report may include employee name, skills, experience level, and department. With this information, managers can

```
06/25/91                    Titanic Widget Company              Page   1
                               SKILL RETRIEVAL

                                For FRENCH

NAME                     TITLE              DIVISION, DEPARTMENT    HIRE DATE
=========================  =================  =========================  ==========
Brown, Virgil L            Mgr Programming    SOFTWARE, ENGINEERING   05/23/85
    COBOL   DBASE   FORTRAN  MANAGER    FRENCH

Krause, Janet A            Cust Support II    SOFTWARE, SALES         03/11/87
    DBASE   BASIC   TYPING   FRENCH     GERMAN

Thompson, Wendy Q          Cust Support II    SOFTWARE, SALES         06/28/88
    DBASE   COBOL   FORTRAN  TYPING     SPANISH   FRENCH

Total Employees: 3
```

Figure 17–7. Typical skills retrieval report. This report displays all candidates whose records match the search criteria—in this case, COBOL programming experience.
(Source: AbraCadabra Software. Reprinted with permission.)

identify which employees might handle new responsibilities most efficiently or effectively.

Because of the variety of information the skills inventory process usually accumulates, the list of reports based on these data is often defined by the needs of the organization rather than the limitations of the data.

Glossary

Career development   An organization's plans and actions designed to identify, direct, encourage, support, and counsel high-potential employees. Usually directed by human resources staff in conjunction with other managers.

Experience   Work activities in which an individual has participated; in human resources, this term usually refers to job-related activities.

Management training   Training designed to help employees become more effective managers. Usually includes decision-making and analytical skills such as problem solving, oral and written presentation skills, human interaction, and consultative skills.

Skill   An attribute an individual has acquired through education, training, practice, or personal development. Skills may be quantifiable (typing speed) or qualitative (communication skills).

Skills inventory A systematic listing of the skills, experiences, and interests of an organization's employees. May include all employees or only those in certain job families.

Skills training Direct training that conveys practical information that is applicable to a job-related situation. Examples include software courses and bookkeeping training.

Sponsor The institution or group offering a particular training course. Potential sponsors include the training function, other departments, external seminar providers, and colleges and universities.

Supervisory training Training designed to help employees become effective supervisors. May include interpersonal skills, communication skills, time management, and supervisory policies and procedures.

Discussion Points

1. What factors affect the integration of training data with the rest of the HRMS?
2. In what ways can automating the training function improve the cost-effectiveness of training?
3. In what ways can an organization's management use HRMS data to assess the effectiveness of training activities?
4. How does the training function use automation to support its administrative and development roles?
5. Under what circumstances might functions besides training use data that training staff enter into the system?
6. When should an organization develop a computerized skills inventory? When should it not?
7. What steps can the HRSC take to maximize the validity of skills inventory data?
8. How can different kinds of organizations use skills inventories? Consider banks, manufacturers, retail businesses, and school systems.

Further Reading

Albert, M. "Cultural Development through HR Systems Integration." *Training and Development Journal,* September 1985.

Amico, Anthony M. "Computerized Career Information." *Personnel Journal,* August 1981.

Arthur, Diane. "The Human Resources Function and the Growing Company." *Personnel,* November 1987.

Bensu, Janet. "How to Select the Best and the Brightest." *Computers in Personnel,* Spring 1988.

Boudreau, John W., and Cathy Smith. "Education: Masters of the HR Universe." *Computers in Personnel,* Summer 1987.

Broomhead, Harry. "An Approach to Career Planning." In *Computers in Personnel: Business and Technology—Achieving Practical Solutions,* edited by Terry Page. Sussex: Institute of Personnel Management & Institute of Manpower Studies, 1987.

Bruner, John D., and Robert H. Garrison. "Record-Keeping Made Easy." *Training,* November 1985.

Buckley, Suzanne. "Evaluating Media for HRS Training." *Human Resource Systems Management Report,* December 1986.

Ceriello, Vincent R., and Leonard R. Linden. "Management Resource Program." *Journal of Systems Management,* December 1973.

Dukes, Carlton W. "Skills Inventories and Promotion Systems." In *Handbook of Personnel Administration,* edited by Joseph Famularo. New York: McGraw Hill, 1979.

Dunn, Brian D. "The Skills Inventory: A Second Generation." *Personnel,* September/October 1982.

Fahnline, Richard H. "The Skills Inventory Put On." *Journal of Systems Management,* May 1974.

Gentner, Claudia A. "The Computerized Executive Job Seeker." *Personnel Administrator,* August 1984.

Gordon, Jack. "Computers in Training." *Training,* October 1985.

Green, Bob. "Applicant and Job Candidate Ranking and Selection: A Systems Approach." In *Computers in Personnel: Business and Technology—Achieving Practical Solutions,* edited by Terry Page. Sussex: Institute of Personnel Management & Institute of Manpower Studies, 1987.

Green, Hugh. "Matching People to Jobs: An Expert Systems Approach." *Personnel Management,* September 1987.

Grey, James W., and Robert E. Wass. "A Mini Human Resource Inventory System." *Personnel,* November 1974.

Hedberg, B., and E. Mumford. "Computer Systems to Support Industrial Democracy." In *Human Choices and Computers,* edited by E. Mumford and H. Sackman. New York: North-Holland, 1975.

Helfgott, R.B. "Can Training Catch Up with Technology?" *Personnel Journal,* 67 (2), 1988.

Horsfield, Debra. "Succession and Management Development Planning: The Organization Metrics Succession Planning System." *Computers in Personnel,* Fall 1986.

Kaumeyer, Richard A., Jr. "Automated Skills Retrieval: One Company's Program." *Personnel,* January/February 1967.

———. "Thinking of Starting a Skills Inventory System?" *Management World,* September 1976.

Kirrane, D.E. "Training: HR's Number One Priority." *Personnel Administrator,* December 1988.

Lavin, Mary J. "HRDIS: A Computerized Human Resource Development Information System." *Human Resource Planning,* Spring 1981.

Linkow, Peter. "HRD at the Roots of Corporate Strategy." *Training and Development,* May 1985.

Madlin, Nancy. "Computer-Based Training Comes of Age." *Personnel*, November 1987.

Mahoney, T.A. "Computerized Simulation: A Training Tool for Manpower Managers." *Personnel Journal*, December 1975.

Marangell, Frank. "The New Language of Skills." *Personnel Journal*, April 1971.

Mayer, John H. "Keeping Records on File: Software for the Management of Training." *Data Training*, May 1986.

Meyer, Gary. "Computer Costs: Hardware Fails; Training Goals." *Personnel Manager's Policy and Practice Update*, August 1985.

———. "Should Your Organization Be Using PCs to Train Employees?" *Personnel Manager's Policy and Practice Update*, September 1985.

Seamans, Lyman H. "What's Lacking in Most Skills Inventories?" *Personnel Journal*, February 1973.

Sperling, Kenneth L. "New Software Bridges Training Gaps." *Personnel Journal*, August 1987.

Thomsen, David J. "Keeping Track of Managers in a Large Corporation." *Personnel*, November 1976.

Toigo, J.W. "Don't Dismiss CBT." *Computers in Personnel*, Winter 1989.

Walter, V. "Self-Motivated Personal Career Planning: A Breakthrough in Human Resource Management." *Personnel Administrator*, March 1978.

Yarusso, Lowell. "Practical Microcomputer Applications." *Performance & Instruction Journal*, May 1985.

Zemke, Ron. "12 Ways to 'Micro-Manage' the Training Function." *Training*, July 1983.

Zemke, Ron, and John Gunkler. "Managing by Micro: A Software Review." *Training*, September 1985.

18
Human Resources Planning

> When you can measure what you are speaking about and express it in numbers, you know something about it; but when you cannot measure and when you cannot express it in numbers, your knowledge is of a meager and unsatisfactory kind.
>
> —Lord Kelvin

To anticipate upcoming human resources issues before they become problematic (and make present solutions obsolete), many human resources departments have established a special function to identify, analyze, forecast, and plan for changes and needs in human resources. Many departments refer to this function as *human resources planning* or *planning and development*. In the past, organizations frequently used the term *manpower planning;* perhaps a third of the organizations that still refer to human resources as personnel administration still use this term. In this book, the term *human resources planning* is used.

A commitment to comprehensive human resources planning offers several crucial benefits. Proper planning can help the organization retain desired employees longer and keep them functioning more productively and at reasonable cost. Specifically, this function can do the following:

- Reduce labor costs associated with attrition
- Reduce recruiting replacement costs
- Focus training resources appropriately
- Increase the ability to take advantage of new business opportunities
- Improve employee morale and satisfaction
- Increase the ability to cope with shifts in employee populations
- Control rapid expansion or reduction in force
- Monitor staffing and retention policies

The HRMS In Human Resources Planning

Computerized support of planning began to appear in the 1960s, when human resources planning had relatively simple statistical requirements. At that time, human resources paid much less attention to the impact of gender, race, and other social factors on work force decisions. Compensation and benefits were relatively straightforward. Thus, someone who had reasonable statistical skills could do human resources planning. As human resources evolved to include issues such as career path planning, organization design and restructuring, affirmative action, and turnover and replacement analysis, human resources planning became correspondingly more complex.

At first, because of the compartmentalization of human resources functions, management relegated planning and forecasting applications to operations research staff and statisticians. These professionals could handle advanced statistics, but they often had minimal understanding of human resources planning issues and procedures. Correspondingly, the staff of human resources did not have sufficient quantitative backgrounds to handle automated forecasting on a sophisticated level.

Computerized planning is enjoying increasing prevalence in human resources departments. In the mid-1960s, about one-third of *Fortune 500* firms probably performed some form of human resources planning. By 1985, less than half of all companies had such a function, with sophistication and techniques varying widely among these operations. Currently, all but a few start-up companies and very small firms have some type of human resources planning function or are considering implementing one as an aid to strategic planning and corporate development. This growth has been engendered partially by the growth in the capabilities and prevalence of microcomputer-based systems for planning and forecasting applications.

A few systems support specific aspects of planning and forecasting, such as succession planning, managerial appraisal and assessment, and organization design. Most serious planning and forecasting, however, requires significant custom creation from basic vendor-supplied software packages. Only a few vendors offer programs specifically designed for human resources planning, and these are primarily designed for microcomputer environments.

Planning normally adds little or no data to the HRMS, so it does not necessarily need to use the same computer system as the rest of human resources. A few vendors offer stand-alone planning systems, but these tend to be generic in nature and directed toward specific applications, such as staffing or succession planning. Human resources planning may choose the most appropriate planning and forecasting software, then determine whether it can electronically port data such as name, job classification, gender, race/ethnicity, grade, training status, and job history from the HRMS. In a few cases, these data must be entered into the planning system manually.

Role of Human Resources Planning

Many human resources departments have established special functions to address planning and forecasting needs. Sometimes this function handles only

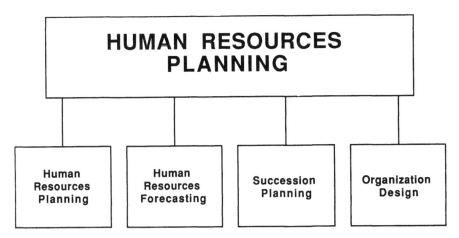

Figure 18–1. Principal roles of the human resources planning function.

operational planning, such as projecting changes in population size or planning for new facilities staffing. Sometimes this function reports directly to a strategic planning function rather than to human resources, providing information for overall strategic decision making. If human resources planning is strategically oriented, other human resources functions may use simple spreadsheet and forecasting software to do their own operational forecasting and planning, consulting with human resources planning staff for guidance as needed.

Occasionally, a human resources department may centralize planning, with each function coming to the planning group via requests. Firms may choose this alternative if other human resources functions lack the computer knowledge and statistical skills that planning requires. A proactive planning function with a responsive computer system often handles an increasing share of strategic and operational planning processes at both the human resources and corporate levels.

Several human resources activities have particularly complex ongoing planning and forecasting needs. These include recruiting, compensation planning, benefits planning, training and development, and retirement planning. Other planning needs may arise periodically depending on the size and pace of the organization.

A well-run organization plans ahead to meet the inevitable, but often unpredictable, need to find replacements for employees in high-level positions. *Succession planning*, sometimes referred to as *replacement planning*, is a special type of career development activity designed to ensure that the firm has qualified employees who are prepared to move into key positions that become available because of retirement, promotion, transfer, separation, or expansion.

Some human resources departments include succession planning within the human resources planning function, in part because this activity depends on supply, demand, and availability data. In some firms, the training function includes career development not only for most line and administrative staff but also for top management. In others, training handles only line personnel, and a separate management development function performs succession planning for higher levels of management.

More and more vendors now offer software dedicated to succession planning. This software usually interfaces with the main HRMS employee data base to include personal and demographic data and to ensure consistency of data between the systems.

Organization design sometimes also falls within the responsibility of the planning function. Organization design's closest association with the HRMS comes via organization charting. Planning (or corporate communications) often creates the most common product of organization design—"org charts." A similarly titled but separate function, organization development (OD), includes management intervention, team building, and other techniques designed to improve work-group productivity. OD is primarily behavioral science oriented and may be assigned either to human resources planning or to the training and development function.

Steps in Human Resources Planning

Regardless of the level of automation, the human resources planning process takes place in definite phases:

1. Consider the organization's strategic and tactical plans.
2. Collect and organize data to measure and analyze relevant factors.
3. Perform human resources forecasting based on these data elements.
4. Develop human resources objectives based on these forecasts.
5. Initiate action programs designed to meet the plans and objectives.
6. Monitor the forecasts to compare them with what actually occurs; adjust forecasting procedures and human resources objectives accordingly.

Of these steps, three involve the computer—data collection, forecasting, and program monitoring. The other steps are primarily human processes with little or no mechanical contribution. These steps must take place in a particular order. The human resources planning function can know what data to collect only if it understands top management's strategic and tactical plans for the organization. Forecasting may be very simple, using only one or two variables, or it may require a large body of data. Human resources objectives and action plans follow from analyses that deal with business challenges and opportunities. Responsive planning requires comparing forecasts with actual experience, to refine the techniques used to project images of the future.

To ensure credibility and promote the human resources planning function, planners need adequate computer tools, facility and staff resources, and computer training. Sometimes, however, human resources planning gets these resources only after it has proved its efficacy. To get this process on the right track, the human resources planning function must have credibility and the ability to sell planning concepts and programs to management. For this reason, human resources planning staff should have significant skills and experience in working with management at all levels.

Advantages and Limitations of Computerized Planning

Contemporary human resources planning inevitably requires computer support, as planning and forecasting require numerous mathematical computations on large amounts of data. Most human resources planning issues involve many variables, and firms cannot do such complex modeling manually.

Many human resources planners use microcomputers that have sufficient capacity to manipulate needed data and perform calculations. If the resultant analyses are not uploaded to a central processor, planners may treat a microcomputer-based planning and forecasting system as a stand-alone application. Because mainframe-based forecasting tools tie up computer resources, mainframes are not as suitable as smaller computers for human resources planning. When doing forecasting, the user must interact often with the computer. The computer prompts the user; the user makes adjustments to data or variables; the computer prompts again. This process works especially well if the user is working on a stand-alone microcomputer. On mainframes, such frequent interaction often is more difficult because the planning and forecasting application is contending with other applications for computer processing time.

Acquiring a working planning module generally involves more customization than do most other human resources functions. Planning and forecasting system design and implementation require a project team with both computer sophistication and general human resources knowledge. Because of these complexities, many firms pay consultants and vendors to provide this customization, although human resources planning staff participate in this process. Customization takes place primarily during design of the module. A well-planned and properly implemented system should require only minor modifications.

Operating this module requires more computer experience than do most other human resources modules. In addition, developing useful data such as future exit rates, future growth rates, and promotability patterns requires a deep and broad understanding of human resources operations and the internal and external business environment. Because the model itself is only as effective as its users' skills in interpreting the data, those skills make a crucial difference in how others perceive the model.

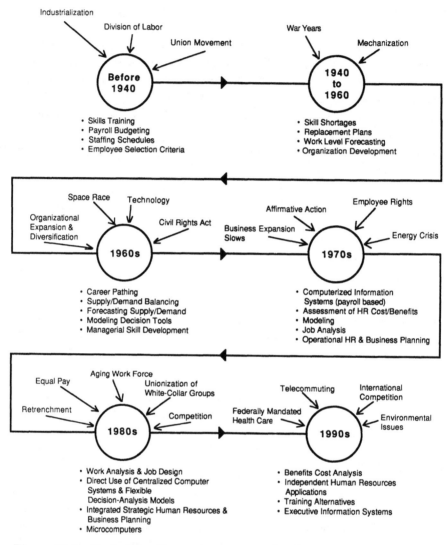

Figure 18–2. Evolution of human resources planning techniques.
(Source: Adapted from *Computers in Personnel*, Auerbach Publishers, New York. Copyright © 1987. Warren, Gorham & Lamont, Inc. Reprinted with permission.)

Firms experience significantly more success with computerized planning and forecasting when many people understand and can manipulate the models and other planning tools. This group should include staff from areas other than human resources planning. Managers also should make certain that this module includes extensive documentation.

These powerful computer programs help skilled professionals increase the accuracy of their forecasts, but even the most well-conceived application cannot eliminate risk and uncertainty from organization decision making. Planners should remember (and remind others who use their reports) that forecasts are probabilistic rather than deterministic—that is, they can estimate future conditions within the most likely ranges but cannot provide exact values with certainty.

Computer Models for Planning and Forecasting

The core of planning and forecasting is computer modeling. A model is a relationship or set of relationships among variables. A modeling program allows users to manipulate data mathematically to simulate different possible future events. *Modeling* refers to the process of establishing those relationships by analysis and experimentation; *simulation* refers to running the model with a set of independent variables or inputs to determine the model's impact on the dependent variables or outputs; *manipulation* involves altering parameters and variables, then examining how these changes affect the resulting data projections.

Computer Model Selection

Computerized planning and forecasting offer many types of human resources models. Human resources planning must begin the model-building process by establishing what kinds of forces are driving human resources management in a particular organization and business environment. The staff must then determine the kinds of computer expertise and resources that are available for human resources planning and forecasting. They then must agree on the kinds of reports and outputs wanted and possibly identify future human resources requirements and resources. Sometimes the staff may try to determine how much one particular factor may influence the future or ascertain the relative importance of various factors. Based on these factors, planning staff can work with system designers to determine the best type of model to use. Because data requirements vary, human resources planning staff normally should begin collecting data only after selecting the type of model it will use.

Planners often consider forecasting to have two major forms—supply and demand. Both types have internal and external influences. For example, a key input to supply forecasting is the prediction of attrition. The attrition rate may be influenced by internal factors (organization policies, quality of supervision, promotional opportunities, or salary levels) or external factors (labor market demand, the local economy, or competition). Both types of forecasting use some of the same data, matrices, algorithms, and techniques, but they often

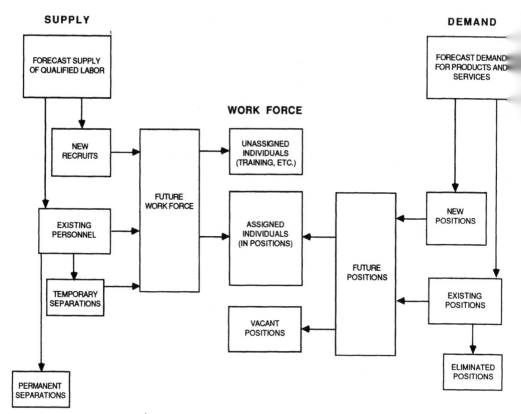

Figure 18–3. Supply and demand work force flows. Forecasting an organization's work force needs usually involves supply or demand forecasting. Supply forecasting concentrates on the availability of labor; demand forecasting emphasizes the market for products and services, which, in turn, translates into positions. As shown in this figure, human resources can use either approach to derive forecasts of employees and positions.
(Source: MacCrimmon, Kenneth R., "Improving Business Decision Making with Manpower Management Systems," *The Business Quarterly*, Autumn 1981.)

address different issues and work most successfully under different circumstances. If the organization has problems filling positions with qualified employees or anticipates such problems, human resources decisions are demand driven. If, however, human resources planning issues involve trying to retain and motivate staff and treat employees equitably when the organization has no control over turnover and internal transfer and promotion, human resources planning is supply driven.

Demand and supply model styles differ significantly enough and are so complex that most human resources planning functions must commit to using only one form or the other. The choice depends on the labor and economic environment in which management believes their firm will operate in the future. The job of human resources planning is to forecast the organization's total need for people (demand forecasting) and the supply of people likely to be available to meet that expected need (supply forecasting). Because projected supply rarely equals projected demand, there almost always is a surplus or a shortfall, which is referred to as net demand. Human resources planning's job is to come up with action programs to minimize the surplus or shortfall. The types of human resources planning and related issues best served by these two approaches are presented here.

Supply Forecasting. If human resources planners and management determine that the most important factor in employee movement is the supply, or availability, of appropriate employees, they will concentrate on building models to measure availability. Supply-push forecasting assumes that a supply of talent is readily available to replace incumbents who are lost through attrition or pushed to higher levels—in many cases before they are ready to assume more responsibility.

Supply forecasting involves predicting the number of employees who will possess certain skills or occupy certain positions that an organization may have in the future. It also may involve predicting the availability of qualified individuals in the labor market. Planning uses supply forecasting to describe the internal career paths of employees occupying each position and to check for continuous availability and flow. This information helps many different human resources functions implement their plans: Employment can refine the criteria for evaluating new hires under consideration for particular positions; training can develop and promote classes that build skills and experience; compensation can adjust the reward system to retain and promote key employees who have valuable experience or potential; and EEO/AA can set goals and timetables according to future demand and supply. Managers can then focus on developing available appropriate talent to meet future staffing needs.

Supply forecasting relies on both external and internal data. On the external side, planners consider sources of supply of qualified candidates, competitor analysis, and relevant labor markets. On the internal side, they work with job families, job classifications, and employee records developed or maintained by other human resources functions. Planners rely on existing employee records for information on promotions, transfers, terminations, retirements, layoffs/recalls, and leaves of absence. Examining the past rates of such activities in various job classifications forms the basis for making future predictions of employee supply.

Demand Forecasting. Demand forecasting assumes that employee migration to new positions results from the movement of other employees to higher positions or out of the organization. Thus, planners consider every position vacated by a promotion or transferred employee as a gap to fill. If human resources planners and management believe that the organization can meet its need for appropriate individuals at any level through external recruitment and hiring, they will concentrate on demand forecasting.

In the most general terms, demand forecasting seeks to estimate the number of employees who have particular skills or are in particular job classifications that an organization will need at a certain future time. In a 1986 survey of 220 major U.S. business organizations, the most common human resources planning modeling application was for recruitment planning.

Most firms also used HRMS planning for internal promotion, which is closely related to demand forecasting. For instance, succession planning is a form of demand-pull modeling. A human resources planning function with a strong mandate to produce responsive succession planning programs is likely to use demand forecasting for its overall human resources planning modeling.

Some planners consider demand forecasting a relatively difficult form of modeling that produces results with a high degree of uncertainty. This uncertainty stems from the dependence of an organization's demand for employees on many external, often unreliable, forecasts, as well as on tactical and strategic planning within the organization. Demand forecasting is an inexact science because organizational success depends on many factors that are difficult to define. These include customer or client responses, actions of competitors, government regulatory changes, and technological developments. Demand forecasting also must consider how future organizational activities, such as product development, shift in services provided, and changes in sales volume, may affect human resources. To establish values for these variables, planning staff must participate directly in the strategic planning and development activity of the enterprise.

Types of Models. Planners in different fields construct many different kinds of models. Human resources planners have developed a variety of approaches to modeling. Some of the most popular human resources planning models follow:

- Network flow model. A network flow model looks at individual career path projections, then forecasts likely job movement in the future. This model type requires access to consistently maintained historical data about jobs, positions, families, and skill groups and permits sophisticated "what if" analyses. Although network flow models are driven by individual career path projections, they can relatively easily include intake and outflow factors such as transfers, hiring into higher job grades, and terminations for a variety of reasons. Many planners believe that this reflects American job patterns fairly accurately.

- Renewal model. A renewal model traces job groups while assuming a pull, or flow, of individuals through the organization. This model works best with large numbers of employees in homogeneous groups or families and in situations that have predictable career paths.

- Markov model. A Markov model tracks employees along predictable, linear career paths in a stable organization. Markov models assume that employees will remain with the organization throughout their working years. They also assume a push of staff through the organization by the continuous availability of replacements.

- Cohort analysis. In cohort analysis, human resources planning follows a group of employees whom the organization hired at approximately the same time. The models tracks losses and changes throughout the internal

---

The Limitations of Markov Models

Markov models represent a matrix of career paths. From each position, employees progress to certain other positions within the organization. A Markov model is a traditional but complex form of human resources planning. This approach enjoyed some popularity when first introduced by the U.S. armed forces during World War II, but fewer planners use it today, for several reasons. Developing a Markov model for an organization of any size usually requires a skilled statistician. These models apply best to cultures and industries in which employee patterns of progression are well established and employees tend to stay with one organization for their entire working career. Because American workers change jobs with relative frequency and promotional patterns are often fluid and unpredictable, Markov models have limited application in U.S. firms.

In such circumstances, demand-pull and supply-push models offer more accurate forecasts. These models allow for inclusion of factors such as attrition, retirement, mergers, and acquisitions—factors that create demands and supplies in deployment of human resources.

employment life of these employees, from hiring to termination. This model may use cohorts within departments or job functions. It works best for measurement and analysis of turnover.

Building a Human Resources Planning Model

Every computer model is a combination of software, data, and mathematical routines. Although human resources planning and forecasting systems have many individual characteristics, a typical planning package is profiled here.

Human resources planning and forecasting applications often start with standard spreadsheet packages. To these, the vendor, designer, or consultant adds statistical routines that can perform mathematical computations not included in the package. The designer then creates subroutines to complete the analysis. With spreadsheet macros or subroutines, designers can include numerous IF/THEN/ELSE capabilities in the application. For instance, IF the retention rate is less than or equal to 10 percent, THEN the movement of employees into certain positions follows the patterns for file 3A, ELSE the movement follows the patterns for file 3B.

A human resources planning model contains numerous types of data files. Many of these files are best depicted in matrix form, appearing as tables with one human resources-related characteristic in rows and another in columns. These file types usually include the following:

- Starting population (typically a matrix of job grades by service, job classification, training experience, or other field carried in the employee master record)
- Exit rate (matrices of exit rates for each population subgroup identified in the matrix of starting population)
- Growth rate (matrix of growth rates for each population subgroup identified in the starting population)
- Promotion patterns (matrices of movements into and out of each position)
- Any other variables or data that affect the population size and composition

Human resources planning programs often have several matrices of each type. A program may have one exit rate matrix with just historical data, one based on maintaining the status quo, one based on an economic downturn, and one based on a prediction of organizational growth. More likely, the program has a single matrix that users can alter dynamically to reflect these conditions.

Most human resources planning models are rather simple. The challenge is knowing where to place the data in the model—that is, the most useful

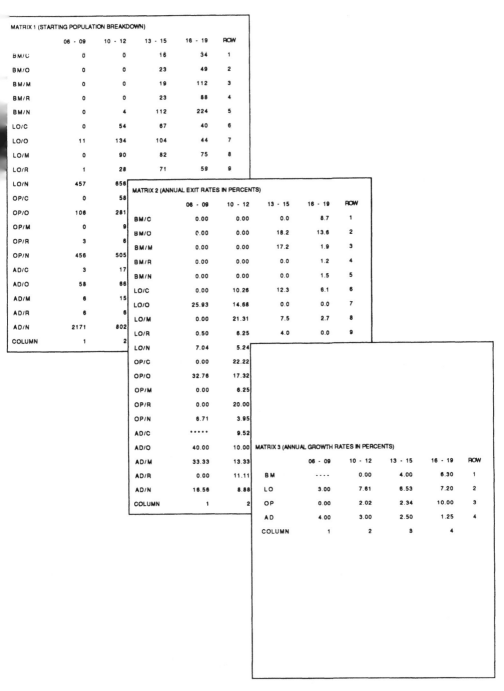

Figure 18–4. Sample matrices. A sample starting population matrix (top), sample exit population matrix (middle), and matrix of population growth rates (bottom).

designations for rows and columns, the impact of external forces, and which values or weightings to assign to variables.

When building a model, planners often start with a small data sample. The computer performs the forecast, and the planner performs the same calculations manually or with another, tested method. Developers and potential users can compare these results to evaluate model validity. They can then adjust factor weightings or algorithms before directing the computer to perform a large-scale forecast that they could not reasonably check manually.

Using the Computer Model

A user begins the forecasting process on a working model by opening one of the model's matrix files, typically a spreadsheet file. Within each matrix, the user can alter any cell, or entry in a row or column. Each cell represents a value (percentage or number), usually relating to a particular employee population subgroup. For instance, the user may want to alter attrition rates to reflect an anticipated downturn in overall economic conditions. The user can employ spreadsheet functions to modify a group of cells as well as individual cells. He or she may have the program increase all the cells in row 3 by 3.5 percent or increase all the cells in column 2 by 10. Normally, users do not alter the cells in the population unless they have some need to experiment with reality, which, in this case, is the starting population of employees in the subject group.

The user continues to open and alter more files until all the files needed for a particular forecast are open and ready. He or she then requests a menu of execution options and chooses a routine. The list may include options such as employee turnover, retention, or promotion flow or number of training program graduates. The user also may choose the length of time covered in the forecast, usually one to five years.

The program then performs calculations, invoking particular statistical operations as needed. After completing the calculations, the system displays the results on the screen. The user may continue to preview the results, altering data or assumptions, then request a report of the results.

Creating "What If" Analyses. Planning staff may create a series of "what if" analyses, which are alternate scenarios of the future. The user first develops a baseline set of matrices and forecasts, then alters one or more variables and runs another forecast. Comparing the results shows the impact of possible future scenarios. One scenario might model the effect of maintaining the same level of college-graduate recruitment; another would model the effect of doubling recruitment efforts; still another might model the effects of an early retirement campaign compared with a freeze on internal transfers and promotions. Some planners refer to "what if" scenarios as simulations.

Using Error Messages and Calculation Limits. A well-designed program notifies the user when certain data prevent completion of the requested calculation. Compared with most human resources functions, the human resources planning module produces fewer lists but performs more calculations. Because of the multiple calculations often required by one algorithm, this module tends to issue error or warning messages more frequently than do other modules. It may identify the specific erroneous value, or it may indicate how far it could carry its calculations before encountering a barrier.

Planners often use this barrier-notification attribute to determine the minimum or maximum acceptable limit for certain variables. For instance, human resources planning may want to determine the optimal movement of trainees into the main employee population. The user creates a matrix of the number of new hires who enter the training program within a specified period of time. The user also gives retention rates for trainees in each relevant employment category and the growth rate for each employment category. The computer model may find, however, that the number of retained trainees and employees exceeds the available positions at that specified growth rate. If so, the user just reduces the values of entering trainees incrementally and orders the computer to execute the routine again, repeating this process until the program can successfully complete the analysis. Having obtained the number of trainees needed, employment and training can refine their hiring and training plans.

Data Requirements and Sources

Human resources planning may use the HRMS to determine trends for virtually any type of data about employees that the system tracks. If a moderately comprehensive HRMS already serves most major human resources functions, human resources planning can concentrate on manipulating data rather than accumulating it. Most planning and forecasting does not deal with individuals but with entities (such as vacancies, promotions, transfers, and leave status). Data requirements and sources depend on the type of planning management requires, but most data come from segments of the HRMS already maintained by other human resources functions.

Starting Population

Planning may assemble several sets of starting population matrices. Each matrix may cover just one job family. It lists the number of employees at the beginning of the period by job classification within the family. Planning may build matrices for each quarter in the planning horizon, which may be a period of one or more years. The system can use these files to calculate the percentage of change from period to period.

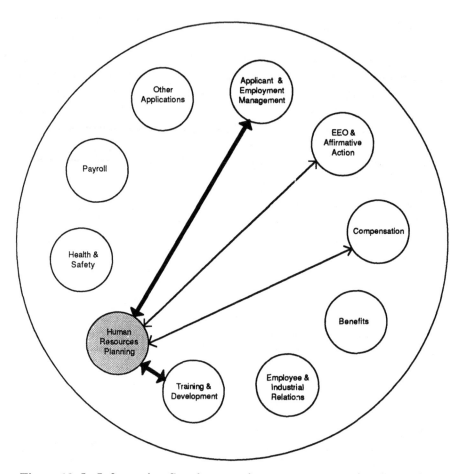

Figure 18–5. Information flow between human resources planning and other human resources functions.

Planning extracts these data from the HRMS. The usual default population is all active, full-time, regular employees. The user may, however, request that the system create a new file containing a specific subset of the population, such as female employees or employees at job grade 20 and above. The occupational focus depends heavily on labor market conditions and organizational plans for expansion or restructuring. Depending on the type of forecasting needed, required starting population data may include job grade, job classification, gender, race/ethnicity, age, service, performance, training, and skills and experience information.

Historical Data. For some forecasting projections, human resources planning may need to extract additional information from the HRMS data base, usually in summary or report form. Staff members use this information for two purposes.

First, they use it to create historical matrices and establish bases for extrapolations—for example, population size, population attributes, or rates of change within the population.

Second, they use this information to determine correlations among various factors. With this information, planning staff can establish which factors to track when projecting future trends. For instance, one bank planner investigating turnover predictions discovered that marital status and number and ages of children served as good predictors of whether employees were likely to remain with the organization. By tabulating marital and dependent data for each population cell, the planner could develop a prediction of turnover rates for the population by job group.

Derivative Data. Planning seldom adds data to the HRMS, with the possible exception of derivative data. For instance, human resources planning may add fields that indicate the positions to which an employee in this position is likely to migrate. Similarly, planning staff may add an index of attrition to the job classification or position code to indicate the relative likelihood that an employee in this position will leave the organization. This information can be useful not only to human resources planning itself but also to line managers and employees during career counseling.

Exit Rates and Other Human Resources Variables

Planning staff set values for variables based on historical patterns, knowledge of upcoming events, and information from human resources functions that have experienced similar trends or events. The information they use covers trends both within and outside of human resources. In addition to starting population, a relatively complete forecasting model would contain internal human resources data that indicate the following:

- Exit rates (from unit, division, region, or company)
- Growth rates (normal and accelerated)
- Promotional patterns (into and out of each position)
- Rate of promotion to management positions not covered by the model
- Trainee retention rate
- Percentage of incumbents having completed the training program

Planners also may consider special collections of HRMS data. They may use skills inventory information to identify employees with the potential for filling critical positions or staffing new projects. When working on determining the supply of employees available to fill particular positions, planners may look at position control data, such as open requisitions or budgeted versus actual positions.

Planning sometimes accesses other HRMS data as well. For instance, to predict future payroll obligations, planning uses not only individual employee records but wage and salary tables and projections of future earnings. The model also may include factors such as overtime, bonuses, and benefits.

Few human resources departments have sufficient resources to tackle such a comprehensive prediction. More simply, most models can estimate and compare future total payroll obligations under various scenarios. For instance, if an organization needs to increase work output by 20 percent, human resources planning can compare the cost of hiring new people, paying current employees overtime, and using temporary staff who do not receive benefits.

Sometimes human resources planning needs historical data, such as types of staffing the organization required in the past in order to meet certain output or service goals. Planners may not be able to transfer this information directly from the HRMS because job tables have changed and the employee population has experienced significant turnover. Instead, they must accumulate it manually from old reports and archived files.

When creating future scenarios for these types of data, human resources planning usually consults with the function that is responsible. For instance, before simulating the effect of proposed new salary rates, planners consult with compensation; before testing affirmative action hiring goals, they consult with EEO/AA.

Some forecasts compute the length of time required until certain events or processes have taken place, so time is part of the answer. Other types of forecasts prompt the user to choose a time horizon for the projection. These horizons usually run one to five years. The longer the horizon, the more uncertain is the simulated result.

If the forecasting routine requests a planning horizon, planning sometimes makes this choice. Sometimes, however, top management or another human resources function will request a specific time line. The length of the desired forecast period often depends on how stable and predictable management judges the market or environment to be. Often such requests involve organizational budgeting cycles.

Although some planners do not feel comfortable with projections that extend more than one year into the future, the effects of a one-year plan often take longer than that to be significant. For instance, every October one company sets the recruitment quotas for its upcoming budget cycle, which corresponds to the calendar year. In January, recruiters start working to hire college graduates. Those hired will complete school in June and may not start work until July or August, so they will have been on board only a couple of months by October, the time for the next budgeting cycle. Thus, human resources cannot reasonably evaluate the results of this staffing and selection process until sometime in the second year. For these reasons, even short-term planning may benefit from using a rolling cycle, constantly placing the present as the first quarter and adjusting subsequent quarters as needed.

Planners' first-year forecasts are generally more accurate than their second-year ones because the former are based on actual data, while the latter rely partially on the accuracy of those first-year estimates. This extrapolation compounds the effect of any inaccuracies in the general model design itself or the values of specific variables.

Variables Outside Human Resources

To function properly, human resources planning depends on data from corporate strategic planning, marketing, sales, finance and other functions outside human resources. In fact, human resources planning often produces more accurate results if its computerization follows the adoption of automated financial planning, production planning, sales and marketing projections, or other corporate planning. This works to even better advantage if human resources planning has the ability to integrate these data directly into its forecasting models.

To predict how management decisions will affect work force needs, human resources planning must have data on those management plans. These may include sales projections, expansion or relocation plans, and merger or acquisition plans. For instance, human resources planning may use sales projections to determine the number of employees of various types the organization will need to produce a specific array and volume of products. To extrapolate, planners need historical data on the number and types of staff required to achieve particular goals in the past. These may include average sales per sales representative and the ratio of sales representatives to marketing analysts.

Forecasting also may need management information on proposed changes in employee relations policies, such as flextime, early retirement, telecommuting, or job sharing. For instance, when exploring how flextime might affect human resources staffing needs, planners will get input from human resources cohorts in other similar organizations that already use flextime. They will try to determine in what job grades flextime is most popular and its effect on exit rates. By revising exit-rate matrices based on this information, human resources planning can forecast the effect of flextime on employee retention. Thus, management can consider the quantitative effects of flextime on recruitment and training costs.

Planners generally do not need to gather additional information, just analyze already accumulated data. When assigning values to external variables such as inflation, interest rates, unemployment rates, work force growth, international market opportunities, and population demographics, planners may need to gather projections from regulatory agencies, tax authorities, market researchers, external data bases and independent futurists.

For instance, in response to a predicted downturn in oil prices, an energy company may forecast a need for more service station attendants because consumers will drive more. But the company also may predict fewer employees at the bulk wholesale and refinery levels because lower prices will reduce the marginal profitability of many oil sources and tend to reduce production.

As another example, human resources planning may need external labor market data when projecting the future availability of qualified new hires. If EEO/AA or employment has already obtained labor-market information, human resources planning can use that information. Sometimes planners must look beyond their own resources for data from government agencies, competitors, or third parties, such as professional survey firms.

Succession Planning

Succession planning begins by identifying target positions, usually high-level positions critical to the organization's continuity and success. Training and development or management may need to generate this list manually if the job classification or position control modules cannot do so. They may use the HRMS to produce a preliminary list, then do final revisions manually. The computer may sort by one or more categories, such as job family, job classification, title, age, or service.

Succession planners usually use the HRMS employee records to identify potential successors to each position. They can develop algorithms to estimate the probability of an individual's succeeding in a specific position, given certain job parameters, individual background, experience, education, and so forth. Some commercial succession planning packages come with built-in processes for creating these algorithms. Developing the algorithms requires a great deal of care and often the services of external experts.

Succession planners also study internal career paths that lead to the target positions. To do so, they look at the career paths of individuals with experience in similar positions. This information helps them to select potentially qualified individuals for each slot in the succession planning scheme. Firms that alter titles and structures with some frequency often find this task particularly difficult; they must use a more manual and interpretive approach.

Organization Design

Those responsible for organization design often use organization charts as a base. In these charts, each manager or individual appears in a box, connected by lines to superiors and subordinates. Organization charting programs are

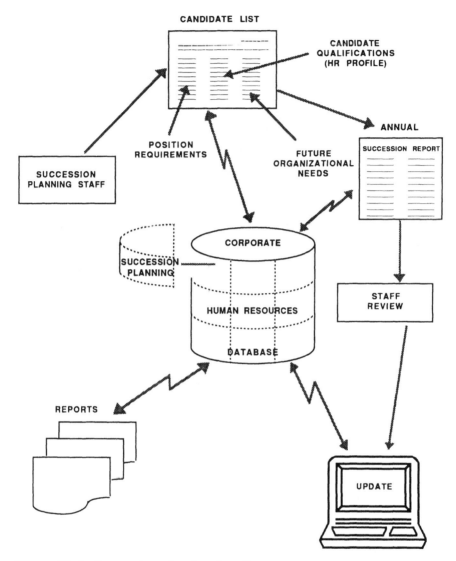

Figure 18–6. Succession planning data flow.
(Source: Andrew O. Manzini and John D. Gridley, *Integrating Human Resources and Strategic Business Planning*, AMACOM, 1986. Reprinted with permission.)

CODE

11   Outstanding performer ready now for promotion (2-3 grades).

12   Outstanding performer capable of promotion with 1-3 years additional experience or training.

13   Outstanding performer who will probably stay in present assignment more than 3 years.

21   Superior performer ready now for promotion (2-3 grades).

22   Superior performer capable of promotion with 1-3 years additional experience or training.

23   Superior performer who will probably stay in present assignment more than 3 years.

31   Good performer ready now for promotion (2-3 grades).

32   Good performer capable of promotion with 1-3 years additional experience or training.

33   Good performer who will probably stay in present assignment more than 3 years.

44   Individual should be reassigned.

Figure 18–7. Promotability index. In some firms, succession planners may assign a promotability code to each employee included in the succession plan. In the two-digit code index shown, the first digit indicates whether performance is outstanding (1), superior (2), or good (3). The second digit indicates readiness for promotion: now (1), within one to three years (2), or longer than three years (3).

basically specialized graphics software. Although most programs use boxes and lines, some use an indented structure to list individuals in tabular form. Such programs create organization charts from data already in employee master files, such as title, supervisor, responsibilities, and division. Simple programs require manual entry of such information, while more sophisticated programs can accept it from the master file if it is compatible with the HRMS.

Reporting Requirements

Reports by human resources planning usually go to three major destinations. Their use depends not only on their subject matter but also on the arrangement, culture, and politics of the organization itself. These major audiences are executive management, human resources management, and managers of other human resources functions (particularly EEO/AA, employment, and training).

Most computer-generated planning reports are in table or graphic form. When a manager or other decision maker receives a report from human resources planning, that report includes the tables used to generate the requested forecast data. The first set of tables may show starting population for the entire organization or by division, department, or other subgroup. Other tables provide historical data for the variables in each cell of the employee population. These variables may include exit rates, percentage of college graduates, trainee retention rates, and so forth.

These matrices provide background data, but not all recipients of planning and forecasting reports look at this information. They focus on the portion of the report that gives the results of the model and computations. This matrix may compare the starting array of employees or positions with subsequent arrangements, status, or quantities at various future points in time. The following discussion of planning reports concentrates on the results or interpretation portion of such reports. It assumes that each report also may include model matrices or cross-tabulations.

Human Resources Planning Reports

More than any other HRMS activity, human resources planning needs to produce an unpredictable and seemingly endless variety of reports. As with some other modules, these reports may cover a specific population or all employees, retirees, or other members of the human resources universe. They also may subdivide employee groups according to various criteria, such as gender, race/ethnicity, pay grade or level, training status, or time in position. Reports should have sufficient flexibility to address virtually any human resources issue and to report on past, present, or future trends and patterns.

To the extent that the training and development function concentrates on training rather than on analyzing data and employment concentrates on recruiting and hiring rather than on analyzing data, human resources planning is more likely to create historical reports and forecasts in support of these functions. Human resources planning usually needs this background as a basis for its own forecasts anyway.

The format of human resources planning reports may vary somewhat depending on whether the function uses primarily demand or supply forecasting. Some reports combine both views. Depending on the computer modeling approach selected, planning reports may be Markov chains, cohort analyses, or in some other format.

Demand Forecasts. A typical demand forecast report predicts the number of employees the organization will need. The report may list number of employees by job classification, job grade, department, division, or other variable. It gives the net number of openings predicted or net requirements for staff on the basis of one or more of the causes of work force demand, such as transfers, promotions, and voluntary terminations. For external recruitment, human resources planning may produce a position openings forecast listing the level of recruitment and hiring activity required to respond to the work force demand.

As a measure of internal demand, human resources planning may produce a promotion patterns report. This report shows promotion patterns among various positions. On this basis, planners can then predict the future demand in positions vacated through promotions, as well as the supply of qualified individuals in feeder positions. Planning also can create a promotions forecast, examining the results of changes in certain variables, such as compensation, training, or turnover rate.

Employee turnover is one cause of human resources demand. A turnover analysis report categorizes employee departures according to factors such as division, job grade, gender, race/ethnicity, age, location, reasons for leaving, or specific skills or experience. As a demand forecasting tool, this report allows human resources planning to predict the number and types of replacements required, assuming that total requirements remain constant.

Demand forecasting allows decision makers to evaluate specific plans for reducing unwanted turnover. For instance, human resources planning may compare exit rates for employees of comparable skill levels but in different job classifications. If planners identify a variance, management can develop corrective plans, such as training, job rotation, or supervisory changes. Human resources planning then estimates the projected improvement in exit rate and produces a report that forecasts the number of exiting employees under the new plan. With reduced turnover, the organization will need to hire fewer new employees; thus, the resulting lowered recruitment and orientation costs will justify the investment in the remedial programs themselves.

Supply Forecasts. Supply forecasts usually predict the number of qualified employees available to fill particular positions, jobs, job families, or other training and development programs. From those figures, planners can extract the number of similarly qualified applicants that the organization will need. A training status report presents the number of employees expected to have a certain level of training experience at particular points in the future. A length of service report presents the number of employees by length of service or seniority. This report often appears as a series of graphs, each showing a different point in time, such as the present, one year ago, and one year in the future.

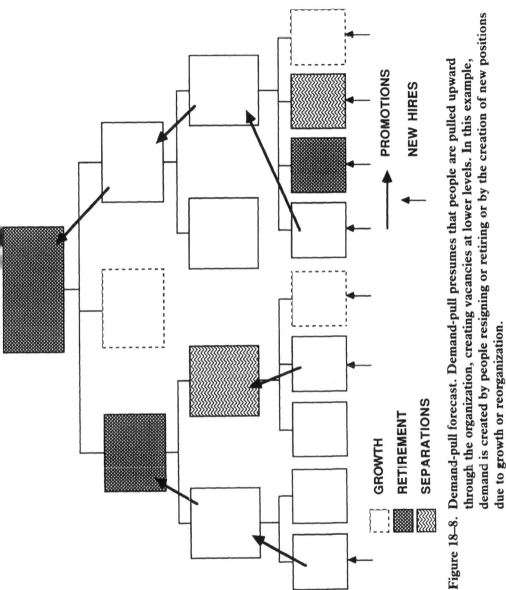

GROWTH
RETIREMENT
SEPARATIONS

PROMOTIONS

NEW HIRES

Figure 18–8. Demand-pull forecast. Demand-pull presumes that people are pulled upward through the organization, creating vacancies at lower levels. In this example, demand is created by people resigning or retiring or by the creation of new positions due to growth or reorganization.

More complex supply forecasts analyze the effects of potential human resources activities on the supply of qualified employees. For instance, an employee retention report may present several alternative retention scenarios based on human resources and management plans to increase employee retention rates. Depending on the specifics of these proposals, each scenario may use different values for factors such as salaries, wages, training availability, and benefit options. The resulting supply in each scenario illustrates the likely effects of these plans on employee retention rates.

Demand/Supply Comparisons. Sometimes human resources planners compare the expected demand for certain types of employees with the expected supply. The report lists the number of employees human resources planning predicts the organization or unit will need and the number available at points in the future. Planners refer to the difference between these supply and demand figures as the variance. This variance identifies the issues human resources and management must address to keep the organization productive and employees satisfied. Demand/supply forecasts might identify issues such as the following:

- Job classifications or management positions that may experience a surplus or shortage
- Recruitment activity needed (additions and replacements to staff)
- Training and development programs needed (new or transferred employees)

Some human resources planning departments use demand and supply forecasts that concentrate on the employees who come and go. This type of report, known as an intake and outflow report, lists the numbers of new and departed employees. *Intake* occurs as the result of hiring, rehiring, returns from leave, transfers from other units, and other sources. *Outflow* marks the exit of employees due to various types of voluntary and involuntary terminations, transfers, and leaves. Specific organization and planning projects may track special types of intake and outflow, such as entry from training programs or exit due to layoffs.

Planning often creates historical reports on this subject because no other human resources function takes responsibility for all these data. To this extent, intake and outflow reports are planning tools rather than forecasting tools. This is an important distinction because such reports sometimes indicate a situation that management anticipates will change or believes will improve by itself. Planning may then use this report as a forecasting tool, estimating future intake and outflow based on estimates of changes in certain factors, such as aging of work force, shifts in compensation practices, or altered retirement policies.

Planning Evaluation Reports. The human resources planning function sometimes prepares reports that compare previous forecasts with actual values. One of these reports might compare the projected number of turnovers in a particular year with the number of turnovers that actually took place that year. These comparisons may involve time-series analysis, a series of observations taken at different points in time. They also may identify other intervening factors, such as natural disasters, regulatory changes, and unexpected shifts in management or executive control.

Planning may use these results, if favorable, as a self-promotion tool to show the effect and accuracy of planning. Many plans do not remain viable, however, and planners do not remain with the organization for more than a few years, so results often do not compare readily with forecasts of several years earlier.

Succession Planning Reports

Human resources planning or training and development usually prepares a package of reports for management's use in developing succession plans. Some of the most common reports are discussed here.

Succession Planning Positions Report. For each position under consideration for succession planning, this report generally lists job title, grade, location, supervisor, current job incumbent, and scheduled retirement date. It also may list succession planning status (potential, in process, suspended, or complete) and personal characteristics. Management staff may use this report to finalize choices of positions to include in succession planning, or they may use it to track the succession planning process.

Qualifications and Capabilities Report. Human resources planning must determine the necessary or desirable preparation for each job having a succession plan. To do so, planners may produce reports that synopsize the career development histories of individuals who have held that position. For each individual, this report may list educational background, external job experience, jobs held within the organization, skill levels, and training courses.

Another form of this report lists certain types of qualifications and identifies their frequency among past position occupants. For instance, the report might show that five of the last six people to hold the position of sales manager had an MBA, two also had engineering degrees, and two had served in marketing departments earlier in their careers. This information helps planners

578

NAME: Barbie Laws

RATING GROUP: District Managers

SIZE OF GROUP: 115

RATING DATE: 2/1/89

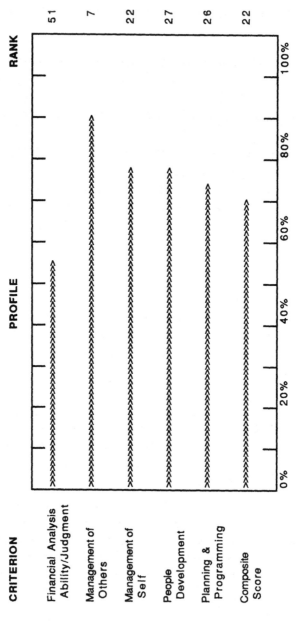

Figure 18–9. Management skills profile. For each person under consideration for a particular portion of the succession plan, staff may provide a profile to show that individual's standing within the group of candidates. Management often can interpert graphic presentations such as this more effectively than they can interpert a table of numbers.

decide which qualifications and capabilities potential candidates should have. Sometimes this report includes information on candidates' career goals and aspirations expressed as interest in specific positions.

Candidates Report. A summary report may list potential successors to a position. To prepare this list automatically, the system must have the capacity to request and sort on multiple attributes, such as job classification, salary, service, and skills. A more detailed report on each candidate may include employee name and other basic employee information, such as job title, location, supervisor, performance history, and promotability indexes.

With this information, the planning or training function can determine the additional career development or training that these individuals require to be ready to fill the positions for which succession is being planned. In turn, training and development may produce an individual career development report for each candidate.

Succession Planning Chart. Succession planning reports often involve a significant amount of graphics. Planners often use charts to show the effects of various succession options. These charts help management understand the ramifications of such options. For instance, one chart might show that if the CEO leaves, the vice president of marketing becomes CEO, the sales manager becomes vice president of marketing, and the head of public relations becomes sales manager. Another chart might still show the vice president of marketing becoming CEO but an executive recruited externally becoming the new vice president of sales and all other positions remaining unchanged.

Organization Reports

Organization reports may come in either chart or book form. Most programs include a variety of graphic designs for the charts; some allow users to create custom designs. A complete organization chart is frequently a series of charts, each showing a portion of the organization (for example, each unit or department) with a separate box for each individual. Solid lines, dotted lines, arrows, and other symbols indicate the relationship among these employees. Each box may note just employee name and job title, or it may contain more data, such as job grade, location, or internal telephone number.

Most organization charting programs can create book-style charts. This report usually uses indenting structures to indicate supervisory and reporting relationships. The name of each manager is followed by those whom that manager supervises; each of those names is indented several spaces. If any of these individuals has subordinates, those people are indented even further under the name of the person to whom they report.

TITANIC WIDGET COMPANY
SUCCESSION PLAN

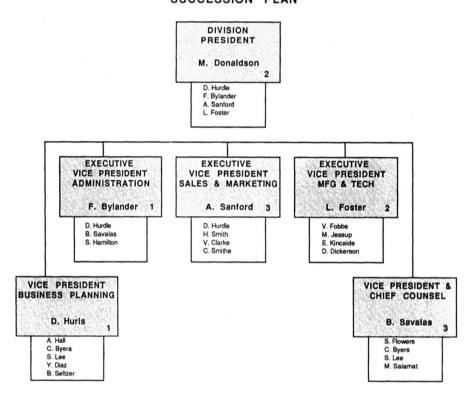

1 = Ready Now
2 = 1-2 Years
3 = 3-5 Years
4 = > 5 Years

Figure 18–10. Typical succession planning chart. Each major box in the succession planning chart lists a position, an incumbent, and a promotability index for the incumbent. The chart also lists possible successors for that position.
(Source: Criterion, Inc. Reprinted with permission)

Glossary

Cohort analysis A type of human resources model that tracks losses and changes among a group of employees whom the organization hired at approximately the same time.

Demand forecasting An organization's total requirements for staff regardless of where they come form. This forecasting approach addresses issues in which the movement of employees is driven primarily by promotions, transfers, and terminations.

Demand-pull model In a demand-pull model, human resources flow upward to satisfy vacancies at the highest levels. Intake includes required staff levels, entry flows, and exit flows. Outflow refers to promotion flow within job groups and to the number of employees who will remain in their present positions for the relevant time period.

Exit rate The rate at which employees leave a particular group. This group may be the organization itself or a particular position, job, job grade, or unit. Employees may move elsewhere in the organization or leave altogether.

Human resources planning The process of determining an organization's human resources needs using forecasting and statistical analysis techniques and preparing scenarios to meet those needs.

Markov chain A form of renewal model that tracks the flow of employees from one time period to the next. Presumes a reasonably stable work force.

Matrix In human resources planning, a form of report that arrays data in rows and columns. These data can be combined along these rows and columns to form sums or products. A matrix report allows display of a large volume of information on a single page or screen.

Model A mathematical, logical, graphic, or written representation of a real-life or hypothetical situation. A computer model allows users to manipulate variables to assess potential changes.

Modeling The manipulation of current data and variables to simulate possible future situations.

Network model A type of human resources planning model that resembles a Markov chain but works with individual rather than group career path projections, including the effects of various inflow and outflow factors.

Planning horizon The length of time to which a plan or forecast applies. These horizons usually run one to five years.

Renewal model A type of human resources planning model that traces job groups through a model that assumes a demand-pull environment and predictable career paths.

Replacement planning The process of determining the types and number of individuals required to fill positions that become vacant during the planning period because of terminations or other unplanned actions.

Succession planning A formal program to identify and prepare qualified successors to assume high-level positions vacated because of promotion, transfer, or scheduled retirement.

Supply forecasting A forecasting approach that addresses issues of availability and flow of qualified individuals. Human resources planning may use this information to develop plans for retaining and motivating staff when the supply of available individuals exceeds the number of appropriate positions for promotion and transfer.

Supply-push model A supply-push model assumes a constant flow of human resources over time. As inventories grow, the flow increases proportionately. Intake includes population levels for promotions, entry, and exit at a certain time. Outflow includes predictions of future human resources inventories for each job at future dates.

Variance In human resources planning, the difference between the number of employees an organization will need and the number that will be available.

Discussion Points

1. How can various human resources functions best use human resources planning to support their activities? Consider employment, EEO, training, compensation, benefits, and safety.

2. Describe various economic, social, regulatory, and political issues that apply to human resources planning. Describe how they may influence human resources planning needs.

3. Describe various types of models used in human resources planning and forecasting. Which ones apply to supply situations and which to demand situations? Why?

4. Which steps in human resources planning involve little or no computer work? What skills do they involve instead?

5. What kinds of steps can human resources planners take to maximize the accuracy of predictions?

6. In what ways has the increased use of computers in human resources planning changed the ways in which managers use forecasting?

7. Under what circumstances might human resources planning need historical data from the HRMS? What historical data might they want?

8. How could a computer system aid human resources planning in selecting target positions to include in succession planning?

Further Reading

Baird, L., and I. Meshoulam. "The HRS Matrix: Managing the Human Resource Function Strategically." *Human Resource Planning*, 1984.

Barocci, T.A., and P. Cournover. "Analyzing Human Resource Flows: Uses and Limitations of the Markov Model." In *Human Resource Management and Industrial Relations*, edited by T.A. Kochan, and T.A. Barocci. Boston: Little, Brown, 1985.

Beal, Richard, Austin Bendall, and Mike Smith. "A Computer-Based Personnel Development System." In *Computers in Personnel: Towards the Personnel Office of the Future*, edited by Terry Page. Sussex: Institute of Personnel Management & Institute of Manpower Studies, 1983.

Bright, W.E. "How One Company Manages Its Human Resources." *Harvard Business Review*, January/February 1976.

Burack, E.H. *Creative Human Resource Planning and Applications: A Strategic Approach*. Englewood Cliffs, NJ: Prentice-Hall, 1980.

Burack, E.H., and N.J. Mathys. *Human Resource Management: A Pragmatic Approach to Staffing and Development*. Lake Forest, IL: Brace-Park Press, 1980.

Camillus, J.C., and A.L. Lederer. "Corporate Strategy and the Design of Computerized Information Systems." *Sloan Management Review*, Spring 1985.

Ceriello, Vincent R., and Richard B. Frantzreb. "A Human Resource Planning Model." *Human Factors*, February 1975.

Clark, Harry L., and Donna R. Thurston. *Planning Your Staffing Needs: A Handbook for Personnel Workers*, Washington, DC: U.S. Civil Service Commission, Bureau of Policies and Standards, 1977.

Director, Steven, *Strategic Planning for Human Resources*, Oxford: Pergamon, 1985.

Dyer, L. "Linking Human Resource and Business Strategies." *Human Resource Planning*, 7 (2), 1984.

———. "Strategic Human Resources Management and Planning." In *Research in Personnel and Human Resources Management*, edited by Kendrith M. Rowland and Gerald R. Ferris. Greenwich, CT: Jai Press, 1985.

Feuer, Michael J., Richard J. Niehaus, and James A. Sheridan. "Human Resource Planning: A Survey of Practice and Potential." *Human Resource Planning*, Summer 1984.

Flamholtz, Eric G. *Human Resource Accounting: Advances in Concepts, Methods, and Applications*. San Francisco: Jossey-Bass, 1985.

Flamholtz, Eric G., and R.A. Kaumeyer, Jr. "Human Resource Placement Cost Information and Personnel Decisions: A Field Study." *Human Resource Planning*, 1980.

Frantzreb, Richard B. "Human Resource Planning: Forecasting Manpower Needs." *Personnel Journal*, January 1981.

———. *The Human Resource Planner's Yearbook*, Roseville, CA: Advanced Personnel Systems, 1984.

Glueck, William F. *Business Policy: Strategy Information and Management Action*, New York: McGraw-Hill, 1976.

Gridley, John D. "Who Will Be Where When? Forecasting the Easy Way." *Personnel*, May 1986.

Grinold, R.C., and K.T. Marshall. *Manpower Planning Models*, New York: North-Holland, 1977.

Grosskopf, Theodore E., Jr. "Human Resource Planning Under Adversity." *Human Resource Planning*, Spring 1978.

Haire, Mason. "Approach to an Integrated Personnel Policy." *Industrial Relations*, February 1967.

Heiken, B.E., J.W. Randell, and R.N. Lear. "The Strategic Implications of HR Planning." *Computers in Personnel*, Winter 1987.

Horsfield, Debra. "Succession and Management Development Planning: The Organization Metrics Succession Planning System." *Computers in Personnel*, Fall 1986.

―――. "The Labor of Supply and Demand." *Computers in Personnel*, Fall 1987.

Jennings, Eugene E. *The Mobile Manager: A Study of the New Generation of Top Executives*, Ann Arbor, MI: Bureau of Industrial Relations, 1967.

Kazanas, H.C. *Strategic Human Resources Planning and Management.* Englewood Cliffs, NJ: Prentice-Hall, 1988.

Kiddoo, K.R. "Redeploying Professional and Technical Workers." *Industrial Relations*, March/April 1977.

Kochan, T.A., and T. Barcocci. *Human Resource Management and Industrial Relations.* Boston: Little, Brown, 1985.

Lee, A.S. "What Human Resource Planning and the Research on OR/MS/MIS Can Learn from Each Other." *Human Resource Planning*, 1986.

Malloch, H. "Manpower Modeling With Computer Spreadsheets." *Personnel Management*, May 1986.

Manzini, Andrew O. "Human Resource Planning and Forecasting." In *Human Resources Management and Development Handbook*, edited by William R. Tracey. New York: AMACOM, 1984.

―――. "Human Resource Planning: Observations on the State of the Art and The State of the Practice." *Human Resource Planning*, 7 (2) 1984.

Mayhem, Leslie, "Manpower Profiling." In *Computers in Personnel: Business and Technology - Achieving Practical Solutions*, edited by Terry Page. Sussex: Institute of Personnel Management & Institute of Manpower Studies, 1987.

Milkovich, G.M., and T.A. Mahoney, "Human Resources Planning and Policy." In *Handbook for Personnel Administration and Industrial Relations*, edited by Yoder and Heneman. Washington, DC: Bureau of National Affairs, 1979.

Morrissey, C.A. "Long-Range Planning in Personnel: Impact of the Computer." *Personnel Administrator*, March 1968.

Niehaus, Richard J. *Computer Assisted Human Resource Planning.* New York: John Wiley & Sons, 1979.

―――. *Strategic Human Resource Planning Applications.* New York: Plenum Press, 1987.

Patten, Thomas H. *Manpower Planning and Development of Human Resources.* New York: John Wiley & Sons, 1971.

Reid, D.M. "Human Resource Planning: A Tool for Development." *Personnel*, 54, 1977.

Rowland, Kendrith M., and Michael G. Sovereign. "Markov-Chain Analysis of Internal Manpower Supply." *Industrial Relations*, October 1969.

Rudary, Robert F., and J. Garrett Ralls, Jr. "Manpower Planning for Reduction in Force." *University of Michigan Business Review*, November 1978.

Russ, C.F., Jr. "Manpower Planning Systems: Part II." *Personnel Journal*, 1982.

Schein, Edgar H. *Human Resource Planning and Development: A Total System*. Boston: MIT, Sloan School of Management, 1978.

Smith, R.D. "Information Systems for More Effective Use of Executive Resources." *Infosystems*, April 1978.

Tichy, N.M. *Managing Strategic Change: Technical, Political and Cultural Dynamics*. New York: John Wiley & Sons, 1983.

Traum, Richard. "Reducing Headcount through Attrition and/or Terminations." *Personnel*, January/February 1975.

Vroom, Victor H., and Kenneth MacCrimmon. "Towards a Stochastic Model of Managerial Careers." *Administrative Science Quarterly*, June 1968.

Walker, Alfred J., and Thomas P. Bechet. "Management Succession Planning: Just in Time?" *HRSP Review*, First Quarter 1987.

Walker, James W. *Human Resource Planning*, New York: McGraw-Hill, 1980.

Wegner, Trevor, "A Microcomputer-Based Decision Support System for Manpower Planning." *Managerial and Decision Economics*, June 1986.

19
Occupational Health and Safety

Salus populi suprema lex ("The people's safety is the highest law").
—Anonymous

Every employer has the legal responsibility to provide a safe, secure workplace; it is also good business. The human resources department generally maintains an occupational health and safety function to promote these goals. Its activities traditionally have focused on monitoring and ensuring compliance with laws and regulations pertaining to workplace safety. In recent years, many firms have broadened this function to include oversight of any potential health hazard in the workplace. The health and safety function also may handle such diverse issues as industrial hygiene, health physics, toxic substance exposure, ergonomics, and human factors engineering.

Occupational Health and Safety in an HRMS

The specific role of safety (as this function is usually called) depends primarily on the type of business or service the organization provides. The safety concerns of manufacturers differ greatly from those of insurance firms, which differ greatly from those of universities. The development of safety as an HRMS function usually reflects those differences in organizational perspective.

Role of the Safety Function

Safety originally operated as a visual system, looking for problems such as slippery floors, blocked emergency exits, leaking gas lines, and open file cabinets. In those days, the safety function might not have taken action to correct problems but simply written up incident reports for line management to handle.

With the increased use of hazardous materials in the workplace, the awareness of the toxic potential of such materials, the promulgation of a diverse body of safety laws, and an increasingly litigious society, many firms now accord the safety function a more prominent and active role. Safety often has not only

Figure 19–1. **Principal roles of the occupational health and safety function.**

a monitoring function but also a proactive role. Its responsibilities include the following:

- Monitoring workplace safety
- Complying with federal and state regulations
- Tracking employee health
- Handling worker complaints about health and safety issues
- Updating programs for regulatory changes
- Providing documentation in legal actions involving Occupational Safety and Health Administration (OSHA) issues
- Administering workers' compensation programs
- Orienting new employees about work-related safety and health issues
- Promoting safety and health, mostly in work-related issues but also in terms of general employee wellness
- Facilitating or requiring hazard-related health screenings and certification of appropriate employees
- Overseeing medical surveillance programs
- Providing some medical services on-site, perhaps a first-aid station, nurse, doctor, or field infirmary

Evolution of Safety in the HRMS

Historically, some human resources departments deemed other issues to be more important than safety. Among these were cost containment of compensation and benefits, EEO/AA, COBRA, retirement benefits administration, and strategic planning. The Occupational Safety and Health Act of 1970 established a federal agency (OSHA) to oversee worker safety. OSHA places three major requirements on employers:

1. Meet safety standards set by OSHA.
2. Submit to OSHA inspections.
3. Keep records and make reports on occupational injuries and illnesses.

In response to the monitoring and reporting aspects of these requirements, many organizations have become interested in computerized safety applications. The growing number and cost of lawsuits in this area have increased management's inclination to invest in computer systems that can provide information to prevent or mitigate problems. Moreover, public and business awareness of the significant potential for exposure to hazardous materials in workplace environments that previously were considered low risk has grown considerably.

In the broadest sense, the internal health and safety function manages a variety of physical, chemical, radiological, and biological hazards. The industrial hygiene function identifies, evaluates, and recommends corrective actions for hazards in the workplace. A health physicist is sometimes employed to manage risks in areas of potential radiological hazard. In this book, all these areas are referred to simply as safety. The information system that monitors this function may operate as a module within the HRMS or as a stand-alone application limited to safety-related data. Safety software purchased from vendors different from those providing the rest of the HRMS may be difficult to integrate. In such cases, HRMS developers may need to develop interfaces to the main system or elect to maintain a separate system.

In fact, the safety function itself sometimes is not a part of human resources. The more complex the organization's safety issues, the greater the possibility of serious risk to employees, and the greater the potential cost to the organization, the more likely it is that the safety function will be outside human resources. Safety sometimes reports to human resources only nominally. It may stand alone or report to legal services, public safety, administrative services, or risk management.

Many safety applications have limited scope. Some departments satisfy their needs by adding a few data fields to the existing HRMS to allow safety staff to track incidents of work-related illness and injury. Many human resources system vendors have concentrated on employee-related data rather than data about facilities and the work characteristics of positions. Most vendor software focuses on the capability to record incidents. These programs can produce reports and logs that fulfill the basic administrative requirements associated with government regulations.

Taking Responsibility
for Facility Safety

Many of the responsibilities of the health and safety function relate directly to employees. Among these are incident reporting, first aid, employee medical testing, and employee safety record keeping. In a diverse, potentially hazardous environment, the safety function handles numerous additional tasks that pertain more specifically to facilities and materials. These include the following:

- Facilities audits
- Accident investigation and analysis
- Waste disposal programs
- Potential-hazard communication programs
- Material safety data sheets (MSDS)
- Polychlorinated biphenyls (PCBs) abatement
- Asbestos abatement
- Environmental monitoring (for exposure to regulated substances)
- Pollution control engineering
- Clean Air Act programs
- Emergency response to hazardous-materials spills
- Government liaison and reporting

Few software programs include monitoring or analytical functions designed to help reduce the number and severity of safety incidents. A thorough safety information system tracks and monitors data on employee demographics, incidents of injury and illness, workplace hazards, and health and safety promotion activities. The system also provides a basis for evaluation of safety activities by generating data that safety staff and management can analyze. Only a few vendors offer comprehensive safety software. Some have begun offering programs that monitor hazardous materials exposure. Others offer special software for certain high-risk industries, such as automobile manufacturing, pharmaceuticals, chemicals, and heavy construction. A few vendors offer applications geared specifically to workers' compensation. Most organizations, however, consider themselves so specialized that they generally customize a system.

Commercial Hazardous-Materials Data Bases. Several institutions offer comprehensive computer data bases of hazardous materials. Such a data base is referred to as a hazardous material inventory (HMI). A thorough HMI for a manufacturer or other relatively high-risk facility requires so much data that organizations almost universally subscribe to an external service rather than constructing their own data base. Organizations often use these data bases on a dial-up basis, receiving information and updates as needed. Scientists are developing new materials and chemicals almost daily, so vendors must update their data bases frequently to maintain accuracy and completeness. Having imported the data base, an organization may add information about materials it uses that the data base does not list or remove chemicals to which it does not need access.

HMIs may apply not only to safety but also to environmental engineering, materials control, and other line operations. In many cases, organizations find advantages in having all such functions use the same data base. HMI purchasers should keep in mind, however, that data about a chemical and its properties may not necessarily provide information about its toxic effects on humans. Material safety data sheets (MSDS) provide comprehensive information and are generated (as required by law) by the manufacturer of such materials. Data bases for MSDS are available externally, may be designed in-house, or may be custom designed.

Vendors have encountered problems in making hazardous-materials applications commercially viable. Because the number of possible materials is so large, no firm can use the complete listing. But subscribing firms want comprehensive information on the specific substances relevant to their own circumstances, so vendors must prepare large amounts of information for which few clients are willing to pay. Moreover, most departments consider this information ancillary to their most important goals. Only about 10 percent of HRMS include a good safety module, and fewer include a hazardous-materials data base.

Building a Safety Module. Human resources departments find safety modules among the most difficult to implement for several reasons. First, each workplace has special safety characteristics because of its activity, size, context, and location, so each requires customization. Second, a safety module often must integrate numerous disparate components. A well-developed safety module must interface with the HRMS yet also maintain other data that are completely independent of individual employee records, such as hazardous-materials characteristics and workplace conditions.

To establish a safety module, the project team needs to work with experts. Management should look for vendors that are able and willing to interpret safety regulations. These vendors should know not only their systems but also the special requirements of health and safety laws. The users provide the necessary information about the specific data needs of the organization. Based on this, the vendor develops the general framework for the safety module, including customized file formats, screens, and tables.

Advantages and Limitations of Computerization in Health and Safety

In spite of the difficulty of computerizing safety, departments that do undertake this process enjoy several advantages:

- Automatic conversion of employee health data and workplace injury data into logs and other reports that meet OSHA and other government regulations
- Easy, consistent, and complete tracking of health and safety incidents
- Automatic flagging of statistically significant occurrences, to minimize health problems, lost work time, and cost to the organization.

Fitness Systems

Some organizations take the "health" part of health and safety very seriously. The employee health function may offer fitness classes, a running track, a PAR course, a fitness center, aerobics, and a fully-equipped gym. As a special benefit, some organizations provide executives with fitness monitoring, including diagnostic and prescriptive recommendations. As part of such programs, some health and safety functions now use fitness-oriented software.

In some cases, a stand-alone minicomputer or microcomputer helps monitor and maintain employee health and wellness. Data from the fitness system usually does not get transferred to the safety computer system. Employees often access such a system at the fitness site itself, using a plastic card (like a credit card) or password. Upon query, the system prints out current health statistics for the individual. This may include height, weight, blood pressure, resting heart rate, and working heart rate. Either health and safety staff, fitness trainers, or the employee input and maintain this information. On some systems, if the user provides information on exercise activities—miles jogged, laps swum, or sets of tennis played—the system calculates the number of kilocalories burned since the last visit.

- Easier monitoring of patterns in work-related injuries and illnesses, to calculate the significance of location, demographics, experience, and other factors.
- A basis for expediting medical and workers' compensation claims

As with every other human resources function, computerization only minimally affects many of safety's important employee-oriented responsibilities. The computer does not significantly affect the surveillance of work activities, although it may issue reminders about inspections and corrections required. Health promotion remains primarily a psychological and interactive process that relies on the knowledge and skills of safety staff and for the most part is unaffected by the automation process.

Data Requirements and Sources

Safety systems often require a comprehensive set of data bases. The system may include data bases for individual employees, job classification tables, location tables, hazardous materials, safety training, and safety equipment. One such arrangement is diagrammed in the accompanying figure and described in the following material. This represents an ideal system, one that would work for an organization with extensive requirements. Most organizations have limited versions of such data bases, reflecting the lower priority accorded the safety function.

Although safety gets data from the individual employee files in the main HRMS, it provides little data for those records and may add only a few codes to tables maintained by other human resources functions. Conversely, those functions tend to need safety data on individual employees only if they need a volume of information that warrants query of the safety module directly.

Employee Status

Safety normally maintains employee records only on people whom it has a specific need to track, although under certain circumstances, the safety system also needs to keep records on applicants, retirees, and terminees. Maintaining safety records for all employees is usually a waste of computer capacity. If only 20 percent of employees ever have work-related injuries or illnesses, the system would maintain 80 percent of its safety records for no reason. If the percentage of employees included approached 50 percent, maintaining minimal records on the entire employee population might be cost-effective.

The individual employee's safety record includes several parts: demographics, job status, health information, known limitations, disabilities, and incident records.

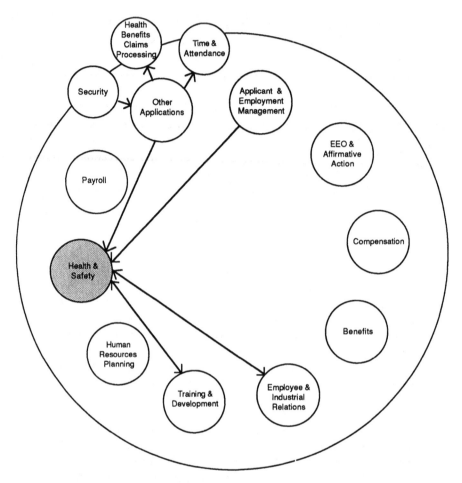

**Figure 19–2. Information flow between occupational health and safety
and other human resources functions.**

Demographics and Job Data. Safety may keep its own employee records, but
it usually imports much of its demographic and job data from the employee
master records in the main HRMS. These include the following:

- Demographics and personal data, including age, sex, address, emergency
  contacts, and personal health data (such as allergies, chemical sensitivities,
  and limitations)

- Job status, including job grade, job classification, location, supervisor,
  salary or wage rate, and length of service

Safety may query the HRMS for data on people who have been involved in reportable incidents or who require other safety monitoring, such as testing. Safety asks for information even if the individual is already in the safety data base, in case changes in wages, address, work location, or other data elements have taken place. Once an employee has experienced a work-related illness or injury, the employee's safety record will build a section for historical, demographic, and job data, such as past salary or wages, work locations, supervisors, and time in position. Safety may periodically archive such data.

Health and Safety Promotion. Safety adds data about health and safety training, equipment issued, and health testing to individual employee safety files. Health and safety promotion data include the following:

- Safety equipment issued
- Credentials or training required for operating potentially dangerous machinery or handling regulated substances
- Type of medical testing or examinations required (such as vision, hearing, blood, neurological, and respiratory)
- Date of last test or examination and results
- Date of next test or examination

Safety staff often are qualified to perform some of these tests, such as visual acuity tests and audiometer readings. Some safety functions contract with audiometrists, optometrists, and other trained health specialists to perform these tests. These specialists then provide safety with the test results, which are entered into the system as appropriate.

Safety usually records data about test results using designations such as excellent, acceptable, passing, or unacceptable. Safety may input actual test results in some circumstances, particularly if it collects baseline data and uses them to validate subsequent results. Some safety functions dedicate a separate subsystem for medical-testing data. This helps ensure the confidentiality of such data and keeps the safety module running more efficiently, since it does not need to maintain data that safety staff seldom use.

Injury and Illness Incident Information

The Occupational Safety and Health Administration (OSHA), an agency within the U.S. Department of Labor, oversees workplace safety in the United States. Most other countries have similar agencies. Many states and provinces have agencies that impose additional regulatory and reporting requirements. OSHA mandates that employers maintain a log of work-related injuries and illnesses. Its regulations define which events the log must track. These are known as reportable incidents. OSHA also dictates specific data that the log must include for each incident. Union agreements may mandate additional reporting requirements. For good business, most companies collect more than the minimum requirements. Safety collects and monitors data on each incident of occupational injury or illness. The system usually records these data in the file of the affected employee.

Each work unit or location usually has a particular safety staff member who handles cases in that area. Based on a request from an employee, supervisor, or medical representative, the safety professional performs direct observation and interviews as required to collect data on each incident. Interviews may include the employee, supervisor, coworkers, and medical staff. The safety representative may log the incident on paper or via a hand-held calculator, then transfer the data to the safety module at a later date. Safety usually cannot make direct observation of vehicle accidents but instead gets data from police reports and from a report by the vehicle operator.

When the user wants to start a file on a new incident, the safety module assigns that incident a unique case number. The user must identify the affected individual. The system opens that employee's safety file, then creates a new set of incident data fields. These data fields prompt for the following:

- Date of injury or date illness was diagnosed
- Time of injury
- Location of injury or exposure
- Type of injury or illness
- Active agent for injury or illness (such as hand tools, vehicle, or ladder)
- Nature of injury or part of body that sustained damage
- License or certificate number
- Weather conditions (coded)
- Time of day
- Day of week (coded)
- Location code
- Date of report
- Person preparing report

This record also may list management's analysis of whether or not the injury was work related, as well as the name and address of the physician and hospital.

Time Lost Due to Illness and Injury

Safety also estimates the costs of time lost to injury or illness. Workers' compensation administrators need such information in order to calculate payments

CODE	HANDICAP CODES
100	Blindness, Both Eyes
110	Blind, Both, <20/200
120	Blind, One <20/200
130	Blindness, One Eye
199	Visual Impairment
200	Deafness, No Speech
210	Deafness, Speech Okay
299	Hearing Impairment
300	Impair 3 or 4 Limbs
310	Impair Multiple Limb
320	Impair of Upper Limb
330	Impair of Lower Limb
399	Limb Impairment, Other
400	Loss Multiple Limbs
410	Loss of Both Upper
420	Loss of One Upper
430	Loss of Lower Extremities
499	Loss Body Parts, Other
500	Psychotic Disorders
510	Psychoneurotic Disorders

CODE	DISABILITY CODES
D01	Occupational Skin Disease
D02	Dust Disease of Lung
D03	Respiratory Condition
D04	Poison-Toxic Material
D05	Disorder-Non-Toxic
D06	Disorder-Trauma
D07	Occupational Illness
H01	External-Lost Body Part
H02	External-No Lost Body Part
H03	Internal-No Lost Body Part
H04	Internal-Body Damaged
H05	Miscellaneous Injury

Figure 19–3. Typical safety codes. The safety function may use code tables such as these to indicate handicap or disabilities. It may use additional tables for causes and conditions that describe the occupational injury incident.
(Source: Cyborg Systems, Inc. Reprinted with permission.)

to affected employees. OSHA sometimes asks for such data, and safety management often use them to prioritize and promote safety promotion programs. This lost-time information usually fills additional data fields in the incident data segment of the affected employee's safety record. These fields contain time lost (hours or days), restricted time (hours or days), and expected return date.

Restricted time means hours or days during which the injury or illness limited the types of work the employee could safely perform. Sometimes safety collects these data independently, but often they import the regular timekeeping and attendance data from the HRMS, or at least use it for corroboration.

Sometimes a separate unit called risk management or workers' compensation handles such issues. This unit takes responsibility for the administrative aspects of the impact of incidents and safety-related problems on the organization. Safety is generally responsible for tracking consecutive days without an incident, time lost to incidents (by employee and work group), and types of incidents. Risk management would handle any workers' compensation obligations, costs of safety improvements, legal ramifications, remedial training, and insurance costs.

Job Hazards

A proactive safety function also maintains information about environmental conditions that could affect employee health and safety. Safety links information about safety issues to particular jobs and locations by placing codes in the job classification table, position control file, and location file. Via the codes for job classification, position, and location, this information also links to each employee's safety record.

Job Classification and Position Tables. Some safety risks and requirements are associated with particular jobs or positions. To identify and track these factors, the safety function contributes certain information to the job classification and position tables in the HRMS. This information is mainly in the form of codes linking jobs and positions to safety's own special tables of risks and requirements. When the safety module imports current information about employees, it also imports the codes for that individual's job and position. These codes include the following:

- Hazardous materials. Within the same organization, different jobs or positions often involve exposure to one or more hazardous materials. Safety lists potential exposures in the job classification or position table either by name or by code. A separate hazardous-materials table (often linked via these codes) provides information about the specific substance.

Workers' Compensation

The federal government and each state have regulations that require employers to provide workers' compensation insurance for employees under most circumstances. Workers' compensation now covers almost 90 percent of all employment. In covered cases of job-related injury or illness, workers' compensation pays all medical expenses. It also covers partial reimbursement for lost wages if the worker does not receive such payments through disability insurance.

Workers' compensation administration primarily involves processing a worker's claim, investigating the claim (often including the worker's health history), deciding whether to approve or deny coverage for that claim, handling financial and other interactions with health care providers (and attorneys), and analyzing causes and costs associated with workers' compensation. Some of these steps resemble benefits administration and claims processing, but the injuries and illnesses covered are already monitored by the safety and health function. Thus, most human resources departments handle workers' compensation within the safety and health function if business conditions, industry type, and incident volume dictate. Most data required are already part of the safety and health module in the HRMS. Workers' compensation administration adds very little data.

States vary in terms of which types of injuries and illnesses workers' compensation covers. For instance, some disallow most claims related to job-related stress, while others allow more latitude. A company operating in more than one state needs to track workers' compensation claims separately for each state in which it does business.

- Other risks. As with hazardous materials, these codes represent other types of exposures, such as high levels of noise, heat, or use of high-risk machinery. These codes link the job or position with a separate table that describes these safety risks.
- Safety equipment. These codes indicate the types of safety equipment required for the particular job or position.
- Safety training. These codes indicate the types or levels of safety training required for the particular job or position.

Safety accesses this information as needed for individual cases and for reports correlating safety incidents with other factors.

Location. The HRMS job classification or position code table usually includes a location code that links each employee's record to a location table. From this table safety staff derive information on the general site (plant or facility) and on the specific location (such as room number, shop name, laboratory, or dock). Safety itself may maintain some data fields in this table, such as the following:

- Maximum and minimum number of employees allowed
- Hazardous substances present at this location (if not coded separately)
- Other risk factors at this location, such as transportation, heat, cold, power tools, and isolation (if not coded separately)
- Locations of safety equipment (such as showers, eyewashes, fire extinguishers, and first-aid equipment)

Some of this location information does not relate directly to human resources issues but links to employee records in case of an incident. Some safety functions perform environmental testing and record test results in the location files. These tests may measure noise levels, air particulate levels, eyesight hazards, heat factors, and so forth. Safety performs these tests to comply with government regulations or union work-rule agreements. Some programs can monitor these values and automatically flag test results that exceed prescribed threshold limits.

To carry out effective monitoring, safety must identify which specific site factors contribute to or indicate the occurrence of a health problem. The 1980s brought increasing concern about workplace health issues such as the presence of asbestos, radon, polychlorinated biphenyls (PCBs), and potential radiation from video display terminals (VDTs). Other potential VDT risks include eyestrain and repetitive motion syndrome. Advocates of preventive measures to reduce potential hazards point out that preventing worker injuries is much more cost-effective than huge health care premiums, workers' compensation, and lost work time. Safety staff must keep informed about such issues and consider which circumstances may bear investigation. For each identified potential risk, a proactive safety function would then collect background information and perform periodic monitoring.

For instance, the *new building syndrome* includes problems such as headaches, dizziness, and respiratory ailments, which some people feel are associated with construction practices related to new buildings. Possible factors in the syndrome's occurrence may include choice of site, ventilation systems, and materials used in furnishing. A company with new or remodeled buildings may need to identify relevant factors in the buildings and scan occupants of them for typical symptoms.

Hazardous Materials and Other Risks

Hazardous materials seem to be everywhere in today's world—asbestos in school buildings, toxins in artists' materials, deadly viruses in health care settings, and pesticides on produce. The job or position table lists codes for potential hazards for each job or position. These codes point to listings in the hazardous substances data base, which the safety function builds and maintains (or has acquired). This data base often contains one file for each relevant hazardous material. It may list information such as the following:

- Chemical composition and properties
- Usual sources of supply
- Exposure route—topical (skin, eyes), by ingestion, or by inhalation
- Definition and effect of each exposure route on both a chronic and an acute basis
- Emergency treatment for each type of exposure (antidotes, washes, and so forth)
- Toxicity levels
- Effects on laboratory animals
- Epidemiology
- Shelf life or expiration date

The table also may list information specific to the use of that substance at this organization, such as the following:

- Date introduced to each location
- Authorized use(s) of material
- Authorized user(s) of material
- Precautions for use of material
- Date discontinued at locations

A computerized safety function may use a separate data base for substances that are not chemicals but do involve significant risk. Every manufacturing operation has its own list, but such tables may include high-speed tools, cutting tools, heavy equipment, heat-producing operations, lasers, vehicles, and other motor-driven equipment.

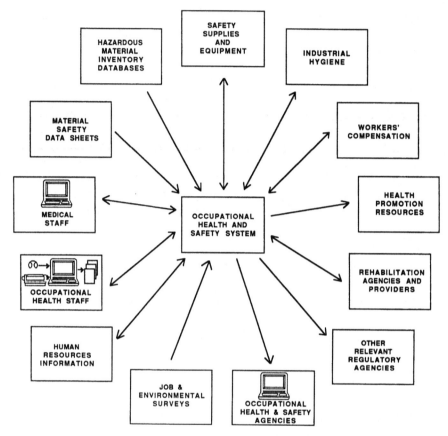

Figure 19–4. Information flow between occupational health and safety and other entities.
(Source: Telecom Australia. Reprinted with permission.)

Safety Equipment

Safety may build a safety equipment table, which links to the job classification table via the safety equipment code. This equipment table lists each type of safety apparatus required for a particular job or position. Usually each code stands for a different array of equipment rather than just a single item. Safety equipment code 0 might indicate no equipment required; code 1 might indicate hard hat required; code 2 might indicate hard hat, steel-toed shoes, and heavy gloves. By using such a table, safety can alter the equipment requirements for each job quickly and efficiently.

Reporting Requirements

The typical safety function defines its reporting needs primarily in terms of government regulatory requirements. Firms whose operations involve higher levels of health and safety risk may want additional reports prepared for internal use.

Government Reports

OSHA does not require employers to make regular filings. Rather, they must keep logs on-site that record each reportable incident of a work-related injury or illness. Occupational health and safety agencies for states, counties, and other countries may have additional reporting requirements. Human resources should ascertain these requirements before contracting for a safety module.

OSHA Form 200. This form, more formally called the Log and Summary of Occupational Injuries and Illnesses, is OSHA's main report requirement. This report contains two parts, log and summary. In the log portion, safety staff must provide information about each case of injury or illness. Cases are listed in order of case number, which usually corresponds approximately to the order in which the cases occurred. The log lists the following:

- Case number
- Date of injury of onset or illness
- Employee name
- Occupation
- Department (work unit)
- Brief description of the injury or illness
- Part(s) of body affected
- Days of work lost
- Days of restricted work
- For illnesses, type of illness (from standard table)

The summary portion of OSHA Form 200 consists of a calendar year total of several of these data elements, such as days away from work, days of restricted work, and types of illness.

Each site must maintain its own Form 200 and make it available for review by government inspectors. OSHA accepts computer-generated logs and summaries if the substitute is as detailed, easily readable, and understandable as the forms OSHA provides.

PAYROLL/PERSONNEL SYSTEM
SUMMARY REPORT
OSHA FORM 200

PAGE NO. 0001
RUN DATE 10/3/1989.

COMPANY 001
DIVISION 1000

TITANIC WIDGET
WESTERN REGION

CASE NO.	INJ/ILL DATE	EMPLOYEE NAME JOB TITLE	DEPT LOC	DESCRIPTION	INJ DAYS OFF	RST	ILL DAYS OFF	RST	OGY CD	TRANS/TERM
252	09/05/89	FISHELL, BEN E. FORK LIFT DRIVER	00100-001	SPRAINED LEFT KNEE	6.00	7.25			18	
253	09/07/89	YUSS, JEANNE WELDER	00100-001	FRACTURED BIG TOE					22	
254	09/12/89	FILLMORE, WINSTON M. INSTRUCTOR	00100-001	ALLERGY TO NITRIC ACID			2.00		02	
255	09/17/89	CANYON, BRYCE ASSEMBLER	00100-001	HEARING LOSS			1.00		06	
256	09/19/89	WILLING, ABEL N. WELDER	00100-001	INHALED POISONOUS GAS			4.50		05	
257	09/27/89	MOBILE, DONNA PARTS MAINT	00100-001	REACTION-SILICA DUST				1.25	04	
580	09/11/89	SALADE, CAESAR INSTRUCTOR	00800-005	REACTION -CHALK DUST			3.00	3.00	04	
449	09/07/89	LYMON, FRANK E. ASSEMBLER	01500-001	FRACTURED RIGHT ANKLE	8.50	7.00	8.50	7.00	22	

Figure 19–5. OSHA Form 200 summary report.

OSHA Form 101. For each work-related injury or illness, safety must prepare an OSHA Form 101, also known as Supplementary Record of Occupational Injuries and Illnesses. In addition to information about the injury or illness already contained in the OSHA Form 200 log, this report lists the following:

- Location of employee when injured/affected
- Activity of employee at time of incident
- How accident occurred
- Detailed description of injury or illness
- Part of body affected
- Agent (object or substance that caused injury)

If first-report-of-injury forms required by workers' compensation already contain all this information, OSHA accepts those reports in lieu of its own. The report should follow OSHA's format but may be submitted in computer-generated form.

Safety Reports

Reports go to safety staff, line managers, union representatives, human resources management, and, infrequently, top management, particularly if potential legal exposure exists. The content of these reports varies. Safety may include a wide variety of data depending on the reasons for the report. Such a report may cover only one site or many sites.

Individual Occupational Injury or Illness Report. This report is basically the same as OSHA Form 101, but internal reports may have additional information and a different format.

Incident Detail Report. A detail report gives some identifying information about each incident, such as employee name or case number. The report organizes these incidents according to any of a number of factors, such as type of incident, type of injury or illness, body part, location, or witness. It sometimes lists job classification of employee, length of service, time of day of incident, and other factors that safety considers potentially relevant.

Incident Summary Report. This type of report gives the number of incidents of each type according to whatever factor the user selects. For instance, a summary report may list the number of incidents in the past year occurring at each site or the number resulting in no time lost, 1 to 2 days lost, 3 to 6 days lost, or 7 or more days lost. Another report may list the number of incidents at a particular location by job classification or by employee's length of service.

OSHA NO. 101
Case or File No. _____

Form approved
OMB No. 44R 1453

Supplemental Record of Occupational Injuries and Illnesses

EMPLOYER
1. Name _____
2. Mail address _____
   (No. and street)   (City or town)   (State)
3. Location, if different from mail address _____

INJURED OR ILL EMPLOYEE
4. Name _____ Social Security No. _____
   (First name)   (Middle name)   (Last Name)
5. Home address _____
   (No. and street)   (City or town)   (State)
6. Age _____   7. Sex: Male_____ Female_____ (Check one)
8. Occupation _____
   (Enter regular job title, not the specific activity he was performing at time of injury.)
9. Department _____
   (Enter name of department or division in which the injured person is regularly employed, even though
he may have been temporarily working in another department at the time of injury.)

THE ACCIDENT OR EXPOSURE TO OCCUPATIONAL ILLNESS
10. Place of accident or exposure _____
    (No. and street)   (City or town)   (State)
    If accident or exposure occurred on employer's premises, give address of plant or establishment in which it occurred. Do not indicate department or division within the plant or establishment. If accident occurred outside employers' premises at an identifiable address, give that address. If it occurred on a public highway or at any other place which cannot be identified by number and street, please provide place references locating the place of injury as accurately as possible.
11. Was place of accident or exposure on employer's premises? _____ (Yes or No)
12. What was the employee doing when injured?_____
    (Be specific. If he was using tools or equipment or handling material,
    _____
    name them and tell what he was doing with them.)
13. How did the accident occur? _____
    (Describe fully the events which resulted in the injury or occupational illness. Tell what
    _____
    happened and how it happened. Name any objects or substances involved and tell how they were involved. Give
    _____
    full details on all factors which led or contributed to the accident. Use separate sheet for additional space.

OCCUPATIONAL INJURY OR OCCUPATIONAL ILLNESS
14. Describe the injury or illness in detail and indicate the part of the body affected. _____
    (e.g.: amputation of right index finger
    _____
    at second joint; fracture of ribs; lead poisoning; dermatitis of left hand, etc.)
15. Name the object or substance which directly injuried the employee. (For example, the machine or thing he struck or which struck him; the vapor or poison he inhaled or swallowed; the chemical or radiation which irritated his skin; or in cases of strains, hernias, etc., the thing he was lifting, pulling, etc.
16. Date of injury or initial diagnosis of occupational illness _____
    _____
17. Did employee die? _____(Yes or No)

OTHER
18. Name and address of physician _____
19. If hospitalized, name and address of hospital _____
    _____

    Date of report _____ Prepared by _____
    Official position _____

Figure 19–6. OSHA Form 101. For each occupational injury or illness, safety must record the information listed in this form. An automated function may generate computer output rather than printing the actual OSHA form.

```
 06/25/91                    Titanic Widget Company              Page   1
                             ACCIDENTS BY EMPLOYEE
                        FOR PERIOD 01/01/90 TO 12/31/90


 OCCURRED
 WC FILED                                      CASE                   DAYS   DAYS
 WC CLOSE   INJURY / BODY PARTS                NUMBER  W/C CLAIM ID    AWAY   RESTR
 ========   ============================       ======  =============   =====  =====
 Adams, Donald A      Employee No: 101 -----------------------------------------
 -------
 01/20/90                                       87  900120-1            0.0   10.0
 01/23/90   FRACTU - Fracture
    /  /    LLEG   - Lower Limbs - Leg, Right
 LOCATION:  ENTRYM - Entry - Main
    CAUSE:  Door swung shut on leg.

 01/03/90                                        3  900103-1            0.0    5.0
 01/04/90   SPRAIN - Sprained
    /  /    BSPINE - Back - Spine
 LOCATION:  STAIR1 - Stair1 - West Staircase
    CAUSE:  Lost footing on stairs

                                                                      ------  -----
                                                SUBTOTALS              0.0   15.0
```

Figure 19–7. **Typical incident report. This report contains all the information requested on OSHA Form 101 in computer-generated form.**

Incident Frequency Report. To calculate the rate of work-related injury or illness, the safety module needs population totals from the main HRMS. For instance, it may query the HRMS for the number of employees in a particular unit having zero through two years of experience, three through five years, or six or more years. The safety module then totals the number of reportable incidents affecting employees in each of those categories. By comparing the figures, safety may learn that proportionally more accidents occur to employees with zero through two years of experience but that no difference exists between three through five years and six or more years.

Individual Employee Safety and Health History. Safety sometimes needs to produce a report that details an individual's safety and health history at the firm. This may occur if the employer disputes the employee's claim for workers' compensation or disability, during grievance proceedings, or in response to employee inquiries. For each injury or illness, this report usually lists position code and title at time of injury or illness, date of injury or illness, description, amount of lost work time, and amount of restricted work time. The report also may include the results of health screenings. OSHA requires that employers keep safety and health records for at least five years. As a good business practice, most employers keep records for the employee's entire tenure with the firm or for life.

Out-of-Range Report and Exception Report. Some systems automatically flag if the number of injuries or illnesses of a particular type exceeds a certain rate or meets other predetermined criteria. Others can, on request, use incident information to look for patterns. Based on such results, the module can generate an out-of-range report or an exceptions report. Because safety staff may take on other responsibilities, they do not do this as often as they could. They often work on this only if an outside agency, union, group of workers, or other circumstances prompt an investigation.

Occupational Injury and Illness Factor Report   Sometimes the safety function looks for correlations between injuries or illnesses and other employment-related factors. These may include seniority, location, job grade, training, and performance appraisal. By identifying such correlations, safety can prepare more effective training, equipment issue, safety programs, facilities design, and procedural revisions as needed.

Occupational Injury and Illness Cost Report. Sometimes safety, line management, or union agreements require lost-time information in greater detail than addressed in OSHA Form 200. For instance, management may want to calculate salary or wage costs associated with lost and restricted time. For such purposes, the safety module may produce a report that lists work time lost

**The Cost of Employee Injury
and Illness**

The following statistics are based on studies conducted by *The Monthly Labor Review* and Medicomp of Virginia, 1987.

- On any given workday in America, 3 to 4 percent of all workers do not report to their jobs due to illness or injury.
- In 1987, 400 million workdays were lost due to illness or injury.
- Productivity lost due to illness or injury is estimated to cost American business $20 billion to $25 billion a year.
- Disabling work injuries totaled 1.8 million in 1987. Of these, about 11,000 were fatal and 70,000 resulted in some form of permanent impairment.
- Back injuries in the workplace are responsible for an estimated 20 percent of all occupational injury cases. This equals about 400,000 disabling back injuries per year.
- The average costs per back injury for workers' compensation cases in 1983 were an estimated $4,489 in wage compensation and $1,581 in medical payments.

(Source: "Employee Absences," Information Center, November 1989.)

according to specific types of injury or illness. Another report may calculate costs by multiplying lost time of each affected individual by salary or wage rate, then producing subtotals by job classification, incident type, month of occurrence, location, or other factor.

Medical Testing and Examinations. Based on an algorithm that computes due dates from date of last examination, the system can produce a report that lists all employees whose deadline for testing is coming up or is overdue. This report may list employee name, location, type of testing required, results of last testing, and due date.

Employee Communications

Test Reminders. Safety often produces health screening and test reminders for employees via a mail-merge function. Based on an algorithm that calculates next test date on the basis of last test date, the system creates files of employees who require notices. The system merges each name (and corresponding address) in these files with a notice tailored to reflect information pertinent to the specific type of test and testing status (upcoming, due date, or overdue).

Determination Report. For workers' compensation to cover health care costs and lost income due to occupational injury and illness, the employer must acknowledge or a state industrial board must determine that the injury or illness is work related. When an incident occurs, safety routes paperwork for such approval through the proper channels. Once that decision is made, safety notifies the affected employee of the settlement. A well-developed safety system can use mail-merge functions to produce both approval and denial notifications as appropriate, as well as to record the distribution of such notification.

Special Circumstances

Safety incidents involving dramatic circumstances, such as explosions, derailments, and fires, receive a lot of publicity. When a worker suffers significant injury or accuses the workplace of contributing to or causing an illness, the public and press pay attention. So do employees, unions, customers and clients, and the government. Although the safety function takes primary responsibility for monitoring and reporting health and safety issues in the workplace, many other internal and external agencies play a role in the satisfactory resolution of such issues.

First, safety should maintain an active but not overbearing presence in the workplace. Safety can collect accurate and complete data more easily if workers and line management cooperate.

Second, safety needs to maintain an ongoing liaison with other human resources functions. Safety staff may deal with these functions and the data they maintain on an ongoing or exception basis. They must interact with benefits in terms of workers' compensation, disability, and death benefits. They work with employee and industrial relations on collective bargaining and grievance proceedings. They may team with training and development on safety promotion, training programs, and certification. Outside human resources, they have contact with the legal department when lawsuits and other claims arise. To facilitate such relationships, safety must respect the data limitations and procedures governing access to and use of other systems and modules. Safety staff should consider the needs of these other functions before making significant alterations in their own module or system.

Finally, to maintain a positive relationship with OSHA and other government agencies, safety must maintain required records scrupulously and be prepared to provide supporting documentation as needed. Because government health and safety regulations change frequently, safety staff must stay current.

Glossary

Ergonomics The study and practice of the relationship between the worker's body posture and motions and the physical arrangement of the workplace. The most common use of this term refers to office environments and objects such as chairs, desks, and computer screens.

Hazardous material Any substance that might be harmful to anyone exposed to it. The reference point is the Resource Conservation Recovery Act (RCRA). Under this law, any substance is a hazardous material if it exhibits characteristics of flammability, ignitability, corrosivity, reactivity, or toxicity; is a listed carcinogen; or causes harm to human health or the environment.

New building syndrome A collection of symptoms, including nausea, dizziness, and respiratory problems, that may occur among employees working in a new or newly renovated environment. Suspected causes include formaldehyde and other chemicals in new carpeting and furnishings or poor ventilation systems that import automotive exhaust or recirculate otherwise contaminated air.

Occupational illness Any abnormal condition or disorder, other than one resulting from an occupational injury, caused by exposure to environmental factors associated with employment.

Occupational injury Any injury, such as a cut, fracture, sprain, or amputation that results from a work accident or an exposure requiring more than first aid or more than a single visit to medical care providers.

Occupational Safety and Health Administration (OSHA) The agency of the U.S Department of Labor that regulates, monitors, and enforces workplace safety standards and provides statistics on safety incidents. OSHA was mandated by the Occupational Safety and Health Act of 1970, which is also known as the Williams-Steiger Act. This act requires employers to provide safe and healthy working conditions. Provisions of the act specifically require firms with twelve or more employees to keep logs of injuries or illnesses stemming from occupational causes.

OSHA See *Occupational Safety and Health Administration.*

Toxic substances A substance produced as the result of a process using hazardous materials that has a measurable toxicity that defines the resulting compound as a toxic substance. These are covered by the Toxic Substance Control Act (TSCA).

Workers' compensation A government-mandated, employer-paid insurance program that covers health care costs, long-term liability payments, and rehabilitation for occupational injuries and illnesses. Insurers assign rates by comparing a firm's incident rate with industry norms.

Discussion Points

1. How can a computerized safety system help an organization comply with the requirements of the occupational safety and health Act?

2. What factors have led to the increased interest in computerizing the safety function?

3. List the data bases that a safety module might include, and identify the data fields that link records from one data base to those in another.

4. Under what circumstances might other human resources functions want access to employee safety records?

5. What kinds of computerized health and safety record keeping and reporting can assist in identifying workplace health issues?

6. What data collection and reporting activities would differentiate a proactive safety function from a reactive one?

7. In what ways might on-site medical services interact with an HRMS safety module?

8. Describe several possible safety-related incident summary reports, including the relevant data fields each might include.

Further Reading

Allred, J.K. *Computer-Integrated Robotic Assembly Systems and Their Potential for the Factory of the Future.* Dearborn, MI: Society of Manufacturing Engineers, 1985.

Ashford, Nicholas A. *Crisis in the Workplace: Occupational Disease and Injury.* Cambridge, MA: MIT Press, 1976.

Beach, Dale S. *Personnel: The Management of People at Work.* New York: Macmillan, 1980.

Boddy, D., and D.A. Buchanan. "New Technology with a Human Face." *Personnel Management,* 17, 1985.

Brown, Bernard M. and Douglas G. Hoffman. "The Workers' Compensation Problem." *Risk Management Reports,* Volume V, 1978.

Chapnik, Elissa-Beth, and Clifford Gross. "Visual Display Terminals: Health Issues and Productivity." *Personnel,* May 1987.

Davis, Ronald H. "Safety and OSHA." *Personnel Administrator,* 25, 1980.

Gomez-Mejia, Luis R., and David B. Balkin. "Classifying Work-Related and Personal Problems of Troubled Employees." *Personnel Administrator,* November 1980.

Kolman, H. Felix. "The Future of Risk Management." *Risk Management Reports,* Volume VI, 1982.

Liker, J., and R.J. Thomas. "Prospects for Human Resource Development in the Context of Technological Change: Lessons from a Major Technological Renovation." In *Handbook of Technology Management,* edited by D. Kocacglu. New York: John Wiley & Sons, 1987.

Lipstreu, O., and K.A. Reed. "A New Look at the Organizational Implications of Automation." *Academy of Management Journal*, Volume 8, 1965.

Majchrzak, Ann. "The Effect of CAM Technologies on Training Activities." *Journal of Manufacturing Systems*, Volume 5, 1986.

———. *The Human Side of Factory Automation.* San Francisco: Jossey-Bass, 1988.

Majchrzak, Ann, T.C. Chang, W. Barfield, R.E. Eberts, and G. Salvendy. *Human Aspects of Computer-Aided Design.* London: Taylor & Francis, 1987.

Mayer, Steven J. "EDP Personnel Systems: What Areas Are Being Automated?" *Personnel*, July/August 1971.

Northrup, Herbert R., et al. *The Impact of OSHA.* Philadelphia: University of Pennsylvania Press, 1978.

Preston, Robert D. "Employee Benefits and Risk Management: A Holistic Future." *Risk Management Reports*, Volume X, 1983.

Richard-Carpenter, Colin. "Medical Records—New Possibilities." *Personnel Management*, August 1986.

Turner, J.A., and R.A. Karasek. "Software Ergonomics: Effects of Computer Application Design Parameters on Operator Task Performance and Health." *Ergonomics*, Volume 27, 1984.

U.S. Department of Labor. *Recordkeeping Guidelines for Occupational Injuries and Illnesses.* Washington: Bureau of Labor Statistics, 1986.

Walton, R.E. "New Work Technology and Its Work Force Implications: Union and Management Approaches." Harvard Working Paper 84–13. Boston: Harvard University, 1983.

Weber, Austin. "Minimizing VDT Health and Safety Risks Demands a Proactive, People-Oriented Approach." *Human Resources Professional*, May/June 1989.

Zarley, Craig A. "PCs Doing Duty as Tools in Firms' Wellness Programs." *PC Week*, December 1986.

20
Payroll

A fair day's wages for a fair day's work.

—Thomas Carlyle

The paycheck is the logical end of human resources record keeping, the end of the reward-management process. Payroll is a highly visible function; every employee receives a paycheck (and is understandably upset if that paycheck is incorrect). Thus, payroll must be accurate and timely. A properly designed HRMS aids that process.

Payroll is not always part of human resources. Initially, payroll was the primary function of human resources, which was then called personnel administration. Employers merely hired and paid employees; they did not provide fringe benefits and were not concerned about employee relations. As legislation and social change increased the importance of other areas of personnel, organizations either moved payroll to an accounting function or relegated it to part of record keeping within personnel. Sometimes payroll functions not as a subset of human resources but as a coequal. No matter where payroll resides, gross pay (wages or salary) remains a human resources responsibility; payroll takes responsibility for calculating gross-to-net pay based on wage and salary policies and procedures, taxes, and other deductions.

An organization that has payroll as a separate function may use the term *human resources* to refer to all human resources functions except payroll. Some firms use the term *personnel* to refer to these nonpayroll functions. Some have no special term, particularly if payroll remains within the human resources department. For clarity in this chapter, the term *personnel* refers to the nonpayroll human resources functions.

Payroll in an HRMS

Most businesses, even small ones, have computerized the payroll function internally or use a service bureau. All except the smallest firms have some sort of automated payroll because accurate payroll involves tracking so many types of tax regulations.

In fact, because of the highly quantitative nature of the work involved in payroll, payroll systems preceded personnel systems as automated applications. Moreover, payroll systems generally have a longer viable life because their purpose and structure remain fairly stable over time.

Roles of Payroll

Payroll tends not to make decisions but to administer and calculate financial data related to employee wages, salaries, and deductions. To carry out this responsibility, payroll must handle several processes:

- Capture time worked by all employees who must report it
- Compute gross pay, deductions, and net pay for each employee for each pay period
- Distribute payments, accompanying statements, and year-end records to each employee
- Facilitate or arrange for the timely transfer of appropriate monies into accounts on which payroll writes checks
- File all necessary tax reports and payments to federal, state, and local tax authorities
- Report to the appropriate human resources or accounting functions amounts collected for benefits and other deductions
- Conduct fundamental audits of all payroll-related transactions
- Distribute labor costs according to project, account, or cost center

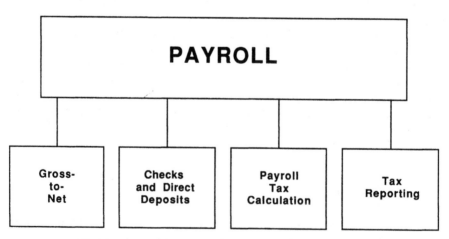

Figure 20–1. Principal roles of the payroll function.

Advantages and Limitations of Computers in Payroll

As a largely clerical task that involves sizable transaction volume, payroll can take great advantage of the speed and data-handling features of computers. Payroll also requires easy auditability of records. A well-designed computer system can provide complete audit trails of every phase of payroll processing, such as time verification, editing and validating transactions, gross calculation, gross-to-net processing, and report generation.

Payroll must make calculations with complete accuracy, and computers certainly increase the accuracy of quantitative data. They eliminate arithmetic as well as human errors that result from inadvertently looking at the wrong table or making the wrong calculation. Edit and validation functions further reduce the error rate.

Vendors offer comprehensive payroll programs, and the market for payroll systems is quite mature, so there is seldom any advantage in building a payroll system internally. Payroll systems should include complete tax tables, tax calculation procedures, and government reporting forms. These tables and formulas often are complicated and exacting to build and maintain. Most vendor systems provide updates to keep the system in compliance with government regulations. This update provision alone prompts many firms to use commercial payroll applications.

In computerized payroll operations, staff often face their greatest challenge maintaining positive relationships with personnel and accounting. Payroll deals with both types of operations. No matter which department encompasses payroll, the entry, update, and interface of data often work less smoothly than they should. To minimize dissatisfaction, payroll managers and system developers must consult with appropriate parties from all these areas during the system planning process. They should discuss issues such as system interdependency, data definitions, processing cycles, and procedures for system interfaces.

The Computerized Payroll Process

To process a payroll, the system follows a lengthy set of algorithms that may reside in a massive decision table of all rules for calculating gross-to-net pay or may be input as options for each cycle. Each type of earning or deduction has its own set of computation rules. A sample portion of a payroll decision table is shown in figure 20–2. During system installation, the vendor provides criteria for definitions and choices for each computation. Payroll decision makers select appropriate choices from these variables. After completion and installation of this table, only payroll and authorized HRSC staff can access or alter this table.

618

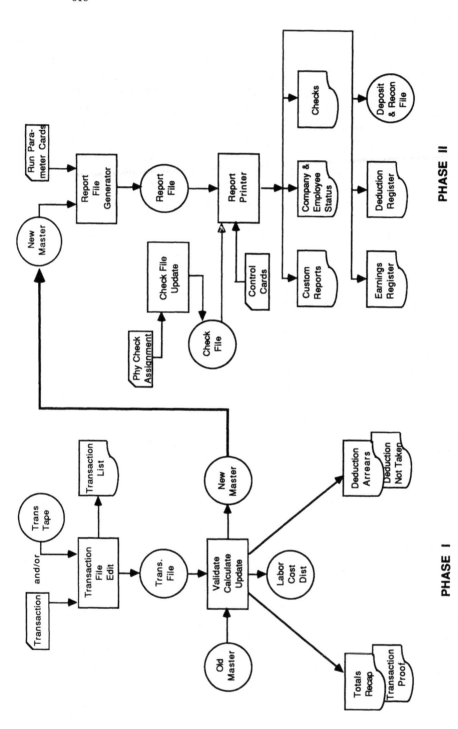

PHASE I

PHASE II

Figure 20–2. Two phases of a modern payroll system. Phase I programs check the validity of input, process transactions, calculate earnings, and update master files. In phase II, the system generates payroll reports and paychecks.

Based on this decision table, the program retrieves data from individual records and various tables, performs particular arithmetic calculations, and enters the resulting information in the appropriate files. Each algorithm may include IF/THEN/ELSE statements that indicate independent and dependent variables, as well as the circumstances under which the system should perform the calculation. For each employee or paycheck, these steps usually include the following:

1. Calculate the gross pay for the period by calculating the gross pay of each earnings type (such as regular wages, overtime, salary, bonuses, and commissions)

2. Calculate tax withholding liabilities for the employee for each applicable taxing authority; update the appropriate amounts in the employee's file and in the appropriate payroll tax file

3. Calculate authorized deductions. These include benefits plan contributions, retirement or pension plan contributions, 401(k) contributions, and others; the rule indicates whether to base calculations on gross pay or after-tax pay; the system enters the deduction in the employee's record and in the file that tracks accumulated credits and distributions for that type of deduction

4. Subtract all deductions to determine current net pay; record the net pay in the employee's file; total all transactions for each type of gross pay and each type of deduction

5. Report the total amount required to cover payroll obligations, tax payments, and each type of deduction; for any amounts for which payroll handles payment, also arrange for funds transfer to bank or brokerage account as required

6. Issue paychecks and direct deposits; most systems have a provision for actual check writing and mailing (or internal distribution) and for automatic deposit to one or several accounts

Stand-Alone, Integrated, and
Other Approaches to Payroll Automation

The relationship between payroll computer operations and those of the rest of human resources usually plays a critical role in payroll system selection and creation. To choose the most efficient payroll system, planners should consider the needs of both operations. Payroll and personnel have some similarities, but they also have significant differences that can affect computer system requirements. Such differences are synopsized in figure 20–3.

Payroll and personnel share some common data but not much compared with the entire HRMS. Commonality is usually around 10 to 20 percent. Per-

DEMOGRAPHICS: Marital Status and Dependents for Tax Purposes, Home Address

EARNINGS: Types, Rates, Hours, Pay Basis

TAXES: Types, Calculation Rules, Covered Gross, Withholding

DEDUCTIONS: Types, Amounts, Covered Gross, Frequencies, Limits

PAYMENT DATA: Bank Account, Check Number, Check Address

REPORTING INFORMATION: 941, W-2, 1099, Bank Reconciliation

ACCUMULATIONS: Current Pay, Month, Quarter, Year-to-Date

PAYROLL NEEDS

DEMOGRAPHICS: Name, Address, Birth Date

EMPLOYMENT STATUS: Category, Status, FLSA Status, Work Shift

COMPENSATION: Pay Rate, Type

TIME AND ATTENDANCE DATA: Accumulations and Usage

BENEFITS: Plan Participation, Contribution Rate

BOTH NEED

DEMOGRAPHICS: Spouse/Emergency Information

EMPLOYMENT STATUS: Job Classification, Position, Locations

COMPENSATION: Salary/Wage Ranges, Salary History

EMPLOYEE AND INDUSTRIAL RELATIONS: Performance Review Data, Work History

EEO DATA

BENEFITS: Coverage Amounts, Beneficiaries, Accrual Rates

TRAINING AND DEVELOPMENT DATA: Skills, Experience, Career Objectives

SAFETY AND HEALTH DATA

PERSONNEL NEEDS

Figure 20–3. Overlapping personnel and payroll data needs. Payroll and personnel have some data needs in common, but most are unique.

sonnel staff seldom need much of the employee data that payroll maintains. Benefits occasionally wants deduction information if questions arise about benefits contributions. Employee relations may need information on net pay if that function provides financial planning counseling.

Sometimes payroll and personnel use different definitions for the same data element. For instance, personnel may want first, middle, and last name, but payroll may need the name listed as last name and first and middle initials to conserve space. The two systems also have different data-handling and storage requirements. Personnel deals with weekly, monthly, or annual salary and records this in the employee master record; payroll deals with the actual pay

Issue	Payroll	Personnel
System Orientation	Production	Maintenance
Data Structure	For update	For inquiry
Cycles	Rigid timing	Flexible
Transaction Volume	Large	Generally smaller
Record Sizes	Generally small	Larger
Accuracy	Critical	Less critical
Data Content	Determined by processing requirements	Determined by information needs
Routines	Arithmetic	Data manipulation

Figure 20–4. How payroll and personnel system needs differ. The processing cycles, data maintenance, and reporting of these two applications differ greatly, leading some organizations to develop separate payroll and personnel systems.

period earnings, which may be weekly, biweekly, semimonthly, or monthly. Personnel archives (or purges) historical data off-line; payroll often needs to keep cumulative historical data on-line.

The two functions need different screen types and reporting tools. Payroll inputs a large amount of new data every pay period, so it needs screens and reports structured for updating. Personnel makes comparatively fewer changes but checks a wider variety of employee data, therefore requiring data structured for access and query. Personnel staff often need to bring up more than one screen for inquiry, a feature that payroll seldom needs.

Payroll has fairly rigid cycle requirements. It must issue payroll checks on time, in accordance with wage and hour laws. Personnel functions have more flexible processing and reporting cycles. Payroll has a high transaction volume, as the system makes calculations and reports for each employee in each transaction cycle.

These considerations often lead companies to set up an independent computer system for payroll. In fact, payroll is probably the most likely human resources–related function to operate its own system. Some choose stand-alone systems, some integrate the two functions into a single system, some interface the two systems, and some use an external service bureau to help solve such problems. Depending on the circumstances of the specific organization, any of these approaches can work successfully.

Stand-Alone Systems. Some payroll functions use a computer system that has no connection to the HRMS used by other human resources functions. Personnel periodically issues a printed report of all changes in personnel records transactions. This report lists all records in which personnel made changes during the preceding period, with the from and to status for each change. Then payroll transcribes and keys the relevant changes into its own system.

This approach has some advantages. Because payroll does not have to share the system, processing time decreases. With smaller files, payroll can use computer equipment that has less capacity, thereby reducing costs without sacrificing performance. More important, payroll and personnel have clearly defined responsibilities.

These separate systems almost certainly have to maintain some redundant data, however. Moreover, in some cases, a user must access more than one system to obtain needed information. This separation often leads to discrepancies between the two master files. Payroll and benefits generally have quite

---

Stand-Alone Payroll and Personnel Systems

Advantages	Disadvantages
Less time required to process each payroll	Discrepancies between separate master files
Smaller files require minimal computer capacity	Common data redundant on computer files and input forms
Personnel responsible for personnel data; payroll responsible for payroll data	To obtain information, users often must access more than one system

a bit of data that must correspond. To be most useful, corresponding data must not only contain accurate information but also reflect the same point in time. Although accurate record keeping requires reconciliation of two sets of files, data definitions and error-checking procedures make this process difficult, if not impossible.

To operate a stand-alone system successfully, payroll must have clear communication lines with personnel. Everyone involved must understand and agree on how information from line managers and employees pertaining to personal transactions reaches both personnel and payroll in a timely, accurate manner. If data elements for two systems have identical definitions, they may be able to share a common data-input form. If the functions use a common input form, personnel and payroll each receives a copy of the completed form, then keys this information into a separate data base. As well as reducing data discrepancies between the two systems, this approach also reduces employee frustration with human resources paperwork. However, separate personnel and payroll systems most often use different input forms, particularly if the systems are from different vendors, homegrown, or of different generations.

Integrated Systems. In an integrated system, payroll functions as a module or an equal subsystem within the HRMS. Such systems virtually eliminate discrepancies and duplications between payroll data and personnel data, since they use the same master data base. This eliminates data redundancy and offers several other advantages: HRSC staff have fewer programs to write and

Integrated Payroll and Personnel Systems

Advantages	*Disadvantages*
Less chance of discrepancies between separate payroll and personnel master files	Processing each payroll requires more computer time
Common data (such as name, sex, and race) not redundant on computer files and input forms	Larger single computer file requires more computer capacity
Fewer programs to write and maintain	Programs are larger and more complex
Single source of all payroll and personnel information	Personnel access to personnel data and payroll access to personnel data—who is responsible?

maintain; human resources staff can consult a single system to obtain both payroll and personnel information; and, once implemented, an integrated system has lower operating costs because of reduced machine use, integrated staff resources, and more accurate data and reports.

Systems generally function more efficiently with all transactions flowing through the personnel subsystem first rather than having the payroll subsystem as the front end of the HRMS. Designers must make this decision early in system development. Otherwise, future changes in documentation and forms design could be costly. Implementing an integrated system is more difficult than implementing other options. Using a single vendor for all applications helps ensure common file architecture, field conventions, and coding structures. Even different generations from the same vendor can pose problems for integrated systems.

Payroll processing time generally increases somewhat with integrated systems. Computer capacity must increase to handle the larger record size. Programs, though fewer, are often larger and more complex. Most important, virtually every organization that allows payroll and personnel functions access to one another's data, as with an integrated system, has problems with responsibility for data accuracy and timeliness.

Firms often do not realize that an integrated system may force an organizational redesign concerning the way people think about issues such as records storage and security. They sometimes learn the hard way that the systems were separated in the first place because they involve such different operations or data requirements. Without efforts to promote a common vision of data use, integration makes the situation worse.

A successful integrated system demands clear policies about who enters specific data and when. If an organization has a working environment in which personnel and payroll follow such policies and procedures, integration may work the way system planners and designers intended.

At present, midrange and mainframe-based systems may integrate payroll into the HRMS, but few microcomputer systems do. Historically, payroll systems and records were so large compared with those of other business needs that only large computers could handle integrated applications. Payroll traditionally handles high-volume, high-speed transactions in a production environment, while microcomputers are designed for ad hoc processing or special-purpose applications.

Microcomputers offer a few options for integrated personnel/payroll systems. The systems available operate efficiently by making full use of large data bases and the newest, most powerful processors. Microcomputer systems sometimes use an integrated network in which multiple human resources applications share a common file server, with one node of the network dedicated to payroll. More often, firms using microcomputer-based personnel systems have a stand-alone payroll system or use a service bureau.

Interfaced Payroll
and Personnel Systems

Advantages	Disadvantages
Eliminate discrepancies between separate payroll master and personnel master	Common data redundant on computer files
Common data not redundant on input forms	To obtain information, user often must access more than one system
Less time required to process each payroll	
Smaller files require minimal computer capacity	
Payroll responsible for payroll data; personnel responsible for personnel data	

Interfaced Systems. Sometimes personnel uses one computer system, payroll uses another, and the two systems interface for periodic electronic data interchange. Every time personnel enters changes to certain fields in employee records, the personnel system tags that change and adds it to a special transaction file. Personnel periodically transfers that file to the payroll system, usually on a batch-processed basis. This exchange usually takes place at least once every pay period via disks or modems using special conversion programs. The system usually contains a routine that performs this exchange automatically during nonwork hours a certain number of days into each pay period.

Because interfacing software packages that come from two different vendors inevitably poses problems, human resources departments commonly use a vendor-supplied system for personnel and a system created in-house for payroll. Some firms find themselves trying to interface a payroll system that is ten to twenty years old with a state-of-the-art personnel system that has a totally different architecture. This can be an obstacle to getting data exchange working smoothly.

Interfaced systems offer some of the same advantages as integrated systems, such as fewer discrepancies and less redundancy of input and forms. Interfacing also has some of the advantages of separate systems, such as smaller files, reduced computer capacity requirements, and separation of responsibility. However, the two systems may have some common redundant data, and users may need to access more than one system. The data in the two systems (particularly wages, salaries, and earnings) must balance at intervals based on audit requirements.

Overall, interfacing is often the least costly and most efficient approach to payroll and personnel. A department considering this option should consider the interface issues discussed in chapters 2 and 3. In particular, they should make sure that the RFP gives vendors complete interface requirements and that the contract establishes responsibility for defining the interfaces.

Payroll Service Bureaus. Many banks and other vendors offer an external service that processes payroll, issues paychecks, and generates payroll tax reports. In a 1986 survey, the VRC Consulting Group estimated that more than half a million firms in the United States use payroll service bureaus for paycheck calculation and preparation.

If an organization has a service bureau arrangement, the in-house payroll function is responsible for providing payroll transaction data on time and in the required form. Payroll extracts the relevant transactions on employee data from personnel records. Payroll may do some preliminary record formatting, then transmit the data to the service bureau in paper or electronic form. Sometimes a service bureau provides time sheets and input forms, but most clients enter their own attendance data, then provide detail reports of that data.

Often the service bureau keeps master files on each employee; personnel contributes only updates on pay-period wage and salary increases (or decreases) and any changes in relevant data such as address, pay location, taxes, and other deductions. In some cases, a service bureau may ask its clients to provide a complete set of employee personnel data each period for reconciliation purposes.

The service bureau calculates gross pay, tax withholdings, and other deductions. The bureau may even print and distribute paychecks and handle direct deposits. Payroll receives some acknowledgment of calculations and disbursements, such as a detail report and a copy of each check or direct deposit advice. An organization that uses a bank as a service bureau usually maintains its payroll checking account with that institution. In some arrangements, the service bureau provides electronic files containing the paycheck information, and the client needs to print its own paychecks. The service bureau also maintains the payroll history of each employee whose paycheck it prepares.

Many organizations use service bureaus to relieve their payroll and IS staff from concern about processing deadlines and accuracy. The service bureau also takes responsibility for updating tax tables and calculation methods to comply with revisions to government regulations. Moreover, the cyclical nature of payroll creates peaks and valleys of staff and computer resource needs; such variances can reduce overall efficiency. A payroll service bureau minimizes those peaks and valleys. With a service bureau, an organization needs fewer staff to process payroll. In some cases, it may not even need a separate payroll unit. Moreover, by establishing a contract with a service bureau, payroll often can predict (and control) processing costs more accurately than it could with internal processing. Once a department has used an external service bureau successfully, staff sometimes hesitate to accept the additional pressures and uncertainties of handling this operation internally.

Service bureaus offer little flexibility in deadlines, input forms, report formats, data element descriptions, and sort and total sequences. Payroll managers must consider whether service bureau standards meet the organization's business and information needs. Payroll and HRSC staff may find ways to increase the productivity of internal applications, but they have few ways of increasing efficiency or otherwise reducing the costs of bureau services.

Selecting an Approach. The reasons for choosing one type of payroll system over another often pertain to an organization's culture. Some personnel departments want very little to do with payroll, whereas some companies want personnel and payroll unified. Providing appropriate data security for payroll data is easier if the payroll function uses a separate system rather than operating within the HRMS.

To Integrate or to Interface?

HRMS planners and designers considering the inevitable link between personnel records and payroll accounting must address and resolve a number of issues before deciding between an integrated system and separate systems linked through an interface. The most important issues involve standardization and agreement on which function will take responsibility for the integrity of each system. The HRMS planning team must accomplish the following tasks with either path:

- Standardize data definitions
- Standardize data formats
- Agree on sources of data
- Agree on maintenance responsibilities
- Consider processing cycles
- Consider volume of transactions
- Plan system implementation carefully

Each organization should consider its own payroll accounting needs. A payroll system that works well for an international bank may not fit a small manufacturing firm. A multicity law firm needs a different system than a school district. Complex payroll requirements often result from factors such as high turnover, a large employee base, a large short-term employee population (temporary or prime-time help), a high percentage of hourly or incentive-based employees, interstate operations, international operations, and unions (particularly multiple unions).

HRMS planners should consider vendor options that are compatible with existing applications. Some firms use a payroll application from the same vendor that provided their accounting packages, especially when integration between payroll and accounting functions is more important than between payroll and personnel. This often occurs when the accounting function needs payroll figures for the general ledger or for shop floor control or labor-cost distribution.

Size, convenience, and existing service bureau relations are other important factors. If the organization's bank offers a payroll service, a shift to its payroll processing might take place relatively smoothly. Service bureaus tend to attract firms with fewer than 1,000 employees, but firms of 5,000 or more employees also use service bureaus. The acquisition of a new HRMS frequently spurs a human resources department to consider bringing payroll processing in-house. However, if an existing arrangement meets most of a firm's present needs, this probably is not a good idea. If payroll processing is already internal, planners must consider the age of the system, the technology, and the degree of redundancy between the payroll and personnel systems. If users are frequently demanding ad hoc payroll-related reports, how well can the current system handle such requests?

Data Requirements and Sources

Basically an accounting function, payroll receives and reacts primarily to data from transactions that take place in other human resources functions. Payroll builds and uses tax tables and tables of other variables. Payroll staff have few degrees of freedom in data manipulation but are greatly concerned with accuracy and timely processing.

The heart of payroll data storage is individual employee payroll records. Each record contains an abbreviated form of that employee's master record plus present and historical data on gross pay, deductions, and net pay. The payroll module also contains files that track totals for each type of deduction, as well as check-register files that track paychecks and other payroll disbursements.

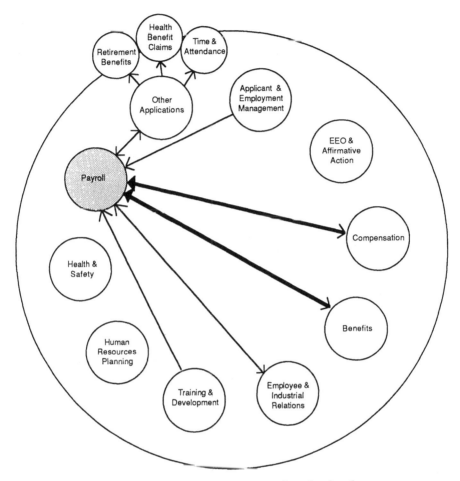

Figure 20–5. Information flow between payroll and other human resources functions.

Employee Information

Payroll needs some basic employee information, which it usually obtains from the HRMS but may collect itself if the data fields do not correspond. This includes the following:

- Employee name (payroll may capture the name as the employee wants it on the paycheck)
- Pay location (address to which the paycheck should be sent, which may

differ from the employee's residence; for instance, it may list a post office box or a company mail stop)

- Home address (payroll must mail tax information to the employee's street address, not just a post office box, company mail stop, or bank address)
- Social security number
- Employee number (if different from social security number)
- Employee category (regular, part-time, or contractor)
- Employee status (active, retired, on leave, or separated)

Earnings

The payroll function for a large, diverse corporation may track as many as 200 types of earnings; even small systems often require more than 20. In the payroll system, each earnings type has a unique code, name, and set of rules for calculation. The earnings determination routine calculates each type for each employee, accumulates the results of each calculation in the employee's file, and totals these earnings as gross pay. Payroll also may process deferred earnings and adjust net pay accordingly. It then performs the entire set of earnings calculations for each employee in turn until it has computed all gross earnings for this pay period.

If most employees receive only a few common types of earnings, the system will work more simply. It may first run the earnings calculation process using algorithms for the common earnings types. A secondary operation would access other earnings calculation algorithms for employees whose current records show timekeeping data for special earnings types, such as incentives, bonuses, and commissions.

To perform these earnings calculations, payroll must gather several types of input from personnel, particularly pay rate and frequency, timekeeping data, and effective dates.

Pay Rate and Frequency. Compensation provides data on pay frequency (such as weekly, biweekly, semimonthly, or monthly), which is also known as pay basis. Some systems allow payroll to select different frequencies for different pay types or job grades. Payroll uses this pay-rate information as part of the algorithm for each earnings type.

Payroll gets the following data from the compensation segment of each employee's master record:

- Type of pay (such as salary, commission, or hourly)
- Commission type, if applicable (if the organization has several commission structures)

Number	Type	Frequency	Conversion	Algorithm
01	Hourly Regular	biweekly	1.0	Base pay x hours (0 to 40) = gross pay
02	Overtime	biweekly	1.5	Base pay x hours (40+) x 1.5 = gross pay
03	Holiday Pay	biweekly	2.0	Base pay x holiday/night shift hours x 2.0 = gross pay
04	Hazardous Duty	biweekly	1.5	Base pay x hours (40+) x 1.5 = gross pay
05	Sick (hourly)	biweekly	1.0	Base pay x sick hours = gross pay
06	Sick (exempt)	monthly	1.0	If sick hours >40/year, then sick hours x (monthly pay/173) = reduction in gross pay
07	Vacation (hourly)	biweekly	1.0	Base pay x vacation hours = gross pay
08	Vacation (salaried)	monthly	1.0	(Monthly salary/days in month) x vacation days = gross pay
09	Salaried	monthly	1.0	Monthly salary = gross pay
10	Commissions (5%)	monthly	1.05	Individual gross salary x 1.05 = gross pay

Figure 20–6. Typical earnings table. This table reflects different types of earnings and the formulas used to derive them.

- Pay rate (salary rate may be amount per year or per month; wage rate may be amount per hour or day)
- Deferred compensation (amount and date payable)

To calculate actual payments, payroll also imports compensation tables such as the following:

- Salary tables
- Wage-rate tables, including steps and levels
- Commission tables
- Incentives tables
- Piece-rate tables

Time and Attendance. To calculate paychecks, particularly for hourly workers, payroll needs data from the timekeeping function. For nonexempt employees, data include hours worked and types of hours. For exempt employees, information may be reported on an exception basis. Employee relations may track this information, or a separate timekeeping function in each line or operating unit may handle it. To eliminate data-transfer problems, payroll itself sometimes handles these responsibilities. In such cases, these operations are often referred to as timekeeping because payroll pays comparatively more attention to hours worked and less to attendance. The term *time and attendance* is frequently used to refer to a separate function. This function is discussed in chapter 21.

Commissions. To calculate commission payments for salespersons and others, payroll needs information from sales. In some situations, the payroll system can accept sales results electronically; if not, this information arrives in printed form. In retail environments, the sales function may receive commission-related information through a point-of-sale recording device, such as a computerized cash register. If the employee's commission depends on individual sales results, the sales information is extracted from each employee's file. If commissions depend on department or territory sales results, each employee's file may have a code that ties it to a table of sales results that payroll updates each pay cycle.

Tips. Sometimes service businesses that employ workers who receive tips, such as hotels and restaurants, record those tips for reporting to the government. If employees pool their tips, the shift manager totals each shift's tips and divides them according to a set ratio (servers, buspersons, cook, and so forth). The shift manager documents these calculations on a form submitted to payroll.

Bonuses. Normally, management declares a bonus as a distribution of profits. Bonuses are almost always discretionary, though they may relate to some other business condition, such as sales, breakage rates, or loan-loss ratio. Compensation, as authorized by management, provides payroll with data on upcoming bonuses. This report lists the following:

- Pay cycle or cycles in which to award the bonus
- Job grades to receive the bonus (all employees or only a specific group)
- Bonus type (dollar amount, percentage of pay rate, or a combination)
- Actual dollar amount or percentage
- Gross or net payment (if management wants the bonus to be a net amount after taxes, some systems can perform net-to-gross conversions)

Pensions. Payroll deals with pensions in two basic areas: pension distributions and pension contributions. Increasingly, payroll does not handle the management or distribution of pensions and other retirement benefits. More likely, benefits, a separate retirement benefits administration function, the treasurer's office, or an external specialist handles this function. As pensions have become more complex, firms have begun using trustees or banks to handle them. Sometimes, even if another human resources function handles the administration of retirement benefits, payroll will take care of pension payments and annual tax statements, since these functions resemble ordinary payroll functions. To do so, retirement benefits administration furnishes payroll with a paper or electronic report of recipients and gross amounts.

Payroll still administers the calculation of pension contributions from employee pay. To have payroll calculate these deductions, pension administrators must provide pension participation and contribution data. After each pay cycle, payroll may, in turn, provide retirement benefits administration with data on the amount contributed by or on behalf of each employee.

Contractor Earnings. Contractors must submit time records. The personnel data base may include contractors and other nonemployee earnings recipients depending on the nature of the organization and the extent to which it uses contractors. If included, the employee status field contains a code for contractor. This signals the payroll system not to calculate gross-to-net earnings but rather to issue a check for the entire amount. Sometimes the government requires that contractors who work exclusively for a particular client be treated as employees with respect to benefits and tax withholding. If contractors are not in the personnel or payroll systems, they appear in the accounting function or a separate tax function.

Some firms refer to certain contractors as leased employees. The term *leased* means rented or borrowed on a full-time or nearly full-time basis. The government considers leased employees statutory employees who should have amounts withheld for taxes and, in some cases, benefits.

Deductions

There are several types of payroll deductions, the most notable of which is federal income tax withholding. Other major types include state income tax withholding and employee contributions for benefits. The average company has 100 to 200 types of deduction categories. As with earnings types, each type of deduction has a unique identifier, name, activation cycle, and algorithm arrayed in a deductions table. The algorithm indicates whether to base each deduction on earnings, before or after taxes, and whether to include the deducted amount as taxable income.

A deduction algorithm also may include an accumulation limit, such as a maximum contribution per year. When the year-to-date accumulation reaches a set amount, it deactivates this deduction for the balance of the year.

Tax Withholding Allowances. In determining tax liability, the IRS considers the number of dependents in an individual's household. Possible qualified members of a household include self, spouse, dependent children, and other dependents; each qualified member entitles the individual to one withholding allowance. The IRS requires that each employee submit to the employer a Form W-4 listing marital status and number of withholding allowances for tax purposes. Marital status for taxation purposes pertains to tax exemptions and may differ from actual marital status.

Taxes. Payroll handles all employee-related taxes. Employers must withhold part of employees' earnings for payment directly to the government for several types of taxes:

- Federal income tax (FIT)
- State income tax (SIT) (where applicable)
- Social security tax (required by the Federal Insurance Contributions Act, also known as FICA)
- State disability insurance (SDI) (where applicable)
- Local income taxes (where applicable)

Based on employee earnings, firms also must calculate and make payments for employer contributions to social security, state unemployment insurance (SUI), and federal unemployment insurance (FUI) where applicable.

To determine the proper amounts to withhold, the payroll system uses a series of tax tables, tax rates, and calculation rules. Payroll systems must in-

Abbreviation	Title	Paid by Employee	Paid by Employer
FICA (Social Security)	Federal Insurance Contribution Act	X	X
FUI	Federal Unemployment Insurance		X
FIT	Federal Income Tax	X	
SIT	State Income Tax	X	
SDI	State Disability Insurance	X	
SUI	State Unemployment Insurance		X

Figure 20–7. What the government takes. These are the standard federal and state payroll taxes withheld from an employee's gross earnings or paid by the employer.

clude tables for all places where the organization has operations. For a large organization, this may include many states, counties, and even foreign countries. Firms operating internationally require an entirely different set of tables to handle the withholding requirements of other countries and locales in which they employ locals, third-country nationals, or expatriates. Vendors should provide timely updated tax tables, calculations, and reporting changes promptly. Because of the size and complexity of these tables, most payroll functions use commercial packages rather than building and maintaining their own tax tables.

Benefits. Payroll takes deductions from earnings to cover employee contributions for a variety of benefits. These may include dependent health care coverage, retirement plan contributions, additional life insurance, or dozens of other options detailed in chapter 15. For each employee and each benefit, the benefits function tracks employee participation, amount of contribution, and frequency of contribution. Depending on the system, payroll accesses benefits data directly, transfers it electronically on a batch basis, or reenters it manually from information provided by benefits.

Garnishments. If the organization has received a legal order to garnish an employee's earnings and make corresponding payments to a third party, payroll handles the processing of this garnishment. The order lists the total amount of the garnishment, frequency of payment, amount per payment, name of payee, and address of payee. Some arrangements have limits (as with tax garnishments), and some are indefinite (as with child-support garnishments). Once the computer has information on total due, it automatically makes the garnishment as ordered.

Charitable Contributions. Payroll may administer United Way and other charitable contributions. For an employer-supported campaign, a participating employee signs a contribution pledge. This pledge lists either a specific amount, an amount per pay period, or a percentage of gross pay. This form may go directly to payroll or be routed via benefits, employee relations, or a special contributions function within the organization.

Union Dues. Sometimes the union collects dues from its members directly. Other times an organization collects its employees' union dues via payroll deductions and passes them on to the union or makes a direct deposit. The job code table usually includes data about whether the job is covered by the union contract. If so, union representatives can solicit union enrollment from a new employee entering that position. The enrollment process includes an authorization for payroll withholding, which the union representative submits to industrial relations or to payroll directly.

Safety Equipment. Employees sometimes pay for safety equipment via payroll deductions. This occurs most often when the job mandates certain equipment that the company does not generally issue. The company may adopt this policy if employees need equipment that they can use outside the work environment but that the employer cannot reuse (such as special shoes or uniforms).

The firm may charge a set amount per equipment item, then deduct a portion of this amount each pay period until the employee has contributed the total purchase price. In other circumstances, the organization may take a deduction every pay period on an ongoing basis, in exchange for which the employer takes responsibility for maintenance (such as uniform cleaning and scheduled replacement).

To initiate a safety equipment deduction, an employee signs an authorization form that goes to payroll. Each type of equipment has a code, which is connected to a price/cost table. Within the employee's payroll record, each equipment purchase contains fields for deduction authorization status, deduction authorization date, equipment code, cost (amount paid by employer), price (amount charged to employee), rate of deduction, frequency of deduction, equipment return date, and historical information on date and amount of each payment.

Additional Deductions. Payroll tracks all other individual deductions. The types are seemingly endless but may include reimbursement of moving expenses, partial reimbursement of temporary housing costs, and reimbursements for purchases of company products or through company stores.

Accumulations

For each type of deduction payroll handles, the payroll module builds a file that tracks accumulations and distributions. Accumulations are the cumulative amounts deducted from an employee's pay and credited toward this deduction. This file contains the following information on each transaction: employee name and number, job classification, effective date, and amount. Payroll also sums all contributions of that type for a particular period.

Payroll uses this file to calculate totals, compare individual employees with others, or analyze trends and patterns of the cost of certain deductions by group. This process creates duplicate information in employee records and in files for each type of deduction or other charge. Payroll also uses these files to reconcile its accounts.

Distributions

The payroll module generally includes files that function as check registers. Payroll may use one account just for paychecks and direct deposits, one for tax payments, and one for other payments, such as benefits premiums (if not paid by other functions). Each check-register file pertains to a particular bank and bank account number. As a user enters a new payment, the program prompts for the following data:

- Check number (generated by the program)
- Payee
- Issue date (or a current date default)
- Distribution method (paycheck, direct deposit to checking or savings account)
- Account code (from general ledger system)

The finance and accounting department, which maintains the corporate general ledger, has an established chart of accounts that indicates the type of payment and the account, project, or cost center to which it is applied. This department also may maintain a table of distribution codes to multiple accounts, particularly if the employer is a municipality, school district, or other public-sector entity. Payroll typically uses these codes for employee payroll cost accounting and for allocation of taxes to the proper account, but it also may have codes for insurance premiums, union disbursements, pension payments, and garnishee payments.

When the HRMS produces computerized paychecks, it generates most of this information itself, without significant user intervention. Once it produces the paychecks, it stores the data about each payment in the check register for the account on which it draws the payments and in the payroll record of the employee or other payee.

For employees who request direct deposit, the HRMS makes automatic deposits to the employee's bank, using bank number (for interbank transfers), bank account number, and appropriate amounts and dates. The system may track deposits to multiple accounts simultaneously, such as an employee's personal checking and savings accounts, individual retirement account (IRA), 401(k), or other retirement account.

Some programs include a routine for check reversal in case of error. Many payroll functions still perform check reversal manually, but some systems now automate this activity. If incorrect checks have already been distributed, the check reversal makes corrections in the next cycle. The system maintains a record of checks voided and transactions reversed. Even in a manual correction system, a routine may prompt the user for correction date, number of voided check or reversed transaction, amount of initial check, corrected amount, and reason for reversal.

Reporting Requirements

Whether part of human resources or finance and accounting, payroll makes few reporting decisions. Its job is to generate accurate, complete, timely reports that are largely mandated by federal and state regulations, benefits contracts, management policies, standard accounting practices, and banking procedures.

Employee Communication

Paychecks and Direct Deposit Advice. Each paycheck (sometimes called a warrant in the public sector) must include date of issue, net amount in both

```
┌─────────────────────────────────────────────────────────────────────────┐
│                      * * * PAYROLL PROFILE * * *                          │
│                                                                           │
│  SEARCH VALUE   ABC50000000000000005          SEARCH TYPE     G           │
│                                                                           │
│  EMPLOYEE KEY   ABC50000000000000005                                      │
│                                                                           │
│  NAME E PANKHURST                                                         │
│                                   SALARY    980.00                        │
│  JOB# 15211                       RATE    11.3086                         │
│                                   NORM HRS   86.66                        │
│  HIRE DATE   05-01-84             PAYMENT METHOD   D      PACKET CNTR.  0  │
│  GROSS YTD 1,842.40               ACTUAL STATUS    A      STAT CHG 02-15-88│
│  RECORD STATUS 0                  PENDING STATUS   A      VAC CYCLES    0  │
│                                                                           │
│  PART. SWITCH      ADD. WITHHOLDING      YTD WAGES      YTD TAX           │
│                                                                           │
│  FICA     0           656.78            1,960.00        140.14           │
│  FEDERAL  0            20.00            1,842.40        308.60           │
│  STATE    0                             1,942.40        115.96           │
│                                                                           │
│  ACCESS PATHS: PF1 - EMPLOYEE KEY, PF2 - S S NUMBER, PF3 - NAME,          │
│   PF4 - ACCESS PATH4, PF5 - ACCESS PATH5                                  │
│                                                                           │
│  RETURNS: PF9 - PAYROLL INQUIRY MENU, PF10 - PAYROLL MENU,                │
│  PF12 - ALL-SCREEN MENU                                                   │
└─────────────────────────────────────────────────────────────────────────┘
```

Figure 20–8. Typical payroll profile. This screen depicts the fundamental payroll data maintained on a given employee.
(Source: Genesys Software Systems. Reprinted with permission.)

numeric and alphabetic form, check number, and valid endorsement. The paycheck stub notes the period for which that paycheck applies. It lists current and year-to-date information on each type of gross, each type of deduction, and net pay. Some firms also use the pay stub as a communications vehicle, including notes about upcoming holidays, deadlines for benefits changes, and number of vacation and sick hours remaining.

A notice of direct deposit, called a deposit advice, contains exactly the same information, but without the check number or endorsement. It may look like a check but have "Not Negotiable" printed boldly or watermarked on the check form.

Sometimes computer limitations lead payroll to contract for external check-writing. In such cases, payroll furnishes the necessary data, and the service issues the checks or warrants.

Wage and Tax Statement. In the United States, the IRS requires that the employer create an annual report for each employee that lists amount of taxable wages and amounts withheld for federal, state, and local taxes of several types. Payroll prepares these reports, known as W-2s, then sends one copy to the IRS, one copy to the state taxing authority, and three copies to the employee. This report used to be fairly simple, but it has become more compli-cated because of rules for reporting ancillary forms of compensation, such as reimbursement for educational expenses, as well as reporting requirements for 401(k) and related plans. To ensure that W-2s are correct before distribution to employees, payroll often prepares trial versions of these statements for in-ternal review before issuing the final reports.

Payroll must prepare these reports by the end of January of each year for any employee who received wages or salary during the preceding year, so the payroll system must include not only current employees but also employees who were terminated or on leave of absence at the end of the year. The law requires employers to mail W-2s to the employee's home address, not to a post office box or company mail stop.

The government requires a similar report for pension distributions. The IRS pension distribution form W-2P resembles the W-2 but with a few differ-ent categories. It includes information on distributions from 401(k) plans, IRAs, and other retirement vehicles.

Miscellaneous Income Reports. Taxing authorities also mandate reports on compensation to nonemployees, such as contractors. The IRS requires that firms annually furnish this information to the contractor and the IRS on Form 1099-MISC if an individual receives more than $600 in nonemployee compen-sation. This report also applies to rents, royalties, prizes and awards, payments in lieu of dividends or interest, and other forms of income. The report lists the recipient's social security number or other identification number, the re-cipient's home address, the amount of income, the payer's address, and the payer's federal identification number. If accounting or other functions have made payments to these contractors or others during the year, accounting may take responsibility for preparing these reports, depending on where the re-quired data reside.

Transaction-Correction Notice. If an employee receives a check for an in-correct amount and payroll is correcting this mistake, a well-designed system includes provision for informing the employee about these circumstances. The notice should list the corrective action taken (such as check reversal or reduc-tion from next paycheck), the reason for the action, and the amount of the reversal.

Government Reports

Payroll has primary responsibility for making accurate, timely tax payments to various government agencies. Penalties for late payments and other forms of noncompliance can be severe and costly.

Filings. The IRS requires employees to make biweekly or quarterly tax payments as well as annual filings. The system may track the frequency of required reporting. The IRS has a variety of forms—940, 941, 941A, and others—depending on the size of the firm, its past tax history, and so forth. These filings list the accumulated amount of income tax withholdings, the amount of social security withholdings, and the amount of each type of employer-paid taxes. Payroll makes similar reports on similar schedules to state taxation authorities and other jurisdictions as required.

Copies of Reports to Employees and Other Payees. Payroll also must send revenue authorities copies of several forms distributed to or filled out by employees. These include the following:

- Copies of wage and tax statements (W-2s, W-2Ps)
- Copies of miscellaneous income reports (1099s)
- Copies of withholding allowance statements (W-4s) (for employees who claim ten or more withholding allowances)

Tax Payments. Payroll or accounting takes responsibility for writing checks for employee-related taxes. Sometimes the system can generate these checks automatically based on the accumulations files and the reports on employer tax liability. One check usually covers several types of taxes, such as income tax withheld from employee pay, unemployment insurance withheld, disability insurance premiums, and both employee-paid and employer-paid social security contributions.

Internal Reports

A modern payroll system can produce current and historical reports on any kind of earning, deduction, or tax withholding category. Although payroll itself is the most common user of such reports, sometimes finance and accounting, employee relations, or line management needs this information.

Individual Earnings History. For each payment to a particular employee, a complete individual earnings history report lists job classification, cost center or account, location, payment date, number of hours at each rate of pay (if applicable), pay rate, gross pay (total earnings), amounts for each deduction, total deductions, net pay, check amount, and check number. This report includes check reversal and prepayments. Payroll can produce an abbreviated history report that includes fewer elements, such as gross, net, and issue date.

COMP. 90001   CONSUMERS' WORLD, INC.   REPORT 03   PAGE 1

PAYROLL DEDUCTION REGISTER
08/29/89

DEPARTMENT CODE		PENSION	UNTD-WAY	SAVINGS	CHECKING	TOTALS
1006 4 SALLY ODAY	100 200 31					
	CUR	5.55	0.00	25.00	112.71	5.55
	YTD	22.05	10.00	0.00	0.00	32.05
		EMP 401K				
1000 0 MOLLY MANTLE	100 300 40					
	CUR	188.31				188.31
	YTD	188.31				188.31
		DEP MED	EMP 401K			
3000 8 SHELLY SWARTZ	500 600 60					
	CUR	0.00	21.08			21.08
	YTD	2.00	61.27			63.27
		GARNISH				
3009 7 LESTER LAWTON	500 600 62					
	CUR	114.71				114.71
	YTD	300.00				300.00
		EMP 401K				
SECTION 40 TOTAL						
	CUR	188.31				188.31
	YTD	188.31				188.31
		EMP 401K				
DEPARTMENT 300 TOTAL						
	CUR	188.31				188.31
	YTD	188.31				188.31
		PENSION	UNTD-WAY	EMP 401K	SAVINGS	CHECKING
DIVISION 100 TOTAL						
	CUR	5.55	0.00	188.31	25.00	112.71	193.86
	YTD	22.05	10.00	188.31	0.00	0.00	220.36

Figure 20–9. Typical deductions register. This report provides detailed information on the voluntary employee deductions withheld during a given pay cycle.

Accumulation and Distribution Reports. Payroll may need accumulation reports, such as those that list current obligations in federal employment-related taxes, state taxes, or particular deductions. Other reports can provide information about historical distributions in such categories.

Tax Distribution Summary. This special form of distribution report lists how much the organization has paid in taxes and to whom. A typical report lists month-to-date, quarter-to-date, and year-to-date figures for gross taxable income and payments for each type of employment-related tax, as well as number of employees paid. It lists these figures for federal taxes and for each state for which the organization must withhold taxes.

Check Registers. Payroll may keep several check registers—one specifically for payment of wages and salaries, another for tax liability, and another for benefits payments and other distributions. On a periodic basis, the system prints a report of activity in the check register during the preceding time period. Payroll then uses these to reconcile statements from the banks and other financial institutions.

Reconciliation Report. This report lists the results of reconciliation of each account payroll handles. The reconciliation process itself balances each check or other charge in the check register numerically with those in the bank statement. The report includes the date of reconciliation, a list of corrections made, and reasons for correction (coded). This report also goes to accounting to check on duplicate payments, interest received from interest-bearing accounts, and so forth.

Audit Reports. Many kinds of payroll audit reports exist. The most common is the transaction summary, which shows the before and after image of each transaction processed by batch, employee, or time period. This provides a check and balance not only on the accuracy of transaction processing but also on the performance of payroll data entry staff. Sophisticated audit reports use rules, formulas, or algorithms to identify exceptions. In a simple system, the report lists the status of the record before and after processing but does not flag obvious errors.

Reversal Update Report. This report lists all checks issued in error and transactions recorded incorrectly. The report usually includes payee name, employee number (if employee), check number, issue date, amount, reversal date, and reason for reversal (coded). As a further audit, it may include the payroll staff member who entered the reversal.

External Reports

Sometimes payroll must report on its financial transactions to other functions both within and outside human resources. The most common of these are reports to the treasury function and to finance and accounting.

Reports to General Ledger. Depending on organizational structure, payroll may track but not pay certain accounts. It may pass these figures to accounting for entry in the general ledger and payment. To do so, payroll issues a report on authorized payables. This may apply to benefit carriers, union dues, charitable contributions, and pension deductions.

Payroll also must report periodically, usually quarterly, to treasury or the department that has fiduciary responsibility for pensions and other benefit payments. The report lists each payee, issue date, checking account, check number, and code from a chart of accounts. Sometimes the check register is used for this purpose; otherwise, treasury may need a separate report.

Payment Authorization and Contribution Reports. Sometimes payroll sends reports on benefits-related deductions to the benefits function for review, approval, and payment. For each benefit type, this report lists contributions by each employee and amount and date of payment, as well as totals. Retirement benefits administration may receive payroll reports on individual deductions made as contributions to stock options, pension plans, and other retirement vehicles.

Union Dues Report. If payroll collects union dues, it must periodically provide the union with a report on which individuals made dues payments, when, and how much. The system may be able to organize these detail reports according to location, job classification, union, or other designation. Sometimes the union receives this report and payment every pay cycle, and sometimes it receives these monthly or quarterly.

Management and Planning Reports

Payroll generally produces financial planning reports on an ad hoc basis. For instance, it may produce a labor-cost distribution report of employee costs and hours by project, job, product, or other criteria. The system uses attributes contained in the job table to produce such reports. If sorting by project, the system can use a code from the employees' time card. Some firms use this information to pass employee time and expense charges on to clients.

Automated Labor-Cost Distribution

Some payroll systems include a labor-cost distribution function, which is sometimes referred to as labor distribution (LD). Organizations that must track allocation of time and salary dollars to specific projects, cost centers, or accounts can use an LD module to do so efficiently. As a cost accounting function, LD usually provides results in percentage or dollar form.

Following are some of the functions and features generally included in an LD module:

- Optional fixed distribution percentage
- Unlimited overrides
- Unlimited time card input
- Unlimited historical accumulation
- Calendar of fiscal period accumulations
- Budgeting capability
- Job-cost or project accounting
- User-defined unique labor definitions
- Full general retrieval capability
- Standard reporting (by dependent, cost center, or project)
- Labor posting and reporting

Special Circumstances

Personnel often regards payroll as that "necessary nuisance" at the end of the record-keeping process. To mitigate this negative attitude, payroll must strive for scrupulous accuracy, working hard to minimize the mistakes that inevitably occur in a high-volume operation. Everyone concerned should understand how payroll gets the information on which it bases its calculations and should acknowledge that payroll can be only as accurate as the quality of the data received.

Payroll develops a calendar to determine how many days before checks are written the system must have pertinent data. Based on this, it establishes policies and procedures for cutoff dates for submission of transactions. Payroll should inform line managers, compensation, and other human resources functions of these deadlines by publishing a payroll activity calendar. Payroll gains considerable goodwill by having procedures for retroactive changes in special circumstances so employees do not have to suffer because of delays or errors by management, human resources, or payroll.

If a problem develops, such as incorrect paychecks or excessive overtime charges, payroll interacts with line management. Such problems usually result from procedural or administrative errors rather than technical malfunctions.

Payroll should maintain open communication with compensation and benefits. Compensation keeps payroll informed of mass adjustments that may include one-time payments or affect a specific employee population. Benefits should inform payroll of new programs and policies.

Glossary

Accumulation The amount of money deducted from employees' pay and credited toward a particular deduction.

Chart of accounts An accounting and bookkeeping table that is part of the general ledger system. This table assigns codes to categories of expenses, such as employee net wages, federal withholding tax, and insurance premiums.

Deduction Money withheld from an employee's gross earnings for contributions or payments toward income tax withholding, benefits, charitable organizations, union dues, equipment, credit union savings accounts or loans, and other employee obligations or commitments.

Direct deposit A form of electronic funds transfer in which employees authorize their employer to transfer their net pay to their personal bank account. Computer tapes are processed through the Automated Clearing House (ACH), a nationwide banking network linked to the Federal Reserve system.

Earnings The various forms of compensation for which employees may be eligible. Includes not only salary or regular hourly pay but also overtime, commissions, tips, severance pay, bonuses, and other forms of compensation.

Federal Insurance Contributions Act (FICA) The federal statute that mandates employer and employee contributions to social security.

Federal Unemployment Tax Act (FUTA) Requires employers to file federal Form 940 to report taxable wages and deposits of FUTA taxes annually. Must file for employees whose wages were $1,500 in any quarter or who worked some part of at least one day in 20 different weeks.

FICA See *Federal Insurance Contributions Act.*

FUTA See *Federal Unemployment Tax Act.*

Gross-to-net The calculation of net pay from gross pay by determining all deductions and subtracting them from gross pay.

1099 A series of IRS forms for providing information on income other than wages, salary, and tips. Payroll most often uses Form 1099-MISC for reporting nonemployee compensation (such as payments to independent contractors). The payee receives a copy of the 1099, as does the IRS.

Wage and tax report The total amount withheld from all employees' earnings for a particular deduction but not yet paid to the eventual recipient of the deduction, such as the government or an insurance carrier.

W-4 The withholding allowance statement on which an employee lists marital status and number of withholding allowances for tax purposes. Employers must distribute blank IRS forms and collect these data from each employee at the time of hire.

Withholding allowance A person whom the IRS considers a qualified member of an individual's household. Possible withholding allowances include self, spouse, dependent children, and other dependents. Withholding allowances reduce an individual's taxable income. Each employee submits a W-4 form to indicate the number of withholding allowances to use in calculating tax liability.

W-2 A wage and tax statement distributed to each employee annually. The report, distributed on a form furnished by the IRS, lists the amount of taxable wages paid and the amounts withheld from the employee's wages for federal, state, and local taxes of several types.

W-2P A form similar to a W-2 but used for retirement plan distributions.

Discussion Points

1. In the average organization, which generally has higher priority—payroll or personnel applications? What are the reasons for this?
2. Should both the payroll and personnel functions be part of human resources, or should each be organizationally separate, with payroll part of finance?
3. Under what circumstances should payroll and personnel applications be integrated, interfaced, or maintained as independent systems?
4. Under what circumstances would an organization benefit most from using a payroll service bureau?
5. Assuming that an organization is developing an integrated HRMS, which function would it probably implement first—payroll or personnel? Why?
6. How does timekeeping affect payroll systems? What implications does this have for attendance and absenteeism policies and procedures?

7. How do payroll systems differ among banks, manufacturers, retailers, and service organizations?

8. When might payroll want to produce audit reports? Describe several specific kinds of audit reports that might be useful.

Further Reading

Anderson, Carol. "PAYE: A Working Guide for the Small Business." London, UK: *Telegraph Publications*, 1988.

Bennison, M. "Computers in Personnel: The Crunch Issues." *Personnel Management*, September 1982.

Berleth, G., K. Reilly, and D. Risteau. *The American Payroll Association's 1988 Basic Guide to Payroll*. Englewood Cliffs, NJ: Prentice-Hall Professional Newsletters, 1988.

Ceriello, Vincent R. "The Integration/Interface of HR with Other Automated Systems: Part I." *Personnel News*, May/June 1988.

———. "The Integration/Interface of HR with Other Automated Systems: Part II." *Personnel News*, July/August 1988.

Council on the Economic Status of Women. *Pay Equity and Public Employment*. St. Paul, MN: 1982.

Edwards, Tim. "Personnel and Payroll on a Microcomputer." In *Computers in Personnel: Towards the Personnel Office of the Future*, edited by Terry Page. Sussex, UK: Institute of Personnel Management and Institute of Manpower Studies, 1983.

Fogel, W. *The Equal Pay Act: Implications for Comparable Worth*. New York: Praeger, 1984.

Gillin, Paul. "First-Time User of T-S Payroll-Personnel Service Cites Cost Savings." *Computer Decisions*, June 1983.

Hierl, Michael. "It's Not Just Payroll Anymore." *Software News*, August 1984.

Lung, Dieter. "No Single Solution." *Payroll Exchange*, October 1984.

Milkovich, G.T., and R. Broderick. "Pay Discrimination: Legal Issues and Implications for Research." *Industrial Relations*, 21, 1982.

Miller, Bonnie, and Sidney H. Simon. "Applications: HRMS—Who Should Have Control, Personnel or Payroll?" *Software Magazine*, August 1988.

Morley, Ann L. "HRMS Has Come a Long Way Since Payroll." *Software News*, March 1984.

National Committee on Pay Equity. *Pay Equity: An Issue of Race, Ethnicity, and Sex*. Washington, DC: 1987.

Patten, Thomas H., Jr. *Pay: Employee Compensation and Incentive Plans*. New York: Free Press, 1977.

———. "Pay Cuts: Will Employees Accept Them?" *National Productivity Review*, 1, 1981.

Reeve, J.T. "An Operational Audit of Payroll." *Automation*, February 1984.

Reichenberg, N. "Pay Equity in Review." *Public Personnel Management*, 15, 1986.

Reid, Allan T. "Automate Time and Attendance Recording." *Personnel Journal*, March 1988.

Richard-Carpenter, Colin. "Toward Integrated Records." *Personnel Management*, October 1986.

———. "Time to Link Clocking to Payroll." *Personnel Management*, October 1987.

Rumac, B., L. Holter, and S. Livacz. A Summary Report on an Executive Survey of Payroll and Human Resource Issues. Roseland, NJ: Automatic Data Processing, 1988.

Salam, D.J., and L.K. Price. Principles of Payroll Administration. Paramus, NJ: Prentice-Hall Information Services, 1988.

Simon, Sidney H. "Time-Efficient Software Evaluation: Integrating HRIS and Payroll Data." *Personnel Journal*, September 1986.

Thayer, Warren. "Computerized Payroll Pays Off." *Progressive Grocer, June 1988.*

VRC Consulting Group. "Payroll and Personnel: The Controversy Continues." *Human Resource Management Systems Report. Los Altos, CA:* December 1985.

21
Other HRMS Applications

Information, its communication and use, is the web of society; the
basis for all human understanding, organization, and effort.
—John Diebold

An automated HRMS can accommodate an almost endless number of
applications besides those covered in the preceding chapters. The
HRMS can handle virtually any data that users can define or quantify.
For any potential addition, the HRMS function should perform a requirements analysis to define or validate the users' needs for data and reports. To
the extent that high volume, speed, accuracy, or complexity of analysis indicates that the function should have computer support, this application becomes part of the overall HRMS plan.

Additional applications may include sales incentives, pension and retirement benefits administration, health benefits claims administration, time and
attendance record keeping, employee clubs and activities, premises security,
quality assurance, and the human factors aspects of facilities planning. Even
among the most comprehensive HRMS packages, few contain the complete
assortment of applications, but some are available as specialized software packages. Departments that choose to integrate special-purpose applications into
the HRMS must invest in the development of new programs or interfaces, or
at least develop user-defined fields, routines, and reports. Increasingly,
users choose stand-alone, microcomputer-based applications that run
independently.

Solid demographics form a firm basis for almost any HRMS application.
Additional required data may be numerous and unpredictable in content, format, and structure. Many applications simply require definition of new data
fields in employee records. Additional fields might include parking lot assignments, tool crib access, safety gear, company equipment, and auto leases. If
users need only an additional records segment, the manager should plan for
adaptation of the main HRMS. If the additional module requires a large
amount of data not otherwise needed by human resources, a separate system
often works best. Separation also has advantages in cases of software incom-
patibility, time constraints, and security needs.

Since some of these activities lie outside the usual responsibilities of a
typical human resources department, external resources and special-purpose

software may become involved. For instance, facilities and premises consultants might access the HRMS data base as part of designing new buildings. Security firms may use pertinent data from the HRMS to verify building access authorizations. In such cases, system designers must make special efforts to protect the records of individuals against possible invasion of privacy. With the more complex of these functions, such as claims processing and retirement benefits administration, the firm does not need to make an all-or-nothing decision about whether to handle this function in-house or externally. Sometimes an in-house system produces an extract file—a subset of the master file—for forwarding or electronic transmission to an outside system. Sometimes an in-house system handles daily records management, but a specialist firm provides statistical analysis, plan administration, and claims processing analysis. The more complex the specific activity, the more likely it is that an external resource can obtain useful results more efficiently than in-house staff.

This book cannot detail each of the possible ancillary applications, but this chapter presents some examples of how to integrate into an HRMS applications not normally considered part of human resources.

Security and Access Control

In the context of a specific HRMS module, *security* refers to the safeguarding of facilities, equipment, and individuals, not to data security. Data security is part of the development of the HRMS, as discussed in chapter 3. Responsibility for physical security may rest outside human resources with security, property management, or facilities planning. To the extent employee records are involved, human resources handles the link to the HRMS. Even if another department provides most of the input, the methods and procedures for how information links to the master HRMS data base should rest within human resources. Sometimes the safety and health function handles site security, particularly if the most important safety risks involve physical security, the firm has relatively few occupational safety issues, and security does not involve much highly confidential material.

Security usually needs a complete, current listing of employees, so a link with the HRMS usually works better than a stand-alone system. Designing a security module usually requires the addition of a relatively small records segment to employee and position records in the HRMS. Analysis and reporting requirements are usually straightforward. A firm may consider a separate system if it has particularly tight security requirements or if its security tracking covers relatively few employees.

Sometimes the security function wants to automate its record keeping but must wait behind other human resources and departmental functions before IS can address its needs. Because of the power and capabilities of microcom-

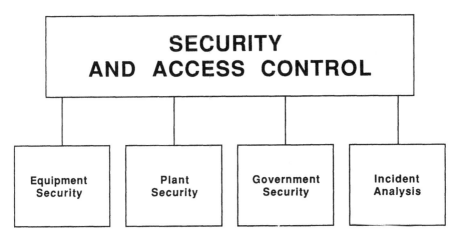

Figure 21–1. Principal roles of the security and access control function.

puter systems, security may decide that it can get on-line faster and more cheaply by getting its own little system.

Plant security includes two types of data—data on the security privileges of employees and data on the security requirements and status of physical premises. To the extent that security is a function of identifying and monitoring who has access to what facilities, when, and under what conditions, an HRMS can help deal with the security of operations and facilities via employee records and job classification tables. A security module may track authorization and status of issues such as government security clearances, industrial and plant security, parking lot assignments, and bonding. (Mandated security clearances are discussed in chapter 12.)

To add a security module, the HRMS project team must devise methods and procedures for determining who has what types of security access. Many firms base potential authorization on job classification; for defense and other government security work, authorization attaches to the specific employee or contractor rather than to job classification. Jobs that may involve access to restricted areas include corporate management, maintenance technicians, contract program administrators, defense industry employees, and medical staff.

Industrial and plant security refers to access not only to the site itself but also to computer centers, special clean rooms, laboratories, supply stores, tool cribs, and any areas in which government classified or proprietary work takes place. It also includes access to and authorization to use specific equipment. A security function may need to make relevant information available to security guards regarding gate access, loading docks, identification badges, and equipment registration.

Large organizations often institute parking security, particularly if the facility has limited parking or if certain employees require special parking be-

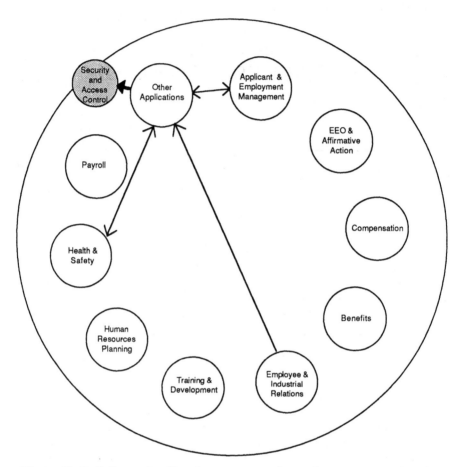

Figure 21–2. Information flow between security and access control and other human resources functions.

cause of assignment, shift, or status. In such arrangements, the security function must keep track of which vehicles (or individuals) are authorized to park in which specific lots or spaces. To do this, they may use vehicle registration numbers, stickers, individually assigned numbers on parking stickers, cards with magnetized strips, or other identifiers.

Security also includes monitoring the bonding status of individuals who handle corporate or customer accounts. Most companies have at least a few employees whose jobs involve handling large amounts of money, such as those handling employee stores, credit unions, or charitable contributions. In banks, insurance companies, brokerage houses, and credit unions, large numbers of employees may have some authorized fiduciary responsibility. Bonding insures the organization against loss if employees use these funds in an unauthorized or unlawful manner.

Security Data Requirements

Security data include information from employee master records, the security function, and, depending on industry and government contract status, certain external agencies.

Employee Records. The security module may link its files on employees to HRMS master files via employee number or another identifier. Security often needs information on job classification, job grade or management level, location, and work schedule from those master files. If the systems are not integrated, human resources and security must work out a system of electronic or paper interfacing that keeps security informed of relevant data updates.

Security may need these data in order to derive additional data. For instance, job classification may correlate with types of security clearances available. Some organizations choose to assign this level on an individual basis, since it is the employee who is cleared, not the position occupied.

If security needs employee vehicle registration numbers, driver's license numbers, or other information the employee controls, the employment function generally collects this information as part of the hiring process or during new-employee orientation. These data may reside only in the security system or may be part of the employee master data base in the HRMS. Security should establish procedures for checking this information periodically, since employees may change status or vehicles or have temporary assignments that affect security privileges.

In some cases, the security function may collect personal data on employees that the rest of human resources does not need. For instance, government security clearance applications ask for lifetime residence, school attendance, and law enforcement history. Some organizations input these data in their systems; others just keep a file copy of the application, since this information does not affect other aspects of the employee's relationship to the organization. Because of the sensitive nature of these data, most organizations do not include such information in the HRMS.

Security Function Data. The security function itself also generates data for employee security tracking. These include authorization codes, passwords, physical access authorization, and status. Usually human resources enters these directly into the records of specific individuals. In some cases, security may create tables that relate security authorization to existing data fields, most commonly job classification, job grade or management level, or location. The security module also has information related to specific locations and facilities, such as equipment registration, serial numbers, keys, and lock combinations.

External Data. Sometimes security must perform background checks on incumbents in (or those under consideration for) sensitive positions. These checks may include investigation into prior employment, vehicle registration, driver's license status, criminal record, and prior government clearance. External data also include the results of clearance investigations performed by government agencies, such as the U.S. Department of Defense or the Nuclear Regulatory Commission.

In keeping with requirements for protection of personal privacy (and to avoid wrongful termination suits), this information becomes part of the security data segment only if the content affects the employee's job responsibilities. Usually entries simply note the status of the investigation (requested, pending, or completed) and the results (passed, rejected, or conditional).

Bonding. Tracking bonding status requires only a few data fields. Several fields may note bonding status and dates for each action. Choices may include application submitted, pending, approved, or denied. Other fields may indicate reason for bonding (coded) and effective dates. Most bonding data, such as bond amount, cost of bond, and renewal date, are maintained by the policy issuer. These are not included in the HRMS. Firms that require bonding for most of their employees often contract for a bonding policy that automatically covers all employees upon hire unless an individual is specifically excluded. Bonding data can be maintained in the employee's master record in the HRMS, as this information is highly static in nature.

Security Reports

Security data are usually very restricted, so any reports containing such data receive very limited and specific distribution. In such cases, security has its own dedicated printer to avoid jeopardizing security during the output process.

Security Status Reports. Security guards need immediate access to current information about each individual's authorized access and related privileges. Each security post or office usually has a printout (or terminal) that the guard or appropriate security staff member can use to access any individual's security record. The detail list or screen may include employee name, position code, work location, supervisor, authorized restricted locations, parking lot assignment, equipment authorized to use (such as certain restricted computers), hours of access to restricted area, and so forth. A detail report may list every

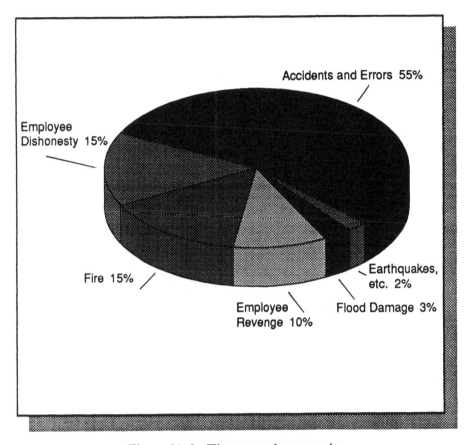

Figure 21-3. Threats to data security.

individual; a summary report provides the number of individuals having each type of security or parking access.

Incident Reports. A security incident report functions much like a law enforcement log. The report lists events as line items, noting time of incident, date of occurrence, incident, location, and outcome. Some may list individuals involved in the incident. Each firm's needs dictate the kind of information this report should include. The function may issue a profile report for each incident or prepare a summary for each day, week, or month that lists the number of each type of incident. Security usually maintains these reports in special restricted-access files. They may or may not eventually file them with the employee's work records.

In some cases, an incident relevant to law enforcement authorities may take place involving company property or assets or in the course of an employee's work duty. For instance, an employee may have a car accident in the parking lot or may be suspected of stealing office computers. In such cases, security may prepare an incident report for external distribution.

Security History Report. In some cases, management or an outside agency has a legitimate need to know about the security status and history of particular employees. Law enforcement authorities may be investigating embezzlement of company funds; government agencies may be checking on potential security risks; management may want to take corrective action against chronic violators of security policies and procedures. When these circumstances arise, security may produce a profile report on a specific individual.

Government Security Reports. The U.S. Department of Defense, the Nuclear Regulatory Commission, and many other government agencies require periodic reports on clearances. Each agency has its own timetable, data requirements, and formats. An organization must work closely with relevant agencies to ascertain that the security package will meet the requirements of all agencies to which the organization must report.

Contract administrators may need reports that list the current access privileges for each employee working on a particular project, including times, locations, and circumstances of permitted access. When planning assignments for projects that require government clearance, management and agency representatives may want a list of employees who meet certain security criteria, such as former clearance to particular levels or with certain types of equipment. When deciding what information on employees to provide government representatives, human resources managers and staff should use considerations based on a need to know.

Retirement Benefits

A good retirement plan offers many important benefits to both employees and employers. An effective retirement plan not only helps employees prepare for the future but also provides them with significant tax advantages. It also helps the organization attract and retain good employees while obtaining significant tax advantages of its own. Not only are contributions to a qualified retirement plan tax deductible, but so are costs for establishing, installing, and maintaining such a plan.

The benefits function tracks eligibility and participation in many types of benefits, but in most cases, having ascertained the number of participants, benefits simply makes a payment to a carrier, then employees make claims as

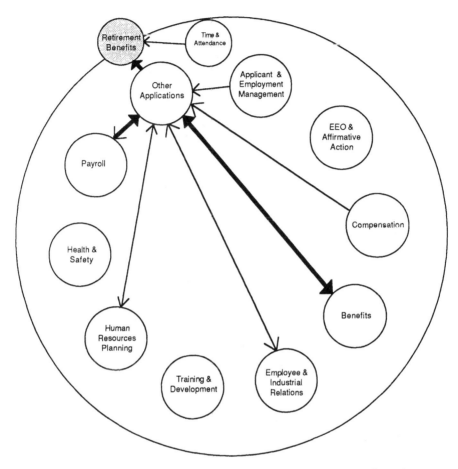

Figure 21–4. Principal roles of retirement benefits administration.

needed. In the case of pension plans and other financial retirement benefits, however, some function must take responsibility for managing the funds contributed to the plan, then handle their later distribution, not as a one-time claim but on a regular basis for years. Performing such tasks inappropriately has great cost for the firm and its employees. These more complicated requirements keep all but the largest, most sophisticated firms from administering their pension plans and other retirement benefits themselves.

In the vast majority of cases, firms have outside specialists administer such funds. The in-house staff may track eligibility and contributions, but outside groups handle fund investment, management, and disbursement. Only the largest firms handle this complicated area in-house, and usually only if their own business already requires that they have significant financial management expertise in-house.

Four major advantages of internal retirement plan administration lead organizations to choose this approach:

1. It is less expensive than hiring a third-party administrator.
2. It provides improved plan confidentiality and control.
3. It provides improved retirement plan communication with employees.
4. It has more flexibility than outside administration.

Administering a plan internally means that sensitive plan data stay within the organization's control. Outsiders are not privy to employee, company, and plan data. In addition to keeping plan information confidential, most human resources departments like the idea of controlling plan administration tasks.

Perhaps the most important advantage of in-house administration is improved employee communication. Running the plan internally means the employer can control the development of creative, timely, and explicit communication with employees regarding their retirement benefits. Improved communication can stimulate interest and participation.

External administration has some less obvious economic disadvantages. For example, many insurance companies, banks, and brokerage houses provide free or low-cost plan administration as an inducement to buy their insurance or investment products. This locks the client into products that may be less favorable than ones they could select on their own. Thus, third-party administration of retirement plans can be costly, inefficient, and inflexible.

A firm that handles this process internally may have a special retirement benefits administration function that takes responsibility for all aspects of retirement benefits as well as the other human resources aspects of its retired employees and beneficiaries. This function often uses its own data base, which is separate from the main HRMS, because individuals receiving pensions are no longer active employees. Upon retirement, the employee's status code reflects this change, and the system routes the relevant elements of that employee's record to a transaction file periodically transferred to the retirement benefits administration system. This system has only a nominal connection to personnel records, since it usually involves a one-time transmittal of data from the HRMS.

The retirement benefits administration function, which may or may not be part of the benefits unit, may take responsibility for the following areas:

- Pension accounts, including 401(k), simplified employee pension (SEP), IRA, or other retirement plans
- Pension payments to retirees

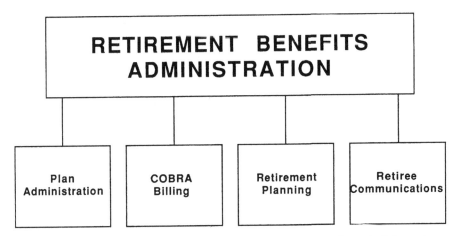

Figure 21–5. Information flow between retirement benefits administration and other human resources functions.

- Payments to surviving annuitants (beneficiaries of the retiree)
- Consolidated Omnibus Budget Reconciliation Act (COBRA) billing management (After separation, COBRA extends eligibility for certain benefits to terminated and retired employees and their dependents. To participate, the individual requests conversion of coverage and pays the individual premium.)
- Extended benefits to retirees (medical, dental, or life insurance)
- Retirement planning (Employees may consult with retirement specialists to learn their current retirement benefits eligibility and status, as well as to make changes in their retirement plan, such as shifts in voluntary contribution rates for pension plans.)
- Other forms of financial planning and savings, such as stock options, stock purchase plans, and estate planning

Because human resources may not handle retirement benefits administration and the complexity of this function varies widely among firms, HRMS vendors have a reduced incentive to offer packages for handling these data. Therefore, vendors do not generally create their own packages but provide an interface to various pension administration systems offered by actuaries, consultants, trusts, and other external services. These programs may be administered by large accounting firms, capital management firms, or plan administration specialists who develop and use plan-management software themselves. They may then license portions of it to their clients. In some cases,

HRMS vendors do not own the software but license it. The owner now has access to a new user, to whom it can offer its consulting services.

Because of the complexity of retirement benefits administration, a firm that handles these operations in-house almost always requires a mainframe computer. Even if the data base fits on a microcomputer, the enterprise may not have enough employees to warrant having specialized financial management staff handle the pension plan accounting.

Because retirement benefits management programs require such complicated algorithms and processing routines, most users adopt packaged programs rather than create customized ones. Firms that provide pension accounting prefer to have their trained staff manually perform some of the steps they could incorporate into a custom program if they were willing and able to make the required investment. They prefer to limit their involvement to personal, individualized account management.

Another downside to in-house retirement benefits administration pertains to compliance and regulation issues. The need to stay current with complex compliance issues and regulations often is the critical factor in deciding whether to bring plan administration in-house in the first place and then whether to build or buy the system. Key selection criteria when buying the system are the vendor's ability and commitment to update it. Retirement plan software vendors and consultants spend considerable time and money keeping themselves and their software up-to-date so clients do not have to interpret new regulations and guidelines. In other words, staying current with compliance issues and regulations does not need to be an additional burden for the human resources department. The service provider should handle it.

Types of Retirement Benefits

Many organizations offer several retirement benefits options. The federal Employee Retirement Income Security Act (ERISA) contains extensive requirements for the offering and administering of benefits plans in order to qualify for tax deferral. These regulatory complexities have prompted most human resources departments to consult ERISA specialists when developing, revising, or computerizing such plans. Plans may include the following:

- Pensions. Pensions may be any of a variety of investment plans. They may include both employee and employer contributions or only employer contributions. The contributions are managed in the form of stocks, bonds, mutual funds, or other investment vehicles. The benefit amount often depends on the employee's seniority and salary in the period preceding retirement.
- 401(k) plans. Both employee and employer contribute to an individual retirement plan; the employee's contribution is taxed only at withdrawal.

What to Look for
in Retirement Plan Software

Retirement plan software can respond more effectively to management needs if it can perform the following tasks:

- Administer investment diversities in dollar amounts, percentages, and shares
- Weight account balances when calculating gains and losses
- Accommodate various vesting schedules such as cliff, 10-year, 15-year, sliding scale, class year, and incremental
- Handle various termination processes, such as joint and survivor clauses, lump-sum payments, and annuity purchases
- Generate benefits statements and other employee communications
- Modify standard reports, forms, letters, and statements
- Generate a variety of management reports, including eligibility, qualification analysis, tax summaries, plan costing models, and top-heavy determination
- Generate or make use of standard output for government reporting

This list is not inclusive. As with any HRMS software, the project team should consider general selection factors such as training, support, user groups, software updates, system flexibility, conversion, documentation, and vendor stability.

- IRAs. The employee may contribute up to $2,000 per year in tax-deferred income to an IRA. No monies are available until the IRA matures and the individual reaches the age of 59½. Financial institutions provide IRAs in a wide range of both defined benefit and defined contribution instruments. Employers used to offer IRAs, but few do today because of changes in tax laws, although they may still administer accounts previously established. Depending on the number and complexity of plans, human resources may choose to administer them using brokers or trustees. If the plans are administered internally, the HRMS tracks each IRA choice for participating employees.

- SEP plans. A SEP plan is similar to a 401(k) plan but is available only to companies having twenty-five or fewer employees. To accommodate small firms, SEP regulations have fewer administrative requirements than 401(k) plans.
- Savings and stock investment plans. The employee contributes a percentage of his or her salary toward savings or stock purchases, and the organization may match those funds according to some established formula. The organization invests these contributions in the employee's choice of investment vehicles or in the company's own stock, depending on the plan.
- Tax-deferred annuities. Public schools, colleges and universities, and charitable organizations may provide qualified tax-deferred annuity plans to their employees. These plans may involve contributions by just the employee or by the employer as well. Tax-deferred annuities may involve various distribution options, such as periodic payments for life.
- Social security. Companies do not administer payment of social security benefits, but many firms report to the employee anticipated social security benefits based on current rates and conditions projected to his or her expected retirement date. Some include this information in individual employee benefits statements as a reminder that the employer as well as the employee makes regular social security payments. Moreover, some firms track social security benefits because these entitlements are considered supplemental to other employer-paid plans.
- Universal life and whole life insurance. Universal or whole life insurance has higher premiums than term insurance but also acquires a cash or loan value, which an employee can later surrender or borrow against to meet retirement needs. A firm that operates in the insurance field may offer such a plan to employees, perhaps even including low-interest loans to pay premiums.

Retirement Benefits Data Requirements

Independent of the benefits function in human resources, retirement benefits administration may handle data on employees, dependents, beneficiaries, and actual benefit plans. If the retirement benefits administration module is part of the HRMS, it uses a combination of data from the employment, compensation, benefits, and payroll modules. This function also generates additional data to analyze assets, investments, forfeitures, and disbursements.

Basic Employee Data. If the retirement benefits administration module operates separately from the HRMS, the system must record some of the basic employee data the HRMS contains. This includes name, basic job information such as salary or wage rate, length of service, age, expected and actual retirement dates, and beneficiaries. Most of this information can come directly from the HRMS.

Retirement Benefits Calculation Data. For each retirement benefit, the HRMS includes routines composed of rules and calculation formulas. These routines calculate financial participation, accrued benefits, and projected benefits for each eligible individual.

To calculate the retirement contribution rate for employees and employers, the system must contain information such as that described in chapter 15, including accumulated hours and earnings, eligibility dates, and eligibility rules. As a basis for auditing individual accounts, the system will normally contain calculation formulas for employee and employer contributions even when these are administered externally. It also considers vesting rules, earnings rules, and the like.

- Eligibility rules. The eligibility formula factors in age and seniority (and perhaps other variables) to determine an individual's eligibility and projected eligibility date. Each job classification or job family also may point to an attribute that shows which retirement plans an incumbent may choose.
- Vesting rules. The program uses a similar procedure to determine vesting status. Vesting refers to the percentage of the retirement benefits to which an employee is currently entitled and that the individual would retain if he or she left the organization before retirement. The HRMS may derive the vesting percentage from a separate table that assigns a percentage to various levels of seniority. Some firms use vesting formulas based on age as well as seniority.
- Earnings rules. Many plans limit the annual contribution level. For instance, 401(k) tax-deferral provisions apply only to the first $7,000 (indexed to the inflation rate) in employee contributions. Other limits apply to employer contributions. The HRMS uses earnings rules when calculating deductions, employer contributions, and so forth. The system may set up maximum payroll deductions for such retirement plans in the same way that social security maximums operate.
- Social security tables. Increasingly, systems track social security benefits by including tables of contributions according to income and tables of projected benefits.

Retirement Benefits Status. Based on the rules for calculating security benefits, each individual's record includes information relating to each plan. In addition to standard benefits information, such as eligibility, employee contribution, and employer contribution, each individual's record also contains information such as the following:

- Enrollment date
- Normal retirement date
- Projected retirement date
- Credited service (based on attendance records)
- Dates to/from breaks in service (based on scheduled layoffs, recalls, and various leaves of absence)
- Employee contribution to date
- Employer contribution to date
- Vesting level
- Final retirement base pay
- Maximum pension payable
- Retirement value (This is the estimated monthly retirement payment based on total contributions to date, current salary, and seniority. Depending on the type of plan, the employee's record also might include guaranteed ROI and actual ROI.)

If a surviving spouse or other dependents would be eligible for pension benefits, employee records should include relevant information. The module also may include a field that indicates whether a survivor is currently receiving benefits from the organization's retirement system, with appropriate flags denoting to whom payments should be disbursed, contingent beneficiaries, and payment frequency.

Information about plan participation, beneficiaries, and employee contribution rate may be input from data supplied by the employee. Most other data are calculated fields based on payroll information and algorithms that compute contribution rates. These values may be in dollar amounts, percentages, or shares depending on the provisions of the retirement system.

Retirement Benefits Contributions. The payroll function plays a key role in retirement benefits administration. The retirement benefits administration function provides payroll with data on the rate or amount to use in calculating plan contributions for each participating employee and data on amounts to pay to retirees or their survivors. Every time payroll staff perform these calculations as part of the process of preparing paychecks, they provide retirement benefits administration with a report on relevant deductions taken. The payroll system should be able to export such information periodically or at the end of each payroll cycle to the HRMS and to external plan administrators and actuaries. Increasingly, firms are installing data kiosks similar to bank automatic teller machines (ATMs). At these terminals, employees can inquire about retirement benefits and input data about contribution rates, beneficiaries, and other employee-determined variables.

Check and Tax Data. Any of several sources might write the actual pension distribution checks, including retirement benefits administration, accounts payable, or the financial institution that holds the funds, such as a bank. If an internal function writes those checks, the system must track data related to check writing, direct deposit, taxation, and other accounting activities.

The data requirements are basically the same as those for generating paychecks (see chapter 20). Additionally, the check-writing function should include fields indicating the reasons for the disbursement, such as pension distribution, pension liquidation (in the case of a terminated, nonvested employee), forfeitures, or transfer of funds to different accounts. Another field should indicate the relationship of recipient to employee (employee, spouse, parent, child, or nonrelative) because of state laws governing this area.

If an outside trustee handles fund distribution, the in-house group may not import and maintain data on disbursements to individuals but leave that to the trustee or bank. Human resources or treasury simply receives summary information indicating total distributions, contributions, and income for the period.

Pension Asset Management Data. Most organizations use specialists to manage their pension funds. Occasionally, some sophisticated organizations have a retirement benefits administration function handle investment and management of these funds internally. To do so, it must track information such as investment vehicle, current assets, rate of return, and investment maturity date.

This information remains completely separate from human resources data because it does not relate to employees or jobs but rather to the actual fund assets. Finance or treasury, rather than human resources, typically takes responsibility for this information.

Stock Options and Purchases. For many employees, stock options and purchases serve as retirement benefits plans. Although the simplest administration of such a plan would require just a few more data fields in the benefits segment, the complexities of administration usually require a separate module. Management of stock options and purchases requires access to data such as eligibility, issuance and execution dates, trust accounts, and reinvestments. In most cases, stock option or purchase programs operate independently of the HRMS. In fact, this responsibility may reside outside human resources. Several vendors offer such packages, which are usually for microcomputers or are tied to administration by bureaus or banks.

Retirement Benefits Reporting Requirements

The retirement benefits administration function uses many of the same types of reports as the benefits function that administers medical, life, disability, dental, and other insurance coverage. Some of the notable differences are discussed in the following sections.

Individual Retirement Benefits Statement. Firms that offer retirement benefits must provide the individual with a periodic statement describing those benefits. Whichever entity handles retirement benefit administration usually also provides the individual statements. For each plan in which the individual participates, the retirement benefits statement lists current rate of employee and employer contributions, dates of contributions, contribution amounts, and year-to-date contributions.

The statement may include projections of retirement value at several different retirement dates and contribution rates. Depending on the type of plan, it may list current ROIs and other financial data to assist potential retirees in making investment decisions. The report also may include a projection of social security benefits.

Pension and Retirement Plan Status Reports. Plan administrators usually must prepare several types of periodic reports on the funds entrusted to them. They must report to the firm's treasurer or accounting department about amount contributed, amount invested, change in asset valuation, amount of disbursements, and dates of contribution, disbursement, and change. If the firm has investments of several types, each type requires a separate report. Employees, retirees, and other plan contributors also receive periodic reports on fund assets and disbursements. These are generally summary reports, but each individual also receives an annual or quarterly summary of the account, with contributions and distributions listed. Most systems also can generate historical reports covering the employee's entire tenure with the firm.

Eligibility and Enrollment Reports. Enrollment reports help retirement benefits administration track financial obligations incurred through pension administration. As with other benefits, these reports list employees eligible, not eligible, and participating in a particular plan. They may contain enrollment status, enrollment date, employee contributions, employer contributions, age, service, and anticipated retirement date. A summary form of this report may list contributions and employer obligations by actual retirement age, type of plan, date, or other criteria.

```
*****************************
EMPLOYEES ELIGIBLE FOR RETIREMENT
          THROUGH 1990
*****************************
```

BIRTH DT	LAST NAME	FIRST NAME	SOC.SEC.NO	SERV DT	DEPT	JOB TITLE	RETIRE DT
03-29-27	BONAVENTURE	JOSEPH	207-36-9843	06-15-65	A784	FINANCIAL ANALYST	03-29-87
07-15-29	CAMPBELL	MARYANN	564-98-2073	10-13-76	A133	PROGRAMMER	07-15-89
12-24-27	SCHULTZ	HERMAN	108-43-9624	05-01-60	D237	ACCT CLERK III	12-24-87
10-11-28	STENGEL	JOHN	204-29-3366	10-15-77	B237	CASHIER	10-11-88
04-11-30	CALLAHAN	CAROLYN	439-26-1145	07-19-68	D684	MGR ENGINEERING	04-11-90

```
NUMBER ELIGIBLE IN 1986    37
NUMBER ELIGIBLE IN 1987    24
NUMBER ELIGIBLE IN 1988    20
NUMBER ELIGIBLE IN 1989    28
NUMBER ELIGIBLE IN 1990    37

146
```

Figure 21–6. Retirement eligibility report. This report lists employees who will be eligible for normal retirement during the period 1986 to 1990. In this case, the report lists eligible employees alphabetically. It also could list them by eligibility date, department, or job classification.

Pension Checks and Tax Reports. Sometimes the retirement benefits administration function writes the pension checks for retirees. It also may prepare the data for annual individual statements of gross pension distribution, tax withholdings, and other deductions. (In the United States, this statement is a W-2P.) Retirement benefits administration provides these data to payroll so that payroll can issue the checks and W-2P statements. These are discussed further in chapter 20.

Government Reports. In the interest of ensuring equity in retirement benefits options within organizations, the IRS and other agencies mandate numerous periodic reports on pension plans and other financial retirement benefits. These include various reports required by ERISA, such as the 5500 series reports described in chapter 15.

The Pension Benefit Guaranty Corporation (PBGC) works with ERISA, the Department of Labor, and the IRS in supervising pension funds. Federal regulations require employers who offer a defined benefit retirement plan to submit an annual report (known as PBGC-1). This accompanies payment of premiums that insure a certain percentage of each employee's basic pension

401(k) Participation
(Number of Employees and Dollar Value)

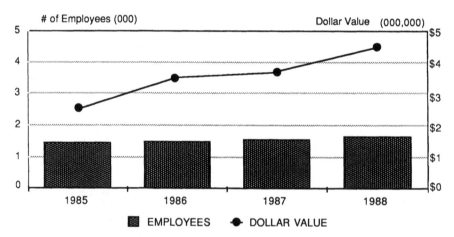

Figure 21–7. 401(k) plan participation report. The retirement benefits
administration can use a graphic report to summarize trends
in the number of participants in a particular plan and the
dollar value of that participation.

benefits. Organizations must make the payments quarterly but file the report annually. The frequency of payments and reports is likely to change.

Health Benefit Claims Processing

Health benefits include medical, dental, hospitalization, surgical, prescription, and vision care insurance. As discussed in chapter 15, the benefits function tracks eligibility, participation, and contributions for each of these benefits. However, relatively few firms require the benefits function to handle administration of employee claims.

Claims processing involves a complicated set of computer procedures that are completely separate from other benefits tracking. This function includes logging, acknowledging, and evaluating claims; notification of claims decisions; distribution of payments; and tracking of claims history—all of which are more pertinent to insurance systems than to human resources systems. Therefore, claims processing software has more in common with insurance software than with HRMS software. Claims processing involves a massive amount of data—at least one set for each medical event, with the potential for additional data on coinsurance, deductibles, preauthorization, and so forth. The need for accuracy keeps many firms from handling their own claims processing. Much of this information is not needed for any human resources activity other than claims processing, so bringing these tasks in-house does not benefit human resources unless volume and business conditions dictate.

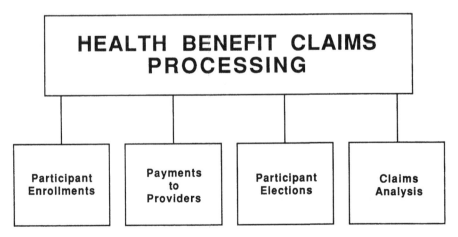

Figure 21–8. Principal roles of the health benefit claims processing function.

User Requirements Questionnaire
for Evaluating Medical Claims Systems

The following questionnaire formed part of an RFP used by a major manufacturing firm in selecting a vendor for an in-house medical claims processing system.

1. How do you identify
   a. employee?
   b. spouse?
   c. retiree?
   d. dependent?

2. How do you handle
   a. changes to the plan?
   b. multiple plans?
   c. divisions/groups?

3. How do you track
   a. eligibility?
   b. canges to HMO or PPO?
   c. part-time change?
   d. self-pay premium?

4. How do you process
   a. terminations?
   b. death?
   c. retirement?
   d. extended benefits?
   e. transfers?
   f. promotions?

5. How do you handle
   a. on-line adjudication?
   b. diagnosis codes?
   c. accident coding?
   d. prepaid amount?
   e. duplicates?
   f. "reasonable and customary" changes?
   g. bills with assignment?

6. How do you handle
   a. cost of benefits?
   b. cost of benefits with other carriers?
   c. calculation of bank/credit reserve?

d. application of primary payment?
e. tracking of maximum benefits?
7. How do you handle
a. inquiries?
b. employee medical status?
c. claim status?
d. access to previously processed claims?
e. status of pending claims?
f. history of claims?

Because claims processing requires intensive administration and dedicated labor, usually only firms with some special need or experience handle it internally. Most firms have insurance carriers and claims processing handle this function. The major exceptions are self-insured firms and very large organizations. In situations such as union environments, some firms may track the claims payments to each individual. Demonstrating this part of the "hidden paycheck" to the employee can help an employer emphasize the amount of its investment in its workers. Occasionally, if a firm is engaged in a potentially risky activity, such as bridge or tunnel construction, in-house claims processing helps management monitor types of claims made or abuses by employees or providers.

A firm does not need to process claims information itself to obtain detailed information needed in special circumstances. For instance, if a firm is exploring particular workplace health issues, it may ask a carrier to report on claims pertaining to certain medical issues. Some companies ask carriers to provide information on employees with claims totals over a certain dollar value. The benefits function can request case-by-case reports from carriers as needed.

In-house claims processing usually takes place on mainframes because most firms that choose this option have a large employee population. Most firms that take this route use a commercial claims processing package. Some HRMS vendors offer claims processing systems as an add-on to the HRMS. Although some human resources departments do develop their own claims systems, few have special needs not met by commercially available claims processing packages administered by professional claims processors.

If a firm decides to do medical claims processing in-house, it usually handles all forms of health insurance claims, including dental, hospitalization, prescription, vision, and surgical. The same function sometimes also processes disability insurance claims, especially if workers' compensation is involved. Most firms still contract with outside carriers for claims processing for life insurance, accidental death and dismemberment insurance, and long-term disability, since such claims are less frequent and involve one-time settlements.

Health Benefit Claims Data Requirements

The claims processing system needs to obtain information from the master files on employee (and former employee) demographics and benefits status, including covered dependents, but it does not generate much information that the HRMS needs in return. Claims processing itself generates a large amount of additional data that the independent system must track with great accuracy and timeliness.

Benefits Eligibility and Participation Data. The claims processing function imports data on a regular basis from the benefits data segments that pertain to health benefits. When an employee (or former employee) files a claim, the claims processing function must establish whether the patient has relevant coverage. The benefits records provide information on eligibility, participation, and enrollment dates, as well as basic demographics such as age and address. Claims processing requires less information from benefits if the type of coverage is automatic than if employees elect coverage from various options.

Claims Form Data. To make a claim, an employee usually files a claim form with the employee benefits claims office. The most basic information in this form identifies the individual who received treatment. Employees may make claims for themselves as well as for covered dependents. Typically, all covered family members are part of the same record, but each claim contains data fields that identify the family member who received treatment: patient name, patient date of birth, and patient relationship to employee.

The provider usually includes a diagnosis code on the treatment form submitted with the claim form. Most claims processors use these codes to standardize diagnoses and treatment procedures, to monitor actual experience, and to control costs. Many now specifically use a system of classification known as diagnosis-related groups (DRGs) in order to be consistent with the federal government's insurance programs for the elderly and indigent. To participate in coinsurance programs, insurance administrators must use this system. Within the HRMS, the particular code in a DRG data field determines the maximum reimbursement or payment allowed for the corresponding treatment.

The claims adjustment record must capture information on each medical event, including employee name, patient, date of treatment, location, provider, diagnosis, treatment description, and treatment cost. PPO and HMO plans also track whether the service provider is a member of the preferred or another acceptable group.

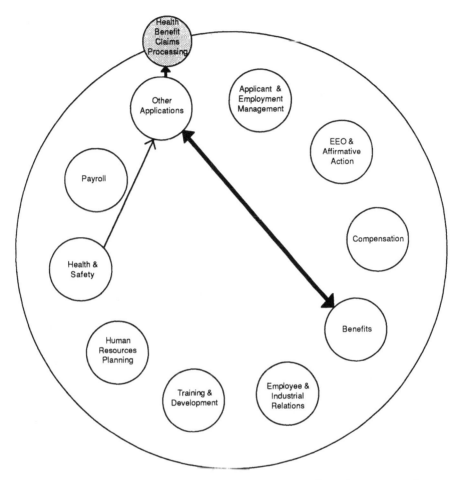

Figure 21-9. Information flow between health benefit claims processing and other human resources functions.

Each type of health insurance has its own forms with its own questions. Hospital claim forms provide claims processors with data such as admission date; release date; reason for hospitalization; name, address, and phone number of hospital; rates or charges for individual services and medication. Prescription claims have their own set of data, such as prescription number, name of medication, pharmacy, date of prescription, and issuing physician.

Claim forms also ask the employee to provide information about any other insurance carrier whose coverage may apply to the incident, such as insurance carried by a spouse or another employer. They request information on other providers who may have given treatment for the incident or condition. Coinsurance data include insurance carrier name, address, and phone; covered individual; and group number. As a claim proceeds, the system may track coinsurance payments, including amount, date, and payee.

Preauthorization Request. Sometimes a covered individual may seek preauthorization for some health care treatment. This preauthorization ensures the patient and the provider that the carrier will pay an established amount for the service. To obtain this authorization, the individual often has the health care provider submit a form to the insurance carrier. This form contains the same information as a claim form, with the exception that the form indicates that it is a preauthorization request.

Health History. Some firms have new employees fill out an extensive medical history questionnaire; others keep their questions to a few record-keeping items maintained in a manual file. In either case, other than demographic information, human resources transfers little of the medical history onto the computer system. The only exception may be to list medical problems that the employee and his or her dependents have had within the past six to twelve months. Many carriers do not cover preexisting conditions for a prescribed period or permanently. For example, an employee who is pregnant when hired often will be ineligible for expenses related to her pregnancy and delivery.

Health history also takes place during the employee's tenure with the insurance carrier. The system must track and tally all claims for each type of coverage for each employee for the current claims year. Most claims systems have provisions for maintaining a complete claims history on any covered employee or dependent. If the policy has a lifetime cap or limit for certain types of coverage, the system must include accumulator fields that keep a running total of payments made over the entire length of time the individual is covered. Employees generally receive coverage throughout their service period; for dependents, some age limit generally applies. After a certain time, such as two years, the system may archive the details of these claims for off-line storage, perhaps retaining a skeletal record on-line, such as treatment dates only.

Claims Settlement. A claims program contains algorithms and other routines for calculating deductibles and payments under a full range of circumstances. These complex routines provide information to numerous dependent data fields, such as covered amount, individual or family deductible, payment, claims credited against deductible, and claims paid to date.

Automated claims settlement involves sophisticated computer processes. For instance, many plans use a fifteen-month year in which claims in the last quarter of the previous calendar year also count toward the next year's deductible. As another example, in PPO coverage, the program may incorporate several different types of payment schedules depending on whether the covered patient uses a medical practitioner within the PPO or another provider.

As the claims process proceeds, the module must track claims adjustment information. This includes date submitted, date approved or rejected, reason for rejection, payment approved, payee, date of claims decision, date of notification to employee, and date of payment.

Health Benefit Claims Reporting Requirements

Claims administration requires numerous reports. Some are for internal control purposes; some are communications to the employee, health care provider, or coinsurer. As is the case with other aspects of data handling for claims administration, any reporting mistake usually results in an administrative problem, an unhappy employee, or a drop in productivity of the benefits or claims function. Effective reports can mitigate this situation.

Individual Claim Report. This report gives a full listing of information about a specific claim. The claims processing function may send such a report, with a mail-merged cover letter, to a coinsurer when seeking information about the other firm's coverage and payment. It also may use the report to answer employee inquiries or when investigating cases that involve complex issues or potential fraud.

Notice of Claim Settlement. Once claims processing determines coverage and payments, it sends a notice of claim settlement to the employee and the care provider. This states the basic data about the event, such as applicable coverage, claim amount credited against deductible, claim amount paid, and date of payment. For any amount not covered or reimbursed, the statement provides the reason for the rejected claim, usually coded, with a table of codes and explanations printed on the statement form.

Checks. Claims processing also sends checks to providers and to reimburse employees for out-of-pocket payments made for covered services.

Annual Claims Statement. Some firms have the system provide individual annual claims statements as part of the overall individual benefits statement discussed in chapter 15. The claims portion of that statement might list health services used and reimbursements or payments provided. Some claims processing systems issue a separate claims statement annually.

Pending Claims Report. Claims processing may need a periodic accounting of pending claims on a monthly or quarterly basis, depending on volume. A

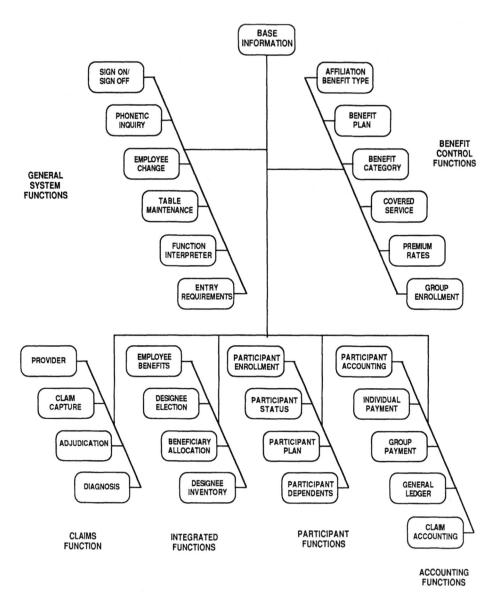

Figure 21–10. Functions of a comprehensive claims processing system. A comprehensive system can track, analyze, and report claims by employee, plan, and rate of contribution.
(Source: Tesseract Corporation. Reprinted with permission.)

summary report would list number of claims, types of claims, cost of requested reimbursement, and payments. A detail report would list each claim, including date of claim, employee name and number, whether the claim is for the employee or a dependent, provider, type of treatment, and amount of reimbursement or payment requested.

Claims Analysis Reports. Internal handling of claims processing provides firms with a tremendous amount of data that they can use to monitor claims requests and thereby reduce fraud, inaccuracy, and inappropriate use of health benefits. By reviewing the number, type, and sizes of claims, the firm can identify misuse of the system, design benefits that meet the legitimate needs of employees, and obtain cost-effective coverage. These analyses may tally claims by diagnosis code, job classification, location, provider, or any other field related to demographics, care, or cost.

Preauthorization Report. In response to a request for preauthorization of a particular charge for a particular treatment not yet performed, claims processing usually sends a letter to the employee and the provider. The notice lists basic information about the treatment, amount of coverage provided, and reasons for denial or limitations of such coverage.

Time and Attendance

The attendance and timekeeping process involves two complementary responsibilities—tracking the hours and days each employee works and tracking each employee's time off and the reasons for that time off. For nonexempt employees, firms generally do both kinds of record keeping, primarily because labor laws require employers to track overtime. For exempt employees, they may track only time off.

The human resources and payroll functions use attendance and timekeeping data to perform several important tasks:

- Calculate payroll, since time worked and time off affect earnings
- Calculate seniority or length of service
- Determine eligibility for benefits (For instance, part-time employees become eligible for benefits if they work more than a certain number of hours weekly or annually.)
- Monitor deliberate abuses, such as extra days off, misuse of sick days, or consistent use of sick days before or after a holiday

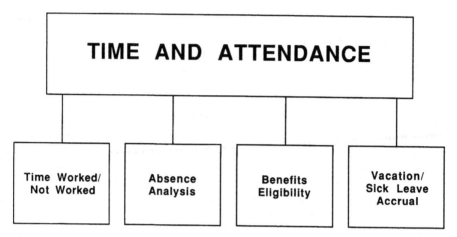

Figure 21–11. Principal roles of the time and attendance function.

- Identify problems that the EAP function should address (Certain patterns of absence or tardiness may point to workers who need EAP counseling for issues such as chronic illness, transportation, or child care.)
- Analyze productivity by comparing production or sales statistics with available person-hours during a given time period

Time and attendance data are a critical part of several human resource areas, but nobody owns all of the attendance and timekeeping data management process. In fact, although many functions want access, few want the responsibility. Benefits monitors myriad programs, so it often tries to have another function handle attendance and timekeeping. Employee relations often deals with the productivity issues related to absenteeism and tardiness but may be insufficiently staffed to handle the massive amounts of data that attendance and timekeeping entail.

Essentially, attendance is an individual productivity function that belongs to line management. If a supervisor allows an employee to take time off, the supervisor should already have taken into account the unit's potential need for a replacement as well as the contribution of the trained individual to the unit compared with that of the untrained replacement. Line managers then keep careful track of these data, or take responsibility for making sure that their individual employees do so, on a positive or exception basis. Human resources may not collect the data or see the input but may apply those data to several different issues.

Because hours and days worked may affect the size of a paycheck, even for salaried employees, payroll is the most basic user of timekeeping data. Even payroll, however, may not input attendance and timekeeping records but merely use such data in calculating correct paychecks. A separate timekeeping function or data entry unit may handle entry of time-related data. This separation of functions permits payroll to perform an audit of attendance and timekeeping data, checking the amounts input against authorized figures for each employee for each category—vacation, regular time, sick leave, overtime, personal time off, and so forth.

A time and attendance function does not make any judgments, except to compare time reported with time accrued. It does not decide what to do in cases of conflict but merely reports results to line management or employee relations for resolution. Time and attendance data generally are recorded on an exception basis—that is, unless employees report extra time worked or time not worked, it is assumed that they worked their regular schedule. Time off is reported in many ways, as described below.

Many different programs are available for handling attendance and timekeeping data. Different HRMS programs may attach attendance and timekeeping maintenance to different functions within human resources. In choosing the HRMS, the project team should consider whether the process for recording time and attendance corresponds with how the firm handles these data. Some have a separate system for attendance alone, especially if they use time cards, clocks, or other electronic recording devices.

All functions that use attendance and timekeeping data must work together as a committee to design the rules for a new time and attendance module. Although each function has its own priorities, all functions share the same definitions. They need to agree on rules for time off with pay and time off without pay. They should agree on which functions need which data and on who has responsibility for resolving particular types of problems.

Time and Attendance Data Requirements

As mentioned earlier, attendance and timekeeping may take place on a positive or an exception basis. For either approach, employees enter these data via time cards, time sheets, or a time clock. Some packages provide direct conversion of time clock data to system data. Some use optical character reader (OCR) forms; others require manual entry from handwritten forms.

These entry media usually include codes for type of time. Depending on organization structure and policy, the system may include 20 to 30 types of attendance data, including the following:

- Regular hours
- Overtime hours
- Special shift hours
- Vacation hours
- Sick hours
- Hours leave with pay

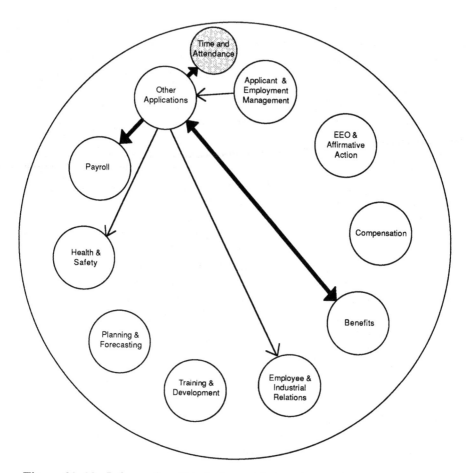

Figure 21–12. Information flow between time and attendance and other human resources functions.

Naturally, all these fields can readily use days or parts of days instead of hours.

The benefits function may establish the categories and codes for these time benefits. It also establishes the algorithms for entitlement that determine the accrual rate for each time benefit. Specific types of time benefits are discussed in chapter 15.

Some vendors offer special software for tracking timekeeping on a project basis. This allows firms to track chargeable hours for billing to separate clients. Consultants, accountants, attorneys, and construction firms frequently require this form of timekeeping. In this case, the employee enters the project code, date, hours worked, and activities (sometimes coded) for each billable or non-billable activity.

Time and Attendance Reporting Requirements

In most cases, human resources functions that use attendance and timekeeping data prepare most of their own reports as needed. Depending on the technical and functional relationship between time and attendance and other activities, however, the time and attendance module also may generate reports.

Time Benefits Accrual and Usage Reports. Employees receive information on time benefits accrual and usage from several different sources. More often than not, no matter who handles attendance data, benefits still takes responsibility for reporting employees' status on vacation, sick leave, and other time reports. It may issue a report to each employee on an annual basis, as well as a report to terminated employees or at the request of managers. Paychecks or deposit advices from payroll have an attached stub that notes the time for which payment is included (not only regular and overtime pay but also pay for vacation, sick days, and holidays).

If the attendance and timekeeping module is separate from the system containing benefits and employee relations data, time and attendance may need to prepare reports on time benefits accrual and usage for those functions. In some cases, that function may even issue individual employee profiles showing patterns of time off with and without pay.

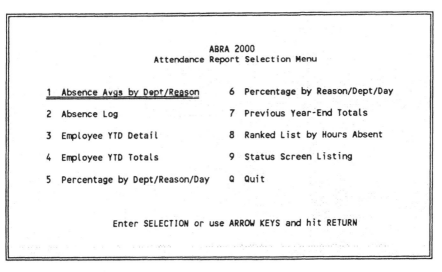

Figure 21–13. Attendance report selection menu. This menu presents the standard attendance reports available with a typical time and attendance module. More complex systems offer thirty or more standard reports in this area.
(Source: AbraCadabra Software. Reprinted with permission.)

EMPLOYEE ATTENDANCE RECORD

EMPLOYEE NAME		SOCIAL SECURITY NUMBER	DATE EMPLOYED	DATE FULL TIME	STATUS	HOURS
Michael V. MacDuff		113-30-6886	09-02-81	09-02-81	FT-R	40
DIVISION/DEPARTMENT NAME	NUMBER	REGION	POSITION TITLE		GRADE E/NE	DATE OF REPORT
Widget Fabrication	3604	Western	Widget Maker		16E	06-01-90

ABSENCE SUMMARY

DAYS ABSENT	SICKNESS PAID	SICKNESS UNPAID	DEATH IN FAMILY UNPAID	JURY DUTY	MILITARY RESERVE	PERSONAL PAID	PERSONAL UNPAID	TOTAL DAYS ABSENT	TOTAL PAID ABSENCE AMOUNT
MONTH TO DATE	0.0	0.0	0.0	0.0	0.0	0.0	0.0	0.0	$ 00.00
YEAR TO DATE	3.0	0.0	0.0	0.0	0.0	1.0	0.0	0.0	$ 270.00
PRIOR YEAR SUMMARY	7.0	0.0	0.0	3.0	0.0	0.0	2.0	2.0	$ 569.10

CURRENT YEAR DAYS OF WEEK ABSENT										TOTAL ABSENCE DAYS	CURRENT YEAR ABSENCES BY LENGTH						DATE EMPLOYEE WAS LAST ABSENT
MON	TUES	WED	THUR	FRI	SAT	SUN	PRE HOL	POST HOL			TOTAL	1 DAY	2 DAY	3 DAY	4 DAY	5+ DAY	
1	0	0	0	2	0	0	0	1		4	3	2	1	0	0	0	04-14-90

ABSENCE HISTORY

DATE ABSENCE BEGAN	REASON FOR ABSENCE	ABSENCE LENGTH	DAY ABSENCE BEGAN	DATE ABSENCE BEGAN	REASON FOR ABSENCE	ABSENCE LENGTH	DAY ABSENCE BEGAN
04-12-90	Sickness-Paid	2.0	Thursday				
02-19-90	Personal-Paid	1.0	Monday				
02-05-90	Sickness-Paid	1.0	Monday				
11-17-89	Sickness-Paid	6.0	Friday				
08-24-89	Sickness-Paid	1.0	Thursday				
07-03-89	Personal-Unpaid	1.0	Monday				
06-12-89	Jury Duty	3.0	Monday				
12-21-88	Personal-Paid	2.5	Wednesday				
02-05-90	Personal-Paid	1.0	Friday				
03-29-88	Sickness-Paid	4.0	Tuesday				

Figure 21–14. Employee attendance record. Large firms often use forms such as this one to print an individual attendance profile. Note that the form allows not only attendance tallies for each type of time benefit but also absence tallies by day of the week and by length.

```
08/29/88                    YOUR COMPANY NAME, INC.                    Page   1
                            ANALYSIS OF ABSENTEEISM
              PERCENTAGES BY REASON/DEPARTMENT/DAY FOR 01/01/88 - 12/31/88


                        -------- PERCENT OF WEEK TOTAL --------  DEPT  COMP
  DIVISION, DEPARTMENT   SUN  MON  TUE  WED  THU  FRI  SAT   PCT   PCT
  ====================== ===  ===  ===  ===  ===  ===  ===  ====  ====
  Compensatory Time
    SALES, SOFTWARE        0   33    0    0    0   67    0   100     1
  REASON PERCENTAGE        0   33    0    0    0   67    0   100     1

  Illness - Excused
    CORP, ACCOUNTING       0   17   26   17   35    4    0    16     5
    CORP, CORP             0   31   23   14   13   20    0    33    10
    ENGINEERING, HARDWARE  0   47    0    3    0   50    0     3     1
    ENGINEERING, SOFTWARE  0   47    6   27   10   11    0    18     6
    SALES, SOFTWARE        0   15   34   24    5   22    0    30     9
  REASON PERCENTAGE        0   27   23   20   13   17    0   100    31

  Jury Duty
    CORP, ACCOUNTING       0    0  100    0    0    0    0    84     2
    CORP, CORP             0    0  100    0    0    0    0    16     0
  REASON PERCENTAGE        0    0  100    0    0    0    0   100     3

  Personal Leave Time
    CORP, ACCOUNTING       0    0    0  100    0    0    0     4     0
    CORP, CORP             0   36   18   36    0    9    0    27     2
    ENGINEERING, HARDWARE  0   42   11   13   35    0    0    17     2
    ENGINEERING, SOFTWARE  0   22   16    0   54    8    0    31     3
    SALES, SOFTWARE        0    7    0   24   45   24    0    21     2
  REASON PERCENTAGE        0   25   12   21   32   10    0   100     9

  Tardy (Late for work)
    CORP, ACCOUNTING       0   33    0   33   33    0    0     9     0
    CORP, CORP             0   50    0    0   17   33    0    18     0
    ENGINEERING, HARDWARE  0    0    0    0    0  100    0     3     0
    ENGINEERING, SOFTWARE  0    0   14   29   14   43    0    21     0
    SALES, SOFTWARE        0   18   12    6    6   59    0    50     1
  REASON PERCENTAGE        0   21    9   12   12   47    0   100     2

  Vacation
    CORP, ACCOUNTING       0   40    0    0    9   51    0    14     8
    CORP, CORP             0   85    0    0   10    5    0    31    17
    ENGINEERING, SOFTWARE  0   43    3   21   12   21    0    25    13
    SALES, SOFTWARE        0   20    6   12   43   18    0    30    16
  REASON PERCENTAGE        0   49    3    9   20   19    0   100    55

  COMPANY PERCENTAGE       0   38   13   13   18   18    0          100
```

Figure 21–15. **Absenteeism analysis report. Managers use this report to examine the extent to which employees are absent on days before and after weekends. Such patterns may indicate some problem that can affect employee predictability and morale.**
(Source: AbraCadabra Software. Reprinted with permission.)

In either case, the system usually can produce these reports as individual detail reports or as summary reports providing information about the amount of time benefits accrual and usage by unit, department, service, or other variable.

Time Usage Out-of-Range Reports. Time and attendance, benefits, or employee relations may issue reports that indicate out-of-range time status situations. For instance, the system may generate review forms to supervisors if an employee reaches certain limits in terms of number of late arrivals within a particular period. It may generate a report that shows all employees whose accrued vacation exceeds a certain limit or who have reported more vacation time used than accrued. Most attendance and timekeeping modules can provide a wide array of standard employee absenteeism and tardiness reports, with additional ad hoc reporting accomplished as necessary.

Other HRMS Applications

The modern human resources significant department includes such diverse and numerous responsibilities that most large organizations have computerized or want to computerize at least one activity not yet mentioned. Here are some other potential applications:

- Suggestion plan administration
- Employee recreation programs
- Human resources accounting
- Medical records
- Service awards
- Productivity measurement

Trying to cover each possibility would take several more chapters, but following are a few examples of how computerization aids in the administration of ancillary human resources functions.

Customer Relations

Some types of enterprises describe those whom they serve as *customers;* others use the term *clients.* Either way, organizations are becoming increasingly aware of the importance of monitoring and optimizing relationships with these consumers. In some organizations, particularly retail operations and service firms, employees have significant interaction with customers. Some human resources departments have begun using computer systems to track customer responses to employee service and communication.

The extent to which HRMS is involved in this area is a function of how the firm measures employee performance and uses it to develop salary incentive schemes. Custom or specialized software based on sales records or other data can perform this function. Human resources may use the system to track the history of communications between each customer and specific employees. It may track by customer, order number, or employee. To be useful to employee relations, these data must eventually become part of the individual employee's record. If the HRMS records employee-related comments, it often does not code or modify them in any way.

Either on a regular basis or when an unusual incident occurs, employee relations may issue a written or electronic mail notice to relevant employees and supervisors. Employee relations may help line managers to use such customer response data to resolve issues of performance, service levels, and incentives as they pertain to specific employees as well as the overall employee population.

Employee Awards

Employee relations sometimes tracks employee recognition for service and community involvement. This may include awards and other forms of recognition for special performance, volunteer work, charity drives, or attainment of five years, ten years, or other levels of service. As well as recording the award in each recipient's record, a system with graphics capabilities may print the award certificates. Some functions print a complete list of recipients for posting and distribution, together with a short description of the reason for the award.

Employee Communications

If human resources has responsibility for creating employee newsletters or bulletins, this production usually takes place on a separate microcomputer-based system because of the need for desktop publishing capability. As an application oriented to text and graphics, newsletter production does not need to interact with the main HRMS data base to obtain information except to perform mail merge and distribution of newsletters. It can import a list of employees as needed for some particular feature, such as a list of award winners or ten-year service employees. A lack of interface with the HRMS poses no problem for this kind of ancillary activity. If the organization wants to distribute the newsletter by mailing it to employees' homes, however, the HRMS must maintain home (as well as mailing) addresses and should produce mail labels or furnish address data on a current, updated basis to a separate mailing system.

Glossary

Annuitant   An individual who receives payments from a pension plan or other retirement income program.

Bonding   Insurance that protects the policy beneficiary from financial losses incurred as a result of unlawful actions on the part of the bonded individual.

Claim   A request that an insurance carrier or other benefits provider pay for part or all of an expense. The most common type of claim is a medical insurance claim, in which the provider is asked to pay for some or all of a test, X ray, or visit to a physician or hospital.

Diagnosis-related group (DRG)   A diagnostic classification system adopted by the federal Medicare program and used by many health insurance carriers. Many carriers now insist that health care providers place each medical encounter in a specific DRG category. Based on the DRG, the carrier assigns a set maximum amount of coverage for that encounter.

DRG   See *Diagnosis-related group.*

Flextime   Flexible hour arrangements in which employees are allowed to set their own schedules, usually around a core time. Such individualized schedules usually add up to full-time workweeks.

401(k)   A salary deferral plan, defined by Section 401(k) of the IRS Tax Code and modified by the Tax Reform Act, that allows employees to put aside pretax earnings—sometimes matched by employers—in savings accounts managed by the employer.

Individual retirement account (IRA)   A savings vehicle to which an employee may contribute up to $2,000 per year in tax-deferred income if the employer does not offer a retirement plan. An IRA may take many investment forms, such as money markets, bond funds, common stock, and government securities.

IRA   See *Individual retirement account.*

PBGC   See *Pension Benefit Guaranty Corporation.*

Pension Benefit Guaranty Corporation (PBGC)   An agency mandated by ERISA to guarantee payment of benefits to participants of defined benefits pension plans that meet IRS qualifications. Requires annual reports (PBGC-1) with premiums for participants.

Retirement value   The estimated monthly payment from a retirement plan; based on total contributions to date, current salary, and seniority.

Security   As distinct from data security, security refers to protecting facilities and equipment from unauthorized access and use. Also, safeguarding employees and other individuals on the premises from assault, burglary, and other unwanted, inappropriate actions.

SEP   See *Simplified employee pension.*

Simplified employee pension (SEP)   A simplified form of a 401(k) plan available only to companies having twenty-five or few employees.

Survivor   A beneficiary who outlives an individual who has been participating in a benefits program. In terms of retirement benefits, survivors usually mean the spouse and children of an employee or former employee.

Vesting   The process whereby an employee acquires rights to the employer-contribution portion of his or her pension benefits regardless of whether the employee remains with the organization. Organizations usually require that an employee attain a certain level of seniority and age before becoming vested with the retirement plan.

Discussion Points

1. Differentiate between *data security* and *physical security and access control* in terms of an HRMS. What factors influence whether a firm needs a specific site security module?

2. What kinds of modifications to employee records help an organization handle facilities security?

3. What aspects of retirement benefits administration is a firm most likely to farm out to an external firm? Why? Which will it most likely do in-house? Why?

4. Under what circumstances should an organization consider administering employee health insurance claims in-house?

5. What human resources and related functions have a stake in time and attendance data? What time and attendance data does each of these functions need?

6. When are certain modules, such as security, retirement benefits administration, and health benefit claims administration, most likely to operate on a stand-alone basis? Why?

7. Describe various types of incentives that could be recorded and maintained in an HRMS.

8. Select a potential HRMS application not specifically discussed. Describe the data requirements and sources for such a module and the reports it might include.

Further Reading

Security and Privacy

Anderson, Kirk J. "Microcomputer Security." *Human Resource Management Systems Report,* November 1985.

Angel, John, and Alastair Evans. "Data Protection and the Subject of Access." *Personnel Administrator*, October 1987.

Chapman, Robert B. "Securing the HR System: An Introduction." *Computers in Personnel*, Fall 1986.

Fernandez, Eduardo B., Rita C. Summers, and Christopher Wood. *Database Security and Integrity*. Reading, MA: Addison-Wesley, 1981.

Hauselt, Denise. "Employee Privacy, Information Needs, and the Law." *Industrial and Labor Relations Forum*, January 1980.

Hoffman, Lance J. *Security and Privacy in Computer Systems*. Los Angeles: Melville Publishing, 1973.

Ledvinka, James. *Federal Regulations of Personnel and Human Resource Management*. Boston: Kent Publishing, 1982.

———. "Privacy Regulations and Employee Record Keeping." *Journal of Library Administration*, Winter 1986.

Lobel, J. "Privacy of Employment and Personnel Information Systems." *Internal Auditor*, October 1977.

Mitsch, Robert J. "Ensuring Privacy and Accuracy of Computerized Employee Record Systems." *Personnel Administrator*, September 1983.

Pasqualetto, Joe. "Staffing, Privacy, and Security Measures." *Personnel Journal*, September 1988.

Personal Privacy in an Information Society: The Report of the Privacy Protection Study Commission. Washington: U.S. Government Printing Office, 1977.

Richards-Carpenter, Colin. "Can Computers Help Security Staff." *Personnel Management*, April 1986.

Stambaugh, Robert H. "HRS Security: Pulling the Pieces Together." *Human Resource Systems Management Report*, December 1986.

———. "Protecting Employee Data Privacy: The Systems Challenges for the '90s." *Computers in HR Management*, February 1990.

Stouffer, Richard. "Computerized Personnel Records Require Confidential Treatment." *Data Management*, December 1985.

Retirement Benefits Administration

Anderson, Kirk J., Nancy Michael, and Debra K. Yarger. "In-House Retirement Plan Administration." *Human Resource Systems Management Bulletin*, October 1987.

Jaquish, Michael P. "Pension Benefit Administration System." Computers in Personnel, Winter 1988.

Michael, Nancy. "Can We Process Our Pension Plan Inhouse on a Micro?" *HRSP Review*, Second Quarter 1986.

———. "Automating Your Retirement Plan in the '80s." *Personnel Administrator*, June 1987.

Schechter, J.H. "The Retirement Equity Act: Meeting Women's Pension Needs." *Compensation and Benefits Review*, Volume 17, 1985.

Williams, David A. "Comparing Your Retirement Options." *Business Software*, July 1985.

Benefits Claim Processing

Fandel, Arthur J. "Cost Control through Claims Control: The 'Tunic' System." *HRSP Review*, Winter 1988.
Handel, B. *New Directions in Welfare Plan Benefits: Instituting Health Care Cost Containment Programs.* Brookfield, WI: International Foundation of Employee Benefit Plans, 1984.
Krakauer, John L. "Slash Health Care Costs with Claims Automation." *Personnel Journal*, April 1985.

Time and Attendance

Bayles, Soni. "Controlling the Hands of Time." *Business Magazine*, June 1985.
Fell, Alan. "Time Loss Analysis and Management." In *Computers in Personnel: Towards the Personnel Office of the Future*, edited by Terry Page. Sussex: Institute of Personnel Management and Institute of Manpower Studies, 1983.
Reid, Allan T. "Automate Time and Attendance Recording." *Personnel Journal*, March 1988.

Miscellaneous

Anderson, Kirk J. "What Can They Do Besides Manage?" *Business Software Review*, June 1988.
Breetwor, Cheryl. "Employee Stock Options: An Incentive That Needs Automation to Motivate." *Computers in Personnel*, Winter 1989.
Maze, Marilyn. "How to Select a Computerized Guidance System." *Journal of Counselling and Development*, November 1984.
Wood, Susan. "Computer Use in Testing." *Journal of Counselling and Development*, November 1984.

General

Albert, Kenneth. *Handbook of Business Problem Solving.* New York: McGraw-Hill, 1980.
Darany, Theodore S. "Computer Applications to Personnel." *Public Personnel Management*, Winter 1984.

Part IV
HRMS Trends
and Resources

A mind once stretched by a new idea never regains its original
dimension.

—Oliver Wendell Holmes

Planning, developing, implementing, and managing an HRMS involves massive information gathering. Some of this process pertains specifically to the organization's own needs and goals, but HRMS planners and managers also must look outside their own firm. They must keep abreast of new technologies, trends, regulations, resources, and tools and techniques likely to affect the HRMS.

Several technological and operational developments that promise to influence HRMS design are introduced in chapter 22. No matter what the field, predicting the future is an inexact science at best. When computers are involved, the accuracy of predictions may become even more uncertain. In the rapidly changing world of information technology, one cannot accurately predict the speed with which a potential development will move from promise to reality, much less the extent to which users will adopt the changes it entails.

The absence of a topic in chapter 22 does not mean that the issue was judged insignificant, merely that only a limited number of topics could be covered. New issues are constantly emerging; every human resources–related journal contains acronymns and terms not in the vocabulary a year or two ago. Ask ten HRMS professionals for a list of five important emerging trends, and each would probably list at least one topic not included by the others. In the end, human resources must make its own judgment about which future-oriented issues to take into account when planning HRMS capabilities.

To evaluate what is happening, HRMS professionls must discuss the trends with others in the field, including peers, competitors, vendors, and consultants. They should keep up with the literature, take courses as appropriate, join professional societies, and participate in other activities. To facilitate information exchange, this book includes lists of these types of opportunities in the appendixes. As with the discussion of emerging trends, these lists cannot possibly be comprehensive. They are meant to serve as catalysts, to inspire individuals to gather their own information about the ever-changing world of human resources management systems.

22
Emerging Trends
and the Future of HRMS

> We should all be concerned about the future because we will have to
> spend the rest of our lives there.
>
> —Charles Franklin Kettering

Although HRMS have been around in one form or another for twenty-five years, during most of that time they were mainframe based, time-consuming to develop and implement, and, therefore, expensive. Before 1982, no one had developed any human resources applications for microcomputers; by 1985, fewer than fifty were offered. Since 1988, the market has exploded, with more than 1,000 packages available today. Lower development costs coupled with increased ease of use have catalyzed these revolutionary changes. Moreover, computer hardware of all types is faster and more complex, and HRMS users have become more sophisticated. For most organizations, human resources computerization is no longer the future but the present.

The next generation of HRMS will include increased functional integration (also called connectivity), high-level computer-assisted decision making, and easier communication between people and computers. To be prepared for the future, human resources professionals must stay informed about developments not just in human resources but throughout the world of technology and automation.

The Coevolution of
Human Resources and HRMS

The term *coevolution* generally refers to the process of nature in which two species evolve together; each changes in response to evolution in the other to allow their mutually dependent relationship to continue. In many ways, the fields of human resources and HRMS are coevolving. Progress in computerization influences how human resources performs, and changes in the field of human resources affect the focus of software developers.

How Technology Advances
Change Human Resources

Technology advances have changed human resources in many ways. Once primarily a record-keeping function, human resources now plays a critical role in many operational and strategic activities. Operationally, these include merit salary budgeting, benefits administration, applicant flow analysis, forecasting, and EEO/AA reporting. In support of strategic decision making, human resources managers use computers to track high-potential employees, monitor long-term trends, and generate models of possible future scenarios. With computer support, management bases decisions on more accurate information than ever before. Managers increasingly expect substantial computer support for human resources programs and plans.

The current generation of HRMS makes comprehensive information available to a much wider range of human resources functions. Although some human resources staff may feel threatened by this development, more enlightened professionals are taking advantage of it. They delegate tasks that only analysts could perform previously, then take on long-range planning tasks for themselves. As more human resources functions become computerized, virtually the entire human resources staff needs to obtain some computer skills. Human resources managers must now consider functional and technical proficiency in making staffing, training, and promotion decisions.

Computer advances have occurred in a wide range of areas, including hardware power and speed, telecommunications, data base management, and approaches to integrating computer applications. Because of these improvements, vendors can now offer features that were formerly unavailable or too expensive. For instance, the past few years have brought tremendous growth in software utilities that translate data and files from one operating system or program to another. With these advances, formerly incompatible systems and programs can now exchange information. Special-purpose applications increasingly include interfaces to comprehensive HRMS software. System integration combines related functions, so a human resources department can consolidate the records of employment, compensation, benefits, training, and other human resources activities into one master employee data base.

How the Evolution of Human Resources
Changes HRMS

Regulatory and operational changes within human resources inevitably lead to changes in HRMS. In response to pressing business issues and increased competitiveness, human resources functions are becoming more complex. This, in

Factors in the Future of Human Resources

The priorities, responsibilities, and needs of a human resources department depend on scores of factors, most of which are outside the control of department staff. A partial list of influences is presented here. Many of these factors are external to the firm, such as laws and regulations, societal developments, and economic conditions. Some are internal, dependent on the organization's position, priorities, and performance.

Laws and Regulations

Changes in federal, state, and local requirements in the following areas often affect human resources. Judicial rulings also have a significant effect.

- Taxation
- Social security
- Unemployment compensation
- EEO and affirmative action
- Immigration
- Fair labor standards
- Minimum wage
- Workers' rights
- Plant closure
- Welfare
- Pensions
- Benefits
- International trade
- Occupational safety and health
- Environment

Societal Developments

The demographics, education, and spending habits of the work force, as well other large-scale societal forces, have a significant impact on human resources.

698

- Evolving technology in many areas
- Effects of office automation on labor needs
- Fewer youth through the 1990s
- Middle-age bulge in the work force
- Migration patterns
- Long-term aging of the American population
- Retirement trends
- Increasing numbers and rank of women workers
- Increasing demand for employer-supported child care
- Rise in two-earner families
- Shifts in consumerism
- Employee attitudes toward work and leisure time
- Existence and reduction of discrimination
- Increase in numbers of minority workers
- Status of labor unions
- Education levels of workers
- Job training programs

Economic Conditions

- Compensation trends
- Changes in interest rates
- Inflation rate
- Unemployment rate
- Rising health care costs
- Changes in public employment
- Benefits trends

Internal Factors

- Increasing emphasis on productivity
- Increasing demand for knowledge workers
- Increasing demand for job satisfaction
- Expansions and reductions
- Restructuring (mergers, acquisitions)
- Relocations/redeployment
- Level of capital investment
- Increasing costs of training and development
- Wage agreements
- Role of labor unions
- Telecommuting

- Flexible work schedules
- Job sharing

---

turn, increases the data management and computational capabilities that sophisticated software must have. For instance, HRMS packages must be able
to perform complicated calculations relative to benefits administration. With
the rise in two-income families and changing employee demographics, employees have more diverse benefits needs. Some need health insurance for their
dependents, while others have coverage through a spouse. Some need life insurance; those with no dependents may prefer more vacation time instead.
Many younger employees value time off more than they do security-oriented
benefits; conversely, older workers want flexible pension plans. The resulting
employee enthusiasm for flexible benefits has driven the development of more
sophisticated benefits administration software. This trend in flexibility will
continue and inevitably spread to other areas of human resources. For instance, to keep valuable workers, more companies are extending flextime, job
sharing, telecommuting, and personal leave and vacation policies. In response,
human resources time and attendance systems must become more flexible and
responsive yet remain friendly to the typical user.

Federal and state legislative and regulatory changes and judicial decisions
frequently affect human resources. In the past few years, these changes have
prompted vendors and human resources functions of all types to develop or
revise computer modules not only in EEO and affirmative action but also in
benefits, compensation, retirement benefits, and employee and industrial relations. Labor law changes related to wrongful termination, comparable
worth, and sexual harassment have necessitated creation of new data fields,
screens, tables, algorithms, and reports. These mandated changes will continue,
although it is difficult to predict how they will affect human resources. The
increasing frequency, scope, and cost of litigation also will prompt many employers to maintain records as completely and accurately as possible.

The increasing sophistication of HRMS users has both driven human resources programs and allowed them to mature. Once users have sampled simple systems, they begin searching for more powerful applications in their areas
of expertise. Most human resources professionals began their careers without
computer experience or training. Many have had to learn on the job. To take
full advantage of human resources automation, many have brought in specialists with less human resources experience but more computer-related skills. In
some cases, this separation of knowledge has caused conflict and produced

poor results. In other cases, management has worked to include HRSC staff as full partners in the human resources department, with productive results.

Emerging Trends

Although changes in human resources programs and functionality have driven HRMS development, information technology in the broadest sense is an even more rapidly evolving field. For this reason, most of the significant developments in HRMS stem from hardware and software improvements rather than changes in human resources itself. Computers, data base management systems (DBMS), operating systems, and telecommunications have evolved so quickly in recent years that applications software developers and users are usually working well below the capacity of the available technologies. HRMS developers have begun to adopt many innovations in technology and process, including the following:

- Increased role of microcomputers and executive workstations
- System connectivity
- Executive information systems (EIS)
- Fourth-generation languages (4GLs)
- Computer-aided software engineering (CASE)
- Artificial intelligence (AI) and expert systems
- Increased use of computer-based training (CBT)
- Document imaging
- High-resolution graphics and animation
- Voice recognition and speech synthesis
- Expendable and expandable systems

These trends are described in more detail in the following sections. Caveats for their application to HRMS are included, as are suggestions for maximizing their successful implementation and utilization.

Increased Role of Microcomputers and Executive Workstations

The microcomputer explosion has been perhaps the most important business phenomenon in the past decade. This process has involved an ongoing series of major advances, with each change making the previous one relatively obsolete. The industry remains heavily committed to even further advances. For instance, numerous suppliers are working on faster processors, improvements in workstation technology, DBMS, and connectivity. As these developments become commercially available within the next few years, they will catalyze new applications and more thorough integration of microcomputers and workstations into business operations.

Several aspects of microcomputers fuel these changes and their rapid adoption. First, microcomputers are much less expensive than midrange or mainframe computers. Microcomputing power that cost $6,000 to $7,000 less than ten years ago costs under $1,000 today. Even when a new, more expensive generation of microcomputers emerges, those machines still offer more for the money than comparable mainframe computers.

Microcomputer-based systems have a significantly faster implementation cycle than do larger systems. On the average, mainframe systems can require twelve to eighteen months or more to implement completely, while microcomputers can require as little as six to eight weeks. Acquisition and implementation options for microcomputers are proliferating. Today, new users can find vendors who specialize in microcomputer HRMS applications and consultants knowledgeable about implementation of microcomputer-based systems. Taking advantage of this specialization optimizes the investment in outside services. Moreover, system developers have built installation procedures into the systems themselves. The effort of planning, developing, and implementing a responsive HRMS is not a trivial task, but modern tools and techniques make it easier.

Most users welcome the independence microcomputers offer. Users can choose their own organizational scheme, set their own development schedule, and take responsibility for system maintenance, without relying on other departments. Although independence is a two-edged sword, it often complements modern human resources departments. Frequent legal and regulatory changes in human resources lead to revisions in procedures. The need to respond rapidly to these changes impedes the ability of human resources staff to explain their needs to technicians. In such cases, computer-literate human resources professionals will handle changes without the intervention of technicians.

As portable and laptop computers become less expensive, more executives and human resources representatives use them to connect to an HRMS from remote locations. As detailed in the accompanying sidebar, telecommuting is a growing influence on the HRMS. Telecommuters must pay special attention to data security, however. Someone who uses a computer outside the organization's offices may inadvertently leave disks or drafts of sensitive data where they are available to competitors.

The executive workstation concept also has been gaining a foothold in large organizations. Although these units are more expensive compared with stand-alone, single-user microcomputers (by a ratio of as much as 10 to 1), they have many beneficial features, such as embedded word processing,

The HRMS and Telecommuting

Today working at home means more than stuffing a few papers into a briefcase to review in the evening. In the past decade, hundreds of U.S. firms have adopted or experimented with telecommuting, allowing employees in certain jobs to work usually at home. Telecommuters avoid the stress and time demands of commuting. Skipping the commute often has particular appeal to employees who want flexible schedules or more time with their families, as well as to physically disabled employees. The companies themselves often experience reduced employee turnover and lower costs of office space and furnishings as well as increased productivity.

In 1989, experts estimated that at least 20,000 individuals were full-time telecommuters. Los Angeles's Center for Futures Research estimates that 600,000 corporate employees work at home. The number will continue to grow, perhaps to as high as 5 million by 1995.

An organization that undertakes telecommuting invariably finds that the human resources department and the HRMS both affect and are affected by it. The human resources department is responsible for establishing standards for which types of jobs and individuals are eligible for telecommuting. Telecommuting usually works best with knowledge workers and employees who do not have public contact rather than with production or retail employees. Telecommuting typically involves jobs such as developers and planners, computer programmers, word processors, data entry clerks, and documentation writers. Telecommuting also may alter criteria used for measuring employee productivity, which in turn may affect the standards used in performance reviews.

The HRMS must translate these standards into coded fields. The HRMS may use fields to maintain eligibility data related to telecommuting based on job family, location, or time period. In this segment, the system tracks which employees and positions are involved in telecommuting, their telecommuting schedules, and dates telecommuting begins and ends. It also may include changes to evaluation criteria for performance reviews. If the human resources department has primary responsibility for the telecommuting program, it may need to track additional data, such as special costs (and cost avoidance) related to telecommuting.

In many cases, telecommuters occupy positions that require use of computers. In fact, the advent of microcomputers has provided one of the most important spurs to the development of telecommuting. If human resources staff participate in telecommuting, they often selectively access HRMS data at home as well. HRSC staff may interact with the HRMS via modems and personal microcomputers or simply import or export data via disks. The HRSC should ensure that the system's data security policies, procedures, software, and equipment provide sufficient safeguards against unauthorized HRMS access or tampering via remote microcomputers and against contamination with bad data or programs.

The ranks of telecommuters will undoubtedly continue to increase. At least one state government, faced with significant highway funding constraints and environmental concerns, now requires private employers to reduce the number of car trips its employees make. Telecommuting allows employees to avoid long commutes and the high cost of housing near big cities. Employers can hire additional employees but avoid having to relocate them from the communities in which they live. In the years to come, telecommuting may become as much a part of human resources management as flexible benefits.

---

spreadsheets, DBMS, voice and electronic mail, message switching, and automatic dialing. Still, many managers continue to use their workstations just for word processing or message switching. Many enterprises face the challenge of how to motivate executives to use more of these features to maximize their own productivity. Some firms use training to meet this challenge; others encourage experienced users to become trailblazers.

The newest generation of microcomputers and workstations is based on powerful new microprocessors that are five to ten times faster than previous machines. These machines now have the data-handling capacity of the early mainframes, a feature of potential importance to users who have sufficient computer systems skills to be able to handle independence from the typically centralized mainframe environment.

Most HRMS users do not need more speed or power. They actually spend much of their time entering data or generating reports rather than waiting for the computer to manipulate data; they are input/output bound. Microcomputer speed really matters only to users who require a significant amount of computational and statistical analysis or who must handle very large volumes of records and transactions quickly.

Most new human resources software runs in the traditional DOS environment because most users still operate in that sphere. The release of new microcomputer operating systems and DBMS has opened up opportunities for new power, flexibility, and accessibility for users. Some developers offer systems for Unix, Xenix, OS/2, A/UX, DR. DOS 5 and other operating systems to run on IBM-compatible personal computers, the Apple Macintosh series, the Hewlett-Packard Vectras, Digital Equipment Corporation's MicroVax, and others. However, most HRMS software has yet to take advantage of these advances, primarily because software development is so costly and vendors are unsure which DBMS and operating environments will survive. As these systems achieve success in the general business computer market, more vendors will offer HRMS packages in these emerging data base and operating system environments. This trend should expand considerably in the near future.

The increased power and lower cost of microcomputers are leading many human resources departments to treat them as single-function systems. In this scheme, each human resources function, such as employment, training, or benefits, has its own completely independent microcomputer-based system. Some applications that need high-powered security in handling sensitive data (such as stock option administration or executive compensation) are natural candidates for this functional separation.

Many human resources departments have yet to address the limitations of microcomputers. Too many "power" users manage complex data but fail to perform regular file backup and thus risk losing entire data bases. As microcomputers become more commonplace, HRICs will be able to provide microcomputer users with adequate and reliable support so they can remain independent.

Many human resources departments also will expand their use of peripheral devices. A human resources department that begins computerization with a single microcomputer and printer may find itself five years from now with an entire network of computers, complete with distributed processing, office automation support, telecommunications, and remote printing. Business users can expect increasingly faster communication, more sophisticated report generators, and flexible location arrangements to accommodate telecommuters and multisite operations.

Executive Information Systems

Some firms have expanded the executive workstation concept even further. Hardware and software vendors, as well as internal systems analysts, have

Information Kiosks:
The Future Is Now

Many human resources professionals have expressed enthusiasm about having information kiosks located in convenient spots, such as the company cafeteria or employee lounge. As with automated teller machines (ATMs) at banks, an employee can access his or her own personnel record privately by using a coded identification number or an access card, then select an activity from a menu. The employee might check the accuracy of personal data, change his or her address or other demographic information, inquire about benefits or compensation status, or even compare the provisions of various retirement or deferred compensation plans.

Kiosks will come with familiar keyboard-based terminals, but some HRMS planners are already experimenting with touch-sensitive screens, and they envision eventually adopting voice activation. The system should include graphics, probably a color monitor, and perhaps printing capability. The installation should have some provision for privacy.

The software should be fun and easy to use. For instance, in benefits planning, each session may start with a basic set of questions about income expectations, dependents, and so forth, which the employee can answer with a minimum of keystrokes. The employee can then select from a menu the type of benefits he or she wishes to consider. The module then illustrates possible scenarios, giving additional choices as the employee proceeds. For instance, an employee can project the level of retirement income in one year or five years. An employee can look at the long-term effects of numerous options. When the session is complete, the employee can choose to have the results printed.

Bringing interactive software and information kiosks into wider use will require improvements in data security and more widespread employee computer training. For data security reasons, the terminal or computer may not be linked to the mainframe-based HRMS. Setting up hardware that meets these needs is a relatively minor issue. Now that ATMs can dispense cash and travelers' checks, human resources kiosks can certainly be programmed to handle basic personnel transactions. Organizations that already have credit union ATMs may be able to adapt them to serve as human resources information terminals.

begun integrating powerful but disparate elements of computer technology into systems that allow executives to take advantage of special-purpose computer applications within their organization. Experts refer to these systems by several different names; the most popular of these are executive information systems (EIS) and decision support systems (DSS).

The EIS approach uses a microcomputer, terminal, or workstation to give an executive access to data from many parts of the enterprise—sales, production, finance, and human resources. Generally speaking, the system accesses strategic rather than operational data. For instance, an executive might need information from the HRMS on the skills, experience, positions, and salaries of employees but not need payroll or time and attendance data. Often the EIS presents summary information only; as needed, executives can access more detailed information immediately via a process commonly referred to as *drilling down*. The executive user generally views and analyzes these data but makes no changes. Some EIS actually block executive users from making changes.

Sometimes managers need primarily statistical or analytical tools. In these cases, they may benefit from using a DSS. The DSS may contain statistical analysis packages, modeling programs, and some form of expert system. A DSS may pertain to only one data base or to more than one. In some cases, middle managers may be the primary users of a DSS.

In contrast, an EIS involves more wide-ranging (and expensive) capabilities. A full-fledged EIS generally contains sophisticated color graphics viewing and printing capabilities, linkages among several data bases, DBMS with sophisticated query languages, and electronic conferencing, or at least electronic mail (E-mail). Some firms use the term *EIS* to refer specifically to systems accessed only by high-level executives and *DSS* to refer to systems used by mid-level managers as well. Others do not distinguish between EIS and DSS.

Creating an EIS involves technical and personal communication challenges. For instance, each department in the firm may use a different operating environment: the HRMS has a 4GL, accounting uses COBOL, and engineering has UNIX. An EIS requires so much planning, compromise, and trust that most firms that have implemented these systems recommend that other firms undertake them only if top management commits wholeheartedly to sponsoring the EIS project. The HRSC manager should help executive users determine for themselves the data they need in the EIS.

To implement an EIS that includes the human resources data base, the HRSC manager often must struggle to coordinate HRMS data with data from other systems. After an initial start-up period, however, an EIS often fosters a feeling of teamwork among participating managers, who find that they share common goals across department lines. In many cases, the EIS results in more executives becoming familiar with human resources data and thus gaining an increased appreciation for the value of these data and of the HRMS overall.

Until recently, firms that wanted an EIS had to invest in significant custom development. New vendor products are available that can reduce this investment, but even these new tools and programs require users to commit to linking software to their existing data sources, customizing reports, and making procedural alterations in order for the EIS to meet the organization's needs.

System Connectivity

More and more human resources departments have found that linking microcomputers to mainframe and midrange computers gives them the best of both worlds. This platform combines the speed and power of the mainframe and midrange systems with the responsive input/output capability and independence of the microcomputer. In a linked or connected system, users typically have the central computer handle storage, production, maintenance, and high-volume printing; users perform data entry, queries, and summary reporting remotely using microcomputers or workstations.

Connectivity happens in several ways. Many human resources departments use local area networks (LANs) to connect stand-alone human resources microcomputers to one another. The capabilities of networks will continue to grow. Emerging technology promises an increase in the number of simultaneous users permitted in a single LAN environment. File servers with increased capabilities also are becoming more popular. In a file-server scheme, one central processor serves as the mass storage facility or repository, with links that enable other microcomputers to access common data but use their own facilities to manipulate and analyze those data.

Connectivity refers primarily to linkages between systems of different types (such as microcomputers to a mainframe), but it also may refer to emerging standards and linkages in operating systems, DBMS, telecommunication protocols, and applications. Hardware and software vendors have made significant progress in these areas, but they continue to search for and struggle with standards. With increasing frequency, vendors are offering packages for microcomputers that, to the user, appear identical to the version that runs on mainframe systems.

Some hardware vendors now offer a single package that can run programs using DOS, UNIX, or Macintosh-type operating systems. Macintosh and DOS systems are beginning to look more similar, as Macintoshes use function keys as alternatives to the mouse and some DOS systems use the mouse to access icons and windows. In fact, object-oriented programming, such as that pioneered with the Macintosh, is beginning to emerge on a wider variety of products. Some DOS-based vendors now offer object-oriented programs. The

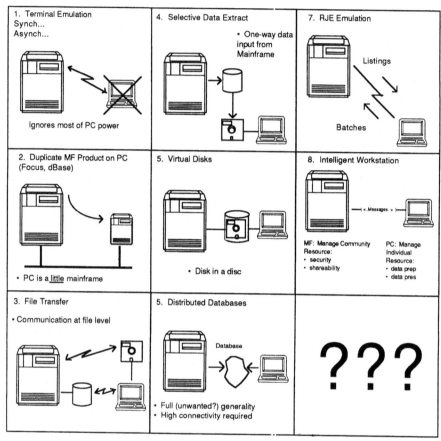

Figure 22–1. Microcomputer-to-mainframe linkage options. Once an organization decides to link microcomputers to a mainframe, it faces a significant technical question: which type of link to provide. As shown here, some links provide for one-way communication, others for two-way. Some treat microcomputers simply as mainframe terminals, others as intelligent workstations. Some have them emulate mainframe operations independently. Making these choices requires computer expertise as well as a thorough understanding of users' needs and skills.

(Source: Kinexis, 1988. Reprinted with permission.)

object-oriented approach is a significant feature of some emerging operating systems, such as Hewlett Packard's NewWave, IBM's Office Vision, and NeXt, Inc.'s NextStep.

Connectivity also is occurring in computer graphics. Until fairly recently, users who wanted to create charts and graphs had to input summary data from the HRMS to independent graphics packages. Now more and more data base management, word processing, and spreadsheet programs offer internal graphics capabilities, so users can obtain graphics output directly without having to transfer data. This connectivity, generally referred to as graphical user interface (GUI), also allows stand-alone graphics packages to import data directly from HRMS applications with no additional data entry.

In response to the proliferation of linkage options and user demands for connectivity, some HRSCs have begun adapting network software and netware to make it easier to use. For instance, some have created linkage menus, including default values for common connections. In the coming decade, many more organizations will network the HRMS with systems in other functions, such as finance, marketing, and production. These network arrangements may involve a mix of systems: mainframe to mainframe, mainframe to midrange, mainframe to microcomputer, and midrange to microcomputer.

Among human resources departments, several types of mainframe-midrange-microcomputer connectivity will become more prominent:

- Downloading (or exporting) data from mainframe to midrange or microcomputer for manipulation and retention at the microcomputer level
- Downloading data to midrange or microcomputer for manipulation, then uploading (or importing) results to mainframe
- Accessing mainframe or midrange on-line and using microcomputer as a real-time terminal

Download linkages provide an opportunity for greater security and access control, since only the data pertinent to a particular application need be exported from the mainframe to the microcomputer. However, they also may increase the threat to data integrity. Because users are not always isolated, access control and corresponding data security may be more difficult to enforce.

These advances have not solved all connectivity problems. In fact, the proliferation of technology has exacerbated rather than alleviated connectivity problems. Integration of systems having different architectures will remain difficult and expensive because of technical differences in data base management, file structures, teleprocessing, and operating system environments. This applies particularly to mainframe and midrange computer systems. Some programs will remain mutually incompatible or will require purchasers to modify source code, develop complex interfaces, or acquire specialized hardware to achieve connectivity. However, some interface standards have been emerging, and these promise to facilitate the interchanges between different systems.

Increasing Role of 4GLs

In the past few years, more than a few human resources departments with computer experience have streamlined the planning and implementation of new applications by developing or acquiring systems based on 4GLs. As described in chapter 4, the command language of 4GLs more closely resembles English-language statements than do those of earlier generation languages such as COBOL and FORTRAN. With 4GLs, human resources functions can achieve more productive results from upgrades and new applications. Moreover, everyone using the HRMS will benefit because the HRIC is more likely to be qualified to support these languages. Although both end users and IS staff can use 4GLs, these languages remain primarily the province of technicians because their syntax and protocols still require technical support.

At present, the benefits of 4GLs in HRMS software packages accrue largely to microcomputer-based systems. Increasingly, human resources departments have begun to encourage users by providing training that allows them to utilize the full potential of 4GLs. The next five years will undoubtedly see a significant increase in 4GLs for HRMS applications as they become more widespread and approach the status of standard languages.

Computer-Aided Software Engineering

Applications developers use 4GLs primarily to generate program code. CASE, a new set of programming tools and technologies, involves computers in many more aspects of program development. It incorporates computers into software development, from planning to maintenance. CASE products build a data base of information about the desired program or system and the data the system will use.

Already vendors offer hundreds of CASE tools. Some, often called *upper CASE*, address higher-level concerns, specifically planning and design stages. Developers use them to produce diagrams and charts of the relationships and data flow the system will support. Other tools, called *lower CASE*, cover program code generation, testing, and maintenance. They bear significant resemblance to 4GLs and other programming tools.

CASE products promise faster development time, standardized results, easier program updates and customization, and reduced dependence on computer programmers. Some experts estimate that CASE tools may reduce labor costs for applications development by as much as 90 percent (and labor accounts for three-quarters of software development costs).

The adoption of CASE places additional demands on IS staff, however. CASE requires that programmers and systems analysts change many aspects of how they plan and design projects. To use CASE tools, they must identify, develop, and agree upon consistent structures and methodologies for software. Most CASE tools require access to a mainframe computer for code generation, although similar capabilities for midrange computers and microcomputers are emerging.

According to one CASE specialist, "The move to CASE requires tremendous cultural changes. When you tell your star COBOL programmer that he's going to have to give up all the little tricks he's learned over the years that make his style of programming unique—that's a frightening thing. But the biggest problem with CASE is understanding the enterprise's business requirements, not the coding. The ideal individual has an even mix of technical and analysis skills. We think of it in terms of moving the creativity up the life cycle away from coding towards analysis and design" (Mark Kindley, "CASE: The Promise Approaches Reality." *VARBusiness*, April 1990).

Human resources may soon see HRMS products developed via CASE. In fact, some sophisticated HRSCs may select a CASE-based system so IS staff can learn to customize applications more easily.

AI and Expert Systems

Computer professionals also have been discussing fifth-generation languages, more commonly known as artificial intelligence. AI refers to a high-level communication between user and machine. It tries to create computer systems that emulate the way people think and interact with each other. The ideal AI computer system has the massive data storage and logical powers of the human mind as well as its power to question, extrapolate, place information in a context (or domain), and "learn" patterned responses. AI can include robotics, computer vision, expert systems, and a process called natural language, but most often it refers to expert systems.

Expert systems are computer programs designed to simulate the decision-making process of human experts. They incorporate a knowledge base, a means of receiving incoming data, and logical paradigms based on past knowledge. An expert system has the ability to learn from expert users. The user makes a request, then the computer uses an extensive lexicon and complicated IF/THEN/ELSE information paths to develop a patterned response or query, requesting clarification as necessary. As an expert system interacts with an

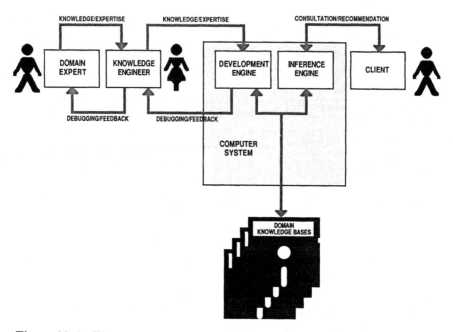

Figure 22–2. Elements of an expert system. Building an expert system requires ongoing interaction among specialists in computer systems development, programmers, and specialists in the area the system will cover. Some of the terminology of expert systems is unique. Terms such as *domain expert* and *inference engine are* used almost exclusively to describe expert systems development.
(Source: *The Office*, February 1987. Reprinted with permission.)

expert, it accumulates information about trends. In response, it develops rules of interaction and information retrieval. The AI process may reason forward to a goal or backward to a cause, and it may follow multiple analytical paths. Having reached a conclusion, an expert system can provide the basis for its findings, recommendations, and alternatives. Eventually the system adds this conclusion to its ongoing knowledge base, perhaps with some human intervention and modification.

AI has been a promised computer development for years, but expert systems require significantly more sophistication, time, and financial investment than conventional systems. For these reasons, the most common applications have been in equipment routing and scheduling (such as trains and airlines), some geological research, and a few specialized medical diagnostic areas. Although AI application generally remains part of the research world rather than part of sophisticated business enterprises, manufacturers, banks, insurance companies, and other commercial entities have begun exploring its application to their information-handling needs.

Vendors now offer AI for systems ranging from mainframes to microcomputers, with choices of general AI languages, specialized languages, and shells. A shell is an expert system designed to work with certain types of knowledge and reasoning but that contains no knowledge to start with. An AI installation requires significant customization and sophisticated users.

The biggest technical challenge in developing an AI application is development of a lexicon on which users can agree. This includes not only each possible word but its synonyms, homonyms, and connecting words. An effective lexicon uses normal human speech patterns, while the computer interprets these statements and asks for clarifications as needed. For instance, an AI system must be able to interpret "Give me" as synonymous with "Load" or "Retrieve." When a user asks for earnings, the system queries which type of earnings the user wants—payroll earnings, base salary earnings, net earnings, year-to-date earnings, noncash earnings, or some combination of these.

A few vendors offer high-powered information-retrieval systems that simulate many of the characteristics of AI, and these likely will enhance human resources functions in the foreseeable future. A few scattered human resources departments have tried such applications. For instance, one vendor offers an expert system that screens the résumés of job applicants. In another case, a major financial institution has used an expert system to correlate the activities and tasks comprising each job, a process known as activity analysis. With this analysis, human resources staff can establish accurate job descriptions, productivity standards, and career paths for employees.

Expert systems are just beginning to find significant application in human resources, but they seem to be starting in relatively sophisticated areas having the attention of top management, such as succession planning. For instance, succession planning experts could create a complex set of IF/THEN/ELSE interactive statements for the computer to use in assessing how to flag problem situations. For instance, IF candidate has five years of management experience and more than four years of education beyond high school, THEN preselect candidate and analyze patterns of experience versus those of other candidates having more or less experience and education; ELSE modify criteria and other variables based on the number of candidates preselected.

A properly developed expert system could aid in employee performance evaluations. For instance, a supervisor might make notes and interview an employee under review, then sit at a terminal to respond to a guided set of computer-generated questions. The supervisor's responses would influence which additional questions the system would pose, helping the supervisor identify exactly which aspects of employee performance deserve commendation or need improvement. Based on this expert knowledge, the system would then suggest actions to help improve the employee's performance. The system

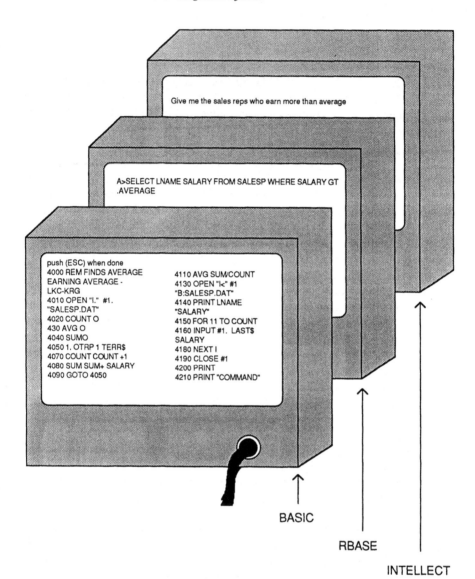

Figure 22–3. AI resembles human communication patterns. This is an example of how a conventional programming language (BASIC), a data base language (R:base), and an AI language (Intellect) handle a typical inquiry.

might even suggest wording that the supervisor might use in discussing the performance review with the employee.

Developments in CBT

In chapter 9, computer-based training was described as a tool for training human resources staff how to use the HRMS. Employees also can use CBT to learn about numerous other operations via computer tutorials or programmed instruction. Typically, these operations involve the computer, such as word processing, records maintenance, claims processing, and bookkeeping procedures. Thousands of college professors have developed and assign courseware to accompany lectures, demonstrations, experiments, and self-paced instruction. In business, more and more training departments are working with internal human resources staff and departmental management throughout the enterprise to develop, implement, administer, and evaluate CBT.

CBT is expensive to create but usually offers a worthwhile improvement in staff productivity through increased efficiency and reduction of training resource requirements. Once an organization has made the initial investment in CBT development, it can save significant resources because CBT requires less staff to administer and maintain it than do some other forms of training. CBT may be cost-effective as a tool for training multiple users simultaneously when having an instructor present is not practical. This frequently applies when trainees are in different locations. CBT allows trainees to schedule their own training sessions. By keeping the trainees at their regular jobs when demand is high yet freeing them for training when time permits, CBT helps improve employee productivity.

The highly procedural, sequential restrictions of CBT may frustrate some users. Although few expert systems for CBT have emerged to date, future technology promises to overcome the cost constraints and other restrictions that have discouraged many firms from developing CBT applications. New software and audiovisual devices will give trainees more on-line choices. CBT needs to incorporate more sophisticated evaluation techniques for deciding the level of training or practice a particular user needs.

CBT's major disadvantage is the absence of a human monitor to answer questions and help users over rough spots. This may reduce the user's confidence and comfort level. Numerous organizations have adopted some form of CBT, but widespread acceptance awaits a sociological evolution and more cost-effective techniques. Users have become more accustomed to computer training in the form of vendor-supplied tutorials but still prefer and are more comfortable with human interaction and conventional classroom instruction. As employees gain more exposure to computers in their professional, educational, and personal lives, they will probably become more comfortable with training via computer-assisted technologies such as CBT.

Document Image Processing

In spite of the information technology explosion in the past decade, many organizations still find themselves overwhelmed by paperwork. Some experts estimate that computers handle only 1 percent of the information generated or used in U.S. business enterprises. Much of the rest resides on paper—applications, memos, reports, invoices, reminders, letters, notices, confirmations, manuals, diagrams, charts, drawings, and so on. Human resources departments especially suffer under this "paper weight."

Some firms, particularly large corporations and many public-sector agencies, have begun using a combination of new technologies to convert much of their paper source documents and computer outputs to electronic images for storage, handling, and retrieval via computer. Some call this approach document image processing; others refer to it as electronic imaging or document imaging. Sometimes document image processing includes only image storage and retrieval; other times it also may encompass document processing. In the latter case, the system integrates the data from the paper input into a data base for processing, modification, and analysis.

A single system often integrates many types of hardware and software, such as high-speed image scanners; intelligent character recognition systems; optical disks, microfilm, and magnetic media for storage; bar code and optical character recognition (OCR) technology for automated indexing; and local area and wide area networks for data communication.

Many organizations remain intimidated by the high costs of document image processing technology and the need to fit together the diverse hardware, software, data, and user requirements this type of system entails. Document image processing applications usually require a mainframe, which prevents smaller firms from considering it cost-effective. Finally, because relatively few firms have adopted document image processing, they do not have staff with imaging experience; thus, they hesitate to enter the field.

Groups that have adopted this technology have reduced operational costs (by reducing needs for mailroom, records, and library staff), increased productivity, improved information cycle times, reduced storage costs, and benefited from having more information integrated and easily retrievable. Frequently, these enterprises have started by converting only one part of their operations to document image processing. For instance, an airline used imaging for maintenance manuals, drawings, and records. It postponed converting core activities such as ticketing and scheduling to document image processing until it had time to develop internal experience and expertise with this approach.

For similar reasons, human resources may serve as an appropriate document image processing pioneer in some organizations. Management may feel more comfortable believing that central record-keeping activities are not im-

How Many Filing Cabinets
Can You Fit on a Disk?

Activities such as document imaging, computerized claims processing, and AI often require massive amounts of data storage. In many cases, optical-disk storage systems offer the most compact, convenient storage for high-volume activities. Storage capacities of conventional paper filing systems and of optical-disk filing systems in a variety of sizes are compared in the following table.

File Size (8.5″ × 11″ Images)	Paper File		Optical-Disk Files (Compressed Images)
	Paper Stack	Filing Cabinet	
1	Single side of page		50 kilobytes (KB)
5,000	10″ to 20″	1 drawer	250 megabytes (MB), or one side of 5″ to 6″ disk
10,000	20″ to 40″	1 to 2 drawers	500MB, or both sides of a 5″ to 6″ disk
20,000	3′ to 7′	2 to 4 drawers	1 gigabyte (GB) or one side of a 12″ disk
50,000	8′ to 17′	4 to 8 drawers	2.5GB, or both sides of a 12″ disk
130,000	22′ to 44′	12 to 24 drawers	6.5GB, or both sides of a 14″ disk
6,000,000	1,000′ to 1,200′	600 to 1,200 drawers	300 GB, or a 120-disk "jukebox"

(Source: John Murphy, "Document/Image Management Systems: Their Advantages Are Not Optical Illusions," *Today's Office,* April 1990. Reprinted with permission.)

pacted by major changes taking place in information technologies, while still experiencing first hand how this approach improves productivity in their organization. Some firms initiate the process by transferring archived material to electronic images. This allows staff to become familiar with the process and work out any communications issues before handling current, time-sensitive material. Human resources document image processing may encompass diverse and voluminous paperwork in areas such as applications, new-hire forms, benefits and claims forms, status-change notices, and time and attendance cards.

Even well into the 1990s, only a small percentage of human resources departments will have adopted document image processing. This percentage will continue to grow, however, because of the productivity and retrieval advantages of this approach.

High-Resolution Graphics and Animation

Computer applications in human resources are based primarily on words and numbers, but graphics have improved the ease with which users can analyze and interpret data. In the future, sophisticated systems will have sufficient computer power and speed to generate computerized animation to carry the power of graphics even further. For instance, planners will be able to combine color and computer animation to display flow rates of individuals through jobs within the organization over time. By hitting a single key, they can command the VDT (or a projection screen) to display images in which different-colored lines represent different types of employees and line width indicates the number of employees; through animation, the change in line width in real time on the screen indicates the change in number of employees during some future time period.

High-resolution graphics also allows computers to store color photographs. Future HRMS will be able to include a color photograph as part of each employee's record. A system that can store and reproduce photographic images could even create photo ID cards. In turn, employees could use their photo ID cards not only for physical identification but also to initiate noncritical transactions (such as address changes) in a graphics-sensitive system. This direct entry would reduce the need for paper to process status changes.

Voice Recognition and Speech Synthesis

Both voice recognition and speech synthesis have the potential to speed up interactions between people and machines. Their ability to process transactions can reduce paperwork to the extent that internal auditors allow them to do so and may hold the further promise of a paperless office. A computer with voice recognition responds to spoken commands and input. The primary difficulty in this rapidly evolving field has been getting computers to understand different voice inflections. Speaker-dependent voice recognition systems can recognize relatively large vocabularies by many users, but each user must create his or her own special data base so that the computer can recognize the peculiarities of that individual's pronunciation. To the extent that voiceprinting has reliability equal to fingerprinting, this technique offers the potential for increased security and access controls for the HRMS. It also may bring reductions in human resources paperwork. One possible human resources application involves creating transaction input via voice. The supervisor or manager simply speaks the transaction change into a device that recognizes his or her voice and approves the transaction based on system-maintained authorization tables similar to the privilege matrix described in chapter 3.

If large numbers of employees (or customers) have access to the system, a speaker-independent voice recognition system may work best. This technology can understand almost anyone's voice without separate user data bases but only within a limited vocabulary. These systems must use password security to control access to potentially sensitive data.

Speech synthesis is the converse of voice recognition; using very different technologies, the computer generates understandable language. Some companies are already using these techniques in applications such as direct marketing and paging. Some school districts use speech synthesis to have robotic devices notify teachers and bus drivers regarding school closures, work availability, alternate routings, or the need for substitutes. Schools can look forward to the day when systems have the capability to search the entire master file, then contact only those teachers who meet certain criteria. Some airline frequent-flyer programs now use systems that recognize participants via direct telephone keypad entry but generate account balance information using speech synthesis.

The most general application of speech synthesis for human resources would be for transaction acknowledgment. In some newer HRMS, users have begun generating verbal reports on specific personnel transactions by interspersing set phrases with the individual social security number, dates, and amounts from the records of a specific employee. The system also can issue verbal warnings if a user inputs a salary figure that exceeds the authorized salary range limits. This area will probably find significant application within HRMS, thus further reducing paperwork.

Expendable and Expandable Systems

In the past few years, some human resources functions not yet ready to make a major financial or staff investment in computer systems have chosen to start with a small-scale, expendable system. Other departments without experience and expertise may start out with a beginner system and expand it as staff needs and volume dictate.

A department may acquire an expendable system to serve only certain human resources functions. One or two disks can probably hold the entire application, and the operations manual can be quite brief. These expendable

Up-and-Coming Computer Buzzwords

There are essentially three sources of software buzzwords. Each of the following factions is already actively backing its nominations:

- The entrepreneurs who sell promising new ideas to practitioners whether they are helpful or not.
- The academics who sell brilliant new ideas to research funding sources whether they are helpful or not.
- The technology-transfer specialists who sort through the work of the entrepreneurs and the academics looking for ideas worth passing on to the practitioners whether they are ready for them or not.

What are the buzzwords these groups propose?

Information engineering is the first nomination of the entrepreneurial faction. To understand it, take the top-down notion of the '70s structured revolution and apply it to the corporate institution and not just to software. This one looks like a sure winner—hardly anyone ever argued that top-down approaches to software were bad.

Enterprise is the second nomination of the entrepreneurs, and it is linked to the first. "Information engineering will improve the data processing of the enterprise," we will all learn to say. We used to say "corporate institution" (or "organization") or some such phrase, but it's a new decade and we can all learn a new way of expressing ourselves.

Paradigm is the first nomination of the academics. It has just the right touch of mystery and exclusiveness—and only the in-group will be able to pronounce it (hard "i," silent "g"). It means "a model of how things should be done," and who can argue with the need for more of those?

Metaphor is the next candidate of the academics. It means "something that represents something else for the purpose of comparison or analogy." There is a distant family relationship to the earlier academic buzzword "abstraction," and thus metaphor has a leg up in the buzzword derby.

Repository is a blockbuster candidate, say the entrepreneurs. After all, it builds on the "data dictionary" buzzword of a decade or two ago, and who can resist a hopped-up version of an old favorite?

Oracle is a dark horse academic nominee. It means some kind of authority figure, and don't we all wish we had one of those close at hand? (Note: Oracle is unlikely to catch on as a buzzword because at least one vendor and several products already bear this name.)

Process is the nomination of the technology-transfer people, heretofore silent in our nominations. However, there is a method to this single-nominee madness; after all, process covers just about all of the other buzzwords in this list. A generic buzzword could be the winner this decade.

Object-oriented is the last-but-not-least nominee of the academics. The bandwagon for this nominee is already well under way. This may be a top candidate for the 1990s. In fact, it is the only buzzword nomination that is nominated by one group (the academics) and seconded by another (the entrepreneurs).

There you have it. Now don't just chuckle or frown and forget these words—work on them a little bit . . . . The *information engineering* success of the *enterprise* may well depend on your placing these *objects* in your personal *repository.* At least, they will determine the success of the *paradigm* that you as an *oracle* choose to employ. It will only be through the *process* of trying to master them that you will realize that they represent a *metaphor* for real success in the software business, 1990s style.

(Source: Robert Glass, "Announcing Finalists for the 'Buzzword of the '90s'," *Computerworld,* February 1990. Reprinted with permission.)

---

systems have a low initial cost but also a significant functional limitation in their lack of flexibility. They have fewer total screens and manipulate less data, so implementation proceeds quickly. They also have no screen generator and no report writer, so users cannot change data element definitions, captions, headings, or report formats.

Users can, however, learn and use expendable programs easily. This allows them to become accustomed to and informed about computerization before making a significant investment of time and money. A department may use such a system to gain computer literacy and define its overall (or emerging) computer needs more precisely.

In the process of querying and receiving reports from this simple system, management becomes accustomed to and more readily accepting of automation. Even a simple system can eliminate incorrect or inconsistent information by editing and validating data transferred from manual files. This forces users to develop and use consistent terminology and coding schemes. A human resources department can use an expendable system to clean up data in preparation for transfer to a larger system.

Eventually the human resources department as a whole, or at least some of its functions, may be ready for a more sophisticated system that permits modifications and additions to fields, record types, screens, and reports. By then, users are better prepared to specify, select, and develop a system that matches their needs and resources. When the new system is ready and system operators have converted data from the old format to the new, users simply discard the beginner system or relegate it to very limited use.

Vendors may not appreciate the idea that clients consider an HRMS package merely a temporary expedient. They would rather that clients invest heavily right away to experience the full benefit of a system. Since some low-cost systems are generally marketed on a mail-order or value-added reseller (VAR) basis, they offer little or no support beyond telephone inquiries.

Expendable systems also may have certain disadvantages. They postpone the inevitable financial and time commitment of developing a full-scale system, and some departments may become frustrated because of limited flexibility or absent expansion capabilities. These limitations may lead some users and managers to lose confidence in the ability of computerization to address human resources management tasks.

Some departments may hang on to a start-up system long after it has outlived its usefulness. They may lack the time or resources to investigate and plan for a new system. Users and managers may fear letting go of a known system, or they may accept its benefits as all they require. They may even hesitate to use the flexibility, expandability, or system upgrades that the vendor does offer. Others may take on a new and bigger system without reevaluating their requirements or adopting a methodology for converting from the old system to the new. Many managers consider the transition trivial, but planning plays a significant role in the adoption of a new system.

Using Present Capabilities Fully

Numerous developments that experts consider emerging trends in HRMS are already possible with current technology. They await managers who have enough expertise and resources to make full use of the capabilities present in the technology already available.

For instance, although many human resources departments already have the hardware and software to link to external data bases, few take advantage of linkages for information on relevant labor markets. Sophisticated use of public and subscription data bases can provide information not only on new regulations, laws, and technology reviews but also on competitors. By understanding other firms' practices, the human resources department can build more effective recruitment, compensation, and management development strategies. As users become more comfortable with electronic data transmission internally, they may become more interested in reaching outside the organization for electronic information.

As another example, although human resources generally develops and publishes personnel policies and procedures, some departments have begun making them available on-line to human resources staff and line managers. By using on-line policies and procedures rather than printed manuals, a human resources department can provide employees and supervisors with information that supports new management decisions, revised government regulations, and recent labor law developments. A human resources function that networks its terminals and microcomputers with a mainframe computer or file server could review and revise on-line policies and procedures with no technical changes to the system. Human resources can use electronic mail to have authorized individuals review and approve proposed changes, and after approval, the network can distribute updated policies and procedures with minimal additional effort.

Some potential developments, though already technically possible, realistically apply only to systems and user communities with substantial computer sophistication. For instance, an automated transaction review process known as activity queuing involves electronic mail, widespread distribution of terminals, and (usually) a mainframe. With activity queuing, once a user processes a transaction, the system routes the transaction via electronic mail to supervisors and managers who should review or approve that transaction. This process works only as well as the communication between human resources staff (who understand the department's manual transaction approval processes) and the technicians who develop paths for automated transaction routing.

Every HRMS consultant has opinions about which predictions are most likely to become widespread and which will remain novelties, unaffordable or too sophisticated for most users. The HRMS manager should not aim to develop a system that includes all of these emerging features but should consider the usefulness and applicability of potential features when planning, developing, or modifying a system.

Future HRMS Needs

Achievement of these promises does not preclude developing another HRMS wish list. Some needs will remain, not only because of technical and financial limitations or the reticence of HRMS developers, but also because of the constant evolution of the field of human resources. As in the past, HRMS software

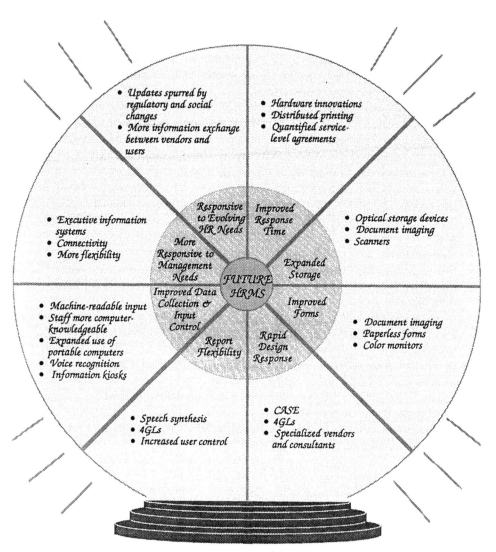

Figure 22–4. The future of HRMS. Planners can user two related methods to build an image of future HRMS. First, they may consider the needs an HRMS should meet (indicated in the inner circle). From those observations, they may predict the enhancements and innovations that will evolve to meet those needs. Alternatively, they may look at pending and potential developments in computer systems and human resources (indicated in the outer circle). Most HRMS planners use a combination of these two approaches to help users, managers, and developers plan for the future of HRMS.

developers will strive to offer enhancements that reflect relevant changes in regulations, industry standards, and employment markets.

Human resources managers must work with computer professionals and trainers both in the HRSC and in IS to increase HRMS user literacy. As employees become more aware of the advantages and potential of computers, they will demand more responsiveness from human resources systems. They will want portable pension accounting systems, human resources information kiosks, individual and group pay-for-performance plans, more flexibility in benefits packages, and customized career development plans. Software in these areas must become more sophisticated without becoming too complicated for the HRMS end user.

HRMS managers can look forward to numerous hardware and software enhancements that aid user accessibility. Many expect that human resources software packages will increasingly support the point-and-click approach to transaction processing and information retrieval made possible by the mouse. Mouse utilization may then augment more sophisticated screens and menus. A mouse allows users quicker selection and scanning of records and other computer choices because the human operator does not need to memorize keyboard protocols and function keys. Human resources users also will benefit as future software provides more on-line help instead of relying on reference to manuals. Human resources users are welcoming increased access to windows that allow users to view several screens simultaneously. With multiple screens, human resources users can compare present and past data, compare records, view multiple tables simultaneously, get on-line help while continuing to view the open file, and transfer data from one segment of the HRMS to another with increased accuracy.

Amidst the barrage of new programs and technical advances, human resources managers must develop more expertise in allocating financial and staff resources for computerization projects. Computers and their peripherals, software, and staff support will require more investment and commitment than many business and government enterprises realize. Decision makers must temper their inclination to adopt technological innovations with a thorough consideration of how each innovation fits into long-range strategic plans for the human resources department.

A human resources professional who uses or is considering developing or acquiring an HRMS can make significant contributions only by remaining in touch with emerging trends in HRMS. The journals, professional groups, data bases, and other resources listed in the appendixes provide a basis for access to this knowledge.

Human resources professionals should investigate trends before making any software or hardware acquisitions. The HRSC should make a special effort to keep up with recent enhancements and how others have applied them as well as with forthcoming innovations. An organization might consider holding on to outdated or outgrown technology for months or years longer than practical and not take advantage of new modules while awaiting further advances. This analysis paralysis only exacerates the problem. What is the opportunity cost of *not* doing something when the technology is available? This rhetorical question carries one important warning: Features and release dates can and will change significantly between announcement of pending availability and actual delivery.

Hardware and software vendors invariably announce the availability of new functions and features or the support of new technologies well before they release them. In part, this is an effective tactic for judging market acceptance. Vendors also use this tactic to demonstrate that they are ahead of their peers in terms of functional and technological enhancements. As we have implied elsewhere, *caveat emptor.*

Whether a human resources department builds a system or buys one, technological considerations are often the least of their worries. They can always find newer and better tools and techniques, no matter when the project proceeds. Participants should strive for the best possible system, then accept its inevitable limitations. The most important variable in system success is the motivation of users, technicians, and managers to work together to maximize the system's effectiveness.

Glossary

Activity queuing   An automated transaction review process. Once the computer system receives a transaction, it automatically routes that transaction to each appropriate user for review or approval.

AI   See *Artificial intelligence.*

Artificial intelligence (AI)   High-level communication between user and machine requiring massive data storage, sophisticated logic, and the power to learn. AI is an attempt to create computer systems that simulate the way people think and act with each other.

CBT   See *Computer-based training.*

Coevolution   The process by which two species (or systems) evolve together; each entity changes in response to evolution in the other, to allow their mutually dependent relationship to continue.

Computer-based training (CBT)   A form of software-based instruction in which trainees at a computer terminal or microcomputer learn at their own pace via tutorials or programmed instruction. The training may relate to general-purpose software (such as word processing or spreadsheets) or to specific HRMS processes (such as transaction input, query, and table maintenance).

Connectivity A term that refers primarily to linkages that facilitate information interchange among computers of different scale, such as linkages between microcomputers and mainframes. May also refer to emerging standards and linkages in operating systems, DBMS, telecommunications protocols, and applications.

Decision support system (DSS) A computer system designed to provide managers with analytical tools. A DSS may contain statistical analysis packages, modeling programs, and perhaps some sort of expert system. A DSS may pertain to only one data base or to many.

DSS See *Decision support system.*

EIS See *Executive information system.*

Executive information system (EIS) A computer system that uses a microcomputer, workstation, or terminal to access data from multiple internal (and possibly external) data bases from various departments. Usually includes data needed by strategic decision makers. An EIS often includes extensive graphics capabilities and decision-support tools to facilitate accessibility and analysis.

Expandable system A basic or specialized computer system that has expansion capability to handle additional data fields, tables, peripherals, modules, or other features in order to respond to evolving user and management needs.

Expendable system A generally inflexible computer system with limited functions and features that meet users' needs only partially. An organization may use an expendable system for certain human resources functions or as a transition from a manual or outdated system to a more sophisticated system. This latter route often applies when users are not yet ready for the complexity or cost of a more comprehensive system.

Expert system A computer system designed to imitate the decision-making process of human experts in a specific field. Expert systems incorporate a knowledge base formed with the assistance of subject-matter experts, a means of processing incoming data, and logical paradigms based on prior knowledge that the system has acquired.

Graphical user interface (GUI) An interface that facilitates links between applications data and graphics production. In one form of GUI, applications packages include graphics capabilities so that users can generate graphics directly from data within the application. In another form of GUI, stand-alone graphics packages import data from applications packages directly rather than requiring additional data entry.

GUI See *Graphical user interface.*

Robotics A process using a computer-controlled device to manipulate physical surroundings. For instance, in HRMS applications, robotic devices may manipulate phone, tape, and digital speech devices to notify large numbers of people about an event.

Speech synthesis The process by which a computer generates understandable spoken words, names, and numbers. It uses a combination of software and hardware specifically designed for this purpose.

Telecommuting   An increasingly popular employment alternative in which an employee works off-site (at home or at a work center) rather than at a central office. Telecommuters frequently (though not always) use computers and modems to communicate with the office. They may or may not spend some time in the office on a periodic basis.

Voice recognition   The process by which a computer recognizes and processes spoken or synthesized voice commands and input.

Discussion Points

1. Which is more likely to affect future HRMS developments—changes in human resources or changes in information technology? Why?
2. What advantages will increasing use of microcomputers and workstations bring to human resources departments?
3. What forms of connectivity are applicable to HRMS development?
4. Under what circumstances might CBT offer advantages over other forms of training?
5. What contributions might CASE tools make to HRMS development?
6. How can a human resources department avoid depending on an expendable system for too long?
7. What future trends may lead to a paperless human resources department? What factors might limit the evolution of a completely paperless office?
8. What economic and sociological forces are likely to influence future HRMS? In what ways will they influence these systems?

Further Reading

Microcomputers and Executive Workstations

Alperson, Burton L. "Choosing Data Management Software." *PC World*, July 1984.
Kull, David. "DB2: Built for Comfort and Speed?" *Computer Decisions*, October 1985.
Nardoni, Ren. "The Building Blocks of Successful Microcomputer Systems." *Personnel Journal*, January 1985.
Perry, Robert L. "Relational DBMS Takes Off." *Computer Decisions*, February 1985.
Phillips, John R. "Multiple Approaches to Multiuser Database Management." *PC*, November 1985.

Telecommuting

Castro, Janice. "Staying Home Is Paying Off." *Time*, October 1987.

Edwards, Lynne. "Everything You Wanted to Know about Telecommuting—But Were Afraid to Ask." *NCHRC Quarterly*, Spring 1990.

Fleming, Lis. *The One-Minute Commuter*. Davis, CA: Acacia Books, 1989.

Hawkins, Michael D. "Micros and Mainframes: Emerging Systems to Support HRP's Newer Roles." *Human Resource Planning*, November 1988.

Johnson, Maryfran. "For the Disabled, Home Is Where the Future Is." *Computerworld*, March 1990.

Levy, Joel, and Robert Miller. "Taking the Guesswork Out of Networking." *Today's Office*, January 1990.

Martin, Arlene. "There's No Place Like Home . . . To Work." *Human Resource Executive*, July 1989.

Moody, H. Gerald. "Out-of-Touch Telecommuters." *Computers in Personnel*, Fall 1987.

Executive Information Systems (EIS), Artificial Intelligence (AI) and Expert Systems

Altieri, Raymond P. "A Memo to the EIS User." *Information Center*, February 1990.

Beall, Ronald. "Decision Support Systems: What Are They and How Can They Help Me?" *School of Business Journal* (San Francisco State University), Fall 1986.

Chorafas, Dimitri. *Applying Expert Systems in Business*. New York: McGraw-Hill, 1986.

Jarvis, Pamela. "Artificial Intelligence: It's Time to Get Ready." *The Office*, August 1988.

Kull, David. "Expert Systems: Programming, Not Magic." *Computer Decisions*, December 1986.

Ladsen, Martin. "Decision Support Systems: Mission Accomplished?" *Computer Decisions*, April 1987.

Miller, Robert. "Executive Information Systems Help You Conduct Your Business." *Today's Office*, April 1989.

Newquist, Harvey P., III. "A Maturing AI Is Finding Its Way in the World." *Computerworld*, February 1990

Paller, Alan, and Richard Laska. *The EIS Book: Information Systems for Top Managers*. Honewood, IL: Dow-Jones Irwin, 1990.

Rockart, John F., and David W. DeLong. *Executive Support Systems: The Emergence of Top Management Computer Use*. Honewood, IL: Dow Jones-Irwin, 1988.

Runge, Larry. "Prototype That EIS!" *Information Center*, February 1989.

Settanni, Joseph A. "Artificial Intelligence: Next Evolution of Software." *The Office*, February 1987.

Seymour, Jim. "Artificial Intelligence: From Academia to Corporate America." *Today's Office*, November 1987.

Shoor, Rita. "When a Buzzword Becomes Reality." *Infosystems*, February 1986.

———. "The New Breed of Executive Information Users." *Infosystems*, June 1986.

Sprague, R.H., and E.D. Carlson. *Building Effective Decision Support Systems.* Englewood Cliffs, NJ: Prentice-Hall, 1984.

Wallach, Rachel Meltzer. "The EIS State." *Computer Systems News*, March 1990.

———. "Executive Systems: Tools or Costly Toys?" *Computer Systems News*, March 1990.

Wilson, Christopher J., and Gary J. Kochler. "Pros and Cons of Expert Systems." *Business Software Review*, December 1986.

Winston, Patrick. *Artificial Intelligence.* Addison-Wesley Publishing, 1984.

Winston, Patrick, and Karen Prendergast. *The AI Business: Commercial Uses of Artificial Intelligence*, MIT Press, 1984.

Wohl, Amy D. "Executive Information Systems Give You the Big Picture." *Today's Office*, April 1990.

System Connectivity

Crawford, Verlaine. "Communications Software for PC to Mainframe Links." *List*, June 1984.

Delaney, Chester. "Integrated Powerhouses." *HRMagazine*, March 1990.

Foster, Ed. "The Department Linkup: Defining the Need." *Personal Computing*, November 1984.

Gabel, David. "The Mainframe Connections." *Personal Computing*, September 1984.

Gregory, Rosemary A. "Local Area Networks." *InfoSystems*, October 1985.

Hannan, James. "A Primer on Micro-Mainframe Links." *InfoSystems*, February 1986.

Kustoff, Marc. "Is It Time to Network Your PCs?" *Personnel Journal*, July 1990.

Levy, Joel, and Robert Miller. "Taking the Guesswork Out of Networking." *Today's Office*, January 1990.

Pollak, Bill. "New Technologies Provide Exciting Opportunities for HRIS Function." *The Review*, Spring 1990.

Schlobin, Roger C. "Computer Communications: An Idea Whose Time Has Come." *List*, June 1984.

Thurber, Ken. "Departmental Solutions, LANs or Multi-User Systems." *Micro Communications*, September 1985.

Fourth-Generation Languages (4GLs)

Brett, Charles. "SAA: Toward Co-operative Processing. Part I." *Tech Exec*, September 1989.

Cortino, Juli. "The Market Grows for 4GLs." *VARBusiness*, March 1990.

Davis, Jack M. "On the Road to Client/Server Computing." *Technical Support*, April 1990.

Feigenbaum, Edward, and Pamela McCorduck. *Machines Who Think.* New York: McGraw-Hill, 1979.

Friedman, Selma. "Fourth Generation Languages Becoming More Comprehensive." *InformationWeek*, March 1986.

Herbert, Martin, and Curt Hartog. "MIS Rates the Issues." *Datamation*, November 1986.

Kindley, Mark. "Software Metamorphosis." *VARBusiness*, March 1990.

Kneisel, Paul. "Talking Data." *Inbound/Outbound*, October 1989.

Kindley, Mark. "Software Metamorphosis." *VARBusiness*, March 1990.

Kneisel, Paul. "Talking Data." *Inbound/Outbound*, October 1989.

Martin, James. *Fourth Generation Languages*. Englewood Cliffs, N.J.: Prentice-Hall, 1985.

Payne, Robert. "Electronic Data Interchange." *Computerworld*, March 1990.

Schussel, George. "Shopping for a Fourth Generation Language." *Datamation*, November 1986.

Snyders, Jan. "Fourth Generation Languages: The Reality and The Promise." *Info-Systems*, November 1986.

Whitmyer, Claude F. "Focus on Software." *The Office*, October 1989.

Computer-Aided Software Engineering (CASE)

Boone, Greg. "The Paradox of CASE." *Database Programming and Design*, May 1989.

Boddie, John. "The Case against CASE." *Tech Exec*, October 1989.

Bouton, Robert H. "Reverse Engineering—An Approach to Migrating Existing Systems to a CASE Environment." *The Review*, Spring 1990.

Kindley, Mark. "CASE: The Promise Approaches Reality." *VARBusiness*, April 1990.

Lyon, Lockwood. "CASE and the Database," *Database Programming and Design*, January 1990.

Merlyn, Vaughn, and Greg Boone. "CASE Tools: Sorting out the Tangle of Tool Types." *Computerworld*, March 1989.

Computer-Based Training (CBT)

Colby, Wendelin. "Computer-Based Training: Letting Users Learn at Their Own Pace." *InfoSystems*, September 1985.

Gery, G.J. *Making CBT Happen*, New York: Weingarten, 1987.

Heck, William C. "Computer-Based Training—The Choice Is Yours." *Personnel Administrator*, February 1985.

Mahoney, Francis X., and Nancy L. Lyday. "Design Is What Counts in Computer-Based Training." *Training and Development Journal*, July 1984.

Pepper, Jon. "Creating Corporate Training Courseware." *PC Magazine*, January 1986.

Schwade, Stephen. "Is it Time to Consider Computer-Based Training?" *Personnel Administrator*, February 1985.

Vogt, Eric. "PC Education: Which Road to Take." *Personnel Administrator*, February 1985.

Zemke, Ron. "Evaluating Computer-Assisted Instruction: The Good, the Bad, and the Why." *Training*, May 1984.

Document Image Processing

Paznik, M. Jui. "Optical Character Readers and Image Scanners Can Reduce Workload." *Administrative Management*, July 1986.

Webb, Dave. "The Image Is the Message." *Computer System News*, March 12, 1990.

Graphics

Barron, Donna. "Graphics Presentations at Your Fingertips." *The Office*, July 1990.

Bove, Robert. "Visual Magic." *Training and Development Journal*, July 1985.

Gore, Andrew. "Graphics: New Media." *Macintosh News*, July 23, 1990.

Stahr, Lisa B. "Presentation Graphics." *Personal Computing*, September 1984.

Wohl, Amy D. "Graphical User Interfaces Make Computing Child's Play." *Today's Office*, May 1990.

Office Automation

Gantz, John. "Office Automation and DP: A 40-Year Side Trip." *TPT Magazine*, November 1987.

McManis, Gerald L, and Michael L. Leibman. "Upgrading Office Technology." *Personnel Administrator*, October 1988.

Miller, Robert. "Marshal Your Resources with Project Management Software." *Today's Office*, January 1990.

Nardoni, Ren. "The Personnel Office of the Future Is Available Today." *Personnel Journal*, February 1982.

———. "Personnel Applications of Micro-Based Video." *Personnel Journal*, January 1988.

O'Malley, Christopher. "Realizing the Office Linkup." *Personal Computing*, December 1984.

Risman, Barbara J., and Donald Tomaskovic-Devey. "The Social Construction of Technology: Microcomputers and the Organization of Work." *Business Horizons*, May/June 1989.

Voice Recognition

Kneisel, Paul. "Talking Data." *Inbound/Outbound*, October 1989.

Kemske, Floyd, and Nancy J. Weingarten. "A Memo From the Future: Data Training in 1999." *Information Executive*, Winter 1990.

Wood, Lamont. "Voices in the Wilderness." *Computer Decisions*, April 1986.

General

Amico, Anthony M. "Critical Human Resource Issues of the 1980s." *Human Resource Planning*, Vol. 6, No. 2, 1983.

Arthur, Diane. *Managing Human Resources in Small and Mid-Sized Companies.* AMACOM, 1987.

———. "The Human Resources Function and the Growing Company." *Personnel*, November 1987.

Frantzreb, Richard. *The Personnel Software Census.* Roseville, CA: Advanced Personnel Systems, 1988.

Hyde, Albert C., and Jay M. Sharfritz. "Introduction to Tomorrow's System for Managing Human Resources." *Public Resource Management*, March/April 1977.

Knapp, Jeffery. "Trends in HR Management Systems." *Personnel*, April 1990.

Kustoff, Marc. "Assembling a Micro-Based HRIS: A Beginner's Guide." *Personnel Administrator*, December 1985.

Lee, A.S. "Despite Microcomputer Proliferation, Mainframes are Still Preferred." *Computers in Personnel*, Winter 1988.

London, Manuel, and John Paul MacDuffie. "Technological Innovations: Case Examples and Guidelines." *Personnel*, November 1987.

Lu, Cary. "Coping with Chaos." *Inc.*, September 1988.

Magnus, M., and M. Grossman. "Computers and the Personnel Department." *Personnel Journal*, April 1985.

McCorduck, Pamela. *The Universal Machine: Confessions of a Technological Optimist.* New York: McGraw-Hill, 1985.

Miller, Robert. "Marshal Your Resources with Project Management Software." *Today's Office*, January 1990.

Misrok, Donna. "Moving the HR Information System to the Line." *The Human Resource Professional*, July/August 1989.

Moad, Jeff. "Large Systems Are Hot!" *Datamation*, May 1990.

Numec, M.M. "Workforce 2000: Dramatic Changes and a Shortage of Skilled Workers." *Industrial Engineer*, January 1987.

Palmer, Scott D. "10 Forces That Will Shape the Next 20 Years." *Business Software Review*, July 1986.

Ruth, Stephen R. "Personnel and EDP in the 1980s." *MSU Business Topics*, Summer 1980.

Shoshana, Zuboff. *In the Age of the Smart Machine: The Future of Work and Power.* where: Basic Books, Inc., 1988.

Tomeski, E.A., B.M. Yoon, and G. Stephenson. "Computer-related Challenges for Personnel Administration." *Personnel Journal*, June 1976.

Walker, Alfred J. "Human Resources: Preparing for the Next Century." *Personnel Journal*, November 1987.

Zimmerman, George. "Getting Down to Business with MIS." *Tech Exec*, September 1989.

Epilogue

Change is the process by which the future invades our lives, and it is important to look at it closely, not merely from the grand perspectives of history.

—Alvin Toffler, *Future Shock*

T he rate of change is accelerating at a rapid pace; each of us has a personal stake in keeping up with these developments lest we be buried in what Alvin Toffler in *Future Shock* describes as "massive adaptational breakdown."

The computer, though most assuredly not the focus of this book, empowers and enables this book. And the computer is almost a metaphor for change itself. No one would care to read about manual systems to support personnel record keeping and reporting. Like it or not, the computer is only a tool that permits us to perform certain tasks quickly and accurately—if we have instructed it properly and provided good raw data.

At this point in the evolution of human resources, we have come to take the computer's presence for granted. Frankly, this is good news. We *should* take the computer for granted. It is only a high-speed superclerk that can perform functions faster and more consistently than a person. But only by viewing HRMS as having considerably more power than a high-speed clerk can human resources professionals make optimal decisions in regard to system planning, development, and implementation. To be prepared for the rapid changes taking place in both human resources and HRMS, we must take a broader view of these systems.

We have used the term human resources management system (HRMS) many times throughout this book. We should point out that this term is more than merely an acronym for a computer application. It contains three component parts, each of which provides a valuable perspective on the responsibilities and opportunities offered by the combination of computers and human resources information. These parts—
HUMAN RESOURCES
                    RESOURCES MANAGEMENT
                                MANAGEMENT SYSTEMS
give HRMS a whole new meaning.

The first component, *human resources,* refers to the function to which the system is applied. This term has evolved to describe employee or human relations, replacing the largely obsolete but still ubiquitous term *personnel.*

The third component, *management systems,* could refer simply to the automation of the human resources function, but actually it means more than that. The term *information systems* focuses primarily on the computer and its surrounding technology. In contrast, *management systems* takes into account not only the hardware, software, data, and outputs but also the staffing, training, policies, and procedures that drive the modern HRMS. In a nutshell, it broadens our focus to include the management process.

The second component, *resources management* is intriguing. Generally speaking, this term refers to the control of aspects of an environment with the objective of sustaining or increasing the viability of an enterprise or environment. The resources may be natural or manufactured, or abstract. Today, everyone can relate to concerns about managing our air, water, and ground resources. People have always been able to relate to the managing of our autos, homes, and machines. But any discussion about managing of human resources still conjures up the old stereotype of personnel administration.

The management of human resources, however, includes more complex processes than earlier administrative operations permitted. Resources management encompasses the managing of the people, financial, facilities, and other tactical resources of the enterprise. It includes the hiring, firing, paying, training, welfare, and nurturing of employees. For instance, contemporary resources management for the human resources function involves proactive planning for the organization's needs and goals. It involves planning for the proper use of the potential of each employee. A human resources department that believes in resources management can optimize its firm's investment in employees. By adopting this broad view of resources management, planners, decision makers, and other professionals can see information resources such as HRMS as tools for handling the present and preparing for the future.

In this book, we have covered the past and the present and have attempted to discuss the future. Many of these discussions have focused on technology, but we must emphasize once again that computers do not, and should not, control human resources management. In the final analysis, this book is as much (or more) about the management of people resources as it is about the automation process. Automation, after all, merely provides tools and techniques. Successful strategies and tactics depend on understanding the knowledge, values, and needs of the people in the enterprise.

HRMS Resources

Knowledge is not in the knowing, but in the ability to find out.
—V.R. Ceriello

I don't know, but I'll find out. At more than one point in the development of any system, someone utters these words. With luck, he or she will come up with appropriate, accurate, and complete information. One of the most important attributes of a successful professional is skill in discovering where to locate pertinent information. The purpose of the material in the appendixes is to make that job somewhat easier.

No listing of resources in a field that is changing as rapidly as human resources can include all relevant information. As soon as a list of vendors, consultants, or professional societies is developed, several firms move, merge or develop joint ventures, new ones emerge, and one or two cease operations altogether. Although we have tried to offer comprehensive, up-to-date information, readers should view these listings as a beginning. Inclusion does not necessarily indicate approval; exclusion has no negative connotation. Suggestions for listings in future editions are welcome.

Appendix A:
Professional Organizations

V irtually everyone involved in planning, developing, implementing, or managing an HRMS can benefit from networking with other professionals in the field. Several organizations foster such opportunities. All the organizations listed here have at least an annual meeting. Many have local chapters that meet monthly. Chapters can be contacted through national headquarters, which are listed. Some of these groups operate internationally as well.

In large metropolitan settings, individuals may have numerous organizations from which to choose. Human resources and professionals in a quandary about which meetings to attend may want to consider that the value of many of these organizations lies as much the networking opportunities as in the professional development opportunities. In these cases, individuals may make choices based on where and when local chapters hold their meetings, which peers and coworkers belong, and the quality of the programs the organization offers.

Most of the organizations of interest to human resources and HRMS professionals are included in the following list. They are national or international in scope. Local chapters and regional organizations are not included, although these are often of more value to human resources and HRMS professionals than their national counterparts.

Administrative Management Society (AMS), 4622 Street Road, Trevose, PA 19047; (215) 953–1040. General management. Performs surveys (including salary and business trend surveys); publications and videos; professional certification.

American Arbitration Association (AAA), 140 W. 51st Street, New York, NY, 10020; (212) 484–4000. Labor relations. Designs and administers dispute resolution procedures for all types of conflicts, including labor-management issues; provides training in the processes used to resolve them.

American Association for Affirmative Action (AAAA), 11 E. Hubbard Street, Suite 200, Chicago, IL 60611; (312) 329–2512. Equal employment oppportunity and affirmative action. Promotes affirmative action in the workplace.

American Association of Industrial Management (AAIM), Stearns Building, 293 Bridge Street, Suite 324, Springfield, MA 01103; (413) 737–8766. Industrial relations. Provides assistance in labor and industrial relations management; performs research.

American Compensation Association (ACA), 14040 Northsight Boulevard, Scottsdale, AZ 85260; (602) 951–9191. Compensation. Courses and seminars for compensation professionals; conferences; publications.

American Institute of Management (AIM), 45 Willard Street, Quincy, MA 02169; (617) 472–0277. General management. Research; education; appraises efficiency, methods, and management performance.

American Management Association (AMA), 135 W. 50th Street, New York, NY 10020; (212) 586–8100. General management. Promotes management education; provides wide range of courses and publications.

American Society for Healthcare Human Resources Administration (ASHHRA), American Hospital Association, 840 N. Lake Shore Drive, Chicago, IL 60611; (312) 280–6434. Personnel and human resources. Professional services for human resources executives and professionals in hospitals and other health care institutions.

American Society for Industrial Security (ASIS), 1655 N. Fort Myer Drive, Suite 1200, Arlington, VA 22209–3198. (703) 522–5800. Security. Professional services; professional certification program.

American Society for Public Administration (ASPA), 1120 G Street, NW, Suite 500, Washington, DC 20005; (202) 393–7878. Public administration. Professional services; standards, education, and promotion; has a special-interest group for personnel and labor relations.

American Society for Training and Development (ASTD), 1630 Duke Street, P.O. Box 1443, Alexandria, VA 22314; (703) 683–8100. Training and development. Publications and information services; sponsors two annual conferences.

American Society of Pension Actuaries (ASPA), 2029 K Street, 4th Floor, Washington, DC 20006; (202) 659–3620. Employee benefits. Educational programs.

American Society of Safety Engineers (ASSE), 1800 E. Oakton Street, Des Plaines, IL 60016; (312) 692–4121. Safety. Provides safety experts with opportunities for professional development; educational programs;

technical resources; representation in government, academia, and the media; safety standards development.

Association for Systems Management (ASM), 24587 Bagley Road, Cleveland, OH 44138; (216) 243–6900. Systems management. Computer and manual systems; methods and procedures management.

Association for the Development of Computer-Based Instructional Systems, Miller Hall 409, Western Washington University, Bellingham, WA 98225; (206) 676–2860. Systems management. Advances the investigation and utilization of computer-assisted instruction systems; promotes the interchange of information, programs, and materials; reduces redundant efforts among system users; specifies requirements and their priority for hardware and software development.

Association of Computing Machinery (ACM), 11 W. 42nd Street, 3rd Floor, New York, NY 10036; (212) 869–7440. Management training. Special-interest group on computer personnel research; EDP personnel; compensation; research.

Association of Human Resources Systems Professionals, Inc. (HRSP), P.O. Box 801646, Dallas, TX 75380–1646; (214) 661–3727. Human resources systems and data processing. Independent chapters; seminars; publications; national conference; referral service.

Association of Labor-Management Administrators and Consultants on Alcoholism, Inc. (ALMACA), 4601 N. Fairfax Drive, Suite 1001, Arlington, VA 22203; (703) 522–6272. Employee assistance. Nonprofit, international organization of professionals involved in occupational alcoholism and EAPs; public and private sector advocate for support and development of EAPs.

Association of Private Pension and Welfare Plans (APPWP), 1331 Pennsylvania Avenue NW, Suite 719, Washington, DC 20004; (202) 737–6666. Employee benefits. Lobbying group; legislative developments regarding pensions.

Canadian Association of Human Resources Systems Professionals, Inc. (CHRSP), 2 Bloor Street W Suite 100/197, Toronto, Ontario M4W 3E2, Canada; (416) 975-4360. Canadian affiliate of Association of Human Resources Systems Professionals, Inc.

Classification and Compensation Society, 810 18th Street, NW, Rm 601, Washington, DC 20006; (202) 783–4847. Compensation. Promotes improvements in government personnel systems; compensation, position classification, and job and organization analysis; training courses; seminars; publications and conferences.

College and University Personnel Association, 1233 20th Street NW, Suite 503, Washington, DC 20036; (202) 429–0311. Personnel. Publications; workshops; national conferences; information exchange.

College Placement Council, Inc. (CPC), 62 Highland Avenue, Bethlehem, PA 18017; (215) 868–1421. Employment and recruitment. Provides communication and interaction between institutions of higher education and employers of college graduates.

Computer Security Institute, 500 Howard Street, San Francisco, CA 94105; (415) 267-7651. Information systems security. National conference, workshops and seminars.

Council on Employee Benefits (CEB), c/o Goodyear Relief Association, 1144 E. Market Street, Akron, OH 44316; (216) 794–4008. Employee benefits. Information clearinghouse; lobbyist; placement service.

Data Processing Management Association, 505 Busse Highway, Park Ridge, IL 60068; (312) 825–8124. Data processing. Research; on-line referral service; professional education programs; management development seminars.

Employee Assistance Society of North America, P.O. Box 3909, Oak Park, IL 60303; (312) 383–6668. Employee assistance. Promotes individual employee health, wellness, and productivity; studies the impact of chemical dependence and other personal problems.

Employee Benefits Research Institute (EBRI), 2121 K Street NW, Suite 600, Washington, DC 20037–2121; (202) 659–0670. Employee benefits. Research, education, and public policy; educational materials; policy forums; publications.

Employers Council on Flexible Compensation (ECFC), 927 15th Street NW, Suite 1000, Washington, DC 20005; (202) 659–4300. Flexible benefits. Lobby for flexible (cafeteria) benefits; 401(k) plans; benefits surveys; research; seminars; publications.

Employment Management Association (EMA), 5 W. Hargett Street, Suite 1100, Raleigh, NC 27601; (919) 828–6614. Personnel. Clearinghouse; educational services; research on personnel matters; surveys; publications.

Equal Employment Advisory Council, 1015 15th Street NW, Suite 1220, Washington, DC 20005; (202) 789–8650. EEO and affirmative action. A nonprofit association formed to monitor federal equal employment, litigation, and legislation.

ERISA Industry Committee (ERIC), 1726 M Street NW, Suite 1101,

Washington, DC 22036; (202) 833–2800. Employee benefits. Information; lobbyist for employee benefits issues.

HR Canada, 111 Queen Street E, Suite 355, Toronto, Ontario, Canada; (416) 367–5900. Human resources planning. Provides a vehicle for communication and cooperation, joining public and private efforts to address human resources issues.

Human Factors Society, P.O. Box 1369, Santa Monica, CA 90406; (213) 394–1811. Personnel management. Promotes understanding of the strengths and limitations of individual patterns of temperament, character, mentality, and physique to increase productivity and effectiveness.

Human Resource Planning Society (HRPS), P.O. Box 2553, Grand Central Station, New York, NY 10163; (212) 490–6387. Human resources planning. Independent chapters; programs related to manpower forecasting and other human resources planning activities; annual conference.

Human Resources Research Organization, 1100 S. Washington Street, Alexandria, VA 22314; (703) 549–3611. Personnel research. Research for clients and sponsors on a nonprofit basis.

Industrial Relations Counselors, Inc., P.O. Box 1530, New York, NY 10101; (212) 764–4198. Industrial relations. A nonprofit research and educational organization; advances the knowledge and practice of human relationships in industry, commerce, education, and government.

Industrial Relations Research Association (IRRA), 7226 Social Science Building, University of Wisconsin, Madison, WI 53706; (608) 262–2762. Labor and industrial relations. Research and educational association; issues publications.

Industry-Labor Council on Employment of Handicapped Individuals, National Center on Employment and Disability, Human Resources Center, Albertson, NY 11507; (516) 747–6323. Affirmative action. Assistance in planning and implementing affirmative action efforts for handicapped individuals; information provided on accessibility, recruiting, legislation, and reasonable accommodation.

Institute of Manpower Studies, Mantell Building, University of Sussex, Falmer-Brighton, Sussex, BN19RF, UK; (0273) 686751. Personnel and human resources. Manpower management; interests include labor markets, employment, and training policies; guidance available for manpower and labor-market problems.

Instructional Systems Association (ISA), 10963 Deborah Drive, Potomac, MD 20854; (301) 983–0783. Training and development. Promotes research; disseminates information; conducts programs; monitors legislation.

International Association for Personnel Women (IAPW), 5820 Wilshire Boulevard, No. 500, Los Angeles, CA 90036; (213) 937–9000. Personnel and human resources. Issues specific to women in personnel field.

International Federation of Training and Development Organizations, Ltd., Brigham Young University, HC Box 1721, Laie, HI 96762–1294; (808) 293–3787. Training and development. Training and human resources development, including professional training organizations, government bodies, universities, training institutions, and multinational organizations.

International Foundation of Employee Benefit Plans (IFEBP), 18700 W. Bluemound Road, P.O. Box 69, Brookfield, WI 53008–0069; (414) 786–6700. Employee benefits. U.S.-Canadian; research; certification; clearinghouse for employee benefits plans; seminars; publications.

International Industrial Relations Association (IIRA), IIRA Secretariat, c/o LEG/REL International Labour Office, CH-1211, Geneva 22, Switzerland; (022) 99 68 41. Industrial relations. Consortium of national associations, research institutes, and individuals; promotes the advancement of knowledge of industrial relations.

International Personnel Management Association (IPMA), 1617 Duke Street, Alexandria, VA 22314; (703) 549–7100. Personnel (government). Education; research; placement services; legislative advisory activity. Independent affiliates in Australia, New Zealand, and the United Kingdom.

International Society of Pre-Retirement Planners, 11312 Old Club Road, Rockville, MD 20852–4537; (301) 881–4113. Preretirement planning. Professional society interested in the multidisciplinary approach to preretirement planning.

Mainstream, Inc., 1030 15th Street NW, Suite 1010, Washington, DC 20005; (202) 898–1400. Affirmative action. Nonprofit organization that provides employers and service providers with technical information on mainstreaming persons with disabilities into the workplace.

National Association for Career Planning, Placement and Recruitment, 62 Highland Avenue, Bethlehem, PA 18017; (215) 868–1421.

National Association of Corporate and Professional Recruiters, Inc. (NACPR), 146 Blackberry Drive, Stamford, CT 06903; (203) 329–2349. Employment. Develops and promotes standards and ethical practices in the recruitment, evaluation, and referral of candidates.

National Association of Manufacturers, Industrial Relations Department, 1331 Pennsylvania Avenue NW, Suite 1500-N, Washington, DC 20004; (202) 637–3000. Industrial relations. Promotes American industrial interests, a strong defense posture, and the betterment of relations between employer and employee; encourages private markets and sound economic growth.

National Association of State Personnel Executives (NASPE), c/o Council of State Governments, P.O. Box 11910, Iron Works Pike, Lexington, KY 40578; (606) 231–1877. Personnel administration. Standards for personnel management and administration in government.

National Association of State Training and Development Directors, Kentucky State University, Government Services, 505 Deaderick Street, Nashville, TN 37219; (615) 741–5546.

National Employee Benefits Institute (NEBI), 2445 M Street NW, Washington, DC 20037; (800) 558–7258. Employee benefits. Lobbies for employee benefits.

National Foundation for the Study of Employment Policy, 1015 15th Street NW, Suite 1220, Washington, DC 20005; (202) 789–8685. EEO and affirmative action. Research on the development of policy and law designed to eliminate employment discrimination.

National Institute of Pension Administrators, 145 W. First Street, Suite A, Tustin, CA 92680; (714) 731–3524. Employee benefits. Education; accreditation.

National Management Association (NMA), 2210 Arbor Boulevard, Dayton, OH 45439; (513) 294–0421. Management. Professional services; middle management; supervisors.

National Retail Merchants Association (NRMA), 100 W. 31st Street, New York, NY 10001; (212) 244–8780. Personnel (retail). Retailers' organization; conferences; literature; advisory services.

National Safety Council, 444 N. Michigan Avenue, Chicago, IL 60611; (312) 527–4800. Safety. Education to influence society to adopt safety and health policies; practices and procedures to prevent human and economic losses arising from accidents and adverse occupational and environmental health exposures.

National Society for Performance and Instruction (NSPI), 1126 16th Street NW, Suite 102, Washington, DC 20036; (202) 861–0777. Training and development. Dedicated to increasing productivity in the workplace through the application of performance and instruction technologies.

National Society for Sales Training Executives (NSSTE), 203 E. Third Street, Sanford, FL 32771; (407) 322–3364. Training. Educational conferences; training clinics; awards; statistics.

Newspaper Personnel Relations Association (NPRA), 11600 Sunrise Valley Drive, Reston, VA 22091; (703) 648–1000. Personnel. Organization for newspaper personnel executives; research; membership; education.

North American Congress on Employee Assistance Programs, 2145 Crooks Road, Suite 103, Troy, MI 48084; (313) 643–9540. Employee assistance. Meets annually to exchange knowledge, skills, techniques, and resources to help implement and operate EAPs.

The Organization Development Institute, 11234 Walnut Ridge Road, Chesterfield, OH 44026; (216) 461–4333. Organization development. Applications of organization development; productivity improvement; quality of work life; placement; ethics; education of organization development professionals; certification.

Profit Sharing Research Foundation, 20 N. Wacker Drive, Suite 1722, Chicago, IL 60606; (312) 372–3416. Profit sharing. Gathers and disseminates information regarding the experiences of companies with profit-sharing, employee stock ownership, and participative programs.

Risk and Insurance Management Society, Inc., 205 E. 42nd Street, New York, NY 10017; (212) 286–9292. Safety. Sponsors educational forums amd competitions; bestows awards; conducts research programs; compiles statistics.

Safety-Health Educators & Training Association, P.O. Box 2213, Brockton, MA 02403; (617) 587–4984. Training and development. Safety, health, and environmental training and resources.

Society for Advancement of Management (SAM), 2331 Victory Pkwy., Cincinnati, OH 45206; (513) 751–4566. Education. Management education; international management; administration; budgeting; collective bargaining; distribution; incentives; materials handling; quality control; training; seminars; conferences.

Society for Human Resource Management (SHRM), formerly American Society for Personnel Administration, 606 N. Washington Street, Alexandria, VA 22314; (703) 548–3440. Personnel and human resources. Seminars; publications; information sharing; on-line data base; research services.

Society of Professional Benefit Administrators (SPBA), 2033 M Street NW, Suite 605, Washington, DC 20036; (202) 223–6413. Employee benefits. Benefits lobbying; ethics of member firms; research; education.

World Future Society, 4916 St. Elmo Avenue, Bethesda, MD 20814–5089; (301) 656–8274. Future. Clearinghouse for ideas about the future, including forecasts, recommendations, and alternative scenarios.

Appendix B: Professional Publications

I n a field that changes as rapidly as HRMS, periodicals provide an excellent means of staying current. They cover emerging trends, pending and recent legislation, technological developments, guides for system development, management, and system success stories. Many magazines offer software reviews; some even have an annual issue that focuses on a thorough comparison of many vendor offerings.

Many human resources periodicals offer either occasional or regular, though not exclusive, coverage of HRMS specifically. The ones listed here feature articles on computer applications and issues. Some publications deal specifically with HRMS. New periodicals are undoubtedly emerging, while several others have ceased publication in the past year. Not only are human resources and HRMS undergoing change, so is their media coverage.

Professional Journals

Benefits, Applied Benefits Research, Inc., 3255 U.S. Highway 19N, Clearwater, FL 34621; (813) 787-2558. Bimonthly

Benefits & Compensation International, Pension Publications Ltd., 11 Tufton Street, London, SWIP 3QB, UK: (1) 222-0288. Monthly.

Benefits Canada, Maclean-Hunter Ltd., 777 Bay Street, Toronto, Ontario M5W 1A7, Canada; (416) 596-5959. Ten issues/year.

Benefits Law Journal, Executive Enterprises Publication Co., Inc., 22 W 21st Street, New York, NY 10010-6904; (212) 645-7880. Quarterly.

Benefits News Analysis, P.O. Box 4033, New Haven, CT 06525; (203) 393-2272. Ten issues/year.

Benefits Quarterly, International Society of Certified Employee Benefits Specialists, Inc., Box 209, Brookfield, WI 53008-0209; (414) 786-8771. Quarterly.

Benefits Today, The Bureau of National Affairs, Inc., 1231 25th Street NW, Washington, DC 20037; (800) 372–1033. Biweekly.

BNA's Employee Relations Weekly, The Bureau of National Affairs, Inc., 1231 25th Street NW, Washington, DC 20037; (800) 372–1033. Weekly.

Bulletin to Management, The Bureau of National Affairs, Inc., 1231 25th Street NW, Washington, DC 20037; (800) 372–1033. Monthly.

Bulletin on Training, The Bureau of National Affairs, Inc., 1231 25th Street NW, Washington, DC 20037; (800) 372-1033. Monthly.

Business & Legal Reports, Bureau of Law & Business, 64 Wall Street, Madison, CT 06443; (203) 245-7448.

Business Software, M & T Books, 501 Galveston Drive, Redwood City, CA 94063; (415) 366–3600. Monthly.

CBT Directions, 38 Chauncey Street, Boston, MA 02111; (617) 542-0146.

Compensation & Benefits Management, Panel Publishers, 14 Plaza Road, Greenvale, NY 11548; (516) 484–0006. Quarterly.

Compensation and Benefits Review, American Management Association (AMA), 135 W. 50th Street, New York, NY 10020; (212) 586–8100. Bimonthly.

Compensation Planning Journal, The Bureau of National Affairs, Inc., 1231 25th Street NW, Washington, DC 20037; (800) 372–1033. Semi-annually.

Computer & Security, Elsevier Advanced Technology Publications, 52 Vanderbilt Avenue, New York, NY 10017. Monthly.

Computer & Software News, Lebhar-Friedman, Inc., 425 Park Avenue, New York, NY 10022; (212) 371-9400. Weekly.

Computer Decisions, P.O. Box 1046, Southeastern, PA 19398-1046; (215) 630-9323. Monthly.

Datamation, Cahners Publishing Co., 249 W. 17th Street, New York, NY 10011; (212) 645-0067. Semi-monthly.

EEO Report, Panel Publishers, 14 Plaza Road, Greenvale, NY 11548; (516) 484-0006. Monthly.

EEO Review, Executive Enterprises Publication Co., Inc., 22 W. 21st Street, New York, NY 10010-6904; (212) 645-7880. Monthly.

Employee Benefit Plan Review, Charles D. Spencer & Associates, Inc., 222 W. Adams Street, Chicago, IL 60606; (312) 236–2615. Monthly.

Employee Benefits Journal, International Foundation of Employee Benefit Plans, 18700 W. Bluemound Road, Brookfield, WI 53005; (414) 786–6700. Quarterly.

Employee Benefits Report, Warren, Gorham & Lamont, Inc., 210 S Street, Boston, MA 02111; (800) 922–0066. Monthly.

Employment Alert, Research Institute of America, Inc., 90 Fifth Avenue, New York, NY 10011; (212) 645–4800. Biweekly.

HRMagazine (formerly Personnel Administrator), Society for Human Resource Management (SHRM), formerly American Society for Personnel Administration, 606 N. Washington Street, Alexandria, VA 22314; (703) 548-3440. Monthly.

HR Reporter, Buraff Publications, Inc., a subsidary of The Bureau of National Affairs, Inc., 2554 M Street NW, Suite 275, Washington, DC 20037; (202) 452–7889. Monthly.

The Human Resource, Croscan Publishing, 1252 Lawrence Avenue East #206, Don Mills, Ontario, M3A 1C3, CANADA; (416) 433-0371.

Human Resource Development Quarterly, Jossey-Bass Inc., 350 Sansome Street, San Francisco, CA 94104; (415) 433-1767.

Human Resource Executive, Axon Magazine Group, 747 Dresher Road, Suite 500, P.O. Box 980, Horsham, PA 19044–0980; (215) 784–0860. Monthly.

HR Magazine, Society for Human Resources Management (SHRM), formerly American Society for Personnel Administration, 606 N. Washington Street, Alexandria, VA 22314; (703) 548-3440. Monthly.

Human Resource Management Journal, School of Business Administration, University of Michigan, John Wiley & Sons, Inc. 605 Third Avenue, New York, NY 10158; (800) 526–5368. Monthly.

Human Resource Management Reporter, Warren, Gorham & Lamont, Inc., 210 S Street, Boston, MA 02111; (800) 922-0066. Monthly.

Human Resource Management System Report, VRC Consulting Group, 289 S. San Antonio Road, Los Altos, CA 94022; (415) 948-1513.

Human Resource Planning, Human Resource Planning Society (HRPS), Box 2553, Grand Central Station, New York, NY 10163; (212) 490-6387. Quarterly.

The Human Resource Professional, 106 Fulton Street, New York, NY 10038; (212) 766-7800.

Human Resources Management Ideas & Trends Newsletter, Commerce Clearinghouse, Inc., 4025 W. Peterson Avenue, Chicago, IL 60646; (312) 583-8500. Biweekly.

ICP Business Software Review, International Computer Programs, Inc., 9000 Keystone Crossing, Suite 200, Indianapolis, IN 46240; (317) 844-7461. Monthly.

International Foundation of Employee Benefit Plans Digest, International Foundation of Employee Benefit Plans, 18700 Bluemound Road, Brookfield, WI 53005; (414) 786-6700. Monthly.

Impact: Information for Managers on Personnel & Current Trends in Human Relations, Prentice-Hall, Inc., Information Services Division, 240 Frisch Court, Paramus, NJ 07652; (800) 562-0245. Biweekly.

Information & Records Management, PTN Publishing Corp., 101 Crossways Park W, Woodbury, NY 11797; (516) 496-8000. Monthly.

Information Management, Auerbach Publishers, Inc., One Penn Plaza, New York, NY 10119; (800) 257-8162. Bimonthly.

Information Management, Center for Management Systems, Box 208, Sioux City, IA 51102; (712) 568-3370. Monthly.

Information Management, PTN Publishing Corp., 101 Crossways Park W, Woodbury, NY 11797; (516) 496-8000. Monthly.

Information Strategy: The Executive's Journal, Auerbach Publishers, Inc., One Penn Plaza, New York, NY 10119; (800) 257-8162. Quarterly.

Information Systems: Databases—Their Creation, Management & Utilization: An International Journal, Pergamon Press, Maxwell House, Fairview Park, Elmsford, NY 10523; (914) 592-7700. Six issues/year.

InfoWorld, CW Communications Inc., 1060 Marsh Road, Suite C-200, Menlo Park, CA 94025 (415) 328-4602. Weekly.

Institute of Personnel Management Digest, Institute of Personnel Management, IPM House, Camp Road, Wimbleton, London SW19 4UX, England; (01) 940-2658. Monthly.

Into the 21st Century: Long-Term Trends Affecting the US, World Future Society, 4916 St. Elmo Avenue, Bethesda, MD 20814. Monthly.

Journal of Compensation and Benefits, Warren, Gorham & Lamont, Inc., 210 S. Street, Boston, MA 02111; (800) 922-0066. Bimontly.

Journal of Information Systems Management, Auerbach Publishers, Inc., One Penn Plaza, New York, NY 10119; (800) 257-8162. Quarterly.

Journal of Management Development, MCB University Press Ltd., P.O. Box 10812, Birmingham, AL 35201; (205) 911 6920.

Journal of Systems Management, Association for Systems Management, 24587 Bagley Road, Cleveland, OH 44138; (216) 243–6900. Monthly.

Legal-Legislative Reporter, International Foundation of Employee Benefit Plans, 18700 W. Bluemound Road, Brookfield, WI 53005; (414) 786–6700. Monthly.

Lotus, Lotus Publishing Company, P.O. Box 9123, Cambridge, MA 02139-9123; (617) 494-1192.

Management Review, American Management Association (AMA), Subscription Services, P.O. Box 408, Saranac Lake, NY 12983; (518) 891-1500, ext. 240.

Management Technology, International Thomson Technology Information, Inc., 135 W. 50th Street, New York, NY 10020; (212) 247–6540. Monthly.

Management World, Administrative Management Society, 4622 Street Road, Trevose, PA 19047; (215) 953-1040.

Occupational Health & Safety, Medical Publications Inc., 225 North New Road, Waco, TX 76710; (817) 776-9000.

MIS Quarterly, Society for Information Management, 111 E. Wacker Drive, Suite 600, Chicago, IL 60601; (312) 644–6610. Quarterly.

MISWeek: The Newspaper for Information Management, Fairchild Publications, 7 E. 12th Street, New York, NY 10003; (212) 741–4000. Monthly.

PC Accounting, formerly Business Software, M & T Publishing, Inc., 501 Galveston Drive, Redwood City, CA 94063-4728; (415) 366-3600. Monthly.

PC Magazine, Ziff-Davis Publishing Co., One Park Avenue, New York, NY 10016; (212) 503-5100. Biweekly.

Pension Plan Summary Guide, Commerce Clearing House, Inc., 4025 W. Peterson Avenue, Chicago, IL 60646; (312) 583–8500. Weekly.

Personal Computing, VNU Business Publications, Inc., Ten Holland Drive, Hasbrouck Heights, NJ 07604; (201) 393-6000. Monthly.

Personnel, American Management Association (AMA), Subscription Services, P.O. Box 408, Saranac Lake, NY 12983; (518) 891–1500. Monthly.

Personnel Journal, A.C. Croft, Inc., 245 Fischer Avenue No. B2, Costa Mesa, CA 92626; (714) 751–1883. Monthly.

Personnel Management, Bailey Bros. & Swinfen Ltd., Warner House, Folkestone, Kent CT19 6PH, England. Monthly.

Personnel Management, The Bureau of National Affairs, Inc., 2554 M Street NW, Suite 275, Washington, DC 20037; (202) 452-7889. Biweekly.

Personnel Manager's Legal Reporter, Business & Legal Reports, 64 Wall Street, Madison, CT 06443; (203) 245–7448. Monthly.

The Personnel News, 4701 Patrick Henry Drive, Suite 1301, Santa Clara, CA 95054; (408) 988–8991. Ten issues/year.

Personnel Policy Briefs, Business Research Publications, 817 Broadway, New York, NY 10003; (203) 245–4700. Semimonthly.

Personnel Psychology, Personnel Psychology, Inc., 9660 Hillcroft, Suite 337, Houston, TX 77096; (713) 728–3078. Quarterly.

Personnel Review, MCB University Press Ltd., P.O. Box 10812, Birmingham, AL 35201; (205) 991-6920.

Personnel Today, Institute of Personnel Management—Australia Incorporated, Victorian Division, Industry House, 4th Floor, 370 St. Kilda Road, Melbourne, Australia 3004; (613) 699–3930. Monthly.

Perspective, Catalyst, 250 Park Avenue S, New York, NY 10003; (212) 777–8900. Monthly.

Public Personnel Management, International Personnel Management Association, 1617 Duke Street, Alexandria, VA 22314; (703) 549–7100. Quarterly.

The Review, Association of Human Resources Systems Professionals, P.O. Box 801646, Dallas, TX 75380-1646; (512) 454-5262. Quarterly.

Software Digest Ratings Newsletter, 1 Winding Drive, Philadelphia, PA 19131; (215) 878-9300. Annually.

Software Journal, Software Journal, Inc., 600 First Avenue, Suite 427, Seattle, WA 98104; (206) 624–4267. Monthly.

A Survey of Personnel Policies in the Workplace, Washington Legal Foundation, 1705 N Street NW, Washington, DC 20036; (202) 857–0240. Monthly.

Systems and Software, Hayden Publishing Co., Inc., 10 Mulholland Drive, Hasbrouck Heights, NJ 07604; (201) 393–6000. Monthly.

Systems Development, Applied Computer Research, P.O. Box 9280, Phoenix, AZ 85068; (800) 234–2227. Monthly.

Training, Lakewood Publications, Inc., 731 Hennepin Avenue, Minneapolis, MN 55403; (612) 333–0471. Monthly.

Training and Development Alert, Advanced Personnel Systems, P.O. Box 1438, Roseville, CA 95661; (916) 781–2900. Bimonthly.

Training and Development Journal, American Society for Training and Development (ASTD), 1630 Duke Street, P.O. Box 1443, Alexandria, VA 22314; (703) 683-8100. Monthly.

Training and Development Yearbook, Prentice Hall, Business & Professional Division, Englewood Cliffs, NJ 07632; (201) 767-5054. Annually.

Work in America, Buraff Publications Inc., 150 Connecticut Avenue, NW, Suite 1000, Washington, DC 20036, (202) 862-0990.

Newsletters Published by Consultants

Benefits and Executive Compensation Bulletin, Pillsbury, Madison & Sutro, 235 Montgomery Street, San Francisco, CA 94104; (415) 984–1000. Monthly.

Compensation and Benefits File, Wyatt Company, 1990 K Street NW, Washington, DC 20006; (800) 424-3083. Monthly.

HR Planning Newsletter, Wargo & Company, Inc., 250 Regency Court, Waukeska, WI 53186; (414) 785-1211. Ten issues/year.

HR/PC, DGM Associates, 330 Washington Street, Suite 700, P.O. Box 10639, Marina Del Rey, CA 90292; (213) 578–1428; (213) 578–1428. Eight issues/year.

Letter, Towers Perrin Forster & Crosby, 1500 Market St, Centre Square W, Philadelphia, PA 19102. Monthly.

Management Memo, Hay/Huggins Co., Inc., 229 S. 18th Street, Philadelphia, PA 19103. Monthly.

Mercer Bulletin and Mercer Report, Mercer-Meidinger-Hansen, Inc., Three Embarcadero Center, Suite 1250, Box 7440, San Francisco, CA 94120; (415) 393-5200. Monthly.

Special Report, Hewitt Associates, 100 Half Day Road, Lincolnshire, IL 60069; (708) 295-5000. Monthly.

SURVEY, Saratoga Institute, Box 412, Saratoga, CA 95071; (408) 446-4788. Annually.

Abstracting and Indexing Services

Personnel Literature, U.S. Office of Personnel Management, U.S. Government Printing Office, Washington, DC 20402; (202) 783–3238. Monthly.

Personnel Management Abstracts, University of Michigan, Personnel Management Abstracts Publishers, 704 Island Lake Road, Chelsea, MI 48118; (313) 475–1979. Quarterly.

Training and Development Alert Index, Advanced Personnel Systems, P.O. Box 1438, Roseville, CA 95661; (916) 781–2900. Annually.

Work Related Abstracts, Information Coordinators, Inc., 1435–37 Randolph Street, Detroit, MI 48226; (313) 962–9720. Monthly.

Appendix C: Sources of HRMS Vendors

To attempt to list all the HRMS vendors would be a thankless and Herculean task. Undoubtedly, someone would be inadvertently omitted or listed with an incorrect address or contact name. Moreover, to be useful, the list should indicate the types of computers, operating systems, applications, and utilities each vendor supports.

Fortunately, several publications and other specialists provide this information. Some of the organizations and publications listed here issue annual software directories; others provide specialized or one-time directories; a few conduct software product reviews. The title of the most recent known relevant issue is included where available.

Human resources departments considering software or vendor changes may want to consider the potential usefulness of consultants in identifying potential vendors. Consultants who are unaligned with any specific vendor get to know hundreds of vendors of all sizes and varieties. Sources of consultants are listed in appendix D.

Advanced Personnel Systems, P.O. Box 1438, Roseville, CA 95661; (916) 781–2900. *The Personnel Software Census*, 1989; *Microcomputers in Human Resource Management*, 1990, annual.

American Management Association, 135 W. 50th Street, New York, NY 10020; (212) 586–8100. *1990 Directory of Human Resource Services, Products, and Suppliers*; *Personnel*, (annual).

Charles D. Spencer & Assoc., Inc., 222 W. Adams Street, Chicago, IL 60606; (312) 236–2615. *Employee Benefits Software Directory*, 1989.

Computer Economics Inc., 2121 Palomar Airport Road, Carlsbad, CA 92009. *Computer Economics Sourcebook*, 1989.

DataPro Research Corporation, 1805 Underwood Boulevard, Delran, NJ 08075. *Payroll & Personnel*, June 1988.

HRMagazine (formerly Personnel Administrator), Reprint Services, P.O. Box 1183, Minneapolis, MN 55458; (612) 633-1214. "The Microcomputer-Based HRIS: A Directory," December 1987; "Microcomputer Software: What's New in HRM?" July 1987.

HRS:Net, Inc., 20 Park Plaza, Boston, MA 02116. *Human Resources Selection Network*, 1989.

Human Resource Executive, 747 Dresher Road, P.O. Box 980, Horsham, PA 19044–0980; (215) 784–0860. "1988 HRIS Buyers' Guide," October 1988; "What's Hot in Specialty Software," April 1989; "Specialty Software Buyers' Guide," April 1989.

International Computer Programs, Inc., 9100 Keystone Crossing, Suite 200, Indianapolis, IN 46240; (317) 844–7461. *ICP Business Software Review*, monthly.

The Kimberly Organization, P.O. Box 31011, St. Louis, MO 63131. *Recruiter Computers*, 1989.

Pension World, Software Product Directory, 6255 Barfield Road, Atlanta, GA 30328. "1990 Software Product Directory."

Personnel Administrator, Reprint Services, P.O. Box 1183, Minneapolis, MN 55458; (612) 633–1214. "Microcomputer Software: What's New in HRM?" July 1987; "The Microcomputer-Based HRIS: A Directory," December 1987.

Personnel Journal, 245 Fischer Avenue, No. B2, Costa Mesa, CA 92626; (714) 751–1883. "HRIS Software Buyer's Guide," April 1989.

Prentice-Hall, Business & Professional Division, Englewood Cliffs, NJ 07632; (201) 767-5054, Training and Development Yearbook, 1990.

VRC Consulting Group, 289 S. San Antonio Road, Los Altos, CA 94022; (415) 948–1513; fax (415) 948–1513. *Microcomputer Applications for HRMS: A Comparative Analysis*, April 1990 (directory produced on a semiannual basis.).

Warren, Gorham & Lamont, Inc., 210 S. Street, Boston, MA 02111; (800) 922–0066. *Handbook of Human Resource Information Systems; HRIS Product Directory.*

Appendix D: Sources of HRMS Consultants

As with vendors, any list of HRMS consultants would certainly exclude newer firms. The following sources probably include listings of the most prominent HRMS consultants. Sources of consultants include consultant organizations, consultant directories, and consultant referral specialists. Additional guidelines for locating and selecting HRMS consultants are covered in chapter 7.

Alan Armstrong and Associates, 7276 Park Road, London, NW14SH, UK. *Directory of Management Consultants in the United Kingdom.*

American Association of Professional Consultants, 9140 Ward Parkway, Kansas City, MO 64114. *Who's Who in Consulting.*

American Business Lists, Inc., 5707 S. 86th Circle, Omaha, NE 68127. *Business Consultants Directory.*

American Consultants League, 2030 Clarendon Boulevard, Suite 206, Arlington, VA 22201. *Consultants Directory.*

American Management Association, 135 W. 50th Street, New York, NY 10020. *1990 Directory of Human Resource Services, Products, and Suppliers, Personnel.*

American Society of Training and Development (ASTD), 1630 Duke Street, Box 1443, Alexandria, VA 22313. *ASTD Buyer's Guide & Consultants Directory.*

Anderson Group, Inc., P.O. Box 508, Madison, NJ 07940. *University Consultants Network Register.*

Association of Data Processing Service Organizations, Inc. 1925 N. Lynn Street, Arlington, VA 22209.

Association of Management Consulting Firms (ACME), 230 Park Avenue, New York, NY 10169.

Consultants News, Templeton Road, Fitzswilliam, NH 02447. *Directory of Management Consultants.*

Counsel of Consulting Organizations, 230 Park Avenue, New York, NY 10169.

Data Processing Management Association, 505 Busse Highway, Park Ridge, IL 60068.

Datapro Research, 1805 Underwood Boulevard, Delran, NJ 08075. *Directory of Management Consultants.*

Directory of Management Consultants, Templeton Road, Fitzwilliam, NH 02447.

Duns Marketing Service, 3 Century Drive, Parsippany, NJ 07054. *Duns Consultant Directory.*

Gale Research Company, Book Tower, Detroit, MI 48277–0748. *Consultants and Consulting Organizations Directory.*

Independent Computer Consultants Association, P.O. Box 27412, St. Louis, MO 63141.

Institute of Management Consultants (IMC), 19 W. 44th Street, Suite 810–811, New York, NY 10036.

Institute of Manpower Studies, Mantell Building, University of Sussex, Falmer-Brighton, Sussex, BN19RF, England.

International Association for Personnel Women (IAPW), 5820 Wilshire Boulevard No. 500, Los Angeles, CA 90036.

San Francisco Redevelopment Agency, 939 Ellis Street, San Francisco, CA 94109. *Directory of Minority Management Consulting Firms.*

TFPL Publishing, 22 Peters Ln., London, EC1M 6DS, England. *Directory of Management Consultants in the United Kingdom.*

Appendix E: Data Bases and Networks

T he number of external data bases and networks has increased rapidly in the past few years as more and more firms adopt telecommunications, increase their computer memory and storage capacity, and begin to understand the efficiency of using electronic information sources. Such organizations are using these outside resources to find out about competitors, trends, publications, regulations, and other issues. Managers can use data base information to compare their own firm with related organizations in employment patterns, compensation, benefits packages.

Because of the rate of growth in this field, the following list cannot possibly be complete. Those interested may wish to contact business libraries, professional organizations, and telecommunications specialists for additional sources of external electronic information sources.

Human Resources/HRMS Data Bases and Networks

ABCS, American Business Computer Society, 544 Main Street, Worcester, MA 01608; (800) 343–0939.

HRM*Net, Society for Human Resource Management (SHRM), formerly American Society for Personnel Administration, 606 N. Washington Street, Alexandria, VA 22314; (703) 548-3440. Over 35,000 citations from various periodicals, newsletters, magazines, and surveys. Also information on conferences and seminars.

Human Resource Information Network (HRIN), Executive Telecom System, Inc., 9585 Valparaiso Court, College Park N, Indianapolis, IN 46268; (800) 421–8884. HRIN has a specific Training and Development Network that features bibliographic data bases and on-line publications; includes two on-line training newsletters, *Employment and Training Reporter* and *Bulletin on Training.* The bibliographic data base known as

Training and Development Alert contains thousands of abstracts of human resources articles largely addressed to the training, development, and human resources planning communities. This data base is compiled from the newsletter of the same name, published by Advanced Personnel Systems.

Management Contents, Information Access Corp., 11 Davis Drive, Belmont, CA 94002; (800) 227–8431.

General Business and Information Data Bases

ABI/Inform, UMI/Data Courier, Inc., 620 S. Fifth Street, Louisville, KY 40202; (800) 626–2823.

ABSTRAX/400, Ageline, Bibliographic Retrieval Service, 1200 Route 7, Latham, NY 12110; (800) 833–4707.

Accountants, and Management & Marketing Abstracts, Pergamon ORBIT InfoLine, Inc., 8000 Westpark Drive, McLean, VA 22102; (800) 421–7229.

Ageline, BRS, 1200 Route 7, Latham, NY 12110; (800) 833–4707.

American Business Computer Society, 544 Main Street, Worcester, MA 01608; (800) 343–0939.

Business Software Database, Information Sources, Inc., P.O. Box 7848, Berkeley, CA 94707; (800) 433–6107.

Canadian Business & Current Affairs, DIALOG On-line System, DIALOG's Knowledge Index, 3460 Hillview Avenue, Palo Alto, CA 94304; (800) 334–2564.

Chase Econometrics, 150 Monument Road, Bala Cynwyd, PA 19004; (214) 896–4720.

CompuServe, CompuServe Information Services, Consumer Information Services, 5000 Arlington Centre Boulevard, Columbus, OH 43220; (800) 848–8199.

Computer ASAP, Computer Database, and Management Contents, Information Access Corp., 11 Davis Drive, Belmont, CA 94002; (800) 227–8431.

Computer Database, Information Access Corp., 11 Davis Drive, Belmont, CA 94002; (800) 227–8431.

Computer Directory, Ziff Communications, Ziff-Davis Publishing Co., One Park Avenue, New York, NY 10016; (212) 503–4400.

Dialog On-line System, DIALOG's Knowledge Index, 3460 Hillview Avenue, Palo Alto, CA 94304; (800) 334-2564.

Dow Jones News/Retrieval Services, Dow Jones & Company, P.O. Box 300, Princeton, NJ 08540; (800) 257-5114.

INFO GLOBE, 444 Front Street W, Toronto, Ontario M5V 2S9, Canada; (416) 585-5250.

ITT Dialcom Services, Dialcom, 1109 Spring Street, Silver Spring, MD 20910; (301) 588-1572.

Mead Data Central, 9333 Springboro Pike, P.O. Box 933, Dayton, OH 45401; (800) 227-4908.

Menu—The International Software Database, Menu Publications, P.O. MENU, Pittsburgh, PA 15241; (800) THE-MENU.

Microcomputer Software Guide, R.R. Bowker Co., 245 W. 17th Street, New York, NY 10011; (800) 323-3288.

MicroSearch, CompuServe Information Services, 5000 Arlington Centre Boulevard, Columbus, OH 43220; (800) 848-8199.

Micro Software Directory, Online, Inc., Weston, CT (203) 227-8466.

Newsnet, 945 Haverford Road, Bryn Mawr, PA 19010; (800) 345-1301.

One Point Electronic Catalog, One Point, 2835 Mitchell Drive, Walnut Creek, CA 94598; (800) 222-2250.

PAIS International, Public Affairs Information Services, Inc., 11 W. 40th Street, New York, NY 10018; (212) 736-6629.

Price Data Bases, Interactive Data Corporation, 486 Totten Pond Road, Waltham, MA 02254; (617) 890-1234.

PTS International Forecasts, PTS Promt, PTS U.S. Forecasts, and PTS U.S. Time Series, Predicasts, Inc., 11001 Cedar Avenue, Cleveland, OH 44106; (800) 321-6388.

PTS Promt, Predicasts, Inc.,11001 Cedar Avenue, Cleveland, OH 44106; (800) 321-6388.

PTS U.S. Forecasts, Predicasts, Inc.,11001 Cedar Avenue, Cleveland, OH 44106; (800) 321-6388.

PTS U.S. Time Series, Predicasts, Inc., 11001 Cedar Avenue, Cleveland, OH 44106; (800) 321-6388.

Standard & Poor's News On-Line, Standard & Poor's Corp., 25 Broadway, New York, NY 10004; (212) 208-8000.

Warner Computer Systems, 605 Third Avenue, New York, NY 10158; (212) 986–1919.

Publications Data Bases

Bibliographic Retrieval Service (BRS), 1200 Route 7, Latham, NY 12110; (800) 833–4707.

Book Review Index, Economic Literature Index, Dialog's Knowledge Index, 3460 Hillview Avenue, Palo Alto, CA 94304; (800) 227–1927.

Business Periodicals Index, WilsonLine, H.W. Wilson Co., 950 University Avenue, Bronx, NY 10452; (800) 367–6770.

Computer Literature Index, Applied Computer Research, Inc., P.O. Box 9280, Phoenix, AZ 85068; (800) 234–2227.

Economic Literature Index, DIALOG's Knowledge Index, 3460 Hillview Avenue, Palo Alto, CA 94304; (800) 227–1927.

Legal Resources Index, Magazine Index, Hot Tips in Review, and Product Evaluation, and Newsearch & Magazine Index, Information Access Corp., 11 Davis Drive, Belmont, CA 94022; (800) 227–8431.

Magazine Index Hot Tips in Review and Product Evaluation, Information Access Corp., 11 Davis Drive, Belmont, CA 94022; (800) 227–8431.

Management & Marketing Abstracts, Pergamon ORBIT InfoLine, Inc., 8000 Westpark Drive, McLean, VA 22102; (800) 421–7229.

Mead Data Central (Nexis), Mead Data Central, 9333 Springboro Pike, P.O. Box 933, Dayton, OH 45401.

Microcomputer Index, Learned Information, Inc., 143 Old Marlton Pike, Medford, NJ 08055; (609) 654–6266.

Newsearch & Magazine Index, Informatin Access Corp., 11 Davis Drive, Belmont, CA 94002; (800) 227–8431.

Trade & Industry Index, Information Access Corp., 11 Davis Drive, Belmont, CA 94002; (800) 227–8431.

Appendix F: Schools Offering Courses Covering HRMS

Traditionally, most HRMS professionals had to learn their specialty on the job. Few colleges or universities offered instruction in this new and rapidly changing field. Although many schools included courses in human resources as part of their business school programs, as recently as a few years ago, only a handful provided courses specifically on HRMS. Today HRMS courses are becoming increasingly popular, especially as graduate and contemporary education offerings.

Some of the colleges and universities in this list offer a single HRMS-related course; others offer advanced degree programs that require an HRMS course. Because schools are constantly changing their offerings in this area, the list below is acknowledged to be incomplete. The level of attention most institutions pay to HRMS is expected to accelerate rapidly.

In 1989, VRC Consulting Group conducted a survey of 250 schools, colleges, and universities offering or planning to offer HRMS-related courses. Institutions responding numbered 66, or 26%. Of these, 27, or 41%, indicated they already offered (or were planning to offer) one or more courses in HRMS-related subjects. An asterisk preceding the school indicates that the institution responded to the VRC survey.

The following listing of higher-education institutions offering degree programs in HR may be useful. The Guidance Information System (GIS) data base may also be helpful.

Abilene Christian University, School of Management, Abilene, TX 79699.

Adelphi University, School of Business, Garden City, NY 11530.

American College, Richard D. Irwin Graduate School of Management, Bryn Mawr, PA 19010.

American International College, School of Business, Springfield, MA 01109.

American Technological University, Department of Management, P.O. Box 1416, Killeen, TX 76541.

American University, Ward Circle, Building 215, Washington, DC 20016.

Arizona State University, Graduate College, Tempe, AZ 85287.

Auburn University, College of Business, Auburn, AL 36849.

Azura Pacific University, School of Management, Azusa, CA 91702.

Baker University, School of Business, Baldwin City, KS 66006.

Ball State University, School of Business, Muncie, IN 47306.

Baylor University, Graduate Studies and Research, Waco, TX 76798.

*Boise State University, Department of Management, Boise, ID 83725.

Boston College, School of Business, Chestnut Hill, MA 02167.

Boston University, Graduate School of Management, Boston, MA 02030.

*Bowling Green State University, Department of Management, Bowling Green, OH 43403.

*Bradley University, School of Business, Peoria, IL 61625.

Brandeis University, Heller School, Waltham, MA 02254.

Brigham Young University, 730 TNRB, Provo, UT 84602.

*Brown University, School of Business, Providence, RI 02912.

Bucknell University, School of Business, Lewisburg, PA 17837.

*California Polytechnic State University, 3801 W. Temple, Pomona, CA 91768–2414.

California Polytechnic State University, Department of Management, San Luis Obispo, CA 93407.

California State College, School of Business, Bakersfield, CA 93311–1099.

California State University, Butte Hall, No. 407, Chico, CA 95929–0031.

*California State University, 800 N. State College, Fullerton, CA 92634.

California State University, 18111 Nordhoff Street, Northridge, CA 91330.

California State University, 5500 University Pkwy., San Bernardino, CA 92407.

California State University, 801 Monte Vista, Turlock, CA 95380; (209) 667–3122.

*California State University, Department of Mangagement, Hayward, CA 94542.

California State University, School of Business, Carson, CA 90747.

California State University, School of Business, Long Beach, CA 90802.

California State University, School of Business, Los Angeles, CA 90032.

*California State University, School of Business & Administration Sciences, Fresno, CA 93740.

*California State University, School of Business & Public Administration, Sacramento, CA 95819.

*Carnegie Mellon University, School of Urban & Public Affairs, Pittsburgh, PA 15213.

Case Western Reserve University, Industrial Relations Division, Cleveland, OH 44106.

Catholic University of America, School of Business, Washington, DC 20064.

Catholic University of Puerto Rico, School of Business, Ponce, PR 00732.

Central Connecticut State University, School of Business, New Britain, CT 06050.

Central Michigan University, School of Business, Mount Pleasant, MI 48859.

Chicago State University, School of Business, Chicago, IL 60628.

City University of New York, Baruch College, New York, NY 10010.

Claremont Graduate School, Business Administration Department, Claremont, CA 91711.

Clarion University of Pennsylvania, School of Business, Clarion, PA 16214.

Clark University, School of Business, Worcester, MA 01610.

Clarkson University, Graduate School, Potsdam, NY 13676.

Clemson University, Graduate Studies, E-106 Martin Hall, Clemson, SC 29634.

Cleveland State University, University Center Building, Room 517, Cleveland, OH 44115.

College of William & Mary, School of Business, Williamsburg, VA 23185.

Colorado State University, College of Business, For Collins, CO 80523.

*Colorado Technical College, School of Business, Colorado Springs, CO 80907.

Coppin State College, School of Business, Baltimore, MD 21216.

*Cornell University, Graduate School, P.O. Box 1000, Ithaca, NY 14851–0952.

*Creighton University, The Graduate School, Omaha, NE 68178.

Dartmouth College, Graduate Office, 305 Wentworth Hall, Hanover, NH 03755.

Delaware State University, School of Business, Dover, DE 19901.

De Paul University, 25 E. Jackson Boulevard, Chicago, IL 60604.

DePauw University, School of Business, Greencastle, IN 46135.

Detroit College of Business, School of Business, Dearborn, MI 48126–3799.

*Drake University, School of Business, Des Moines, IA 50311.

Drexel University, 32nd & Chestnut, Philadelphia, PA 19104.

Duke University, Fuqua School of Business, Durham, NC 27706.

*Duquesne University, Graduate School, 600 Forbes Avenue, Pittsburgh, PA 15282.

East Central Oklahoma State University, Graduate Studies, Ada, OK 74820-6899.

Eastern Michigan University, 1215 Huron River Drive, Ypsilanti, MI 48197.

Eastern New Mexico University, College of Business, Portales, NM 88130.

East-West University, School of Business, Chicago, IL 60605.

Emory University, School of Business, Atlanta, GA 30322.

Fairleigh Dickinson University, School of Business, Madison, NJ 07940.

*Ferris State University, Department of Management, Big Rapids, MI 49307.

Fisk University, School of Business, Nashville, TN 37218.

*Florida Atlantic University, P.O. Box 3091, Boca Raton, FL 33431.

Florida Institute of Technology, School of Applied Technology, Melbourne, FL 32901.

*Florida State University, College of Business, Tallahassee, FL 32306.

Fordham University, Graduate School of Business Administration, Lowenstein 619, New York, NY 10023.

Framingham State College, School of Business, Framingham, MA 01701.

Furman University, School of Business, Greenville, SC 29613.

Georgetown University, Old North NW, Suite 315, Washington, DC 20057.

George Washington University, School of Educational & Human Development, Washington, DC 20052.

Georgia Institute of Technology, College of Management, Atlanta, GA 30332.

*Georgia State University, Institute of Personnel & Employee Relations, Atlanta, GA 30303.

*Golden Gate University, School of Management, 536 Mission Street, San Francisco, CA 94105.

Grambling State University, Division of Graduate Studies, P.O. Drawer 584, Grambling, LA 71245.

Hardin-Simmons University, School of Business, Abilene, TX 79698.

Hofstra University, Associate Provost of Graduate Studies, Hempstead, NY 11550.

Houston Baptist University, School of Business, Houston, TX 77074.

Howard University, School of Business & Public Administration, Washington, DC 20059.

Humboldt State University, Department of Business Administration, Arcata, CA 95521.

Idaho State University, School of Business, Pocatello, ID 83209.

Illinois Benedictine College, School of Business, Lisle, IL 60532.

Illinois Institute of Technology, School of Business, Chicago, IL 60616.

*Indiana Institute of Technology, School of Business, Fort Wayne, IN 46803.

Indiana State University, School of Business, Terre Haute, IN 47809.

Indiana University, Poplars 630, Bloomington, IN 47405.

Indiana University, 2101 Coliseum Boulevard E, Fort Wayne, IN 46805.

Indiana University of Pennsylvania, College of Business, Indiana, PA 15705.

Iona College, School of Business, New Rochelle, NY 10801-1890.

Iowa State University of Science and Technology, School of Business, Ames, IA 50011.

Ithaca College, School of Business, Danby Road, Ithaca, NY 14850.

*Johns Hopkins University, 1 Charles Plaza, 2nd Level, Baltimore, MD 21201.

Keller Graduate School of Management, 10 S. Riverside, Plaza, Chicago, IL 60606.

*Kent State University, Graduate School, Kent, OH 44242.

*Kentucky State University, School of Public Affairs, Frankfort, KY 40601.

La Salle University, School of Business, Philadelphia, PA 19141.

Lindenwood College, School of Business, St. Charles, MO 63301.

Loma Linda University, School of Business, Riverside, CA 92515.

Long Island University, The Brooklyn Center, University Plaza, Brooklyn, NY 11201.

Louisiana State University, School of Business, Baton Rouge, LA 70803.

Louisiana Technical University, P.O. Box 10318, Ruston, LA 71272.

Lynchburg College, School of Business, Lynchburg, VA 24501.

Marygrove College, Graduate Admissions Office, 8425 W. McNichols Road, Detroit, MI 48221.

Marymount University, School of Business, Arlington, VA 22207-4299.

Massachusetts Institute of Technology, E52–580, Cambridge, MA 02139.

Memphis State University, 202 Business Building, Memphis, TN 38152.

*Miami University, School of Business, Oxford, OH 45056.

*Michigan State University, School of Labor & Industrial Relations, East Lansing, MI 48824.

*Mississippi State University, P.O. Drawer MG, Mississippi State, MS 39762.

Montclair State College, Graduate Studies Office, Upper Montclair, NJ 07043.

Mount Saint Mary's College, School of Business, Emmitsburg, MD 21727.

National University, School of Business, San Diego, CA 92108-4194.

*New Jersey Institute of Technology, 323 High Street, Newark, NJ 07102.

New School for Social Research, Graduate School of Management and Urban Professions, 66 Fifth Street, New York, NY 10011.

New York Institute of Technology, School of Management, Old Westbury, NY 11568.

*New York University, 100 Trinity Place, Merrill Hall 509, New York, NY 10006.

*North Carolina State University, 640 Poe Hall, Raleigh, NC 27695–7881.

North Dakota State University, School of Business, Fargo, ND 58105.

North Texas State University, The Graduate School, Denton, TX 76203.

*Northeastern University, 304 Hayden Hall, Boston, MA 02115.

Northern Arizona University, School of Business, Flagstaff, AZ 86011.

*Northern Illinois University, College of Business Administration, Dekalb, IL 60115.

Northwestern University, Kellogg Graduate School of Management, Evanston, IL 60201.

*Nova University, 3301 College Avenue, Fort Lauderdale, FL 33314.

*Oakland University, School of Business Office, Rochester, MI 48063.

*Ohio State University, 1775 College Road, 319 Hagerty Hall, Columbus, OH 43210.

*Ohio University, College of Business, Athens, OH 45701.

Oklahoma State University, School of Business, Stillwater, OK 74078.

Old Dominion University, School of Business, Norfolk, VA 23508.

Oregon State University, School of Business, Corvallis, OR 97331.

Pace University, Graduate Office of Admissions, 55 Church Street, White Plains, NY 10601.

Pacific Lutheran University, Graduate Studies Office, Tacoma, WA 98447.

Pennsylvania University, 901 Liberal Arts Tower, University Park, PA 16802.

Pepperdine University, School of Business, Malibu, CA 90265.

Pomona College, 333 College Way, Sumner Hall, Claremont, CA 91711.

Portland State University, P.O. Box 751, Portland, OR 97207.

Purdue University, Department of Management, West Lafayette, IN 47907.

★Rensselaer Polytechnic Institute, The School of Management, Troy, NY 12189–3590.

Rice University, Department of Management, Houston, TX 77251.

Rivier College, The Graduate School, Nashua, NH 03060.

Rochester Institute of Technology, School of Business, Rochester, NY 14623.

Russell Sage College, Graduate Studies, Troy, NY 12180.

★Rutgers University, Institute of Management & Labor Relations, New Brunswick, NJ 08903.

Saint John Fisher College, Graduate School of Management, 3690 East Avenue, Rocher, NY 14618.

Saint Mary's College, Graduate School, Winona, MN 55987.

Saint Thomas University, Graduate Admissions Office, 16400 NW 32nd Avenue, Miami, FL 33054.

Sam Houston State University, School of Business, Huntsville, TX 77341.

San Diego State University, School of Business, San Diego, CA 92182.

San Francisco State University, Department of Management, 1600 Holloway, San Francisco, CA 94132.

San Jose State University, School of Business, 2797 Lena Drive, San Jose, CA 95124.

★Santa Clara University, Leavey School of Business & Administration, Santa Clara, CA 95053.

School for International Training, Department of Business, Kipling Road, Brattleboro, VT 05301.

Seattle Pacific University, Graduate Studies, 3307 3rd Avenue W, Seattle, WA 98119.

*Seattle University, School of Business, Seattle, WA 98122.

*Seton Hall University, South Orange Avenue, South Orange, NJ 07079.

Shenandoah College and Conservatory of Music, 1460 College Drive, Winchester, VA 22601.

Somona State University, Graduate Studies, Rohnert Park, CA 94928.

Southeastern Louisiana University, School of Business, Hammond, LA 70402.

Southern Illinois University, College of Business Administration, Carbondale, IL 62901.

*Southern Methodist University, Edwin L. Cox School of Business, Dallas, TX 75275.

Stanford University, Old Pavilion, Stanford, CA 94305.

State University of New York, 1400 Washington Avenue, Albany, NY 12222.

*State University of New York, 271 Jacobs Management Center, Buffalo, NY 14223.

*State University of New York, 8 Swetman Hall, Oswego, NY 13126.

State University of New York, Empire State College, 2 Union Avenue Saratoga Springs, NY 12866.

State University of New York, School of Business, Binghamton, NY 13901.

State University of New York, School of Business, Brockport, NY 14420.

State University of New York, School of Business, Cortland, NY 13045.

State University of New York, School of Business, Geneseo, NY 14454.

State University of New York, School of Business, New Paltz, NY 12561.

State University of New York, School of Business, Old Westbury, NY 11568.

State University of New York, School of Business, Plattsburgh, NY 12901.

State University of New York, Potsdam College, Potsdam, NY 13676.

Syracuse University, Graduate School, Syracuse, NY 13210.

*Temple University, School of Business and Management, Philadelphia, PA 19122.

Texas A&M University, School of Business, John R. Blocker Building, Room 321, College Station, TX 77843.

Texas Women's University, Department of Management, Denton, TX 76204.

Towson State University, Graduate School, Baltimore, MD 21204.

Trenton State College, Division of Graduate Studies, Trenton, NJ 08650–4700.

Tulane University, The Graduate School, New Orleans, LA 70118.

Tuskegee University, Office of Development Affairs, Tuskegee, AL 36088.

United States International University, School of Business, 10455 Pomerado Road, San Diego, CA 92131.

*Universite de Montreal, C.P. 6128-Succ A, Montreal, Quebec H3C 3J7, Canada.

University of Alabama, 1900 University Blvd., 215 THT, Birmingham, AL 35294.

University of Alabama at Huntsville, School of Graduate Studies, Huntsville, AL 35899.

*University of Alaska, School of Business, Fairbanks, AK 99775–0060.

University of Arizona, Graduate College, Tucson, AZ 85721.

University of Arkansas, College of Business Adminstration, Fayetteville, AR 72701.

University of Baltimore, Charles at Mount Royal Avenue, Baltimore, MD 21201.

University of Bridgeport, Graduate Admissions, Bryant Hall, Bridgeport, CT 06602.

*University of British Columbia, Faculty of Commerce & Business, Vancouver, British Columbia V6T 1Z2, Canada.

University of California, 350 Barrows Hall, Berkeley, CA 94720.

University of California at Davis, County Road 79 & California Avenue, Davis, CA 95610.

*University of California at Irvine, Division of Graduate Studies and Research, Irvine, CA 92717.

University of California at San Diego, 501 MAAC 0-016, La Jolla, CA 92093.

University of California at Los Angeles, Anderson Graduate School of Management, Los Angeles, CA 90024.

University of California at San Francisco, Department of Management, Box 0400, San Francisco, CA 94143.

University of California at Riverside, Department of Management & Business, Riverside, CA 92521.

University of California at Santa Barbara, School of Business, Santa Barbara, CA 93106.

University of California at Santa Cruz, School of Business, Santa Cruz, CA 95064.

University of Chicago, 1101 E. 58th Street, Chicago, IL 60637.

University of Cincinnati, Department of Economics, ML 37–1, Cincinnati, OH 45221.

University of Colorado, Graduate School Office, P.O. Box 7150, Colorado Springs, CO 80933.

University of Colorado, 1100 14th Street, Denver, CO 80202.

*University of Colorado, School of Business Administration, Boulder, CO 80309.

*University of Connecticut, 368 Fairfield, P.O. Box U41, Storrs, CT 06268.

University of Dayton, Office for Graduate Studies, Dayton, OH 45469.

*University of Delaware, School of Business, Newark, DE 19716.

*University of Denver, 2020 S. Race Stret, Denver, CO 80208.

University of Detroit, School of Business, Detroit, MI 48221.

*University of Florida, 219 Business Building, Gainesville, FL 32611.

*University of Georgia, College of Business Administration, Athens, GA 30602

University of Hartford, Graduate Studies Office, 200 Bloomfield Avenue, West Hartford, CT 06117.

*University of Hawaii-Manoa, 2404 Maile Way, Honolulu, HI 96822.

University of Houston, School of Business, Box 13, Houston, TX 77058.

University of Idaho, School of Business, Moscow, ID 83843.

University of Illinois, Urbana-Champaign, Human Resource Management, 504 E. Armory, Champaign, IL 61820.

University of Illinois, School of Business, Chicago, IL 60680.

*University of Iowa, School of Business, 651 Phillips Hall, Iowa City, IA 52242.

*University of Kansas, School of Business, 206 Summerfield, Lawrence, KS 66045.

University of Kentucky, Graduate School Office, Lexington, KY 40506.

University of La Verne, College of Graduate and Professional Studies, La Verne, CA 91750.

University of Louisville, School of Business, Louisville, KY 40292.

University of Maryland, School of Business, College Park, MD 20742.

University of Maryland, School of Business, College Park, MD 20770.

University of Massachusetts, 125 Draper Hall, Amherst, MA 01003.

University of Massachusetts, School of Business, Boston, MA 02125.

University of Miami, School of Business, P.O. Box 248106, Coral Gables, FL 33124.

University of Michigan, Graduate School of Business, Ann Arbor, MI 48109.

*University of Michigan, School of Business, Dearborn, MI 48128.

*University of Minnesota, 271 19th Avenue S, Minneapolis, MN 55455.

University of Minnesota, 1994 Buford Avenue, St Paul, MN 55108.

University of Mississippi, School of Business, University, MS 38677.

*University of Missouri, 303D Middlebush Hall, Columbia, MO 65211.

University of Missouri, School of Business, Kansas City, MO 64110.

University of Missouri, School of Business, Rolla, MO 65401.

University of Missouri, School of Business, St. Louis, MO 63121.

University of Montana, Department of Business & Management, Missoula, MT 59812.

University of Nebraska, School of Business, Lincoln, NE 68588.

University of Nebraska, School of Business, Omaha, NE 68182.

University of Nevada, 4505 Maryland Pkwy, Las Vegas, NV 89154.

University of Nevada, School of Business, Reno, NV 89557.

University of New Haven, Graduate School, 300 Orange Avenue, West Haven, CT 06516.

University of New Mexico, Robert O. Anderson School of Management, Albuquerque, NM 87131.

*University of North Carolina, School of Business, Greensboro, NC 27407.

*University of North Dakota, Management Department, Box 8050, Grand Forks, ND 58202.

University of North Florida, Academic Affairs, Jacksonville, FL 32216.

University of Northern Colorado, School of Business, Greeley, CO 80601.

*University of Notre Dame, School of Business, Notre Dame, IN 46556.

University of Oklahoma, School of Business, Norman, OK 73019.

University of Oregon, Gilbert Hall, Eugene, OR 97403.

University of Pennsylvania, Graduate Group in Industrial Relations, Philadelphia, PA 19104.

University of Pittsburgh, Graduate School, 276 Mervis Hall, Pittsburgh, PA 15260.

University of Rhode Island, Adams House, Kingston, RI 02881.

University of Rochester, 260 Crirenden, Box 636, Rochester, NY 14627.

*University of San Francisco, 2130 Fulton Street, San Francisco, CA 94117.

University of Scranton, Graduate School, Scranton, PA 18510.

University of South Carolina, College of Business Administration, Columbia, SC 29210.

University of South Dakota, School of Business, Vermillion, SD 57069–2390.

University of Southern California, School of Business, University Park, Stonier Hall 244–1142, Los Angeles, CA 90089.

University of South Florida, School of Business, Tampa, FL 33620.

University of Tampa, School of Business, Tampa, FL 33606.

University of Tennessee, School of Business, Chattanooga, TN 37403.

University of Tennessee at Knoxville, Graduate School, 218 Student Services Building, Knoxville, TN 37996.

University of Texas, Graduate School, CBA 4–202, Austin, TX 78712.

University of Texas at Dallas, School of Management, P.O. Box 688, Richardson, TX 75080.

University of Texas, School of Business, El Paso, TX 79968.

University of the Pacific, School of Business, Stockon, CA 95211.

University of Toledo, 2801 W. Bancroft Street, Toledo, OH 43606.

University of Toronto, Centre of Industrial Relations, Toronto, Ontario M5S 1A1, Canada.

University of Utah, 108 Business Classroom Building, Salt Lake City, UT 84112.

University of Vermont, School of Business, Burlington, VT 05405.

*University of Virginia, McIntire School of Commerce, Charlottesville, VA 22903.

University of Washington, Department of Management Science, DJ-10, Seattle, WA 98195.

University of Wisconsin, 4226 SS Building, 1180 Observatory, Madison, WI 53706.

University of Wisconsin, 929 N. Sixth Street, Milwaukee, WI 53203.

University of Wisconsin, Graduate Office, Roseman #2047, 800 W. Main Street, Whitewater, WI 53190.

University of Wyoming, Department of Business Administration, Laramie, WY 82071.

U.S. Air Force Academy, School of Business, Colorado Springs, CO 80840.

U.S. Military Academy, School of Business, West Point, NY 10996–1797.

Utah State University, UMC 35, Logan, UT 84322–3500.

Villanova University, School of Business, Villanova, PA 19085–1672.

Virginia Commonwealth University, School of Graduate Studies, Box 568, Richmond, VA 23298.

Virginia Polytechnic Institute, School of Business, Blacksburg, VA 24061.

Wake Forest University, School of Business, Winston-Salem, NC 27109.

Washington State University, College of Business & Economics, Pullman, WA 99164.

Washington University, School of Business, St. Louis, MO 63130.

Wayne State University, School of Business Administration, Detroit, MI 48202.

West Virginia University, School of Business, P.O. Box 6025, Morgantown, WV 26506.

Western Connecticut State University, Graduate School, Dansbury, CT 06810.

Western New England College, Coordinator, Graduate Studies, 1215 Wilbraham Road, Springfield, MA 01119.

Western New Mexico University, Graduate Division, National Avenue, Las Vegas, NM 87701.

Westminster College at Salt Lake City, 1840 S. 1300 E., Salt Lake City, UT 84105.

Wichita State University, College of Business Administration, Wichita, KS 67208.

Widner University, Graduate Studies, Kapelski Building, Chester, PA 19013.

Williamette University, Graduate Studies, Salem, OR 97301.

Wilmington College, School of Business, 320 Dupont Highway, New Castle, DE 19720.

Worcester Polytechnic Institute, Graduate Studies, Boynton Hall, Worcester, MA 01609.

Yale University, School of Business, New Haven, CT 06520.

Yeshiva University, School of Business, New York, NY 10033.

Appendix G: Sources of HRMS-Related Seminars and Workshops

Many of the organizations listed below offer seminars and workshops related to HRMS. Others simply maintain listings of upcoming events and serve as clearinghouses.

Seminar Data Bases

EdVENT, Timeplace, Inc., 460 Totten Pond Road, Waltham, MA 02154; (617) 890–4636. Lists 120,000 seminars and conferences in the United States, Canada, and overseas; focuses on management, technical, and personal development topics; can search by subject, date, geography, sponsor, facility, or instructor.

EdVENT II, Timeplace, Inc., 460 Totten Pond Road, Waltham, MA 02154; (617) 890–4636. Same information as EdVENT but fewer search criteria (subject, date, or other data); less extensive than EdVENT; available through CompuServe.

Electronic Registrar, Solution Associates, Inc., P.O. Box 177, College Park, MD 20740; (301) 982–0823. Produces information and seminars, conferences, videotapes, audiotapes, self-study materials, and computer-based courseware; covers fewer seminars than EdVENT but provides more detail on listed items.

1st Seminar Service, 88 Middle Street, Lowell MA 01852; (617) 452–0766. Custom seminar search service; no fee to user; receives a commission from seminar providers.

Human Resource Event Calendar, Executive Telecom System, Inc., 9585 Valparaiso Court, Indianapolis, IN 46268; (800) 421–8884 or (317) 872–2045. Covers 2,500 to 3,000 human resources management seminars and related events.

Seminar Clearinghouse International, 630 Bremer Tower, St. Paul, MN 55101; (612) 293–1044. Information on 50,000 program instructors and 9,000 regular seminars.

Seminar Information Service, 17752 Skypark Circle, Suite 210, Irvine, CA 92714; (714) 261–9104. Publishes a directory of seminars; available on-line through Human Resource Information Network (HRIN).

TRAINET, American Society for Training and Development (ASTD), 1630 Duke Street, P.O. Box 1443, Alexandria, VA 22313; (707) 683–8100. Similar to EdVENT II but less expensive; available only to ASTD members.

UA Consulting & Training Services, University Associates, Inc., 8380 Miramar Mall, Suite 232, San Diego, CA 92121; (619) 552–8901. Offers public and inhouse workshops in strategic planning, organizational change, internal consulting, group dynamics, and models for management.

HRMS Seminar and Workshop Providers

In addition to the groups included here, many professional organizations and some HRMS consultants listed in the preceding appendixes offer workshops, seminars, and conferences.

American Compensation Association (ACA), 14040 Northsight Boulevard, Scottsdale, AZ 85260; (602) 951–9191.

American Management Association (AMA), 135 W. 50th Street, New York, NY 10020; (212) 586–8100.

American Society for Training and Development (ASTD), 1630 Duke Street, P.O. Box 1443, Alexandria, VA 22314; (703) 683–8100.

Association of Human Resources Systems Professionals (HRSP), P.O. Box 801646, Dallas, TX 75380–1646; (214) 661–3727.

Canadian Association of Human Resources Systems Professionals, Inc. (CHRSP), 2 Bloor Street W, Suite 100/197, Toronto, Ontario M4W 3E2, Canada; (416) 975-4360.

Classification and Compensation Society, 810 18th Street NW, Room 601, Washington, DC 20006; (202) 783–4847.

Group Health Association of America, 1129 20th Street NW, Suite 600, Washington, DC 20036; (202) 778-3228.

Human Resource Planning Society (HRPS), P.O. Box 2553, Grand Central Station, New York, NY 10163; (212) 490–6387.

International Foundation of Employee Benefit Plans (IFEBP), 18700 W. Bluemound Road, P.O. Box 69, Brookfield, WI 53008-0069; (414) 786-6700.

University Associates, 8380 Miramar Mall, Suite 232, San Diego, CA 92121; (619) 552-8901.

VRC Consulting Group Inc., 289 S. San Antonio Road, Los Altos, CA 94022; (415) 948–1513; fax (415) 948–1339.

Index

DOS. *See* Disk operating system
Dot matrix printers, 161, 175
DSS. *See* Decision support system

EAPs. *See* Employee Assistance
Programs
Earnings, payroll and, 630–634
Edit and validation rules, 79–80
EEO. *See* Equal employment
opportunity
EEOC. *See* Equal Employment
Opportunity Commission
EIS. *See* Executive information systems
Electronic data processing (EDP) audit,
313–315
Electronic mail (E-mail), 131, 175, 706
Electronic output, 104
Electronic storage devices, 155–156, 175
Employee(s): awards, 687; background
checks, 656; category, 376, 400;
communications, 609–610, 638–639,
687; compensation and employee
files, 447–450; data requirements
and sources for, 376–380; files, 70;
history, 391; information for payroll,
629–630; new-hire forms and
reports, 389–390; number, 376, 400;
profile, 391; records and security,
655; referral bonus report, 390–391;
relations with, 357–358; status, 376,
400; surveys, 522
Employee and industrial relations:
compensation and, 466; computers
in, 505, 507; data requirements and
sources for, 507–514; definition of,
503, 522, 523; disciplinary action,
510, 517, 519; Employee Assistance
Programs, 509–510, 517, 522;
performance reviews and reports,
508–509, 517; reporting
requirements for, 515–521; role of,
504; specific industrial relations
issues, 512, 514; terminations, 510–
512, 519; terminology used with,
522–523; time and attendance data,
507
Employee Assistance Programs (EAPs),
509–510, 517, 522
Employee Retirement Income Security
Act (ERISA), 495–496, 498, 662

Employment: activity reports, 394; data
and EEO/AAP functions, 409–413;
management reports, 391–394. *See
also* Applicant and employment
management
Equal employment opportunity (EEO):
advantages of computerization, 408–
409; applicant and employment
management and, 397–398; audits
and, 430; background of, 403–405;
comparable worth and, 431, 432;
compensation and, 465–466; data
requirements and sources for, 409–
417; definition of, 406, 432; disabled
and, 411; external data bases and,
416–417; occupational categories,
413; purpose of, 407–408; reporting
requirements for, 417–430; test data
and, 414–416; who is covered by,
405–406
Equal Employment Opportunity
Commission (EEOC), 403, 432
Equal Pay Act (EPA), 432
Equity participation, 454
Ergonomics, 169–170, 175
ERISA. *See* Employee Retirement
Income Security Act
Error messages, 127
Evaluating: another system, 47;
consultants, 218–222; current
systems, 25, 46–47; training, 277–
278; vendors, 54, 202–208
Evaluation: administrative, 53–54, 62;
compensation and job, 438, 440–
450, 467; by consultants, 306;
economic, 54–55, 58, 60–61, 63; in-
house, 304–306; maintenance, 321–
322; technical, 52–53, 64
Executive information systems (EIS),
704, 706–707
Executive workstations, 700–701, 703–
704
Expandable systems 719, 721–722, 727
Expendable systems 719, 721–722, 727
Expert systems, 711–715, 727
Expert users, 281, 283

Fair Labor Standards Act (FLSA), 467
Family Educational Rights and Privacy
Act, 104

About the Authors

Vincent R. Ceriello is president of VRC Consulting Group in Los Altos, California, and founder of VRC Consulting Australia in Melbourne, Australia and Auckland, New Zealand. He is a frequent lecturer on human resources management and data processing for the American Society for Personnel Administration, the American Management Association, Human Resource Systems Professionals, the Administrative Management Society, the Association for Systems Management, and the American Electronic Association as well as for various university management development centers.

In addition to this book, Mr. Ceriello has authored numerous articles in the *Journal of Systems Management, Human Factors Journal, Personnel News*, and *Personnel Journal*. He has also served as keynote speaker for the Institute of Personnel Management Conferences in Melbourne, Australia, and Auckland, New Zealand, and for the British Payroll Managers' Association in London.

Mr. Ceriello is former vice president and director of human resource management systems for a subsidiary of Hay Associates, where he was responsible for developing systems to support compensation, manpower planning, benefits, EEO/AA, and personnel record-keeping and reporting. His operation served over two hundred U.S. and Canadian firms in the planning, design, and implementation of their automated systems.

He has also served as vice president of Manpower Planning and Development at the Bank of America in San Francisco, where he supervised the creation of management appraisal, succession planning, career development, and manpower forecasting programs. His duties included the development of a computer-based manpower simulation model, their first affirmative action programs, and a system for career development and counseling.

Mr. Ceriello was also involved in the development and installation of personnel information systems with Information Science Incorporated (InSci). This included project management responsibility for the Bank of America, Atlantic Richfield, CPC International, and over fifty other organizations. He established the first InSci regional office in San Francisco.

Prior to this, he was with Ford Motor Company as a personnel system analyst in the personnel and organization staff. His responsibilities included job evaluation and salary administration and management of the computer services budget for the automated personal records (APR) system. He developed the first engineering skills inventory, which became the prototype for a company-wide system.

Mr. Ceriello's educational background includes a bachelor of arts in psychology and master's degree in personnel services from the University of Colorado. He was formerly a director of the Northern California Human Resources Council, and a member of the Association of Human Resource Systems Professionals. He teaches a graduate-level course on human resource management systems at Golden Gate University, San Francisco, and is on the editorial board of *The Informationist.*

Christine Freeman had headed her own freelance writing and editing business for over seven years. During this time, she has written on a wide variety of technical subjects ranging from computers to health to energy production. She specializes in presenting technical information in a way that nonspecialists can understand. Her clients include the National Nursing Review, the Electric Power Research Institute, Intel, AMD, Decision Focus, several public relations firms, media producers, and consulting engineering firms.

Ms. Freeman has served as writer and editor on several nonfiction books with both publishers and authors as clients and has provided feature articles and applications stories for public relations agencies, computer firm magazines, an energy journal, business periodicals, and general interest magazines. She has also created software documentation. She did substantial technical writing while working for Energy Systems Planning, Inc., a mechanical and electrical engineering consulting firm specializing in energy-related projects. She researched and analyzed economic, environmental, fuel, and regulatory aspects of major energy projects. In her capacity as project manager and research associate, she supervised creation of feasibility study reports and specifications.

Ms. Freeman has extensive experience in presenting information in visual form. She has written and produced a videotape for the Electric Power Research Institute as well as numerous slide productions for Bay Area media firms. While at Panorama Productions and the Johnny Vaughn Organization, Ms. Freeman wrote, edited, and produced dozens of film and slide productions, including programs featuring five or more simultaneous images. She handled over twenty programs for education, training, public relations, and promotion. Several of these assignments involved presenting scientific material in terms and format appropriate for nontechnical audiences. She has also produced supporting multimedia for several theatrical productions.

Ms. Freeman has a bachelor's degree in communication from Stanford University and has taken additional coursework in writing and technical subjects such as database management and energy auditing.